DATE DUE

Handbook of
Management Accounting

Handbook of Management Accounting

Fourth edition

Edited by
JULIA A SMITH

AMSTERDAM • BOSTON • HEIDELBERG • LONDON • NEW YORK • OXFORD
PARIS • SAN DIEGO • SAN FRANCISCO • SINGAPORE • SYDNEY • TOKYO

ELSEVIER
CIMA Publishing is an imprint of Elsevier

CIMA
PUBLISHING

CIMA Publishing is an imprint of Elsevier
30 Corporate Drive, Suite 400, Burlington, MA 01803, USA
Linacre House, Jordan Hill, Oxford OX2 8DP, UK

First published 2007

British Library Cataloguing in Publication Data
A catalogue record for this book is available from the British Library

Library of Congress Cataloguing in Publication Data
A catalogue record for this book is available from the Library of Congress

ISBN: 978-0-7506-8596-2

For information on all CIMA publications visit our web site
at http://books.elsevier.com

Printed and bound in Great Britain

07 08 09 10 11   10 9 8 7 6 5 4 3 2 1

CONTENTS

PART A – INTRODUCTION

1. *Introduction*

2. *Strategic Management Accounting*

3. *Strategic Management Accounting in the Small Business*

PART B – PLANNING

4. *Management Accounting and the 'New Finance' Function*

5. *Strategic Financial Management*

6. *Dynamic Budgetary Control*

7. *Competitor Analysis*

8. *Research and Development Performance Measurement*

9. *Budgeting*

10. *Cash Budgeting and Management*

11. *Capital Budgeting*

12. *Zero-base Budgeting*

13. *Activity-based Budgeting*

14. *How to Implement Activity-based Budgeting: Lessons from Three Case Studies*

15. *Change in Management Accounting*

PART C – COSTING

16. *Standard Costing*

17. *Cost System Design and Profitability Analysis*

18. *Quality Costing*

19. *Product Life Cycle Costing*

20. *Contract Costing*

21. *Engineered, Committed and Discretionary Costs*

26. *Cost Tables*

PART D – DECISION MAKING

27. *Cost Management*

28. *Activity-based Cost Management*

29. *ABM in Practice – A Case Study*

30. *Using Activity-based Information*

31. *Implementing ABC in a Service-driven Business – DHL Worldwide Express*

32. *Business Process Re-engineering*

33. *Throughput Accounting*

34. *Environment-related Management Accounting*

35. *Pricing*

36. *Transfer Pricing*

37. *Shareholder Value in Practice*

38. *Outsourcing or Subcontracting*

39. *Case Study of Outsourcing and Management Accounting*

40. *Value Chain Analysis*

41. *Supply Chain and Management Accounting*

42. *Management Accounting for New Product Design and Development*

43. *Management Accounting and Human Resource Management*

PART E – CONTROL

44. *Financial Control*

45. *Financial Control in a Rapidly Changing Business Environment*

46. *Management Control*

47. *Corporate Governance*

48. *Financial Performance Measurement*

49. *Multi-dimensional Performance Measurement*

50. *Case Study: Development of a Non-financial Performance Measurement System*

51. *Tableau de Bord*

52. *Information Management Delivering Business Intelligence*

TABLES AND FIGURES

ABBREVIATIONS

ABB	Activity-based budgeting
ABC	Activity-based costing
ABCM	Activity-based cost management
ABI	Activity-based information
ABM	Activity-based management
ABT	Activity-based techniques
AICPA	American Institute of Certified Public Accountants
APA	Advance pricing agreement
APV	Adjusted present value
ARR	Accounting rate of return
ASB	Accounting Standards Board
ASP	Application service providers
B2B	Business to Business
B2C	Business to Customer
BCCI	Bank of Credit and Commerce International
BCG	Boston Consulting Group
BI	Business intelligence
BPR	Business process re-engineering
CAPM	Capital asset pricing model
CBI	Confederation of British Industry
CBS	Computer-based system
CCA	Cost contribution arrangement
CIMA	Chartered Institute of Management Accountants
CIO	Chief Information Officer
CM	Cash management
CMG	Cost Management Group
c-o-c	Cost of conformance
CPS	Crown Prosecution Service
CPSI	Customer Perception Satisfaction Index
CRM	Customer relationship management
CSF	Critical success factor
DCF	Discounted cash flow
DETR	Department of the Environment, Transport and the Regions
DFMA	Design for manufacturing and assembly
DPM	Divisional performance measurement
DSS	Decision support system
DTI	Department of Trade and Industry

EAI	Electronic Application Integration
EC	European Community
ECB	European Central Bank
ED	Exposure Draft
EDI	Electronic data interchange
EFS	Environmental financial statement
EFT	Electronic funds transfer
EIP	Enterprise information portal
EIRMA	European Industrial Research Management Association
EIS	Enterprise information system
EPS	Earnings per share
EQL	Economic quality loss
ER	Employee relations
ERP	Enterprise resource planning
EU	European Union
EVA	Economic value added
FAME	Financial Analysis Made Easy
FAST	Function analysis system technique
FCA	Functional cost analysis
FDI	Foreign direct investment
FRS	Financial Reporting Standard
FRSSE	Financial Reporting Standard for Smaller Entities
FTSE	Financial Times and London Stock Exchange
GATT	General Agreement on Tariffs and Trade
GDP	Gross domestic product
GEC	General Electric Company
GP	General Practitioner
HCA	Historical Cost Accounts
HR	Human resources
HRG	Health resource groups
IAS	International Accounting Standard
IASB	International Accounting Standards Board
ICAEW	Institute of Chartered Accountants in England and Wales
ICAM	Integrated Computer Aided Manufacturing
ICAS	Institute of Chartered Accountants of Scotland
IDEF	ICAM Definition
IMF	International Monetary Fund
IRR	Internal rate of return
IRS	Internal Revenue Service (US)
IT	Information technology

JIT	Just in time
KM	Knowledge management
KPI	Key performance indicator
LDZ	Local district zone
MA	Management accounting
MADE	Manufacture and design evaluation
MAI	Multilateral Agreement on Investment
MDPM	Multi-dimensional performance measurement
MDPMS	Multi-dimensional performance measurement system
MIP	Metalik International plc
MIS	Management information system
MMC	Monopolies and Mergers Commission
MNC	Multinational company
MPS	Manufacture process system
MRP	Manufacturing resource planning
MV	Market value
MVA	Market value added
NAFTA	North American Free Trade Agreement
NBV	Net Book Value
NFPM	Non-financial performance measure
NHS	National Health Service
NOPAT	Net operating profit after tax
NPD	New product development
NPV	Net present value
NTS	National transmission system
OECD	Organisation for Economic Co-operation and Development
OFCOM	Office of Communications
OFGEM	Office of Gas and Electricity Markets
OFR	Operating and Financial Review
OFT	Office of Fair Trading
OFWAT	Water Services Regulation Authority
OLAP	Online analytical processing
OPT	Option pricing theory
ORR	Office of Rail Regulation
p-a-f	Prevention, appraisal and failure
PBB	Priority-based budgeting
PBIT	Profit before interest and tax
PDV	Purpose, direction and values
P/E	Price: earnings
PM	Performance measurement

PMS	Performance measurement system
pos	Point of sale
PPBS	Planning, programming and budgeting systems
PPRS	Pharmaceutical Price Regulation Scheme
QFD	Quality function deployment
R&D	Research and development
RC	Replacement Cost
RDF	Results and determinants framework
RI	Residual income
RMEC	Royal Mail Executive Committee
RMS	Risk measurement service
ROC	Return on capital
ROI	Return on investment
ROS	Return on sales
SBU	Strategic business unit
SCM	Supply chain management
SCNI	Scotland and Northern Ireland
SEM	Strategic Enterprise Management
SHQ	Royal Mail Strategic Headquarters
SMA	Strategic management accounting
SP	Share price
SSAP	Statement of Standard Accounting Practice
SVA	Shareholder value added
SWOT	Strengths, Weaknesses, Opportunities and Threats
TCA	Total cost assessment
TNC	Transnational corporation
TOC	Theory of constraints
TPA	Transfer pricing system
TPS	Transfer pricing system
TQM	Total quality management
UNCTAD	United National Conference on Trade and Development
VA	Value analysis
VE	Value engineering
WACC	Weighted average cost of capital
WTO	World Trade Organisation
XML	Extensible Mark-up Language
ZBB	Zero-base budgeting

RELEVANT FINANCIAL REPORTING STATEMENTS AND STANDARDS

Financial Reporting Statements

FRS1	Cash Flow Statements
FRS3	Reporting Financial Performance
FRS10	Goodwill and Intangible Assets
FRS11	Impairment of Fixed Assets and Goodwill
FRS12	Provisions, Contingent Liabilities and Contingent Assets
FRS14	Earnings Per Share
FRS15	Tangible Fixed Assets
FRS19	Deferred Tax
FRSSE	Financial Reporting Statement for Smaller Entities

International Accounting Standards

IAS1	Presentation of Financial Statements
IAS2	Inventories
IAS7	Cash Flow Statements
IAS11	Construction Contracts
IAS12	Income Taxes
IAS14	Segment Reporting
IAS16	Property, Plant and Equipment
IAS33	Earnings Per Share
IAS38	Intangibles

Statements of Standard Accounting Practice

SSAP5	Accounting for Value Added Tax
SSAP9	Stocks and Long-Term Contracts
SSAP13	Accounting for Research and Development
SSAP19	Accounting for Investment Properties
SSAP25	Segmental Reporting

Part A

Introduction

1. **Introduction**

1:1 Readers

It is expected that the readership of this Handbook will include management accountants in both small and large organisations from both the manufacturing and service sectors. It is a reference book with extensive cross-referencing so that readers are directed to topics of related interest. As with many other areas of business and management today, management accounting is going through a period of rapid change and readers need to be able to assess which developments are relevant for their own organisation.

1:2 Knowledge Assumed

This Handbook assumes a prior knowledge of management accounting such as that included in the textbook by Drury (2004). However, each chapter can be read on its own although there are links made between the chapters with the cross-references.

1:3 Contributors

The contributors are a mix of academics and practitioners. However, the academics have been selected for their ability to communicate with management accounting practitioners. For example, a number of the academics specialise in management accounting case study research which involves going into organisations and finding out what is happening in practice.

Many of the developments in management accounting are taking place in practice. One such example is the activity-based approach (*see* **Chs 13, 22, 28, 29, 30** and **31**) which was developed in practice but publicised by the academics, Cooper and Kaplan, who found the activity-based approach being used during their case studies.

John Innes and Julia A Smith

1:3.1 Research Findings for Practitioners

Most management accounting practitioners do not have the time or inclination to read the academic management accounting literature which is basically written in a style aimed at other academics. One aim of this Handbook is to make readers aware of some of the management accounting reseach findings in a form and style which is easily accessible. Given the rate of change in management accounting, just as organisations need to monitor the rapidly changing external environment, so management accounting practitioners need to monitor developments in management accounting in other organisations to ensure that they are providing the best possible information for managers in their own organisation.

1:4 Themes

There are a number of themes running throughout this Handbook but perhaps the two most important are:

1   cost commitment during the design process;
2   external focus of management accounting.

1:4.1 Cost Commitment During the Design Process

Most product costs may be actually incurred during the manufacturing stage but most cost-commitment decisions are made during the planning and design stages for new and updated products. It is critical therefore that management accountants play an active role as a team member or in some other capacity during the design process. Some organisations have found that more than 70% of their costs are committed during the design process. The question for management accountants is how much of the management accounting resource is spent on the design process?

It is sometimes suggested that management accountants consider that they lack specialised techniques for the design process. This Handbook covers the following ten techniques which can all play a useful role during the design process:

*1.   strategic management accounting (**Chs 2 and 3**);*
*2.   competitor analysis (**Ch.7**);*
*3.   research and development performance measurement (**Ch.8**);*

4. *product life-cycle costing (Ch.19);*
5. *target costing (Ch.24);*
6. *functional costing (Ch.25);*
7. *cost tables (Ch.26);*
8. *cost management (Ch.27);*
9. *environment-related management accounting (Ch.34);*
10. *design (Ch.42).*

Some other techniques such as dynamic budgetary control (**Ch.6**), budgeting (**Ch.9**), capital budgeting (**Ch.11**) and activity-based budgeting (**Ch.13**) also have some relevance to the design process.

1:4.2 External Focus of Management Accounting

Historically management accountants have tended to concentrate internally within their organisation and rather ignored the external environment. Strategic management accounting (*see* **Ch.2**) has begun to change this emphasis and management accountants in some organisations are now integrating both an internal and external focus so that they can report the most relevant information (financial and non-financial) to their managers.

Strategic management accounting is now considered to be so important that it is included in the introductory section as **Chapter 2** together with strategic management accounting in the small business in **Chapter 3**. Many of the techniques in this Handbook have strategic management accounting elements but perhaps the most important are:

(a) *strategic financial management (Chs 5 and 6);*
(b) *competitor analysis (Ch.7);*
(c) *research and development performance measurement (Ch.8);*
(d) *target costing (Ch.24);*
(e) *environment-related management accounting (Ch.34);*
(f) *outsourcing (Chs 38 and 39);*
(g) *value chain analysis (Ch.40);*
(h) *design (Ch.42);*
(i) *performance measurement (Chs 48 and 49);*
(j) *benchmarking (Ch.53).*

Chapter 4 on management accounting and the new finance function also includes material relevant for strategic management accounting.

1:5 A Note on Financial Reporting

While this book is intended as a handbook for management accountants, it is difficult to escape the fact that, if you work in practice, then financial reporting standards will have an influence over the reports you provide, even as a management accountant. Indeed, management accounts often form the basis for the financial accountants that reach the public domain. This new edition therefore gives reference to relevant financial reporting standards, wherever relevant, throughout the text. These include the financial reporting standards and statements of recommended practice issued by the Accounting Standards board (ASB) in the UK.

Since 1 January 2005, reporting under the auspices of international accounting standards has been compulsory for all domestic listed companies in the UK. Further reference in this text is given, therefore, to the International Accounting Standards issued by the International Accounting Standards Board (IASB), for companies that are now liable to report under this regime. Helpful guidance on the implementation of international standards is contained in the book by Alfredson et al (2005).

1:6 Overview of Handbook

This Handbook has this introduction and two chapters on strategic management accounting (Part A) followed by four sections on:

- planning (Part B);
- costing (Part C);
- decision making (Part D);
- control (Part E).

However, there are links between these four different sections and this is emphasised by the cross-referencing within each chapter to other relevant chapters. The index to this Handbook also provides another means of finding relevant material.

Chapter 2 on strategic management accounting defines the topic and considers eight relevant techniques being two in each of planning, costing, decision making and control. These techniques are:

(a) planning:
    (i) competitor analysis;
    (ii) research and development;

(b) *costing:*
    (i) *target costing;*
    (ii) *cost tables;*
(c) *decision making:*
    (i) *value chain analysis;*
    (ii) *design;*
(d) *control:*
    (i) *performance measurement;*
    (ii) *benchmarking.*

Chapter 3 discusses strategic management accounting in the small business.

1:6.1 Planning

The introductory chapter in Part B (**Ch.4**) sets the scene by considering management accounting and the new finance function. Topics discussed include:

(a) *leadership;*
(b) *business risk management;*
(c) *finance function strategy;*
(d) *finance function organisation;*
(e) *functional process integration;*
(f) *benchmarking the finance function;*
(g) *re-engineered new finance function.*

Chapters 5 and **6** discuss the proactive, forward-looking and outward-looking strategic financial management with its emphasis not only on the cost of capital but also on values. Another outward looking chapter is that on competitor analysis (**Ch.7**) again linked to an organisation's strategy and how competitors may react given their strengths and weaknesses.

Chapter 8 is one of these chapters which might have been included in another section, namely Control, but it concentrates on the neglected aspect of the performance measurement of research and development. However, measures for evaluating research and development are also critical in the budgeting of R&D in order to link inputs and outputs.

Chapters 9 to **13** emphasise different aspects of budgeting from an overview of budgeting including the different roles of budgets, the budgeting process and the behavioural aspects of budgeting in **Chapter 9** to the more detailed but very important cash budgeting and cash management in **Chapter 10**. It is still surprising how many small, profitable organisations go out of business because of inadequate cash budgeting and management.

Capital budgeting is covered in **Chapter 11** including such topics as:

(a) *setting a discount rate for a company;*
(b) *setting a project-specific discount rate;*
(c) *international investments;*
(d) *risk analysis;*
(e) *post-audit of investment projects.*

Chapters 12, 13 and **14** consider two relatively specialised aspects of budgeting, namely zero-base budgeting and activity-based budgeting. Zero-base budgeting is a technique which assumes a zero base, meaning that all proposed expenditure must be justified instead of taking this year's actual expenditure and adding a percentage for next year's budget. Activity-based budgeting is a different approach to the budgeting of overheads based on activity cost pools and cost drivers. **Chapter 15** discusses the critical aspect of changes in management accounting and how to manage such changes.

1:6.2 Costing

Part C begins with **Chapter 16** on standard costing which remains a very popular technique in practice. **Chapter 16** discusses variance analysis in the context of variable costs, fixed costs and activity-based costs. The criticisms and future of standard costing are also considered. **Chapter 17** discusses cost system design and profitability analysis. **Chapter 18** considers cost accounting and quality (including prevention, appraisal and failure costs), the management accountant's role in quality costing and two case studies of quality costing in practice. Quality costing is a technique which has become increasingly important with the development of total quality management.

Product life-cycle costing in **Chapter 19** is a longer-term view of costing throughout all the stages of a product's life cycle from conception to disposal of the product and this chapter also considers how such product life-cycle costs can be estimated. A specialised costing technique which has become more widespread in recent years is that of contract costing, which now applies not only to construction contracts but also to the provision of services by external contractors (*see* **Ch.20**). **Chapter 21** discusses engineered, committed and discretionary costs. Activity-based costing in **Chapter 22** is a different approach to costing overheads for unit product costing purposes with activity cost pools instead of departments and cost drivers instead of more traditional bases such as labour hours.

For some organisations energy costs have become an increasingly important cost and **Chapter 23** on energy costing considers ways of reducing such costs and the environmental impact together with various suggestions for energy management. Target costing in **Chapter 24** is a different approach from traditional costing because it begins with a future market price and works back to what the target cost should be. Target-cost management is also discussed in this chapter.

Chapter 25 on functional costing concentrates on the various functions of a product rather than on the individual parts as in traditional costing. For example, the functions of a staple remover could include separate paper, collect staples and not tear paper. Functional costing can also be applied to overheads. Cost tables in **Chapter 26** are probably most developed in Japan where both internal and external cost information is held in a computer database so that managers' 'what if?' questions can be answered. There are both approximate and detailed cost tables which are also useful when negotiating with suppliers and subcontractors.

1:6.3 Decision Making

In Part D **Chapter 27** pulls together the cost management aspects of many of the techniques in this Handbook. One specific cost-management technique for overheads, namely activity-based cost management, is discussed in **Chapter 28** with categories such as core, support and diversionary activities or value-added and non-value-added activities to be managed. **Chapter 29** is a case study of activity-based management in practice. **Chapter 30** discusses the use of activity-based information. **Chapter 31** has a case study on implementing activity-based costing in a service-driven business, namely DHL Worldwide Express. A development from activities crossing departmental boundaries is to rename these processes, and **Chapter 32** considers business-process re-engineering. This chapter discusses the principles of business-process re-engineering and also how it operates in practice.

Management accounting textbooks have tended to neglect materials, but **Chapter 33** on throughput accounting is one approach which emphasises the importance of sales less variable costs (often mainly material costs) and the question of how to maximise this per unit of limiting factor or constraint. The decision is then how to remove such constraints. Of increasing importance for many organisations is the environmental impact of their operations. **Chapter 34** considers the need for environmental-management accounting, environmental costs and benefits and current initiatives in environment-related management accounting.

Chapters 35 and **36** discuss pricing and transfer-pricing decisions. **Chapter 35** considers both cost-based and market-based pricing together with some key problems associated with cost-based pricing and some possible solutions. With taxation authorities throughout the world becoming increasingly interested in transfer-pricing policies, **Chapter 36** is very topical. It considers the context of transfer-pricing, accounting aspects of transfer pricing together with transfer-pricing manipulations and gives an integrated, illustrative example. **Chapter 37** discusses shareholder value in practice.

Another very topical subject is that of outsourcing or subcontracting. **Chapter 38** gives examples of outsourcing, considers the short-term and long-term reasons for outsourcing and the possible pitfalls of outsourcing. **Chapter 39** discusses the effect of outsourcing on management accounting in practice, within the setting of a large and successful retail business. Just as outsourcing decisions involve looking outside the organisation, so value-chain analysis in **Chapter 40** involves examination of where and how much value is added in the chain from original suppliers to final customers. Such a value chain perspective can also be useful for cost-management purposes. **Chapter 41** discusses the relevance of management accounting to supply-chain management. **Chapter 42** emphasises that it is during the design process that a high percentage of total costs are committed and when management accountants can play an important role either as a design team member or as an active adviser. The role of management accounting in relation to human-resource management is discussed in **Chapter 43**.

1:6.4 Control

The first three chapters in Part E consider financial control and management control. **Chapter 44** on financial control discusses financial control of assets and also financial controls for the product portfolio. **Chapter 45** discusses financial control in a rapidly changing environment. **Chapter 46** on management control considers managerial behaviour in relation to management control, conflicts in management control and the management control of divisions. **Chapter 47** discusses the need for good corporate governance within organisations, and the various guidance on the topic that is available to practitioners.

The financial and non-financial aspects of performance measurement are discussed in **Chapters 48** and **49**. The reasons for measuring financial performance, the key questions in performance measurement and the use of ratios and divisional performance measurement are all considered in **Chapter 48**. This chapter also examines shareholder value analysis and market value added together with the problems of financial performance measures. **Chapter 50** is a case study of the development of a non-financial performance measurement system.

The French *'tableau de bord'* system is outlined in **Chapter 51**. This is a self-reporting and self-measurement performance and control system involving both financial and non-financial performance measures with links up through the hierarchy of an organisation. **Chapter 52** provides an overview of information management including Enterprise Resource Planning and a case study on Anglian Water Services.

The chapter on benchmarking emphasises one theme of this Handbook, namely the importance of management accountants also having an external focus. **Chapter 53** explains how benchmarking can be used to improve an organisation's performance. Various approaches to benchmarking and different types (internal, industry and cross-industry) are described. The question of how to select the key processes, sources of data and a ten-step approach to process benchmarking are discussed. **Chapter 54** discusses in detail how to implement a balanced performance measurement system for an organisation.

Reference

Alfredson, K., Leo K., Picker R., Pacter P. and Radford J. (2005) *Applying International Accounting Standards*. Sydney, Australia: John Wiley and Sons Ltd.

Drury, C. (2004) *Management and Cost Accounting (6th edn)*. London: Thomson Learning.

2. Strategic Management Accounting

2:1 Definition of SMA

Historically management accounting has tended to neglect the provision of information to support the strategic decisions of organisations. The relatively new term of strategic management accounting is an approach to support such strategic decisions. Capital investment appraisal is one area where management accountants have contributed to the strategic planning of organisations for many years. However, the emphasis of management accounting has tended to be at the management control and operational level with techniques such as cash budgeting and standard costing.

Managers often complain that they have too much data but too little relevant and useful information. In a survey in 1990 of information provided to executive boards KPMG found that this information was:

(a) *biased to financial indicators;*
(b) *concentrated on internal, self-determined comparisons.*

Strategic management accounting attempts to rectify such weaknesses by including:

(a) *both financial and non-financial indicators;*
(b) *both internal and external information and comparisons.*

This Handbook covers a number of techniques which contribute to strategic management accounting and this chapter discusses several of these with more detailed information available in the individual chapters. Most of these techniques such as competitor analysis (*see* **Ch.7**), target costing (*see* **Ch.24**) and value chain analysis (*see* **Ch.40**) have both strategic and operational elements. Before discussing some of these techniques in relation to strategic management accounting, the topic of strategic decisions will be considered briefly.

2:1.1 Strategic Decisions

If strategic management accounting is about providing information to support strategic decision making, what are strategic decisions? Strategic decisions usually involve the longer term, have a significant effect on the organisation and, although they may have an internal element, there is also an external element. Examples of big strategic decisions include:

- takeovers;
- divestments;
- development of new line of business;
- major new investments (e.g. new factory).

However, many other decisions have smaller strategic elements such as R&D decisions (*see* **Ch.8**), design decisions (*see* **Ch.43**), capital investment decisions (*see* **Ch.11**), budgeting decisions (*see* **Ch.9**), performance measurement (*see* **Chs 48, 49 and 54**) and human resource decisions (*see* **Ch.43**).

There is, of course, a vast amount of literature on setting strategy and strategic decisions. Given the above reference to the KPMG 1990 survey, one point to make is that middle managers as well as the board of directors 'make' strategic decisions. For example, in Japan there is very much a respect for age and often it appears that strategic decisions are taken by the oldest and most senior managers or directors. The reality is very different. In Japan in those organisations with a job for life policy, it is middle managers in their forties who generally 'make' the strategic decisions. The thinking is that managers who are going to be with that organisation for the next 20 years will certainly take the long-term view.

In the West organisations need to consider how best to ensure that the long-term view is taken into account when there are so many short-term pressures on directors and managers. Strategic management accounting can play a small part in helping to ensure that the long-term view is taken into account by presenting relevant information to managers (*see* **Ch.3, para.3.3** and **Ch.18, para.18:1.5**). Strategic decision processes are usually very complex and are also dynamic. The internal and external environments of most organisations are changing quite rapidly.

One way of considering strategic decisions is in terms of three stages:

1. *recognising that a problem exists;*
2. *generating various alternative solutions;*
3. *choosing one of these solutions.*

Management accountants are familiar with the above in relation to capital investment decisions (*see* **Ch.11**). Very often the most important (and difficult) stage is the first one of recognising that there is a problem (*see* **Ch.18, para.18:4.3**) and **Chapter 15** discusses how to manage change in management accounting. Of course, in addition to relevant external, financial information, external, non-financial information is important for strategic decisions including competitors' actions, changes in demand, technological developments and government actions.

2:2 SMA Techniques – Planning

Most of the planning techniques in the Handbook have at least an element of strategic management accounting. For example, **Chapter 3** on strategic management accounting in the small business and **Chapter 4** on strategic financial management include the word 'strategic' in their title. **Chapter 4** on management accounting and the new finance function emphasises the external aspect of management accounting. Similarly, all the budgeting chapters have strategic implications such as **Chapter 6** that considers dynamic budgetary control. **Chapter 10** on cash budgeting and management is perhaps the least strategic although, of course, without cash no organisation will continue in existence for long. However, the two chapters which will be discussed in relation to strategic management accounting are Competitor Analysis (**Ch.7**) and Research and Development (**Ch.8**).

2:2.1 Competitor Analysis
(*See* **Ch.7**.)

Competitor analysis is a good example of a management accounting technique which:

(a) *has primarily an external focus;*
(b) *integrates financial and non-financial information.*

Historically management accountants have generated internal cost–volume–contribution calculations but, although these can still be useful, it is now generally recognised that such calculations are inadequate as a basis for decisions. Competitors' possible reactions need also to be taken into consideration.

The management accountant can play an important role in competitor analysis usually as part of a team. One important way in which the management accountant can contribute significantly is in undertaking an assessment of competitors' strengths and weaknesses (*see* **Ch.7, para.7:2.4**). These strengths and weaknesses will include a lot of non-financial information but will also include competitors' financial strengths and weaknesses. This is an overall assessment of competitors but part of the information for this overall assessment will come from an analysis of competitors' products.

At this point it is important to mention that nothing illegal is being proposed. This is not industrial espionage. In most organisations a lot of information is known about competitors (*see* **Ch.3, para.3:3.2**). The problem is that not many organisations are good at collecting such competitor information in a systematic way and reporting it so that managers who would find such information useful can access it easily. Again management accountants have an expertise in collecting and reporting information to managers in a usable format and this may be another contribution which management accountants can make.

Another specific role for management accountants in the area of competitor analysis is as a member of a multi-disciplinary team which buys competitors' products, breaks these down and analyses them. Such a team might have members from engineering, marketing, production and purchasing as well as someone from management accounting. The objective is to understand the competitors' product strengths and weaknesses and to see if anything can be learnt from these products. One important element of such an analysis is an estimate of the material, labour and overhead costs of competitors' products. Again the management accountant has the expertise to play a critical role in costing competitors' products.

Such competitor analysis is now very widespread. One danger of such an approach is that all organisations try to copy each other's products so that in a particular industry it becomes very difficult to distinguish one manufacturer's products from those of other manufacturers. It is important that the information from competitor analysis is used wisely. One benefit can be that it highlights your own organisation's strengths so that they can be built on in the future.

2:2.2 Research and Development

(*See* **Ch.8.**)

Research and development is an area where, in some organisations, management accountants are not involved at all. In others, management accountants have only a control function and then often only a financial control function. In some organisations the future survival of the business depends on good research and development for its future products. Where large amounts of money are spent on research and development, it is at least reasonable to ask whether the management accountant can play a useful role.

Two potentially useful roles are:

1. *planning of research and development expenditure;*
2. *performance measurement system to assess the research and development department.*

Strictly speaking, performance measurement is a control aspect but it will be discussed here briefly. The planning of research and development expenditure involves deciding not only the total amount to be spent but also the amount to be spent on individual projects. In many ways these decisions are similar to capital investment decisions (*see* **Ch.11**) with generally greater uncertainty involved. Again, management accountants may be able to contribute usefully to such decisions.

Reporting actual research and development expenditure against budgeted expenditure poses some problems, but these are not insurmountable. However, a performance measurement system based on such expenditure inputs has limited usefulness. The real test of a performance measurement system for research and development (*see* **Ch.8**) is how to assess the outputs in relation to the inputs. Historically, management accountants have tended to avoid assessing the outputs from research and development because of the problems involved. Nevertheless, some experience is now available in this area and **Chapter 8** gives more details of this.

2:3 SMA Techniques – Costing

As with the planning section of this Handbook, several of the costing techniques have strategic elements. However, the two costing techniques which will be highlighted in relation to strategic management accounting are target costing (**Ch.24**) and cost tables (**Ch.26**).

2:3.1 Target Costing
(*See* **Ch.24.**)

Traditionally costing has had an internal focus building up from material, labour and overhead costs. For example, a unit product cost would be calculated by adding together a unit material cost, a unit labour cost and the overheads associated with a unit. There is little, if any, external focus in traditional costing.

In contrast target costing has an external market focus. Instead of building up internal costs, target costing begins with a future estimated market price, deducts the expected profit margin and works back to the target cost. **Figure 2:1** compares traditional costing with target costing.

Figure 2:1 **Comparison of traditional unit cost and target unit cost**

Materials per unit	+	Labour per unit	+	Direct expenses per unit	+	Variable overheads per unit	+	Fixed overheads per unit	=	Traditional unit cost
Estimated future market price per unit			−	Required profit margin	=	Target unit cost				

Figure 2:1 illustrates the external emphasis of target costing. It is really a very simple idea but a very different approach from traditional costing. With target costing the emphasis switches to achieving the target cost. Indeed a better term than target costing is target-cost management. Setting the target cost is difficult (*see* **Ch.24** for more details) but the real problem with target costing is managing costs so that the required target cost is met in practice. The essence of target costing is that it ensures that the costing system has an external focus by incorporating market information into the costing system.

2:3.2 Cost Tables
(*See* **Ch.26.**)

Traditional costing systems concentrate on costs within an organisation. In contrast, cost tables are designed as databases to answer managers' 'what if?' questions. Perhaps the most important strategic element of the cost tables is the fact that the cost tables include details about materials and manufacturing processes which are not used at present by the organisation. In other words, an organisation's cost tables include information from the external environment. Indeed in Japan there are companies which sell such information.

Such cost tables are useful when designing new products. In Japan some organisations have incorporated their computerised cost tables with their computer-aided design system so that designers can see for themselves the cost implications of different design alternatives.

Cost tables can also play a part in strategic cost management with their external focus. When managers are considering strategic alternatives, again an organisation's cost tables can give comparative cost information about the different alternatives. Furthermore, by including cost information from outside the organisation, there is always the possibility that such information from the cost tables may encourage managers to explore alternatives which they were unaware of before being informed by the cost tables.

2:4 SMA Techniques – Decision Making

As with the planning and costing sections there are a number of chapters in the decision-making section of this Handbook with direct relevance to strategic management accounting. For example, one element of cost management is strategic cost management. A more recent and increasingly important aspect of management accounting is in relation to the environment. However, the two chapters which will be discussed in relation to strategic management accounting are Value Chain Analysis (**Ch.40**) and Design (**Ch.42**).

2:4.1 Value Chain Analysis
(*See* **Ch.40**.)

The basic idea underlying value chain analysis is for management accounting to look externally and to analyse the 'value chain' from suppliers to final customers into strategically relevant activities to manage the costs. Each link in the chain should add value. For example a value chain for the paper industry could be the following:

- forestry;
- logging;
- pulp manufacturing;
- paper manufacturing;

- conversion manufacturing of paper;
- distribution;
- use by final customer.

Having identified the costs involved in the various activities and the value added at each stage in the chain, an important question is how to maintain and develop sustainable competitive advantage. Management accountants have an important role to play in helping managers to identify the values and costs involved. Value chain analysis is another example where management accountants need to pay as much attention to values as to costs.

In terms of costs, just as with the activity-based approach (*see* **Chs 13, 22** and **28**) it is almost certain that factors in addition to volume of output will drive costs in the value chain. Factors such as complexity of the value chain and use of capacity at each stage of the value chain are factors which may drive costs within the value chain. Understanding such drivers of costs will help the management of the value chain. The two basic questions are:

1. *Can costs in this activity be reduced without diminishing value?*
2. *Can value be increased from this activity without increasing costs?*

Another link with strategic management accounting is that value chain analysis can also be combined with competitor analysis. In other words, competitive analysis can be performed using the value chain approach. The value chain of competitors can be analysed to identify similarities and differences from an organisation's own value chain. Furthermore, the values and costs in competitors' value chains can also be compared with an organisation's own values and costs.

2:4.2 Design
(*See* **Ch.42.**)

Design is one of the areas of many organisations where management accountants have not contributed very much. However, for many organisations it is at the design stage where most costs are committed by decisions made by designers. Experience has shown that 60% to 90% of the total costs of a new product may be committed by the end of the design stage, although only a small percentage of the total costs have actually been incurred. Most expenditure is usually incurred during the actual production stage. So there is an important strategic cost management aspect of design where management accountants can contribute as part of a team.

In many organisations designers may be wary of having management accountants involved during the design process. Management accountants, therefore, need to show how they can help designers by providing cost information about different design options. If 60% to 90% of the costs are committed during the design stage, an interesting question for management accountants to ask themselves is: 'how much of the total management accounting time is spent on the design process? If it is less than 60% to 90% of the time, what is the justification for this?'

There may be three main reasons for this lack of involvement of management accountants in the design process:

1. *designers prefer to exclude accountants in case designers' creativity is stifled;*
2. *management accounting textbooks and education tend to ignore the design process;*
3. *management accountants are uncertain how they can contribute to the design process.*

Obviously it is not being suggested that management accountants should drive the design process but rather that a management accountant should be a member of the design team. At the basic costing level there is evidence to suggest that designers understand material and labour costs much better than they understand overhead costs. Management accountants could contribute their costing expertise to the design team. In some cases different costing information may change some of the design features of a new product.

In addition to their basic traditional costing expertise, management accountants can contribute a number of techniques which may be useful to the design team such as:

(a) *activity-based costing (see **Ch.22**);*
(b) *capital budgeting (see **Ch.11**);*
(c) *competitor analysis (see **Ch.7**);*
(d) *cost tables (see **Ch.26**);*
(e) *functional costing (see **Ch.25**);*
(f) *product life-cycle costing (see **Ch.19**);*
(g) *target costing (see **Ch.24**).*

2:5 SMA Techniques – Control

As with most management accounting, it is important that there is a control loop so that the strategic management accounting plan can be compared against the actual results so that directors and managers can consider what, if any, action is required. The two control chapters which will be discussed in relation to strategic management accounting are Performance Measurement – Financial and Performance Measurement – Non-financial (**Chs 48, 49, 50** and **54**) and Benchmarking (**Ch.53**).

2:5.1 Performance Measurement

(*See* **Chs 48, 49, 50** and **54**.)

Performance measurement in relation to strategic management will probably involve a combination of financial and non-financial performance measures. One difficult area for managers and management accountants is the trade-off between different performance measures, that is, improving one may worsen another. A second problem area is the relationship between non-financial and financial performance measures. Very often for organisations it is a matter more of hope than anything else that improving its non-financial performance measures will also improve its financial performance. Management accountants need to gather such evidence and, if necessary, inform managers that the links between non-financial and financial performance measures are not direct one-to-one effects.

Many organisations now identify critical success factors which managers consider will affect the future success of the organisation. It is important that management accountants measure and report on such critical success factors as part of their performance measurement system. Very often these critical success factors can be difficult to measure and management accountants need to do their best and develop their expertise at measuring such critical success factors. As a broad generalisation, management accountants are generally much better at measuring costs rather than values. However, managers may need information about values (such as value to the customer or value of an advertising campaign) as much as they need information about costs. Management accountants may need to develop their expertise in measuring and reporting on values – particularly in the area of strategic management accounting.

2:5.2 Benchmarking

Benchmarking is a specific form of performance measurement. It is particularly relevant for strategic management accounting because of its external focus. The basic idea is to move away from critical comparisons and to benchmark your performance (both overall performance and specific aspects of performance) against other organisations. An organisation may wish to benchmark itself against another organisation which is considered to be the best in its class. Such a comparison will enable comparisons to be made so that similarities and differences can be identified leading to corrective action and hopefully improvements in the organisation's area of weakness.

Benchmarking is another example of how, by looking outside the organisation, new information can be gathered which leads to new comparisons. This encourages managers to view their own organisation in a slightly different light, to ask new questions and to aim for higher levels of performance.

In addition to illustrating the external focus of strategic management accounting, benchmarking also illustrates the integration of financial and non-financial indicators of strategic management accounting. Benchmarks can include both financial and non-financial performance measures. This is another way in which managers can try to test the links between non-financial and financial performance measures.

2:6 Conclusions

This chapter has considered a number of management accounting techniques in relation to strategic management accounting such as:

- competitor analysis (*see* **Ch.7**);
- management accounting for research and development (*see* **Ch.8**);
- target costing (*see* **Ch.24**);
- cost tables (*see* **Ch.26**);
- value chain analysis (*see* **Ch.40**);
- management accounting for design (*see* **Ch.42**);
- performance measurement (*see* **Chs 48, 49, 50** and **54**);
- benchmarking (*see* **Ch.53**).

This Handbook includes a number of other techniques which also have a role to play in strategic management accounting. However, it would be wrong to think of strategic management accounting as being merely techniques driven.

Techniques are an important aspect of strategic management accounting but equally as important is the attitude of management accountants towards providing information for managers as one of their bases for strategic decisions. Like much of management accounting this will involve a dialogue between managers and management accountants in terms of the information to be provided. Perhaps the most important elements of strategic management accounting as far as management accountants are concerned are:

(a) *long-term focus;*
(b) *integration of financial and non-financial indicators;*
(c) *focus outside the organisation.*

Each organisation must decide the most appropriate information for its strategic management accounting given its own particular context and circumstances.

3. Strategic Management Accounting in the Small Business

3:1 The Small Business Information System

Ask small business owner-managers whether they produce management accounts, and they will often answer 'no, I haven't got the time', or 'they are of no use to me'. Indeed, a number of studies confirm the findings of Holmes and Nicholls (1998: 58) that, in small businesses, 'the preparation of anything other than statutory information is limited'. However, delve a little deeper and you will usually discover, at the very least, a basic information system which, essentially, is a nascent management accounting system. Probe further still and you will even find that, yes, very often, small businesses do have a means of using information generated by their firm to pursue the aims of management accounting *viz.* planning, decision making and control.

A similar response will often be obtained if you ask small-business owner-managers whether they undertake any form of strategic planning. Young firms, in particular, find it very difficult to plan far ahead. Usually, they are so concerned with the day-to-day running of the company, the marketing of their product or service and the establishment of an initial customer base, that strategy formulation is put to the bottom of the agenda. This is to neglect an important area. In fact there is evidence to prove that small businesses who adopt an early strategic viewpoint, and who create long-term plans, will ultimately experience superior performance.

Julia A. Smith

Mitchell *et al.* (2000: vii) found two major uses of accounting information in the small firm, as follows:

> First, for the successful, growing firm, in a dynamic and competitive environment, it is used to integrate operational considerations within long-term strategic plans. Second, for the struggling firm, it is used to manage short-term problems in areas such as costing, expenditure and cash flow, by appropriate monitoring and control.

Kaplan and Norton's 'Balanced Scorecard' (see definition below) goes some way to addressing the issues mentioned above, although its main use has been in large organisations. However, Chow *et al.* (1997) investigated the applicability of this technique to the small firm, finding (p.22) that 'a key advantage of the Balanced Scorecard is that it puts strategy, structure and vision at the centre of management's focus'.

Definition of The Balanced Scorecard
'The Balanced Scorecard (*see* **Ch.15, para.15:4.1.4, Ch.30, para.30:3.7** and **Ch.47, para:47:2.3**) is a management tool designed to articulate, execute and monitor strategy using a mix of financial and non-financial measures. It is more than a performance measurement tool and, if implemented appropriately, should help an organisation to align and focus all its resources on its strategy.'
Source: CIMA (2001) 'Developing and Promoting Strategy', Technical Briefing, Chartered Institute of Management Accountants, London.

Raymond and Magnenat-Thalmann (1982: 10) concur that small businesses:

> face many of the same problems and decisions as big firms but without the benefit of staff expertise and multiple managerial levels. Thus, the top manager or managers must shoulder a much broader decision making burden both horizontally (marketing, production, finance) and vertically (strategic planning, management control, operations control). As a consequence, information to support managerial decisions should be as important, if not more, to the small business manager as to his large firm counterpart.

While the Balanced Scorecard does not enable us to produce a generic strategy to suit any organisation, its strengths lie in the fact that it can provide a unique template tailored specifically to meet the needs of an individual company. Further, Chow *et al.* (1997: 27) find that:

the scorecard also appears to be a concept that helps management direct its attention to those goals and objectives, and the measures that drive the company toward achieving those goals and objectives, that will allow the company to re-engineer or restructure to meet the needs of the 21st century.

The management accountant in a small business therefore has a very important role to play. As Labrack (1994: 38) observes:

> the ... accountant in today's small firm must be familiar with a myriad of issues, ... it is almost impossible to avoid frequent contact with co-workers, ... (and) accountability is direct and personal without departmental boundaries to obscure normal operations.

The aim of this chapter, then, is to link the evidence on strategic planning in the small firm with that of small business management accounting information systems. While management accounting and business strategy together encompass many aspects of business and financial management, the goal here is to highlight those particular techniques and activities which have been shown, through empirical investigation and academic research, to assist in building superior performance.

3:1.1 Small Business in the Economy

In order to understand why it is important to consider small to medium-sized enterprises (SMEs) separately, we should examine briefly the statistics on these organisations. Definitions vary, but the European Commission has recently adopted the definitions given in **Table 3:1**.

Table 3:1 **EC Definition of SMEs**

Source: European Commission (2007)
http://ec.europa.eu/enterprise/entrepreneurship/facts_figures.htm

Criterion	Micro	Small	Medium
Maximum number of employees	< 10	< 50	< 250
Maximum annual turnover	≤ €2m	≤ €10m	≤ €50m
Maximum annual balance sheet total	≤ €2m	≤ €10m	≤ €43m
Maximum percentage owned by one or several enterprise(s) not satisfying the same criteria	—	25%	25%

Note: To qualify as an SME both the employee and independence criteria must be satisfied, plus either the turnover or the balance sheet criteria.

In the UK, SMEs have assumed increasing importance in recent years, where they are seen as sources of innovation and economic growth. They account for 99% of all businesses in the UK and 58.7% of private sector employment (see National Statistics, 2006). Thus it is clear that SMEs are very important to the well-being of the economy. Given their special characteristics, in terms of ownership, size, organisational form, and so on, they have very specific needs, which differ from those of larger organisations. This is relevant to management accounting as much as it is to financial reporting, staff management, marketing, and to every other function that contributes to the overall success of an enterprise.

3:2 Why Management Accounting is Important

Management accounting is an important integral part of the strategic process. It has inputs at every stage, as we can see from **Figure 3:1**. Stage 1 is to gather an initial body of evidence. This might be both financial and non-financial, and could come from both external and internal sources. This is our first step in planning for the future – we need to know the current state of the environment, in order to start making decisions about where we want to be.

Stage 2 requires us to generate alternative courses of action that will help us to achieve our goals and then to evaluate each of these options in turn. Analysis might be quantitative or qualitative, and can use techniques such as, for example, relevant costing. Stage 3 is then to develop a strategy for the chosen option. At this stage, management accounting standards are employed to create budgets and set a planned idea of what will happen. Information technology can be used to good effect to examine the impact of alternate strategies on business performance.

Stage 4 is the implementation of strategies. Management should be continually monitoring actual results and comparing them with the planned budget. Finally, stage 5 introduces the control aspect of management accounting. This might be undertaken by the use of variance analysis and investigation, followed by correction of any problems. The feedback loop returns to stage 1: strategy should be an ongoing process, and not simply treated as a one-off exercise.

Figure 3:1 **Management Accounting in the Small Business Strategic Planning Process**

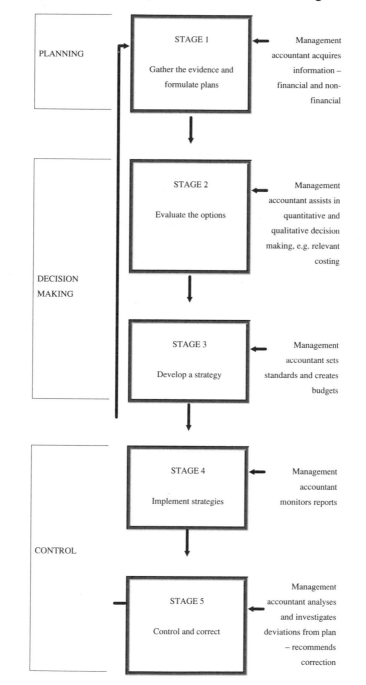

PLANNING

STAGE 1

Gather the evidence and
formulate plans

Management
accountant acquires
information –
financial and non-
financial

STAGE 2

Evaluate the options

Management
accountant assists in
quantitative and
qualitative decision
making, e.g. relevant
costing

DECISION
MAKING

STAGE 3

Develop a strategy

Management
accountant sets
standards and creates
budgets

STAGE 4

Implement strategies

Management
accountant
monitors reports

CONTROL

STAGE 5

Control and correct

Management
accountant analyses
and investigates
deviations from plan
– recommends
correction

3:3 Planning

Without realising it, small business owner-managers often have at their disposal a wealth of information that might be of use to them. While they may see financial reporting (i.e. the production of statutory balance sheets and profit & loss accounts) as a necessary evil, management accounting would be arguably of more use to them, as the users of such information are internal to the organisation. Information can help small-business owner-managers to make decisions, or to improve efficiency. It deals with the future, and so aids planning. However, it must be provided quickly, if management are to act upon it.

Aram and Cowen (1990: 65) recommend:

> the existence of satisfactory internal and external financial reporting, systems, including some experience with budgeting, (because) effective planning often relies on the existence of reliable and accessible financial information.

In this regard, recent developments in information technology and software support have helped enormously, as the costs of access to such resources have rapidly diminished.

The planning process, of which, as we have seen, management accounting is a key element, is crucial to the enhanced performance of a small business. It relies on having an appropriate database of relevant information on which to base the plan. In fact, as Gobeli and Seville (1989: 8) found:

> the alarming rate of small business failures each year can ultimately be traced to ineffective management ... (and) one root cause is a lack of good management information – especially financial information.

So where might a small business gather its information, and what form might we expect it to take? (*See* **Ch.7, para.7:3.**)

Figure 3:2 **Sources of Information to a Small Business**

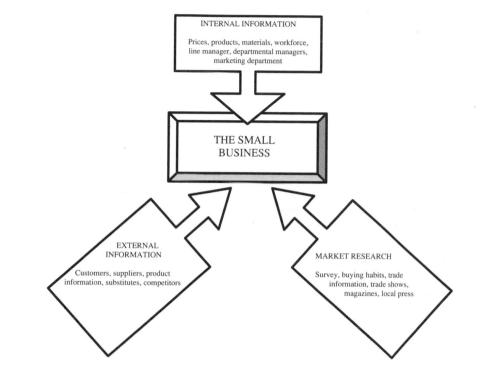

There are three generic headings under which we might classify information sources: internal, external and market research (*see* **Figure 3:2**), and we analyse these below.

3:3.1 Internal Sources of Information

This heading refers to the information that is generated simply through the process of running a business on a day-to-day basis. Such information may be generated without any particularly proactive effort. It might come from the workforce, departmental managers, or from the marketing department. Or it could relate to sales, purchases, and/or personnel matters. Such information might be quantitative or qualitative. Examples are given in **Table 3:2**.

Table 3:2 **Internal Sources of Information**

Source	Quantitative Examples	Qualitative Examples
Workforce	Number of days off sick	Opinions on quality of supplies
Departmental manager	Percentage of material wasted	Quality of labour employed
Marketing manager	Increase in turnover due to new advertisement	Assessment of impact of new product on the marketplace
Sales manager	Analysis of trends in sales over time	Customer feedback on products
Purchasing manager	Quantity of inputs (kg/litres etc.) bought for production	Quality of materials input to production

3:3.2 External Sources of Information
(*See* **Ch.7**.)

External information may be volunteered freely, or obtained relatively easily, from a number of sources. These include customers and suppliers. It might also be derived from observation of the impact of new products on the marketplace, or through the development of alternative or substitute products by rivals, in response to the introduction of new products by the business itself. Again, such information may be either quantitative or qualitative. Some possible examples are given in **Table 3:3**.

Table 3:3 **External Sources of Information**

Source	Quantitative Examples	Qualitative Examples
Customers	Number of customers per day	Feedback forms for opinion gathering
Suppliers	Quantity of materials sold to rivals	Information on new developments
Competitors	Prices of products or services	Competitors' image compared with own

3:3.3 Market Research

The third source of useful information comes from proactive market research. This can take multiple forms in the small business. For example, it may be sought out by market surveys, an analysis of customer buying habits, trade magazines or shows and the local press, to name but a few. Examples are given in **Table.3:4**.

Table 3:4 **Market Research**

Source	Quantitative Examples	Qualitative Examples
Trade magazines	Size of market sector, in £ Sterling	New products/developments in the sector
Market survey	Percentage of sales by geographic location of customers	Customer perception of the company
Local press	Prices of competitors	Sales or promotions by rivals

3:3.4 Formulating Plans

Once the evidence has been gathered, the small-business owner-manager can begin to use it to develop a plan of action to take his business forward. This plan should be designed to help the firm achieve its aims and objectives, and may consist of a number of different alternatives. Typically, in a young, small business, these objectives will be closely aligned to the personal ambitions of the owner-manager. As Bamberger (1983: 26) observes, 'the implicit image that the manager has of the firm's future development overlaps with his/her values'.

A study by Peel and Bridge (2000) examines planning and capital budgeting in a sample of SMEs. Their work compared the strategic orientation of a sample of Japanese, German and UK SMEs, by reference to their objectives. UK-based companies thought improving profitability was the most important objective, while German SMEs were most likely to be striving for cost reduction and Japanese SMEs for sales growth. Management accountants could obviously play an important role in assisting companies to achieve such objectives. Another important finding of their work is that 'investment planning horizons tend to be shorter for domestic SMEs than for their German and Japanese counterparts' (Peel and Bridge (2000: 363)). In order for planning to work, however, the owner-manager must expect a pay-off from his investment of effort: 'if the owner-manager does not perceive that his/her company is better off for having planned, he/she will no longer allocate resources to planning' (Shuman and Seeger (1986)).

Studies have shown that proactive planning does in fact lead to higher performance. For example, in an empirical study of small businesses, it was found that 'of the high performers, 80% had detailed formal plans, which were updated when required, for expansion, moving premises, or reformulating budgets' (Smith (1998: 865)).

While strategic planning is important, it is a huge area of study and not the main focus of this chapter. However, it is useful to summarise the recommendations of Smith (1998) in relation to small business planning and strategy. These findings are based on an empirical study of small businesses, which experienced superior performance in their early life-cycle.

(a) **Set clear, long-term objectives:** *The management accountant can help here by identifying the feasibility of the firm's objectives, in relation to the resources available and anticipated. He should also be involved in developing written plans for the business, as 'the large majority of fast-growth firms do create written business plans as a product of strategic planning' (Baker et al (1993, p.87)).*

(b) **Set business, rather than personal, goals:** *Management accountants can take a detached view and offer alternative suggestions to owner-managers who are too close to the company. This is important if the small business wishes to grow. As Mount et al. (1993: 114) discovered, 'for many small business owners, the sharing of decision-making is an [sic] anathema. Resistance to doing so can result in a long and stressful transition; at worst it may bring about the demise of the business as schedules are missed, employees quit in frustration and similar problems occur'.*

(c) **Aim for long-term profit and a high rate of return:** *Management accountants can help to identify cost-cutting opportunities and to determine the most profitable product mix, according to available resources. Evidence has shown that such an aim is important, as 'seeking the best return on investment has a positive and significant impact on performance' (Reid and Smith (2000a: 166)).*

(d) **Target a specific niche and concentrate on developing your business within it:** *The management accountant can help to identify profit-making opportunities, and to determine the extent of the niche market to be targeted. A **differentiation strategy** would mean that 'the firm seeks to distinguish a business or its products from competitors by other characteristics than low costs, such as, for example, product features quality or high technology, superior service or technical assistance, a strong brand name, company image, a good location, a particular distribution system or a broad product line' (Bamberger (1989: 80)).*

(e) **Cut costs where possible:** *The management accountant should be aware of processes and procedures which are inefficient and alert management to areas for improvement. **Cost leadership** is a possible strategy, whereby the small business 'aims at the lowest cost position in the industry and market. The development of this ... type of competitive advantage may include the pursuit of economies of scale, experience curve effects, low cost product design and tight cost and overhead control' (Bamberger (1989: 80)).*

(f) **Have quantifiable financial goals:** *Management accountants can help to formulate budgets that can be used as a target or benchmark, and which can provide motivation for employees. Bear in mind the advice of Bhide (1994: 159)* that '*back-of-the-envelope, short-term cash forecasts and analyses of breakevens can keep the entrepreneur out of trouble*'.

3:4 Decision making

Once data have been gathered and analysed, and a potential plan or plans of action have been developed, then management must evaluate the various options before deciding upon a definite strategy that the company will follow.

3:4.1 Evaluate the Options

In order to evaluate the various options that are open to a small business, the management accountant should help to identify costs (and revenues) that are *relevant* to that decision. Costs which have already been incurred are *past* or *sunk* costs, and are considered to be irrelevant to that decision. *Opportunity* costs, which represent the next best alternative use of a resource (for example, materials), are *relevant* to the decision. *See* Drury (2000: Ch.9) for more detail. We can examine some of the types of decision that may be confronted by small business owner-managers under a number of headings, as below.

3:4.1.1 Produce In-house or Outsource?

Manufacturing companies may have the opportunity to subcontract all or part of their production – a so-called 'make-or-buy' decision. Likewise, a service company could choose to outsource some of its core activities. In each case, the management accountant will be required to evaluate both the costs of continuing to produce or provide the service in-house *and* the likely costs of subcontracting, in order to make an informed comparison.

Example 3:1
A small family business makes lamps in a small, rented warehouse, buying in parts such as shades, wooden and ceramic bases, and all of the electrical components required. The business is doing well, but the three family members who work in the company spend more time making the products than promoting them. Another manufacturer has made an offer to produce the lamps for the firm, so that the family can devote more time to sales and advertising.

Management Accounting Considerations

1. *What does it currently cost to produce a lamp? Family members' time should be valued, in addition to the costs of the individual components.*

2. *How much will it cost to subcontract the work?*

3. *What is the 'value-added' to be gained from releasing family members from the day-to-day work of production, in order to promote their company, and perhaps better utilise their existing skills?*

4. *Will the expected additional revenue exceed the cost of subcontracting?*

3:4.1.2 Discontinue Product Line

When a company delivers a number of products to its customers, there may be a time at which a certain product line becomes no longer viable. For example, it may come to the end of its product life cycle, either through dated technology, or simply because it has just gone out of fashion.

Example 3:2

Using the same company as in **Example 3:1** – the company now thinks that its standard lamps are proving too costly to produce and wonders whether to discontinue the line.

Management Accounting Considerations

1. *What is the contribution made by the product (i.e. its selling price less variable costs) to fixed overheads?*

2. *If it costs more to produce than it brings in sales, are there other benefits from continuing to produce the standard lamp? For example, is it a so-called 'loss-leader' that brings in customers who subsequently also buy other, higher-contribution, goods?*

3. *What 'signal' would the discontinuation of the product line give to the market? For example, might it suggest that the company is doing badly?*

3:4.1.3 Ideal Product Mix

In any number of situations there may exist factors which constrain the organisation's ability to meet overall demand. For example, a small company faced with a large order may be restricted by the availability of skilled labour or a shortage of materials might mean that demand cannot be met. Further, overall capacity might be constrained by the speed at which the company's current machinery can work. In such situations, the recommendation is to maximise the *contribution per limiting factor*, as in **Example 3:3** below.

Example 3:3

Consider a small engineering company which has the ability to make two components, A and B. It finds that capacity is limited by the 1,500 machine hours available. If demand is expected to be 500 units each for components A and B (in other words, demand will exceed the maximum the company can supply), what product-mix should the company produce?

At first glance, component B looks preferable: it has both a higher selling price and a higher contribution per unit than component A. However, component B takes five machine hours per unit to make, compared with two hours for component A. The resulting *contributions per limiting factor* are £8 for B and £9 for A, thus giving preference to production of A (*see* **Table 3:5**).

Table 3:5 **How the management accountant can help with product-mix decisions in a small company**

	Component A	Component B
Selling price	£50	£60
Variable costs	£32	£20
Contribution per unit of output (selling price less variable costs)	£18	£40
Machine hours required per unit	2	5
Contribution per limiting factor	£9	£8
Ranking	1	2

The company should therefore make as much as possible of component A, and use the remaining machine hours to make component B, as in **Table 3:6** below.

Table 3:6 **Optimal Product-mix**

	Component A	*Component B*
Demand	500	500
Machine hours per unit	2	5
Production	<u>500</u>	<u>100</u>
Total machine hours	1000	500
Total contribution	£9000	£4000

3:4.2 Develop a Strategy

The third stage in our strategic planning process (**Figure 3:1**) is the development of a strategy that will enable the company to achieve its goals. This should take the form of a plan of action, which incorporates forecasts of, for example, expected demand and anticipated costs. At this point, the management accountant will be involved in setting standards and creating budgets. This is also the stage at which information technology can become an important tool.

3:4.2.1 A Plan of Action

Having a plan in itself is not necessarily an indicator or predictor of success. Furthermore, if the owner-manager of a small business does not perceive any benefits from planning, they will stop allocating resources to this activity. Thus it is important to create a plan that the organisation can use, rather than hide away in a filing cabinet, and understand, if they are to make sensible decisions, based on that plan.

Table 3:7 contains some clear goals set by the owner-managers of high-performing small businesses. These better-performing companies have clear strategic ambitions, which are in line with Michael Porter's (1985) recommendations for achieving sustained profitability.

Table 3:7 **Goals of high-performing small companies**

Source: Smith (1998) 'Strategies for start-ups', *Long Range Planning*

- Increase the number of branches
- Develop a higher profile
- Gain more clients and more business
- Make more money
- Provide an opportunity for the employees to develop

Management accountants should be able to examine the feasibility of achieving each of these goals, and to develop budgets that will facilitate their success.

3:4.2.2 Setting Standards and Creating Budgets

Only a minority of small firms set budgets. This gives them an edge over their rivals. However, these budgets tend to be at a very basic level, for example, based on what they want their bank balance to be at the month end. In the small business, cash flow is crucial; you can survive for a while without making any profits, but if you run out of cash you are lost. In order to monitor cash flow, Welsh and White (1981: 26) recommend that small companies prepare and update on a monthly basis 'the future operations of the business in a simultaneous portrayal of the income statement of receipts and disbursements over successive short time intervals for the coming 6 to 12 months'.

Table 3:8 shows some of the standards a small business might wish to establish, in order to assist them in preparing budgets for forthcoming periods.

Table 3:8 **Small business standards**

Standard	Example	Measured in
Quantity of material per unit of output	Paint	Litres per unit
	Metal	Kg per unit
	Electric cable	Metres per unit
Quantity of labour per unit of product	Skilled solicitor	Days per job/contract
	Unskilled machine operative	Labour hours per unit

Standards may also be set relating to, for example, the number of machine hours per unit, or the recommended mix of inputs for a given output. The information required to produce these standards could come from a number of sources, including:

- *expert opinion;*

- *market reports;*

- *trade journals;*

- *departmental managers;*

- *past performance reports;*

- *averages;*

- *suppliers of materials.*

Standards are very helpful for companies who have repeated operations, in that they enable firms to forecast expected costs for a given level of demand and, subsequently, to better control of cash flow. They may also be used by a small firm wishing to implement an activity-based costing (ABC) system, which can help management to obtain 'an accurate picture of the real cost of producing each product or providing each service' (Hicks (1999: 41)).

3:4.2.3 The Use of Information Technology

Information technology (IT) has developed rapidly over recent years. Sophisticated computer hardware and software have enabled small businesses to compete on an even playing field with their larger rivals. These developments have facilitated the installation and implementation of detailed management accounting systems in even the smallest company, and those who have embraced the technological benefits have experienced the greatest rewards.

Obviously, the first stage of our strategic planning process will generate a huge amount of qualitative and quantitative data, the analysis of which is eased by technology. Smith (1999) found that the greater the use of IT in a small firm, in particular to run an accounting information system, the greater the firm's performance. This study concluded that the owner-managers of small firms considering implementing a strategy for IT should ask themselves the following questions:

(a) ***What kind of information will I be gathering?*** *We have discussed above (see Para. 3:3) the nature of information that might be gathered. This will have an impact upon the nature of the information system, and therefore the IT, to be installed. From the very beginning, though, management accountants should be included. As Kole et al. (1988: 35) find: 'the decision to computerise managerial planning and control in smaller service firms must have the full support an involvement of all key people. The objective should be not just to answer today's need but to provide the groundwork for an integrated accounting system that will serve the firm for many years. Management accountants, whether inside the firm or outside, should guide the implementation of a database system for planning and control'.*

(b) ***How should I transmit information?*** *If information is likely to be needed quickly, then pagers or mobile phones may be appropriate for daily communications. Design companies might prefer to provide their experts with laptops, so that they can have drawings, price lists, and client records to hand on site visits. Retail outlets might consider point of sale technology, to enable instant bar-code reading.*

(c) ***What should I use to store information?*** *Even today a basic DOS-based computer might be powerful enough to meet the needs of a small business. There is no point in spending money on the most up-to-date technology, if most of it will not be used. Small businesses should consider second-hand equipment and the opportunities available for future upgrade, when deciding which hardware and software to use.*

(d) ***How do I intend to process information?*** *The IT system should be appropriate to the needs of the users. If data are only to be stored, then basic spreadsheets might suffice. On the other hand, if the small business owner-manager wishes to use the information generated to produce accounts, generate invoices and forecast sales, then he might prefer to install a fully-integrated database management system (DBMS) alongside accounting packages like Sage (see below).*

Depending on the company, it might be appropriate to have designed and installed a custom-made system, such as that suggested in the Sage advertising, to meet specific user needs. Although, as McMahon and Holmes (1991: 27) observe:

> simpler solutions may be more effective. For example, cash-based accounting systems may be perfectly adequate and provide for an acceptable level of financial control in smaller enterprises.

Sage advertising

Sage's industry-leading accounting solutions contain rich functionality and the latest internet-related technologies, having been developed to meet the needs of today's small and medium-sized businesses. All solutions are designed to be easy to use and whilst they are tailored to meet localised accounting needs they accommodate future growth possibilities by enabling customers to migrate to larger and more powerful Sage business solutions.

Source: Sage (2003): www.sage.com/solutions/IntAccounting.htm

3:5 Control

The third major role of the management accountant is to assist in control of the organisation. Within the strategic planning process this function becomes important as soon as strategies are implemented.

3:5.1 Implement Strategies

When a new strategy is undertaken, the management accountant cannot afford to assume that everything will go smoothly. Very rarely does anything go to plan, so it is advisable to monitor new strategies in order to check how they match up with expectations. Smith (1998: 866) found that high performing firms were those which were characterised by forward-thinking owner-managers whose strategies included 'creating and maintaining a profitable core that will drive forward growth', and 'always trying to increase the market, [having] built up a bit of finance that can be invested'.

Three issues stand out when it comes to the implementation of strategies: timing, communication and cost management.

3:5.1.1 Timing

Once the decision has been made to follow-up a strategic plan, it is important to make sure that it **is** actually implemented, and that this is done quickly, according to high-performing small businesses. **Table 3:9** provides evidence of some of their recommendations:

Table 3:9 Recommendations on strategy implementation by high-performing firms

Source: Smith (1998) 'Strategies for start-ups', *Long Range Planning*

- If you believe in it and stay the course, then you've got to follow it through
- You must expect that things don't go right
- You've got to be fairly swift if you make a decision

3:5.1.2 Communication

To facilitate speedy implementation of new strategies, there must exist within the small business an effective means of communication. The management accountant can help by ensuring that the accounting information system is updated regularly and works efficiently. Reid and Smith (2000) found that certain events, or contingencies, would affect the development of a management accounting system in the small firm. These include:

1   *The point at which the firm experiences its most severe cash-flow crisis.*

2   *The point at which a severe shortfall of finance most seriously restricts strategic investment in the firm.*

3   *The point at which the most significant innovation is made in the firm.*

At times, therefore, where cash flow or growth capital are in short supply, or when innovation is taking place, management accountants should pay particular attention to ensuring that records are kept up to date, as the data thereby generated may prove invaluable for future strategic purposes. If owner-managers are in any doubt that effective management accounting systems are not worthwhile, then they should heed the warning of Day and Taylor (2002: 130) that:

> financially distressed companies that we examined showed strong evidence of poor-quality management accounting information, ... (and) a lack of attention by senior managers/directors to improving this aspect of financial control.

3:5.1.3 Financial Management

Expanding on the points made above, probably the most important thing for any new or young business, especially at times of growth or innovation, is the management of finances. When investments are being made and stock built up, it is very easy to tie up all the cash and be left short of funds to pay a key creditor. High performers realise this and, for example, 'do deals with our suppliers to extend trade credit, and monitor stock – we're sensible' (Smith, 1998: 866).

Other recommendations by high performers are:

- *cash flow is the most important thing (and) it's essential that it's done daily;*

- *analyse margin and sales per product group (because) the product mix is important in terms of the well-being of the company.*

This concurs with Thurston's (1983) recommendation that:

> no capable manager should find surprising news in the monthly financial report (and) the manager for each area of responsibility should have daily and weekly running figures on how that responsibility is performing against plan.

Reid and Smith (2002) investigated management accounting systems in small companies and found evidence of a U-shaped relationship between business performance and information system development, as shown in **Figure 3:3**. That is, those who are performing poorly require information on a crisis basis and those who are doing well need information to plan ahead. Those better performing firms might be classified as 'adaptive'. They have been shown to plan strategically, while not becoming bogged down in too much detail and subsequently achieve higher growth and increased market share. Thus the development of a system for monitoring data on a regular basis is justified.

Figure 3:3 Information system development and business performance in small firms

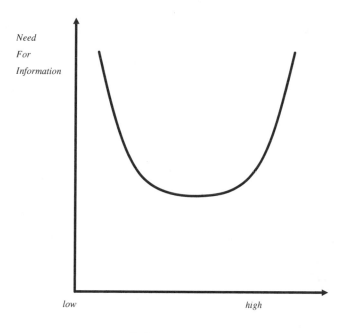

Performance

3:5.2 Control and Correct

High-performing small firms are those which have established methods for evaluating performance and controlling and correcting for deviations from plan. Engle and Dennis (1989: 6) state that 'an active, concerned owner-manager is vital to the control system of most small business and there are many tasks which can appropriately be accomplished by this individual'. Examples of some of actions taken by small business owner-managers in practice are given in Smith (1998: 867) as follows:

- *We ask ourselves, does it fulfil the financial targets and budgets we've set, and do people enjoy working here?;*

- *We plot graphs of growth – for example, this year versus last year;*

- *We analyse the mix for everything – volume and sales;*

- *We do a client analysis, which gives us the sales figure per client for 12 product groups, and tells us what we're doing right and wrong;*

- *We do product analysis using stock reports and gross margin on a monthly and yearly basis.*

3:5.2.1 Control Charts

One easy method of analysing performance, using a graphical measure, is that of control charts. Recall Examples 3:1 and 3:2, the small business which makes and sells lamps. Imagine that sales of standard lamps are, on average, 100 a week. The owner-manager, worried that sales are declining, has decided to withdraw these lamps when sales drop by 10%, i.e. when they fall to a level of sales of 90 units a week. He decides to monitor sales on a weekly basis, and draws up the control chart shown in **Example 3:4** below.

Example 3:4 **Control chart for standard lamps**

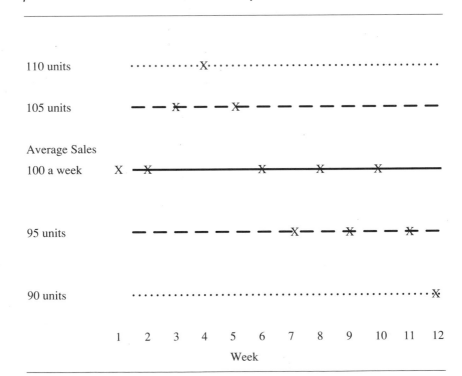

This chart allows the owner-manager to plot average sales, sales 5% above, and sales 5% below average. At the end of each week, he puts a cross against the relevant amount. By the twelfth week of monitoring, the owner-manager can see that sales have dropped to 90 units a week, the point at which he has decided to withdraw the lamps from sale. Control charts such as this are a very useful method for monitoring performance and implementing controls, subject to pre-determined criteria. They allow the user to identify trends, and to take action when potential problems are observed. In this case, the owner-manager decides to withdraw the standard lamps from sale and to focus on more popular products instead.

3:5.2.2 Variances
(*See* **Ch.6, para.6:4.**)

The analysis of variances is another technique which enables management accountants to control an organisation's behaviour. Essentially, a variance is a difference between budgeted or planned performance, and actual performance. In order to report financial performance, small companies now have the opportunity to adopt the *FRSSE: Financial Reporting Standard for Smaller Entities*, and there is talk of international developments in this area. In our example above, sales of 90 units give a variance of 10 units from expected (average) sales. Thus profit will be lower than expected. The difference between budgeted and actual profit can be explained by a number of factors, as below:

(a) *A difference in the number of units sold, compared with plan.*

(b) *A difference in the selling price of each unit.*

(c) *A difference in the quantity of materials used to make each unit.*

(d) *A difference in the combination of materials used (for example, more plastic, less wood) compared to plan or standard.*

(e) *A difference in the price of materials (i.e. it differs from the standard price used in budgeting).*

The procedures for calculating variances are more detailed than can be accommodated here, but see for example, Drury (2000) for a detailed explanation.

The management accountant can help the business to identify the root cause of the variance arising. For example, if a variance arises because the number of units sold is fewer than budget, then the sales or marketing manager should be approached first for an explanation. If the materials price variance is unfavourable, then the production manager should be asked whether, perhaps, materials were wasted, or a more expensive supplier was used and, if so, why. On the basis of this analysis, corrective action may be taken and the small firm might avoid the pitfalls of a lack of control identified by Fleming and Kim (1989: 39):

> Small businesses are vulnerable to cash mismanagement because their accounting systems are easier to manipulate, cash is easier to appropriate, and the loss of a relatively small amount ... might bankrupt the firm.

3:6 Back to the Beginning

As mentioned at the start of this chapter, management accounting and strategic planning should be an ongoing process. A company should not go through this process as a one-off experiment, but rather should find that strategy, information systems and the use of management accounting evolve organically over time. Thus for strategic management to work, it must be adopted as part of the company's philosophy, with all members of the organisation involved in striving towards a common goal.

3:7 Conclusion

While small business owner-managers might initially consider management accounting to be an unnecessary drain on their time, it has been proven that using management accounting to support strategic planning in a small firm has a positive and significant effect on performance. Even from an early stage, or in a sole tradership, a basic information system might be developed. Over time, as the company grows, then so too should the accounting information system. Then it can be used to support future plans and strategies, to assist in decision making and to act as a control mechanism by providing a benchmark against which performance can be assessed.

References

Aram, J.D. and Cowen, S.S. (1990) 'Strategic planning for increased profit in the small business', *Long Range Planning* 23(6), 63–70.

Baker, W.H., Addams, H.L. and Davis, B. (1993) 'Business planning I successful small firms', *Long Range Planning* 26(6), 82–8.

Bamberger, I. (1983) 'Value systems, strategies and the performance of small and medium-sized firms', *European Journal Small Business Journal* 1(4), 25–39.

Bamberger, I. (1989) 'Developing competitive advantage in small and medium-sized firms', *Long Range Planning* 22(5), 80–8.

Bhide, A. (1994) 'How entrepreneurs craft strategies that work', *Harvard Business Review*, 72(2), 150–61.

Chow, C.W., Haddad, K.M. and Williamson, J.E. (1997) 'Applying the balanced scorecard to small companies', *Management Accounting*, August, 21–27.

CIMA (2001) 'Developing and promoting strategy', Technical Briefing, Chartered Institute of Management Accountants; London, UK.

Day, J. and Taylor, P. (2002) 'Accounting: SMEs - the accounting deficit', *Accountancy*, January, 130.

Drury, C (2000) *Management & Cost Accounting (5th edn)*, Business Press; London, UK.

DTI (Department of Trade and Industry) (2003) Small and Medium Enterprise (SME) – Definitions: www.sbs.gov.uk/statistics/smedefs.php

Engle, T.J. and Dennis, D.M. (1989) 'Benefits of an internal control structure evaluation in a small business audit', *The Ohio CPA Journal*, Spring, 5-11.

Fleming, M.M.K. and Kim, K. J. (1989) 'Where did the cash go?' *Management Accounting*, July, 39–43.

Gobeli, D.H. and Seville, M.A. (1989) 'The small business – CPA interface', *Journal of Small Business Management*, October, 8–16.

Hicks, D.T. (1999) 'Yes, ABC is for small business too', *Journal of Accountancy*, August, 41–3.

Holmes, S. and Nicholls, D. (1998) 'Analysis of the use of accounting information by Australian small business', *Journal of Small Business Management*, April, 57–68.

Kole, M., Oberheim, S. and Wood, L. (1988) 'Controlling costs with a database system', *Management Accounting*, June, 31–35.

Labrack, B.D. (1994) 'Small business controller', *Management Accounting*, November, 38–41.

McMahon, R.G.P. and Holmes, S. (1991) 'Small business financial management practices in North America: a literature review', *Journal of Small Business Management*, April, 19–29.

Mitchell, F., Reid, G.C. and Smith, J.A. (2000) *Information System Development in the Small Firm: the use of management accounting*, CIMA Publishing; Chartered Institute of Management Accountants, London; UK.

Mount, J., Zinger J.T. and Forsyth G.R. (1993) 'Organizing for development in the small business', *Long Range Planning* 26(5), 111–20.

National Statistics (2006) *Statistical Press Release* URN 06/402, 20 December 2006.

Peel, M. and Bridge, J. (2000) 'Planning, business objectives and capital budgeting in Japanese, German and domestic SMEs: some evidence from the UK manufacturing sector', *Small Business and Enterprise Development*, 350–65.

Porter, M.E. (1985) *Competitive Advantage: creating and sustaining superior performance*. Free Press: New York.

Raymond, L. and Magnenat-Thalmann, N. (1982) 'Information systems in small business: are they used in managerial decisions?', *American Journal of Small Business* VI(4), 20–6.

Reid, G.C. and Smith, J.A. (2000) 'The impact of contingencies on management accounting system development', *Management Accounting Research* 11, 427–50.

Reid, G.C. and Smith, J.A. (2000a) 'What makes a new business start-up successful?', *Small Business Economics* 14(3), 165–82.

Reid, G.C. and Smith, J.A. (2002) 'The bigger picture', *Financial Management*, January, 24–6.

Sage (2003) website: www.sage.com/solutions/IntAccounting.htm

Shuman, J.C. and Seeger, J.A. (1986) 'The theory and practice of strategic management in smaller rapid growth firms', *American Journal of Small Business* 13(1), 7–18.

Smith, J.A. (1998) 'Strategies for start-ups', *Long Range Planning* 31(6), 857–72.

Smith, J.A. (1999) 'The behaviour and performance of young micro firms: evidence from businesses in Scotland', *Small Business Economics* 13, 185–200.

Thurston (1983) 'Should smaller companies maker formal plans?' *Harvard Business Review* 61(5), 162–88.

Welsh, J.A. and White, J.F. (1981) 'A small business is not a little business', *Harvard Business Review* 59(4), 18–32.

Part B

Planning

4. Management Accounting and the 'New Finance' Function

4:1 Introduction

4:1.1 Background

The finance function and those who work in it now face a constantly changing and challenging future. Amidst all the changes that are taking place there are still basic values and qualities that accountants are expected to deliver to a high standard. These include integrity, independence and objectivity. This chapter explores some of the key issues that are impacting on and influencing what changes are being made. From a finance function perspective, it also explores how the changes are being planned and actioned to create the so-called 'new finance'.

The business world is now characterised by:

(a) *shifts towards the globalisation of businesses and industries;*
(b) *intense international competition;*
(c) *a post-quality environment, where quality is taken as given and additional selling features are demanded by customers;*
(d) *a turbulent commercial and political environment where dramatic changes can unfold unexpectedly in any part of the world and have significant business implications anywhere.*

These characteristics require ever more detailed and sophisticated analysis of financial and non-financial business information (*see* **Chs 48** and **49**) to provide the decision support needs of managers. This information need is being met, in part, by accountants and finance functions reinventing and reconfiguring themselves to:

(a) *be proactive and forward looking and shake off the 'beancounter' and backward-looking image;*

(b) *be responsive to both internal and external finance function customer needs;*

(c) *be open as opposed to closed in their thinking about new ideas;*

(d) *contribute generally to leadership of the whole business;*

(e) *do the basics of financial management excellently;*

(f) *act in a challenging yet constructive way to improve overall business efficiency and effectiveness.*

4:1.2 Delivering Performance

In many businesses these qualities are already becoming well embedded. The impetus for this may come from a variety of sources. First, top management is under pressure to deliver shareholder value improvements (*see* **Ch.48, para.48:6.2**); and second, there is a need for everyone in the business to increase their value adding contribution. There is also pressure from other stakeholders, including customers, suppliers and bankers. While the attainment of these performance criteria requires detailed consideration, there are moves towards simplification and transparency in the way financial management works, in so far as individual employees are concerned. Not surprisingly, there are moves towards consensus building rather than confrontation. In this changed culture and business environment, efforts are also being focused on initiatives for employees to share control and responsibility with senior management and adopt higher levels of self-control. None the less, ultimate control and responsibility resides with top management who cannot abrogate these duties.

4:1.3 Targets and Stepping Stones

With all the changes being demanded by shareholders, customers and other stakeholders, the finance director may turn to performance data generated from external sources, for example, benchmarking data, in order to set targets (*see* **Ch.53**). The question then is to decide which data are appropriate to select for the particular business in question. Subsequently, stepping stones need developing to move the finance function towards the selected targets. These developments may entail, for example, changed finance function processes and headcount reductions as well as the introduction of new technology. In making these changes into the unknown, finance directors may be learning as they go, and so a healthy regard and openness to not knowing can be a distinct advantage.

4:2 Leadership

4:2.1 Changing Role of the Finance Director

In the UK the finance director has traditionally been a key partner of the managing director in developing and tracking organisational strategy and its implementation through budgetary planning and control procedures. These are important leadership roles. They have to be accommodated together with related work that includes acquisitions, divestments, reporting to and dealing with the outside financial community. While the emphasis may be expected to vary from time to time, research has revealed trends towards more time being spent by finance directors on strategic work (*see* **Ch.2**), partnering business colleagues and less time being spent on internal transaction handling, and 'scorekeeping'-related work.

The transformation of finance functions around the world which finance directors have had to plan and lead have largely been aimed at refocusing the function and reducing the resources required. Results of a recent global survey of leading multinationals world-wide suggest the trends as shown in **Fig.4:1**. The features to note particularly are:

(a) *major increase in decision support and analysis work;*
(b) *major decrease in transaction processing work.*

These changes have as a background:

(a) *major headcount reductions in the finance function;*
(b) *major investments in new IT hard and software technology;*
(c) *reprofiling the staffing skills and competencies of the finance function.*

Figure 4:1 **Refocusing the resources of the finance function**
Source: Price Waterhouse (1997)

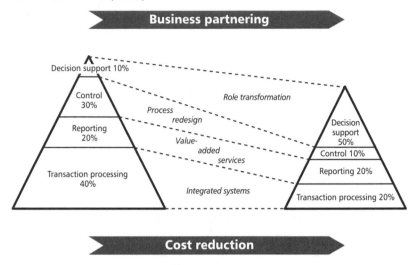

4:2.2 Joint Role with Managing Director

The finance director now has to spend more time working with the managing director in order to meet the demands for increased shareholder value and business performance generally. This has resulted in the need to develop better ways of communicating and expressing, for example, value-based management improvement ideas throughout the business. It still remains a key responsibility of finance directors to ensure overall finance viability of the whole business (*see* **Chs 5, 40** and **48**). Financial markets and managing directors are extremely averse to 'nasty financial surprises' and so basic financial controls for the whole business have to operate to a high standard. There is now public concern and pressure for higher levels of financial propriety and corporate governance.

4:2.3 Business Risk Management

The 'Combined Code' contains principles of good governance and the Code of Best Practice, derived by the Committee on Corporate Governance, from the Committee's Final Report, and from the Cadbury and Greenbury Reports (*see* **Ch.47**). Related to corporate governance developments, it is increasingly the norm for finance directors to be given a leading role in developing approaches for overall and integrated business risk management improvement initiatives. The fact that these business risk management reviews and assessments have been made has to be documented as do the steps that have been taken to manage the risks. Risk management has to be a board responsibility and is not one that should be centred on the financial director alone.

4:2.4 Integrated Top Management

In the new finance approach to financial management, a close working relationship of the financial director with the managing director and senior colleagues responsible for non-finance functional areas is essential. Organisationally this means finance function staff working in multi-discipline teams (*see* **Chs 7, 8, 24, 25, 42 and 53**) and through business processes that may cut across a number of different functions. To achieve this, finance functions probably need to:

(a) *ensure that the right staff are available, and in the right place and at the right time;*

(b) *deliver what non-accounting colleagues want in terms of analysed and interpreted information where they want it and at the right time. In doing so the trust of non-accounting colleagues will be earned;*

(c) *create a culture where the finance function staff are seen as co-leaders, business partners and proactive.*

4:2.5 Finance Function Staff

The new finance function is characterised as having fewer, but more relevant and competent staff, who are focused on providing relevant decision support and analysis, efficient transaction handling facilities and financial controllership. Businesses are moving towards creating 'transaction factories' and using all kinds of sophisticated IT to help to achieve this. Broadly, the finance function staff are allocated between business support and 'transaction factory'-related work. It is important to note that neither set should be regarded in any sense as being of less importance to the business than the other.

While staff in the decision support and analysis areas may be more visible outside the function, and their work may appear more glamorous, what they can do and achieve is built upon the excellence in the transaction handling and stewardship areas of the finance function. If the primary data are for example, corrupted or inaccurate, all subsequent work done on them will be of little value. Research shows that worries about inadequate data feeder and handling systems are a major concern to finance directors. It is therefore important that well-trained and senior staff oversee, develop and control the inputs to, and workings of, the 'transaction factory'. Tasks related to general ledger, sales and purchase ledgers, payroll and treasury have to be handled accurately and efficiently as does financial reporting and taxation conformance work. Inadequacies in these areas will alarm third parties and throw doubt on the general financial management of the whole business.

In the analysis and decision support area accountants can act as well-informed and objective business analysts and consultants to help line managers everywhere, both organisationally and geographically, within the business. To break out of the finance function into this work they may need to achieve some well-publicised examples within the business, where they have really added value to management decision making. These decisions may range from new product development decisions (*see* **Ch.8**), to strategic management (*see* **Ch.2**), to helping to re-engineer business processes (*see* **Ch.32**). In doing this type of work well they will earn the trust and respect of non-finance line managers and create acceptance and requests for 'repeat' work.

4:2.6 Integrity, Objectivity and Independence

Integrity, objectivity and independence are key attributes of the finance function staff. These attributes position the finance function staff to constructively challenge and show business leadership as members of decision-making groups. Care must be taken not to compromise these attributes. Finance directors need to set core values and principles for the function and support their staff. For their part, finance function staff must develop interpersonal skills that enable them to be accepted proactive team players in groups outside the finance function, yet conform to its core values and principles in all their activities. This can be enabled through:

(a) *careful staff selection alongside meaningful job descriptions;*
(b) *developing functional coherence and staff co-operation;*
(c) *carefully constructed and delivered staff development and training programmes.*

4:2.7 Engaging in Delivery of Strategy

New finance is built around finance staff and their skills being used proactively in a forward-looking way. To achieve this they must work towards ensuring that there is a seamless connection between business strategy and operations (*see* **Chs 2 and 4**). This requires a move away from the preoccupation of traditional management accounting with budgetary planning and control, and recognises the equal importance of regular and meaningful tracking of strategy. By definition, this involves being more understanding and analytical about strategic factors in the external environment, including technology, markets and changing global economic climates. Strategic management accounting ideas are very relevant to this work and are developed in **Chapter 2** so will not be detailed here.

4:2.8 Leading Business Transformations

Finance directors and finance function business support staff are frequently called in to join business re-engineering task forces (*see* **Ch.32**). In this work, business processes are analysed and individual activities costed and checked as to their overall value-adding (or waste) characteristics. These analyses and assessments can be very important in guiding top-management decision making and reshaping targets for the business.

Finance function staff engaged in these exercises need to preserve their independence, objectivity and challenging approach in order to facilitate good quality and rational decision making. To some extent they also need to break out of the narrow mould of traditional accounting and adopt more lateral-thinking perspectives. The finance function itself may well be in the vanguard of an overall business re-engineering project and we will examine related issues later in this chapter. In these projects, it is important to remove thinking in terms of rigid functional boundaries and allow cross-fertilisation of ideas.

4:2.9 Marketing the Finance Function

Once the finance director has defined, organised, staffed and equipped a new finance function, then it is important that it and its staff are effectively marketed within the organisation. All other functions and processes must be treated as customers and be offered high levels of service and quality from a competitive base. If this is not done then the finance function will be vulnerable to external market testing, which may result in a decision being taken by top management to outsource the whole or part of the function.

A change in culture, whereby individuals in the finance function market not only the function but also themselves, is one that can be very useful. By following this approach, which includes individuals networking themselves around the business, the needs of different non-finance colleagues for finance function assistance can be better understood and developed.

4:2.10 Learning Organisation

In the new finance environment, it is important for the finance director to create and foster within the function a continuous learning culture. This means much more than attendance at seminars and lectures, although these may be part of the process. It is an open-mindedness to listening and trying to understand how the different people and workings of the business can impact together upon and enhance the work of the function. It involves an element of lateral and cross-functional thinking and is part of a move to get accountants to 'think outside the box' of accounting. The finance director needs to create opportunities where ideas can be brought forward for:

(a) *presentation;*
(b) *discussion;*
(c) *creation of action plans, where ideas which are considered appropriate, are tested and implemented.*

4:3 Finance Function Strategy

4:3.1 Integrating Strategies

It is essential that the strategy of the finance function closely integrates with and supports the overall business strategy. This should be facilitated by the finance director working closely with the top management team, and managing director in particular, in developing the corporate strategy of the business. Traditional longer-term financial targets that might be set for a business could include return on capital employed and residual income. These targets are accounting-based and involve significant areas of judgement. There is evidence that shareholders are looking for cash-based performance measures more and more. One increasingly popular measure is **shareholder value** (*see* **Ch.48, para.48:6.2**) which is defined as:

Shareholder value = corporate value – debt

where:

$$\text{corporate value} = \frac{\text{future free cash flow}}{\text{discounted by the weighted average cost of capital}}$$

In the financial press, league tables list companies in terms of the value they are 'creating' or 'destroying' for their shareholders. The finance director is now required to ensure that:

(a) *people in the business understand what shareholder value is and what its drivers are;*

(b) *people understand the business processes sufficiently well to know where shareholder value is being added to or destroyed.*

Only when these points are addressed and answered, will people be able to factor the idea of creating or destroying shareholder value into their decision making.

This shift in fashion in different performance measures means that the finance function needs to be able to respond by not only having the information to respond in providing excellent traditional financial reporting for statutory purposes, but to concurrently develop a whole new way of thinking, planning and reporting based around an integrated set of value added and other performance measures.

4:3.2 Expanding Performance Measures

Strategic targets are of little value to the business unless they can be clearly understood, prioritised and measured. Work on shareholder value analysis is in addition to that connected with the expanding range of external and forward-looking financial information that the finance function now needs to collect and analyse as part of its measurement systems development. Strategic financial management (*see* **Ch.5**) is a developing area, and methodologies are constantly developing. The aim must be to avoid duplication and confusion among measures. The balanced scorecard (*see* **Ch.49, para.49:2.3**) is an example of an approach where a total business performance picture is developed that embraces the following types of measures:

- financial and non-financial;
- strategic and operational;
- internal and external.

4:3.3 Core Values of the Finance Function

To support and further business strategy by developing and reporting upon different measures, the finance function itself needs to develop a finance function strategy. As part of establishing a finance function strategy, a useful step is to establish a set of core values.

Core values specified might include:

- technical excellence;
- integrity;
- continuous improvement;
- open communication;
- learning culture.

Having specified what the cores values are, it is important that they are clear, supported by the business top management, subscribed to by all in the finance function and that they are actively reinforced and nurtured and used to guide day-to-day activity.

4:3.4 Strategic Plans and Policies

In order to make the finance function activities meaningful and purposeful, plans and policy guidelines need to be developed. These plans and guidelines may by promoted through:

(a) *regular staff conferences and programmed technical courses;*
(b) *preparation of a finance function manual;*
(c) *newsletters;*
(d) *staff appraisal and feedback;*
(e) *staff career planning.*

All plans and guidelines should be realistic and take account of contextual needs and differences. However, a common basis and set of principles must be in place throughout the business to enable reliable, accurate and coherent reporting and consolidation of financial data. Overall, the strategy of the finance function may be expected to be aimed at:

(a) *helping to ensure the overall business mission is achieved;*
(b) *reducing the cost of the finance function;*
(c) *shifting the emphasis from transaction handling, stewardship and conformance reporting towards business partnering work that provides analysis and decision support for managers.*

4:4 Finance Function Organisation

4:4.1 Organisational Form

The organisation of the new finance function should be designed to enable:

(a) *customer-friendly analysis and decision support;*
(b) *efficient and reliable transaction processing, financial control and reporting.*

Increasingly, businesses are co-locating finance staff with non-finance function managers, to provide the latter with analysis and decision support. Efficient and speedy transaction handling is being achieved in some cases through moves to using shared service centres. As already suggested, it is essential that finance function staff who are handling what may be perceived as basic transaction processing are not regarded as less valuable than those working as business analysts. The accuracy and efficiency of the work of what are increasingly being termed 'transaction factories' is vital to the work of everyone who uses these data.

One might expect the general form of the overall business organisation to be heavily influenced by the traditions of the organisation and style adopted by top management. The former is something the organisation has, the latter may come and go. Not surprisingly, therefore, the same organisation can undergo major changes when responding to the styles of new top management. This added dimension of change has to be handled by the finance function through, for example, redesign of accounting responsibility centres, meeting demands for new types of financial information and timetables for its provision.

4:4.2 Organisational Location

The physical location of the finance centre and the finance director can be very important for the operational effectiveness of the business overall. As already noted, it is important that the finance director can meet frequently with the managing director and this generally means co-location. Clearly, the decision on where to locate other finance staff and facilities will depend upon the overall business organisation structure.

Where there are major business units and subsidiaries then senior finance staff will probably need to be allocated to local management teams. Certain aspects of financial management, for example, transaction handling, payroll and treasury may be handled centrally for efficiency reasons. Carefully prepared finance function guidelines will be needed so that local finance activities conform to overall business standards and established principles, yet at the same time ensure that local finance staff are not viewed as finance centre 'spies' and so are not trusted locally by non-finance colleagues.

Given the cultural and other differences that can exist in global businesses, more than written policies and procedures are required to give the finance function as a whole coherence. This is sometimes termed 'socialisation' and involves careful recruitment procedures for staff and regular, structured staff training and development programmes to be designed and operated.

4:4.3 Role of the Finance Centre

Given the pressure for all business activities to add value, the finance function has constantly to re-examine where, what and how it does its work. Some businesses have a reputation for being 'financial control' businesses, meaning top managers, particularly the managing director, place great emphasis on sound, tight financial control. This does not necessarily mean that the headcount in the finance function is large in these businesses compared to other types of businesses. It does mean, perhaps, that greater 'value' is placed on their work.

It has been argued that greater globalisation of businesses can make highly centralised decision making less desirable. Reasons for this include:

(a) *the need for decision makers to be close to where key and relevant information is produced;*
(b) *the need to respond quickly.*

At the same time, it has to be recognised that a well-connected corporate centre can truly have a global overview that will probably not be available to dispersed business units. Whatever arrangements are made, the finance centre has to be fully informed to effectively contribute to decisions which are fundamental and have strategic implications.

Overall, there is a need to build constructive entrepreneurialism amongst business unit managing directors and their management teams. This should be consistent with overall business strategies and management styles set by central top management. The finance function should enable and not stifle this. At the same time, the finance director has a particularly important responsibility in external relations exercises with shareholders and market analysts and needs assurance that all that is presented externally comes from a sound financial base.

It is hard to be specific about how large or small central finance or business unit finance functions should be. With the pressure for all areas of a business to demonstrate how they add value to the business and for business units to be allocated some of the central costs, then there are enormous pressures to make finance functions, wherever they are located, small. Certain work that should usually be undertaken at the centre includes:

- treasury;
- taxation;
- financial reporting;
- corporate audit.

Management accountants may be expected to continue to be closely involved in their traditional activities in the future, for example:

(a) short-term budgetary planning and control (see Chs 9 and 10);
(b) contributing to strategic planning (see Chs 2 and 4);
(c) performance-related work (see Chs 48 and 49);
(d) managing the finance function (see Chs 4 and 5);
(e) developing accounting systems (see planning section and Ch.49).

The emphasis and content of the work of management accountants will vary to focus on areas perceived to be of key concern to businesses. This may happen in a number of areas, for example:

(a) developing 'balanced scorecard'-type performance portfolios that include financial and non-financial measures, short and long-term measures, internal and external measures (see Chs 48 and 49);
(b) developing improved project management and reporting systems (see Chs 5, 8, 11, 19 and 20);
(c) developing improved focus upon and accuracy of customer and product profitability (see Chs 13, 19, 20, 24, 26, 28 and 40).

When looking at what financial management can be centralised and what is best undertaken at business units, a careful balance is needed between the costs involved and the service that is being offered to different managers *(see Ch.5).*

Shared service centres, for example, where all accounting transactions are processed, offer the possibility of offering better service levels across different business units and geographies together with achieving economies of scale. Having reduced the workload of experienced finance function staff through the use of shared services and new technology, then certain experienced and trained finance function staff may focus more on discussing business issues with local management teams, and on helping them to make better decisions. This growth in business partnering enabled through refocusing and reorganising is one of the key features of the new finance function.

4:5 Functional Process Integration

4:5.1 Managing Through Business Processes

With the rise in interest in activity-based costing (ABC) ideas (*see* **Chs 13, 22** and **28**) has come the move to better understanding and management of business processes. Increasingly, businesses are not viewed as being comprised essentially of compartmentalised functions, that vertically rise like 'stove pipes' from the bottom to the top of the organisation. Rather they are seen as horizontal activity streams of business processes, that may cross through traditional functional boundaries in a seamless way.

With the business process management approach (*see* **Ch.32**) the overall business can more conveniently be managed across different products and geographic groupings. Also, overall business processes can be broken down into subprocesses. The aim is to facilitate the efficient and effective operation of processes with defined initiation points, resources and outputs. In this regime, the finance function is required to deliver relevant cost and revenue information to business process managers, coupled with a range of financial and non-financial information including information on the drivers of costs and sources of revenues. In this way value adding and non-value adding activities may be clearly identified, and views developed and decisions made about how to handle and manage them; the basic idea being to remove or reduce non-valuing activities and streamline the business.

With an activity-based management (ABM) approach (*see* **Ch.28**), what might have been seen previously as impenetrable overheads become more transparent, understandable and manageable. This is particularly important in businesses where overheads represent a substantial and possibly rising proportion of overall costs.

4:5.2 Differing Information Needs

The different information needs of process and functional managers have to be considered by the specialist finance decision support staff. These staff have to consider the way that data originating from a common data base is converted into relevant and useful decision-making information for the different user groups and presented in an appropriate way. For example, business process managers may want a particular focus on product costs, geographic-related costs and costs related to new product developments measured against some project time scales. On the other hand, functional managers may focus more on operational costs and human resource management issues related to the regular budgetary planning and control periods. This is an area of work where finance specialists can bring their 'coaching' skills into action and work with the managers as the latter get involved more in understanding and defining their own information needs.

Finance function staff, with their overview of the business are well placed to act as central information logistics managers. To operate in this role effectively, they need to have a very clear grasp of the operation and rationale of business processes and functions and the key business competencies.

4:5.3 Business Process Re-engineering

Business process re-engineering (BPR) (*see* **Ch.32**) has become popular in recent years. In theory it offers a blueprint for radical changes to be made in the way businesses operate. Generally teams from different functions and disciplines are drawn together to undertake the task of 'mapping out' the business processes. This work can be very time consuming and detailed. To be successful, BPR projects need to be supported by top management, preferably with the clear support of the managing director.

The support of top management is needed to enable not only the analysis for a BPR to be undertaken, but also the creation and execution of any subsequent plans for redesigning the business, or parts of the business. Because the results of BPR often result in radical changes, careful consideration needs to be given to:

- people issues;
- systems issues;
- overall organisational issues.

Insofar as systems are concerned, careful consideration needs to be given to internal and external integration of functional systems, and the ways in which legacy systems should be handled. This is particularly important in the finance areas where systems may have been acquired historically, on an *ad hoc* basis, to handle separately, for example, the general ledger, payroll, fixed assets, and so on. The work involved in conversion and rationalisation of systems may involve considerable direct and indirect costs, all of which need to be planned and fully costed.

4:5.4 Documenting Processes

From a clear understanding of overall business strategy, financial function strategy and operations, a 'map' can be prepared which defines the processes by which the finance function delivers its work to different internal and external customers. The process mapping of the finance function should be designed to reveal:

(a) *value adding and non-value adding activities;*
(b) *duplications and gaps in how activities are organised to deliver given outputs;*
(c) *a framework against which comparisons with benchmarking partners could be made.*

Examples of finance processes to be examined include fixed asset management, purchasing, sales and payroll. Moreover, the contribution made to wider business processes, for example, new product developments (*see* **Ch.8**) should also be mapped.

Through the better understanding of what the finance function does and how it goes about its work, the following benefits can be achieved:

(a) *rationalisation of information systems;*
(b) *compatibility of systems;*
(c) *steps to overcome legacy system problems;*
(d) *moves towards overall business cost and operational effectiveness and efficiency.*

4:5.5 IT: Developments and Data Requirements

A number of new off-the-shelf IT systems abound to meet the demands of different user groups for financial management information (*see* **Ch.3, para.3:4.2.3**). Care must be taken in selecting these to ensure:

(a) *they will actually meet the needs of users;*
(b) *users are capable of using the outputs and that the interfaces are 'user friendly'.*

An important consideration is that the data feeder systems are in place, or are concurrently planned to be in place, to meet the new system requirements. Meeting these requirements needs the active co-operation of people in other functions. If that co-operation is not achieved, then the new systems may well be useless or perform well under specification. Therefore, finance systems developments should be fully discussed at the start with relevant colleagues in non-finance areas. There will probably need to be a shared agenda for progressing the work.

4:5.6 Embedding the Finance Function

Considerable reference is made by finance professionals to 'embedding the finance function'. In general this means ensuring that what the finance function does, can do and how it goes about its work is well understood around the business. In this way the co-operation of non-accounting colleagues can be obtained by demonstrating that the finance function is proactive, and by showing a willingness to get involved with them in a positive way.

By gaining general acceptance of the finance function and its staff throughout the business, the development of new systems and solving day-to-day operational problems that arise can be facilitated. General communication barriers can be broken down, and the increased exchange of informal information can supplement that from formal sources and improve the quality of decision making.

4:5.7 Supporting Concurrent Engineering

Concurrent engineering is the term used to describe the organised coming together, at the outset, of teams drawn from relevant people from different functions who have a common purpose in achieving a new initiative (*see* **Chs 7, 8, 19, 24, 25, 34, 40** and **42**). The functions involved might include:

- design;
- production engineering;
- manufacturing;
- sales and marketing;
- finance.

These teams may have as their purpose, for example, new business development or new product development. The aim is to break down functional barriers and ensure a 'through the business' process approach to managing the particular initiative in hand. By adopting this approach it is recognised that the emphasis required from people in the different functions may vary over the life of the initiative. It essentially avoids the barriers created between functions and the consequent communication and time problems that arise in the alternative, sequential approach. The sequential approach can result in tasks taking much longer to complete than planned and increase the chance of misunderstandings between different functions.

Concurrent engineering can reduce new product development costs and times-to-market significantly, compared with a sequential approach. With a sequential approach expensive mistakes can be locked in to a project at the design stage and only manifest themselves in manufacturing when the problems can be very expensive to put right or may even be intractable.

The finance function can provide valuable inputs at all stages of development: design through to product support. This change, with the new finance approach, represents a major shift from the traditional management accounting emphasis, which existed at the manufacturing stage of the product development cycle.

4:6 Benchmarking the Finance Function
(*See* Ch.53.)

4:6.1 Leading Change

In order to identify what changes may be necessary, many businesses are turning to benchmarking their activities and processes against other, external businesses. In this way they seek to compare performance and the way others go about achieving it. However, identifying what may be possible targets to aim for is only part of the process of achieving business transformations. Basic questions remaining include:

(a) *Which targets to choose?*
(b) *How to prioritise?*
(c) *What are the stepping stones to be from where the business is now?*

The search for 'best practice' and modelling a business to match what may be termed 'world-class' standard has become a growth industry in itself. As an alternative to looking to external standards, some large and already successful businesses are now internally benchmarking sub-business units against one another. They then set targets for improvement for those sub-business units that lag in performance behind the best. This is done with the view that it is better to raise the general standards across all their business rather than try to match what may be some external and abstract targets drawn from external businesses where there may be enormous variability in contingent factors.

4:6.2 Benchmarking Collaborations

It is not unusual for subprocesses of particular business functions to be benchmarked externally to subprocesses in entirely different functions in partnering businesses. In respect of benchmarking the finance function, collaboration does exist, for example, between the Hackett Group and the Institute of Chartered Accountants in England and Wales (ICAEW) and the American Institute of Certified Public Accountants (AICPA). This group argues that benchmarking the finance function:

(a) *creates a definite baseline against which improvements can be measured;*

(b) *enables the size of the gap between current and external performance to be established;*

(c) *creates a driver for the formulation of improvement goals;*

(d) *enables the targeting of processes based on priorities related to savings and increasing value added;*

(e) *facilitates creation of objective and measurable cost, productivity and service levels to give to customers of finance function services;*

(f) *is consistent with total quality management ideals of benchmarking with the best.*

4:6.3 Comparability of Benchmarking Data

In order to be useful, the data collected for benchmarking must be obtained on a comparable basis and validated carefully. Therefore sets of data must be categorised and codified. The Hackett–ICAEW–AICPA finance best practice benchmark group categorises processes as follows.

Transaction processes including:

- accounts payable;

- fixed assets;

- customer billing;

- external reporting;

- cost accounting;

- tax accounting;

- payroll.

Control and risk management processes including:

- budgeting;
- business performance reporting;
- cash management;
- treasury management;
- internal audit.

Decision support processing including:

- business performance analysis;
- new business/pricing analysis;
- cost analysis;
- strategic planning support;
- finance function management.

4:6.4 Output from Benchmarking

The Hackett–ICAEW–AICPA finance function benchmark group believes that by engaging in it finance directors can obtain the following comparative data:

(a) *finance costs as a percentage of revenue;*
(b) *percentage of cost and staff time for each of the identified processes;*
(c) *the mix of staff as between management, professional and clerical;*
(d) *labour rates for different types of staff;*
(e) *costs per transaction and productivity measures for certain processes;*
(f) *measures for the utilisation of information technology.*

4:6.5 Setting a Course for Change

By engaging in a benchmarking study, a finance director is not automatically going to have the 'right' targets and a route map for change. What will be made available is an analysed set of information and access to a network of like minded people with whom a useful dialogue and idea exchanges can be developed.

4:7 The Re-engineered New Finance Function

4:7.1 Aims of the New Finance Function

The new finance approach is aimed at transforming the traditional finance function from one which is mainly backward looking and has a transaction processing emphasis towards one that is forward looking and is an active business partner. Some of the main accounting trends that are driving the changes are summarised in **Fig.4:2**.

Figure 4:2 **Accounting trends**
Source: adapted from trends prepared by the AICPA and modified by ICAEW research feedback

---

- The emergence of truly global capital and investment markets, coupled with innovative financial schemes and business practices.

- An acute and growing demand on the finance function to supply strategic decision support information as a crucial competitive weapon.

- Rapid acceptance of desktop and network information technology as both the enabler and driver of the change.

- Fundamental and massive changes in how transaction processing, record keeping and basic financial reporting are accomplished.

- The greatly enhanced and expanding role of finance in strategic development and overall leadership within business.

- Dramatic shifts in organisation and human behaviour systems towards flat management structures with informed thinking and empowered workers.

The AICPA envisage the new finance as:

(a) *providing better information, cheaper;*
(b) *providing insight, not merely citing facts;*
(c) *planning the future, not concentrating on the past;*
(d) *being change agents;*
(e) *acting globally;*
(f) *generating new business;*
(g) *reducing costs;*
(h) *providing better decision support.*

The AICPA see a benchmarking study of the type outlined in the previous section:

(a) *identifying high-leverage change opportunities;*
(b) *establishing clear priorities;*
(c) *building widespread support in the business for change.*

Making any changes to the existing finance function requires:

(a) *a sound IT platform, capable of efficiently and effectively handling the different user group requirements. Efficiency may well be improved by moving to a 'one touch' data system. In this type of system data is only handled once on entry into what has been specifically designed as an integrated, overall IT business system;*
(b) *the creation of a 'toolbox' of relevant accounting and finance techniques and practices from which selections can be made as appropriate to meet the demands of different business processes;*
(c) *a reskilled finance function workforce, trained and empowered to work in the new finance environment.*

4:7.2 Deploying New Techniques and Practices

In this Handbook a range of new accounting techniques and practices are referred to, including:

- activity-based costing (*see* **Ch.22**);
- strategic management accounting (*see* **Ch.2 and Ch.3**);
- quality costing (*see* **Ch.18**);
- target costing (*see* **Ch.24**).

The development of so called new accounting techniques and practices gained momentum in the 1980s, largely as a response to claims about the inadequacies and irrelevance of existing ones which were then widely used. This criticism was mainly directed at manufacturing businesses that were starting to use advanced manufacturing techniques and practices which were aimed at improving speed, flexibility and quality.

There is evidence from research that accounting changes have frequently lagged behind advances in other functional areas. For example, in manufacturing, total quality management may be introduced without quality costing.

In this case, relevant financial management information might not be made available to support decision makers. More generally, if business processes are being examined in the business with a view to redesigning, the absence of relevant activity-based costing information relating to both activities and drivers, might seriously undermine the whole project. Through the concurrent engineering approach, accountants are increasingly being proactively involved at the inception of change by being key players in change management teams.

In terms of the deployment of individual accounting techniques and practices, it should not be forgotten that they require integration into wider financial and general management systems. Care needs to be taken to ensure that adequate feeder systems are in place, implying concurrent systems developments in all relevant functions, and that any legacy system problems are properly handled. All this requires that accountants who are involved with the strategic development of systems and their implementation and operation should be selected on the basis of their possessing the relevant skills and competencies. The effort put into developing a new finance approach will largely be wasted if managers as its customers, users and suppliers do not clearly understand, use and want what it does.

4:7.3 Key Skills and Competencies

With the shift in emphasis in finance functions towards analysis and decision support, finance directors are carefully considering the key skills and competencies that they want from the people they employ in their functions. Studies suggest that the profile of what are increasingly being termed 'business analysts' rather than accountants include:

(a) *a positive attitude to hard work;*
(b) *excellent interpersonal skills;*
(c) *leadership capabilities and a proactive approach;*
(d) *good at listening and understanding what is being said;*
(e) *good oral and written communication skills;*
(f) *good IT skills.*

These are in addition to excellent financial management skills, in terms of individual accounting techniques and practices and the incorporation of them into well-designed systems. To achieve this, individuals must have a good grasp of the workings of the overall business.

Where do these icons come from in practice? To some extent this may be influenced by the history of the business. Those businesses which have historically been innovative in process and administration, including the finance area, may well have a track record in recruiting individuals with already relevant profiles and have been training and developing people in this way already. Other businesses have the more difficult task of recruiting new people. In this case there are issues such as culture change to overcome and assimilation with existing staff, among whom the new staff may have to act as catalysts for change.

Creating a learning organisation approach where new ideas and insights can be cross-fertilised is essential. This will happen to some extent informally, but the finance director also needs to plan, energise and sustain the process by means of workshops and staff seminars where both internal and external speakers provide inputs.

4:7.4 Outsourcing
(*See* Ch.38.)

The 'new finance' function may have to handle outsourcing issues both:

(a) *where non-finance activities are outsourced by the business; and*
(b) *where activities of the finance function itself, to a greater or lesser extent, are outsourced. These may include, for example, internal audit and transaction processing.*

Generally great care is needed to define the nature and working of the arrangement. The details of the making of these arrangement are not simple and need the time and close ongoing attention of senior staff if they are to work well. Importantly, senior finance staff should be involved in providing what is essentially 'make-or-buy' finance information to aid both decisions to outsource and the terms of related deals that are made. Detailed consideration of outsourcing issues is outside the scope of this chapter.

4:8 Useful Contacts/References

Hackett–ICAEW–AICPA Finance Function Benchmarking Group, ICAEW Faculty of Finance and Management, PO Box 433, Chartered Accountants' Hall, Moorgate Place, London EC2P 2BJ.

Management Accounting Guideline, No. 43 (1997) *Redesigning the finance function.* Ontario, Canada: Society of Management Accountants of Canada.

Price Waterhouse (1997) *CFO: Architect of the corporation's future.* New York: Wiley.

The Committee on the Financial Aspects of Corporate Governance, *The Financial Aspects of Corporate Governance* (The Cadbury Report), December 1992.

The Study Group on Directors' Remuneration, *Directors' Remuneration: Report of a Study Group Chaired by Sir Richard Greenbury*, (The Greenbury Report), July 1995.

Acknowledgements

Bob Sweeting would like to acknowledge the collaboration of John Morrow and John Fisher of the AICPA and financial support of the ICAEW Research Board in his work on new finance developments.

5. Strategic Financial Management

5:1 Terminology

5:1.1 Strategic

For the purposes of this chapter, the words 'strategy' and 'strategic' relate to decisions as to *what* to do: the capital structure to establish, the business(es) to be in, the products to offer, the markets to serve, the facilities to use, etc. Two subsets are worthy of identification:

1. *business strategy, which is concerned with individual dimensions of strategy (e.g. the degree of production flexibility, the breadth of the product range) and the blending thereof to maximum effect (e.g. a very flexible production process coupled with a wide product range);*
2. *corporate strategy, in which businesses are combined, such that the whole is worth more than the sum of the parts (e.g. as a consequence of economies of scale in shared services, or synergies arising from the transfer of knowledge) and an appropriate capital structure determined.*

The contrast is with the words 'tactics' and 'tactical', which relate to decisions as to *how* to do what is to be done: how high a price to charge, how long a lead time to quote, how much stock to carry, etc. As the rate of change in the business environment increases, strategic issues surface more frequently, and need to be dealt with more rapidly, than ever before.

5:1.2 Financial Management

The expression 'financial management' is used to describe the proactive forward-looking, outward-looking and dynamic subset of accountancy. It embraces subjective judgements about an uncertain future, and is capable of assessing values.

The contrast is with the passive, backward-looking, inward-looking and static subset known as 'accounting', which sets out to identify the objectively verifiable truth about a certain past, and is rooted in costs.

The skills required for the financial management task are quite different from those required for accounting, to the point that individuals tend to be good at, and enjoy, one or the other but not both.

5:1.3 Strategic Financial Management

The more strategic and proactive accountants become, the more they see that the traditional accounting model and its derivatives are worse than useless as a basis for control, that is, that they are potentially misleading. The sheer power of budgets which focus on the current year's profits/earnings per share/return on assets impedes the formulation of a sound strategy and damages the long-term financial health of the enterprise.

A key aspect of the problem is the accounting model's understandable inability to embrace the concept of intangible assets. With outlays on research and development, marketing, training and information being treated as costs to be charged against current revenue, performance measurement and reward systems based on accounting numbers create a significant and adverse bias. In particular, they discourage the very investments which are crucial to survival in a rapidly changing environment, namely those which enhance the three 'a's – awareness, anticipation and adaptation – which, in turn, determine the enterprise's responsiveness to changing needs, its pace of innovation and its reputation as a supplier and an employer.

The expression 'strategic financial management' refers to an approach, which, being focused on long-term financial health, offers an antidote to this short termism. Given that the maximisation of short-run accounting profits is inappropriate, the best starting point is with the question of what constitutes an appropriate financial objective.

5:2 Clarifying the Objective

5:2.1 The Evolution of Enterprise

For any enterprise to survive in the long term, there are some obvious imperatives. It must acquire and develop resources, and deploy them with a view to identifying needs, to satisfying those needs and to offering the prospect of an adequate return. The loop is completed by what amounts to the pivot of the market economy: the fact that those enterprises which can offer the prospect of an adequate return will be able to attract the funds necessary to acquire and develop resources, while those which cannot will not – and may be forced to give up some or all of the funds which they have.

An adequate return is made when the value of outputs exceeds the costs of all inputs. Inputs include capital, the cost of which is a function of prevailing interest rates. In the distributable profit-seeking sector of the economy, value manifests itself in the form of cash receipts from customers. Elsewhere (including the public sector) this is not the case, and an alternative (e.g. opportunity cost or value judgement) is substituted.

Either way, there is a need to heed the external discipline of the market, as regards the prospective rate of return required to justify the employment of funds, and to translate it into an internal discipline as regards their deployment. Reflecting this, strategic financial management comprises two distinct, but interrelated, aspects.

5:2.2 The Treasury Aspect

The external aspect is normally referred to as the *treasury* function, and is located at the centre of an enterprise (e.g. the parent company of a group). It is concerned with the enterprise's relationships with the three financing stakeholders: lenders, taxers and shareholders. The Cadbury Committee (*see* **Ch.4, para.4:2.3**) recommended that companies should include, in their financial reports, a narrative report, called the Operating and Financial Review (OFR). The financial role of the review was, amongst others, to explain the capital structure of the business and its treasury policy (*see also* **Ch.47, para.47:2**).

Echoing the three 'a's mentioned above, the key tasks at the strategic level can be summed up as follows:

1. *awareness – identification of the potential sources of funds, from debt through various hybrids to equity;*
2. *anticipation – quantification of the reward expectations of the various providers of funds, in the form of interest, tax and dividends;*

3. *adaptation – employment of the appropriate amount of funds, in proportions designed to minimise the aggregate reward expectation (otherwise known as the cost of capital).*

5:2.3 The Financial Control Aspect

The internal aspect is normally referred to as the *financial control* function (*see* **Ch.43**), and is usually devolved, for example, to business units within a group. It is concerned with the enterprise's relationships with the other contractual stakeholders: customers, suppliers and employees. Reflecting the three a's again, the key tasks at the strategic level are:

1. *awareness – identification of opportunities to invest (or, in some cases, to disinvest);*
2. *anticipation – quantification of the likely outcomes should the various opportunities be pursued;*
3. *adaptation – deployment of funds to those opportunities which offer the prospect of an adequate return, that is, in excess of the cost of capital.*

5:2.4 Translating the Discipline

As portrayed in **Fig.5:1**, the links between the two aspects are twofold:

1. *the treasurers quantify the rate of return necessary to warrant the employment of funds, which the financial controllers then use as the criterion for their deployment, that is, by way of decisions as regards investment;*
2. *the financial controllers quantify the projected cash flows/values, which prompt the treasurers to modify the amount and mix of funds employed, that is, by way of decisions as regards the raising and/or distribution of funds.*

Harmony is ensured by promulgation of the financial objective of the business as being the maximisation of net present value. In the distributable profit-seeking subset of the private sector, for example, it is the projected cash flows from the company to its shareholders which are discounted. The treasurers major on minimising the cost of capital, the financial controllers major on identifying investment opportunities which show a return in excess thereof.

We need to recognise, however, that decision making is not the only element of control.

Figure 5:1 **Two aspects of financial management**

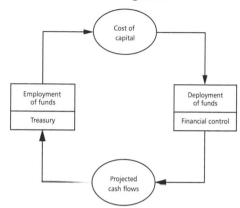

5:3 Control in a Learning Organisation

(*see* Ch.3, para.3:5)

5:3.1 The Three As

The three 'a's mentioned earlier are relevant to control, because they prompt thoughts as to the corresponding information requirements.

1. *Awareness calls for monitoring information, reporting on what is happening (or, more precisely, what has just happened). The accounting model provides inward-looking monitoring information but, increasingly, managers are paying more attention to external information. It is especially important to be alert to developments in technology and changes in customer needs.*
2. *Anticipation calls for (inevitably judgmental) forecasts, of which there are two distinct subsets:*
    (a) *relationship forecasts, for example, the effect of alternative levels of investment in flexible manufacturing equipment on lead times, on the range of products which could be offered and on variable costs. These assessments would then need to be interpreted in terms of the consequential volumes, contributions and ultimately on cash flow;*
    (b) *outcome forecasts, for example, the cash-flow consequences of a decision to invest in a particular degree of flexibility.*

3. *Adaptation calls for decision support information, for example, the distillation of the cash flows associated with the alternative levels of investment in flexibility, into a net present value, and the identification of the one which meets the organisation's chosen objective, that is, which maximises the net present value of the business.*

5:3.2 A Coherent Structure

Those various kinds of information can be linked, as in **Fig.5:2**, so as to provide a coherent structure of control (*see* **Chs 44** and **46**). Decisions are based on forecast relationships, and the specific forecast outcomes are logged, so as to provide a basis for interpreting what happens thereafter. Comparing what is happening with what was forecast to happen when a decision was made provides accountability and the opportunity to learn lessons which will improve the forecasting ability of the organisation.

Figure 5:2 **Elements of control**

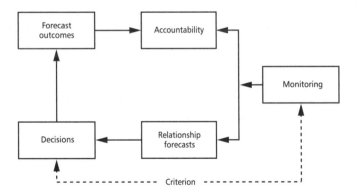

It is important to appreciate the fact that progress monitoring is not a matter of repeated performance measurement: witness how many companies have shown increasing earnings per share right up to the year which ended a few weeks before they became insolvent. To provide a comprehensive indication of progress, it is necessary to combine a measurement of performance with an assessment of the change in potential.

For the structure to be coherent, it is also necessary for the criterion used for monitoring to be the same as that used for decision making. It would be quite disorientating, for example, to make strategic decisions on a financial management basis (i.e. net present value) and then purport to monitor progress on an accounting basis (i.e. profits) because the easiest way to improve profits is to slow down the pace of implementing strategic investment decisions. Before addressing that aspect, however, it is necessary to be clear as to the various inputs to any net present-value assessment.

5:4 Net Present Value

5:4.1 The Entity Focus

It is now widely recognised that a sharp focus on the interests of those people who happen to be shareholders at a point in time (e.g. by setting out to maximise the small lot share price) is not in the long-term interests of the shareholders in aggregate (current loyal ones and new ones), let alone those of other stakeholders. As a consequence of this recognition, we are seeing moves towards a more inclusive approach.

In this context, it is important to note that, whereas published accounts focus on the equity, management accounts have always focused on the entity, and nowhere is this difference more pronounced than in respect of cash flow (*see* **Ch.10**). Strategic financial management adopts the management accountancy viewpoint, and majors on the cash-flow equation:

(a) *as far as the treasurers are concerned, cash generation is seen as the balance of payments between the enterprise and its financing stakeholders, that is, the excess of distributions (interest, tax and dividends) over new financing (increased borrowings and/or share issues) [cf. FRS1: Cash Flow Statements; IAS7: Cash Flow Statements];*

(b) *as far as the financial controllers are concerned, the same cash generation is seen as the balance of payments between the businesses and the other stakeholders, that is, the excess of receipts from customers over payments to suppliers and employees (adjusted, where applicable, for the pass-the-parcel levy known as value added tax).*

The equation springs from the fact that the cash generations of the businesses add up to the cash generation of the enterprise. The financial controllers seek to maximise the net present value of their business to the entity (*see* **Ch.11, para.11:1.3.5**) and, in the distributable profit-seeking sector, the treasurers seek to maximise the proportion of that value which is attributable to the shareholders. As portrayed in **Fig.5:3**, actual cash flows can be measured, up to the minute and unequivocally, and therefore provide a 'real-time' foundation for financial management.

Figure 5:3 **The cash-flow cascade**

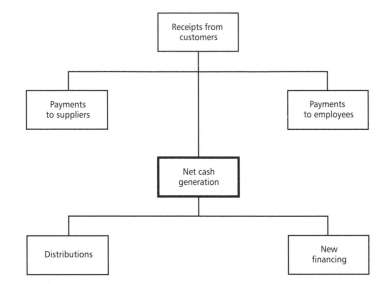

Contrast this with accounting statements which are always in arrears, and subject to equivocation in such areas as the dividing line between capital and revenue, the appropriate rate of depreciation and the extent of provisions for slow-moving stocks and doubtful debtors.

5:4.2 Progress Monitoring

As noted earlier, however, measuring performance is only a part of the progress monitoring task. In addition, there is a need to assess the change in potential. In other words, the profit attributable to a given period comprises the cash generation for the period plus the expansion (or minus the contraction) during the period. Whereas accounting assesses the change in potential by reference to the costs of unconsumed tangible assets, however, strategic financial management assesses it by reference to what is to be maximised, that is, net present value.

Specifically, at any point in time, the net present value of a project (or strategy, or business) can be compared with a benchmark which amounts to the opening net present value, uplifted by the cost of capital but reduced by the cash generation (or increased by the cash absorption) in the interim. If the new value exceeds the benchmark, there is a perceived net strengthening; a shortfall indicates a perceived weakening.

5:4.3 The Cost of Capital
(*See* Ch.11, Para.11:2.4.3.2.)

Strategic decisions are almost invariably trade-offs between time frames – typically an investment now for a return in the future. The rate at which society trades off between time frames is indicated by prevailing interest rates (summed up in the familiar 'yield curve'). From an economic point of view, it is the same for all entities, irrespective of whether they are public or private, and irrespective of their capital structure. Capital structure cannot affect the value of an enterprise to its financing stakeholders in aggregate. It can and does, however, affect the attribution of that value as between them.

This is mainly a consequence of the distortion brought about by taxation [*cf. FRS9: Deferred Tax; SSAP5: Accounting for Value Added Tax; IAS12: Income Taxes*], the two main problems being as follows.

1. *The tax authorities are entitled to a share of the value created by a company, even though they have not provided any of the capital which was employed specifically in earning it. Hence the return expected by shareholders has to be 'grossed up'.*
2. *The tax is calculated as a percentage of profit, rather than of cash generation. Relief for outlays treated as revenue costs is given in the year in which they are incurred but for those classified as capital expenditure it is spread over an indefinite period of time, while investments in current assets (notably stocks and debtors) will not be relieved at all. Consequently, though corporation tax might take around 30% of profits, it often represents more than 50% of the cash generation of a successful business.*

In mitigation, it should be noted that interest payable is an allowable deduction, so – other things being equal – the more highly geared a company is, the less tax it pays. In the treasurers' quest to maximise the present value of projected cash flows to shareholders derived from a given present value of the entity, therefore, capital structure is extremely important.

The situation is complicated by frequent intervention by the Government, in terms of the rules and rates of tax on profits and dividends, and the reliefs for particular kinds of expenditure, but the underlying situation does not change. Corporation tax is likely to continue to take at least as high a proportion of a successful company's cash generation as that taken by dividends, which means that such businesses are worth as much to the Inland Revenue as they are to their shareholders.

Profit figures, tax computations, dividend payments and tax payments are all characterised by single point precision. Cash-flow forecasts, however, are characterised by uncertainty, which induces risk. The two concepts need to be understood and recognised if they are to be managed.

5:4.4 Uncertainty and Risk Aversion

In a financial management context, *uncertainty* is seen as arising from the range of possible outcomes, for example, where the present value of the benefits of a particular endeavour are assessed as £10m +/− £2m (i.e. anything between £8m and £12m). Such uncertainty will vary from strategy to strategy, and according to time frame, for example, the further out the cash flows are, the more uncertain they are likely to be.

Risk arises from the commitment of resources to an endeavour, the outcome of which is uncertain, for example, if the investment required to produce the benefits mentioned in the previous paragraph amounts to £9m, then the net present value of the endeavour will be put at anything from minus £1m to plus £3m.

Whether the managers of the enterprise in question would wish to pursue this particular opportunity depends on their *aversion* to risk. This varies from one management team to another, and from time to time. It is partly a matter of psychology, but is also affected by such things as capital structure and the uncertainty associated with ongoing cash flows. If the company were close to its borrowing limits, and its forecast cash flows were subject to considerable uncertainty, for example, the managers might classify the opportunity as too risky, that is, their fear of losing up to £1m would outweigh their enthusiasm for the prospect of making up to £3m.

There are various ways of expressing risk aversion. In most cases, the most practical is to relate the extent to which the managers' 'aim off' to the margin of error in the projected cash flows, for example, 'one in four', meaning that they would reduce a statistically expected cash flow by one percentage point for every four percentage points in the margin of error. On that basis, the present value of the benefits mentioned above would be taken as £10m minus 20%/4, that is, £9.5m, and the net present value, therefore, would be put at £0.5m.

Where it is a stream of cash flows which is being evaluated, different margins of error, different degrees of risk aversion and different costs of capital (as portrayed in the yield curve) can be applied to the different periods within the forecast. This is in sharp contrast with the academic theory which rolls all three together, and claims to be able to deduce one 'risk-adjusted' rate, to apply to all future periods, from an analysis of past fluctuations in small lot share prices.

Separating these three components, as portrayed in **Fig.5:4**, makes it easier to manage them, for example, it may be possible to phase the investment (at a cost) such that the decision to go ahead with some parts is delayed until the forecasts are considered more robust.

Figure 5:4 **Uncertainty and risk aversion**

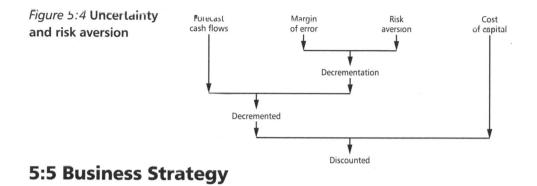

5:5 Business Strategy

5:5.1 Investment Decisions

The key inputs to investment decisions within business units are forecast relationships. In most enterprises, they can be grouped under three main headings:

1. *The relationship between price and volume, otherwise known as the elasticity of demand. At a point in time, this is unalterable, being a function of customers' perceptions of relative quality, etc. In the medium term, however, it can be improved, by what amount to volume inducing outlays, of which advertising is a good example – getting more people to try the current product. In the longer term, it can be improved further by regenerative outlays, such as investments in more flexible production processes which reduce lead times and/or widen the product range.*

2. *The relationship between volume and cost. Again, at a point in time, the incremental outlay associated with a given increment of volume throughput is unalterable, being a function of the degree of mechanisation, the adaptability of employees, etc. In the medium term, however, it can be improved by what amount to volume anticipative outlays such as mechanisation and training. In the long term, it can be improved further by other regenerative outlays such as process development.*

3. *The extent of customer loyalty, that is, the likelihood that current sales will open the door to future sales – thanks both to existing customers 'coming back for more' and new customers being attracted by a good reputation. Again, at a point in time, this tendency is unalterable. In the medium term, however, it can be improved by what amount to volume sustaining outlays, such as improvements in quality, including sales force efforts to identify customers' particular needs. In the long term, it can be improved further by yet other regenerative outlays aimed at enhancing the distinctiveness of what is offered, for example, through superior design (see **Ch.42**).*

Decision support in this area amounts to identifying the feasible alternatives (e.g. different levels of investment in flexible production, or advertising), quantifying their respective impacts on the cash flows of the business/enterprise and highlighting the one which shows the greatest enhancement of net present value.

5:5.2 Don't Think Straight!

Figure 5:5 **Present values**

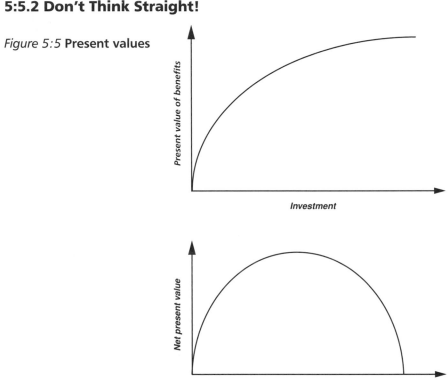

On a practical note, it is important to avoid thinking along straight lines, because most investments will be characterised by diminishing returns: a smaller incremental benefit for each successive incremental outlay. As portrayed in **Fig.5:5**, the net present value will rise up to a point, and then fall back.

Those who remember their calculus will see this as the point at which the gradient of the curve is zero – but use of a 'black-box' approach is unlikely to go down well with colleagues not familiar with the discipline!

Meanwhile, it is impossible to overstate the importance of the interaction between various decisions. Investing in advertising, only for the customers to find that the product is not as good as the competition, is unlikely to show positive net present value.

Improving the quality of the product but not being prepared to support it in terms of marketing is also likely to fail. But improving the product and getting customers to try it, confident that they will like it and come back for more – that is the most likely way to enhance the value of the business. This reflects a significant change in management generally, namely away from the reductionist model based on analysis to a holistic model based on synthesis.

5:5.3 Three Components

Cash-flow forecasts for any business comprise three components:

1. *expectations, that is, those consequent upon past decisions;*
2. *hope, that is, those consequent upon current decisions with specifically identified benefits – usually the medium-term ones mentioned above;*
3. *faith, that is, those made in the belief that they will lead to future decisions with specifically identified benefits but which are, at the present time, vague, for example, investments in research and development.*

Most managers spend most of their time on the operational task of converting expectations into results – outcomes which are susceptible to measurement. It seems to require a conscious and concentrated effort to pay sufficient attention to the tactical task of converting hope into expectations, and the strategic task of converting faith into hope – neither of which outcomes are susceptible to measurement, but both of which need to be quantified.

Contrast the richness of the above language with the poverty of the accounting classification of outlays – material, labour and overheads. They are purely input classifications, whereas financial management is also concerned with forecast outcomes.

5:5.4 Forecast Outcome

The impact of the various decisions can be summarised in a form which emphasises the foundation stones of strategic financial management, namely cash flow and the cost of capital.

For the sake of simplicity, let us assume that:

(a) *a particular business is expected (net of an appropriate decrementation for uncertainty) to generate cash, starting at £1m in year 1 and increasing at 4% per annum constant thereafter (i.e. £1.040m in year 2, £1.082m in year 3, etc.);*

(b) *the cost of capital is also constant at 9.2% per annum – 109.2% being 104.0% plus 5%, such a stream of cash would have a value at the end of year 1 of £1m/5%, that is, £20m. The value at the beginning of year 1 would, of course, be 100/104 of that, that is, £19.231m.*

In a format which is characteristic of, and central to, strategic financial management, these numbers can be summarised as in **Table 5:1**.

Table 5:1 **Cash flow/cost of capital**

	£000
Opening net present value	19,231
Cost of capital 9.2% thereof	1,769
(Cash generation)	(1,000)
Closing net present value	20,000

There are various ways of looking at this. Some, for example, will see the cost of capital of £1.769m as a quantification of the wealth which must be created over the year, in order to warrant the valuation of £19.231m, and the combination of cash flow (£1m) and the increase in net present value (£0.769m) as how it is believed it will be achieved.

Others – especially those preparing their budgets in this format – will see the opening net present value (£19.231m) as being the discounted aggregate of the closing value and the cash flow (i.e. £21m/1.092). Either way, this layout provides a language in which finance can be pictured dynamically, that is, in a way which articulates the key numbers over time.

Some financial managers find it useful (in terms of 'attention directing') to compare the financial management numbers with the corresponding accounting numbers. In the case of our continuing example, for instance, the cash flow of £1m might be interpreted as a profit of £1.500m minus an expansion of £0.500m, to a closing position of £12.500m. In that case, the reconciliation would appear as in **Table 5:2**.

This layout highlights the different approaches to assessing the change in potential: accounting sees the expansion in terms of the increase in the unconsumed cost of tangible assets, whereas strategic financial management sees it as the increase in net present value.

It also draws attention to the intangibles, provides a framework for the quantification of their values, and prompts thoughts about nurturing them. Once upon a time (and still evidenced today in articles of association, borrowing covenants and stock market rules) it was assumed that the value of a business, its financial health, its capacity to borrow and acquire, etc, were a function of the cost of its tangible assets. In a rapidly changing environment, however, tangible assets can be strategic liabilities (the property is in the wrong place, the plant is obsolete and stocks are redundant in a just-in-time environment).

Table 5:2 **Reconciliations**

	£000			
	Historical cost	*Unrealised gains*	*Cost of capital*	*Net present value*
Opening position	12,000	7,231	–	19,231
Cost of capital			1,769	1,769
(Cash generation)	(1,000)		–	(1,000)
Benchmark	11,000	7,231	1,769	20,000
Closing position	12,500	7,500	–	20,000
Profit	1,500	269	(1,769)	–

Conversely, the value of a business, these days, is more likely to be a function of its intangible assets (its pace of innovation, its reputation in the market place, its responsiveness, the flexibility of its workforce, etc.). To emphasise a point made in **paragraph 5:1.3**, such assets are nurtured by investments which are treated as costs in the accounting model – research and development, marketing, information and training. The greater the investment in areas crucial to survival in a changing environment, the lower the short-run profits!

5:5.5 Strategic Monitoring

The sum of the cash flow and closing value of a business should equate with its opening net present value uplifted for the cost of capital. Both the actual cash flow and the closing net present value, however, will almost certainly be different from that forecast at the beginning of the period – on account of new opportunities presenting themselves, on account of outcomes being different from expectations and on account of changes to forecasts.

By substituting the actual cash flow in the framework introduced above, we can establish a benchmark with which to compare the closing net present value. If the closing net present value exceeds the benchmark, there has been a perceived net strengthening; if it falls short, there has been a net weakening.

5:6 Corporate Strategy

5:6.1 Attribution of Value

In the previous section, we built up an example of a business with an aggregate present value, at the end of year 1, of £20.000m. Given the simplicity of the assumptions, this amounted to the forecast year 1 cash flow of £1.000m, divided by the excess of the cost of capital over the growth rate, that is, 5%. Since the cash flow of £1.000m can be attributed, as between the three categories of financing stakeholder, so can the value of £20.000m.

Say, for example, the £0.500m increase in the operating assets during year 1, from £12.000m to £12.500m, reflected the movement on the various capital accounts summarised in **Table 5:3**.

Table 5:3 **Lenders, taxers and shareholders**

		£000		
	Lenders	*Taxers*	*Shareholders*	*Total*
Opening balance	1,923	400	9,677	12,000
Operating profit	177	440	883	1,500
(Distributions)	(100)	(400)	(500)	(1,000)
Closing balance	2,000	440	10,060	12,500

Given the forecast of a constant 4% per annum rate of growth, coupled with a constant 9.2% per annum cost of capital, the value of the business can be attributed as in **Table 5:4**.

Table 5:4 **The value of the business**

		£000		
	Lenders	*Taxers*	*Shareholders*	*Total*
Opening balance	1,923	7,692	9,616	19,231
Cost of capital	177	708	884	1,769
(Distributions)	(100)	(400)	(500)	(1,000)
Closing balance	2,000	8,000	10,000	20,000

The majority of financial managers are active in business strategy, seeking to blend the various dimensions of strategy to maximum effect. A much smaller number are active in corporate strategy, to which we now turn our attention.

5:6.2 Synergies

On the 'control' side of corporate strategic financial management, the focal point is summed up in the question of what businesses the enterprise should be in. In general terms, the answer is those which are worth more to it than to any other enterprise. A common source of such synergy is the opportunity to share services, for example, various businesses defined in product terms could share logistical services (physical distribution, invoicing, sales ledger and credit control).

Say, for example, that the business evaluated in **paragraph 5:5** were, at the beginning of the year in question, to acquire another business of equal value but, because it served the same customers, it could share logistical services such that there would be a saving of £0.5 million per annum (say, commencing in year 1 and increasing at 4% per annum compound thereafter). Assuming a cost of capital of 9.2% per annum again, this means that the synergies would be worth £10m/1.04, that is, £9.615m. In other words, the entity cash flow would be £2.5m + 4% per annum, and hence the aggregate value of the combined business would be £50m/1.04, that is, £48.077m. The gross present value of the acquisition would therefore be £28.846m.

Bear in mind, however, that that figure represents the aggregate value to all the financing shareholders. Its attribution depends on the enterprise's capital structure – which would undoubtedly change in order that the acquisition could be funded. Say, for example, that it was decided that the gearing should remain the same, at 10% of net present value, that is, that £1.923m of the acquisition should be funded by additional borrowings, and the rest by equity.

On that basis, the acquisition would have a (gross) present value, to the shareholders and taxers, of £28.846m – £1.923m, that is, £26.923m. On the basis of the attribution of the pre-acquisition value, approximately 44.4% (i.e. £11.965m) would be attributable to the taxers, and 55.6% (i.e. £14.958m) to the equity. That last figure is the maximum price which our enterprise could pay for the acquisition without its value to its own shareholders being reduced.

Say, for instance, that it paid £13.000m, that is, £1.000m above the historical cost of tangible assets (otherwise, but misleadingly, known as net book value or net worth to the shareholders). The acquisition would have a net present value, to the shareholders and taxers, of £26.923m – £13.000m, that is, £13.923m. Of that, only £14.958m – £13.000m (i.e. £1.958m) would be attributable to its shareholders. The balance

(£11.965m) would be attributable to the taxers (but bear in mind that they would be losing the stream of taxes from the acquired company, worth £7.692m, that is, their net benefit is only £4.273m).

We can now summarise the disposition of the £9.615m worth of synergies as in **Table 5:5**.

Table 5:5 **Synergies**

	£ millions
Shareholders of the acquired company 13.000 – 9.616	3.384
Shareholders in the acquiring company 14.958 – 13.000	1.958
All shareholders (55.6% of total value)	5.342
Taxers 11.965 – 7.692 (44.4% of total value)	4.273
Total	9.615

In a form which is compatible with the strategic monitoring model, the situation can be summarised as in **Table 5:6**.

Table 5:6 **Net strengthening resulting from acquisition**

		£000		
	Lenders	*Taxers*	*Shareholders*	*Total*
Pre-acquisition value	1,923	7,692	9,616	19,231
Cash flow, (i.e. new financing)	1,923	–	13,000	14,923
Effect of cessation of acquired company	–	7,692	–	7,692
Benchmark	3,846	15,384	22,616	41,846
Post-acquisition value	3,846	19,657	24,574	48,077
Net strengthening	–	4,273	1,958	6,231

Every acquisition is unique, of course, but it is hoped that the above example provides a useful starting point. Simple as it is, the need to distinguish between the entity and equity viewpoints is easily overlooked. The high incidence of failure of acquisitions (in terms of enhancing the value of an entity to the acquirer's shareholders) is at least partly due to the price being at a level which looks sensible in terms of the aggregate present value, but is far too high relative to the expected stream of cash flow to the shareholders.

5:6.3 Capital Structure

As indicated in **paragraph 5:2**, capital structure is determined, in practice, by two processes: the raising and returning of new capital and the distribution of profits. The underlying decisions which those practices put into effect relate to the amount, and mix of capital. **Figure 5:6** portrays an extension of the 'cash-flow equation' introduced in **paragraph 5:4**.

Figure 5:6 **The extended cash-flow equation**

In very broad terms, the amount of capital required is assessed by reference to the rate of growth, relative to the rate of return foreseen. Specifically, if the rate of growth is expected to exceed the rate of return, a cash absorption will be forecast, calling for an excess of new financing over distributions. Conversely, if the rate of return is expected to exceed the rate of growth, a cash generation will be forecast, which will enable distributions to exceed new financing.

The mix of capital is determined by the interplay of taxation considerations and risk aversion. The greater the 'gearing', that is, the proportion of capital which takes the form of borrowings, the smaller will be the tax take, and hence the smaller the grossing up of the cost of capital. On the other hand, the greater the proportion of capital which takes the form of borrowings, the greater will be the pre-emption of cash flows for the payment of interest. A given volatility/unpredictability of entity cash flows will therefore translate into greater volatility/unpredictability of cash flows attributable to the shareholders (and taxers).

The lenders will put an upper limit on how much they wish to provide (given that they are lending other people's money, at relatively low rates of interest) and this will be fine tuned by the directors of the enterprise in question, bearing in mind their own attitudes to risk.

The combination of these two relationships (growth/return and gearing/risk aversion) produces four sets of conditions, as follows:

1. *where a company has low gearing relative to risk aversion, and a low rate of growth relative to its return, it makes sense to reduce equity capital – by paying dividends or buying its own shares;*
2. *where a company has high gearing relative to risk aversion, and few opportunities offering the prospect of an adequate return, it makes sense to reduce borrowings;*
3. *where a company has low gearing relative to risk aversion, and a high growth rate relative to its return, it makes sense to fund the growth by way of increased borrowings;*
4. *where a company has high gearing relative to risk aversion, and a high growth rate relative to its return, it needs to increase its equity capital – by way of a rights issue.*

Treasurers need to be clear, at all times, in which category the company is.

5:7 Application

The ideas summarised in this chapter have been exposed in various forums in recent years. The composite reaction is that they amount to common sense but are difficult to apply in many enterprises, on account of institutionalised short termism. Such is the preoccupation with what can be measured (e.g. last year's profits, last night's share price) that consideration of opportunities which can only be quantified by way of a subjective assessment are abhorred. Yet the rapid rate of change in the business environment is putting an even greater premium on flexibility and adaptability – and hence on those investments designed to achieve a degree of continuity, like training and branding.

For those determined to try out the ideas, the advice is to start in a limited area. If they are suitable in a particular situation, they will flourish; if not they will wither away. Among the opportunities which might be taken are the following:

(a) *Raise the issue of the financial objective of the enterprise: what criterion should be used for deciding which of a range of feasible alternatives is optimum. Argue the case for the maximisation of net present value.*
(b) *Emphasise the importance of recognising the value of time, otherwise known as the cost of capital. What is it, at present, and how might it be reduced?*

(c) *Begin to summarise cash flow (within hours of the end of a period) by reference to stakeholders. After a few months' experience begin to forecast on that basis, and interpret the difference between forecast and actual.*

(d) *Use the 'maximising net present value' approach, to help colleagues to decide on the optimum level of investment in research, development, marketing, training etc, not previously evaluated in the way that capital expenditure has been (see Ch.11).*

(e) *Use the monitoring approach to monitor the progress of investments approved on a net present value basis. Given the value claimed at the outset, and the cash that has flowed and the time passed since then, what ought the project to be worth now – and what is it worth now? The net strengthening or weakening can be explained in terms of the key relationships – price/volume, volume/cost, customer loyalty – so as to provide strategic accountability and feedback into the forecasting and decision-making elements of control.*

(f) *Use the monitoring approach to provide a means of articulating successive long-range plans. Assess the value of the business implicit in last year's plan, update it according to the flow of cash and the passage of time, so as to assess what it ought to be worth now – and compare that with a distillation of this year's plan. Likewise, use the monitoring approach to track the progress of a newly acquired subsidiary.*

6. Dynamic Budgetary Control

6:1 The Background

6:1.1 Origins

The CIMA definition of budgetary control has stood the test of time (in the shape of several revisions of its official terminology) and embraces three distinct aspects:

> The establishment of budgets relating the responsibilities of executives to the requirements of a policy...
>
> and the continuous comparison of actual with budgeted results...
>
> either to secure by individual action the objective of that policy or to provide a basis for its revision.

Amongst the benefits it can bring are:

(a) *a pressure to clarify objectives, and the criteria for the making and monitoring of decisions;*
(b) *a structure within which authority, responsibility and accountability are delegated;*
(c) *a means of influencing behaviour;*
(d) *a framework within which to communicate the prevailing strategy;*
(e) *a model for the evaluation of alternatives in support of tactical decisions;*
(f) *the provision of the parameters for day to day operational controls.*

Budgetary control is not a subset of cost accounting, concentrating on the arithmetic of variance analysis; it is a management tool which embraces:

(a) prices and values, as well as costs;
(b) assets and cash flows, as well as profits;
(c) treasury as well as financial control;
(d) decision support as well as monitoring;
(e) physical as well as financial quantifications.

Moreover, it is important to note that the specifics of budgetary control are not imposed from outside (in the way that standards are imposed on accounting) but are customised to the needs of the enterprise concerned.

It is also important to note that, to date, the literature on the subject has been dominated by examples customised to the needs of organisations characterised by the 'old scientific' management culture, which was based on a centralised, confrontational, command and compliance style. Given the relative stability of those days, all the big tactical decisions were made once a year for a year, e.g. prices were negotiated with suppliers and wages with unions, and a selling price list was published. The expected outcome was spelled out in the budget (and reflected in standard costs) and subordinates were told to conform.

Understandably, given its characteristic annuality, the accounting model provided a suitable language in which to express those budgets, with profit (or some derivative thereof, like return on assets) as the focal point. The regular (e.g. monthly) comparison of actual with budget was seen as a measure of the subordinates' performance and often determined their rewards. Significantly, strategic decisions were few and far between: by definition, in an era of stability, questions like 'What business are we in?' did not occupy much managerial time.

6:1.2 Consequences of Rapid Change

As the rate of change in the environment has increased, however, this 'traditional' approach to budgetary control has come under pressure, as has been evidenced by symptoms such as the following:

- The assumptions on which rigid annual budgets are predicated are quickly overtaken by events, to the extent that the most common explanation for a variance therefrom, these days, is that 'the budget was wrong'. Though there is nothing in the CIMA definition to say that budgets have to be set once a year for a year and rigidly adhered to (indeed, the last clause of the definition highlights the fact that a variance might prompt a revision of policy and hence the budget) those at the centres of organisations have often been unwilling to sanction a revision because they feared that they would thereby lose control (command and compliance being the only form of control they know). The truth is, however, that it is becoming increasingly difficult for people in the centre to keep abreast of changing technology, customers' needs, competitive activity, etc. In response, we are seeing the emergence of a 'new scientific' culture based on a devolved, co-operative, trust and commitment style. Managers who are close to the action are empowered to make decisions on the basis of contemporary conditions. An increasing proportion of those decisions are strategic, as businesses acquire new facilities, launch new products, enter new markets, etc., in response to the changing competitive scene. Rigid annual budgets are at best an irrelevance and at worst engender a debilitating short termism.

- Techniques such as Total Quality Management, and the concept of delighting the customer, can be fatally impaired by systems of performance measurement and reward which are based on conformance with an out of date budget. 'What am I supposed to do?' asks the middle manager. 'Delight the customer, or meet the budget? I can't do both.' Meanwhile, the relevance of management accounts is questioned: the material/labour/overhead orientation (inherited from the accounting model) is appropriate for very few businesses these days, and analysing the variance between actual outcomes and an out of date budget provides no meaningful feedback.

- In a rapidly changing world, there is no correlation between the value of a business and the carrying costs of its tangible assets. In many instances, what the accountant calls a tangible asset is seen by managers as a strategic liability (the property is in the wrong place, the technology has been superseded, stock is an embarrassment in a just-in-time context, etc.). Conversely, the value of a business, these days, is primarily determined by its intangible assets (its pace of innovation, its reputation in the market place, the responsiveness of its employees to changing customer needs, etc.). Unfortunately, in this respect, the accounting model treats investments in such assets (research and development, marketing, training, etc.) as costs to be deducted in arriving at current profits. Managers who see profit as the objective will be motivated to skimp on such investments, thereby damaging the long-term health of the business.

For reasons associated with reporting to outsiders, the accounting model sees each year as a discrete campaign but, if this infects budgets, problems are inevitable. Managers ask whether the unspent portion of one year's budget can be carried over to the next and are dismayed by the negative answer. In many cases, the power of projection is overwhelming: failure to spend this year's budget may result in next year's being lower than it otherwise would have been. Such an approach to control is counterproductive and drives a wedge between finance and other functions.

Unsurprisingly, therefore, proactive financial managers no longer sing the praises of integrating management information with accounting numbers. Rather, they use a distinctive financial management model – up-to-the-minute, forward looking, outward looking and dynamic, and capable of accommodating uncertainty, judgements and intangibles.

In these new circumstances, persistence with the traditional approach to budgetary control degenerates into a game in which superiors set arbitrary numerical targets and subordinates build in slack ahead of confrontational budget meetings. Alibi data crowd out genuine decision support and monitoring information, nobody trusts anybody, and the budget ceases to be a valid basis for control.

6:1.3 Some Reactions

In the light of the above, a number of consultants are advocating the abandonment of budgetary control. Headlines in the press, like 'Companies to scrap budgets' and the establishment of a 'Beyond Budgeting Round Table' give the impression that the technique is dead. In the words of Mark Twain, however, such headlines are exaggerated: no examples of abandonment, as such, have been uncovered.

Meanwhile, some management accountants have been hoping that some tinkering, i.e. making small increments of change, offers a solution. Some, for instance, prepare 'updated forecasts' for the current year but this inevitably engenders conflict between the local managers (who welcome the forecasts as an input to current decision making) and those at the centre (who ignore them, on the grounds that to do otherwise would let local management off the hook).

Others have experimented with rolling budgets looking, say, 12 months ahead once a quarter, but:

- if the organisation in question has consistently taken several months to produce an annual budget, moving to a quarterly frequency will not be welcomed;

- if the budget is still locked into the accounting model, then there will be a mismatch, e.g. if the March results are not complete until towards the end of April, which budget provides the benchmark for April?

- comparing quarters 2–5 with 1–4 is not easy and there is a severe danger of data overload.

Yet others have simply shortened the budget period to, say, a quarter, on the grounds that that is as far forward as they can see with any precision. That may be true, but it militates against longer-term considerations – and precision is not a concept which has much relevance in a forward-looking context.

There are even organisations where the budget period has been lengthened, e.g. the UK government's resource budgets, with which ministries are expected to conform for no less than three years. This represents a reinforcement of the command and compliance style, the inappropriateness of which, in a rapidly changing environment, becomes ever more obvious.

If your colleagues are setting out to be more strategic, customer oriented, devolved, aware of the importance of intangibles, etc., you cannot carry on with accounting based budgetary controls. Experience has shown, however, that piecemeal tinkering is no more viable that abandonment. Fortunately, there is a 'third way' which transcends both. It offers a comprehensive solution, based on *revolutionary adaptation*. It is called dynamic budgetary control ('DBC' for short) and will now be described.

6:2 The Framework

6:2.1 Fundamentals

DBC is set in the context of financial management, as defined for the purposes of **Chapter 5**. As such, it starts with the recognition that financial viability is about the value of outputs exceeding the value of inputs. The latter term includes capital but on an economic, rather than accounting basis, so as to include intangibles as well as tangibles. On that basis, the generic financial objective of a distributable profit seeking enterprise (be it privately owned or quoted on the stock market), is the maximisation of the net present value of cash flows between the company and its shareholders: essentially, dividends and share buybacks minus share issues. In turn, this is determined by events in all four spheres of financial management: financing and distributions as well as investment and returns.

More immediately, net cash flows between the company and the shareholders are influenced by two things: the cash flows of the enterprise as a whole (the excess of receipts from customers over payments to suppliers and employees) and the choice of capital structure (which determines how much of the cash flow of the entity is pre-empted for the benefit of taxers and lenders). Budgets should cover all of these aspects, in a way which allows for the fact that there may well be life after the end of the current financial year, i.e. which focuses on the long-term continuum (*see* **Ch.10, para.10:3**).

At this point, however, it is vital to emphasise that nobody *knows* what is going to happen, especially on the outcomes side of the equation. We make our decisions, not on the basis of our knowledge, but on the basis of a synthesis of the judgements of colleagues we trust. The decision-making and monitoring criteria, therefore, must be expressed in terms of forecasts, i.e. the impact on the net present value of *forecast* cash flows.

Thus the focus is on cash flow, the actual version of which is continuously, unequivocally and immediately measurable. At some later date, but only if it is thought useful, cash flow can be analysed into its profit and asset-movement components. The accounting model sees cash flow through the rear-view mirror as the excess of profit over expansion; financial management looks at the events in chronological order and sees profit as the sum of cash flow and expansion. The forecast version can be produced at exactly the same time (but expressed in a way which allows for a margin of error), thereby ushering in the era of real-time financial management.

6:2.2 Scientific Method

The term 'scientific method' refers to the process by which a theory is continuously refined as a result of the application of lessons learned from a comparison of outcomes with those predicted by hypotheses derived from the theory ('If our theory is valid, we should find that …'). If the outcome matches expectations, the theory is reinforced; if not, it needs to be adapted. A theory reflects best understanding at a point in time, but becomes more and more reliable over time.

DBC uses scientific method in a way which puts the management accountant in the position of custodian of the business model. The budget, at a point in time, shows the expected outcome of decisions made and expected to be made, based on a set of interlocking relationships: if we choose option A, we think outcome X will follow: if we choose option B, we believe outcome Y will follow. Identifying the optimum, on the basis of the perceived relationship, is what decision making is all about and, together, these relationships and forecast outcomes amount to a model of the business, analogous to scientific method.

Proof does not precede events, but follows them, when we compare actuals with budgets, and learn lessons. As a result, we may (echoing the last clause in the Institute's definition) resolve to act differently in future, and/or we may choose to amend the model. This corresponds with the 'elements of control' introduced in **Chapter 5**, where accountability was seen to be reflected in a requirement to explain the difference between outcomes and the forecasts used in the making of the decision. Many pundits talk about the concept of a 'learning organisation' but this is a practical manifestation of it.

6:2.3 Key Relationships

The accounting model is concerned with where a business has come from, and therefore classifies outlays on an input basis (firstly is it capital or revenue then, if the latter, is it material, labour or overheads?) People who make decisions, on the other hand, are concerned with where a business is going and are concerned with the impact on future outcomes. This leads to a classification along the lines inferred by the 'forecast relationships' introduced in **Chapter 5**:

> (a) *expectations, i.e. the outcomes of decisions already made:*
>
>> (i) *elasticity of demand, i.e. volume as a function of selling prices;*
>>
>> (ii) *cost responsiveness, i.e. cost as a function of volume;*
>>
>> (ii) *customer loyalty, i.e. the likelihood that customers will 'come back for more'.*
>
> (b) *hope, i.e. the outcomes of decisions foreseen:*
>
>> (i) *volume inducement, e.g. advertising, to improve the elasticity of demand;*
>>
>> (ii) *volume anticipation, e.g. mechanisation, to reduce cost responsiveness;*
>>
>> (iii) *volume sustaining, e.g. the sales force, to increase customer loyalty.*
>
> (c) *faith, i.e. the outcome of decisions not yet specifically identified, e.g. respectively, product development, process development and design.*

These relationships, and their links to net present value are portrayed in **Fig.6:1**.

Figure 6:1   **Business modelling**

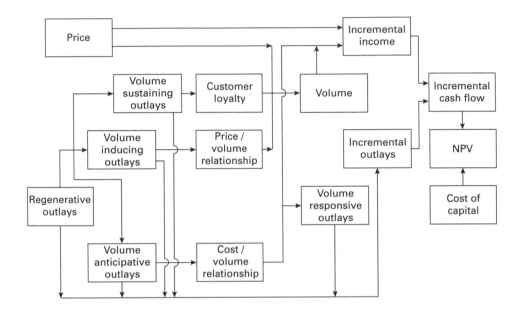

6:3 Optimisation

In order to elaborate on the ideas mooted so far, let us focus on one of the most important decisions to be made in any business – determining selling prices (or, what amounts to the same thing, whether or not to accept an order at a price determined by someone else, e.g. the customer or competitors).

The reason for choosing this one lies in the fact that it enables us to bring out another major trend, namely that towards 'a market segment of one', in which every order is different. Consequently, putting price on the x axis of the elasticity graph makes sense for very few businesses these days. How are we to respond to this trend?

The answer is to relate volume to unit contribution. In a manufacturing concern, for example, this might be done by plotting demand in terms of machine hours, against contribution per machine hour. These usually fit an expression in the $y = 1 - x^2$ family. This can be displayed in spreadsheet format, as in **Table 6:1** (based on a real example, but suitably disguised, and exaggerated, to emphasise the key features), but some managers might feel the need for a graph too.

Table 6:1   **Budgeted elasticity**

x	$1 - x^2$	Average unit contribution £ per machine hour	Volume machine hours	Aggregate contribution £
0.0	1.00	100	2,000	200,000
0.1	0.99	120	1,980	237,600
0.2	0.96	140	1,920	268,800
0.3	0.91	160	1,820	291,200
0.4	0.84	180	1,680	302,400
Optimum		187	1,622	303,314
0.5	0.75	200	1,500	300,000
0.6	0.64	220	1,280	281,600
0.7	0.51	240	1,020	244,800
0.8	0.36	260	720	187,200
0.9	0.19	280	380	106,400
1.0	0.00	300	0	0

The relationship portrayed in **Table 6:1** fits the particular expression:

$$v = 1,500 + 10x - 0.5c^2,$$

where v is the monthly volume in machine hours and c is the contribution per machine hour. Thus, the volume falls away from 2,000 hours per month at an average unit contribution of £100 per machine hour, to zero at £300 per machine hour. On this basis, aggregate contribution fits the expression:

$$£(1,500c + 10c^2 - 0.5c^3).$$

Readers who recall their calculus will be able to deduce that this would be maximised where

$$0.15c^2 - 20c = 1,500,$$

i.e. at £303,314, where unit contribution is £187 per hour. Others prefer trial and error but the most popular approach, these days, is to use a spreadsheet facility.

Whichever approach is adopted, the point is that both the pricing decision and the elasticity expression become key elements in the budget, with which actual outcomes will be compared, in order to learn appropriate lessons.

Readers are encouraged to think how this approach can be applied to other key relationships, e.g. how increasing the level of volume inducing investments (such as advertising) affects the price/volume curve. In all cases, a useful piece of advice is 'Don't think straight!'. Generally speaking, as portrayed in **Fig.6:2**, these relationships are subject to diminishing returns on investment, e.g. each increment of investment in advertising produces a smaller shift in the price/volume curve than the one before. Plotting incremental net present value against incremental investment produces a bell shaped curve, the task being to identify where it turns, i.e. where its gradient is zero.

Figure 6:2   **Don't think straight!**

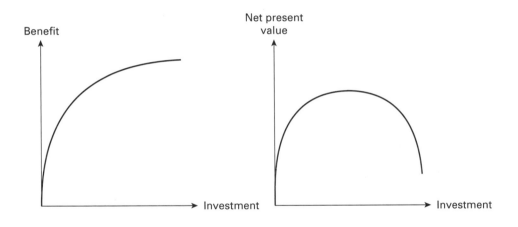

6:4 Variance Analysis

6:4.1 The Old, Static Approach

Once it is recognised that a budget is a model of the business, and comparisons of actual with budget provide the feedback required to refine the model, it will be seen that the traditional approach to variance analysis is totally inappropriate.

Let us imagine, for example, that the standard contribution on actual sales in the month for which we developed the elasticity chart and the pricing decision, was:

1,350 hours @ £210 per hour = £283,500,
as against a budget of
1,622 hours @ £187 per hour = £303,314.

Traditional variance analysis would interpret this as follows.

Budgeted contribution 1,622 hours @ £187 per hour	£303,314
Volume variance (272 hours) @ £187 per hour	(50,864)
Actual volume @ budgeted margin 1,350 hours @ £187 per hour	252,450
Margin variance 1,350 hours @ £23 per hour	31,050
Actual contribution 1,350 hours @ £210 per hour	£283,500

Arithmetically, this is correct, as would the slightly different figures which would be obtained by taking out the price variance before the volume one. Neither, however, provides any useful information. Why report a favourable price variance when the average unit contribution has been higher than was perceived as leading to maximum aggregate contribution?

6:4.2 The New, Dynamic Approach

What is required, from a managerial point of view, is feedback on those two components of the budget, by way of answers to the questions:

- Did we succeed in averaging an average unit contribution of £187 per hour?

- Did we attract the volume we would expect, given our perception of the elasticity of demand and the average standard unit contribution actually achieved?

In our example, we can see that:

- Had our assessment of elasticity been correct, an average unit contribution of £210 would have brought in a volume of 1,395 hours, for an aggregate contribution of £292,950, i.e. an adverse variance on this score of £10,364, in respect of pricing.

- In fact, however, it attracted a volume of only 1,350 hours, indicating that the elasticity of demand was greater than we had believed. This meant an aggregate contribution of £283,500, i.e. a further adverse variance in respect of our perception of elasticity.

This can be expressed in a form which is easy to compare with the traditional layout, as follows.

Budgeted contribution 1,622 hours @ £187 per hour	£303,314
Price variance	(10,364)
Expected contribution @ £210 per hour, per budget	292,950
Elasticity variance	(9,450)
Actual contribution 1,350 hours @ £210 per hour	£283,500

Thus we have relevant feedback and, in line with the Institute's definition, we might aim to get back on track (by pricing less greedily) and/or modify the perception of the elasticity of demand. Neither of these courses of action would be automatic: it would depend on the appropriate manager's explanation of the differences between actual and budget.

In some businesses, a tolerance is agreed, i.e. variances are classified as statistically significant or insignificant, depending on the percentage they represent of the standard.

6:5 Completing the Loop

As indicated above, DBC provides a framework for focusing on short periods of time (standard contribution, and the variances therefrom can be tracked daily if necessary). Every so often (e.g. quarterly), however, the long-term continuum can be updated, and articulated with the previous assessment, by way of strategic monitoring – again compatible with the approach introduced in **Chapter 5** – as in **Table 6:2**.

Table 6:2 **Results of strategic monitoring**

	£ 000
Opening net present value	3,000
plus cost of capital	60
minus cash (generation)	(40)
Benchmark	3,020
Closing net present value	3,100
Net strengthening	80

In this way, the technique provides the links between the three levels of control as portrayed in **Fig.6:3**.

The solid lines indicate the logical sequence of events: decide what you are going to do, then how you are going to do it, before actually doing it. This may sound like common sense but, for many managers, a conscious effort is required to follow the logic; naturally, they are obsessed with the operational level, to the point that they feel guilty taking time out to think of the how and the what of management.

The dotted lines indicate feedback. The lower one answers the question 'How well did we do what we chose to do?' as in the elasticity and pricing example above. The higher one answers the question 'How well did we choose what to do?' and prompts consideration of alternative strategies, e.g. the markets served, the products offered and the facilities used.

Figure 6:3 **Levels of control**

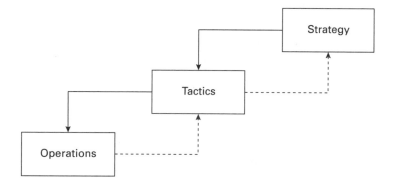

6:6 Summary and Conclusions

6:6.1 A Check List

The above description provides only a brief introduction to the technique, but highlights its distinguishing features. The overall message is that, if their budgetary control systems are to be relevant in today's rapidly changing conditions, management accountants are urged to consider the following check list:

1. *Budgets should flow from strategy, not constrain it. Rejecting an opportunity to enhance the long-term health of the business because it has an adverse effect on short run profits is patently wrong.*

2. *The pressures on budgetary control should be seen in the context of broader managerial trends, e.g. the greater emphasis on strategy, customer orientation, devolution, co-operation, and intangibles. The old management model concentrated on what could be measured; the new model recognises that the most important things in life cannot be measured.*

3. *In particular, the emphasis on measuring past performance needs to be sharply reduced. In a rapidly changing world, less time should be spent on that, to allow more to be spent on the assessment of potential.*

4. *Starting with a clean sheet, it would be impossible, these days, to make a case for expressing budgets in the language of the accounting model. The appropriate language is now that of financial management: forward looking, outward looking and dynamic.*

5. *Specifically, more attention needs to be paid to the value of forecast outcomes, as distinct from the preoccupation with costs which characterises the accounting model.*

6. *This leads to the recognition of the need to focus on outcome-based relationships, e.g. volume as a function of price, cost as a function of volume. These should be explicit in the model of the business and hence in the budget, and should determine the structure of the variance analysis.*

7. *Life needs to be breathed into the concept of 'the learning organisation' by adopting and integrating the elements of control. Accountability needs to be defined in terms of comparing what is happening with what was expected to happen when the relevant decision was made. Reinforcing points made above, such comparisons should be positioned as learning opportunities, not measures of individual performance.*

8. *Underpinning all aspects of control should be a clear statement of the primary financial objective of the organisation, in a form which can be translated into a criterion for the making and monitoring of decisions. For a distributable profit seeking organisation, the appropriate aim is to maximise the present value of projected cash flows between the company and its shareholders.*

9. *Finally, the budget should be seen not just in terms of providing the parameters for operational control, and a model for evaluating tactical alternatives, but also as providing feedback to the strategic level of management, thereby making a seamless link with Strategic Financial Management as described in* **Chapter 5.**

6:6.2 Obstacles

The ideas outlined above have been floated and tested in various situations and proved robust. Readers might welcome an indication, however, of the likely obstacles to their adoption. There are two main streams:

Top Management
One arises where top managers are unwilling to follow the trend towards 'right-brain' thinking, i.e. they are unwilling to devolve authority, or even to spell out the financial objective. 'Let them propose a course of action and I will decide' seems to be their philosophy. As Mr Gorbachev has pointed out, successful revolutions never start from the top, because of the many vested interests in the status quo. If the ideas in this chapter appeal to you, test them in a definable part of the business: if they are worthwhile, they will flourish.

Alternatively, they may be nervous of the pace of change, e.g. thinking that they are so busy implementing their Total Quality Management approach that they cannot think about modifying their budgetary control and performance measurement systems. Therein lies an inevitable conflict. The answer is to stress the holistic nature of management: whereas the old model was built on analysis (breaking things down) the new is based on synthesis (building things up).

The Finance Function
Many accountants are seriously uncomfortable with the uncertainty which characterises forecasts and assessments of potential. 'I deal in facts', they say. 'If there are no facts about the future, can you blame me for spending all my time looking backwards?' The answer here lies in the recognition that our quantitative skills are equally applicable to judgements about the future as to verifiable facts about the past.

Alternatively, they argue that it is impossible for anyone so active in the management of the business as to be involved in the making of decisions to be objective when it comes to reporting. This is true, and explains why, in most businesses now, proactive financial management is seen as quite distinct from passive accounting. There is far more to accountancy than accounting – what a pity the importation of American English has confused the picture as far as management accountancy is concerned!

7. Competitor Analysis

7:1 Introduction

7:1.1 What is Competitor Analysis?

The activities of a firm shape the nature of the issues which arise, and the events which occur in its operating environment. At the same time, the firm's performance and survival prospects are influenced by this environment. As a result most firms monitor and analyse the issues and events which arise and occur in their environment, in order to understand, shape and react to them for the firm's benefit. One set of events and issues which firms monitor and analyse is the activities and intentions of their rivals. This analysis, known as competitor analysis is designed to help answer the question, 'What is my rival likely to do in a given situation?' (Oster, 1994: 392). It involves gathering intelligence about rivals and comparing products, prices, promotions and channels regularly in order to identify actual or potential sources of competitive advantage. If performed properly, the analysis should enable the firm to launch more precise attacks on its rivals as well as prepare stronger defences against their attacks (Kotler, 1994: 224).

7:1.2 Why Perform Competitor Analysis?

The impact of certain events in the global economy on the sources of superior performance provides the rationale for competitor analysis. Firms attain superior performance when they:

(a) *operate in protected environments where entry is difficult;*
(b) *anticipate market changes and rapidly exploit new opportunities – often faster than their rivals; or*
(c) *possess sustainable competitive advantage over potential and actual rivals (Oster, 1994).*

Noel Tagoe   113

The deregulation of markets and removal of national trade barriers have significantly reduced the opportunities for firms to operate in protected environments. At the same time, the rapid diffusion of new technology and the fast competitor response to product innovation has reduced considerably the length of time over which a firm can earn excess returns by exploiting new opportunities and made competitive advantage less sustainable. The effect of these developments is intense global competition. In order to survive and achieve superior performance in the market, a firm must, among other things, gain a profound understanding of the activities, motivations and capabilities of its rivals. That is, for most firms, competitor analysis is now an indispensable tool in the quest for superior performance. The success stories of some global companies illustrate this point. For example, in order to increase and consolidate their global market share, Japanese automobile firms had to penetrate the US market. Their success in doing so is attributed, in part, to their careful attention to competitor analysis (Halberstam, 1986: 310; Aaker, 1995: 64).

7:2 How Competitor Analysis Works

Although the product market is the visible arena of competition, it should not form the starting point or the exclusive focus of competitor analysis. The products on which firms compete are the outcome of various processes. Superior product offerings and success in the market place reflect superior business (including manufacturing and logistic) processes. Since the sources of competitive advantage are located within these processes, competitor analysis must be geared towards producing an informed understanding of the underlying dynamics of the processes.

The following broad sets of issues are normally addressed in competitor analysis:

(a) *Who are my competitors?*
(b) *What are their objectives? How committed are they to these objectives? What are their exit barriers?*
(c) *What strategies are they currently pursuing? What strategies have they pursued in the past? How successful have they been? Which are the successful and unsuccessful ones over time? Why?*
(d) *What are the strengths and weaknesses of each competitor or group of competitors?*
(e) *How will they behave in future either on their own initiative or in response to the actions of others?*

The issues are explained in greater detail below.

7:2.1 Identifying Competitors

A firm will often regard other firms which offer similar products (or close substitutes) as its competitors. Thus, for example, Coca Cola will regard Pepsi as a competitor in the soft-drinks market. This definition focuses on the provision of physically similar products. However, restricting the definition to such direct, obvious and existing competitors can result in 'competitor myopia' (Kotler, 1994: 224). For example, a cinema is not only competing against other cinemas for its audience: it is also competing against satellite television film channels and live theatres, and would ignore these significant sources of competition at its own peril. Hence the definition of competitors must be widened. One way of achieving this is to think of the customer as a purchaser of a group of benefits or attributes rather than a specific product. Thus the real competitors are those who provide the customer with a similar group of benefits even though the product may be physically different (Ward, 1992; Kotler, 1994). **Figure 7:1** shows four main ways by which competitors can be identified.

Figure 7:1 **Levels of competition based on degree of product substitution**

Source: Kotler (1994: 225)

1. *Brand competition:* A company can see its competitors as other companies offering a similar product and services to the same customers at similar prices. Thus Buick might see its major competitors to be Ford, Toyota, Honda, Renault and other manufacturers of moderate-price automobiles. But it would not see itself as competing with Mercedes, on the one hand, or Yugo automobiles, on the other.

2. *Industry competition:* A company can see its competitors more broadly as all companies making the same product or class of products. Here Buick would see itself as competing against all other automobile manufacturers.

3. *Form competition:* A company can see its competitors even more broadly as all companies manufacturing products that supply the same service. Here Buick would see itself competing against not only other automobile manufacturers but also manufacturers of motorcycles, bicycles and trucks.

4. *Generic competition:* A company can see its competitors still more broadly as all companies that compete for the same consumer dollars. Here Buick would see itself competing with companies that sell major consumer durables, foreign vacations and new homes.

Competitor identification must cover potential competitors including:

(a) *new entrants from different geographic regions or from other product markets with technologies and channels that overlap with ours;*
(b) *customers integrating backwards; or*
(c) *suppliers integrating forwards.*

New entrants increase competition and can reduce industry profitability. In order to avoid that situation existing firms must invest in entry barriers. 'An entry barrier can be anything which represents a significant economic disincentive to a new business which is considering entering a particular market or developing and launching a competitive product' (Ward, 1992: 94). It aims to increase the perceived risk or reduce the expected financial returns from the market entry investment. Examples of entry barriers are patents, economies of scale, technology barriers, licences, distribution channels, brands, huge initial investment and learning effects. The investment in an entry barrier should be evaluated financially to cover an appropriate time span. Assuming that the discounted cash flow (DCF) analytical technique is used, the financial evaluation could proceed as follows:

(a) *Calculate the present value of the firm's margins (PV1) in a market without the new competitor as follows:*
    (i) *estimate the size of the market over the relevant time horizon;*
    (ii) *estimate the relative market share of the firm;*
    (iii) *from (i) and (ii) above (together with other relevant information, calculate the expected margins of the firm for each year);*
    (iv) *calculate the present value of the margins in (iii) using an appropriate discount factor. This step should lead to the total present value for the firm without the new competitor (i.e. PV1).*
(b) *Repeat the process in (a)(i) to (iv) above, but this time incorporating the new competitor. The new present value is PV2.*
(c) *Calculate the difference between the two present values to arrive at PV3. That is, PV3 = PV1 − PV2.*

The difference (i.e. PV3) represents the maximum amount that the firm must invest now to prevent the new competitor from entering the market (*see* **Ch.5**).

In a market with many competitors it might not be feasible for a firm to monitor all of them to the same extent. In that event, the firm might monitor only competitors which pose serious threats to its survival and success. The danger with this approach is that a previously insignificant competitor might suddenly become a major player in the market. Since the firm has very little intelligence about this competitor, the firm's ability to attack or defend itself against the competitor can be severely hampered. An alternative way of dealing with large numbers of competitors is to reduce the set to strategic groups. Each strategic group would comprise firms which over time pursue similar strategies in a target market, have similar characteristics and/or have similar assets and skills. These groupings make the analysis more compact and feasible. At the same time very little strategic insight is lost 'because firms in a strategic group will be affected by and react to industry developments in similar ways' (Aaker, 1995: 69).

7:2.2 Competitor Objectives

At this stage the analyst seeks to answer the question: What is each competitor seeking in the market place? It might be useful to assume that each competitor pursues a mix of objectives relating to profitability, market share, cash flow, technological leadership, service leadership, etc. The competitor makes trade-offs between these objectives depending on the relative weights it attaches to them. Knowing a competitor's objectives helps one to assess how satisfied it is with current performance and, therefore, how likely it is to retain its current strategy. It also enables the firm to predict how the competitor will behave on its own initiative or in response to strategic moves in the market place. For example, a firm whose objective is to become a cost leader is likely to react more strongly to a manufacturing process breakthrough by a competitor than to an increase in the advertising budget of that same competitor (Kotler, 1994: 231).

The firm must also form an opinion about the competitor's commitment to that objective. This can be influenced by the level of exit barriers in the industry. An exit barrier is 'anything which increases the perceived cost to the company of leaving the industry and which may therefore affect the strategic decision as to whether to exit or stay in the industry' (Ward, 1992: 100). Exit barriers include legal and moral obligations to customers, creditors and employees; government restrictions; low asset realisation values due to overspecialisation; lack of alternative opportunities; and high vertical integration. High exit barriers increase the commitment of firms who might otherwise leave the market. Since this situation can reduce overall profitability, it might be in the interest of the other firms to lower the exit barriers by offering to buy the competitor's assets, meet its customer obligations, etc (Kotler, 1994: 226–7). Financial analysis for such moves is similar to that for exit barriers.

To determine the objectives of the rival the analyst must ask questions that relate to the rival as business unit and to its parent company levels (Walker *et al.*, 1992). At the business unit level the following questions could be relevant:

(a) *What are the rival's financial and market objectives? What trade-offs will it make between the objectives and between the long term and the short term?*

(b) *What expectations does the rival have of its activities and how do these expectations affect the rival's objectives?*

(c) *How does the rival perceive its position in the market or industry (in terms of market leadership, cost leadership, etc) and what price will it pay to maintain or improve its position?*

(d) *Are there any constraints to the rival's behaviour (e.g. regulatory constraints, prior commitments, etc.)?*

At the level of the rival's parent company the following questions can be asked:

(a) *Does the rival have any strategic value to its parent company? (see **Ch.2**) What is this value and how great is it?*

(b) *How important is the rival in attaining the objectives of the parent company?*

(c) *Has the parent company been successful? How does this success (or lack of it) affect its attitude to the rival's performance?*

(d) *Is there any economic relationship between the rival and any of its sister firms (or divisions)? For example, does this relationship involve shared costs or complementary products? If so, to what extent?*

7:2.3 Competitor Strategy

The firm must review the strategy of each of its competitors over time. The review must cover both past and current strategies in order to establish the rival's pattern of strategic behaviour that might help the firm to predict future strategic moves of its rival. This process also involves studying how the competitor responded to market and industry changes over time and how it is revising (or has revised) its current strategy to meet emerging customer needs. In analysing the current strategy, it is useful to understand the critical resources (or core competencies) on which the success of the strategy hinges. For example, if:

> a differentiation strategy is detected, to what extent does it rely on product-line breadth, product quality, service, distribution type, or brand identification? If a low-cost strategy is employed, is it based on economies of scale, the experience curve, manufacturing facilities and equipment, or access to raw materials?
>
> (Aaker, 1995: 74)

The pattern of investments in physical plants and other capabilities can signal to the firm the strategies its rival is pursuing. Image and market positioning components of competitive strategy can also be seen from the advertising and promotions carried out by the firm's rival. Another valuable source of information could be the recruitment and changes in personnel levels and profile. This human resource information can indicate the skills that the rival is seeking or building and from this the firm can infer what strategies the rival might pursue.

As part of the analysis the firm should look at the success or failure of the rival to date. The rule of thumb is that the rival would keep away from failed strategies. It is important for the firm to understand the underlying reasons for the success or failure of the rival's strategies since these can highlight the strengths and weaknesses of the rival (*see* **Chs 48** and **49**). The measures for success must be broadly related to the objectives and strategies of the rival. These measures might include financial metrics such as profitability, marketing metrics such as sales growth and market shares and technological issues such as quality and product/process innovation.

The main aim of this analysis is to detect the potential strategies a rival could pursue. That is, what alternatives are open to the rival? Under which market and other conditions might a particular alternative be selected? Can the rival switch from one alternative to the other if the original alternative fails or if market conditions change? The answers to these questions would help the firm to plan anticipatory and reactive moves to the competitor.

7:2.4 Competitor's Strengths and Weaknesses

This exercise is closely linked to the identification of the rival's objectives and strategy. It is concerned with whether or not the competitor can carry out its strategy and reach its goals. The answer would depend on the rival's resources and capabilities (or assets and skills). The existence of assets and skills which are relevant to the industry and the strategy represents strengths and their absence indicates weaknesses. The rationale for assessing a competitor's strengths and weakness is to enable the firm to take advantage of the rival's weakness using the firm's strength and to neutralise or bypass the strengths of the rival.

The first step in assessing a competitor's strengths and weaknesses is to gather recent data about the competitor's sales, market share, profit margin, return on investment, cashflow, new investment, capacity utilisation, etc. It might also be useful to identify the assumptions which the rival is making about the business, market and/or industry which are no longer valid. If the firm knows that the rival is operating on a major wrong assumption, it can attack the rival in that area (Kotler, 1994).

Having gathered data about the rival the next step is to identify the assets and skills that are relevant to the industry. The key questions and issues that can help the firm to identify these assets and skills include:

(a) *Over time what assets and skills have contributed to the success of successful businesses? What assets and skills do unsuccessful businesses lack?*

(b) *What motivates the customer? (Customer motivations greatly influence buying decisions and can therefore indicate the assets or skills that can potentially create meaningful advantages.)*

(c) *What value-added stage represents the largest percentage of total costs? (see Ch.39) (This can be revealed by analysing the cost structure of the industry. The rival can gain sustainable competitive advantage if it can obtain a cost advantage in a key value-added stage.)*

(d) *Are there any mobility barriers in the industry? What is their nature? (In addition to both entry and exit barriers, mobility barriers include barriers to moving from one strategic group to another. They arise because of the cost and difficulty in creating assets and skills that can support sustainable competitive advantage.)*

Identifying these skills also alerts the firm to potential entrants into the market. The potential entrants would include firms in other markets who possess the skills and assets relevant to the firm's market. Consequently the firm can monitor the activities of the potential entrants in order to be able to anticipate whether or not they would enter and if so when.

Various aspects of the rival's business are then reviewed to see if they have the relevant assets and skills. **Figure 7:2** gives an overview of those areas.

Finally the analyst needs to construct a competitive strength grid which scales the firm and its major competitors or strategic group of competitors on the relevant assets and skills. The scale could range from strong to weak with intermediate points. This grid summarises the position of the major rivals with respect to each asset and skill. Since competitive advantage can be attained only by gaining and maintaining a superior position on one or more of these assets and skills relative to one's rivals, the grid can be a powerful tool in strategy development. For instance, if a firm does not have the assets and skills relevant to its industry and strategy it must either acquire it or abandon (probably modify) the strategy. The value of the grid for competitive strategy analysis is also enhanced if a longitudinal perspective is adopted. That is, the firm needs to build the grid over time to establish a trend of the changing relevance of various assets and skills and the movements of major competitors in the grid. The trend could be used to spot potential rivals who could pose serious threats to the firm.

Figure 7.2 **Analysis of strengths and weaknesses**
Source: Aaker (1995: 80)

Innovation	*Finance – Access to capital*
Technical product or service superiority	From operations
New product capability	From net short-term assets
R&D	Ability to use debt and equity financing
Technologies	Parent's willingness to finance
Patents	
	Management
Manufacturing	Quality of top and middle management
Cost structure	Knowledge of business culture
Flexible production operations	Strategic goals and plans
Equipment	Entrepreneurial thrust
Access to raw material	Planning/operation system
Vertical integration	Loyalty – turnover
Workforce attitude and motivation	Quality of strategic decision making
Capacity	
	Customer base
Marketing	Size and loyalty
Product quality reputation	Market share
Product characteristics/differentiation	Growth of segments served
Brand name recognition	
Breadth of the product line – systems capability	
Customer orientation	
Segmentation/focus	
Distribution	
Retailer relationship	
Advertising/promotion skills	
Sales force	
Customer service/product support	

7:2.5 Competitor's Future Behaviour

Competitor analysis is all about predicting the rival's most probable future behaviour in terms of their objectives and strategies. Thus it is necessary to develop a behaviour profile of each serious competitor. The key questions to be answered in order to construct this profile are as follows:

(a) *To what extent is the competitor satisfied with its current position?*

(b) *Is the competitor likely to change its current strategy, and if so, what specific changes is it likely to make?*

(c) *How much weight is it likely to put behind such change?*

(d) *What will be the likely response of other competitors to these moves? How will the anticipated responses affect the competitor initiating the changes?*

(e) *Does the competitor provide its close rivals with any opportunities? How long will these opportunities endure?*

(f) *Will the competitor be effective in responding to changes in the market and industry (including moves made by other competitors)?*

The profile 'should help the firm decide which competitors to target within each major segment and which strategies to use' (Walker *et al.*, 1992: 133).

Although each major competitor's profile might to some extent be unique, common patterns of future competitive behaviour can still be identified among competitors. **Figure 7:3** gives a brief overview of four of these behaviour patterns. It must be stressed that these patterns are most valuable when used as heuristics. Each major competitor then needs to be examined in detail.

Figure 7:3 **Common reaction profiles of competitors**
Source: Kotler (1994: 236)

---

1   ***The laid-back competitor:*** *Some competitors do not react quickly or strongly to a given competitor move. They may feel their customers are loyal; they may be milking the business; they may be slow in noticing the move; they may lack the funds to react. The firm must try to assess the reasons for the competitor's laid-back behaviour.*

2   ***The selective competitor:*** *A competitor might react only to certain types of attacks and not to others. It might respond to price cuts in order to signal that they are futile. But it might not respond to advertising expenditure increases, believing them to be less threatening. Knowing what a key competitor reacts to gives the company a clue as to the most feasible lines of attack.*

3   ***The tiger competitor:*** *This company reacts swiftly and strongly to any assault on its terrain. Thus P&G (Procter & Gamble) does not let a new detergent come easily into the market. A tiger competitor is signalling that another firm had better not attack because the defender will fight to the finish. It is always better to attack a sheep than a tiger.*

4   ***The stochastic competitor:*** *Some competitors do not exhibit a predictable reaction pattern. Such a competitor might or might not retaliate on a particular occasion, and there is no way to foretell this based on its economics, history or anything else.*

7:3 Information for Competitor Analysis

Two principal issues arise when discussing information for competitor analysis, namely:

1. *Where can the firm get the information it needs? – information source issues (see* **Ch.3, para.3:3**).
2. *How does the firm organise the information gathering, processing and dissemination functions? - information system issues.*

These issues are dealt with below.

7:3.1 Sources of Information

It is important to note that information for competitor analysis does not come from one source in an organised, well-analysed and neatly packaged form. Rather, the firm scans diverse sources in order to gather raw and often very crude data which need to be processed. Some of the data are readily available whereas some are very difficult to come by. Although the data should be valid and reliable, they need not be precise. The firm should avoid using illegal and unethical means.

There are five main sources of information of competitor analysis. First, information could be gained from ex-employees of the competitor. For example, the firm may have recruited ex-employees of the rival. Secondly, those who do business with the rival can often provide important information about competitors to the firm. Such people include equipment suppliers who can give information about installations, customers and distributors. In addition, the competitor often makes public disclosures to security analysts, shareholders, government legislators and regulators. Thirdly, published material and public documents are an excellent source of information. Such sources include trade magazines, trade shows (for information on innovation and product development), advertising (image and market positioning information), top executive speeches (for intentions and strategic direction), annual reports (for financials, satisfaction with current performance and strategic direction) and computer databases (ranging from free internet sources to commercial databases). Fourthly, observation of competitors and analysing physical evidence. This would include buying competitors' products and pulling them apart to understand both the technology, manufacturing process and cost configuration as in reverse engineering (*see* **Chs 19, 24 and 25**). And fifthly, a firm can generate its own data as in marketing research and customer surveys. Customer perception about the competitor in areas like preferences, brand recognition, quality, ranking of various competitors, etc. could be gained from this source.

7:3.2 Competitive Intelligence System

Since competitor analysis must be carried out regularly, and not on an *ad hoc* basis, the firm must set up a means by which the data required can be gathered, processed, analysed and disseminated to relevant users on time. These information tasks can be performed effectively with a well-designed, well-managed and cost-efficient competitive intelligence system. Such a system will normally be part of the firm's overall management information system (MIS) and should be able to share information efficiently with the other components of the firm's MIS. The importance of such a system is underlined by the observation that though 'the cost in money and time of gathering competitive intelligence is high, the cost of not gathering it is higher' (Kotler, 1994: 237).

To set up the system the firm needs to identify the types of information which are crucial for competitor analysis and identify the best sources for such types of information. This exercise should be reviewed periodically so that current and relevant information types and sources are always used. It is also important to assign the task of administering the system to an individual or a group of persons with the relevant information and co-ordinating skills. Next, data should be collected regularly from the information sources identified. Care should be taken not to use illegal and unethical means. In addition the validity and reliability of the data should be assessed. This assessment can be done via an assessment of the quality and integrity of the information source or by choosing the information which is confirmed by different sources. The systems should then be designed such that valid and reliable data can be analysed, interpreted and organised in an appropriate manner. What is appropriate depends on the needs of the firm in general and key users of the information, in particular. Finally, the information must be disseminated to relevant users on time. The important dissemination issues include defining target users, what means of dissemination (e.g. electronic or paper-based), how regular the information is disseminated and the time span the information or reports should cover.

7:4 Role of Accountants in Competitor Analysis

Competitor analysis is a multi-disciplinary task because the types and sources of information and the analysis required are beyond the scope of any single functional domain. Thus though it is possible to locate the design and management of the competitive intelligence system in one functional department, it is important to note that the main role of that functional department is to co-ordinate the collection and analysis of data. Within this context accountants can play two principal roles. First, they can provide the accounting and financial information and techniques which are vital to competitor analysis. These techniques and information include investment appraisal techniques (e.g. as used in appraising an investment in an exit barrier), product and process cost analysis (as part of reverse engineering effort), financial ratios (used in assessing financial performance) and evaluation of relative ability to raise funds from different sources and their impact on availability and cost of funds. Secondly, in addition to the first role, they can seek to manage the competitive intelligence system. Management accountants are seen as particularly suited for this role (Simmonds, 1981; Ward, 1992) because they:

> have [already] been spending a significant proportion of their time and effort in collecting and estimating cost, volume and price data on competition and calculating the relative strategic position of a firm and its competitors as a basis for forming business strategy.
>
> (Simmonds, 1981: 26)

Simmonds envisaged this coordinating role taking place within the ambit of strategic management accounting (*see* **Ch.2**) which he defined as:

> the provision and analysis of management accounting data about a business and its competitors for use in developing and monitoring the business strategy, particularly relative levels and trends in real costs and prices, volume, market share, cashflow and the proportion demanded of a firm's total assets.
>
> (Simmonds, 1981: 26)

Whether or not accountants are given this co-ordinating role will depend on how well they understand the manufacturing and marketing processes of the organisation – in particular what the firm's own distinctive capabilities and sources of competitive advantage are. The situation will differ from organisation to organisation.

References

Aaker, David A. (1995) *Strategic market management*, 4th edn. New York: John Wiley & Sons.

Halberstam, David (1986) *The reckoning*. New York: William Morrow.

Kotler, Philip (1994) *Marketing management: Analysis, planning, implementation and control*, 8th edn. Englewood Cliffs, NJ: Prentice-Hall International.

Oster, Sharon M. (1994) *Modern competitive analysis*, 2nd edn. New York: Oxford University Press.

Simmonds, Kenneth (1981) 'Strategic management accounting', *Management Accounting* (UK), March: 26–9.

Walker, Orville C., Boyd, Harper W. and Larreche, Jean-Claude (1992) *Marketing strategy: Planning and implementation*. Homewood, IL: Irwin.

Ward, Keith (1992) *Strategic management accounting*. Oxford: Butterworth-Heinemann.

8. Research and Development (R&D) Performance Measurement

8:1 Introduction

8:1.1 Pressures for R&D Performance Evaluation

Many factors are changing the way that R&D is managed. Considerations of cost, risk, time, available expertise and the diversity of technologies needed to create new products are just a few of the factors increasing the pressure to manage R&D activity in a much more systematic, market-oriented and integrated way. The escalating expenditure on R&D that many companies must now incur simply to maintain a fast response capability is causing managers to question the productivity and effectiveness of their R&D budgets. Although the corporate-funded R&D of UK companies is currently over £9 billion, nevertheless the evidence of *The UK R&D Scoreboard*, 1996, shows that UK companies have been consistently investing at a lower intensity than their major competitors. The OECD reported in 1989 that: 'The UK was the only country [of the 24 OECD member countries] where growth in R&D expenditure was lower than growth in GDP' (OECD, 1989: 14).

The growing interest in R&D performance evaluation in the UK is an acknowledgement that a loss of competitiveness is almost inevitable unless UK companies can counter a lower rate of R&D expenditure with a more effective management of R&D than their higher-spending rivals.

Yet for all the attention that has been focused on performance measurement (PM) systems in the last few years and the various competing models of PM that have emerged, such as 'the performance pyramid' (Lynch and Cross, 1991) (*see* **Ch.49,**

Para.49:2.2) and 'the balanced scorecard' (Kaplan and Norton, 1992) (*see* **Ch.49,** **Para.49:2.3**), the measurement of R&D productivity and effectiveness has received relatively little attention in the management control and accounting literatures.

It is non-accounting organisations like the European Industrial Research Management Association (EIRMA), the Industrial Research Institute of the United States and the American Productivity and Quality Centre which are taking the initiative in promoting studies and conferences on R&D PM. However, the activities and publications of these organisations have a low profile in the mainstream management literature, especially in the strategic management area. Most of the work on R&D evaluation is, to judge from the literature and conference proceedings, being carried out by scientists, engineers, research managers and economists. The technical, non-financial, nature of these R&D PM systems (all of which have cost, contribution, cash-flow and risk implications) are more suitable for operations control and project management than for strategy formulation and product portfolio planning.

The need to link technical and financial metrics of R&D performance is not just a matter of internal communication and integrating strategy and operations. In the USA R&D directors report that: 'the pressure to do more with less has caused significant changes in their R&D practices' (Gupta and Wilemon, 1996: 506). In Britain shareholders have begun to demand more information about the precise contribution of R&D to corporate performance and are increasingly unhappy with explanations that: 'We do not know what they do, except that the money disappears, but now and again a good idea comes out' (Weinstock, 1991: 266).

8:1.2 Information Needs of Investors

Institutional investors, in particular, have stated that they cannot attribute a proper value to a company's reported R&D expenditure unless information is also provided that indicates its effectiveness. *SSAP13: Accounting for Research and Development* gives guidance on the issue. The relevant international standard is *IAS38: Intangibles*, which defines research as 'original and planned investigation undertaken with the prospect of gaining new scientific or technical knowledge and understanding', and development as 'the application of research findings or other knowledge to a plan or design for the production of new or substantially improved materials, devices, products, processes, systems or services before the start of commercial production or use'. On the premise that information on successful innovation in the past is indicative of the likely success of current and future (R&D) expenditure, the Institutional Shareholders' Committee (1992) suggested that they would find it especially useful to have information on:

(a) *the split between research and development;*

(b) *the allocation of total R&D expenditure to different company divisions;*

(c) *the proportion of current sales attributable to products introduced in the last three to five years; and*

(d) *case histories of any R&D-led successes in recent years.*

This kind of external pressure is, independently of other competitive pressures, forcing CEOs to demand better ways of measuring the return on R&D expenditure, if not quantitatively then at least qualitatively (e.g. explanation of the contribution of R&D to competitive advantage in particular product groups). Evidence from the literature on R&D management and product innovation, from related conference proceedings and empirical research undertaken by the author, suggests that more companies are now attempting to overcome the difficulties that have in the past deterred them from measuring and baselining R&D effectiveness.

8:2 Difficulties of R&D Performance Evaluation

One major difficulty in evaluating R&D activities is that successful innovation requires many performance and structural characteristics that no one function can completely control. Other constraints on attempts to measure R&D performance include:

(a) *the complexity of R&D activities, which may range from applied research in pursuit of new knowledge to the development that seeks applications for this knowledge;*

(b) *the long time lag (between research, invention and innovation) that is almost inevitable in some R&D areas, for example, the pharmaceutical and aerospace industries;*

(c) *the R&D process is a sub-system of the organisation with its own inputs (e.g. people, funds, equipment, information, ideas), activities (e.g. research, developing, testing, reporting) and outputs (e.g. patents, publications, information, technology, projects completed, products, processes);*

(d) *the belief that: 'We still need unfettered research' (Odlyzko, 1996: 9).*

However, the practical difficulties and limitations of R&D evaluation are, to judge from growing interest in R&D PM, outweighed by the benefits to be gained from carefully conducted evaluation in terms of better communication, consensus building and more effective decisions.

8:3 Some Possible Methods of Evaluating R&D Performance

The literature on R&D management identifies not only a broad array of quantitative, semi-quantitative and qualitative approaches but also provides some guidance, based mostly on case histories, of those system features that should be adopted and those that are best avoided. The EIRMA report, based on 21 in-depth case studies and an extensive literature review, identified over 100 R&D methods of R&D evaluation in 14 broad classes (*see* **Table 8:1**). The report concluded that it is especially important to note that:

(a) *whichever method is used, the most important outcome of a properly structured evaluation is improved communication;*

(b) *no single approach to pre-evaluation (ex-ante evaluation) meets all circumstances. This is because an R&D measurement system must be consistent with 'the way R&D is organised, planned and budgeted, including the management structure, decision-making process, links to other functions and prevailing R&D culture' (EIRMA, 1995: 46).*

Table 8:1 **Classes of R&D evaluation methods**

Source: EIRMA, 1995

Classes	R&D evaluation methods
1	Ratio methods
2	Economic score index methods
3	Financial score index methods
4	Mixed score index methods
5	Mathematical methods
6	Matrix methods
7	Checklists
8	Relevance trees
9	Multi-criteria and table methods
10	Consensus methods
11	Project appraisal method (PAM)
12	Quality function deployment
13	Experience-based methods
14	Vision

8:4 Which Measures are Appropriate?

The literature and practical experience of PM and R&D evaluation suggest that the choice of measures and the way they are used in specific situations are influenced by at least five factors:

1. *Top management views on R&D measurement; for example, if top management believes that trying to predict the likely future benefits of R&D is largely futile then that company's R&D measurement system is likely to place greater emphasis on ex-post, historic, evaluation than on ex-ante assessment.*
2. *Different perspectives that need to be accommodated and balanced; for example, the 'balanced scorecard' (see **Ch.49, Para.49:2.3**) suggests the financial (shareholder), customer, internal business process, learning and growth perspectives. Other perspectives that might need to be made explicit are those of employees and suppliers, who may have to meet tight schedule and cost targets set by the company, as well as research collaborators, 'strategic alliance' partners and environmentalists.*
3. *The risks inherent in R&D; for example, technological, commercial, financial, management, project, portfolio and personal risks for those involved.*
4. *Features specific to certain industries; for example, nature of entry and exit barriers, number and size of strategic groups, intensity of competition.*
5. *Specific organisational features and arrangements including, for example, the organisational 'climate'; conventional wisdom suggests it is extremely difficult to implement new measures successfully in a period of downsizing.*

8:5 R&D Risks and Capital Investment Appraisal Techniques

A recurring theme in the R&D PM debate is the need to match the evaluation criteria and measures to the stage of development and in particular to distinguish between high-risk pioneering research and more incremental development. It is frequently argued that conventional capital investment appraisal techniques, including discounted cash flow (DCF) and payback methods, constrain investment in R&D and new technology because they:

(a) fail to deal explicitly with the implications of not pursuing research – the opportunity cost concept; and

(b) are systematically biased towards the short term.

However, when such claims are viewed in the context of the typically protracted 'stage-gate' process (Cooper, 1993) that new product development (NPD) necessitates it usually means simply that these appraisal techniques are being applied too early. In the idea generation stage, or so-called 'fuzzy front end', of NPD the consequences of *not* investing (in terms, for example, of lost market share as products mature) and the costs and potential benefits of proceeding to the next stage and keeping options open (the option pricing theory concept) are more appropriate methods of dealing with uncertainty than the more commonly applied DCF methods (*see* **Ch.11**). The latter approach is likely to be most valuable when future cash flows, both receipts and payments, can be predicted with reasonable reliability as, for example, most near-market developments of a product and service for which the risk dimensions are well known.

Part of the current appeal of option pricing theory (OPT) in the context of R&D and financial management is that it advocates a cautious step-by-step approach that maps well onto the intensive and extensive discussions, which the risk-reduction/consensus-building process of most innovative projects entails. The OPT approach is suitable not only to the high uncertainty that prevails in the early stages of innovative projects but it also supports the trend away from developing products one at a time and towards developing technology platforms for a family of products, that may span several generations (*see* **Ch.19, Para.19:1.1**). A DCF-based approach to evaluating platform technologies is likely to filter out numerous downstream opportunities that could be potentially valuable; the OPT perspective, by contrast, recognises that such expenditures are intended to create opportunities to generate a stream of new products. OPT is therefore, not only consistent with NPD practice but it also offsets the short-term bias of DCF.

8:6 Effective R&D Performance Measurement

8:6.1 Measures of R&D Performance that Work

Certain features of effective R&D PM systems appear to have fairly general application although most of the relevant literature emphasises the dominant influence of specific situational factors and the need to ensure that the system is consistent with: 'the way that R&D is organised, planned and budgeted, including the management structure, decision-making processes, links to other functions and prevailing R&D culture' (EIRMA, 1995: 46).

There is broad agreement that an effective R&D PM system usually has the following features:

(a) *a strategic orientation. R&D outputs such as patents obtained, papers published, research proposals written, awards won, projects completed are relatively easy to measure in an objective way and relate to variables that the R&D team can influence; however, without a measure of their quality and value to the organisation such immediate R&D outputs are unlikely to support the attainment of strategic objectives. The goals on which the R&D PM system focuses must be clearly seen by top management to be closely linked to corporate objectives; without such an evident link the R&D activity is more likely to be perceived as a service function that might be outsourced than as a strategic core competency;*

(b) *supports the achievement of critical success factors (CSFs). In many innovative projects it will not be possible to precisely define the CSFs until a good deal of the technological and commercial uncertainty has been reduced. In general the CSFs reflect the performance, quality, functionality, time-to-market and life-cycle cost requirements of customers. Definition of these needs is the basis for articulating more precisely the technical and financial goals that must be achieved; these goals are the basis of the PM systems and the means of balancing the customers' cost and value needs with the company's contribution and cash-flow requirements;*

(c) *has a balance of financial and non-financial measures (see* **Chs 48 and 49**). *This need arises partly because in the early stages of innovative projects much of the information is of a qualitative nature; in part also the need reflects the communication, co-ordination and collaboration that must take place among the many disparate participants in NPD projects. Case study evidence suggests that in the idea generation/concept development stage the performance criteria and measures are more strategic, qualitative and subjective; the measures become more operational, quantitative and objective as progress is made towards a final design;*

(d) *is simple. It is frequently asserted that: 'The best [R&D] performance measurement systems are based on the collection of data on six to eight key indices. Those indices should be a combination of quality, quantity and cost measures' (Brown and Svenson, 1988: 58). Another factor that tends to increase the number of measures is the power of the informal information system relative to the formal system; the more reliable, extensive and current the formal system the less dependence is placed on formal measures. A further influence on the relative simplicity/complexity of the PM system is the emphasis that top management places on* ex-ante *and* ex-post *evaluation respectively and on project team performance vis-à-vis the contribution of participant disciplines within the team;*

(e) *encourages collaboration among the internal multi-disciplinary team members and between the team and other product development team members like the customer, suppliers, research collaborators and financiers.*

In one small company that relies on constant product innovation for survival top management carefully evaluates proposed R&D expenditure by reference to:

(a) *the consequences of deferring or not proceeding with the expenditure in terms of the effect on the company's competitive strength, market share, future opportunities and growth;*

(b) *the risks involved; the joint managing directors (an engineer and a marketeer) believe that they need to be very conservative and therefore take a very incremental approach to risk management that employs the principle of OPT. Only when the perceived risk is reduced to an acceptable level, and the value of the option to defer is therefore low, is a commitment made to full-scale development;*

(c) *the degree of consistency between the proposed R&D expenditure and the company's core technologies and competitive strategies.*

8:6.2 Metrics to Support Collaboration

However, once a project is undertaken the focus of the measurement system shifts entirely to support the attainment of project goals and no attempt is made to evaluate the performance of any single function on the grounds that it is the success of the project that is important to the company and that responsibility for managing CSFs cannot be allocated exclusively to any single function. Like the managers of the Japanese industrial manufacturer, Komatsu, this small engineering company does: 'not measure success one department at a time. They know that the market-place does not reward an outstanding component, only an outstanding integrated design' (Cooper, 1995: 94). This premise promotes the collaboration, openness, trust and confidence that top management seeks to foster; there is a wealth of empirical evidence that indicates that these organisational attributes are essential to successful innovation. There is also a broad consensus that these features are difficult to develop and maintain; they are easily eroded by performance measures that are inappropriate and/or incorrectly used.

One of the major changes that has occurred in the management of R&D in the last decade, driven, in part, by the need to do more with less, is that: 'business strategy is shaping technology to a much greater extent than the other way around' (Gupta and Wilemon, 1996: 502). A related development is that increasingly: 'Both the tactical and strategic value of R&D to the business must be marketed and sold effectively if business investment in R&D is to be sustained' (Lever, 1997: 39). Management accountants can play a vital role in developing R&D PM systems that both: (a) help to create synergy between technology and business strategies; and (b) evaluate R&D expenditure as an investment rather than to simply treat it as an expense of the period in which it is incurred, which is the practice for fiscal and external reporting purposes. Such a role, however, requires a good understanding of the R&D management process and of the many factors that influence the commercial exploitation of technology; it also requires management accountants to transcend functional boundaries in order to be effective participants in multi-disciplinary teams.

Acknowledgements

The author is grateful to the Design Council, London, for funding the research on which this chapter is based. Sincere thanks are also due to my co-researcher, John Innes, who provided an invaluable contribution at every stage.

References

Brown, M.G. and Svenson, R.A. (1988) 'Measuring R&D productivity', *Research-Technology Management*, July–August, reproduced in Industrial Research Institute (IRI) (1994), *Measuring and improving the performance and return on R&D*, Washington, DC: IRI.

Cooper, R. (1993) *Winning at new products: Accelerating the process from idea to launch*, 2nd edn. Reading, MA: Addison-Wesley Publishing Company.

Cooper, R. (1995) *When lean enterprises collide: Competing through confrontation*. Boston, MA: Harvard Business School Press.

European Industrial Research Management Association (EIRMA) (1995) *Evaluation of R&D Projects*. Paris: EIRMA.

Gupta, A.K. and Wilemon, D. (1996) 'Changing patterns in industrial R&D management', *The Journal of Product Innovation Management, 13(6)*, November: 497–511.

Institutional Shareholders' Committee (ISC) (1992) *Suggested disclosure of R&D expenditure*. London: ISC.

Kaplan, R.S. and Norton, D.P. (1992) 'The balanced scorecard – Measures that drive performance', *Harvard Business Review*, January–February: 71–9.

Lever, O.W. (1997) 'Selling and marketing of R&D', *Research-Technology Management, 40(4)* July–August: 39–45.

Lynch, R.L. and Cross, K.F. (1991) *Measure up: Yardsticks for continuous improvement*. Cambridge, MA: Blackwell Publishers.

Odlyzko, A.M. (1996) 'We still need unfettered research', *Research-Technology Management, 39(1):* 31-7.

OECD (1989) *Science and technology indicators report,* No.3. Paris: OECD.

Weinstock, A. (1991) in oral evidence to House of Lords Select Committee on Science and Technology, *Innovation in Manufacturing Industry.* London: HMSO.

9. **Budgeting**

9:1 Introduction

9:1.1 Relationship Between Budgeting and Long-term Planning

Every organisation needs to plan and consider how to confront future potential risks and opportunities. In most organisations this process is formalised by preparing annual budgets and monitoring performance against the budgets. Budgets are merely a collection of plans and forecasts. They reflect the financial implications of business plans, identifying the amount, quantity and timing of resources needed.

The annual budget should be set within the context of longer-term plans, which are likely to exist even if they have not been made explicit. Long-term planning involves strategic planning over several years (*see* **Chs 2, 3** and **5**) and the identification of the basic strategy of the firm (i.e. the future direction the organisation will take) and the gaps which exist between the future needs and present capabilities. A long-term plan is a statement of the preliminary targets and activities required by an organisation to achieve its strategic plans together with a broad estimate for each year of the resources required. Because long-term planning involves 'looking into the future' for several years the plans tend to be uncertain, general in nature, imprecise and subject to change.

Annual budgeting is concerned with the implementation of the long-term plan for the year ahead. Because of the shorter planning horizon budgets are more precise and detailed. Budgets are a clear indication of what is expected to be achieved during the budget period whereas long-term plans represent the broad directions that top management intend to follow.

The budget is not something that originates 'from nothing' each year (*see* **Ch.12**) – it is developed within the context of ongoing business and is ruled by previous decisions that have been taken within the long-term planning process. The budget process is not, however, one where the activities for individual years, included in the long-term plan, are merely added together. When the activities are initially approved for inclusion in the long-term plan, they are based on uncertain estimates that are projected for several years. These proposals must be reviewed and revised in the light of more recent information.

This review and revision process frequently takes place as part of the annual budgeting process, and it may result in important decisions being taken on possible activity adjustments within the current budget period. The budgeting process cannot therefore be viewed as being purely concerned with the current year – it must be considered as an integrated part of the long-term planning process.

9:2 The Different Roles of Budgets

9:2.1 Multiple Functions of Budgets

Budgeting is recommended as an important technique which helps management in at least six ways:

1. *by forcing managers to plan ahead and reduce the number of ad hoc decisions;*
2. *by aiding communication as management set out objectives and lower management indicate the problems and opportunities they perceive. Everyone in the organisation should have a clear understanding of the role they are expected to play in achieving the annual budget. This process will ensure that the appropriate individuals are made accountable for implementing the budget. Through the budget, top management communicates its expectations to lower-level management, so that all members of the organisation may understand these expectations and can co-ordinate their activities to attain them;*
3. *by aiding co-ordination as separate functional departments provide inputs that have to be reconciled during the budget process. A sound budgeting system helps to co-ordinate the separate activities and ensure that all parts of the organisation are in mutual harmony;*
4. *by setting clearly defined targets which (if set at an appropriate level of difficulty and accepted by managers) aid motivation. If individuals have already participated in preparing the budget, and it is used as a tool to assist managers in managing their activities, it can act as a strong motivational device by providing a challenge. Alternatively, if the budget is dictated from above, and imposes a threat rather than a challenge, it may be resisted and do more harm than good;*
5. *by providing standards and plans which can be employed as part of the control process. By comparing actual results with the budgeted amounts for different categories of expenses, managers can ascertain which costs do not conform with the original plan and thus require their attention;*

6. *by providing a yardstick against which managers can be evaluated. A manager's performance is often evaluated by measuring his or her success in meeting the budgets.*

The multi-functional role of budgets provides an apparently overwhelming case for employing them and, despite the well-documented dysfunctional behavioural consequences which budgets tend to generate, most companies do set budgets. For example, a survey by Puxty and Lyall (1989) of 453 UK companies reported that 94% of the responding companies operated budgeting systems.

9:2.2 Conflicting Roles of Budgets

Because a single budget system is normally used to serve several purposes there is a danger that they may conflict with each other. For instance the planning and motivation roles may be in conflict with each other. Demanding budgets that may not be achieved may be appropriate to motivate maximum performance, but they are unsuitable for planning purposes. For these a budget should be set based on easier targets that are expected to be met.

There is also a conflict between the planning and performance evaluation roles. For planning purposes budgets are set in advance of the budget period based on an anticipated set of circumstances or environment. Performance evaluation should be based on a comparison of actual performance with an adjusted budget to reflect the circumstances under which managers actually operated. In practice, many firms compare actual performance with the original budget (adjusted to the actual level of activity, i.e. a flexible budget), but if the circumstances envisaged when the original budget was set have changed then there will be a planning and evaluation conflict.

9:3 The Budgeting Process

9:3.1 The Budget Period

The conventional approach is that once per year the manager of each budget centre prepares a detailed budget for one year. The budget is divided into either 12 monthly or 13 four-weekly periods for control purposes.

An alternative approach is for the annual budget to be broken down by months for the first three months, and by quarters for the remaining nine months. The quarterly budgets are then developed on a monthly basis as the year proceeds. For example, during the first quarter, the monthly budgets for the second quarter will be prepared; and during the second quarter, the monthly budgets for the third quarter will be prepared. The quarterly budgets may also be reviewed as the year unfolds. For example, during the first quarter, the budget for the next three quarters may be changed as new information becomes available. A new budget for the fifth quarter will also be prepared. This process is known as *continuous or rolling budgeting* and ensures that a 12-month budget is always available by adding a quarter in the future as the quarter just ended is dropped. In contrast, when budgets are prepared once per year the period for which a budget is available will shorten as the year goes by until the budget for the next year is prepared. Rolling budgets also ensure that planning is not something that takes place once a year when the budget is being formulated. Instead, budgeting is a continuous process, and managers are encouraged to constantly look ahead and review future plans.

9:3.2 Stages in the Budget Process

The important stages are as follows:

(a) *communicating details of budget policy and guidelines to those people responsible for the preparation of budgets;*
(b) *determining the factor that restricts output;*
(c) *preparation of the sales budget;*
(d) *initial preparation of various budgets;*
(e) *final acceptance of budgets;*
(f) *monitoring of actual results against the budget.*

9:3.3 Communicating Details of Budget Policy and Guidelines

It is essential that all those staff who are responsible for preparing the current year's budgets are made aware of the policy of top management for implementing the long-term plan so that common guidelines can be established. Policy effects might include planned changes in the sales mix, or the expansion or discontinuation of certain activities. In addition, other important guidelines that are to govern the preparation of the budgets should be specified. For example, planning assumptions such as changes to be made for inflation, exchange rates and productivity.

9:3.4 Determining the Factor that Restricts Output

In every organisation there is some factor which is a binding constraint on the profitability for a given period. In the majority of organisations this factor is sales demand. However, it is possible for production capacity to restrict performance when sales demand is in excess of available capacity. Prior to the preparation of the budgets, it is necessary for top management to determine the factor that restricts performance since this factor determines the point at which the annual budgeting process should begin.

9:3.5 Preparation of the Sales Budget

The volume of sales and the sales mix determine the level of a company's operations, when sales demand is the factor which restricts output. For this reason the sales budget is the most important plan in the annual budgeting process. This budget is the most difficult to produce because the outcome is dependent on external factors such as the state of the economy and the actions of competitors.

9:3.6 Initial Preparation of the Budgets

The managers who are responsible for meeting the budgeted performance should prepare the budgets for those areas for which they are responsible. The preparation of the budget should be a 'bottom-up' process. This means that the budget should originate at the lowest levels of management and be refined and co-ordinated at higher levels. The justification for this approach is that it enables managers to participate in the preparation of their budgets and increases the probability that they will accept the budget and strive to achieve the budget targets.

9:3.7 Negotiation of Budgets

To implement the participative approach to budgeting, the budget should be originated at the lowest level of management. The management at this level should submit their budget to their superiors for approval. The superior should then incorporate this budget with other budgets for which he or she is responsible and then submit this budget for approval to his or her supervisor. The manager who is the superior then becomes the budgetee at the next higher level and so on. This process has been described by Sizer (1989) as a two-way process of a top-down statement of objectives and strategies, bottom-up budget preparation and top-down approval by senior management.

The negotiation process is of vital importance in the budgeting process, and can determine whether the budget becomes a really effective management tool or just a clerical device. If managers are successful in establishing a position of trust and confidence with their subordinates, the negotiation process will produce a meaningful improvement in the budgetary process and outcomes for the period.

9:3.8 Co-ordination and Review of Budgets

As the individual budgets move up the organisational hierarchy in the negotiation process, they must be examined in relation to each other. This examination may indicate that some budgets are out of balance with other budgets and need modifying so that they will become compatible with other conditions, constraints and plans that are beyond a manager's knowledge or control.

During the co-ordination process, a budgeted profit and loss account, a balance sheet and a cash-flow statement should be prepared to ensure that all the parts combine to produce an acceptable whole. Otherwise further adjustments and budget recycling will be necessary until an acceptable whole is produced.

9:3.9 Final Acceptance of Budgets

When all the budgets are in harmony with each other, they are summarised into a master budget consisting of a budgeted profit and loss, balance sheet and cash-flow statement (*see* **Ch.10**). After the master budget has been approved, the budgets are then passed down through the organisation to the appropriate budget centres. The approval of the master budget is the authority for the manager to carry out the plans contained in each budget.

9:3.10 Monitoring Actual Results Against the Budget

At frequent intervals (normally monthly) for each budget centre a report should be prepared comparing actual results with budgeted results. Budget performance reports enable management to identify items that are not proceeding according to plan and to investigate the reasons for the differences. If these differences are within the control of management corrective action should be taken to avoid such inefficiencies occurring again in the future. However, if the differences are due to the actual conditions during the budget year being different from those envisaged when the budget was prepared the budgets for the remainder of the year may have to be amended to reflect the change in conditions.

9:4 Incremental and Zero-base Budgeting

9:4.1 Incremental Budgeting

Budgets are normally prepared on an incremental basis. This means that existing operations and the current budgeted allowance for existing activities are taken as the starting point for preparing the next annual budget. The base is then adjusted for changes (such as changes in product mix, volumes and prices) which are expected to occur during the new budget period. Hence, the budget process is concerned mainly with the increment in operations or expenditure that will occur in the forthcoming period. The major disadvantage of the incremental approach is that the majority of expenditure, which is associated with the 'base level' of activity, remains unchanged. Thus, past inefficiencies and waste inherent in the current way of doing things are perpetuated.

9:4.2 Zero-base Budgeting
(*See* **Ch.12.**)

An alternative to incremental budgeting is zero-base budgeting (also known as priority-based budgeting). This approach requires that all activities are justified and prioritised before decisions are taken relating to the amount of resources allocated to each activity. Besides adopting a 'zero-based' approach zero-base budgeting (ZBB) also focuses on programmes or activities instead of functional departments based on line-items, which is a feature of traditional budgeting.

ZBB works from the premise that projected expenditure for existing programmes should start from base zero, with each year's budgets being compiled as if the programmes were being launched for the first time. The budgetees should present their requirements for appropriations in such a fashion that all funds can be allocated on the basis of cost-benefit or some similar kind of evaluative analysis. The cost-benefit approach is an attempt to ensure 'value for money'; it questions long-standing assumptions and serves as a tool for systematically examining and perhaps abandoning any unproductive projects. ZBB is best suited to discretionary costs and support activities. Direct production and service costs where input/output relationships exist are more suited to traditional budgeting using standard costs.

9:4.3 Decision Packages

ZBB involves the following three stages:

1. *a description of each organisational activity in a decision package;*
2. *the evaluation and ranking of decision packages in order of priority;*
3. *allocation of resources based on order of priority up to the spending cut-off level.*

Decision packages are identified for each decision unit. Decision units represent separate programmes or groups of activities that an organisation undertakes. A decision package represents the operation of a particular programme with incremental packages reflecting different levels of effort that may be expended on a specific function. One package is usually prepared at the 'base' level for each programme. This package represents the minimum level of service or support consistent with the organisation's objectives. Service or support higher than the base level is described in one or more incremental packages. For example, managers might be asked to specify the base package in terms of level of service that can be provided at 70% of the current cost level and incremental packages identify higher activity or cost levels.

Once the decision packages have been completed, management is ready to start to review the process. To determine how much to spend and where to spend it, management will rank all packages in order of decreasing benefits to the organisation. Theoretically, once management has set the budgeted level of spending, the packages should be accepted down to the spending level based on cost-benefit principles.

9:4.4 Advantages of ZBB

The benefits of ZBB over traditional methods of budgeting are claimed to be as follows:

(a) *Traditional budgeting tends to extrapolate the past by adding a percentage increase to the current year. ZBB avoids the deficiencies of incremental budgeting and represents a move towards the allocation of resources by need or benefit. Thus, unlike traditional budgeting the level of funding is not taken for granted.*
(b) *ZBB creates a questioning attitude rather than one that assumes that current practice represents value for money.*
(c) *ZBB focuses attention on outputs in relation to value for money.*

9:4.5 Usage of ZBB

ZBB was first applied in Texas Instruments in 1969. It quickly became one of the fashionable management tools of the 1970s and, according to Phyrr (1976), there were 100 users in the USA in the early 1970s including the State of Georgia whose governor was ex-president Jimmy Carter. When he became the US President, he directed that all federal agencies adopt ZBB.

During the 1970s many articles on ZBB were published but they declined rapidly towards the end of the decade, and by the 1980s they had become a rarity. ZBB has never achieved the widespread adoption that its proponents envisaged. The major reason for its lack of success would appear to be that it is too costly and time consuming. The process of identifying decision packages and determining their purpose, cost and benefits is extremely time consuming. Furthermore, there are often too many decision packages to evaluate and there is frequently insufficient information to enable them to be ranked.

Research suggests that many organisations tend to approximate the principles of ZBB rather than applying the full-scale approach outlined in the literature. For example, it does not have to be applied throughout the organisation. It can be applied selectively to those areas about which management is most concerned and used as a one-off cost-reduction programme. Some of the benefits of ZBB can be captured by using priority-based incremental budgets. Priority incremental budgets require managers to specify what incremental activities or changes would occur if their budgets were increased or decreased by a specified percentage (say 10%). Budget allocations are made by comparing the change in costs with the change in benefits. Priority incremental budgets thus represent an economical compromise between ZBB and incremental budgeting.

9:5 Activity-based Budgeting
(*See* Ch.13.)

9:5.1 Deficiencies of Conventional Budgeting

The conventional approach to budgeting works well for those activities where there are well-defined input–output relationships such that the consumption of resources usually varies proportionately with the volume of final output of products or services. Flexible budgets can be used to control the costs of these activities. For those indirect costs and support activities where there are no clearly defined input–output relationships, and the consumption of resources does not vary with the final output of products or services, conventional budgets merely serve as authorisation levels for certain levels of spending for each budgeted item of expense. Budgets that are not based on well-understood relationships between activities and costs are poor indicators of performance and performance reporting normally implies little more than checking whether the budget has been exceeded. Conventional budgets therefore provide little relevant information for managing the costs of support activities.

9:5.2 Activity-based Budgeting

To manage costs more effectively and evaluate the performance of support activities the principles of activity-based cost management have been extended to budgeting. The distinguishing features of activity-based budgeting (ABB) are:

(a) costs are analysed by activities and expense categories;
(b) a physical output measure is identified for each activity.

The physical output measure is known as a 'cost driver'. Cost drivers are the forces that are the significant determinants of the cost of activities. For example, if the cost of the production scheduling activity is caused by the number of production runs that each product generates, then the number of set-ups could represent the cost driver for production scheduling.

The conventional approach to budgeting analyses costs by expense categories for each budget centre but does not provide any information on the anticipated outputs or outcomes arising from the expenditure. In contrast, ABB analyses costs by activities and thus provides management with information on why costs are being incurred and the output (in terms of the cost driver) measured by the number of times the activity is undertaken. Activity-based budgets are presented in a matrix format similar to the format illustrated in **Fig.9:1** which shows the budget for an order receiving department. In **Fig.9:1** the major activities are shown in each of the columns and the resource inputs are listed by rows. The cost-driver activity levels are also highlighted. The major advantage of ABB is the enhanced visibility arising from showing the outcomes from the budgeted expenditure. This information is particularly useful for planning and estimating future expenditure.

Figure 9:1 **Activity-based budget for an order receiving department**

Activities	Handle import goods	Execute express orders	Special deliveries	Distribution administration	Order receiving (standard products)	Order receiving (non-standard products)	Execute rush orders	Total cost
Expense accounts								
Office supplies								
Telephone expenses								
Salaries								
Travel								
Training								
Total cost								
Activity measures	Number of customs documents	Number of customer bills	Number of letters	Number of consignment notes	Number of standard orders	Number of non-standard orders	Number of rush orders	

When ABB is first introduced the activities must be identified by undertaking an activity analysis of the work performed in a department. Cost drivers for each activity must also be established. For a detailed discussion of these two stages you should refer to **Chapter 13, paragraphs 13:2 and 13:3.** The next stage is to determine the current planned resources that are committed to the activity. This will normally be the resources that are currently available. In addition, the capacity that can be supplied, expressed in terms of cost driver activity levels, from the current planned resources committed to the activity must be determined. For example, assume that in **Fig.9:1** the budgeted salary costs committed to the processing of the receipt of standard customers' orders activity are £150,000 for the year, and six staff are currently employed on the activity. If each member of staff can process on average 50 orders per month then the actual capacity supplied in terms of the cost-driver level is 3,600 orders (6 staff × 50 orders × 12 months).

The next stage is to convert the budgeted production into the budgeted activity usage for the cost driver. Let us assume that in order to meet budgeted production it is estimated that 3,000 orders will be required. Thus, attention is drawn to the fact that there is an excess supply of staff resources with only 831/3% of the capacity supplied (3,000/3,600 orders) being utilised. Management is therefore made aware that the budget could be reduced by £25,000 by transferring one member of staff to other activities where staff resources need to be expanded or, more drastically, making them redundant. The decision, however, should be based on long-term considerations and not a reaction to short-term excess capacity. Nevertheless, the ABB approach highlights in advance excess resources and the need for management to focus on the long-term consequences and the actions required.

Some of the expenses (such as office supplies and telephone expenses) listed in **Fig.9:1** for the processing of customers' orders activity are more likely to vary in the short term with the number of orders processed. With conventional budgeting the budgeted expenses for the forthcoming budget would normally be based on the previous year's budget plus an adjustment for inflation. Assuming that the level of activity for the previous budget period was 3,600 orders then the budget for those expense items that vary in the short term with the number of orders processed should be reduced by one-sixth to reflect the predicted decline in activity to 3,000 orders.

ABB therefore provides a framework for understanding the amount of resources that are required to achieve the budgeted level of activity. By comparing the amount of resources that are required with the amount of resources that are in place, upwards or downwards adjustments can be made during the budget setting phase. For some resources, however, a lengthy time lag may be required to adjust the supply to the anticipated level of demand, and adjustments may not be possible within the current budget period.

Periodically actual results should be compared with a budget flexed to the actual output for the activities (in terms of cost drivers) to highlight both in financial and non-financial terms those activities with major discrepancies from budget. Assume that practical capacity for salaries for the processing of customers' standard orders activity was maintained at 3,600 orders, even though budgeted activity was only 3,000 orders, and the actual number of orders processed during the period was 2,800 orders. Also assume that the actual resources committed to the activity in respect of salaries was £150,000 (all fixed in the short term). The following information should be presented in the performance report shown in **Fig.9:2**.

Figure 9:2 **Performance report**

	£
Flexed budget (2,800 orders x £41.67)	116,676
Budgeted unused capacity cost (–3,600 – 3,000) x £41.67	25,000
Capacity utilisation variance – Actual unused capacity (3,000 – 2,800) x £41.67	8,333
	150,000

The cost driver rate of £41.67 per order processed is calculated by dividing the £150,000 budgeted cost of supplying the resources by the capacity supplied (3,600 orders). The variances highlight for management attention the potential reduction in the supply of resources of £33,333 (£25,000 expected and £8,333 unexpected) or, alternatively, the additional business that can be accommodated with the existing supply of resources.

9:6 The Behavioural Aspects of Budgeting

9:6.1 Introduction

For the successful operation of a budget system attention needs to be given not only to the technical characteristics but also to the so-called 'behavioural aspects' of budgeting. If the behavioural aspects of budgeting are ignored there is a danger that budgets may encourage undesirable behaviour that hinders the accomplishment of the organisation's objectives. Much research has been conducted into the behavioural aspects of budgeting. **Paragraphs 9:6.2** to **9:6.6** summarise the major findings relating to how people behave in relation to budgeting in respect of the following:

(a) *the effect of budget levels on performance;*
(b) *the dysfunctional consequences of performance measures;*
(c) *managerial use of budget information in performance reporting;*
(d) *participation in the budgeting process;*
(e) *contingency theory approach to budgeting.*

9:6.2 The Effect of Budget Levels on Performance

There is substantial evidence from a large number of studies that the existence of a defined, quantitative goal or target is likely to motivate higher levels of performance than when no such target is stated. Furthermore, the more difficult and demanding the goal that is set in general the better the resulting performance although extremely difficult goals may lead to a decline in performance. Such goals are likely to be seen as unattainable causing a person to give up and produce a performance that is worse than if a less demanding goal had been set. The highest level of performance is likely to result from the most difficult goal that will be accepted by a manager and thus internalised as his or her personal goal or aspiration level. The fact that budgets represent definite, quantitative goals means that they have a strong motivational potential, but standards must be accepted by budgetees if they are to motivate high levels of performance.

Figure 9:3 derived from Otley (1987), shows the research findings relating to the effect of budget levels on aspiration levels and performance. As the level of budget difficulty is increased both the budgetee's aspiration and performance increases. However, there becomes a point where the budget is perceived as impossible to achieve and the aspiration level and performance decline dramatically. It can be seen from **Fig.9:3** that the budget level which motivates the best performance may not be achieved. However, a budget that is expected to be achieved (i.e. the expectations budget in **Fig.9:3**) will motivate a lower level of performance. Therefore if budgets are to be set that will motivate individuals to achieve maximum level of performance, adverse budget variances are to be expected. In such a situation it is essential that adverse budget variances are not used by management as a punitive device, since this is likely to encourage budgetees to obtain easier budgets by either underperforming or deliberately seeking to negotiate easily attainable budgets. This may lead to fewer adverse variances, but also to poorer overall performance. To motivate optimal performance demanding budgets should be set and small adverse variances should be regarded as a healthy sign and not something to be avoided.

Figure 9:3 **The effect of budget difficulty on performance**

Source: Otley (1987)

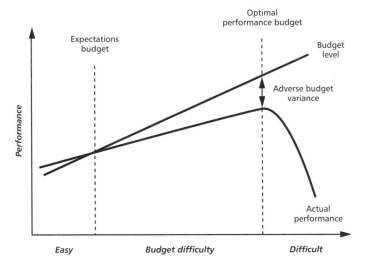

9:6.3 Dysfunctional Consequences of Performance Measures
(*See* **Chs** 48 and 49.)

Dysfunctional consequences arise when performance measures motivate managers to engage in behaviour that is not in the best interests of the organisation. The behavioural literature is replete with evidence of performance measures that have dysfunctional consequences. **Figure 9:4** derived from Otley (1987), illustrates why performance measures do not necessarily motivate desirable organisational behaviour. This exhibit shows that those aspects of behaviour on which individuals are likely to concentrate to achieve their personal goals (represented by circle B) may not correspond with the behaviour that is required for achieving organisational goals (represented by circle A). In an ideal accounting system the measured behaviour (represented by circle C) should completely cover the area of desired behaviour (circle A). Therefore if a manager maximises the performance measure, he or she will also maximise his or her contribution to the goals of the organisation. In practice, however, it is unlikely that perfect performance measures can be constructed that measure all desirable organisational behaviour, and so it is unlikely that all of circle C will cover circle A. Assuming that managers desire the rewards offered by circle C, their actual behaviour (as represented by circle B) will be altered to cover more of circle C and, to the extent that C coincides with A, more of circle A.

Figure 9:4 **The measurement reward process with imperfect measures**

Source: Otley (1987)

Notes: A, behaviour necessary to achieve organisational goals
B, behaviour actually engaged in by individual manager
C, behaviour formally measured by controls systems

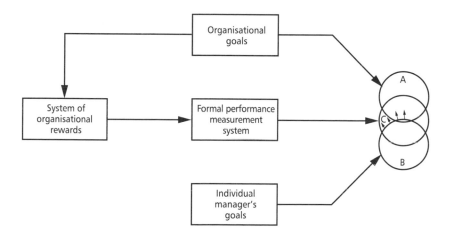

It is likely that a performance measurement system, supported by an appropriate reward structure, will motivate actions that will improve the performance measures. However, organisational performance will be improved only to the extent that the performance measure is a good indicator of what is desirable to achieve the organisation's goals. Given that perfect performance measurement is unlikely to be attainable there is a danger that they may encourage dysfunctional behaviour as represented by that part of circle C that does not coincide with circle A. It is therefore possible that employees will concentrate only on what is measured, regardless of whether or not it is organisationally desirable. Furthermore, actual behaviour may be modified so that the desired results appear to be obtained, although they may have been achieved in an undesirable manner which is detrimental to the organisation. For example, return on investment (ROI) is a widely used accounting performance measure. However, the use of this measure for performance evaluation may motivate managers to reject potential investments if acceptance will lower their ROI, even if the investments are in the organisation's best interests. Such situations might occur where a manager's existing ROI is 30% and projects are rejected with a return of less than 30% but with a return in excess of the organisation's cost of capital.

9:6.4 Managerial Use Of Budget Information in Performance Evaluation

Some of the dysfunctional consequences that arise from the use of accounting information may not be due to the inadequacy of the information, but rather from the way the information is used. If accounting information is to lead to organisationally desirable behaviour, it is essential that it is interpreted and used appropriately. A classic study on how budgets are used in performance evaluation was undertaken by Hopwood (1976) over 20 years ago. It is still relevant today. Hopwood observed the following three ways in which accounting information was used for performance evaluation:

1. A budget-constrained style. *Performance is evaluated primarily on a manager's ability to meet the budget. Not achieving budget targets results in punishment whereas achievement results in rewards. Thus, budget data is used in a rigid manner for performance evaluation.*
2. A profit-conscious style. *Budget data is used with care and in a flexible manner, with the emphasis for performance evaluation on contributing to long-term profitability rather than short-term rigid evaluation of performance. Given good reasons for over-spending, non-attainment of budgets can still result in rewards.*

3. A non-accounting style. *Accounting data play a relatively unimportant part in evaluating a manager's performance. The budget is relatively unimportant because rewards and punishment are not directly associated with its attainment.*

The evidence from Hopwood's study indicated that both the budget-constrained and the profit-conscious styles of evaluation led to a higher degree of involvement with costs than the non-accounting style. Only the profit-conscious style, however, succeeded in attaining this involvement without incurring either emotional costs for the managers in charge of the cost centres or defensive behaviour that was undesirable from the company's point of view. The budget-constrained style gave rise to a belief that evaluation was unjust and resulted in manipulation and undesirable behaviour. Managers' relationships with supervisors deteriorated. They also sought to improve their own reports, regardless of the detrimental effects on the organisation, and then tried to pass on responsibility by blaming their colleagues. In contrast, Hopwood found that the profit-conscious style avoided these problems, while at the same time it ensured that there was an active involvement with the financial aspects of the operations.

9:6.5 Participation in the Budgetary Process

Participation has been advocated by many writers as a means of making tasks more challenging and giving individuals a greater sense of responsibility. For many years participation in decision making was thought to be a panacea for effective organisational effort but this school of thought was later challenged. The debate has never been resolved. The believers have never been able to demonstrate that participation really does have a positive effect on productivity and the sceptics have never been able to prove the opposite (Mackintosh, 1985). The empirical studies have presented conflicting evidence on the usefulness of participation in the management process. For every study indicating that participation leads to better results and improved performance, an alternative frequently exists suggesting the opposite.

A number of studies of the role of participation within the budgeting process have been undertaken. Here also, the findings appear to be in conflict. The differences in the research findings have led to a number of studies that have attempted to specify the conditions under which participation appears to be effective. For example, Brownell (1981) examined the role of the personality variable, locus of control (i.e. the degree to which individuals feel they have control over their own destiny), and its effect on the participation–performance relationship. Budgetary participation was found to have a positive effect on those individuals who felt they had a large degree of control over their destiny, but a negative effect on those who felt their destinies were controlled by luck, chance or fate. Brownell suggests that where an organisation has discretion over the level of participation given to its members, role descriptions relating to participation should be adjusted to suit the individual characteristics of the role occupants. For example, participation appears to have a positive motivational effect only upon those managers who are confident in their ability to cope with the many factors influencing job performance. Conversely, managers who lack confidence are likely to find that participation only serves to increase their feelings of stress and tension due to uncertainty.

Mia (1989) examined how job difficulty interacts with participation to influence managerial performance. Performance was found to be high when the amount of participation was proportionate to the level of job difficulty. In contrast, performance was found to be low when the amount of participation was disproportionate to the level of job difficulty. Mia's findings suggest that participation in budgeting should be used selectively. In cases where perceived job difficulty is high, encouraging managers to participate in budgeting is likely to improve their performance whereas participation is unlikely to increase performance where perceived job difficulty is low. In the latter situation prescribed rules, policies and standards may be more effective in the pursuit of improved performance.

The evidence from the various studies is that budget participation must be used with care. It is therefore necessary to identify those situations where there is evidence that participative methods are effective, rather than to introduce universal applications into organisations.

9:6.6 A Contingency Theory Approach to Budgeting

A contingency theory approach suggests a different type and mode of operation for accounting systems for different sets of circumstances, rather than a universal theory that applies to all circumstances. The contingency theory approach seeks to identify specific organisational features that influence the design of accounting information systems. See, for example, Reid and Smith (2000). Three major contingent categories have been identified in the literature – the environment, organisational structure and technology. Environmental factors that have been identified include the level of uncertainty, complexity and degree of competitiveness. Technology factors that have been considered to be important include the nature of the production process and the amount of task variety. Organisational structure factors that have been suggested include size, interdependence and decentralisation.

The contingency approach applied to budgeting seeks to identify those circumstances that will result in the budgetary system being operated more effectively. For example, research suggests that a rigid use of budget data, adopting a budget-constrained style of evaluation, may be more acceptable to managers if they perceive that they are able to exercise control over their performance outcomes. This is likely to occur in organisations composed of independent parts or where tasks are characterised by low uncertainty. Alternatively, a more flexible style of budget evaluation appears to be more appropriate in organisations consisting of interdependent parts and/or where managers are faced with high levels of environmental or task uncertainty. In these circumstances, managers may perceive themselves as having less than full control over their outcomes. Research also suggests that the effectiveness of budget participation is dependent on contingent factors.

Insufficient empirical evidence, however, has been found to support or refute accounting information contingency theories. Most of the connections that have been suggested in the literature have only been tentative and, at present, contingent theories tend to represent normative theories rather than an explanation of real-world behaviour.

References

Brownell, P. (1981) Participation in budgeting, locus of control and organizational effectiveness, *The Accounting Review*, October, 944-58.

Hopwood, A.G. (1976) *Accountancy and human behaviour*. Prentice-Hall.

Mackintosh, N.B. (1985) *The social software of accounting and information systems*. Wiley.

Mia, L. (1989) 'The impact of participation in budgeting and job difficulty on managerial performance and work motivation: A research note', *Accounting, Organizations and Society, 14(4)*, 347-57.

Otley, D.T. (1987) *Accounting control and organizational behaviour*. Butterworth-Heinemann.

Phyrr, P.A. (1976) Zero-base budgeting – Where to use it and how to begin, *S.A.M. Advanced Management Journal*, Summer: 5.

Puxty, A.G. and Lyall (1989) *A survey of standard costing and budgeting practices in the UK*. Chartered Institute of Management Accountants.

Reid, G.C. and J.A. Smith (2000) 'The impact of contingencies on information system development', 2000, *Management Accounting Research* 11(4), 427-50.

Sizer, J. (1989) *An insight into management accounting*. Ch.9. Penguin.

10. Cash Budgeting and Management

10:1 Introduction

It is not very unusual for a profitable company to go out of business due to poor cash management. For example, it may have carried too much stock and extended such generous credit terms that it found itself without sufficient cash to pay wages and creditors.

Conversely, a company making modest losses could stay in business for years by selling off surplus fixed assets, minimising stock levels and paying creditors on the latest allowable dates.

Without adequate cash, a company cannot expand its markets, train its staff or implement capital expansion programmes. Good cash management is key to company survival and the cash budget should reflect the cash-flow implications of management's plans over the budget period.

In this chapter, we will:

(a) *examine the cash budgeting process;*
(b) *construct a cash budget for an example company;*
(c) *show how the cash budget ties into the wider process of cash management; and*
(d) *explore briefly the elements of cash management.*

10:2 The Role of the Cash Budget

The cash budget shows the planned opening balance, inflows, outflows and closing balance of cash by interim period (usually a week or month) for the budget period (usually a year) (*see* **Ch.9**). The preparation of the cash budget should be a central

Figure 10:1 **Cash budget in annual budgeting cycle**

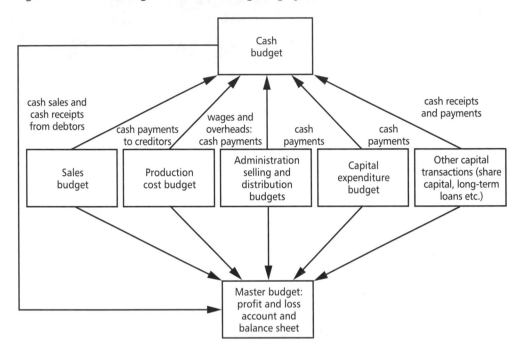

element of the annual budgeting cycle. The way in which a company's cash budget is integrated into the budgeting cycle is shown in **Fig. 10:1**.

A well-prepared cash budget will:

(a) *show the planned cash balance at the end of each interim period;*
(b) *identify cash surpluses (for investment) and shortages (for which loans need to be arranged);*
(c) *establish a solid planning base for all aspects of cash management (see **para. 10:6.2**); and*
(d) *facilitate co-ordination of cash management with working capital, sales, expenses, investments, assets and liabilities management.*

10:3 Developing a Cash Budget

10:3.1 Cash Inflows and Outflows

Preparation of the cash budget focuses on establishing the **cash inflows** and **cash outflows** arising from the activities planned in each period of the budget. Therefore, its construction usually involves a detailed analysis of other budgets (e.g. sales, production and capital expenditure budgets) to assess their impact on cash inflows and outflows.

10:3.2 Cash Management Targets

During the process of cash budgeting, in order to calculate the cash inflows and outflows associated with many budget items, cash management targets are agreed, for example:

(a) *the debt collection period;*
(b) *the creditor payment period; and*
(c) *interest rates for short-term deposits and borrowings.*

Normally, past experience is an important input to the setting of these targets [cf. *FRS1: Cash Flow Statements; IAS7: Cash Flow* Statements] but it ought not be the only input. For example, unless the company has changed its terms of sale or its incentives for prompt payment, it would be reasonable to assume that customer payments would follow broadly the same pattern as in the past. However, cash management targets must be as demanding as other standards in the budget (e.g. sales price and volume targets). Every opportunity should be taken to find cost-effective ways of:

(a) *speeding up the cash collection process;*
(b) *slowing down the cash payment process; and*
(c) *reducing net interest costs,*

which should then be reflected in cash management targets incorporated into the cash budget.

Areas which might be examined to achieve this include:

(a) *the time lag between the dispatch of goods and invoicing;*
(b) *costs and savings associated with discounts given for early payment;*
(c) *the credit-review process which ensures that bad risks are not granted credit; and*

(d) *the time lag between payment by customers and availability of cash in the company's bank account (e.g. this might be reduced by wider use of electronic funds transfer).*

Once agreed, the achievement of each cash management target will be the specific responsibility of an individual manager as is the case with all other targets and standards in the budget.

10:4 Worked Example of a Cash Budget

Relevant extracts from Manu Ltd's 2006 expenses and revenues budgets and supporting information are given in **Table 10:1**. We will now use that information together with appropriate cash management targets and adjustments for non-cash transactions (such as depreciation) to calculate the company's cash budget for the first three months of 2006.

Table 10:1 **Manu Ltd: Extracts from 2006 budget and supporting information**

(a) *Budgeted expenditure and revenues are as follows:*

	October (£)	November (£)	December (£)
		2005	
Expenses			
Direct:			
Materials	50,000	45,000	60,000
Wages	40,000	36,000	44,000
Overhead:			
Production	15,000	14,000	18,000
Administration	10,000	9,000	12,000
Selling and distribution	6,000	5,000	8,000
Research and development	4,000	5,000	5,500
Revenues			
Sales	160,000	200,000	240,000

(cont'd)

(Table 10:1 *cont'd*)

	January (£)	2006 February (£)	March (£)
Expenses			
Direct:			
Materials	40,000	30,000	35,000
Wages	32,000	24,000	28,000
Overhead:			
Production	20,000	16,000	18,000
Administration	10,000	11,000	12,000
Selling and distribution	6,000	5,000	7,000
Research and development	6,000	6,500	7,000
Revenues			
Sales	200,000	160,000	160,000

(b) *Excluded from the above are:*

1. *a commission of 2.5% is paid on sales;*
2. *taxation of £180,000 is to be paid in February 2006;*
3. *in March 2006 a net dividend of £40,000 is to be paid to ordinary shareholders;*
4. *the company has been approved for a training grant for training carried out in previous years which will result in £50,000 being received in February 2006; and*
5. *a new computer is to be installed in January at a cost of £100,000 and will be paid for in March 2006.*

(c) *The cash balance on 1 January 2006 is forecast as £40,000. Manu Ltd currently has no borrowings. It budgets to receive 5% on cash surpluses and pay the same rate on overdrafts.*

10:4.1 Cash Inflows (Receipts)

Cash inflows arise from transactions such as cash sales, payments by debtors for credit sales and sale of fixed assets. A review of **Table 10:1** reveals that Manu Ltd has only two sources of budgeted cash inflows in the first three months of 2006, namely:

(a) payments from debtors; and
(b) a training grant.

10:4.1.1 Payments from Debtors

There is no time lag between sales and cash inflows for cash sales. For credit sales, cash inflows are calculated by applying debt collection targets to budgeted sales.

We establish that all of Manu Ltd's sales are made on credit and, after negotiation with credit control, we agree that for 2006:

(a) as in 2005, to encourage prompt payment, a discount of 5% will be allowed if payment is received within one week and 2.5% if payment is made within one month; and
(b) again, as in 2005, debtor collection targets will be 25% to pay within one week of invoicing, a further 60% to pay within one month and the remaining 15% within two months.

By combining this information with the sales budgets in **Table 10:1**, we can construct Manu Ltd's debtor payment schedule as shown in **Table 10:2**.

Table 10:2 **Manu Ltd: Debtor payment schedule**

Note: To simplify calculations, we assumed that sales are invoiced on the last day of each month

	January (£)	Receipts February (£)	March (£)
November (Sales = £200,000)			
15% January	30,000		
December (Sales = £240,000)			
25% x 95% January	57,000		
60% x 97½% January	140,400		
15% February		36,000	
January (Sales = £200,000)			
25% x 95% February		47,500	
60% x 97½% February		117,000	
15% March			30,000
February (Sales = £160,000)			
25% x 95% March			38,000
60% x 97½% March			93,600
	227,400	200,500	161,600

10:4.1.2 Training Grant

The budgeted monthly cash inflows (taken directly from **Table 10:1**) are:

	Jan (£)	Feb (£)	Mar (£)
Training grant	0	50,000	0

10:4.1.3 Cash Inflows Schedule

Manu Ltd's budgeted cash inflows schedule for January, February and March 2006 is, therefore:

| | *Jan* | *Feb* | *Mar* |
Cash inflows	*(£)*	*(£)*	*(£)*
Debtors	227,400	200,500	161,600
Training grant	0	50,000	0
Total inflows	227,400	250,500	161,600

10:4.2 Cash Outflows (Payments)

Cash payments are made for such items as raw materials, direct labour, expenses, capital additions, repayment of debt, taxation and dividends. Having reviewed **Table 10:1**, we have categorised Manu Ltd's budgeted cash outflows for the first three months of 2006 under six headings, namely:

1. *materials;*
2. *wages;*
3. *overheads;*
4. *research and development;*
5. *sales commission; and*
6. *other cash outflows.*

10:4.2.1 Materials

We agree the targets set out below with purchasing and production control. They are identical to the 2005 targets.

1. *The target credit period for suppliers of materials will be two months.*
2. *Two months' stock of materials will be held. This will be achieved by purchasing the budgeted usage of materials two months in advance. For example, January's purchases will equal March's materials budget.*

Combining 1 and 2, we find that for each month, the budgeted cash payments for materials will equal the materials budget, as shown below:

	Jan (£)	Feb (£)	Mar (£)
Trade creditors (materials)	50,000	45,000	60,000

10:4.2.2 Wages

We establish that delay in payment averages a quarter of a month. Therefore, budgeted cash outflow is:

January	£44,000 × .25 + £32,000 × .75 = £35,000
February	£32,000 × .25 + £24,000 × .75 = £26,000
March	£24,000 × .25 + £28,000 × .75 = £27,000

10:4.2.3 Overheads

We agree with purchasing that the target average period of credit on overheads will be one month – the company hopes to be achieving this target by the last quarter of 2005. We also establish that the production overheads include £3,000 per month for depreciation of buildings, plant and equipment. The budgeted monthly cash payments are therefore the previous month's expenditure budget less £3,000 for depreciation (which does not involve the outflow of cash), namely:

	Jan (£)	Feb (£)	Mar (£)
Overheads	35,000	33,000	29,000

10:4.2.4 Research and Development

We agree with purchasing that the target average period of credit on research and development expenditure will be one month. Again, the company hopes to be achieving this target by late 2005.

The resulting budgeted monthly cash payments are:

	Jan (£)	Feb (£)	Mar (£)
Research and development	5,500	6,000	6,500

10:4.2.5 Sales Commission

We establish that the sales commission is always paid in the month following the month of sale. The resulting budgeted monthly cash payments are:

	Jan (£)	Feb (£)	Mar (£)
Sales commission	6,000	5,000	4,000

10:4.2.6 Other Cash Outflows

All other budgeted monthly cash outflows can be taken directly from **Table 10:1**.

	Jan (£)	Feb (£)	Mar (£)
Capital expenditure (new computer)	0	0	100,000
Taxation	0	180,000	0
Dividend	0	0	40,000

10:4.2.7 Cash Outflows Schedule

We can now combine the information on all the outflows to create the company's budgeted cash outflows schedule, namely:

Cash outflows	Jan (£)	Feb (£)	Mar (£)
Trade creditors (materials)	50,000	45,000	60,000
Wages	35,000	26,000	27,000
Overheads	35,000	33,000	29,000
Research and development	5,500	6,000	6,500
Sales commission	6,000	5,000	4,000
Capital expenditure	0	0	100,000
Taxation	0	180,000	0
Dividend	0	0	40,000
Total outflows	131,500	295,000	266,500

10:4.3 Cash Budget

The cash inflows and outflows schedules can be combined to produce the cash budget and calculate the budgeted cash balances (or borrowings) as shown in **Table 10:3**.

The estimated interest income was calculated as follows:

	Jan	*Feb*	*Mar*
	(£)	*(£)*	*(£)*
Opening cash balance	40,000	136,300	92,300
Closing cash balance (borrowings)	135,900	91,800	(12,600)
Average cash balance	87,950	114,050	39,850
Say	88,000	114,000	40,000
Interest at 5% per annum for 1 month*	367	475	167
Say	400	500	200

* *(Average balance × .05 x ½)*

Table 10:3 **Manu Ltd: Cash flow for the first quarter of 2006**

	Jan	*Feb*	*Mar*
	(£)	*(£)*	*(£)*
Cash inflows			
Debtors	227,400	200,500	161,600
Training grant	0	50,000	0
Total inflows	227,400	250,500	161,600
Cash outflows			
Trade creditors (materials)	50,000	45,000	60,000
Wages	35,000	26,000	27,000
Overheads	35,000	33,000	29,000
Research and development	5,500	6,000	6,500
Sales commission	6,000	5,000	4,000
Capital expenditure	0	0	100,000
Taxation	0	180,000	0
Dividend	0	0	40,000
Total outflow	131,500	295,000	266,500
Net inflow/(outflow)	95,900	(44,500)	(104,900)
Opening balance	40,000	136,300	92,300
Closing balance (excluding interest)	135,900	91,800	(12,600)
Estimated interest income	400	500	200
Closing balance *(including interest)*	136,300	92,300	(12,400)

10:5 Computing the Cash Budget

10:5.1 Volume of Calculations

Manu Ltd is a very straightforward example of the preparation of a monthly cash budget. In practice, while the approach and principles remain the same, the volume of calculations increases dramatically in all but the smallest of companies. Reasons for this include:

(a) *the need to consolidate cash inflows, outflows and balances across many subsidiaries and operating units;*
(b) *having to deal with a variety of currencies; and*
(c) *difficulties in agreeing cash management targets.*

10:5.2 Computer Models

Negotiations resulting in frequent changes in targets and budgets are part and parcel of budgeting. **Figure 10:1** showed how the elements of the overall budget are highly interrelated. Even small changes to a functional budget can have significant knock-on effects on the cash budget. In all but the smallest of companies, this gives rise to a high volume of laborious (and, in some cases reasonably complex) calculations. Budget models (usually based on software designed for that purpose or on spreadsheets) are ideal for dealing with these calculations.

10:5.3 Sensitivity Analysis

Another advantage of computer-based budget models is that planners and managers can easily consider 'what if?' questions (e.g. what would the impact on budgeted cash balances be if sales volume dropped by 1% or interest rates increased by 2%?). Varying key estimates or plans in this way is sometimes known as 'sensitivity analysis' and can highlight the variables (e.g. sales prices) which critically impact on cash flow.

10:6 Cash Management

10:6.1 Scope and Objectives

The annual cash budget is a key element in planning a company's cash management activities. But cash management (CM) goes well beyond cash budgeting.

CM may be defined as the planning, monitoring and controlling of an entity's liquid or near liquid resources to ensure that it has sufficient cash to meet its short-term obligations at the lowest possible cost. Specific objectives of CM are to:

(a) *ensure the availability of cash at the right time and place to meet liabilities as they fall due;*
(b) *reduce the cost of short-term borrowings and increase return on temporary cash surpluses; and*
(c) *reduce bank charges.*

10:6.2 Activities and Organisation

To achieve these objectives, CM includes the following activities (each of which will be discussed in more detail in **Paras. 10:7** to **10:10**):

- forecasting and estimation;

- bank account management;

- cash transmission; and

- surplus cash investment.

CM is itself part of a wider set of activities collectively known as treasury management, which, according to the UK Association of Corporate Treasurers, embraces 'the corporate handling of all financial markets, the generation of external and internal funds for business, the management of currencies and cash flows and the complex strategies, policies and procedures of corporate finance'.

The position of CM within treasury is illustrated in **Fig.10:2**. In addition, CM requires close links with many other areas in the company, including marketing, credit control, stock and production control, purchasing and creditor control.

Figure 10:2 **Treasury activities**

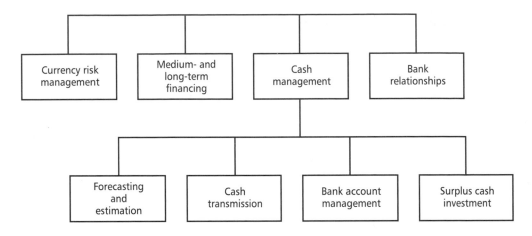

The organisational position, scope and structure of CM varies a great deal between companies. In practice, individual elements of cash management and treasury often merge, especially in small companies. Many companies' cash management is very centralised while that of other companies is quite decentralised. However, the trend in the past decade is undoubtedly towards greater centralisation. This is fuelled by a belief that centralised CM can achieve economies by managing cash on a company-wide basis. Among the factors which influence the structure and organisation of a company's CM (especially its level of centralisation) are:

(a) *size – larger companies can usually justify more CM specialists because of the scale of their cash flows and the complexity of their operations whereas, in very small companies, CM is typically carried out by the accountant;*

(b) *level of internationalisation – generally, the wider the geographic spread of a company's operations, the greater the complexity of its CM (e.g. dealing with many bank accounts in many countries);*

(c) *type and mix of business – companies with short cash cycles (such as supermarkets) give priority to different CM issues (e.g. investing short-term surpluses) to those with long cash cycles (e.g. manufacturing companies) and companies with homogeneous product ranges tend to have more centralised CM; and*

(d) *company philosophy – the more centralised the management of a company is in general, the more centralised its CM is likely to be.*

10:7 Forecasting and Estimating

The budgeting cycle typically takes place annually and establishes the planned monthly cash inflows, outflows and balances for the year ahead. It is good practice to revise the budget periodically, but, because of the workload involved, this rarely happens more than quarterly.

However, CM needs shorter-term (weekly or even daily) and up-to-date cash forecasts. For example, to improve returns, a cash manager would need daily forecasts based on the latest data available of the amount, location and duration of expected cash surpluses. Analysis of variances between budgeted and actual cash flows is a fruitful method of improving the accuracy of short-term cash forecasts and is an important link between annual budgeting and the short-term forecasting of cash.

The creation and maintenance of accurate cash forecasts are only possible if there is good communication between CM and significant users and providers of cash throughout the company (e.g. credit control and purchasing).

Computer-based treasury and cash management systems are available from banks and specialist software suppliers which, in addition to initiating electronic funds transfer (EFT) and other transactions, provide:

(a) *up-to-date information on company transactions and bank balances;*
(b) *cash forecasting models; and*
(c) *a wide range of financial information (money market rates, exchange rates, etc.).*

10:8 Bank Account Management

Bank account management is at the core of cash management. All but the smallest of companies operate multiple bank accounts. This is required, for example:

(a) *to deal with the different banking systems and currencies in overseas branches and subsidiaries;*
(b) *to enhance the operating autonomy of subsidiaries; and*
(c) *for legal and taxation reasons.*

The objective of bank account management is to minimise bank account maintenance charges and net interest costs (interest costs less interest income) while ensuring that the company always has sufficient cash to meet its obligations where and when they fall due. To achieve this, the cash manager addresses:

- processes; and

- flows.

10:8.1 Processes

It should be ensured that the processes negotiated with bankers minimise the cost of operating the company's network of bank accounts, for example, that:

(a) *credit and debit balances across the company's bank accounts can be pooled for the purpose of calculating interest; and*
(b) *cash inflows and outflows to, from and between company bank accounts can be netted, so that only net flows are actually transferred (which reduces interest costs and bank charges – this facility may be administered by the company or its banker).*

10:8.2 Flows

Even with pooling and netting, the cash flows into and out of a company's bank accounts need to be monitored and managed on a daily (or, even hourly) basis (e.g. so that obligations can be met while staying within credit limits and to identify, as early as possible, temporary cash surpluses for investment).

10:9 Cash Transmission

Cash transmission is concerned with the instruments and methods used to collect and pay cash. The major collection and payment systems available to cash managers include:

- cash;

- credit cards;

- cheques and drafts;

- standing orders and direct debits; and

- electronic funds transfer (EFT).

Cash managers seek to minimise the net cost to the company of cash collection and payment. The systems are chosen after an assessment of:

(a) the transaction costs (which are often based on a charge per item (e.g. per cheque, standing order, etc.));

(b) the standing cost of supporting the transmission system (e.g. EFT);

(c) the interest cost associated with clearing transactions through the system (e.g. many EFT transactions yield same day value to the company, while cheques take a number of days to clear); and

*(d) the information system associated with the system (see also **para.10:7**).*

10:10 Surplus Cash Investment

Most companies will, from time to time, generate temporary cash surpluses. The objective of this element of CM is to maximise the risk-free return on those temporary surpluses. The instruments for such investment (e.g. bank deposits, treasury bills and commercial paper) are chosen after considering:

(a) interest rates offered; and

(b) liquidity (how readily they can be converted into cash – an important consideration because cash inflows and outflows cannot be foreseen with certainty).

If the company generates surpluses which will be available for the medium or long term, a decision on their investment is best made in the context of the company's medium- and long-term financing policies. Investment opportunities other than those that are risk free may then be considered.

10:11 Conclusions

We have seen that a company needs adequate cash to ensure its survival. Even companies which survive unexpected cash shortages usually have to raise finance on unfavourable terms and forgo trading opportunities and discounts. It is not surprising, therefore, that cash is often referred to as the 'lifeblood' of business.

The preparation of an annual cash budget and its implementation through the wider process of cash management discussed in this chapter will make a major contribution to a company's survival and prosperity.

11. Capital Budgeting

11:1 Introduction

11:1.1 Capital Budgeting Problems

Capital budgeting is concerned with the appraisal of business projects where the costs and the financial benefits will occur at different times. This covers a wide range of decisions:

(a) the purchase or sale of plant or equipment;

(b) the decision to add or delete products or services offered by the company;

(c) the decision to acquire new premises (by purchase, lease or rental) or to dispose of premises;

(d) the decision to acquire or dispose of subsidiary companies;

(e) the decision to launch a marketing campaign to raise brand image or brand recognition;

(f) the decision to restructure a distribution network or a supply system;

(g) the decision to change the warranty or guarantees associated with a product;

(h) the decision whether to acquire a new asset by purchase, lease or rental;

(i) the decision to exchange an existing asset for a new and improved replacement.

11:1.2 The Objective of Capital Budgeting

Capital budgeting decisions are made in a business environment. We shall assume that the objective of the company, and hence the objective in making capital budgeting decisions, is to create wealth for the shareholders. If the company is quoted and our decision does not involve splitting shares or similar capital adjustments, this objective can be more simply expressed. We are seeking to make decisions that will maximise the market price of the shares.

11:1.3 The Basic Principles

11:1.3.1 Identification of all Credible Alternatives

In capital budgeting there is always at least one alternative. If there is no alternative there is no decision to be made. Often there will be several alternatives, and it is essential to make sure that all serious alternatives are brought into the analysis (*see* **Ch.26, para.26:2.3**). Major companies frequently require that at least three alternatives are presented for analysis.

Restricting the range of alternatives which are put forward for consideration is one of the major ways in which the capital budgeting process can be distorted or corrupted. Any alternative can be made to look good if it is set against a sufficiently poor 'base case'.

The capital budgeting process starts with a diligent and creative search for all the credible ways of exploiting a commercial opportunity.

11:1.3.2 Incremental Cash Flows

Many finance specialists have been trained to measure company achievements in terms of profitability. However, profit numbers are smoothed, adjusted numbers designed to give outsiders an impression of the company's financial performance. For internal-management purposes we need to work with the raw, unadjusted facts. By this we mean the inflows and outflows of cash (*see* **Ch.10**). It is future cash-flow prospects that create stock market value, and the basic data on which capital budgeting decisions are made is the pattern of cash outflows and inflows that the project will generate.

The cash flows must be measured relative to some 'base case'. One of the alternatives (often the decision to reject the project in any form) will be labelled as the base case and the cash flows of each alternative will be measured relative to this.

11:1.3.3 Expected-value Cash Flows

Prudence and conservatism are accounting principles. They are not capital budgeting principles. There is no merit in analysing cash flows which are a downward-biased forecast of the future. The capital budgeting system fails just as much when it rejects a good project as when it accepts a poor one. The process should use, in the first instance, cash flows which are an unbiased estimate of middle of the range of potential outcomes. Techniques of risk analysis will be discussed later in this chapter. Any attempt to base the analysis on hand, guaranteed cash flows will fail. Commercial decisions are taken in an unavoidably risky environment. In many cases, cash-flow estimates will have to be based on judgement supported by experience.

11:1.3.4 Real Options

An investment opportunity is a way of exploiting an economic opportunity. Often the investment starts on a small scale and expands if the opportunity proves fruitful. The initial appraisal of such a project should include an allowance for the value of the opportunity to scale up the project if demand warrants. Such opportunities are termed 'real options', and are analogous to the 'financial options' which are traded in financial markets. An option involves the right, but not the obligation, to make an investment. The Disney organisation, which has already set up Disneyland in California, Disney World in Florida and Disneyland Paris in France has 'real options' to set up additional theme parks in China, Australia, etc. These real options are valuable and are likely to be associated with capital investment decisions. A decision to establish a restaurant offering a novel cuisine would carry with it the 'real option' to open new branches in new markets if the formula proved successful.

There may be other projects, an outsourcing decision for example, where closing down a company's operations in a particular area would throw away 'real options' for future growth.

Financial analysis suggests that a large part of the value of companies on the stock market – more than half in the case of many 'growth' companies – is made up of the value of these real options. If our objective is to create stock market value, we must take real options into account. Estimating the value of these options is likely to be a very rough exercise, but it is better to make a rough estimate than to ignore a significant item altogether.

11:1.3.5 Discounted Cash-flow Appraisal
(*See* Ch.5, para.5:5.4.)

Cash that is going to be received in the future is less valuable than cash received today. Inflation may be one cause; we shall discuss the effect of inflation later (*see* **para.11:2.4**). Even in the absence of inflation there will be a positive interest rate, and an interest rate is nothing other than an exchange rate between cash at two different points of time. An interest rate of 8% (or 0.08) means that £100 now can be exchanged for (i.e. has the same market value as) £108 in one year's time, thus £100 can be called the present value of £108 to be received in a year.

In general, the present value of 1 to be received in n years at an interest rate of r is $\frac{1}{(1+r)^n}$.

If n = 4 and r = 8% = 0.08 then the present value is $\frac{1}{(1.08)^4}$ = 0.7350.

The rate of discount to be applied to a cash flow will depend on how risky it is. Risky cash flows are less attractive than certain ones and so must be discounted at a higher rate.

11:1.4 Structure of the Chapter

We shall see how these general principles can be applied in practice by looking at the issues in more detail. The following topics will be covered:

- defining project cash flows;

- allowing for inflation;

- appraisal techniques;

- setting a discount rate for a company;

- setting a project-specific discount rate.

We shall then look at some further, more specialised, topics as follows:

- international investments;

- risk analysis;

- lease or buy decisions;

- asset life, asset replacement and investment timing decisions,

and we shall end with:

- post-audit of investment projects;

- conclusion.

11:2 Mainstream Issues in Capital Budgeting

11:2.1 Defining Project Cash Flows

11:2.1.1 Principles of Cash-flow Definition

We want to measure the difference between cash flows with the project and cash flows without. Key points to bear in mind are:

1. *Ignore sunk costs. Sunk costs are those that the company has already paid, or is irrevocably committed to paying, and which cannot be claimed back.*
2. *Remember working capital. UK companies have as much money tied up in working capital as they do in fixed assets. Many projects will have working capital implications. The most common pattern is:*

   (a) *an initial cash outflow at the beginning of a project. This will involve filling the 'production pipeline' with raw materials, work-in-progress, finished goods. There will also be changes in creditors and debtors;*
   (b) *small or zero inflows/outflows, as working capital remains roughly constant during the project life;*
   (c) *a final cash inflow as working capital is liquidated at the end of the project.*

3. *Remember terminal cash flows. The economic opportunity may have ended but the plant and buildings it has employed may well have a disposal value. Property in the UK has tended to rise in value over time. However, some projects will have terminal costs, for example, environmental clean-up expenses.*
4. *Ignore depreciation. It is not a cash-flow item. However, writing-down allowances will affect tax payments.*
5. *Look behind overhead items (see Chs 12 and 22). Simple management accounting systems often lump together a number of items as overheads and assign them to units of production by a variety of methods. This approach is inappropriate for capital budgeting. It is necessary to consider specifically whether the project will affect expenditure on overhead items such as floorspace, IT capacity, managerial staff, etc.*
6. *Include knock-on effects elsewhere in the company. Do not look purely at the cash flows within one department or division.*
7. *Include opportunity costs. If assets already owned by the company are committed to a project, they should not be treated as 'free'. The cost to the company is the value they would have provided in their next best use.*

11:2.1.2 Cash-flow Definition – an Example

11:2.1.2.1 Anglian Cable – the Problem

Anglian Cable has just received an offer from Zytex Marketing to take over the task of sending out monthly bills to Anglian's subscribers. Zytex would receive the necessary information daily through a data link and would print and dispatch the bills from its own premises using its own equipment. It would reserve the right to enclose advertising material from other Zytex clients in the same envelope. It would charge four pence (+ postage) per bill and this price would remain fixed during a five-year contract.

Anglian sends out 160,000 bills per month and this number is expected to remain constant. Outsourcing would completely replace the work of the billing department. The billing department has:

(a) *a mailing machine which prints bills and inserts them in envelopes. This machine was purchased for £67,000 five years ago. After subtracting depreciation, the book value is now £36,000. The current market value of the machine is £20,000. If the machine were retained to the end of its useful life in five years' time, its disposal value then would be £5,000. Anglian expects that entirely new technology will make a conventional billing department obsolete at that time;*

(b) *three employees with a total annual wage of £54,000. If they were made redundant they would be entitled to severance payments of £18,000. None of the employees is close to retirement and all have sufficient seniority to qualify for the maximum severance entitlement of four months' pay;*

(c) *a stock of blank billing forms and envelopes with an average value of £3,600. The value of the stationery used each year is £8,000. It would be possible to use up the existing stock while closing the billing department.*

The billing department occupies a large ground floor room of 3,000 sq. ft. The company owns the building, and the cost of rates, heating, lighting, cleaning/maintenance and insurance is reckoned to be £5.50 per sq. ft. If the company paid rent rather than owning the building, the market rental would be an additional £4.00 per sq. ft. For costing purposes Anglian adds an overhead equal to 20% of the cost of direct labour and materials. This covers all company overheads except space costs.

Anglian Cable is planning to set up a new telemarketing operation. The existing building is fully occupied and Anglian has purchased a small plot of land next door where it plans to erect a new 3,000sq. ft. single-storey building for the telemarketing department. The land cost £50,000; the architect's plans (invoice received but not yet paid) cost £15,000; and Anglian has received a tender of £150,000 to erect the building. If billing is outsourced, the telemarketing department can use the vacant space and the new building will not be needed. The land, however, would not be sold. Anglian would keep it so that it could expand in the future at its existing location. Any future building, however, would be likely to have an entirely different use, and need an entirely different design, from the current proposals. Inflation will not affect any of the project cash flows, and we assume a zero-tax environment. (Tax is covered in **para.11:2.1.3.3**.)

11:2.1.2.2 Anglian Cable – the Solution

The 'base case' would be for Anglian to continue running its own billing department. The cash-flow changes included in outsourcing would be as follows.

1. *The payments to Zytex would be:*
   160,000 × 12 × 0.04 = 76,800 (£) annually.
2. *Selling the mailing machine would bring in £20,000. Notice that historic cost, depreciation and book value are all irrelevant here. (Remember our zero-tax assumption. If tax were a consideration the sale of an asset for less than its book value would create a loss and hence a reduction in tax payable.) Notice also that, if the machine is sold now, Anglian will lose a cash inflow of £5,000 that it would have obtained from selling the machine in five years' time.*
3. *Making the employees redundant will save £36,000 in the first year and £54,000 thereafter. The information given implies that the employees would be redundant in five years' time if they are not made redundant now. So the saving in year five will be £54,000 + £18,000 = £72,000.*
4. *The materials saving will be £8,000 annually. There will be an immediate working capital cash inflow of £3,600 as the stationery stock is liquidated, balanced by an incremental outflow in five years of £3,600 because the stock cannot be liquidated at that time.*
5. *The saving on space costs is not calculated on the basis of the costs of the space currently occupied by the billing department. The company would not save these costs by outsourcing. The space will continue to be occupied by telemarketers. The saving is the cash cost of the new building. It:*

   (a) includes the cost of erecting the building (£150,000). However, the proceeds from selling the building (and land) at the end of five years, after moving the telemarketers into the billing department, have been lost. (It may be unlikely that the land and building will be sold, but if the company decides to retain the building after five years this implies that the property is worth at least its market value to the future operations of the company.) If the property is flexible in its use and property value does not diminish with time, this could be estimated at the total cost of the building;

(b) does not include *the architect's fees. These are a sunk cost and irrelevant to the analysis. Even though they have not yet been paid, the commitment to pay them is irrevocable;*

(c) includes *the price at which the land could be sold which is presumably roughly equal to the price at which it has recently been bought. (Ideally the figure should be even higher – the price at which the company would be willing to sell the land and thus give up the opportunity to use it for future expansion. This figure should be used if available.)*

The incremental cash flows from the outsourcing project would therefore be as shown in **Table 11:1**.

Table 11:1 **Incremental cash flows from the outsourcing project**

				(£000)		
Year	*0*	*1*	*2*	*3*	*4*	*5*
Payments to Zytex		(76.8)	(76.8)	(76.8)	(76.8)	(76.8)
Sale of old machine	20.0					(5.0)
Employee savings	(18.0)	54.0	54.0	54.0	54.0	72.0
Materials		8.0	8.0	8.0	8.0	8.0
Changes in working capital	3.6					(3.6)
Building	200.0					(215.0)
Incremental cash flow	205.6	(14.8)	(14.8)	(14.8)	(14.8)	(220.4)

In this example, annual cash flows have been used although in practice, monthly flows are more usual. Payments during a year are treated as if they occurred at the end of the year. Notice that the initial cost of the building is the construction cost (£150,000) plus the opportunity cost of the land (£50,000) which could otherwise be sold. The assumption underlying the exit value for the building is that the market value of the building will include all costs (including the architect's fee).

In addition to calculating their 'hard' cash flows, Anglian Cable would also need to consider the 'real options' that would be created or destroyed by the project. Zytex is planning to enclose advertisements with the bills. Could Anglian purchase additional equipment and get into this business? This 'real option' would be destroyed by outsourcing and Anglian should consider the value of this, and perhaps other 'real options' before making a final decision.

11:2.1.3 Tax and Interest

11:2.1.3.1 Corporate and Personal Tax

Cash flows should be measured after corporate tax but before personal/investor taxes (*see FRS19: Deferred, Tax; IAS12 Income Taxes*). The measurement should be after corporate tax because these payments arise from decisions for which company management is responsible. Personal tax payments are ignored. Company managements usually do not know the personal tax position of their investors and the tax position varies from investor to investor and from time to time.

11:2.1.3.2 Interest

A company can be regarded as a form of 'joint venture' between the shareholders and the debtholders (usually banks), with rules governing the division of cash flow between the two groups.

Projects can be appraised either from the point of view of the shareholders alone or from the point of view of the 'joint venture'.

Example

The initial outlay for a project is £100,000 of which £60,000 will be borrowed and the remainder will come from the shareholders. There is no corporate tax. In the first year the project will generate £20,000 in cash; £4,000 will be paid to the debtholders in interest; and £7,000 will be paid to them as a partial repayment of the project related debt. It is not necessary to consider cash flows in subsequent years.

It is helpful to put the cash flows into a diagram – *see* **Fig.11:1**. The project cash flows can be measured in two different ways, as shown in **Table 11:2**.

Table 11:2 **Measurement of project cash flows**

Appraisal basis	*Initial cash outflow*	*Cash inflow year 1*
'Joint venture' (*Boundary 1*)	£100,000	£20,000
Shareholders only (*Boundary 2*)	£40,000	£9,000

Confusion between the two boundaries (e.g. measuring the cash outflow at boundary 1 and the cash inflow at boundary 2) is a common source of error.

Figure 11:1 **'Joint venture' cash flows**

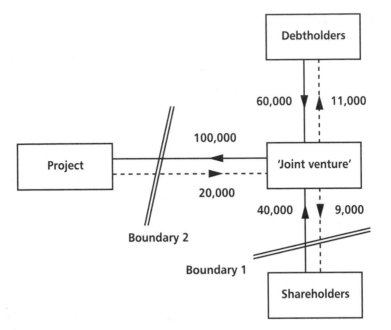

11:2.1.3.3 Cash Flow After Company Tax

Company tax is not paid on cash flows. The two main items that can be deducted in calculating taxable income are capital allowances (writing-down allowances) and interest. It should also be noted that cash flows associated with increases or decreases in working capital are not subject to tax.

Since interest is tax deductible, a company can reduce its tax payments by increasing its use of debt. The term 'tax subsidy' or 'tax shelter' refers to the difference between the full tax charge that would be paid if the project were 100% equity financed, and the actual tax charge.

As a consequence, there are two boundaries at which 'after corporate tax' cash flows can be measured:

1A *After subtracting a full tax charge (i.e. ignoring the interest subsidy).*
1B *After subtracting the actual tax charge (i.e. after taking the interest tax subsidy into account).*

It might seem illogical to use method 1A and to subtract from the cash flows tax payments which will never be paid. In practice, this is a common and useful approach.

In many companies, project appraisal is carried out in departments or divisions which have no contact with or knowledge of the overall debt policy of the company. The divisions and departments are instructed to take off a tax charge that ignores the interest subsidy. The tax advantage of debt is handled by an adjustment to the required return (*see* **para.11:2.4.3.2**).

11:2.1.3.4 Example of Alternative Cash-flow Boundaries – Neotex

Neotex plc is considering purchasing new equipment costing £10,000 for printing designs on T-shirts. The designs will be 'fractal patterns', computer generated, with the unusual selling feature that each design is guaranteed to be unique. As a fashion item, the project is expected to last for two years and the equipment will have zero scrap value at the end of that time.

For the two-year project life the incremental operating cash flows are expected to be as shown in **Table 11:3**.

Table 11:3 **Neotex's incremental operating cash flows**

	Year 1	Year 2
	(£)	(£)
Sales	*48,000*	*38,000*
Raw materials	*(26,000)*	*(20,000)*
Labour	*(10,000)*	*(8,000)*
Distribution and promotion	*(5,100)*	*(3,100)*
Cash flow before interest and tax	*6,900*	*6,900*

Neotex pays corporate tax at a rate of 40%. It will be able to write down (i.e. depreciate for tax purposes) the new equipment on a straight-line basis over two years. Interest can also be deducted for tax purposes. The sum of £4,000 will be borrowed in connection with this project, of which £1,875 will be repaid at the end of the first year and the remaining £2,125 at the end of the second year. Interest at 10% must be paid at the end of each year on the debt outstanding at the beginning of the year.

Solution

Tax-allowable depreciation is £5,000 in both years. So without an interest tax shelter, tax would be $(6,900 - 5,000)0.4 = £760$ each year. The interest subsidy is the amount of interest paid times the tax rate. This is:

1st year	$400 \times 0.40 = £160$
2nd year	$212.5 \times 0.40 = £85$

Hence the cash inflows at the different boundaries are as illustrated in **Fig.11:2**. The Figure shows two numbers for each cash-flow component. The top number relates to Year 1; the lower number to Year 2.

Figure 11:2 **Neotex example: Cash inflows at three measurement boundaries**

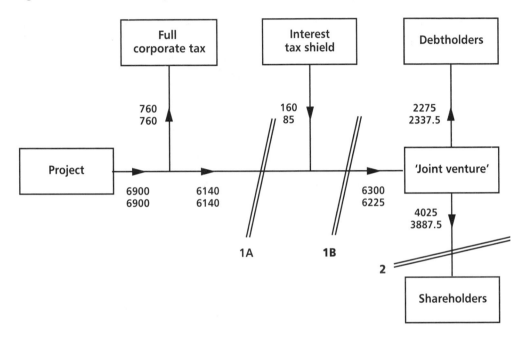

11:2.2 Cash Flows and Inflation

Many of the items that enter into the calculation of project cash flows will be affected by inflation, so that project appraisal will normally require a forecast of inflation.

A forecast of inflation for the UK can be generated by observing the nominal interest rate (N) that can be obtained on conventional gilt-edged securities and the real interest rate (R) that can be obtained from index-linked gilts. These rates are printed daily in the financial press. The forecast of inflation (I) is calculated as follows:

$$I = \frac{1 + N}{1 + R} - 1$$

(The commonly used 'short-cut' formula I = N − R gives a less accurate solution.)

Illustration

In January 2007, a company is appraising a project with a five-year life and requires a forecast of the average rate of inflation over that period. The yields available on gilts which will be redeemed in 2012 are reported as follows:

Treasury 6% 2012 Redemption yield = 6.27% = N
Index-linked 2½% 2012 Redemption yield = 3.18% = R

hence the inflation forecast:

$$I = \frac{1.0627}{1.0318} - 1 = 0.030 \text{ or } 3.0\%$$

All cash flows should be forecast with this rate of inflation in mind. The individual items which make up the project cash flow will relate to inflation in different ways. Wage costs typically rise at about 2% above inflation. Tax allowances associated with fixed-asset investment are fixed in money terms.

Failure to incorporate forecasts of inflation into cash flows will introduce substantial bias into the appraisal of long-lived projects.

An alternative technique, where cash flows are forecast at current price levels and an adjusted 'real' hurdle rate is employed, is not recommended. Among other problems, this approach will fail to make a satisfactory estimate of future tax liabilities.

11:2.3 Appraisal Techniques

11:2.3.1 Net Present Value (NPV)

This technique puts a monetary value on the project. All the cash flows are discounted back to present value and summed.

If the project lasts for n periods, the cash flow in time period t is C_t and the required rate of return is k

$$NPV = \sum_{t=0}^{t=n} \frac{C_t}{(1+k)^t}$$

NPV is the single most useful appraisal technique. If NPV is positive the project will create value for the shareholders and should be accepted. If NPV is negative, the project will destroy shareholder wealth and should be rejected.

If Anglian Cable had a required rate of return of 10% for the outsourcing project described in **paragraph 11:2.1.2.2**, the NPV (ignoring real options) would be:

$$NPV = 206.6 - \frac{14.8}{1.10} - \frac{14.8}{(1.10)^2} - \frac{14.8}{(1.10)^3} - \frac{14.8}{(1.10)^4} - \frac{14.8}{(1.10)^5} - \frac{220.4}{(1.10)^6}$$

$$= 25.09 \ (\pounds 000)$$

So the project adds £25,090 of wealth and should be accepted.

If two or more projects are mutually exclusive, the alternative with the highest positive NPV should be chosen.

11:2.3.2 Internal Rate of Return

A company puts its money into a project and gets money back at a later date. The cash-flow pattern can be compared with putting money into a bank and drawing it out later. The attractiveness of bank deposits are measured by the rate of return they offer. The same can be done for projects.

This internal rate of return (IRR) is calculated as the value of r which solves

$$\sum_{t=0}^{t=n} \frac{C_t}{(1+r)^t} = 0$$

In other words, it is the discount rate at which the NPV is zero.

Using this technique, projects which give an IRR which is higher than the required rate, k, are accepted. Those that give a lower rate are rejected.

IRR is a flawed appraisal technique which can give misleading results.

When choosing between alternatives, the alternative which offers the highest IRR is not necessarily the one which creates the highest shareholder wealth. For example, a very small-scale project might offer an exceptionally high IRR but would still create modest shareholder value. A larger-scale project might offer more value even if its IRR was lower.

IRR cannot be used to identify the best choice from a group of good alternative projects.

IRR assumes a conventional cash flow of outflows followed by inflows – a 'bank deposit' pattern. There will be other projects with 'reverse' cash flows – inflows followed by outflows. Decisions to extend a product warranty, or to save money on maintenance of fixed assets would be in this category. These projects have the same cash-flow pattern as borrowing from a bank – a 'bank-loan' pattern – and a lower rate of return (like a lower interest rate charged on a bank loan) would be preferred.

Notice that the Anglian Cable example is in this category. The project gives an immediate cash-flow benefit with cash outflows coming later. The project has an IRR of 7.20% since:

$$0 = 205.6 - \frac{14.8}{1.072} - \frac{14.8}{(1.072)^2} - \frac{14.8}{(1.072)^3} - \frac{14.8}{(1.072)^4} - \frac{14.8}{(1.072)^5} - \frac{220.4}{(1.072)^6}$$

This is lower than Anglian's required rate of return which we have assumed to be 10%. Because of the 'inflow then outflow' cash-flow pattern a lower IRR is preferred. The fact that the IRR is lower than 10% indicates that the project should be accepted.

More commonly, the cash flow of a project may change sign more than once. In the case of such unconventional cash flow there will be more than one internal rate of return and the IRR appraisal technique becomes unusable.

11:2.3.3 Profitability Index

The profitability index is defined as:

$$PI = 1 + \frac{NPV}{\text{Initial Cash Outlay}}$$

This measure is a variant of the NPV approach. A project with a positive NPV will also have a PI greater than one.

PI is intuitively attractive in that it looks at NPV in relation to the amount of cash invested and put at risk. However, there are other, better, ways of carrying out risk analysis (*see* **para.11:3.2**). It is not an acceptable method of ranking alternatives. Its main use is in capital rationing. If a company has a limited total investment budget, PI measures the efficiency which a project converts the scarce resource (cash for investment) into the desired result (shareholder wealth). Good projects should be ranked in order of PI and projects should be accepted until the available funds are used.

Capital rationing should be a very rare event if a company has access to developed financial markets. If available cash and all available projects are known several years ahead then linear programming techniques can be used. This is even rarer.

11:2.3.4 Payback

Payback is the period of time necessary, after the initial cash investment has been made, for the aggregate cash inflows to match the initial outflow. In simple terms, payback answers the question: 'How long before we get our money back ?'.

Companies set a maximum payback, for example three years, and accept or reject projects accordingly.

Although it is still widely used, payback is a poor method of appraising projects:

(a) it does not apply a discount factor to future cash flows;
(b) it ignores cash flows beyond the payback point. Since it is cash flows beyond the mere recoupment of the initial investment that create wealth for shareholders, this is a serious omission;
(c) there is no theoretical basis on which to choose a maximum payback;
(d) The technique has no relevance when the project has an unconventional cash-flow pattern.

A maximum payback of two or three years is better viewed as a panic cash conservation measure than a serious method of project appraisal.

11:2.3.5 Discounted Payback

With this technique, all cash flows are discounted to their present value equivalent. The payback period is calculated using these numbers. With conventional cash flows, only projects with a positive NPV will have a discounted payback period.

Discounted payback addresses only one of the problems associated with ordinary payback. It is not a recommended technique.

11:2.3.6 Accounting Profitability

Companies often look at $\dfrac{\text{Incremental Profitability}}{\text{Project Investment}}$

There are a variety of ways of calculating this ratio. None of them is appropriate for appraisal purposes. The incremental profitability and the after-depreciation investment will vary from year to year. These techniques break the most basic rules of project appraisal. They do not use cash flows and they do not use discounting.

11:2.4 Setting a Company-wide Required Rate of Return

Both NPV and IRR require companies to specify a required rate of return – sometimes called a 'hurdle' rate or a 'test' rate. Why might investors require a higher return from projects carried out by one company than another? The main explanation would seem to be that different companies have different levels of risk. Investors are risk averse and require higher expected returns to compensate for higher risk.

11:2.4.1 The Logic of Risk-adjusted Required Returns

The return/risk relationship is not a simple one. Investors will not normally place all their wealth in the shares of a single company. They will diversify – spread the risk – by holding a portfolio which would be unlikely to contain less than 20 shares and usually considerably more. Although investors are sometimes unaware of the fact, such a portfolio will move closely in harmony with the movement of the stock market index. The independent movements of the individual shares – that is, the movements that are not linked with the ups and downs of the market as a whole – are diversified away. It is only the tendency of any share to move with the market which is not diversified away. This type of risk impacts on and hurts investors. It needs to be compensated by a higher expected return.

The tendency of any share to move with the market index is measured by its β coefficient.

For any share i, β_i is defined as the expected percentage rise (fall) in the price of share i that is associated with a 1% rise (fall) in the stock market index.

From this definition it follows that the average β of all the shares in the market (appropriately weighted) must be one. If the stock market index goes up 1%, this must mean that the average share has gone up 1% too.

A company with a $\beta < 1$ would be what brokers call a defensive share. In a stock-market downturn it would be expected to fall less than the average. Conversely, in rising markets it would be expected to underperform. Utility companies and food retailers are examples of low β, defensive shares.

The values of fund management companies, on the other hand, are highly sensitive to the level of the market, and these would tend to have high β's.

The β's of individual companies, and the average β's of companies in major market sectors are published regularly by several organisations. The illustrative figures in **Table 11:4** come from the Risk Measurement Service (RMS) published by the London Business School.

Table 11:4 β's **for a small sample of leading UK companies**

Source: **London Business School January – March 1997**

Company	β
Boots Co	*1.00*
British Airways	*1.26*
British Gas	*0.80*
General Electric Company (GEC)	*0.66*
Guinness	*0.96*
Vodafone Group	*1.30*

Finance theory suggests that investors will require a basic rate of return, R_f, even from risk-free investments. On top of this, they will require a premium proportional to the β of the investment.

The size of this premium is best estimated from historic data. In the UK, the average returns on shares, before personal tax, has been 7.4% above the risk-free rate on gilt-edged securities (BZW Gilt-Equity study 1996) – 7.4% is therefore a reasonable estimate of the equity risk premium.

This risk/return relationship is known as the capital asset pricing model (CAPM). Let us use this approach to estimate, as of January 1998, the return that investors require from investing in GEC shares over a five-year horizon.

A. *The redemption yield of a 5-year gilt on 1 January 1998 was 6.3%.*
B. *The* β *of GEC is 0.66 (see* ***Table 11:4****).*

Hence:
required return = risk-free rate + $(\beta \times 7.4\%)$
= 6.3% + $(0.66 \times 7.4\%)$
= 11.2%

11:2.4.2 Required Returns for Shareholders Cash Flows (Boundary 2)

If we were appraising a five-year project for GEC plc in January 1998 and:

(a) *the project were similar in its risk classification to the other operations of the company;*
(b) *the new project were to use the same debt–equity mix as existing operations;*
(c) *the cash flows involved were 'geared' or 'shareholder' cash flows measured at boundary 2,*

then 11.2% would be an appropriate required rate of return to use for appraisal purposes.

11:2.4.3 Required Rates of Return for Cash Flows at Other Boundaries

In order to establish the required rates of return if cash flows are measured at boundary 1A or 1B we need to establish their levels of risk.

Through gearing, a risky cash flow from corporate operations is divided into a low-risk stream for the debtholders and a risk-concentrated stream for the shareholders. We know the β, and hence the required rate of return, for the risk-concentrated stream. We need to calculate the β of the cash flows before the division into debt and equity – the 'ungeared βs'.

Risk is neither created nor destroyed in the gearing process. The risk of the ungeared cash flow is the weighted average of the two components into which it can be divided – in just the same way that the strength of a punch is a weighted average of the strength of its component liquids.

At each boundary it is possible to calculate the risk, β, and hence to set the required rate of return R(β) using the CAPM formula.

11:2.4.3.1 Boundary 1B – the 'Overall Rate' Method

Debt is virtually risk free and its β is normally taken to be zero.

If:

V_D = value of company debt
V_E = value of company equity
β_E = the β of the (geared) equity
β_B = the ungeared β at boundary 1B

$$\beta_B = \frac{V_E}{V_E + V_D} \; \beta_E$$

This formula measures the β at boundary 1B and cash flows at this boundary can be evaluated at the discount rate R (β_B). This rate of return is usually called the overall rate.

11:2.4.3.2 Boundary 1A – the Weighted Average Cost of Capital (WACC) Approach
(*See* Ch.5, para.5:4.3.)

Imagine that the tax subsidy to debt was not paid to the company, in the form of a reduction in tax payments, but was paid directly to the debtholder. The corporate tax rate is t. The debtholders would receive the same interest rate overall, R_D, but would get $R_D.t$ directly from the tax authorities and would lend to the company at a rate $R_D(1-t)$. Because of the subsidy, the value of the loan is still V_D, not $V_D(1-t)$.

With the interest subsidy having disappeared, the boundary 1B cash flow can be evaluated at a weighted average of required return on debt $R_D.(1-t)$ and the required return on equity R_E.

$$R_{WACC} = \frac{V_E}{V_E + V_D}\ R_E + \frac{V_D}{V_E + V_D}\ R_D(1-t)$$

11:2.4.3.3 Boundary 1A – the Adjusted Present Value (APV) Approach

This technique values the cash flows at boundary 1A, but then calculates separately the value of the interest subsidy. The value of the interest subsidy cash flow is calculated at the low-risk discount rate R_D. This is appropriate when we are confident that the company will remain in a tax-paying situation. The value of the tax shelter calculated in this way is S.

The remaining cash flow, at boundary 1A, can be split into a low-risk stream with value $V_D - S$ and a risky stream with a value V_E and a risk level β_E.

The β of these two streams combined will be:

$$\beta_A = \frac{V_E}{V_E + V_D - S}\ \beta_E$$

and $R(\beta_A)$ will be the appropriate discount rate for valuing the cash flows at boundary 1A. This value, plus the value of the interest tax shelter, makes up the total value of the project cash flows.

11:2.4.4 Example of Alternative Required Return Methods

We return to the Neotex example from **paragraph 11:2.1.3.4**. We assume that the β_E of Neotex's equity is 1.081 and the risk-free rate is 10%. The cash inflows at the different boundaries are shown in **Fig.11:2**. The initial cash outflow was £6,000 from shareholders and £4,000 from debtholders. The NPV can be calculated in four ways.

Boundary 2   shareholder cash flows
These are equity cash flows and should be valued at the rate appropriate for equity risk.
    Using the CAPM formula:

$R[B_E] = 10\% + [1.081 \times 7.4\%] = 18.00\%$

The initial cash outflow by the shareholders was £6,000. The cash inflows are measured at boundary 2. On this basis the NPV is:

$$-6,000 + \frac{4025}{1.18} + \frac{3887.5}{(1.18)^2} = 203$$

Boundary 1B – the 'overall' method
The β of the cash flows at boundary 1B is:

$$\beta_\beta = \frac{V_E}{V_E + V_D} \quad \beta_E = \frac{6203}{6203 + 4000} \; 1.081 = 0.657$$

The required return is therefore:

$R[\beta(\beta)] = 10\% = [0.657 \times 7.4\%] = 14.86\%$

At this boundary the initial investment has been 10,000 so the NPV is:

$$-10,000 + \frac{6300}{1.1486} + \frac{6225}{(1.1486)^2} = 203$$

Notice that V_E is the value of the cash flows coming back to shareholders and not the amount (6,000) that they put in. The analysis here makes it appear that the 'overall' method' cannot be used unless the boundary 2 method has been used first. In practice, however, the value of $\frac{V_E}{V_E + V_D}$ is very often measured for the whole company (not an individual project) and when this is done V_E and V_D can be directly observed.

Boundary 1A – the weighted average cost of capital
From the formula in **paragraph 11:2.4.3.2**:

$$R_{WACC} = \frac{6203}{10203}\,0.18 + \frac{4000}{10203}\,0.10[1 - 0.40] = 0.1330 \text{ or } 13.3\%$$

Hence the NPV using this method is:

$$-10,000 + \frac{6140}{1.1330} + \frac{6140}{(1.1330)^2} = 203$$

Boundary 1A – adjusted present value
The value of the interest subsidy, calculated at the risk-free rate is:

$$\frac{160}{1.10} + \frac{85}{(1.10)^2} = 216$$

The β of the cash flows at boundary 1A is therefore:

$$\beta_A = \frac{6203}{6203 + 4000 - 216}\,1.086 = 0.671$$

The discount rate for these cash flows is:

$$R[\beta_A] = 0.10 + [0.671 \times 0.074] = 0.1496 \text{ or } 14.96\%$$

and the NPV is:

$$-10,000 + \frac{6140}{1.1496} + \frac{6140}{(1.1496)^2} = -13$$

Add the value of the interest subsidy to get:

Overall NPV = 216 – 13 = 203

In this example the NPVs are identical when calculated by all four methods. In other cases, they will not be identical, but the four methods all give closely similar results and can be recommended accordingly.

11:2.4.5 Required Return When A Company β is Unavailable

Unquoted companies will not have a published equity β. Other companies may have a published β, but feel that the number is unreliable because the company has been through a transformation and its risk characteristics in the past are a poor guide to its risk in the future.

In this case it is appropriate to use an industry β. β's for the stock exchange sectors are calculated and published by RMS. Alternatively the β of a 'notional industry' could be calculated by averaging direct competitors. These methods would produce an equity β for the industry.

Note that the risk levels (and hence required returns) of companies with similar business operations would be expected to be the same at boundary 1A. The risk levels at other boundaries would be affected by gearing policies. The appropriate technique, therefore, is to adjust the equity β, using industry gearing to calculate the β for the industry at boundary 1A. Assume that this is the appropriate required return for your own company and then make the appropriate gearing adjustments depending on which of the four cash-flow definitions you have decided to use.

11:2.4.6 Required Returns and Company Size

There is substantial evidence that equity investors receive higher returns from investing in companies with a lower stock market capitalisation. Banks also charge higher interest rates to smaller corporate customers. While the logic behind these relationships is not clear, they are sufficiently significant and well established to warrant the addition of a small-firm premium to required rates of return. The adjustment can be no more than a rough estimate, but a premium on the scale shown in **Table 11:5** would seem appropriate.

Table 11:5 **Premiums to required rates of return**

Source: Hirst 'Business Investment Decisions', updated

Market capitalisation	Return premium (%)
>£100M	0
£30M – £100M	1
£10M – £30M	2
£3M – £10M	3
<£3M	4

For a private company, the market capitalisation figure must be an estimate of the value the company would have if it were quoted on the stock exchange.

11:2.5 Project-specific Required Rates of Return

The arguments above suggest that required rates of return should be related to risk. We have shown how required rates can be calculated taking into account differing company risk levels. However, within a single company it is unlikely that all projects will have the same risk level. Logically, required rates of return should be set for individual projects related to their own risk characteristics.

11:2.5.1 Project-specific Required Returns – APV

The most straightforward way to do this is to use the APV method. The value of the interest tax shelter will not depend on the risk characteristic of the project (although it will depend on the amount of debt associated with the project and it may be appropriate to impute different debt ratios to different projects). The project-specific adjustment will relate to the valuation of the boundary 1A cash flows.

For each project it would be necessary to estimate:

(a) *Revenue sensitivity – the revenue sensitivity of a project, T, is the percentage rise (fall) in the revenue for this project that would be associated with a 1% rise (fall) in the overall revenue of the company.*

(b) *Relative operational gearing – operational gearing measures the importance of fixed costs in the cost structure of the project. It is defined as the percentage change in cash flow associated with a 1% change in sales. The determinant of this is the significance of fixed costs (F) relative to variable costs (V) in the production process.*

Operational gearing = $1 + F/V$

The relative operational gearing, P, is the operational gearing of the project divided by the operational gearing of the company overall. The fixed costs here are cash costs. Depreciation is not part of fixed cost.

Both of these factors affect the risk level of a project's cash flow. Instead of discounting the boundary 1A cash flows at $R[\beta_A]$ we can make allowances for the project's individual risk characteristics by using the discount rate $R[\beta_A.T.P]$. The beta coefficient is multiplied by both T and P to incorporate the particular risk characteristics of the project.

The adjustments are not easy to calculate. They need to be average figures over the life of the project. While some analysts will wish to undertake the necessary calculations others will note the factors that influence required rates of return and make rough adjustments accordingly.

11:2.5.2 Examples of a Project-specific Approach to Required Returns

• A car manufacturer is appraising a new car project. It normally uses a single company-wide rate, but the analyst notes that this is a luxury car project. Sales of luxury cars are much more sensitive to economic conditions than the sales of more basic models. Revenue sensitivity will be significantly greater than one and this would justify a higher discount rate.

• A conference organisation company in London is considering setting up a new subsidiary in Edinburgh. In London the company has a printing department which pays an annual rental for printing equipment and also employs a full-time printer. The proposed subsidiary would contract out its printing work. In this case the subsidiary has a lower fixed component in its cost structure and the required rate of return could justifiably be lowered as a result.

11:2.5.3 Simple Project Risk Adjustments

A much simpler approach is to add or subtract directly from the required rate accordingly to the project category.

Cost reduction projects tend to be low risk, and fixed cost reduction projects tend to be particularly low risk because the gains are made whether output is high or low. Capacity expansion is generally in a higher risk category, since the cash flows depend on achieving an increase in sales. New ventures tend to be the riskiest projects. A way of implementing this approach is shown in **Table 11:6**.

Table 11:6 **Project category adjustment**

Source: Hirst 'Business Investment Decisions'

Project category	Adjustment to required rate (%)
Fixed cost reduction	−3
Variable cost reduction	−1
Purchase of company in same industry	0
Capacity expansion	+1
Initial venture into new business field	+3

11:2.5.4 Simplicity Versus Complexity in Setting Required Returns

There is a large amount of literature on the selection of required rates of return. It is worth remembering that the error of measurement of the equity risk premium is 2–3% either way. It is sensible therefore, to check whether the appraisal of a project is robust for changes of this magnitude in the required rate of return. Elaborate minor adjustments to the required return may be hard to justify. The WACC approach with rough adjustment for major project risk categories may be sufficient for many fixed-asset investments.

Errors in the identification of relevant cash flows usually pose a greater risk to successful project appraisal than the use of unsophisticated hurdle rates.

11:3 Specialised Techniques for Capital Budgeting

11:3.1 International Investments

Investing across national boundaries raises two main problems.

11:3.1.1 Cash-flow Definition for International Investments

Typically an overseas investment is undertaken by a foreign subsidiary. The subsidiary may not be 100% owned by the parent, and is likely to have debt of its own. Project cash flows can be measured either as the outflows and inflows to the parent company or as the outflows and inflows to the subsidiary.

For projects in developed economies, it generally is preferable to use the second of these methods. The subsidiary measures the project cash flows just as if it was an independent company in the foreign country appraising the project, and measures these using an appropriate rate. Overseas subsidiaries sometimes have unusually high debt levels, acceptable to bankers only because of a parent company guarantee, as a way of reducing currency exposure. It may help with the tax bill too. In such a case it is best to use an APV approach based on evaluating operating cash flows at a risk-adjusted rate. It is assumed that cash flows will be forecast in foreign currency.

In less developed economies there are often exchange controls or restrictions on remittances or difficulty in gaining 100% control of a subsidiary. In such a case it is better to appraise the project on the potential for dividends, royalties and other cash flows that can be remitted.

11:3.1.2 Required Returns for International Investments

An overseas project will normally generate cash flows in foreign currency. Using the CAPM approach described earlier, the appropriate risk-free rate will be the foreign currency rate. The difference between the foreign and the domestic rate will largely reflect different inflation expectations.

The equity risk premium is not easy to measure in many countries, where the stock exchange may have a shorter history than the UK, and in any case it is not certain that a foreign risk premium is appropriate for an investment by a UK company. It is probably best in most cases to use the same β and same risk premium for the required rate of return at boundary 1A as would be used for a similar project in the UK.

It would not, in general, be true that a higher risk premium should be charged just because the project is 'foreign'. Nor should a lower premium be charged because foreign operations, through diversification, reduce the overall riskiness of a company's operations. This point follows from the earlier discussion of the logic of risk-adjusted required returns.

11:3.2 Risk Analysis

Risk analysis of projects takes two different forms which have quite different objectives.

11:3.2.1 Sensitivity Analysis

The objective of sensitivity analysis is to identify the major sources of project risk. Consideration can then be given to redesigning the project so that these risks are reduced or controlled.

The NPV of a project will depend on some factors which are fixed and others which are uncertain at the time the decision is made. Consider a project to construct a dam to generate hydro-electricity. A fixed price might be tendered for the construction of the dam and the installation of the generating equipment. Risks would remain relating to:

(a) *the average rainfall in the catchment area;*
(b) *the average price of electricity;*
(c) *the period of time before the turbines require replacement.*

For sensitivity analysis it is necessary to estimate 'bounds' for each of these variables. The 10% upper bound is a value so high that the probability that it will be exceeded is only 10%. The 10% lower bound is similarly defined.

Sensitivity analysis looks at each variable in isolation. For rainfall, a range of NPVs would be calculated as rainfall variable moved from its lower to its upper bound. Turbine life and electricity prices would be held at expected values throughout. The result would normally be shown in the form of a graph plotting NPV against rainfall.

The same procedure is then carried out for each of the other two variables.

Figure 11:3 shows three illustrative graphs that might be produced in this way. The negative NPV zones, often called the 'danger triangles', are shaded. They indicate, in a rough visual way, the risk associated with each variable. From the graphs it appears that uncertainty about rainfall is the main source of risk. The electricity price is less important and turbine life is not a very significant risk factor.

This information would concentrate management thinking on rainfall risk. Could the risk be reduced by commissioning a computer simulation of rainfall patterns in the area? Could the company explore the possibility of taking out an insurance policy against low rainfall in the early years of the project?

The electricity price risk is also significant. Would it be possible to sell part of the output forward at a fixed price? Management should consider all available risk-control techniques.

Sensitivity analysis requires extra information compared with analysis based on expected values. However the same process of estimation that produced the mid-point of the range of outcomes can also be used to produce other points, including the 10% and 90% points.

Figure 11:3 **Sensitivity analysis**

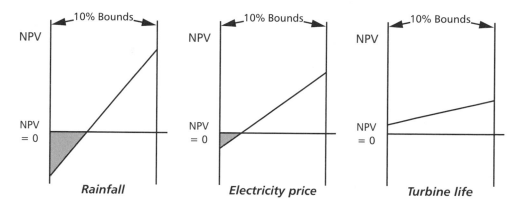

11:3.2.2 Monte Carlo Simulation

This technique looks at the combined effects of all risk factors on project NPV. The intention is to indicate the range of possible gains and losses from the project. The technique is particularly useful when the project is large in relation to the size of the company. Could a poor outcome be absorbed without corporate financial distress threatening the development of the rest of the business? Simulation also encourages management to consider exit strategies if the project performs poorly.

Simulation requires more detailed information than sensitivity analysis. It requires an approximation of full probability distributions. For turbine life, for example, the probability distribution might be as shown in **Table 11:7**.

Table 11:7 **Probability distribution of turbine life in Monte Carlo simulation**

Life before major rebuild	Probability
8 years	0.10
9 years	0.20
10 years	0.40
11 years	0.20
12 years	0.10

For simulation purposes, values can be drawn from this distribution using a single-digit random-number generator. Any one number, say zero, could be assigned to eight years. There is a one-in-ten chance of picking zero and hence a one-in-ten chance of drawing an eight-year life. Nine years would have two numbers allocated (say one and two) to give a 20% chance of selection. Ten years would have three numbers, and so on.

Each simulation would require three random numbers, one for each variable. Having 'simulated' the variables, the NPV is calculated. This is done, perhaps 500 times.

This information answers commonly asked questions. What is the probability that we shall lose money on this project? If, from 500 simulations, 60 gave negative NPVs the answer would be 12%. It is possible to quantify the probability of getting more, or less, than any specific NPV value.

The outcome of Monte Carlo simulation can be presented in graph form as illustrated in **Fig.11:4**. NPV is on the X-axis and probability on the Y-axis. Each simulated NPV is plotted against the probability (i.e. the proportion) of higher NPVs in the overall simulation exercise.

Figure 11:4 **Monte Carlo simulation**

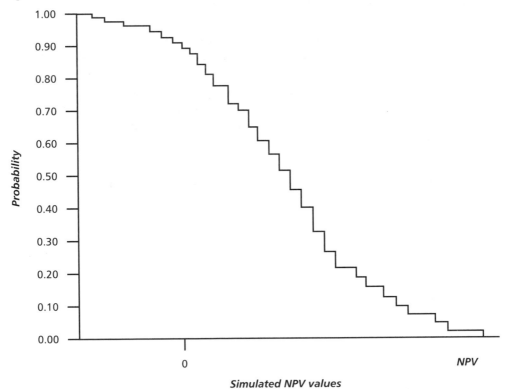

From the graph the probability of exceeding any specific NPV can be read.

Performing 500 simulations is not an onerous task. In simple examples, a simulation requires a single row on a computer spreadsheet:

(a) *The random number is generated for each variable.*

(b) *Look-up tables are used to convert the random numbers into variables.*

(c) *Appropriate formulae, probably using a PV function, are used to create the NPV.*

(d) *This process is copied down for 500 rows, giving 500 NPVs.*

(e) *Arrange the column of NPVs in ascending order. Graph them against a column that starts at 1.000 and moves down in units of 0.002.*

Standard spreadsheets are well suited to simple simulation analysis.

In the example described above all three variables were independent. This will not usually be the case. A housebuilding company will find that the success of a site in a particular year depends on several variables: number of houses sold; the price it can sell them for; and the financing cost for unused land. In simulating this situation it would be important to recognise that if the Government chose to cool the economy with high interest rates all these variables would go wrong simultaneously. Links between the different variables often need to be built into the model. More sophisticated models will allow for early termination of a project if the out-turn is unfavourable.

11:3.3 Asset Life and Asset Replacement

11:3.3.1 Assets and Projects

It is easy, but wrong, to associate a project with a specific asset such as an item of production equipment. Assets and projects are quite different things. The life of an asset ends when it corrodes, runs its bearings, fails to hold its tolerances, becomes unreliable, etc [*cf. FRS15: Tangible Fixed Assets; FRS11: Impairment of Fixed Assets and Goodwill; IAS16: Property, Plant and Equipment*]. A project is an economic opportunity. It will last until the market changes, the economic environment changes or the company loses its competitive advantage.

Computers often have a life of less than five years. It does not follow that projects which involve the purchase of computers should not project cash flows beyond five years. The project – adopting the company's operations to use the potential of information technology – is a long-term one for most firms and cash flows should be assessed accordingly. When computers leave the building it is usually because a new and more powerful machine is coming in.

11:3.3.2 Alternative Assets with Different Lives

This common situation is best illustrated by an example. A company uses a fleet of vehicles to deliver its services to customers. Two types of vehicle can be purchased as shown in **Table 11:8**.

Table 11:8 **Comparative example considering two types of vehicle**

	Type A	*Type B*
Initial cost	£24,000	£18,000
Annual (end of year) maintenance cost	£800	£1,000
Life	7 years	5 years
Scrap value	£4,000	£3,000

Other costs would be unaffected by the choice of vehicle, and we assume that the company expects to stay in business for the indefinite future.

It would be a mistake to compare the NPV of the company's operations over the next seven years using vehicle type A with the NPV over the next five years using B. The vehicles will be replaced and the underlying project is long term.

The correct approach is to ask which alternative will do the job more cheaply on an annual basis. To do this, calculate the equivalent annual cost, a notional annual rental payment, made at the end of each year during the vehicle's life, which will cover the costs of purchase and maintenance, less the scrap value. If the required rate of return is 10%, the equivalent annual cost (X) for a type B vehicle is calculated from:

$$\frac{X}{1.10} + \frac{X}{(1.10)^2} + \frac{X}{(1.10)^3} + \frac{X}{(1.10)^4} + \frac{X}{(1.10)^5}$$

$$= 18,000 + \frac{1,000}{1.10} + \frac{1,000}{(1.10)^2} + \frac{1,000}{(1.10)^3} + \frac{1,000}{(1.10)^4} - \frac{2,000}{(1.10)^5}$$

and X = £5,257.

By a similar calculation, the annual cost of vehicle A is £5,308. B is therefore the cheaper option.

The same result could have been obtained by comparing the present value over the next 35 years (35 being the lowest common multiple of five and seven) of a sequence of five type A vehicles or seven type B vehicles.

Implicitly, this analysis assumes zero inflation, so that a new vehicle will cost the same as the one it replaces. In an inflationary environment, therefore, a slightly different approach is needed. An equivalent annualised cost is calculated which is constant in real or purchasing power terms (but rises in money terms each year in line with inflation). This can be done by using a required real rate of return in the annualised cost calculation.

11:3.3.3 Optimal Asset Life and Replacement Cycles

In the vehicle example above it was specified that a type A vehicle would last for seven years before replacement and a type B vehicle five years. Where do these numbers come from? How is an optimal life calculated?

The answer is straightforward. The optimal life is the one that gives the lowest annualised cost. A seven-year life for vehicle A has to prove itself cheaper on an equivalent annual cost basis than six years or eight years.

11:3.3.4 Replacement Timing

Annualised cost is calculated by considering the total cost over a number of years and converting this into a constant annual amount. With further information, it is possible to calculate separate annual costs for each year of an asset's life. Suppose, for example, that the sale value of a type A vehicle would be £20,800 at the end of the first year.

C_1, the cost of ownership in the first year, is the end-of-year payment which equates the cash from selling the asset at the beginning of the year to the present value of cash flow from maintaining it and selling at the end of the year.

$$24{,}000 = 20{,}800 - 800 + \frac{C_1}{1.10} \quad C_1 = \pounds6{,}400$$

The cost of keeping the asset for the second and subsequent years can be calculated in the same way. Assume that the cost of holding on to the equipment rises as its reliability deteriorates.

Now suppose that an opportunity arises to replace the old equipment with new technology that has recently been developed which would perform exactly the same task. The annual cost of owning the new equipment can be calculated by the annualised cost method.

Each year the cost of keeping the old machine can be compared with the annualised cost of owning the new machine. The switch to the new machine should be made as soon as its annual cost of ownership falls below the existing equipment.

In the literature on replacement decisions the existing piece of equipment is called the 'defender' and the potential replacement the 'challenger'. Using this technique, it is possible to calculate, not just whether the challenger should replace the defender, but when.

11:3.3.5 Lease or Buy

Acquiring the use of an asset by agreeing to make payments under a full-payout lease is very similar to buying the asset and agreeing to make payments on a 100% loan. The similarity is so great that accounting standards now require, under certain conditions, that they should be given similar accounting treatment. The view of the tax authorities is that, if it is appropriate to account for a lease as if it were a loan, it is also appropriate to tax it like a loan.

This would not be welcome to finance directors, and the leasing industry has shown ingenuity in designing contracts that keep leased assets off the balance sheet and qualify for concessional tax treatment.

A lease-or-buy decision is a choice between two alternative patterns of future cash flow (*see* **Table 11:9**). As such, it should be appraised using NPV or another appropriate technique. A major reason for cash-flow differentials is the tax treatment.

Table 11:9 **Making a 'lease-or-buy' decision**

	Cash flows	
	Buy/borrow	*Lease*
Pay asset cash price	✓	✗
Borrow purchase price	✓	✗
Make loan repayments	✓	✗
Obtain tax shield on interest	✓	✗
Obtain tax shelter on capital allowances	✓	✗
Benefit (after tax) from terminal value of asset	✓	Lease terms vary
Make lease payments	✗	✓
Obtain tax shelter on lease payments	✗	✓

The preferred alternative is the one with the lowest NPV of outflows.

Notice that, assuming the company remains taxpaying, almost all the cash flows included in the analysis are low risk. The single exception is the terminal value of the asset, which in many cases will not differ much between the two financing methods. For this reason, it is usual to use a low, debt-based discount rate in the evaluation.

11:4 Post-investment Analysis

There are two main aspects to post-investment analysis. The first is to confirm that the target dates and budgets for the project have been met. Throughout the initial stages of sizeable projects it is normal for the project manager to report progress, costs and deviations from plan monthly.

The second type of analysis begins when the project starts to generate cash flows. It will often become clear quite quickly whether the forecasts of revenues have been optimistic or pessimistic. Risk is inevitable and substantial deviations from forecasts will not necessarily be a cause for blame.

It is important, however, that the company should extract the maximum knowledge dividend from all investment projects whether successful or unsuccessful. For many companies, their knowledge assets, in terms of understanding their markets, are a key component of competitive advantage.

For example, retailers, public house operators, hotels and airlines all have, at the heart of their operations, models that predict the business potential at different locations or on different routes. Each new project gives an opportunity to improve the accuracy and sophistication of these models. All projects, successful and unsuccessful, give an opportunity for corporate learning.

11:5 Conclusions

The techniques of capital budgeting can be used successfully to make a wide range of business decisions. In every case the analysis is based on forecasts of future cash flows. This chapter has shown how to identify relevant cash flows; it has discussed the range of appraisal techniques available; and it has demonstrated different ways of calculating a required rate of return. It has also looked at some more specialised techniques such as risk analysis and asset replacement decisions.

A good understanding of all these topics is required. But the identification of relevant incremental cash flows is the most challenging and gives rise to the most serious errors. It is recommended that the capital budgeting process should be centred on this activity. Nice refinements in the calculation of a risk-adjusted required rate of return are entirely unproductive if the cash-flow analysis is not soundly based.

12. Zero-base Budgeting

12:1 Background

It is generally accepted that Texas Instruments first applied zero-base budgeting in the late 1960s. Phyrr (1970) publicised this new budgeting technique in an influential article in the Harvard Business Review. Phyrr (1976) claimed that there were more than 100 American organisations using zero-base budgeting. One organisation which was using zero-base budgeting was the State of Georgia whose governor was Jimmy Carter who, when he became President, ordered all federal government agencies to adopt zero-base budgeting.

Zero-base budgeting was developed to try to overcome a common weakness in traditional budgeting that only new developments are given very close scrutiny. Traditional annual budgeting (*see* **Ch.7**) tends to take an incremental approach with the current year's budget or the current year's actual results being used as the basis for next year's budget. Such a basis is adjusted for forecast changes for next year but basically most of the existing expenditure is taken as given for next year. It is not a zero base but a current year base for budgeting. What then is zero-base budgeting?

12:1.1 Definition

Zero-base budgeting is also known as priority-based budgeting. As its name suggests, zero-base budgeting begins with a base of zero. It does not begin with the current year's budget or with the current year's actual results. Priorities must be decided not just for new initiatives but also for all ongoing activities.

This means that equal attention and consideration is given to all activities both existing and projected. There is no question of resources being allocated to existing activities just because these have always been funded in the past. The underlying assumption is that the organisation is starting from a zero base or starting again from scratch. Everything is up for reconsideration and no activity is sacrosanct. Obviously this can be a very difficult approach for some managers to accept because it can threaten the continuation of their own activities.

12:2 Decision Units and Decision Packages

Zero-base budgeting starts with what are technically called 'decision units' – namely the lowest level of budgeting units in an organisation concentrating on activities. Such subunits may be different from existing budget departments because the activities involved may cross departmental boundaries giving rise to new budgeting or 'decision units'.

Each decision unit prepares a set of 'decision packages' which include both existing and future activities. Managers then evaluate and rank these decision packages in order of priority in terms of cost–benefit to the organisation. This means that some new activities may be ranked higher than some existing activities. In other words, some existing activities may cease to allow new activities to begin.

This cost–benefit evaluation of decision packages involves a number of difficult questions such as:

(a) Are these activities really necessary?
(b) Can some of these activities be combined?
(c) Can these activities be performed in a different way?
(d) Can an activity be discontinued?
(e) What is the minimum required level for each activity?

Indeed usually each decision unit prepares a number of decision packages for different levels of each activity resulting in different costs for each package. The base package is the minimum level for that activity taking into consideration the objectives of the organisation.

Morden suggests the following for each decision package:

(a) a description of the activity
(b) a statement of the targets or objectives of the activity
(c) performance assessment and measurement criteria
(d) the alternative methods and costs of performing the activity
(e) the benefits achieved at different levels of funding
(f) the consequences of not funding the activity. (1986 : 43)

After each decision unit has prepared its decision packages and its own rankings, these will be evaluated by higher level managers who will complete a final ranking for all decision packages based on the organisation's objectives. These decision packages will be ranked in order of diminishing benefits to the organisation. The basic idea is that given the budget available and using cost–benefit analysis, the decision packages will be agreed in terms of the ranking. This means that all the top priority decision packages will be accepted and the cut-off point will be the budgeted expenditure available.

12:3 Problems with Zero-base Budgeting

Since the 1970s it appears that the use of full zero-base budgeting systems has declined. The problems with zero-base budgeting can be summarised as follows:

(a) *The managerial time involved in producing the information for a zero-base budgeting system is much greater than in a traditional budgeting system. Instead of just considering new developments as under many budgeting systems, managers need to assess all their activities, that is, start from a zero base.*

(b) *The use of decision units is inappropriate. Decision units concentrate on activities and this can mean that decision units cross departmental boundaries. This is fine for setting the zero-base budget but, unless this is accompanied by some form of reorganisation, causes problems in terms of holding individuals responsible for the actual results because these individuals are in different departments.*

(c) *The preparation of decision packages for different levels of each activity causes problems. Managers associated with a particular activity are not happy about specifying a base package for the minimum level of that activity.*

(d) *There is a lot of extra work involved in setting several decision packages for different levels of each activity.*

(e) *The ranking of different decision packages can be difficult. Relating decision packages to the objectives of the organisation is not as easy as it may seem. Very often there is a lack of information to enable a proper cost-benefit analysis to be undertaken of different decision packages.*

(f) *Zero-base budgeting, as with many other management accounting techniques, usually requires the support of top management to be successful. However, zero-base budgeting is a technique which requires a lot of time from top management – for example, for ranking all the decision packages. Top management are often unwilling to give such time and support to zero-base budgeting.*

12:4 Advantages of Zero-base Budgeting

Although relatively few organisations have full zero-base budgeting systems, more organisations have applied it on a one-off basis or to different parts of their organisation each year where there are problems. Such organisations are trying to benefit from the following advantages of zero-base budgeting:

(a) *Existing activities are as carefully scrutinised as proposed new activities.*

(b) *Activities are reviewed in relation to the objective of the organisation.*

(c) *Alternative ways of achieving the organisation's objectives are considered.*

(d) *By concentrating on activities rather than on departments, the budget encourages communication between managers in different departments.*

(e) *The budget forces an organisation-wide review of resource allocation.*

(f) *Managers are forced into careful consideration of their priorities by the required ranking of their decision packages.*

(g) *The cost–benefit analysis means that the relationships between resource inputs and outputs have to be clearly stated. This can lead to improved performance measures in terms of outputs.*

12:5 Conclusions

Zero-base budgeting has been used by organisations in both the public and private sectors. However, it tends to be a partial rather than a full zero-base budgeting system. For example, Pendlebury (1985) found that almost half of local authorities used a form of zero-base budgeting by using its principles to review the base estimates for each department. In other words, it is accepted that it is as important to review existing activities as it is to review new activities.

Perhaps the major contribution of zero-base budgeting is that it has raised questions about the traditional incremental budgeting approach (*see* **Ch.9**). Zero-base budgeting encourages managers to consider different ways of achieving their objectives. Another hybrid system, namely priority incremental budgeting, has been developed from zero-base budgeting. Priority incremental budgeting asks managers to consider what they would change if their budget was decreased by 10% or increased by 10%. Again the basic idea is to force managers to consider their priorities taking account of both existing and new activities.

For all organisations it is worth considering whether or not zero-base budgeting has any role to play in their budgeting system. Experience suggests that its role is most likely to be on a one-off or partial basis. Perhaps the main contribution of zero-base budgeting is to assume a zero base so that existing activities are examined as much as any new activities.

References

Morden, A.R. (1986) 'Zero-base budgeting: A potential revisited', *Management Accounting*, October: 42-3.

Pendlebury, M. (1985) *Management accounting in local government*. London: Chartered Institute of Management Accountants.

Phyrr, R.A. (1970) 'Zero-base budgeting', *Harvard Business Review*, November/December: 111-21.

13. Activity-based Budgeting

13:1 Overhead Costs

13:1.1 Increasing Importance of Overheads

During recent years overhead costs have become an increasing percentage of total costs for many organisations because of reasons such as increased automation, more robotics and information technology developments. For example, in a 1990 survey by the Confederation of British Industry, overheads exceeded 30% of total costs for 70% of the companies surveyed. Furthermore, from 1970 to 1990 overhead costs had increased by 50% in real terms.

During the last 20 years or so, in the manufacturing sector, material costs have remained a reasonably constant percentage of total costs but direct labour costs have fallen and overhead costs have risen as a percentage of total costs. Furthermore, in the service sector with almost no material costs, overhead costs have always been a very significant percentage of total costs. Surveys have shown that the activity-based approach is used both in manufacturing and service organisations.

13:1.2 Traditional Approach to Overheads

Both the traditional budgeting approach to overheads (*see* **Ch.9**) and the activity-based approach to budgeting need to be linked to an organisation's overall strategic plan (*see* **Chs 2** and **5**). However, the traditional approach to budgeting for overhead costs is to budget on the basis of overhead departments such as the purchasing department, maintenance or stores. Generally the starting point has been the overhead expenditure for the past and current year and, taking account of factors such as forecast inflation or forecast volume changes for the next year, some adjustment is made to determine the budgeted overheads by department for the following year. In the past overhead costs have tended to be treated as a black box, and less attention has been paid in some organisations to the overhead costs with most effort being concentrated on the budgeted material and labour costs.

In terms of the traditional build-up of the budget, these costs by overhead departments have then been related to production departments and traced to individual product lines using overhead absorption bases such as direct labour hours or direct machine hours. However, overhead absorption bases such as direct labour hours or direct machine hours tend to vary with the volume of output. This is a weakness in the traditional overhead budgeting approach because many overhead costs do not vary with the volume of output. This traditional process is illustrated in **Fig.13:1**.

Figure 13.1 **Traditional overhead budgeting**

Overhead costs	→	Production departments	→	Production volume-based overhead rates	→	Individual product lines

13:1.3 Activity-based Approach

The activity-based approach to budgeting refers to a different approach to traditional budgeting in terms of the overhead costs. The activity-based approach uses the same approach as traditional budgeting for direct materials, direct labour and direct expenses. Activity-based budgeting concentrates on the budgeting of overhead costs.

The first difference from the traditional approach to budgeting is that instead of relating overhead costs to production departments, overhead costs are related to activity-based cost pools such as receiving or material handling. The second difference from traditional budgeting is that instead of using production volume-based overhead absorption rates (such as direct labour hours), activity cost driver-based rates are used to relate the activity costs to individual product lines. Examples of activity cost driver rates are number of receipts for receiving or number of material movements for material handling. The activity-based budgeting approach is illustrated and compared with traditional overhead budgeting in **Fig.13:2**.

Figure 13:2 **Comparison of traditional and activity-based overhead budgeting**

Traditional budgeting

Overhead costs	→	Production departments	→	Production volume-based overhead rates	→	Individual product lines

Activity-based budgeting

Overhead costs	→	Activity-based cost pools	→	Activity-based cost driver rates	→	Individual product lines

13:2 Activities and Cost Pools

13:2.1 Determining Activities

Some organisations have used consultants to help determine their activities, other organisations have used internal managers and accountants with advice from a consultant and other organisations have done the whole process in-house without any assistance from consultants. Whatever approach is used, a critical step is the determination of activities. This step is a basis not only for activity-based budgeting but also for activity-based costing (*see* **Ch.22**) and activity-based cost management (*see* **Ch.28**).

To determine the activities in an organisation, interviewers will ask managers and other employees various questions such as:

(a) *What staff work here?*
(b) *What does each person do?*

Very often too many detailed tasks or subactivities will be identified in the first instance. However, gradually with further interviews the main activities will emerge. Examples of activities include the following:

• purchasing;

• material handling;

- engineering support;

- receiving;

- training;

- accounting;

- customer services;

- shipping.

13:2.2 Activities Crossing Departmental Boundaries

The interviewers will tend to interview by department but it is critical that the interviewers are always thinking of activities crossing departmental boundaries by asking questions such as:

(a) *What links do you have with other departments?*
(b) *What information/products/services do you receive from or send to other departments?*

The fact that activities cross departmental boundaries is a central feature of activity-based budgeting. Sometimes these activities crossing departmental boundaries are described as processes and are the basis of business process re-engineering (*see* **Ch.32**).

An example of an activity which crosses departmental boundaries is purchasing. There will, of course, be a purchasing department which may request competitive bids, choose the suppliers and place purchase orders but purchasing activity takes place also outside the purchasing department. For example, other departments will issue purchase requisitions, the finance department may vet the financial viability of new suppliers, stores will receive the goods ordered and accounts will be involved in paying the supplier. The activity or process of purchasing involves a number of departments. The amount of detail in terms of the number of activities selected will depend partly on the overall objectives including the amount of detail required to meet the budgeting objectives.

13:2.3 Cost Pools and Responsibilities

After selecting the main activities the next step in the budgeting process is to determine the costs involved in each activity. These are called activity cost pools. To determine the costs of each activity, interviewers will ask questions such as:

(a) *What staff are involved in each activity?*
(b) *What equipment is used by each person?*
(c) *What major consumables are used for each activity?*

For budgeting purposes, the first time that an activity-based exercise is conducted, it is obviously important to reconcile the total in the activity cost pools to the existing overhead cost total in the financial ledger to ensure that all overhead costs have been included in the activity-based system. The budgeting system will centre on these activity-based cost pools and one problem to be recognised is that the existing responsibility system based on departmental managers will probably not fit well with the new system because of the fact that some activities will cross departmental boundaries.

A few organisations have been so enthusiastic about the activity-based approach that they have reorganised from a departmental structure to a process-based structure across the organisation. A more common solution is to change to a matrix structure retaining departmental managers but adding managers with responsibility for the activities or process across the organisation as illustrated in **Fig.13:3**.

Figure 13:3 **Matrix organisational structure**

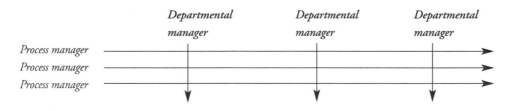

13:3 Cost Drivers

13:3.1 Choosing Activity Cost Drivers

For budgeting purposes, selecting the activities and determining the related cost pools are two important steps, but a third step is to choose the cost drivers for each activity cost pool. The question is what is the main driver of the costs in each activity cost pool? To select appropriate cost drivers, interviewers will ask questions such as the following:

(a) *what determines the amount of time spent on:*

(i) *activity X ?*
(ii) *activity Y ?*
(iii) *activity Z ?*

(b) *What might cause you to require more/less staff?*
(c) *Why is overtime worked?*
(d) *Why does idle time occur?*

Examples of cost drivers include the following:

Activity	*Cost driver*
movement of parts	number of parts
receiving	number of receipts
customer services	number of customer orders

The cost drivers are usually volume-based as in the above examples. However, the above activity cost drivers are very different from the traditional overhead bases such as number of machine hours or number of labour hours which are very closely related to the volume of production.

13:3.2 What Makes a Good Cost Driver?

The starting point is to find out what is the true driver of the costs of an activity. However, other considerations are also important when choosing cost drivers. A second criterion is what will be the effect of that cost driver on employees' behaviour? For example, in Japan some organisations give their designers information about overheads in terms of yen per labour hour because they wish their designers to design labour out of their products. A high overhead add-on in terms of labour hours motivates designers to achieve the desired organisational objective.

A third criterion for a good cost driver is that it is measurable. If not, this can pose problems for budgeting purposes. A fourth criterion is that very often a good cost driver may be the best measure of the capacity of that activity. In summary, the four criteria for a good cost driver are:

1. *incentive for desired behaviour;*
2. *true driver of costs of that activity;*
3. *measurable;*
4. *best measure of capacity of that activity.*

13:3.3 Cost Drivers and Capacity

If the cost driver is a good measure of the capacity of that activity, that is very different from the traditional overhead bases of direct labour hours or direct machine hours which may have very little relationship with the capacity of that overhead. For budgeting purposes the actual capacity used for each cost driver can be compared with the budgeted capacity and this will highlight:

(a) *spare capacity for certain activities where it may be possible to eliminate at least some of that spare capacity and so reduce costs;*
(b) *certain activities as bottlenecks where existing capacity is insufficient and where extra resources may be required to increase the capacity of such bottleneck activities.*

In summary, the cost driver volumes can be used to justify budgeted overhead cost levels. Very often under a traditional budgeting system it is impossible to find such a justification for overhead cost levels because the capacity of such overhead areas has not been considered.

13:4 Budgeted Activity Cost Pools and Drivers

The main steps in an activity-based budgeting system will therefore be:

(a) *determine activities;*
(b) *calculate activity cost pools (actual for current year and budgeted for next year);*
(c) *select best cost driver for each activity cost pool;*
(d) *calculate:*

(i) *actual usage of cost driver volumes in current year;*
(ii) *actual full capacity of cost driver volumes in current year;*
(iii) *budgeted usage of cost driver volumes for next year;*

(e) determine managerial responsibility for each activity cost pool and each cost driver.

The above is an iterative process involving both a top-down and a bottom-up approach. What then are the main benefits of activity-based budgeting because obviously there are costs involved in both setting up and running such a system?

13:5 Benefits of Activity-based Budgeting

A survey by Innes and Mitchell (1995) of the Times Top 1000 companies found that approximately 20% of the respondents used the activity-based approach and 76% of these users rated the ability to set more realistic budgets as the most important benefit from activity-based budgeting. Again this is a reflection that management accountants themselves accept that the activity-based approach to overheads is closer to reality than the traditional approach using direct labour hours or machine hours for all overhead costs.

However, it is not just management accountants who consider that the activity-based approach is closer to reality because another important benefit to emerge from this survey on activity-based budgeting was the greater acceptance of budgets by staff. Managers as well as management accountants appear to prefer activity-based budgeting to the traditional approach of budgeting for overheads.

Respondents to this survey identified the following additional benefits of activity-based budgeting:

(a) better identification of resource needs;
(b) identification of budgeting slack;
(c) linking of costs to outputs and staff performance;
(d) enhanced participation by staff in setting budget;
(e) clearer linking of costs with staff responsibilities;
*(f) improved variance information feedback (see **Ch.16, para.16:4**).*

In a survey of organisations in the financial sector (banks, building societies and insurance companies) Innes and Mitchell (1997) found that these organisations experienced similar benefits from activity-based budgeting. This suggests that activity-based budgeting is as relevant to organisations in the financial sector as it is to manufacturing organisations.

This final benefit (improved variance information feedback) emphasises that, as with traditional budgeting, the one certainty is that the budget will be different from the actual. However, the critical point is the feedback of the actual results against the activity-based budget and this feedback can include not only monetary variances but also physical variance in terms of the activities. The actual usage of the capacity of an activity may be less than the budgeted capacity. For example, the budgeted capacity for material movements for January may be 100,000 but the actual number of such material movements may be only 90,000. As with traditional budgeting variance analysis can be conducted of the actual cost per material movement against the budgeted cost.

13:6 Conclusions

If the accountants or managers in an organisation are unhappy with their budgeting of overheads, it is certainly worth considering changing to an activity-based budgeting system. However, given the amount of work involved in setting up such a system, it is unlikely that activity-based budgeting can exist without at least one other element of an activity-based system such as activity-based costing (*see* **Ch.22**) or activity-based cost management (*see* **Ch.28**). Given the increasing significance of overheads in many organisations it is important to give full attention to their budgeting.

In their ABC surveys in 1994 and 1999, Innes *et al.* (2000) found that 55% and 57% of responding companies used activity-based budgeting. Using a scale of 1 to 5 where 5 = very important/successful and 1 = very unimportant/unsuccessful, Innes *et al.* (2000) found that the importance rating of activity-based budgeting increased from 4.2 to 4.4 and the success rating of activity-based budgeting increased from 3.7 to 3.9 over the period 1994 to 1999.

The four main features and also the major advantages of an activity-based budgeting system are:

1. *determination of budgets by activities in the overhead area;*
2. *fact that budgeted activities cross departmental boundaries;*
3. *collection of budgeted overhead costs by activity cost pools which gives a very different analysis of overhead costs from the traditional ledger analysis;*
4. *selection of cost driver for each budgeted activity cost pool which improves understanding of behaviour of overhead costs.*

However, perhaps the most important advantage of activity-based budgeting is that both accountants and managers generally agree that it is a more realistic system than our traditional overhead budgeting based on departments and using direct labour hours or machine hours. Management accounting is all about trying to report reality as accurately as possible and trying to influence managerial behaviour. Activity-based budgeting tries to do just that.

References

Innes, J. and Mitchell, F. (1995) 'A survey of activity-based costing in the UK's largest companies', *Management Accounting Research, 6(2)*: 137–53.

Innes, J. and Mitchell, F. (1997) 'The application of activity-based costing in the United Kingdom's largest financial institutions', *The Service Industries Journal, 17(1)*: 190–203.

Innes, J., Mitchell, F. and Sinclair, D. (2000) 'Activity-based costing in the UK's largest companies: A comparison of 1994 and 1999 survey results', *Management Accounting Research, 11(3)*: 349–62.

14. How to Implement Activity-based Budgeting: Lessons from Three Case Studies

14:1 Activity-based Budgeting

14:1.1 Activity-based Budgeting Methods

'Activity-based budgeting' (ABB) is a term that refers to the practice of applying activity-based costing (ABC) information to budgeting processes (*see* **Ch.13**). Until now, two main types of ABB processes have been reported in the literature (Brimson and Fraser, 1991; Kaplan and Cooper, 1998).

Management consultants Brimson and Fraser (1991) first proposed a framework for the ABB process shortly after the emergence of ABC in the late 1980s. This framework combines a number of well-proven management practices drawn mainly from priority base budgeting and total quality management (TQM), together with ABC management concepts (Brimson and Fraser, 1991: 42). The main purposes of this ABB framework are to enhance processes for planning and controlling expected activities of an organisation and to derive a cost-effective budget that meets forecasted workload and agreed strategic goals (Brimson and Antos, 1994) (*see* **Fig.14:1**).

Figure 14:1 **The ABB framework as per Brimson and Fraser**
Source: Brimson and Fraser (1991: 42).

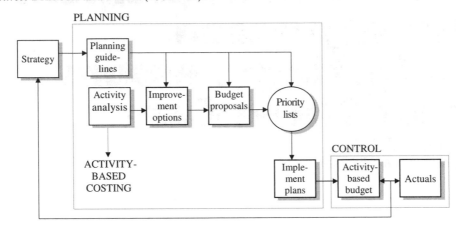

Kaplan and Cooper (1998) described an ABB process as reversing the methods of cost ascertainment following an ABC perspective (*see* **Fig.14:2**). The process starts with generic planning and budgeting, the purpose of which is to estimate the next period's sales and production volumes. It then proceeds with a forecast of the demand for organisational activities to meet the planned targets and the calculation of the resource demands needed to sustain these activities. Next, the actual resource supply needed to meet the calculated activity demands can be determined. Finally the practical capacity of resources to perform forecasted activities can be determined.

Figure 14:2 **ABB process as reverse of ABC process**
Source: Kaplan and Cooper (1998: 303)

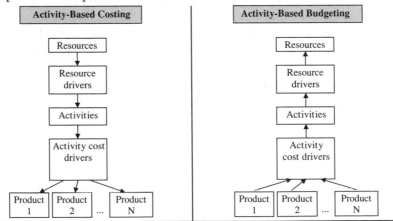

ABB is regarded as an important budgeting technique as it can potentially reduce the pitfalls of conventional budgeting processes, which can include, for example, making cuts across-the-board, creating a lack of linkage between long-term strategies and short-term actions, or by encouraging budget 'padding' or slack (Robinson and Liu, 1998). Its benefits have also been recognised in practice (*see* **Ch.13, para.13:5**). However, it is still unclear how organisations incorporate the above-mentioned ABB framework or process within their organisational structures and business processes.

14:1.2 Need to Clarify the Design and Implementation Issues of ABB Systems from a Practical Perspective

In recent years, business organisations have been motivated to make radical changes to their traditional business thinking and operational methods, in response to changes in the competitive economic environment in which they are operating. The proliferation of internet technologies, for example, has enabled the emergence of 'e-commerce' that radically changes the traditional supply chain and promotes aggressive competition between suppliers trying to produce low-cost and fast delivery services. Business organisations, therefore, have the need to place significant emphasis on lean operations, in order to survive and succeed in the face of fierce competition.

Business operations, especially leaner ones, require careful planning in order to ensure continuity and flexibility of business processes and to achieve optimum utilisation of the organisations' resources. Budgeting contributes to this aim, as it is used by most business organisations as a means of planning and control, to allocate limited resources in order to sustain the business operations and to ensure consistency between long-term objectives and short-term business actions. Therefore, effective, accurate and efficient budgeting paradigms are crucial to many business organisations. Conventional budgeting methods often cannot offer effective solutions to the need for planning and controlling business processes. Hence, there is a perceived need to change or improve conventional budgeting methods. ABB is one method of achieving such change and improvement. The case for considering ABB in this respect is duly addressed in the following sections (**paras 14:1.2.1–1.2.3**).

14:1.2.1 Need to Change Conventional Budgeting Methods

In view of the importance of budgets, attempts have been made over the years to reform the process of budgeting strategically and operationally, in order to optimise resource utilisation, to rationalise business processes and to enable attainment of organisational objectives. In the 1950s, for example, performance budgeting, which sought to tie budgeting to performance, was introduced to organisations in both private and public sectors in the USA and Europe. However, the lack of any long-term consideration in performance budgeting resulted in short-termism (i.e. with no consideration of the effects of actions on long-term objectives). In the wake of its failure, planning programming and budgeting systems (PPBS) were introduced in the 1960s in an attempt to bridge the gap between budgetary planning and decisions to achieve both long-term and short-term objectives. Zero-base budgeting (ZBB) appeared in the 1970s with an attempt to rationalise the input–output link underlying the budgeting process (*see* **Ch.12**). Although the philosophies behind both PPBS and ZBB are to improve the linkage between budgeting processes and organisational objectives, the implementation of these two systems has proven to be relatively costly and highly labour intensive. Thus, the simple line item budgeting (in public service) or other conventional budgeting methods are still widely used in current business practice, despite the various criticisms of their inadequacies (*see* **Table 14:1**).

Table 14:1 **Summary of pitfalls in conventional budgeting**

Purpose of conventional budgeting process	*Emphasis in practice*	*Problem*
Strategic direction making	Historical extrapolation Arbitrary cuts	Not linked to strategy Wrong services cut
Allocate resources	Functional organisation Annual process Cost element focus Investment benefits understated	Allocation depends on budget holders' negotiating skills Inappropriate cycle times Task outputs not visible, especially indirect Surplus resources not reallocated
Continuous improvement	Incremental improvement Costs identified as fixed or variable	Internally driven Fixed costs not reduced
Common objectives	Predominantly top-down Financial measures	Lack of commitment at the bottom level Ignores vital non-financial information, which will lead to a distortion of operational decisions
Add value to business operations	After event reporting of actuals Bureaucratic	Too late to prevent variance Non-value-added to business

The inadequacy of conventional budgeting is often clearly exposed when it is used to support some of the better-known management and performance measurement paradigms (e.g. TQM, just in time (JIT), manufacturing resource planning (MRP)). For example, an MRP system requires adequate information about the resource utilisation in the manufacturing processes. Since the allocation of resources under conventional methods is heavily based on historical financial costing information, conventional budgeting methods provide relatively little support in terms of linking resource deployment with changes made through manufacturing processes. Consequently, variances between budgets and actuals, in a conventional stance, provide relatively little information to reveal the improvement of resource utilisation made before and after adopting the MRP paradigm.

In contrast to conventional methods, information on the likes of 'activity cost', 'output' and 'workload', which is used routinely by ABC and activity-based management (ABM) systems, promotes a growing understanding of business operations that are unveiled by activity analysis. An interest in allocating resources based on ABC information (e.g. the ABB applications) is perceived in practice to address the major limitations of conventional budgeting, and a natural progression from the successful application of ABC.

14:1.2.2 Interest in ABB

Although limited, there is evidence that business organisations are interested in ABB. For example, in their survey of ABC implementation in UK large organisations, Innes and Mitchell (1995) revealed that 29 out of 49 ABC users (60%), had applied ABC techniques to budgeting and considered their use of ABC in the budgeting process to be a fairly important and successful application. On the basis of responses to their survey of 166 ABC users in 132 organisations, Foster and Swenson (1997) also indicated that ABC had been used for budgeting and planning. In their examination of ABC applications within organisations in the logistics sector, Pohlen and Londe (1999) revealed that 19% of 282 organisations surveyed considered ABB to be a progression from the use of ABC information.

Interest in ABB has also been shown by government organisations. For example, the Government of Ireland was considering the application of ABB as a future means of support to the allocation of its foreign aid fund. Owing to constraints on public resources, some government organisations in the UK actively sought better budgeting systems to assist them in allocating and utilising resources more effectively and efficiently. The two organisations in this chapter (i.e. the Crown Prosecution Service (CPS), a government-funded organisation, and BG Transco plc (Transco), a government-regulated organisation) are examples of such interest in ABB.

14:1.2.3 Need to Clarify ABB Design and Implementation Issues

While enthusiasm and interest in ABB exist, both management accounting textbooks and survey reports explain relatively little about:

(a) *The differences of design specifications between ABB, ABC and ABM models. Survey results reveal relatively little about the design specification. A lack of clear specification leads to difficulty in ABB design and implementation. For example, how does an organisation use an ABC cost-allocation model (i.e. using multiple-stage cost drivers to allocate costs from resources, through activities, to products, services or customers) and ABM models (e.g. using 'workload', 'output' measures to trace through the business processes) to form an ABB model? How does an ABB model developed in a manufacturing organisation differ from one in a service organisation?*

(b) *The extent of ABB applications. These survey results give relatively limited insights into the extent of ABB applications (i.e. a full-scale ABB application as prescribed by Kaplan and Cooper (1998) as opposed to a partial implementation that simply adopts some ABC information in a budgeting process).*

(c) *The existence of obstacles in the actual implementation of ABB. Since the existing evidence tends to emphasise the success measures and the extent of ABC applications, it gives relatively little insight into the actual ABB implementation processes. The existence of obstacles, faced by ABB system managers, has not been reported in detail.*

Thus surveys or other management accounting textbooks do not provide a rich description and analysis either of the form of ABB or of the process and impact of its use in a real organisational context.

On the basis of a preliminary investigation into ABB implementation and use, it is clear that organisations pioneering the introduction of ABB have experienced various degrees of difficulty (Robinson and Liu, 1998). A simplified presentation of the results of this investigation is shown in **Table 14:2**. It can be seen from column A in **Table 14:2** that 20 out of 82 organisations (24%) responded positively to the question of 'the adoption of ABB technique' asked during the workshops in 1996–7. This result confirms the relatively high level of interest indicated in the previous section. Despite this level of interest, a follow-up enquiry revealed that only five out of 82 organisations (6%) had actually implemented ABB systems (column B).

The significant difference between the data expressed in columns A and B, as shown in **Table 14:2**, raises some concern about the successful implementation and actual utilisation of ABB in business organisations. Follow-up enquiries to those participating organisations indicate that some difficulties, which almost inevitably include 'teething problems', are encountered by business organisations in their attempts to implement ABB systems.

Table 14:2 **Results of preliminary investigation based on the 'ABM workshops'**

Notes:

[a] Represents organisations that responded 'yes' to the question of 'the adoption of ABB technique' during the workshops

[b] Represents organisations who replied to the follow-up enquiries on whether they have actually implemented ABB systems

Sectors	No. of participants	'Yes' response to adoption of ABB'[a] (A)	Claim of 'implemented ABB'[b] (B)
Manufacturing	28	5	1
Public	10	2	1
Health & pharmaceutical	4	1	0
Financial services	15	4	0
Utilities	4	3	2
Services	16	3	1
Higher education	3	1	0
Research organisations	2	1	0
Total	82	20	5
	100%	24%	6%

Thus it can be concluded that existing ABB reports provide relatively little evidence from a practical stance in respect of the following important issues:

(a) *the technical design specification of an ABB system;*
(b) *implementation of ABB and its role in facilitating business budgeting processes and integrating with management information systems within an organisation; and*
(c) *users' perceptions of the usefulness of an ABB system.*

There is, therefore, a need to address the above issues from an empirical stance so that the impacts of various organisational and human factors associated with the technical aspects of an ABB implementation can be clearly understood. Research has been undertaken by the author in order to fulfil this need. Scottish Courage Brewing Ltd

(SCB), Transco and the CPS have been involved in this research. Their experiences on the implementation of their respective ABB systems are presented in the following three sections. This will help to shed some light on the above-mentioned issues and draw some practical lessons.

14:2 Scottish Courage Brewing Ltd

14:2.1 Company Background

Scottish Courage Brewing Ltd (SCB) originated from two organisations: Scottish & Newcastle Brewing Ltd and Courage Brewing Ltd. Scottish & Newcastle Brewing Ltd belonged to Scottish & Newcastle (S&N) Group plc and in 1995 S&N Group plc acquired Courage Brewing Ltd in order to expand its business activities. After the acquisition, Scottish & Newcastle and Courage Brewing Ltd were merged to become SCB, which is a wholly owned subsidiary of S&N Group plc.

At present, S&N Group plc is the largest brewer in the UK and one of the leading brewers in Europe. There are three sources of business: retail, brewery and leisure (*see* **Fig.14:3** showing its organisational chart, the bold type indicating the parts of the business with which SCB is involved).

Figure 14:3 **Organisational chart of Scottish & Newcastle Group plc**

Note:
  [a] As a result of its restructuring to meet competitive markets, S&N sold its Bristol brewery and its leisure business unit in 2000

As shown in **Fig.14:3**, the beer business unit consists of two main units: the beer production unit and the beer selling unit. SCB is one of two production subsidiaries within the beer production unit, which is involved in the actual manufacturing, packaging and distribution of beer to depots throughout the UK. The beer selling unit is responsible for wholesales to external clients, and the supply of beer to the companies (e.g. pubs, bars and restaurants) in the retail business[1] within the S&N group. The transfer price of beer from beer production unit to beer selling unit is calculated based on a fully absorbed production cost.[2]

The other subsidiary of the beer production unit is the beer malting company, which produces various grades of malts and supplies them to both the breweries within SCB and other external clients. SCB has six breweries, including the three brewing plants previously belonging to Scottish & Newcastle Brewing Ltd and the three previously belonging to Courage Brewing Ltd, acquired as a result of the acquisition in 1995. The main activities carried out at SCB are beer brewing and beer packaging.

14:2.2 Introduction of Activity-based Costing at SCB

An ABC pilot project had been initiated in 1991. The catalyst for this ABC project's initiation was an annual negotiation process between S&N group and supermarkets to which S&N group would sell its canned beers. Instead of a negotiation, supermarkets demanded lower prices. This made S&N's management start to ask questions, such as 'Are we confident about the product costs?'. Despite their confidence in the accuracy of the make-up of their variable costs, they were unsure about the appropriateness of the allocation of the fixed costs to products.

Because of the constant pressure for lower prices exerted by its customers and the uncertainty about the accuracy of its product costs, management at the former SCB (i.e. Scottish & Newcastle Brewing Ltd before S&N's acquisition in 1995) felt the need to ascertain the accuracy of its product costs. The following phases to the introduction of ABC at SCB took place:

1. *A simple prototype model with the assistance from external consultants. After consultation with external management consultants, the ABC method was brought to the attention of the former SCB's management, who then decided to conduct an ABC pilot test. In this ABC pilot project, the external management consultants helped the management to develop a simple prototype model to calculate the product costs. This prototype model consisted mainly of a computer spreadsheet product-costing model that was used to calculate and allocate fixed*

costs to finished products. In this first attempt, variable costs were calculated using individual breweries' existing spreadsheet models.

Benefits: This simple and limited capability ABC model produced results that gave some important insights into the costing system at the former SCB. By highlighting a link between product costs and the work (especially those overheads or sustaining activities) being undertaken in the production process, management at the former SCB began to understand the rationale behind the ABC and recognised the importance and relevance of ABC to the organisation. For example, costs of each production process – fermentation, maturation, canning and transportation – were calculated using identified cost drivers which directly related to the activities, not the direct labour costs or production volume.

2. *A computerised ABC system developed with co-operation between SCB and Quality Production & Research (QPR) Ltd. Following the recognition of ABC from the initial pilot project, the top management of the former SCB then decided to increase the functionality of the ABC model by introducing a computerised ABC system, which could handle fixed and variable costs and be able to produce ABC costs and reports promptly. After assessing a range of commercially available software packages (in 1993), it was concluded that a software package, 'Cost Control' from QPR, a Finnish software company, was to be used as the standard ABC system for the former SCB. The software package 'Cost Control' was designed to handle fixed costs.3 However, QPR agreed to customise its 'Cost Control' by developing a common software suite that could convert variable cost data to a format suitable for 'Cost Control'. The large amount of variable costs in the former SCB, therefore, would still be calculated independently using each brewery's existing spreadsheet models, consolidated and then fed into 'Cost Control' through the customised common software suite.*

   Limitations: A pilot test was conducted in 1994 by using one of the three breweries at the former SCB. It produced some reasonably satisfactory results. However, the roll-out to the other five breweries at SCB in 1995 found that the common software suite, which was used to transfer variable cost data to 'Cost Control', was inadequate in dealing with the large amount of data. To overcome this problem, a customised database interface system was then developed to replace the data-transfer function for variable costs.

3. *A refined ABC 'Cost Control' system. In the final version of SCB's ABC 'Cost Control' system (see **Fig.14:4**), two separate processes were set up. The variable costs were calculated during the first process. This information was then fed into the 'Cost Control' system (i.e. the volumes and costs of the variable items were first calculated using the individual brewery's spreadsheet models before being fed into the 'Cost Control' system via the database interface system). The second process*

involved the input of the fixed costs to the 'Cost Control' system. For example, a number of fixed asset items were first consolidated from the 'Fixed Asset Register' and then fed into the 'Cost Control' system, together with other data such as purchased date and useful life of equipment, so that depreciation charges could be calculated. The depreciation charges were then allocated to individual products using different cost drivers (e.g. floor area usage and number of cans).

Benefits: The product costs produced from the ABC 'Cost Control' system had been generally accepted to be relatively accurate as compared to those produced from the traditional costing system, because the ABC system was able to track costs to activities via the brewing and packaging processes.

Figure 14:4 **Structure of the ABC model at Scottish Courage Brewing**

Note:

ᵃDDE link is the interface database system that transfers volumes and unit costs of variable items from spreadsheet models into the 'Cost Control' system

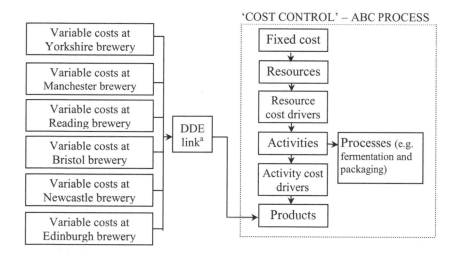

14:2.3 ABB System

14:2.3.1 The Rationale of the ABB System

When SCB's top management considered a full-scale ABC implementation at six breweries at SCB, they set up the following objectives:

- to build a product cost model;

- to build an ABB model; and

- to build a cost management model.

To achieve these objectives, a comprehensive computer model was deemed to be adequate:

(a) *to incorporate both the principles of ABC and ABB within the model;*
(b) *to deliver the product costs and budgets based on the ABC and ABB systems; and*
(c) *to integrate the ABC and ABB data with other organisational systems to provide support for the management decision-making process.*

Apart from utilising the impetus from the introduction of the ABC system (*see* **para.14:2.2**), it was anticipated that the ABB system, once developed successfully, would also solve some problems related to SCB's annual budgeting process, listed as follows:

(a) *the existing budgeting process (i.e. zero-base budgeting) was time consuming – it usually took over two months to complete;*
(b) *the budgeting process was very labour intensive and therefore costly;*
(c) *the process produced rigid budgets and it was difficult to identify savings (e.g. cut for £100,000 was not according to the necessity of activities but in a form of 'across the board');*
(d) *there was a lack of standardisation;*
(e) *the budgeting system was not related to the ABC model;*
(f) *the information from the existing budgeting process could not be used to support 'what-if' analysis.*

These issues (which were associated with its ZBB process) had prompted the management to seek other alternative budgeting methods. The successful introduction of the initial ABC system pointed to an attractive and feasible path – to extend the use of the ABC system to its budgeting process. A feasibility study was subsequently authorised in October 1994 by the finance director and the study was completed with satisfactory results in August 1995. The ABB project was officially initiated in December 1994. A steering committee was formed to set the strategies for the ABB implementation, to monitor the progress of the project and to measure the achievement of the project against the set objectives. This steering committee consisted of a production director, the finance director of SCB and an ABB co-ordinator (who is also the interviewee of this case study). In addition, an ABB implementation team with two full-time members of staff (i.e. the ABB co-ordinator and a management accountant) and part-time members representing each of the breweries was also formed. To ensure a successful implementation, support from top management was sought by the implementation team at the beginning of the implementation process.

14:2.3.2 ABB Model

The conceptual model of ABB used at SCB was based on the 'reverse ABC' model, as codified by Kaplan and Cooper (1998) (*see* **Fig.14:5**). The 'reverse ABC' concept was used to calculate ABB from the fully absorbed product costs and anticipated to derive resource costs and capacity constraints information. Referring to **Fig.14:5**, starting with the sales forecasts, the ABB process worked against the product structures to determine product mix by taking account of various influential factors (brands, packaging and markets). Activity and resource requirements were then determined by taking capacity constraints into consideration. Finally the expected cost influences on the various products or future product costs were then determined and used to feed back to the general ledger to derive (functional) budgets. In this model, simulations of sales forecasts (corresponding to different sales scenarios) could be used as a part of 'what-if' analysis to provide SCB's management with useful costing information.

Figure 14:5 **Conceptual ABB model used at Scottish Courage Brewing**

This ABB model was built on the infrastructure of SCB's existing ABC system with various enhancements. These enhancements included the additional capability for the system to undertake calculations of different volume/mix scenarios and to allow the process to work from sales forecasts towards resource cost influences, which were used to determine revised total resource costs in the general ledger (*see* **Fig.14:6**). A main requirement of this process was to establish activities and resources requirements in relation to production volumes so that relationships (e.g. linear relationships[4] were used in the ABC/ABB models) between these variables were able to be determined. Another requirement was to set capacity constraints for assembly lines/sites. This was achieved by establishing maximum ceilings in resource/activity cost drivers. During the operation, the model should then be able to flag a warning signal if a particular site's capacity was exceeded; the violation of these constraints would invalidate the resultant total cost budget for the site.

The schematics data-flow diagram of the ABB model at SCB is shown in **Fig.14:6**. From **Fig.14:6** it can be seen that the various calculation routines for the variable product costs are carried out by the variable cost spreadsheet model prior to the transfer of these to 'Cost Control' via the DDE link (the database interface system).

Figure 14:6 **Schematic data-flow diagram**

Note:

[a] DDE link is the interface database system that transfers volumes and unit costs of variable items from spreadsheet models into the 'Cost Control' system

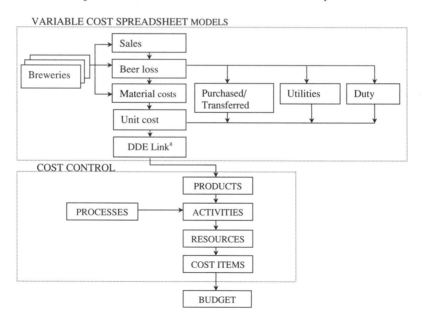

14:2.3.3 Implementation Problems

During the actual implementation, some problems occurred and jeopardised the whole ABC/ABB implementation process. SCB ceased the further development of the ABC/ABB systems. These problems are analysed as follows (Liu *et al.*, 2002).

14:2.3.3.1 Technical Aspect

Differences in model specifications between ABB and ABC systems. SCB's ABB model was designed on the basis of 'ABC in reverse', in line with Kaplan and Cooper's (1998) proposition. This was implemented using a customised dual-purpose computer software model (which was designed to perform both ABB and ABC processes). While this principle was theoretically sound and straightforward, its application was unexpectedly complex. Owing to computer software constraints[5] two computer models (i.e. spreadsheet models to deal with variable cost data and the customised 'Cost Control' model to deal with fixed cost data) were required to handle the combined ABC and ABB processes via a database interface transfer system (i.e. the DDE link, as shown in **Fig.14:6**). While it was able to perform satisfactorily the data aggregation and transfer functions during an ABC process, the system was unable to undertake the reverse calculation exercises during an ABB process (*see* **Fig.14:7**). The data dissemination during the ABB calculation process resulted in a huge number of possible permutations. This slowed down the computational processes to an unacceptable level even for today's high-speed computers.

Figure 14:7 **Differences in model design specifications between the ABC and ABB processes**

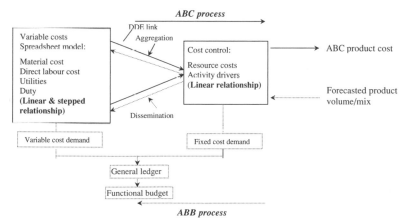

'Linear' v. 'stepped' cost behaviour. As mentioned above, the main assumption made by the implementation team and built into the model was the existence of 'linear' relationships between volume and products, activities and resources. The assumption was actually invalid, because some of the costs had 'stepped' relationships rather than 'linear' relationships (e.g. overtime cost). During ABC calculations, costs with a 'stepped' nature were accounted for manually prior to inputting into 'Cost Control'. The ABB model assumed the existence of 'linear' relationships between variables. For example, in a scenario where the volume of a product was reduced, overtime costs were also reduced based on the assumed 'linear' relationship. This linearly reduced overtime cost was then applied to the ABB 'Cost Control' system to obtain resource costs. The resulting budget was inaccurate and lower than expected. The 'stepped' nature of the overtime cost required that volumes should be reduced below a certain level before an overtime shift could be removed. In this case, a change in volume did not produce a linear change in overtime cost in reality. The difference between these relationships is shown in **Fig.14:8**. Unlike the ABC calculations, human intervention in the ABB calculations (which were performed automatically in the 'Cost Control' system) to correct these erroneous situations was not possible.

Figure 14:8 **Difference in 'stepped' and 'linear' relationship**

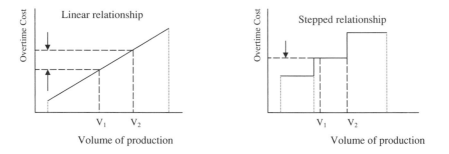

Complexity in systems and data modelling. The ABC/ABB systems developed at SCB consisted of 250 activities, 100 products and 500 types of resources; they were rather complex. Because of the complexity of the ABC system, the possible permutations for a large number of variables, necessary in the ABB process, made the computations for the ABB process formidable even for modern-day computers. For example, 250 activities and 100 products could potentially produce 25,000 possible permutations, and ultimately 12,500,000 possible permutations to cover all possible scenarios, encompassing activities, products and resources. In addition, given the large amount of data that had to be processed and transferred between the spreadsheet models and 'Cost Control' system, the time required to perform these operations was found to be significantly longer than expected.

Another facet of this complexity related to the existence of a variety of systems employed within the company. Some of the systems were based on concepts that conflicted with the principles of the ABC methodology. For example, the financial accounting system was configured using cost codes for reporting financial information in a traditional form. Data from this financial accounting system could not be directly downloaded to the 'Cost Control' system.[6]

14:2.3.3.2 Other Aspects Influencing Implementation

A lack of standardisation. The ABC and ABB projects only involved SCB, which is the production unit of Scottish & Newcastle Group plc. However, sales forecasts were modelled by the beer selling unit, which is a separate unit at SCB. Since no standard guidelines existed for sales forecasts, managers at breweries had their own ways of obtaining sales forecasts. This created a perceived credibility and budget reliability problem since each brewery attempted to obtain favourable sales forecasts data in order to maintain an optimal production level and keep the plant running. In addition, each brewery had its own classification of fixed and variable costs and the format (product volume and mix) of input data varied from one brewery to another. These various sources of non-standardised data, when used in a unified ABB model based only on one pilot site, created difficulties in data conversion and data validation for the purpose of data inputting.

As a consequence, budgets produced by the ABB system were perceived by managers as unreliable and unsuitable for planning, making budget-related decisions and measuring performance.

The impacts of structural change on the ABC/ABB projects. The implementation process coincided with a major acquisition exercise, which resulted in an expansion of the number of breweries from three to six. This acquisition brought inevitable changes to the organisational structure. To the ABC/ABB projects, this meant a possible change of priority, which could affect the commitment and support of top management.

The volatile nature of beer and resort markets in which the company operates requires rapid responses to market signalling. Constant restructuring was taking place in the S&N group in response to the competitive market situation. Managers required systems that could allow them to perform 'what-if' analysis and produce management information in a prompt and accurate manner. This was not possible with the ABB system given the technical difficulties mentioned above. There were other mechanisms used to control costs. For example, the quarterly financial review was an update of departmental annual budget performance. This was based on benchmarking variances between monthly forecasts and actuals of sales and expenses. The annual budget became less important in terms of planning because the monthly forecasts were perceived by managers to be more realistic and accurate targets than those presented in the annual budgets.

Behavioural influences. The ABB system was developed and implemented alongside the ABC system, hence human inertia may have been 'inherited' from the introduction of the ABC system. For example, the use of 'non-value-added' to define activities in some divisions (e.g. maintenance) attracted resentment from those managers concerned. A lack of the line management involvement in the development of the model also contributed to the resentment towards the ABB system.[7]

Training sessions were provided to accountants and managers at the end of the implementation process at each brewery. However, due to the involvement of accountants at the model-building stage, accountants became more familiar with the system than operational managers. Because of the complexity of the ABC and ABB models and a lack of familiarity with activity-based principles, managers would rely upon the accountants to build budgets. Compared to the conventional budgeting process, where managers could participate in the whole budgeting process with relative ease, managers found it hard to participate in the budget preparation and negotiation process under the ABB system. A sense of frustration and resentment occurred, which would inevitably carry adverse behavioural implications for the adoption of an ABB system.

14:3 BG Transco

14:3.1 Company Background

Transco is an organisation that enjoys a monopoly in transporting and supplying gas to end consumers in the UK. Owing to its monopoly position, it is deemed necessary for Transco to be regulated by the Director General of Gas and Electricity Markets, Ofgem. The regulator determines the profit ceiling of the company (which will be x% of Return on Assets, ROA). Ofgem also constantly monitors the cost structure of Transco.

In 1986 British Gas was privatised. Seven years later, after a Monopolies and Mergers Commission (MMC) report issued by the Government, the privatised British Gas (BG) was demerged into two separate organisations – BG Group plc and Centrica, which was the retail section of the old BG. BG Group plc comprised Transco (which operated the

UK's gas pipelines network) and a business unit (which focused on international exploration and production activities). Transco became BG Transco plc in December 1999, but still remained as a part of BG Group plc. In October 2000 another demerger from BG Group plc resulted in Transco becoming a part of Lattice Group plc.[8] The remaining BG Group plc thus concentrates on its international exploration and expansion activities.

Despite the series of organisational privatisation and demerger processes, Transco is still highly regulated due to the monopoly nature of the business activities it carries out. Transco is the owner, operator and developer of a majority of the UK's gas transportation systems. Offshore gas producers supply gas to seven coastal terminals around Britain and then Transco transports the gas on behalf of more than 50 shippers to nearly 20 million industrial, domestic and commercial consumers. It operates a network of 273,000km, or £12 billion, of pipes and infrastructure, and aims to provide a secure and economic gas transportation and storage service in the UK. According to Transco's 1999 Annual Report, Transco employed 16,000 people and its annual turnover in 1999 was just over £3 billion.

Transco's organisational structure (at the time of this case study[9]) consisted of five operating business units (i.e. Asset Business – NTS, Asset Management, Operations Management, Support Services, System Operation) and two main strategic business units (i.e. regulation and strategy and business development). The front-line business operation was undertaken by Asset Business – NTS, Asset and Operations. The two strategic business units and the Support Services unit, which were located at Transco's headquarters in Solihull, carried out strategic business activities and financial services (e.g. finance, accounting and billing) (*see* **Fig.14:9**).

Asset and Operations Management were once a single business unit that was formerly responsible for the operation of the local transmission system within the four area control centres (ACCs) (which are in line with the four local district zones (LDZs) of Asset Management). With an aim to improve competitiveness and efficiency within the front-line business operation, Asset and Operations were separated into three independent business units in 1998. The Asset Business – NTS unit, which was located in Hinkley, focused on management and development of pipeline and other assets within the national transmission system (NTS) and carried maintenance for NTS; Asset focused on management of pipeline networks and other assets within four local transmission systems; and operations focused on the construction, maintenance and replacement of gas pipelines for the four local transmission systems.

A majority of front-line business activities was undertaken by LDZs within Asset and Operations. Normally, Asset received all enquires for new connections to LDZ networks and undertook the design and cost calculation work. Asset was also responsible for demand forecasting, management of gas pipeline infrastructure in compliance with Transco's licence obligations and other relevant legislation. Operations undertook all the essential services at the request of Asset (including construction of new gas pipelines, maintenance and replacement of existing pipeline infrastructure). The relationship between Asset and Operations was primarily that of 'contractor and service provider', or in Transco's terms, 'agent-contractor', 'service-provider' or 'budget holder–budget operator'.

Figure 14:9 **Organisational chart of BG Transco plc[a]**
Note:

   [a] This chart refers to the organisational structure when this study was commenced in 2000. However, Transco has changed this structure since then, after the commercial relationship between Operations and Asset Management was introduced. As a result, the internal structure of these two units has changed significantly

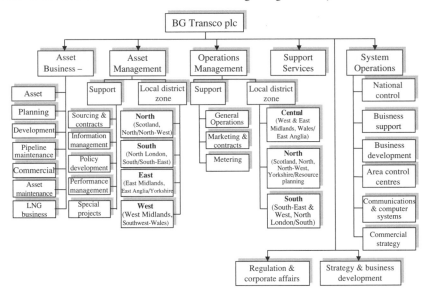

14:3.2 Introduction of Activity-based Costing at Transco

As a privatised monopoly organisation, Transco's cost structure is under scrutiny on a regular basis in order to ensure the achievement of cost-effectiveness as required by both external and internal stakeholders (including Ofgem, consumers and the internal management). This constant pressure had prompted Transco to introduce a better costing paradigm – ABC.

ABC was first introduced at British Gas (BG) during 1992 for the purpose of identification of business activities during the demerger between the old BG and Centrica. The result of this initial ABC information, as it was a top-level analysis, was perceived by both the regulator and internal management to be encouraging, in that it provided a relatively clear justification of cost structure for Transco's core business activities.

A decision to develop a comprehensive ABC system was taken by Transco's top management. The development started by analysing the business processes and activities of a sample district.[10] Since then its ABC model has been improved by mapping business processes and activities within 12 LDZs in the front-line operating units,[11] and has become more sophisticated.

In 1996, Transco made a major improvement to its ABC system. Rather than taking the initial top-level approach, this new attempt was made via a bottom-up approach by building an individual activity model for each of the 12 LDZs and one NTS unit.

This new system was subsequently implemented in 1997 and was in full operation throughout Asset – NTS, Asset and Operations at Transco. ABC information was used to reflect the actual costs in providing the transportation services (as required by Transco's Public Gas Transporter's licence). Since Transco's total revenue was regulated by an agreed price control formula set by Ofgem (i.e. 7% of Return on Assets at the time of this case study), ABC information also helped to rectify the charges made to customers.

14:3.2.1 Transco's ABC Model

This 'bottom-up' ABC process started with the conversion of general ledger data into a form, which represented a view of all the activities undertaken at Transco. In this process, thousands of transaction costs across all the departments within the 32 districts at 12 LDZs and the National Control Centre (NCC) were reorientated to provide one single view of all the activities undertaken by Transco, irrespective of which part of the organisation they occurred in. As a result, 350 core activities and 76 products[12] were established on the basis of ABC principles. An ABC dictionary, containing product description and relevant cost drivers, was also developed, constantly revised and updated, and made available to users via Transco's internal computer network. These 76 products, which are intermediate services, were eventually driven into five main principal services. These principal services, used as a base to the ABC system, are shown in **Fig.14:10**.

Figure 14:10 **ABC service view at Transco**
Source: Transco's activity-based costing review (1999: 3)

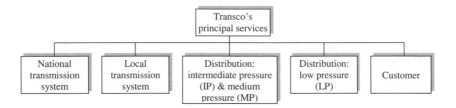

The computational steps undertaken in Transco's ABC process were summarised as follows (Transco ABC review, 1999: 16):

1. *Each LDZ's and centre department's ABC costs were converted from the general ledger data in accordance with the activities they undertook. This involved taking each ledger account (e.g. wages, materials) and assigning it either directly to a single activity, or in the case of support departments, indirectly across a range of activities using templates based on timesheets or other appropriate data.*
2. *These activity costs were then consolidated.*
3. *Activity costs were driven to (76 products eventually) the five principal Transco services. An activity that supported more than one service product would require the use of ABC cost drivers such as the number of employees or lengths of main and Transco's 'Activity Mapping Rules'. However, for a small number of activities no meaningful driver existed – these costs (around 4%, see **Fig.14:11**) were then allocated to services using conventional absorption costing principles.*

In Transco's 1999 ABC model, 70% of resources costs from the general ledger were directly driven to activities while the remaining 30% were templated.[13] In addition, 94% of activity costs were directly attached or driven to a service using ABC cost drivers (*see* **Fig.14:11**).

14:3.2.2 Development of Transco's ABC Computer Software System

Upon completing the development of the conceptual ABC model, the next step was to find a suitable computer software package to implement the tasks identified and specified by the conceptual ABC model.

Figure 14.11 **Transco's ABC model**

Note:

^a UAG stands for 'unaccounted for gas', which is an adjustment occurring due to LDZ shrinkage factor and falling gas prices

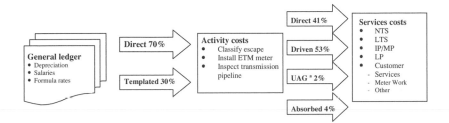

The implementation of the first trial software package was unsuccessful, because it was unable to process a large amount of data (i.e. 350 activities and 76 products) at Transco. This problem had a 'knock-on' effect on the ABC project itself. Shortly after realising the limitation of the first software system, Transco decided to use another commercial software package called Hyper ABC, which was able to perform the required data-processing task satisfactorily. The Hyper ABC was subsequently upgraded to Hyper Metify. The resultant ABC accounts' processing time was reduced from originally D^{14} plus two to three weeks to D plus nine days, which was compatible with the data-processing time for its traditional financial account (which was D plus seven days).

After solving the data-processing problem associated with the software system, Transco was then able to focus its efforts on improving the quality of information that was vital to the utilisation and credibility of the ABC system.

To facilitate efficient data transfer, query and conversion, Transco also utilised another computer software system called EssBase, which was a database management system. Hence data retrievals and queries of various forms could be generated with relative ease via EssBase without causing constant interruptions to ABC data processing in Hyper Metify (e.g. producing various reports and conducting 'what-if' scenarios). The ABC system was centrally maintained by a designated accountant.

With the introduction of the ABC system, two sets of financial information were then available at Transco, traditional and ABC, as shown in **Fig.14:12**. Traditional financial information was processed in SAP™. As shown in **Fig.14:12**, SAP™ produced financial reports that were based on expenditure categories (e.g. salaries, materials, printing) within the cost centres. Variances between traditional expenditure budgets, actuals and forecasts were used to monitor the spending. Transco used ABC information for monitoring actual performances between LDZs in Operations and Asset, identifying performance gaps by using target figures (e.g. forecasts, last year's actual, ABC unit costs for top 26 out of the 76 products).

Figure 14:12 **Transco's ABC computer systems and financial reporting system**

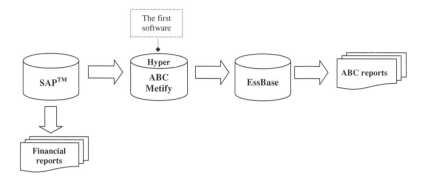

14:3.3 ABB System

14:3.3.1 ABB Model

The conceptual model of the ABB system was developed in 1999, for the purpose of the construction of the Year 2000 product costs budget, primarily for Operations. During the preparation stage for the Year 2000 budget, two types of budgets were being built – traditional and ABB. The traditional budget was used to control each profit centre's (i.e. each LDZ's) costs and spending limits, while ABB was designed to estimate future product costs for the 76 products within the costs limits.

> *(a) Traditional budgeting process. The traditional budget was calculated by extracting expenditure information from the general ledger and applying with a fluctuation of x%. The budgeting process started with a 'Control Total', which was determined by the top management on the basis of forecasts of future workload and the agreed percentage of 'Return on Assets' (with Ofgem). The 'Control Total' was then used to determine a control sum for each business unit's budget. All departments within one business unit were required to propose their departmental budgets. The consolidation sum of the departmental budgets was then required to match with the control sum of the business unit. The calculation of each*

department's budget was undertaken in a 'bottom-up' fashion and based on the nature of expenditures.

(b) *Links between traditional cost items and activity costs. The expenditures were classified into three cost centres (i.e. Capital expenditure or Capex, Operation expenditure or Opex and Replacement expenditure or Repex). Each cost centre consisted of direct costs and overheads. Direct costs had a 'one-to-one' relationship with the 76 products as identified in the ABC exercise, and were linked directly to Operational ABC costs (i.e. unit-driven costs). Overheads had a 'one-to-many' relationship with the products, and were linked to cost items within Non-operational ABC costs (i.e. batch-level costs or technical support costs, sustaining costs which include management, administrative support and manager sustaining costs).*

(c) *ABB process. Instead of conducting a full reverse ABC exercise, which would start from product through activities and eventually to resource costs, Transco's ABB product cost budget was calculated directly by linking products to resources via a matching exercise:*

(i) *The direct costs in its traditional budget were first translated into Operational ABC costs in ABB (i.e. an Operational ABC cost budget = previous year's ABC unit costs x forecasted direct/contract labour hours).*

(ii) *The overheads derived from the traditional budget were matched with Non-operational ABC costs (e.g. those batch-driven costs and sustaining costs) using ABC templating information. The allocation of Non-operational costs to activities was primarily done on the basis of historical ABC template information (i.e. timesheets every manager at each LDZ filled in for themselves and their department) since the majority of these activities were repetitive in nature. The allocation of activities to products was based on Transco's 'mapping rules'. The template information specified the proportion of staff time spent across related products within the 76-product range.*

Based on the above description, a graphical representation of Transco's conceptual ABB model shown in **Fig.14:13**.

14:3.3.2 Implementation Problems

Although Transco has sophisticated computer systems, some problems still occurred during the implementation of the ABB system. This led to the limited use of 2000's ABB product cost budgets at Transco. The problems are explained as follows.

Figure 14:13 **Conceptual ABB model at Operations, Transco**

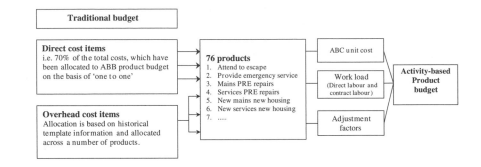

14:3.3.2.1 Technical Aspect

Suitability of the ABB information in meeting budgetary planning purposes. The theoretical concept underpinning Transco's ABB model was relatively straightforward (i.e. multiplication of previous year's ABC unit costs with predicted workloads for Operational ABC cost budget and proportion of overhead costs budget to Non-operational ABC costs budget based on an allocation basis). The assumption of this theoretical ABB model was made on the basis of applying the previous year's ABC performance level to undertake the coming year's workload. Furthermore the ABB product cost budget was restrained by the traditional expenditure budgets for the coming year.

In other words, Transco's ABB product cost budget was a reapportionment of traditional budgets into an ABB format, rather than a budgetary plan for 'should-be' product costs in the coming year. Generally speaking, budgetary planning requires information such as resource demand in order to determine whether or not the current available resource capacity can meet the demand. The resource demand is usually derived on the basis of forecasted workload of products and activity cost drivers. Transco's ABB computation started with the determined resource costs that were derived from the traditional budget and then reallocated to 76 products.

The derived ABB product cost budgets were used to help Asset to obtain an overall picture of product costs at Operations. It was thus considered as suitable by Asset for managing Operations' product performance. However, this ABB budget did not appear to identify resource capacity constraints for planning purposes, which would be useful from Operations' viewpoint. Hence Transco's ABB product cost budget achieved relatively limited success in terms of fulfilling the needs of strategic planning requirement for Asset, but not for Operations.

System complexity from a user's viewpoint. Transco utilised a considerable number of computerised systems to enable the operation of information within such a complex organisation. For reasons of data security and integrity, the ABC system – Hyper Metify – was operated centrally by a designated management accountant. Managers at individual LDZs provided the management accountant with timesheets and templating information. They were then provided with ABC reports that were prepared by the LDZs' accountants, using ABC information extracted from EssBase (which acted as an information generator). From end-users' (i.e. managers at all levels) viewpoints, these activity-based systems were fairly complex. The use of 'Budget Plus' for the ABB purpose just added to the level of complexity. They were not able to construct their own departmental budgets directly using the 'Budget Plus'.

Although some training sessions were provided to enable them to use the ABC systems, some of the users (e.g. front-line managers, middle-level managers at Operations and some management accountants at LDZs level) were still unable to understand the software packages or extract information effectively. This inability would deny them an opportunity to gain direct access to EssBase. Therefore, despite Transco having about eight years of ABC experience (since 1992), there were still significant variations in users' understanding of ABC and ABB principles and practical knowledge about using the ABC and ABB systems.

In light of the level of system complexity and concerns over the ABC knowledge at LDZ level, the Year 2000 ABB product cost budget for Operations was developed centrally by a team of management accountants who had a relatively good understanding of ABC and ABB. The exercise (intended to reduce the complexity involved in the construction of an ABB from a 'bottom-up' approach) did reduce the complexity to calculate the ABB budget. However, it also resulted in some side-effects, indeed, the centralised budget construction exercise brought tension between management accountants and line managers, who perceived the ABB as the accountants' budget.

Thus the ABB approach, which attempted to reduce the system complexity by constructing an ABB product cost budget for the end users, did not achieve its intended objectives.

Representational accuracy of Transco's ABB model for budgetary control purposes. In general practice, a budget is used to measure and evaluate against managers' actual performance. Since Transco adopted the previous year's ABC unit costs in the construction of the ABB budget, the accuracy of this budget largely depended on the accuracy of the previous year's ABC information. However, because of uneven distribution and fluctuation of workload across the LDZs in 1999, the ABC unit cost for one particular product had a large variation of between £615 and £187 in different LDZs. There were seasonal factors, i.e. a significantly heavier workload during the winter months than the workload during the summer months (because of leakage of gas pipelines during the winter months requiring more repair work). In addition, some LDZs that had a greater workload during the year had to cope with the extra workload with the existing workforce (hence stretching the staff overheads limits). Thus the actual ABC unit costs for those LDZs were lower than those for other LDZs. While using the lower ABC unit costs (which were affected by these non-routine factors occurring during the previous year) in budgeting, the derived ABB product cost budgets for those LDZs would be lower than for others. However, these non-routine factors might not occur in the budgeting year. Therefore these ABB product cost budgets would be rendered as inaccurate to be used as a reliable measure for the purpose of controlling product costs and monitoring performance at LDZ level on a monthly basis. As a result, LDZ managers at Operations did not accept ABB budget targets in measuring their performance. They were only used as complementary information, along with traditional budgets, for strategic purposes at Assets, e.g. Assets monitoring Operations' product performance by comparing product costs between last year's actual ABC, ABB and this year's actual ABC.

Compatibility of the ABB system with existing systems. In comparison to the compatibility of its ABC system, Transco's ABB system was relatively incompatible to the existing systems. After a series of improvements to the ABC computer systems were made over the years, Transco's ABC system was now relatively compatible with the traditional ones. For example, information from SAP™ was extracted with relative ease to enable the production of monthly ABC reports on approximately the same time scale as financial reports. This also helped to promote the adaptation of the use of ABC information at the LDZs.

The ABB system, however, did not enjoy the same degree of success as the ABC system, owing to the incompatibility of 'Budget Plus' with existing systems at Operations. Technically, the ABB system 'Budget Plus' was not integrated into the ABC system directly but linked to EssBase. Therefore a lot of time was spent on downloading ABC information from EssBase, and consequently affected the speed of producing an ABB budget. In addition, Operations relied on current ABC performance rather than past performance (e.g. ABB product cost) to control its product performance. Thus, from Operations' viewpoint, ABB which was constructed on an annual basis was quickly out of date. It was considered to be less cost-effective to construct an up-to-date ABB as the labour intensity in the construction of an ABB made updating an onerous task.

The intention of monitoring product costs by comparing ABB and actual ABC results was thus not feasible; the task was therefore replaced by the use of other control mechanisms, e.g. monthly forecast, performance gap analysis and bandwidth analysis[15] using ABC information.

14:3.3.2.2 Organisational Perspective

Influence of administrative arrangements on the implementation of the ABB system. A budgetary reform (e.g. the introduction of an ABB system) needs to encompass all administrative arrangements that impinge on budgetary and financial management. Transco had different administrative arrangements with the two departments to undertake its budgetary planning processes. Support Services Finance at HQ was assigned with the job of overseeing projects to ensure acceptable delivery of its organisational long-term plan. The business planning team at Operations was responsible for developing and executing some short-term plans (including annual budgets). It should be noted that a slight discrepancy existed between the execution of the long-term plans and that of the short-term plans, because the (long-term) planning team at Support Services Finance worked separately from the (short-term) planning team at Operations (as indicated in Operations' short-term planning proposal (internal document)). The development of Year 2000's ABB product cost budget only involved the members of the planning team at Support Services Finance, but did not involve the team members at Operations. This arrangement might explain the limited perceived usefulness of ABB among LDZ managers at Operations.

The discrepancy in administrative arrangements (and differences in opinions resulting from the arrangements) could potentially cause Transco to face some conflicts and inefficiencies in the introduction of any new budget planning and control systems. In realisation of this potential danger, Transco's budget process manager adopted a hybrid approach, i.e. a combined top-down/bottom-up approach to reach the Operations Budget for 2001. Based on a pre-determined control budget total allocated from Transco HQ to Operations, the top-down approach was used to calculate a 'benchmark budget' aimed at closing the performance gap and reducing the cost among LDZs. The bottom-up approach was used in LDZs to review their current performances and to prepare a business case to support their applications for any additional funds. It is thus hoped that the discrepancy of administrative arrangements among the two teams can be properly addressed during this proposed approach.

Suitability of organisational structure for the introduction of the ABB system. The structure of an organisation may influence the implementation of an ABB system, particularly for an ABB product cost budget system. The design of the ABB system was not in line with the existing structure and operational processes, which were in a fairly hierarchical and functional manner. More efforts would be required to co-ordinate between functional departments to ensure the success of the ABB implementation. This requirement became apparent when a lack of co-ordination occurred relating to the two planning teams (i.e. the long-term planning team at Support Services Finance and the (short-term) business planning team at Operations). Furthermore, managers at Transco got used to calculating and managing budgets in a functional way. Therefore, the ABB product cost budgets, which set budgets for 76 products, did not appeal to these managers, particular those at Operations. For example, a front-end team supervisor was only interested in the cost of finishing a job by using his team resource. The overall ABC cost for that job which included other support activities did not seem to be relevant to this supervisor. Furthermore, the ABB product cost budgets did not appeal to those managers at top and middle levels either; evidently those managers still adopted traditional budgets as the predominant form of budgetary control. Given Transco's hierarchical structure, the introduction of ABB product cost budgets encountered barriers arising from the structure and general practices that had been established over the years.

To overcome these barriers, changes to either the construction of the ABB budgets or the structure were needed. There were some indications that Operations was to be separated from Transco to become an independent gas operator, in that it would have to compete with other service providers to bid for contracts from Asset. By then the importance of ABB information would become more apparent to managers at Operations. But until the market competition was formalised at Transco,[16] the structural barriers to the adoption of the ABB product cost budgets still remained as one of the major factors to the success of ABB implementation.

Impacts of restructuring on ABB implementation and training. The restructuring exercises at Transco had some positive and negative impacts on the implementation of the activity-based systems. The positive aspects are that the potential separation between Asset and Operations may make managers more aware of the potential use of its ABC and ABB information.

However, constant restructuring may produce some negative results, i.e. a tendency to use traditional sets of information and loss of expertise. The restructuring resulted in constant updating and maintenance of the activity-based models (which were designed based on the structure prior to restructuring) in order to keep up with the changes. To the managers, particularly front-line managers, the constant changes amounted to additional confusion (i.e. the original confusion arose from the different interpretation between traditional and activity-based information; the additional confusion was the different figures shown in activity-based information before and after the restructuring).

Restructuring may also relate to a loss of expertise and knowledge. This tended to have detrimental impacts on the development and implementation of the ABB system. Transco had a high turnover of experienced management accountants during the restructuring exercise.

The constant restructuring also increased the demand for training. Training was usually given to managers and management accountants at LDZs; however, priorities would normally be given to management accountants. The constant structural changes resulted in ongoing changes to the activity-based models, thus demand for training was increased in order to keep managers and management accountants updated with the changes. However, owing to the high turnover of experienced/trained staff members and increased training demand for updated models, a 'vicious circle' seemed to exist at Transco.

14:3.3.2.3 Other Aspects

Cultural barriers to ABB implementation. A 'set culture' might be in existence among different levels of managers. For example, Operations' line managers perceived the ABB information as less relevant and useful to their daily operations. One reason for this perception was that these managers were accustomed to the use of traditional information and thus were perceived to have a 'set view' (culture) about the way to do things. The existence of the 'set culture' implies that some difficulties are to be expected in the introduction of an activity based approach across the organisation, particularly among the front-line managers.

Since Transco is a large organisation with many functional departments and business units, it is difficult to draw a detailed profile of Transco's culture. On the description given by the interviewees, however, insight into the culture among the various levels of managers[17] at Operations' LDZs is possible. Some of the front-line managers (i.e. team supervisors and departmental managers) with an engineering background were accustomed to the use of traditional financial information. In addition, their performance measurements were also set against their departmental (functional) results. This, in one way or another, tended to promote the continuous use of traditional information and hinder the introduction of new systems like ABC and ABB.

The following possible scenarios may be described as forms of such 'set culture':

1. *The managers at Operations may perceive the constant changes as being irrelevant to their routine operations (i.e. Transco was still being regulated at the time of this research).*
2. *Changes may be perceived to affect the structure at a higher level, and the front-line operational units (or teams) at Operations were not affected by these changes.*

Constant changes brought constant modifications to the ABC model. It may therefore be difficult for the managers to keep up with these changes. As a result they may also choose to continue to use the familiar traditional information.

On the other hand, a gradual change of attitude occurred among middle-level managers (i.e. LDZ managers, business network managers and LDZ marketing managers) who understood the principles of ABC. They were able to make some effective use of the two sets of financial information – traditional and ABC – to support their operational management tasks. It was notable that their requirements from the ABB system were different from those of the front-line managers. They required more influence, autonomy and ownership of the ABB system. Consequently, issues relating to culture (i.e. existing practice and belief) and the ownership of ABB produced tension (even disagreement) among personnel within Operations and between Asset and Operations.

In addition, views on the use of budgets also varied among managers within Asset and Operations. While Operations was more interested in the actual performance among LDZs, Asset, as a budget holder, was more interested in comparing Operations' performance with external service providers. This difference indicated that different beliefs (cultures) existed between Asset and Operations.

In general, the existence of varied cultures within different parts of an organisation (or sub-cultures) may affect the level and extent of using an ABB system. The varying use of ABC information for management purposes (including budgeting) at Transco varied considerably among managers at various hierarchical levels. Thus these variations and the existence of culture differences (i.e. 'set cultures' and subcultures in different departments and business units) made it relatively difficult to introduce ABC and ABB approaches across the whole organisation.

Lack of budget participation in the ABB system. A general sense of participation was regarded as important towards managers' acceptance of the budgets. This was because managers perceived the participation process as a way to understand the construction process of a budget and the steps involved in underpinning their knowledge about their own business processes. However, during Transco's construction of its ABB product cost budget, there was a lack of participation from middle-line managers.

The two approaches involved in preparing traditional and ABB budgets suggested two different levels of participation. Under the traditional bottom-up budgeting process, managers were able to participate in the calculation of their individual functional budgets. However, the ABB product cost budget was calculated based on the derived functional budgets and undertaken at a strategic level. Although the ABB budget was essentially based on the functional budgets, which were prepared with the participation of those LDZ managers, the LDZ managers were not literally involved in the ABB process. As a result, LDZ managers would feel that they were unable to influence the ABB outcomes. Thus they tended to make less use of the ABB budgets.

Some tensions among the accountants and the LDZ managers also occurred as a result of this ABB approach. The accountants felt that the LDZ managers did not have the necessary knowledge to construct the ABB product cost budgets effectively. On the other hand the LDZ managers argued that without active participation they would not be able to gain sufficient knowledge for subsequent use of activity-based information. In contrast to the participative manner used in the functional budgeting process, where managers felt they had greater influence on the final budgets, the non-participative manner used in the ABB process made LDZ managers less motivated and less keen to understand and use ABB information for management purposes. Thus, the participative manner that LDZ managers were accustomed to in the 'bottom-up' budgeting approach created an impediment for managers to adopt an ABB system, which was introduced in a non-participative manner.

Emerging market competition to Transco's business activities. As revealed in previous sections, the likelihood of the introduction of market competition could change the managers' (particularly those at Operations) attitude towards the use of activity-based information. Over the past eight years, managers at Transco have adopted the ABC/ABB systems in a limited and gradual fashion. However, when Operations was to become an independent service provider to Asset, the importance of ABC/ABB information was evidently becoming more apparent. This indicates that the introduction of market competition may be an external force to help managers to adopt ABC/ABB as a useful tool for decision-making purposes.

14:4 Crown Prosecution Service

14:4.1 Company Background

The Crown Prosecution Service (CPS) is a UK government agency that carries out legal justice services to the public against criminal offences in England and Wales. It was created by a governmental policy act in 1985 and was in full operation in October 1986. As a government agency, the CPS is fully funded by the Treasury on the governmental funding principles in a three-year budget cycle (e.g. April 1998 to March 2001).

The CPS's operational structure has changed from time to time. However, regardless of these changes, the constant feature is a geographic network of operational units grouped in Areas. Each Area covers a number of metropolises, cities and rural counties. The nature of CPS work naturally requires the maintenance of close links with the Police Force and the courts (i.e. the magistrates' courts and the Crown Courts). Prior to 1999, one Area was geographically linked with two or three police forces' boundaries. With an aim to improve efficiency, cost-effectiveness and accountability within the criminal justice system, the CPS was restructured in April 1999 into a 42-Area structure to align with the existing 42 police-force boundaries. An exception is the CPS's London Area, which is aligned with the City of London Police and the Metropolitan Police.

The current organisational structure of the CPS comprises two HQs (i.e. one is based in London and the other is in York), 42 Areas and 10 service centres. The HQs manage the whole CPS process to ensure quality and consistency of work and other corporate functions (e.g. corporate planning, strategic management control, human resources and public relations). Within the 42 Areas, the larger Areas consist of a few branch offices. The smaller Areas consist of two teams, rather than branches, to deal with legal work in the crown courts and the magistrates' courts (i.e. the magistrates' court team and the Crown Court team). The CPS has 10 service centres, which had been reduced from 13 in April 2000, and each of them performs various essential supporting functions (e.g. payment of staff payroll, bills, accommodation costs of Areas' premises and management of leasing contracts of those premises) for three or four Areas. Diagrammatically, the CPS's organisational structure is shown in **Fig.14:14**.

Figure 14:14 **Organisational structure of CPS**

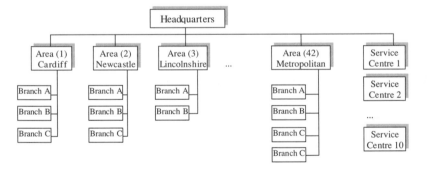

The CPS introduced an ABB model to its annual budgeting allocation of its Areas' running costs for the financial year 2000/01 (excluding HQ's running costs). During this period of introducing the ABB model the CPS also faced a number of constraints:

1. *The Government has introduced a 'value-for-money' policy for public funding. This resulted in a step-cut of the overall budget provisions during a three-year funding period (1998–2001). The funding allocated to the CPS for the year 2000/01 was 4.5% less than the previous year (1999/2000) and approximately 8% less than that for the first year of the three-year funding period (1998/99).*

2. *The CPS's workforce structure was inflexible. Given that more than 85% of the CPS's running costs are staffing costs, the first constraint has resulted in direct consequences for the workforce. The fund for the year 2000/01 was merely enough to pay its workforce.*
3. *The CPS's efforts to improve its performance were constrained by a relatively inefficient interaction between the CPS and other agencies in the criminal justice system.*

As a result, ABB was not used directly to allocate the Areas' budgets for the financial year 2000/01 but as a comparative mechanism to highlight the differences between the budgets based on the ABB allocation and those based on the conventional method. The conventional method used in the actual allocation of the Areas' budgets was an 'across-the-board' cut approach, i.e. a 4.5% cut of the Areas' budgets from the year 1999/2000. However, the value of ABB was soon recognised by the CPS during this budgeting exercise and the management decided that ABB was to be the only method for the following areas of budget allocation (*see* **para.14:4.3** for a detailed explanation):

1. *an additional fund obtained from the Treasury to ease the budget constraints in the financial year 2000/01;*
2. *a special fund to promote new initiatives in 'Performance Improvement Programme' (PIP);*
3. *the Areas' running costs budget starting from the financial year 2001/02.*

14:4.2 Introduction of Activity-based Costing at the CPS

The introduction of an ABB system at the CPS can partly be attributed to the confidence in and the general acceptance of its ABC system. Hence a brief description of the CPS's ABC system is included in this section.

The CPS regards ABC as a system that produces improved staff costing information and provides some links between activities and processes. The main activities in the whole process of prosecution include advice, review and case preparation, presentation at courts and case disposal. The ABC costs are equal to the multiplication of the number of files handled with staff time, or in other words, the total cost of staff time spent on the prosecution process.

The purposes of implementing this ABC system are:

(a) *to identify good practice and more efficient and cost-effective working methods which can improve efficiency;*

    (b) to provide Area managers with a greater understanding of the costs and efficiency of their business processes/practices;

    (c) to help to prevent each Branch/Area 're-inventing the wheel' in their pursuit of efficiency and effective service.

In that sense, only the activities with direct links to the prosecution processes, which are carried out by Areas, are measured by the ABC system.

When ABC was first introduced at the CPS in 1995, there was a significant reduction in reported crime cases (i.e. caseload, not workload[18]) in the UK, accompanied by increases in staff costs. The Treasury raised concerns about this trend. By using ABC information, the CPS was able to demonstrate that a greater case complexity and additional tasks involved accounted for the increases in staff costs during this period. Besides this, two additional factors were also attributed to the CPS's use of ABC:

1. *ABC information helped to improve openness and external accountability. For example, the CPS constantly faced questions on how the CPS's budget was being spent. With ABC information, the CPS was able to demonstrate to the public the cost differences between a motoring offence case and a burglary, or youth cases as opposed to rape cases.*

2. *The use of ABC information offered an opportunity to distribute budgets within the CPS based on need rather than precedent. This issue related directly to the internal distribution of resources. The perceived imbalance in the distribution of resources was common knowledge at the CPS, in that many believed that those who shouted loudest got the most. It was anticipated that ABC was able to address this issue (this was embedded in the attempt to use ABB; see also **para.14:4.3**).*

An ABC implementation team, consisting of two full-time members of staff with expertise in the ABC system (i.e. the two personnel from the activity-based cost management (ABCM) unit who were interviewed during the initial visit) and a few prosecutors and administrative staff, was subsequently formed to commence the initial ABC implementation in 1995. At the same time, arrangements were put in place for staff within the Internal Resource Performance Management Branch to develop an ABC modelling system (that has now evolved to become part of the Corporate Information System. The Corporate Information System would integrate ABC timings with actual case files prosecuted and staff costs so as to inform the budgeting allocation process of the Areas' running costs.

From the lessons learned from the implementation of the other systems, management at HQ decided that the new ABC system would need constant maintenance and updating to accommodate changes and new initiatives at the CPS. In order to do so, an ABCM unit, which consisted of the two full-time members of the ABC implementation team and a few part-time members of staff, was set up. Furthermore, an ABC steering group, which consisted of members from the ABCM unit, Area Business Managers, Areas' Chief Crown Prosecutors and senior executives, was also formed to oversee the implementation process at a strategic level.

The general expectation from the management was that the use of ABC would enable the CPS to model the complexity of the tasks undertaken by the CPS so as to reflect the costs associated with the tasks in a consistent and rational manner. Consequently, any observed increases in costs would be traceable and justifiable. Another use of the ABC information was for the enhancement of the existing performance management index – the Performance Indicator system. Although the Performance Indicator system was introduced before the implementation of the ABC system, staff members generally had positive opinions because 'the ABC information was able to make some elements in the Performance Indicators more meaningful'. Simply put, 'ABC does not replace Performance Indicators but illuminates them to make their message meaningful'.

14:4.2.1 The CPS's ABC Model

The main role of the CPS is the prosecution of alleged criminal offenders in England and Wales. This role includes five main functions:

1. *Advising the police on possible prosecutions.*
2. *Reviewing prosecutions started by the police to ensure that the right defendants are prosecuted on the right charges.*
3. *Preparing cases for prosecution in court.*
4. *Prosecuting cases at the magistrates' courts and instructing counsel to prosecute in the crown courts and higher courts.*
5. *Working with other agencies to improve the effectiveness and efficiency of the criminal justice system.*

These functions thus determine the various activities that the CPS's ABC system needs to monitor and measure.

As described in **paragraph 14:4.1**, many of the 42 Areas have a number of branches. The lowest level of activities reported in the CPS's ABC system reports are at branch level. Thus, a reorganisation of the number of Areas would not seriously affect the ABC system, apart from the regroupings of branches according to the new Area structure.

The starting point of the CPS's ABC system involves the construction of workflow process charts, which show the prosecution activities at the magistrates' courts and the crown courts respectively. This is followed by the calculation of average duration of these activities.

In the construction of an ABC system, the three following bases are considered:

1. *prosecution activities which are directly related to its prosecuting process and can be timed;*
2. *relaxation allowance timing which is related to restoration from prosecution activities and can be timed in percentage terms on the timing of prosecution activities; and*
3. *travelling time.*

The timing of prosecution activities is measured in three ways:

1. *using the Predetermined Administrative Data Systems (PADS) that are internationally recognised timings for basic actions such as reading, writing, filing and so on;*
2. *using Analytical Estimation, obtained from experienced lawyers and caseworkers who provide estimates of time required for actions such as review and court attendance;*
3. *using Observed Timing and Activity Sampling undertaken by the ABC implementation team that can be used to validate estimates, particularly court times.*

In determining the relaxation allowance timing, the CPS allocates an appropriate percentage in relation to the actual timing spent on prosecution activities to the ABC model. The CPS believes that regular periods of rest, recovery and refreshment will complement and enhance performances. Hence, rather than considering it as a 'non-value-added' activity, the CPS uses a timing allowance to take account of time spent on relaxation in its ABC model in order to measure the activity timings in a more realistic manner.

Travelling time relates only to the time taken in travelling to deal with casework (e.g. attending the courts). It represents around 2%–10% of the use of the resource in a branch. There are significant differences in travelling time between Areas located in inner cities and those in counties. For example, for some Areas located within a city, it may only take a lawyer ten minutes on foot to attend a court session and subsequently fewer resources are required in those Areas. In some Areas, lawyers may take up to two hours by car to reach a court. The latter case requires more of a lawyer's time in travelling to attend a court session and incurs a higher cost on travelling expenditure, and consequently a lawyer can attend a smaller number of court sessions. While some mechanisms (e.g. Predetermined Administrative Data Systems) are applied in the derivation of the timing for prosecution activities, timings for relaxation allowance and travelling are determined using averaged values. Different views do exist on the appropriateness of using averaged measures for travelling time and relaxation allowance to allocate resources. None the less, the averaged ABC timings and costs relating to relaxation allowance and travels have been incorporated as standard measurements, called 'Should Take' in the CPS's ABC terms.

Each branch is required to record its own finalised actual cases – its caseload – on a monthly basis, which is then fed into the Corporate Information System for the production of its quarterly ABC report. This caseload volume information, together with 'Should Take' timings and actual payroll costs, allows the Internal Resource Performance Management Branch to conduct ABC analyses. A quarterly ABC comparison report is then produced on the basis of 'Should Take' and 'Did Take' costs. The accuracy of recording the caseload volumes is thus important since it reflects throughput of prosecution services. This can then be used as a standard measurement for the actual use of resources and performance[19] (to a certain extent).

On the basis of 'Should Take' ABC information, an Area's ABC ratio is then calculated by comparing its month-to-date ABC outcomes (i.e. ABC performance, in the CPS's term) to the entire CPS's month-to-date ABC performance. An Area's ABC performance is calculated by multiplying the 'Should Take' ABC costs per case by its caseload volumes (*see* **Table 14:3**; for the purpose of confidentiality, the figures shown are not the actual figures).

Table 14:3 **Sample of CPS's ABC report (December 200x)**

Notes:

ᵃ 'No. of finalised cases' represents the cases that have been finalised in that month. The cases include all types of cases (e.g. shop-lifting, motor offences, murder trial, etc.) being prosecuted at the Crown Courts and magistrates' courts.

ᵇ 'ABC costs' are derived from multiplying different types of cases with respective 'Should Take' ABC timings

	Crown Courts		*Magistrates' courts*		*ABC earnings December)*	*ABC earnings (YTD)*	*ABC ratio*
	No. of finalised cases ᵃ (A)	*ABC cost ᵇ (£000s) (B)*	*No. of finalised cases ᵃ (C)*	*ABC cost ᵇ (£000s) (D)*	*(E)= (B) + (D) (£000s)*	*(F) (£000s)*	*(G)*
42 AREAS	**36**	**4,130**	**2,046**	**3,816**	**7,946**	**26,798**	**100%**
Area 1	3	251	20	231	482	914	3.41%
Area 2	1	131	8	115	246	257	0.96%
Area 3	0	0	10	120	120	193	0.72%
...							
Area 41	5	320	12	138	458	1372	5.12%
Area 42	2	205	6	94	299	308	1.15%

In **Table 14:3**, columns A and C are the quarterly finalised cases in both courts (from October to December). Columns B and D are the 'Should Take' ABC costs. The ABC earnings in column E refer to the quarterly ABC performance. The ABC earnings in column F are the accumulated ABC figures from April to December. Each Area's accumulated ABC earnings are then compared with the total accumulated ABC earnings to derive the ABC ratios in column G.

14:4.3 ABB System

14:4.3.1 ABB Model

The ABC ratio, which is based on the multiplication of 'Should Take' ABC timings, payroll costs and the actual caseloads during the period of 1999/2000, is subsequently made available to be used for the allocation of Areas' budgets for the year 2000/01. Based on this 1999/2000 ABC ratio and the budget provision available for Areas' budget allocation, the process in the ABB system, which is shown in **Fig.14:15**, is fairly simple and straightforward.

Figure 14:15 **ABB process in CPS**

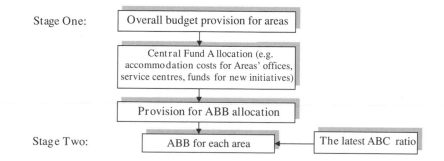

As shown in **Fig.14:15**, the CPS annual budgeting process starts with the overall budget provision for the Areas and decides on a number of funds that are to be centrally retained. The current centrally retained funds are:

(a) Accommodation costs for Areas' premises are to be paid out directly and are not subjected to the rule of ABB calculation.

(b) Costs to run the ten service centres are excluded from ABB calculation.

(c) New initiatives raised by the CPS, the central government and European Union would require additional funding and therefore a contingency fund is reserved for those unforeseen circumstances.

After the deduction of those centrally kept funds, a provision that is subject to ABB allocation can then be derived. At Stage Two, the ABC ratio is used as a standard to calculate budgets for all 42 Areas.

As an illustration, a sample of the CPS's ABB budget is shown in **Table 14:4**.[20]

Table 14:4 **Sample of CPS's budget based on ABB system**

Note:

ᵃ '% share' represents the proportion of an Area's budget to the overall budget allocated in 1999/2000. These budgets were not allocated on the basis of the ABB model

	ABC ratio (see Table 10A:3) (A)	2000/01 Available provision allocated on ABB basis (£'s) (B)	1999/2000 Budget on traditional basis (£'s) (C)	% shareᵃ (D)	Budget reduction (E) [(B) − (C)]/(B) %
42 AREAS	100%	80,000,000	83,600,000	100%	−4.50
Area 1	3.41%	2,728000	2,758,800	3.30%	−1.13
Area 2	0.96%	768,000	710,600	0.85%	7.47
Area 3	0.72%	576,000	744,040	0.89%	−29.17
...					
Area 41	5.12%	4,096,000	4,974,200	5.95%	−21.44
Area 42	1.15%	920,000	919,600	1.10%	0.04

In **Table 14:4**, the ABC ratio is shown in column A, the budget allocated based on the ABB system is shown in column B and the budget allocated in 1999/2000 which was done without using the ABB system, is shown in column C. Furthermore, in column D the percentage share of an Area represents the final proportion of an Area's budget to the overall budget. The ABC ratio shown in column A is derived from the ABC system that uses average ABC timings in conjunction with actual caseloads (*see* **Table 14:3**). It is apparent in column E that despite a 4.5% reduction of the overall budget provision, Areas 1, 2 and 42 would suffer less under the ABB allocation. In fact Areas 2 and 42 could receive higher budgets in 2000/01 than they did in the previous year (i.e. a respective increase of 7.47% and 0.04%), whereas other areas (e.g. Areas 3 and 41) would be severely affected as a result of the overall budget reduction. For example, if a strict ABB system was applied, Area 3's budget would be reduced by 29.17%. Given that more than 85% of an Area's running costs are staffing costs, Area 3 would not have sufficient funds to pay staff salaries. In the light of various budget pressures the CPS faced (*see* **para.14:4.1**) and other difficulties (e.g. the issue of the perceived accuracy of the ABC model; further details are explored in **para.14:4.4**), a compromise approach, i.e. an 'across-the-board', cut or 'equal share of misery between HQ and Areas', was decided by the Chief Executive Management Committee.

Λ minute was circulated to inform Area managers about the Chief Executive Management Committee's budget decisions. This minute stated clearly the various pressures the CPS faced and various considerations/criteria that were taken into account in the derivation of the final budget.[21] The following worksheets were also attached to indicate various budget figures under three different scenarios (i.e. column B is based entirely on an ABC ratio or ABB model, Option 1 on an 'across-the-board' cut and Option 2 on the indicative figures based on various local factors and provisions for staff salaries) (*see* **Table 14:5**).

Table 14:5 **Sample of final budget**

Note:

ᵃ '% share' represents the proportion of an Area's budget to the overall budget allocated in 1999/2000. These budgets were not allocated on the basis of the ABB model

	(A)	2000/01 (B) (£)	1999/2000 baseline		Option 1: Pro rata reduction (i.e. 4.5% cut)		Option 2: Indicative figures	
	Share from latest ABC model 1999	Budget based on straight ABC basis	Budget (C) (£')	% shares	2000/01 budget allocation (£') (D=C x 4.5%)	Change on 1999/2000 budget (£') (E=D–C)	Indicative figures (£') (F)	Change on 1999/2000 budget (£') (G=F–C)
42 AREAS	100%	80,000,000	83,600,000	100%	80,000,000	–3,600,000	80,000,000	–3,600,000
Area 1	3.41%	2,728000	2,758,800	3.30%	2,634,654	–124,146	2,670,340	–88,460
Area 2	0.96%	768,000	710,600	0.85%	678,623	–31,977	643,105	–67,495
Area 3	0.72%	576,000	744,040	0.89%	710,558	–33,482	745,120	1,080
...								
Area 41	5.12%	4,096,000	4,974,200	5.95%	4,750,361	–223,839	4,810,223	–163,977
Area 42	1.15%	920,000	919,600	1.10%	878,218	–41,382	798,410	–121,190

14:4.3.2 Implementation Issues

In comparison to the ABB implementations at SCB and Transco, the CPS's ABB experience can be considered as successful. The factors influencing the CPS's ABB implementation can be analysed as follows.

14:4.3.2.1 Technical Perspective

The CPS's ABB model as a simple and improved basis for budget allocation. Technically speaking, the CPS's ABB model was the simplest among the three organisations. It was based on a method of multiplying the ABC ratio with the Areas' budget provisions for the coming year. Once the ABC information became available, the calculation of Areas' running-cost budgets could be undertaken with the aid of computer spreadsheets in a relatively short period of time (i.e. three days for the financial year 2000/01 and one day for the financial year 2001–2). Moreover, the ABB method was so simple to understand that some Areas applied it in allocating their branches' budgets. Thus it was apparent that the simplicity of this model increased the possibility for adopting ABB at the CPS.

In comparison to the previously adopted budget allocation methods, the ABB model was considered as an improvement over those methods. Such improvement became apparent when the CPS faced some special circumstances. The budgeting process at the CPS was somewhat different from that in other sectors. First of all, the allocation criteria from the Treasury (to fund the CPS's resource need) and the CPS's HQ (to fund the Areas' needs) were not based on any means of forecasts. Thus the CPS's budgeting process was basically an allocation of budget provision to Areas. When the CPS was restructured from a 13- to a 42-Area structure in 1999, the budget allocation across 42 Areas would be more time consuming. This was compounded by a 'who shouts the loudest gets the most' situation that existed in its budgetary negotiation process. Thus, when the CPS Board decided to use a top-down or imposed budgeting approach, a more cost-effective allocation method became an urgent need. In addition, there were internal and external demands for establishing links between resource deployment (expenditure) and performance. The traditional budgeting methods (e.g. line-by-line budgeting) that the CPS adopted did not meet these demands. Thus a more stringent and unified allocation method was required to enable a 'fairer' and cost-effective justification of the resource deployment, utilisation and performance across the 42 Areas. The CPS's ABC information established a causal link between performance (e.g. the number of finalised cases), core activities and resource utilisation at the CPS. Based on past ABC information, the ABB model was considered to be a 'fairer' and more cost-effective means of allocating Areas' budgets than other allocation methods.

Due to the overall budget reduction, the use of the ABB model was limited in its initial budget allocation for 2000/01. However, because of the simplicity and cost-effectiveness of the ABB model, it was used in the budget allocation of (1) the additional budget allocated by the Treasury during 2000/01, (2) the 'Performance Improvement Programme' (PIP) fund and (3) the financial year 2001/02's Area budgets.

The simplicity of the ABB model played an important role in the success of ABB system implementation at the CPS. Because of the simplicity, the ABB model was fine-tuned with relative ease to suit CPS needs and external demands. This, in turn, helped the ABB system to gain general acceptance from the staff members.

Compatibility with the organisational structure and existing systems. The CPS's ABB model was also relatively compatible with its organisational structure and the existing systems. The ABB model was used to allocate the budgets to the 42 Areas, therefore the implementation of the ABB system related directly to its existing organisational structure (i.e. HQ and Areas). Moreover, the ABB calculations were done in a stand-alone computer system by inputting ABC ratio and payroll costs data (which were processed in the Corporate Information System). Thus the interruption between the ABC and ABB systems was kept to a minimum level.

Level of accuracy of ABC variables and budget situations to the use of the ABB model. Area managers generally accepted the relative improvement of the ABB model over other budget methods that the CPS had previously adopted. However, they also recognised that the current ABB model could only provide a generalised (not precise) measure or a 'slice of cake'. When the CPS faced budget scarcity (as experienced in the year 2000/01), this lack of precision ('fairness') became a serious threat to the adoption of the ABB system.

This lack of precision was directly attributed by the variables in the ABC system. Because of the averaged timing measures adopted in the ABC system, some Area managers raised their concerns regarding the accuracy of these variables, particularly timing allowances for travelling and case complexity among Areas. For example, timing allowance for travelling measured the time taken for staff members to travel from offices to courts. It was fixed at 2%–10% of the actual timing for core prosecution activities. The actual travelling cost from office to court differed greatly from one Area to another, ranging from a mere five minutes' walking in an urban Area to a car journey of three hours in a rural Area. The 2%–10% factor adopted by the ABC model was therefore not considered as a satisfactory way to model the diverse range of travel timing in reality.

Case complexity was another ABC system variable that affected the 'fairness' of budget allocation using the ABB model. The case complexity in the CPS's ABC model was measured on the basis of an average timing on case finalisations. Although different weights were built in to differentiate the complexity and seriousness of cases, these weights were not sufficient enough to represent the precise situations at an Area level. For example, some complex criminal cases involving serious offences like murder and trafficking of drugs could take more than a year to be finalised, whereas simpler cases like shop-lifting would require an average of only half a day to be finalised. It was argued that a simple weighting factor applied to a complex case was not able to represent the exact amount of resource, applied in the actual case. As demonstrated in **Fig.14:16**, the ABC timing only modelled the average times in finalising cases. It was weak in measuring activity timings in Areas in which caseloads fell into the two extreme ends, i.e. a large number of simple cases or complex cases. This average timing in the ABC system naturally favoured Areas with a higher proportion of simple cases and penalised Areas with a higher proportion of complex cases.

Figure 14:16 **Demonstration of case complexity in ABC system**

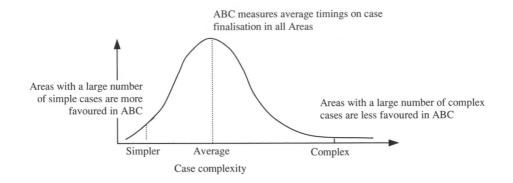

Furthermore, as a result of the increased number of Areas, the size of an Area was reduced significantly and so were the Areas' budgets. Compounded by the overall budget reduction, a fraction of difference (e.g. 0.1%) in the ABC ratio (amounting to £40,000 difference in budgets) would have different impacts on different Areas. To a larger Area with a budget of, say, £7,000,000, £40,000 difference would not result in substantial impacts on the Area's operation. However, to a smaller Area with £250,000, this difference would cause serious consequences (e.g. staff retrenchment). Before the imprecision of system variables was dealt with sufficiently, the CPS was not prepared to impose a budget that could cause such serious impacts. Further evidence revealed that the CPS's adoption of the ABB budget allocation for 2001/02 was partly contributed to by some revisions made to ABC variables. In particular, the major contributor to the adoption was evidently the (relatively substantial) increased government budget for 2001/02.

Hence, on the basis of varying budget situations, the accuracy of ABC variables affected the use of the ABB model to different extents. In the case of budget scarcity, the accuracy of ABC variables had serious impacts on the actual adoption of the ABB model in the budget allocation. When the budget situation was improved, the accuracy of ABC variables became less influential on the adoption of the ABB model.

14:4.3.2.2 Behavioural Aspect

Impact of the implementation of ABB on managerial behaviour – proactive learning and initiatives on process re-engineering. Emphasis on the use of the ABC system was stated in the minutes of 'Areas Budget Allocation 2000/01'. This was the first time that the HQs had stated their inclination to link budget allocation to Areas' ABC performance. This minute caused some concerns, particularly among those Areas with poorer ABC performances and those Area managers who had not previously paid much attention to understanding the ABC information. Following the circulation of this minute, Area managers started to take the ABC figures much more seriously as they realised that their future budgets would be determined by the ABC figures. An observation was that the Area managers made more proactive efforts to learn the ABC principles. They particularly focused on the use of ABC information for management purposes.

Consequently, Area managers, who were accustomed to managing the 'bottom-line' figure, felt the need to change the way that they managed the Areas' activities. Some of them began to use activity information in critically analysing their activities and processes. As a result, some new initiatives were taken in re-engineering business processes. An example of a re-engineered process was the deployment of designated caseworkers, which was an initiative taken by the CPS top management to improve the quality of case finalisation. Under this initiative the designated caseworkers were deployed to deal with less complicated cases so that lawyers could concentrate on preparing more serious cases. As a result, the overall quality of the CPS's service and performance was improved.

Another example of process re-engineering, which involved external co-ordination, also produced a favourable outcome. The ABC information revealed the existence of inefficiencies in some Areas. Area managers found that some of the inefficiencies were attributed externally. For example, if a case file was not prepared properly by the police, a CPS's lawyer would spend more time on revising the case file. The same inefficient situation applied to the arrangement of court sessions. For example, if two court hearing sessions were arranged at the same time, it would take two lawyers to attend the sessions. The above-mentioned two instances demonstrated that an Area's performance was closely reliant on the police and the courts, whose efficiency was considered to be beyond the CPS's control. The significance of the influence on Areas' ABC performance exerted by these uncontrollable external inefficiencies prompted some Area managers to take some proactive actions. A visit to one Area which involved Interviewees H and I, revealed that they had initiated a joint exercise with the police and the crown court. This exercise included a mapping exercise of the entire legal process from the police, the CPS's Area and the Crown Court in an attempt to streamline various interactions (*see* **Fig.14:17**).

Figure 14:17 **Sample of process flow across the UK criminal justice system**

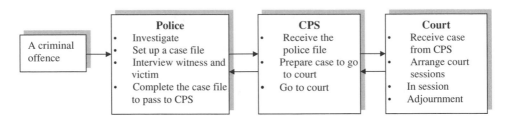

As shown in **Fig.14:17**, the mapping exercise produced a model that depicted the legal process and series of interactions across the three agencies (the police, the CPS and the Crown Court) in that Area. As a result, improvements in the legal process could be introduced and implemented in a holistic manner. Although this exercise was still at its early stage at the time of this case study, some improved interactions between the CPS and the police could be observed. For example, the CPS assigned caseworkers to prepare case files jointly with the police. As a result, the quality of case files was improved and resource utilisation for both agencies was also optimised. Most of all, the mapping exercise helped managers to visualise the three agencies' activities and streamline interactions between them (e.g. reduce duplication of work, improve or eliminate ineffective practices).

In this respect, the introduction of the ABB model had significant impact on managerial behaviour. The managers paid more attention to managing processes and activities and began to take initiatives to improve internal and external processes.

ABB Information as a common communication platform to encourage participation in a top-down budgeting process.

(a) *Job satisfaction and tension reduction through participation. The CPS's top/middle managers did not support the idea of budget participation. Rather, some form of Area representation on the Chief Executive Management Committee and constant dialogues between HQ and Areas were considered to be more effective.*

Area managers were not involved at the budget allocation process before commencing a financial year, but became involved during the financial year, through formal and informal budget-related meetings at national and Area levels. At national level, budget reviews were held formally twice a year: a mid-year and end-of-the-year review. Informal budget-related discussions were also held between Areas and the Internal Resource Performance Management Branch during the year. Evidence suggested that these two forms of discussions helped to reduce some tensions that occurred as a result of the imposed budgets.

(b) *Motivation related to the use of the ABB system and budget pressure. As a result of the 'across-the-board' budget reduction in the year 2000/01, a sense of budget disincentives in using ABC information could be felt. The increased budget pressure also resulted in an increased sense of demotivation among Area managers, as observed during this case study. Although the CPS insisted that non-correlation between budget and performance had been found in the past, the increased budget pressure could still have an impact on Area managers' motivation to learn proactively and improve the quality of service, which was often hard to quantify. However, the demotivation did bring some obvious consequences at the CPS, such as increased stress levels and low morale.*

(c) *Performance, budget pressure and task complexity. The CPS's performance targets, which were built into the Performance Indicators in the CPS's national and Area business plans, were divided into two main categories: financial and non-financial. The financial targets for an Area included items such as 'stay within the budget' and 'reduction of unit cost of accommodation'. The non-financial targets were the main measures of the performance targets, including items such as 'paying witness expense claims within ten days of receipt', 'replying to complaints within ten days' and 'sending out brief to counsel within 14 days of at the receipt'. These targets had no direct links to the budget and resource deployment at the CPS. In other words, the budget pressure would not cause immediate impacts on the quality and performance of work. However, when the budget pressure persisted, tasks such as the achievement of budgetary targets became more difficult, and adverse impacts on the quality of services began to emerge. These adverse impacts had already been manifested in the increased rates of sickness and absence. Results from a 'Staff Survey and Stress Audit' 22 revealed that the stress level at the CPS was one of the highest among the organisations audited. This stress had a detrimental impact on the ability to deliver quality services. For example, when one lawyer was sick, his cases would have to be passed on to another lawyer, who would have to handle more cases on top of his/her own caseload. The consequent chain effects resulted in delays of case finalisation and aggravated the already high stress level. A vicious circle was formed as a result of the budget pressure (see **Fig. 14:18**).*

(d) *The use of ABC/ABB helps to expose the slack. Evidence suggested that the use of ABC/ABB information helped to quantify the existence of slack. For example, within the minutes of 'Budget Allocation 2000/01', to an Area with higher staff costs but a lower level of ABC performance, its slack was represented by an addition23 to the fair share in the ABB budget.*

> *Thus the use of ABC/ABB information provided a transparent measure to highlight the existence of slack in some Areas. The budget allocation based on the ABB model could be used as a reward for managers' commitment.*

Figure 14:18 **Impact of budget pressure on the quality of performance**

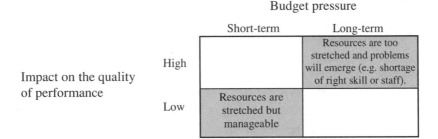

14:4.3.2.3 Organisational Perspective

Top-down budgeting approach and training influenced the implementation of ABC and ABB systems at the CPS. Top management support and training have been identified in the literature as two of the main organisational factors that influence the success of ABC implementation. The finding of the CPS's ABB experience supports this view, in that the top management support acted as a main driving force towards the CPS's ABB infusion.

The CPS's 'top-down' budgeting approach has helped to steer the implementation of both the ABC and ABB systems into their current operational states. Two members of the ABCM unit have revealed that the introduction of the ABC system directly resulted from the requirements of accountability and 'value for money' set by the Government. These requirements prompted the CPS to implement some stringent measures to justify its resource requirement and performance. The implementation of the ABC system received a relatively high level of general support and commitment from the top management. The ABC/ABB systems were also generally perceived as suitable management tools by the CPS's Area managers.

In terms of training, HQ and Area managers remained sceptical about the effectiveness of the training sessions and held different opinions about the extent of appropriate training required. At the CPS, managers' knowledge and understanding of matters relating to practical implications and the use of ABC in management decisions was relatively limited during the ABC implementation process and at the adoption stage of ABB. Two different expectations of the training resulted in perceived conflict. Members of the ABCM unit and top/middle management expected the Area managers to be able to apply the ABC information effectively in making their decisions after they attended the ABC training sessions. A basic assumption was that the Area managers should have general management knowledge and only require training to grasp the essence of the ABC system. However, Area managers who came from a legal profession (as solicitors) and different educational backgrounds did not have sufficient management knowledge. They experienced some difficulties in understanding the application of ABC for management purposes and therefore were not able to use ABC information as an effective management tool.

On the basis of the above analysis, it was notable that the effectiveness of the ABC training was perceived differently by those managers with general management knowledge from those without. To those with general management knowledge, once they understood the ABC principles, they were able to adopt the ABC/ABB information with relative ease. On the other hand, those managers without general management knowledge would require training not only in the ABC principles but also in general management. Otherwise, they were left with two hurdles: one was the interpretation of ABC information and the other was the various applications of ABC information in solving practical problems. Therefore because of different managers' backgrounds, the ABC training had a divergent effect on the Area managers' acceptance and ability to use the ABC/ABB information.

Level of management as a key determinant of the use of ABB information. The ABC/ABB information helped to draw a comparative picture of performance among Areas and establish a causal link with budget allocation. Thus it was perceived to be more applicable to those managers at HQ and Areas who needed to view performance in a holistic manner and allocate budgets on a consistent ('fairer') basis. However, the ABB information, which was generated from the averaged ABC measures, was not able to give the precise indication of situations related to individual Areas and branches. Thus, to those managers who needed more accurate information for their daily operations, the ABB information was perceived as less useful.

The use of ABB information was thus effective for the purpose of budgetary planning. It provided top/middle management with a comparative picture of activities and performance across 42 Areas. This was also applicable at an Area level when the Area Business Managers and Chief Crown Prosecutors wanted to compare performance between branches. The effectiveness decreased when the requirement for accurate information increased, particularly at the branch level. Managers with a full understanding of their operations needed more precise information for their management control purposes. Consequently they were more sceptical about the effectiveness of the ABB information.

Influences of administrative inflexibility and budget availability on budgeting process. From **Table 14:4**, if the budget was allocated on the basis of the 'strict ABB model', the CPS could face some serious and immediate problems in some Areas. At the CPS, the allocated budget was to meet the cost requirement, i.e. salary costs of full-time staff members (i.e. crown prosecutors, caseworkers, Area managers and administrative staff) and other costs including travelling, photocopying, utilities and telephone. Among these costs, the staffing costs accounted for more than 90% of its budget. In addition, as all full-time members of staff the CPS were on permanent contracts, unless they voluntarily chose to resign, the workforce structure generally had little flexibility.

This problem of an inflexible workforce structure derives from some historical reasons. When the CPS was formed in 1986, it was expanded considerably in order to meet increased caseload demands at that period. Thus Area 41 may have recruited a large number of lawyers to deal with the then relatively high levels of caseload. Staff members were also offered permanent contracts. When the caseloads were significantly reduced in recent years, Area 41 became over-staffed (as also indicated by the ABB model). The reduced budget derived from the 'strict ABB model' was thus not feasible to be administered in the CPS's later situation. On the other hand, when the budget was increased to a certain level so that the use of the ABB model would have minimum effects on workforce arrangements, the use of the ABB model then became possible. This was the case in the CPS's budget allocation for the financial year 2001/02. Hence the budget availability and the existence of an inflexible workforce structure at the CPS were the determining factors in the ABB implementation.

Although not applied, the 'strict ABB model' did expose the problem of an inflexible workforce and drew managers' attention to the existence of inefficiency in those Areas with a relatively large number of staff but low caseloads. The resultant pressures forced Area managers and top management to devise an action plan, such as the secondment of staff members to other Areas and the recruitment of short-term contractual staff. Hence, the CPS's ABB information had some positive influences on decision making even though the CPS's cost (workforce) structure was inflexible.

14:4.3.2.4 Cultural Perspective

Evidence suggested that there was a certain divergence in values (which formed a part of the organisational culture) after a series of changes were introduced to the CPS over a number of years (e.g. restructuring from a 13- to a 42-Area structure and implementation of the ABC system). Such divergence in values became more apparent when the decision to link the ABC system with the budget allocation was made.

Although top-level management's support had always been a crucial factor in ensuring the successful introduction of a new system, in comparison to the period before and after 1999, other variables (i.e. the reorganisation, the refinement of the ABC system and the introduction of the ABB system) also played a role in changing the organisational culture, which influenced the successful implementation of ABB after 1999.

Before the implementation of the ABB model, the adoption of the ABC system (which was implemented in 1995) was a slow and controversial process. This slow rate of adoption was also compounded by the old Area structure. Before the reorganisation in 1999, the CPS had 13 larger Areas (as opposed to 42 smaller Areas) for a number of years. Those managers had formed a 'set culture', which had been established from their working practice over the years. However, the implementation of new knowledge (i.e. ABC) posed a challenge to the assumptions and basic values (i.e. the 'set culture') that managers had established over the years. Thus the resistance from those managers to accept an ABC system was high.

After 1999, an increased rate of adoption of the ABC and ABB systems was noticeable. This was due to a number of factors.

1. *The real challenge to the Area managers' assumptions and basic values took place after the reorganisation to 42 Areas. Along with the reorganisation, a set of newly appointed managers was formed in an attempt to establish new working practices. Such an attempt was evident in their search for some suitable and cost-effective tools in assisting their performance, management and decision-making process.*

2. *With top management support and commitment, activities measures and cost drivers in the ABC system were continually refined and updated. Although the ABC system still measured averages, it had already taken account of a more comprehensive range of local variables that had been previously neglected.*

3. *The decision to use the ABB model as an essential reference for Areas' budget allocation was made in the financial year 2000/01. Together with the refined ABB system (i.e. with a 36-month ABC ratio), the decision to use ABB as the only determinant for Areas' budget allocation for 2001/02 was subsequently made.*

Change of culture in the workplace to an open management style (e.g. increased communications between HQ and Areas) was also observed occurring in a logical progression.

Furthermore, the situation of limited co-operation among government agencies started to change as a result of the ABB implementation. The CPS's new initiative to streamline its operations with the police and the courts was, according to the CPS's Area Business Managers, 'a significant move to look at the long-halted process and start to make changes which are long overdue'.

Generally speaking, the formation of the CPS's organisational culture was informed by two aspects: the permanent employees and the nature of being a governmental agency since 1986. The long-established beliefs and values that existed among the employees had inevitable impacts on its organisational culture, which could influence the chosen business practices and systems. Prior to 1999, such beliefs were too strong to allow the ABC system to have any significant effect. In order to introduce change to improve the working practice, more destabilising actions were needed. The CPS's success in the implementation of the ABB and ABC systems was the result of a combination of the reorganisation in 1999, new systems' implementation, changes to organisational culture and flexible managerial attitudes towards new management systems (*see* **Fig.14:19**).

Figure 14:19 **Mixture of cultural influences and ABB implementation at CPS**

Notes:
    '–' represents negative or no influences on ABC implementation
    '+' represents positive or certain influences on ABC and ABB implementation

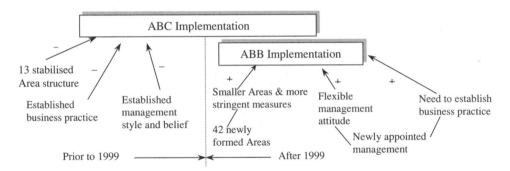

14:4.3.2.5 Other Aspects

Uncontrollable external factors. These were mainly associated with the functional procedures and the fluctuation of the quality of services provided by the police and the two courts. The CPS carries out prosecutions against criminal offences based on case files prepared by the police. The quality of these files, which contain the records, details and evidence of the criminal offences, affect directly the quality and efficiency of the CPS. A well-prepared case file could save significant time on the part of a prosecutor in preparing a court hearing. On the contrary, if a case file were not well prepared the prosecutor would have to spend a significant amount of additional time to revise and validate the case file. The quality of police case files (with sufficient evidence) can also reduce significantly the court time taken to reach final verdicts.

During a court hearing, a prosecutor may have to wait for available court sessions. Because of the courts' arrangement, some unforeseen delays in the hearing can occur. Excessive time delays caused by these factors inevitably demand additional resources (e.g. CPS prosecutors).

In the light of these 'pass-on' inefficiencies that are generated by the police and the two courts, one of the CPS's Areas took proactive action and initiated a process mapping exercise in association with the police and the courts. If implemented successfully, this initiative should have a positive impact on the overall improvement of efficiency in the entire UK criminal justice system.

14:5 Lessons Learnt from the Three Case Studies

In broad terms, ABB refers to the application of ABC in budgeting. This research has found that by applying ABC information in budgeting processes two main types of ABB budgets are derived in practice. One type of ABB budget is the product cost budget, whereby activity information is used in process analysis across functional departments. The other type of ABB budget is the functional budget, whereby activity information is used to determine resource costs, which can then be formulated into budgets for functional departments. The ABB models developed in the three organisations are summarised in **Table 14:6**.

Table 14:6 **Three models' specifications compared**

Notes:

[a] The ABC ratio refers to the ABC performance of one CPS Area over that of the 42 Areas' overall. One Area's ABC performance is the multiplication of average ABC activity standard measures with the Area's actual caseloads

[b] Despite its pilot ABC in 1991, SCB's actual implementation of ABC with full functionality in 'Cost Control' took place at the same period as that of ABB in 1995

	SCB	*Transco*	*CPS*
Nature of organisation	Brewing	Utility service (regulated)	Public service
ABB model	ABC process in reverse	Reallocation of its functional budget on the ABC ABC allocation rules	The use of ABC ratio[a] to allocate Areas' budget provisions

Type of budgets	Functional budget	Product cost budget	Areas' running cost budget (excluding Areas' accommodation cost)
Involvement of functional units in ABB	Production unit (i.e. the six breweries)	Operations & Asset (i.e. the two front-line business units)	42 Areas (i.e. the front-line functional units)
Developed from/link to ABC systems	Yes (developed within the same ABC system)	Yes (linked but independent from the ABC system)	Yes (linked but independent from the ABC system)
ABC knowledge prior to the implementation of ABB	Developed at the same time as ABB[b] introduction	Eight years of ABC experience prior to the the introduction of ABB	Five years of ABC experience prior to the introduction of ABB
Software system specification	'Cost Control' (in-house designed & link with general ledger and breweries' spreadsheet models for variable costs)	Budget Plus' (link with ' ABC systems called 'EssBase' & 'Hyper ABC/Metify')	Computer spreadsheet link with an in-house (built ABC software system called 'Corporate Information System')
No. of activity/ product involved in ABB model	250 activities, 100 products and 500 types of resources	350 core activities and 76 products	130 activities and 11 core products
Complexity/ simplicity	Complex	Complex	Relatively simple
Budget outcome	Unrealistic functional budget information	An approximate product cost budget	An approximate Area (functional) budget

14:5.1 Applicability of Two Theoretical ABB Approaches in Practice

Two ABB approaches have been proposed in the literature, i.e. Kaplan and Cooper's (1998) ABB model that is based on the concept of ABB as 'a reverse ABC process' and Brimson and Fraser's (1991) ABB process model that is a general use of ABC information in a planning and budgeting process. Based on the evidence from the three case study organisations, it can be stated that Kaplan and Cooper's model, under certain circumstances, is impractical. The main drawback of Kaplan and Cooper's approach is that, in the context of SCB, it created major permutation problems (see SCB's case). To overcome these problems an enormous amount of investment would be required, and this would have rendered SCB's ABB system significantly less cost-effective. Similar results were also evident in Transco's first ABB attempt when they tried to implement both ABC and ABB models in one computer system. Another drawback of this approach is concerned with the 'reverse ABC process', where the computerisation tends to magnify any technical drawbacks, associated with an ABC system, in an ABB system (as evident at SCB). Brimson and Fraser's approach, on the other hand, provides a general framework, which promotes the use of ABC information and allows organisations to interpret ABB in different ways. Thus it tends to be relatively more workable in practice. For example, Transco applies ABC information to reapportion the functional budgets into the product cost budgets, whereas the CPS adopts the ABC ratio as a tool to allocate Area budgets.

14:5.2 Budgeting Purposes and Organisational Objectives

The three case studies have demonstrated that the variations in the three ABB system implementations were determined predominantly by two factors: an individual organisation's budgeting purposes and the objectives of a system implementation. The general objectives of the ABB system implementations at SCB, Transco and the CPS were very much the same, i.e. to improve the existing budgeting processes and achieve better budgetary planning and control. The detailed objectives, which are related to different budgetary purposes at SCB, Transco and the CPS, determined their ABB system implementations. SCB's ABB was primarily designed to *replace* its highly labour-intensive ZBB process with a computerised ABB model, which was believed to be able to compute functional budgets in a fraction of the time. Transco's product cost ABB budget was designed to *supplement* its functional budgeting process and to provide useful information for the planning and control of product performance. The CPS's ABB budget was designed to *replace* its less cost-effective traditional budget allocation methods. These objectives determined the particular outputs (i.e. SCB's functional budget, Transco's product cost budget and the CPS's Area budgets) and the varying approaches taken by SCB, Transco and the CPS during the implementation of their ABB systems.

14:5.3 ABB Links to Budgetary Planning and Control

The evidence at Transco and the CPS suggests that the overall and comparative picture provided by ABB information is more suitable for budgetary planning purposes. Transco's ABB product cost budgets helped management to align their plans for future actions with objectives, activities, processes and product costs. The CPS's budgets also helped management to align resource planning with organisational objectives and Areas' activity performance. Furthermore, ABB information provided a clearer causal link between performance requirements, overall business processes and resource deployment at the operational levels. Thus, a cross-functional view of business operations was established to enhance the strategic planning process. The top and middle-level managers at Transco and the CPS confirm that ABB information improves their understanding of business activities at the operational levels. Consequently this improved understanding has helped them to devise better strategic plans.

On the other hand, budgets were drawn up on the basis of past ABC information, which included some non-routine factors related only to the previous year(s). Thus the ABB information may not be accurate for monitoring current operations. The production of both budgets was also on an annual basis. The managers (in particular at the front-line level) at both Transco and the CPS argued that the budgets were 'out of date' for measuring performance and did not provide exact information related to individual functional departments. Therefore the front-line (functional) managers regarded ABB information as less effective and inaccurate for monitoring and evaluating departmental activities/performance. Indeed, this research found that the managers at both organisations were less reliant on ABB information for controlling business operations. Rather, they used what they consider to be simpler and timely measures to assist their control of business operations and performance (e.g. functional budgets for spending control, monthly financial information, such as forecasts, financial accounting and ABC information (if available), and non-financial information for monitoring performance). This finding supports the argument that a set of budgets derived for planning purposes may be unsuitable for motivating performance or performance evaluation (i.e. control purposes).

14:5.4 Influential Factors on Success (or Otherwise) of an ABB Implementation

1. *The general findings from the three case studies suggest that a simpler ABB model tends to have a higher probability of success and is regarded as a cost-effective means of implementation in practice (e.g. the simple model used by the CPS).*

2. *The system design specification should be suitable for an existing organisational structure, compatible with existing systems, and appropriate for budgetary purposes.*

3. *It is notable that behavioural factors (such as top management's commitment and recognition, training, users' involvement, resistance to change and motivation) can have a significant influence on the use of ABB information.*

4. *Organisational factors such as changes to organisational structure, administrative arrangements and a clear demonstration of the interrelationship between organisation goals' and sub goal development can also be substantial obstacles to the success of an ABB implementation.*

5. *The existence of a 'set culture' as opposed to an open culture is evident.*

In addition, some specific factors that emerged from this research are related to ABB experiences. They are addressed as follows:

1. *Top-down v. bottom-up implementation approach. Since the ABB information provides a relatively clear picture of the overall anticipated performance across functional departments, it is perceived by top and middle management to be useful in managing front-line business activities. Hence an ABB approach can be adopted relatively easily and readily in an organisation that uses a top-down budgeting approach. However, the ABB approach may not be adopted readily in an organisation that uses a bottom-up budgeting approach. This is because the front-line managers are familiar with accurate information that represents their departmental operations. More importantly, unless their understanding of an ABB model/system can be substantially increased, they are likely to ask for 'fairer' and more accurate budgets rather than appreciate the 'cross-functional' view provided by the ABB information. Therefore it is relatively difficult to implement an ABB in a bottom-up manner.*

2. *Managerial behaviour in a system implementation, such as acceptance of the system, claim of ownership and resistance to change, is often associated with factors such as users' involvement and training (Innes and Mitchell, 1991; Liu et al., 2002). This research found that the involvement of users through all stages of an ABB implementation process, together with adequate training and support, are related and important to users' acceptance of an ABB system. The users' involvement in system development can act as a form of training and improve users' understanding of such an ABB system. Various forms of training and support, not only on the principles of an ABB system, but also on the applications of ABB in business scenarios, are essential. In addition, as was evident in this*

research, line managers' acceptance and motivation to use an ABB system are also affected by top management's budgetary decisions, which are perceived as an indication of commitment at the top level to such a system.

3. Changes to an organisation's structure with inevitably have an impact on an ABB implementation process. This impact can be either positive or negative, based on the different timings of the implementation and organisational changes. Structural changes may create an opportunity for management to look for new methodologies (e.g. ABB), but may also introduce a sense of instability to an organisation. When an ABB system is implemented just after the organisation reaches a new level of stability, the implementation tends to be more successful. When an ABB implementation takes place during a transitional period (e.g. an acquisition), it is crucial to ensure that the implementation delivers useful results promptly. Otherwise an ABB project is likely to face increased resource competition and conflicts in priorities during such a period. Furthermore, frequent structural changes may result in the need to modify an ABB model constantly, which may significantly increase the difficulty for a user to adapt the system effectively. As a result, users may decide to continue using more familiar and/or simpler methods.

4. Supportive administrative arrangements (e.g. standardised procedures and a clear demonstration of the interrelationship between organisational goal and sub goal development) and budgetary devolution tend to help to define the precise role of an ABB and thus help to pave the way for a smooth ABB implementation. To quote a negative example, data collected from non-standardised procedures may have an adverse effect by unnecessarily increasing the labour intensity in the use of an ABB system. This may then become an impediment to the achievement of the budgeting purposes and organisational objectives for implementing the ABB system. On the other hand, supportive arrangements such as budget devolution can help to promote creative management, which will encourage managers to seek effective management tools and learn to use activity-based information in planning scenarios spontaneously and actively.

5. Culture does play a significant role in an ABB implementation process. Budgets can help to form a particular set of norms (and/or beliefs) to encourage people to work towards organisational goals. However, the existence of a formed organisational attitude towards a given set of budgets may reduce the readiness of an organisation to accept the introduction of another set of budgets such as at the ABB budgets. In this research, two aspects of cultural influence have been observed CPS and Transco. The CPS's restructuring created a group of newly appointed managers throughout the organisational hierarchy. The introduction of ABB budgets tended to help these managers form a new set of norms (or culture). On the other hand, Transco's ABB product cost budget was introduced to complement

its traditional budgets. A 'set culture' on budgeting, such as the use of traditional financial information (including budgets) had already been established among various levels of managers. Simply put, the managers were familiar with the traditional budgeting practice. Thus, it was relatively difficult for Transco to break this 'set culture' to allow for a greater use of ABB.

14:5.5 Other Issues

Evidence from this research suggests that an ABB implementation is also substantially influenced by some external factors, such as political concerns, regulatory pressure, market competition and impacts from/to other government agencies (e.g. in the case of the CPS).

The degree of influence from these external factors varied among SCB, Transco and the CPS, which operate in different sectors. For example, political concerns are of particular importance to the CPS. Since it is one of the government agencies, the CPS is very cautious about accountability and the potential political consequences of its decisions. The CPS's ABB information highlights the significant influence that other government agencies' service quality can have on the CPS's own performance. This identification helps to promote some proactive management actions. One example is the process mapping exercises that the CPS undertook jointly with the police and the courts in an attempt to rationalise processes in the criminal justice system.

In Transco's case, although its ABC implementation was a direct result of the regulatory pressure for a clear justification of its cost structure and costing information, the recognition of the importance of the ABB information is noticeably linked to the introduction of market competition. When Transco was in a monopoly position, cost control was the prime concern of all business units at Transco because of the regulator's focus on the cost structure. The introduction of market competition to one of two key business units (Operations) changed the monopoly nature of the 'contractor and service provider' relationship between these two units. Managers at Operations started to realise the importance of ABB product cost budget information when competing with other service providers in bidding for future contracts. In this respect, the introduction of market competition to Transco has had a positive influence on the use of ABB product costing information.

However, market competition represents a negative influence on SCB's ABB implementation. The volatile and fiercely competitive beer market in the UK and abroad means that SCB needs to make swift responses to the market and monitor performance rigorously. SCB's ABB process (and indeed the budgeting process), which is an annual exercise, can no longer meet these needs.

14:6 Recommendations

- *Two dedicated computer systems to handle ABC and ABB processes separately.* The use of two dedicated systems tends to be more effective and responsive in fulfilling costing and budgeting purposes. As stated in **para.14:2.3.3**, ABC and ABB systems deal with two different types of data processes, i.e. data aggregation in an ABC system and data dissemination in an ABB system. The separation of the two different processes can ensure the relatively smooth operation of data processing in both systems without any interruption. In addition, in order to provide useful information for management planning and decision-making purposes, some analytic and data manipulation exercises, such as 'what-if' analyses, are required in an ABB process. Once separated, these exercises can be conducted in the ABB system effectively without interrupting any data processing operations within an ABC process. Thus this separation increases the efficiency of both systems.

- *Level of detail in activity/process analysis.* It is inevitable that ABB uses ABC information. However, one may ask: 'Does ABB require the same level of detail as ABC?'. SCB had a very detailed ABC analysis which included more than 200 activities and cost drivers. This level of detail in ABC was used in order to achieve accurate product costs. To achieve this level of accuracy, the members of staff, however, were confronted with the time-consuming and laborious task of calculating variable costs using spreadsheet software (which is a comparatively inefficient software in comparison to many purpose-built software packages) and converting/feeding this information to the ABB system. In this respect, a trade-off between efficiency or cost-effectiveness and accuracy together with some kind of compromise is required in order to achieve an optimum benefit.

- *Evaluation of ABB software package.* The following should be considered when evaluating ABB software packages:

- compatibility of an ABB system with existing computer software systems in an organisation;

- the objectives and anticipated outcomes via consideration of the technical specification of an ABB system;

- the investment in both ABB software package and conversion of existing hardware and software packages (if any); and allocation of adequate resources (financial and human) for the implementation, training and maintenance of the proposed ABB project.

- *Users' awareness and behavioural issues.* Sufficient training must be provided to ensure that all users (system managers, team/operation managers and accountants) are familiar with the operation and at ease with the ABB system. In all three case studies, some managers were not computer literate or familiar with management knowledge; this may have contributed to the users' unwillingness to use the system. In addition, constant technical support must also be provided to ensure continuity of the ABB system. A reasonable period of 'parallel run' of new and existing systems is necessary so that all users have sufficient exposure to the new system and gain confidence through its results being validated against the results from the old system. This 'parallel-run' period should be reasonable (usually about six months), otherwise users tend to return to the old system because of their confidence in and familiarity with the old system.

- *Timing of ABB implementation versus changes to organisational structure.* Nowadays, changes to organisational structure are inevitable and become more frequent. Thus the timing of an ABB implementation is crucial to the success of any new system. At SCB, for example, changes to its organisational structure and culture arose due to the acquisition process in 1995, which coincided with the development process of the ABB system. These changes created an interruption and caused instability to the ABB project and severely affected its model-building process. At the CPS, on the other hand, ABB was gradually introduced one year after its reorganisation. This decision was made deliberately to ensure a smoother transition period for both the reorganisation and the ABB implementation.

Notes

[1] The retail business focused mainly on beer retailing to pubs and the housing and tenancy operation of pubs, bars and restaurants.

[2] Before its implementation of ABC, the transfer price was based on the traditional costing method. After ABC was implemented in 1997, the product costs derived from ABC calculations were used as standard costs for transfer price for a consecutive three-year period (i.e. 1997–2000) despite SCB ceasing any further development and use of the ABC and ABB systems. From 2001 onwards, SCB has used traditional accounting systems to inform its costing, transfer pricing and other financial information.

[3] According to SCB, it was common practice for a software company to develop software packages for manufacturing companies that only contained fixed costs. The reason was that the manufacturing industry had various types of variable costs and a unified software package for variable costs was thus not considered as economically viable.

[4] For example, volume increase/decrease of one unit may lead to a 100% increase in an activity which results in a 50% increase in a resource leading to a 150% increase in a cost item.

[5] The computer software was only designed to deal with fixed-cost data, but not costs with a variable and stepped nature. The data from spreadsheet models for variable costs has to be transferred to 'Cost Control' via an electronic data link (i.e. the DDE link) (as shown in **Fig.14:6**).

[6] For example, the 'book value' of a given piece of equipment in the nominal ledger depreciates gradually. Hence, over a period of time, that piece of equipment will eventually have a zero 'book value' in the nominal ledger. Since the 'book value' of a piece of equipment is taken into consideration for product costing in ABC and ABB, the products which use a piece of zero 'book value' equipment in the production process will naturally have a disproportionately low cost as compared to those that use a piece of newer equipment with a relatively high 'book value'. The account codes in the nominal ledger, which were created to fulfil the traditional accounting purpose, are not as detailed as required by ABC and ABB. To perform an ABB process, data from nominal ledger accounts need to be disseminated and converted to an ABC form and then divided into variable and fixed-cost data before inputting into the 'Cost Control' system. This process is rather labour intensive and time consuming.

[7] Due to the time constraint involved in rolling out the ABB system to six brewing plants, the implementation team was not able to consult all managers at individual plants despite its full awareness of the importance of the line managers' involvement.

[8] Lattice Group is the holding company for the group of businesses recently demerged from BG Group plc. Lattice Group comprises Transco and other business units, including telecommunications, property management, a leasing group and energy services, and Advantica.

[9] Transco's organisational structure has constantly adjusted to suit its business needs. This structure represents its structure when this case study took place in 2000.

[10] Transco originally had 32 districts which were organised by either geographical or process-aligned functional units. The 32 districts were later mergered into 12 process-aligned LDZs.

[11] These units include Asset – NTS, Asset and Operations, but exclude those business units at Headquarters (i.e. Support Services, Regulation and Corporate Affairs, and Strategic and Business Development). Costs incurred at these units were recharged to Asset and Operations and allocated to Transco's five principal services on a pro-rata basis.

[12] Products are the types of services that Transco provides, because the nature of Transco's business is to provide gas transportation services.

[13] Transco uses a number of drivers to template its resources costs to activities and then to products. For example, managers are required to fill in timesheets to indicate the proportion of time they spend on a range of activities and products.

[14] D is the closing date for the monthly account.

[15] Based on ABC analysis, bandwidth analysis is to set a 'bandwidth unit cost' as a standard unit cost for each product, and to compare year-to-date unit costs with the 'bandwidth unit cost'. The 'bandwidth unit cost' is a unit cost being an applied certain percentage of a targeted unit cost. It aims to even the variations attributed to factors outside of the LDZs' control (e.g. location variation between South and North LDZs).

[16] During this case study, Transco only gave a limited number of contracts to external contractors if Operations did not have the spare capacity to take them.

[17] Under the organisational hierarchy, one LDZ mainly consists of one LDZ manager who is responsible for the whole of the LDZ's operation and performance, a few business network managers who are responsible for business activities across a few functional departments and directly report to the LDZ manager, departmental managers who are in charge of various functional departments within the LDZ, and team supervisors who lead a team of 10–20 people individually to carry out the fieldwork.

[18] Caseload refers to the number of cases that the CPS deals with. Workload refers to the complexity of work that one case involves. For example, with shop-lifting and murder, the caseload is one for each of the two cases; however, the workload involved for prosecuting the former case is obviously more straightforward and simpler than it is for the latter case.

[19] The CPS's performance is also affected by other criteria, such as the difficulties of cases and court adjournment. Thus caseload is only a part of the measure of the overall performance.

[20] For reasons of confidentiality, the figures used do not reflect the actual CPS figures.

[21] The various considerations and criteria were the different scenarios being worked through during the budgeting exercises, such as the amount of budget to the CPS being reduced by the Treasury and allocation methods being used.

[22] This stress audit was conducted by a consultant firm called Organisational Stress Audit (OSA), which specialises in examining organisational stress in public and private sectors.

[23] The addition was derived by the difference between the budget derived by the 4.5% 'across-the-board' cut and the one based on the ABC (performance) ratio.

References

Brimson, J.A. and Antos, J. (1994) Activity-based management: For service industries, government entities, and nonprofit organisations. John Wiley & Sons.

Brimson, J.A. and Fraser, R. (1991) 'The key feature of ABB', Management Accounting, January: 42.

Foster, G. and Swenson, D.W. (1997) 'Measuring the success of activity-based cost management and its determinants', Journal of Management Accounting Research, 9: 109–142.

Innes, J. and Mitchell, F. (1995) 'A survey of activity-based costing in the UK's largest companies', Management Accounting Research, 6, June: 137–153.

Kaplan, R. and Cooper, R. (1998) Cost and effect. Boston, MA: HBS Press Book.

Liu, L.Y.J., Martin, J. and Robinson, J. (2002) 'Double measures', Financial Management, October: 22–24.

Pohlen, T.L. and Londe, B.J. (1999) '1998 survey of activity-based costing applications within business logistics', Logistics Management and Distribution Report – Logistics Best Practices (online journal available at www.manufacturing.net/lm/), Issue 2, 1 February.

Robinson, J.J. and Liu, L.Y.J. (1998) 'Is it time to consider activity-based budgeting?', paper presented at the 1998 British Accounting Association Northern Accounting Group Conference, Sunderland, UK, 9 September.

15. Change in Management Accounting

15:1 Introduction

Management accounting at the cutting edge has evolved more over the past decade than in the 50 years previous to that. For many years the profession was inward looking and to a degree justified the outsider's view that management accountancy is some sort of arcane black art.

This view of the profession as a black art understandable only to initiates has been fostered to an extent it must be said by the narrow interests of the accounting institutes and their members. For many years accountants, like the guilds of old, have protected their privileged position and their salaries by keeping the organisation and their 'customers' at a distance and in general ignorance. At the same time they have spent considerable time and effort on inward contemplation and detailed discussions about the technical intricacies of costing systems and suchlike.

The combination of the IT explosion and the increasing business literacy of the organisation has over the last decade eroded the walls of these ivory towers and has paradoxically liberated management accountants and provided the enablers through which they can realise their full potential in terms of added value to an organisation.

The aim of this chapter is to pull together the threads of these diverse developments and build a coherent picture of the future of management accountancy.

15:2 The Emergence of the 'Renaissance Accountant'

Remember the adage that: An expert is someone who knows more and more about less and less? For some time this jaundiced view could easily have applied to the accounting profession with some resonance. Over the last ten years or so accountants, and management accountants in particular, have been applying their skills to many areas beyond the traditional budget and balance-sheet analysis.

The emergence on the corporate scene of such processes as total quality, environmental management, lifetime learning and continuous improvement (*see* **Chs 18 and 34**) has provided an opportunity for the management accountants of many firms to apply their analytical skills to many new arenas. At the same time the revolution in information technology has placed in the accountants' hands the tools that they have needed to enable those skills to be applied in a manner much more responsive to the needs of the business than has hitherto been possible.

These developments have resulted in a new breed of management accountant; the old works accountant has now evolved into a much more sophisticated species. This new breed of accountant, freed by technology from the time-consuming analysis of historical data, has been able to widen his horizon to include a far wider range of issues than his forebears. This in turn has produced the 'renaissance accountant'. A formidable and important player on the corporate field, he is as familiar with the tenets of supply chain management and continuous improvement as he is with activity-based management and standard costing (*see* **Chs 28 and 16**). More importantly his focus and role have been, and are being, adjusted. It may not be long before the term 'management accountant' is as anachronistic as 'works accountant'. This does not, however, represent the demise of management accounting but rather the absorption of its techniques and of the management accountant into the mainstream of the business.

What this means for those still in a traditional role is, of course, that they will also in time need to adapt. The following chapter of this Handbook aims to provide an overview of the current developments and to project these forward so that the reader can not only catch up with what has been happening, often unnoticed, but can anticipate the challenges of the future.

15:3 Where Are We Going?

Table 15:1 provides some comparisons between what is still the norm in many companies and what is likely to be the situation in 2010.

15:3.1 The Management Accountant's Role

Table 15:1 **The management accountant's role**

NOW	2010
Functional focus	*Holistic focus*
What?	*Why? and how?*
Inward looking	*Outward looking*
Backward looking	*Forward looking*
Alchemists/scientists	*Analysts and teachers*
Accountants	*Controllers/information managers*
Country based	*Global*
Slaves to technology	*Masters of technology*
Separate overhead department	*Integrated specialists*

15:3.2 A New Role For Accountants

The days of 'beancounters' are over but the need for measurement is not.

The role of the accountant is not just to count the fruit on the tree but to create the conditions for the management and workforce to produce a fertile soil, care for the long-term health of the tree, pick the fruit and get it to market. This will require measuring the fertility of the soil and the condition of the processes of transforming the nutrients into fruit and structural wood.

15:3.3 The Corporate Tree

Figure 15:1 **The corporate tree**

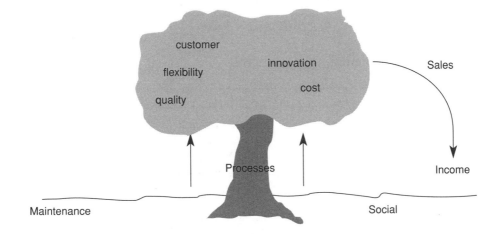

What this means is that the modern management accountant, while still being responsible for the pounds and pence of the bottom line in the profit and loss account (or income statement), finds an increasing amount of his time devoted to performance analysis within the business. This is a very healthy development that rides on the back of the technology which provides fast, high-quality analytical tools.

15:3.4 Non-financial analysis
(*See* **Ch.49.**)

The KPIs (key performance indicators) used in much of the analysis referred to above increasingly take a non-financial form. There are several reasons for this:

   (a) The increasing sophistication of IT has allowed much more direct measurement at every stage of a process in a business. Thus the accountant has access to concrete information which in the past he could only obtain by derivation.

   (b) There is no real need to convert measurements into currency equivalents unless you wish to calculate bottom-line impact. This can be done on a periodic (annual) rather than continuous basis. Managing on the basis of the initial measurement therefore reduces workload.

(c) *Staff often will relate more easily to more tangible figures for which they have some personal reference point than they do to an abstract value based upon someone else's conceptualisation or technical analysis. For example, a storeman can easily comprehend the idea that 'we lose x tons of stock per year through spillages' whereas 'wastages account for 5% of product cost' means far less. The storeman feels a direct responsibility for spillage, but that product cost is not his responsibility.*

(d) *Managing on the basis of primary information eliminates the confusion and obfuscation possible with derived figures. This is especially so when comparing across different locations, business units or countries. Absolute measures cannot be fudged, and allow direct comparisons.*

This increase in the use of non-financial information (e.g. in the OFR) brings with it both opportunity and danger for the management accounting function. The opportunity is that accountants may paint on a much broader canvas: the danger is that other parts of the business also have a base of numeracy analysis and even control mechanisms (audit etc.), for example the quality control department. This means that if accountants resist the new trends someone else will step into the breach and the accounting function will lose some of its pre-eminence and influence on the business.

There is also a danger for the organisation here in that unless the synergies between such departments are realised and capitalised upon an unproductive and damaging power struggle may develop.

The management accounting function is in an ideal position to offer its services in respect of both total quality management, continuous improvement and the impartial monitoring of KPIs. In this role the continental European title of controlling is perhaps more appropriate than that of management accounting.

15:4 Hot Topics

Table 15:2 illustrates some of the potential changes that will occur in the issues facing the management accountants of the future.

Table 15:2 **Hot topics**

NOW	2010
Activity-based management	Management cockpit
Environmental accounting	Browsing the data warehouse
Enterprise solutions	Efficient data mining
Balanced scorecard	Organic periodicity
Shared service centres	Integrating data channels
	3D business models
	Working without budgets

For those unfamiliar with the terms used in the Table these are briefly defined below. Some relatively new concepts are discussed more fully in subsequent subsections of this chapter.

15:4.1 Hot Topics Now

15:4.1.1 Activity-based Management (ABM)
(*See* Ch.28.)

The technique, developed from activity-based costing, whereby a business is managed upon the basis of key activities within each of the main business process areas. Metrics are established for each of these key activities and these are used both to judge performance and steer the business. Very often the metrics are non-financial.

15:4.1.2 Environmental Accounting
(*See* Ch.34.)

A concept originating from that of sustainable development. Environmental accounting seeks to include within the decision-making processes of a business and its measures of performance evaluation the effects of the business's activities on the environment. Life-cycle costing is one example of these type of analyses. As with ABM, metrics are usually a combination of financial and non-financial. In those companies with a real commitment to the environment annual environmental reports are now published.

15:4.1.3 Enterprise Solutions

Enterprise solutions is the name given to large, complex and often modular software systems such as those supplied by SAP, Peoplesoft, etc., which encompass the whole of the business process rather than the component parts. For example, 'supply-chain management' rather than stock management, the second being a small subset of the first and supply-chain management taking in everything from supplier selection through purchasing, payment internal logistics and so on right down to delivery and invoicing of the customer. An enterprise solution can therefore be seen to cut across traditional functional boundaries and is part way towards a holistic management system.

15:4.1.4 Balanced Scorecard
(*See* Ch.49, para.49:2.3.)

A hot topic a few years ago, balanced scorecards can now be regarded as almost mainstream accounting. The principle is that in order to manage the business properly a representative range of metrics is required that reflects not only financial performance but other key non-financial performance parameters as well. The business will select those parameters which are crucial to its success, devise appropriate metrics and use these rather than just the profit and loss account and balance sheet in the daily management of the business.

15:4.1.5 Shared Service Centre

Shared service centres are a direct result of the technology now available to business. The concept is simple, to minimise costs and maximise economies of scale by centralising administrative support both for the organisation's internal functions and often for customers. This centralisation will usually be in a country of relatively low labour cost but with a technological infrastructure capable of providing appropriate links to the rest of the organisation and the customer base. For companies operating in Europe this is often the UK or Eire. The technique is still most common in service industries such as banking, airlines and insurance, but is spreading to multinational manufacturing as well.

15:4.2 Hot Topics 2010

Unlike the listing of items above, these subjects are less likely to have been encountered yet by the majority of management accountants. Therefore fuller definitions are given. Obviously as these issues take off these definitions or the terminology may change.

15:4.2.1 Management Cockpit
(*See* Ch.52.)

This term refers to an on-screen real-time interactive 'desktop' display customised to the needs of a senior executive or manager. Such a display allows interrogation of the company's IT systems and provides hot-key access to critical information groups. The management cockpit may also be linked to non-internal information systems such as on-line services and internet websites. It will usually also contain quick access to email and fax facilities. The aim being that executives have at their fingertips all the necessary information to guide the business together with the appropriate tools to control it. The term derives from the similarity of this situation to an aircraft pilot.

This concept has since the earlier editions of this handbook become a reality within a number of major internationals and is marketed commercially by AtosOrigin.

The aim of the management cockpit is to increase the effectiveness of the process whereby strategy is converted into action. Strategy is important but difficult to implement. Studies show that:

- 68% of top managers believe 'a better translation of strategy into action would improve operating income by 20%'; and

- 32% of top managers believe 'a better implementation of our plans would improve performance by 50%'.

Strategy is important but difficult to implement – and not all employees understand the strategy. The same studies indicated that:

- 71% of executive management understand the company vision/mission;

- 40% of middle management understand it;

- 3% of the line employees understand it.

And that many in the organisation do not even agree with it.

- 50% of middle management cannot identify with the new strategy;

- 20% of middle management thinks the new strategy is completely strange to market.

Figure 15:2 **The management cockpit**

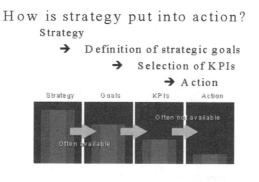

How is strategy put into action?

Strategy
→ Definition of strategic goals
→ Selection of KPIs
→ Action

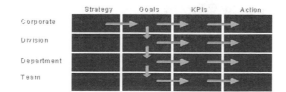

How to align action?

The Management Cockpit

A tool to turn your strategy into action

Figure 15:2 shows the management cockpit developed by the NET research company. The company was founded 10 years ago by human intelligence scientists, bankers and computer scientists and the management cockpit as seen was designed by Professor Patrick M. Georges, MD Director of the Human Intelligence Labs at HEC-Paris, Professor in Management and a Senior Brain Surgeon. Professor Georges' work focuses on human intelligence and using ergonomics to boost the productivity of managers.

The management cockpit is produced by NET and is configured and installed by AtosOrigin a global IT and business consultancy.

15:4.2.1.1 The Elements of the Management Cockpit

1. A board room which can be configured as desired by the company.
For example:

- By area of responsibility:

  – the Corporate Tower;

  – the Business Management Cockpit;

  – the Plant Management Cockpit.

- By function:

  – the Management Cockpit for CFO;

  – the Management Cockpit for CIO.

Figure 15:3 **The board room**

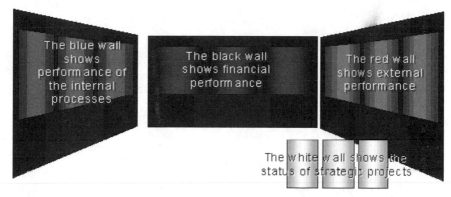

- By industry:

    – the Bank Management Cockpit;

    – the Pharmaceutical Management Cockpit.

2. The board room has four walls.
Each wall contains six logical views which represent the management's most important issues, such as:

- Are we selling harder?

- Are our critical clients moving away from us?

- Are our key projects in good shape?

- What are our competitors doing?

- Are we innovative?

- Are we in danger?

Each logical view contains five visuals, displaying:

- indicators;

- objectives;

- limits;

- benchmarks;

- trends.

For example:

- sales growth rate compared to bid-win rate;

- cost to supervise;

- revenues from new products compared with competitors;

- hot news on competitors;

- absenteeism versus staff turnover.

3. Flight deck.
This contains dedicated information to explain the KPIs. The aim of the management cockpit is to enable the transformation of strategy into action by providing:

- clear communication on:

  - strategy;

  - goals;

  - KPIs;

  - action;

- focusing on key figures;

- presenting effective management information;

- facilitating rapid and effective decision making.

15:4.2.2 Data Warehouse

(This is a term used to describe a large data repository storing information from a wide range of sources for retrieval as required. The analogy is to a physical warehouse but with information 'bins'. In most cases the information is not stored in a directly usable form but in common format that allows a data extraction tool to access the full range of information for downloading into appropriate desktop applications.

The alternative arrangement favoured by some ERP suppliers such as SAP is to incorporate the familiar desktop applications into their standard offering. Typical of this genre is SAP's Business Information Warehouse which incorporates MS Excel into its front end toolset and also provides information extractors for systems other than its own proprietary products. This then provides the user with a tool that can be used across many applications and can pull information into a familiar environment for the user.

15:4.2.3 Data Mining

This refers to the technique whereby the organisation's data banks are trawled for previously hidden or unreported data and relationships. It is currently in its infancy but if current developments continue will come of age in a relatively short time. Currently the technique is usually confined to marketing research by large organisations.

15:4.2.4 Organic Periodicity

Organic periodicity is a concept whereby periods selected for analysis in a business are derived from events or step changes in the business situation rather than the traditional phases of the moon (months). Division of business activity by month is of little direct relevance to the internal workings or performance of the business but is historically of convenience to the accountant. This situation has been changed by IT developments which now allow for single point of entry for data together with the separation of fiscal and management accounting data.

For example, it may be more relevant to look at profitability over time divided not by monthly segments but on the basis of the length of an advertising campaign or price-change steps.

15:4.2.5 Integrated Data Channels

The concept of integrated data channels ties in very closely with the concept of the management cockpit. The basic concept is that the organisation's staff have single-point access to information from all appropriate company systems via an interactive desktop customised to the particular user's requirements. The integrated data channels will allow the extraction and manipulation of data from a variety of subsystems and the communication of the results all from the same platform. The integrated channels will be multi-media based and include both intranet and internet facilities as appropriate.

The more go-ahead and technically aware organisations are now integrating their data channels in a big way creating a seamless 'product' for their employees to use which combines the internal databases of an intranet (procedure manuals, telephone directories, employee CVs, company standard methodologies, news bulletins, etc.) with internet access, webmail and even access to purchased services such as those provided by the *FT*, the *Economist*, Gartner, etc.

15:4.2.6 3D Business Models

Currently most business models are two dimensional and represent process flows along a chosen axis. An organisation and business are, however, three dimensional much like the molecular structure of a chemical compound.

Developments in IT are now creating a situation where it will be possible to create three-dimensional images and models of the business with relative ease. This will in turn allow for more complex relationships to be evaluated and modelled.

15:4.2.7 Working Without Budgets

Increasingly the traditional budget methodologies have been coming under attack as diverting the attention of managers away from their real purpose, adding value to the business. Frequently this results from bad budgeting practice and the tendency for budgets to become set in stone once agreed and for senior management to use them as a crude (and it must be said, ineffective) performance indicator. The development of continuous improvement methodologies, increasing use of non-financial KPIs and rolling forecasts enabled by modern computer technology may sound the death knell of the budget. Already major institutions like the Handelsbank in Sweden have been operating for many years without the use of budgets. Significantly such organisations regularly outperform their more traditionally run rivals.

15:4.2.7.1 Rationale

Budgets are barriers – Budgeting is a barrier to success in the information age. Abandoning it is entirely feasible, the alternatives are better and it is not particularly difficult to achieve.

Principles and practices – There are a number of these, just dismantling the budgeting system is not enough. It will not be effective unless the changes in management principles and practices are seen as an integrated approach with as much emphasis on the 'soft' cultural issues (such as empowerment) as on the hard process issues (such as management reporting).

New steering mechanisms – Alternative steering mechanisms can be used to manage the business more effectively. For example, management information and control is improved with better anticipatory techniques (such as rolling forecasting) leading to more effective control and better decisions.

Organisational levels – The management model can vary according to the needs and complexity of a business and between different levels within an organisation.

Building the new model – The organisation, culture and values are all important. They take time to develop and should be appropriate to the competitive pressures on the business (e.g. decentralisation, process teams and knowledge management systems should be considered).

Implementation – Careful thought needs to be given to implementation.

15:4.2.7.2 Principles and Practices

Targets and target setting – Set targets to maximise long-term value and beat the competition not the budget.

Strategy – Devolve strategy to the front line and make it a continuous and open process, not a top–down annual event.

Growth and improvement – Challenge people to think radically not incrementally.

Resource management – Manage resources on the basis of value creation over the lifetime of an investment, not on the basis of a short-term (budget) allocation.

Co-ordination – Achieve co-ordination by managing cause and effect relationships across business units and responsibility centres (such as processes), not by using departmental budgets.

Cost management – Challenge all costs on the basis of whether they add value, not whether they should be increased or decreased in relation to last year.

Forecasting – Use rolling forecasts for managing strategy and decision making, not only for 'keeping on track'.

Measurement and control – Use a few key leading and lagging indicators to monitor performance, not a mass of detailed reports.

Rewards – Base rewards on company and unit-level competitive performance, not personal financial targets.

Delegation – Give managers the responsibility and freedom to act, do not micro-manage them.

15:5 Darwinism and Management Accounting

It is generally accepted that an organisation can be compared to a complex living organism. By natural extension we can draw a parallel between the survival requirements of commercial organisations and living organisms, this principle also applies to the components of an organisation. Thus the principles of Darwinism are as relevant to the survival of accountants as they are to any living organism.

As was noted in **paragraph 15:1**, the management accounting function must evolve to survive. It must retain those characteristics that have proved their usefulness and discard those which no longer add value.

15:5.1 Darwinism – The Lessons

Dinosaurs that failed to adapt became extinct (the Tyrannosaurs). Those that made only token changes survive in small isolated pockets and remain endangered (the Kommodo dragons). Those that adapted fully to the new conditions survive and multiply (the birds). Note that the most successful adapters do not have the most obvious lineage, they have adapted to the extent that they are regarded as a separate species. Note also that the most successful adapters have, by and large, reduced the size of their organism and at the same time increased their specialism and efficiency.

Key survival factors are:

- a proactive approach;

- willingness to change where it is appropriate;

- speed of adaptation;

- increased efficiency and hence added value;

- reduction in size – doing more with less bulk but more quality;

- continuous learning – both organisations and individuals;

- valuing the team but listening to the individual;

- managing perceptions;

- honesty regarding both the need for, and effects of, change.

Remember it is not the invention or technique that is important, it is how it is applied. It is this fact that makes the management in management accounting so important. It is vital that those implementing new ideas and techniques within their organisations or who undertake to transform the function pay sufficient heed to the human element. The management of staff both within and outside the function is what will ultimately determine the true success of a particular venture.

15:6 How to Adapt

Assuming that you agree with the above analysis the next steps are to consider what in your case requires changing and then how to go about changing it. This first requires the equivalent of a SWOT (Strengths, Weaknesses, Opportunities and Threats) analysis of your department/function.

15:6.1 Questions to Be Answered

- How do you perceive management accounting?

- How does your organisation perceive it?

- How close are these perceptions to reality?

- What is the role of management accountancy?

- How do you go about raising expectations?

15:6.2 Perceptions

To perceive is to see, appreciate, understand, comprehend, be aware of. How much does perception match reality? – Remember that for the individual perception is reality. 'If the doors of perception were cleansed everything would appear as it is – infinite' (William Blake, 1757–1827).

15:7 Managing Change in Management Accounting

This is a huge topic which cannot be covered in full depth in this Handbook, however the following sections will provide in as succinct a format as possible the basic guidelines that should be followed to introduce change successfully into the organisation.

15:7.1 Key Steps

- Recognise the need for change.
- Anticipate the likely changes in your own environment.
- Gear up the organisation:
  - carry out an information needs analysis;
  - map all data use in the organisation;
  - emplacement and training of key personnel;
  - instigate controlled business-driven IT investment.
- Ask yourself the following questions:
  - Given the current state-of-the-art technologies and methodologies and the likely pace of development over the next 12 years, what organisation profile best suits your business?
  - What functions do you envisage in this organisation?
  - Will functions that are today independent have merged or even disappeared?

15:7.2 Business Timetables

- Period ends *will* shrink to one day. In many organisations this is already fact.

- This will affect working patterns and open up the planning of accounting to more effective use. (For example, ask yourself, why do we post 'month-end journals' if the system is responsive enough they can be posted immediately following the previous close, come to that most of them can be virtually automated?)

- Working practices will be business driven and not system driven. (How many times have you heard, or given, the excuse 'we'd love to but the system …'?)

15:7.3 Will Period Ends Still Exist?

- Probably yes, the phases of the moon are convenient to some and understood by all, *but* internal data may well be analysed separately by event-driven periods of more direct relevance to the business.

- Periodicity may vary dependent upon data type and use.

- Period end will cease to be the burden that it now is, becoming a virtually fully automated exercise.

15:7.4 Which Data and How Much?

- More than you can imagine, not only the current types but increasingly integrated shop-floor data.

- Data on data (metadata).

- Increasingly non-financial data.

- Increasingly externally sourced data.

15:7.5 Will the Management Accounting Function Still Exist?

No – not in its current form in leading-edge companies.
Yes – in laggard companies.

The role will evolve, maintaining its underlying principles but becoming almost unrecognisable in their execution. A good analogy being the evolution of the longbowman of old into the modern-day sniper, greater technology, fewer staff, increased range, higher rate of fire but still the same aim.

15:7.6 How Will the Role Change?

- Fewer management accountants.

- More information specialists.

- Increased expertise.

- It will continue to move from number production to number interpretation.

- Skills will be applied over a wider area.

Parallels: 'whatever the technical change it is still the humble infantryman that has to winkle the other bastard out of his foxhole and make him sign the peace treaty' (US General, 1945).

The means may alter, the rationale will not.

ABCM, balanced scorecards, etc., are important developments but are mere pointers to the future. The development of the jet engine, while a great scientific achievement, would have been but a curiosity without the vision that foresaw the possibilities that it created.

We should take time therefore to look beyond the mechanics of accounting. We should realise that at certain points in time a step change is required, when we have reached the point at which merely adjusting the controls no longer yields sufficient improvement.

15:7.7 What's In a Name?

What are the connotations of accounting in the popular mind?

- Know the cost of everything and the value of nothing?
- Old fashioned?
- Beancounters?
- Overhead?

What are the connotations of the words 'controlling' or 'information management'?

- Central positioning?
- Wide ranging?
- In control?
- Up to date?
- Essential?
- Added value?

15:7.8 Resistance Factors

- Conceptual understanding.
- Technophobia or ignorance.
- Political.

The first two of these are matters of education, the third needs greater examination.

15:7.8.1 Political Resistance to Change

There can be several causes of this and the key to overcoming it is, as with all things, to understand it. Common causes are:

(a) *synergy – synergies between departments threaten the position of those departmental managers concerned;*

(b) *new technologies and techniques versus old organisation and reward structures;*

(c) *poor management is often exposed by holistic techniques;*

(d) *inappropriate investment and post-audit evaluation in respect of IT investment;*

(e) *short-term post holding – change initiatives often take some three to five years to fully bear fruit, many career managers change their posts every two to three years, thus they are faced with all the heartache, while the benefits go to the successor.*

Then there is a range of often unpalatable reasons for resistance which many organisations sidestep rather than address. *It is critical that these are recognised where they exist and are dealt with.*

These are:

(a) *Managers' 'pet systems' – one can often find that the systems under critical review were implemented by the senior managers you are seeking to convince when they were in more junior roles. They can therefore be protective particularly if the critique is blunt. Do your homework.*

(b) *Management distrust of staff – in some companies this is endemic, if present it will eventually kill the organisation. Luckily it is often present only in part.*

(c) *Insecure managers hate change.*

(d) *'Baronies' – all barons of whatever type (feudal, cattle or otherwise) dislike change. Anything that threatens the status quo threatens their empire. This is a major cause of failure in many organisations.*

15:8 Communicating Change

Here are some key points to remember:

(a) *frontline supervisors, not senior managers, are the opinion leaders;*

(b) *if you break the rule that values are best communicated through action not words, employees will punish you;*

(c) *to many, company publications have two flaws – they are untrustworthy and incomprehensible;*

(d) *rumours are usually inaccurate but the transmission method is perfect.*

15:8.1 Staff Involvement

When instigating change:

(a) *involve the right staff – those who actually do the work, including secretaries and clerks. Remember the manager will often tell you what should in his opinion be happening or what the procedure says. If you have the trust of the staff they will tell you what actually happens, and more importantly, why;*

(b) *be honest and open with staff;*

(c) *listen to them! Staff always know the inefficiencies of manager-designed systems.*

Table 15:3 **Asking for opinions**

What to do	Why
One manager to eight to ten supervisors.	*Do not give the impression you are afraid and need help.*
One piece of paper with two parts: *(i) what you are willing to change;* *(ii) what you are not willing to change.*	*Do not play games, if you are going to change something, say so.*
Describe the 'not willing' and request recommendations for the 'willing'.	*You are not there to argue, defend, or evaluate, but to hear opinions and report back.*
Never give away the power to decide: this remains with management.	*You want opinions not permission. People get restless – get into it, get it done, get out.*

Table 15:4 **Giving the feedback**

What to do	Why
Same manager, same supervisors.	*Supervisors do not want to deal with an abstraction, they want to deal with a person.*
One piece of paper with supervisors' recommendations. For each a reason why it was accepted or rejected. Answer questions, do not argue or excessively defend.	*You are there to communicate not to convince.*
Distribute the change booklet, describe the major changes.	*You are preparing the supervisors for face-to-face conversation with their subordinates.*

15:9 The Celtic Management Style

- Holistic.
- Environmentally friendly.
- Recognised cause and effect.
- Based upon knowledge specialists using relational databases.
- Information specialists held in high regard.

15:10 Teamwork and Individualism

Teamwork is essential to success but lemmings and sheep do not make for success. This is something of a dichotomy that must be resolved. A balance must be struck that realises the synergies of teamwork while not stifling individual thought and creativity. It is in this area that the management accountant should draw on the proven lessons and methodologies of total quality management that can provide a framework for continuous change (an outlet for individual expression) within a team structure.

Cultivate individual skills and thinking – remember that the lone voice may be right, the Trojans failed to heed Cassandra, and Troy was sacked.

15:11 Holistic Re-engineering
(*See* Ch.32.)

Very often, books directed at the profession are either single subject or, through the division of subjects into chapters, artificially separate subjects. This can often lead to a mindset which follows this pattern and compartmentalises what are, in reality, complementary tools and techniques.

One result of this is business re-engineering projects that are directed primarily at one of three areas: processes, activities or behaviour. In order for the re-engineering of any business activity to succeed it must address all three areas. In order to succeed it should also make use of an appropriately wide mix of techniques and tools. This is holistic re-engineering.

Figure 15:4 **Holistic re-engineering**

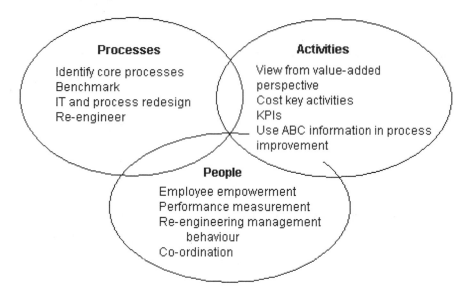

15:12 Change – A Historical Perspective

They must often change who would remain constant in happiness and wisdom.

(Confucius)

There is nothing more difficult to take in hand, more perilous to conduct or more uncertain in its success than to take the lead in the introduction of a new order of things.

The reason is that the innovator has for enemies all those who have done well under the old conditions and lukewarm defenders in those who may do well in the new.

(Niccolo Machiavelli, from *The Prince circa* 1514)

Change is not made without inconvenience, even from worse to better.

(R. Hooker, 1554–1600)

A State without the means of change is without the means of its own conservation.

(Edmund Burke, 1729–1797)

One of the greatest pains to human nature is the pain of a new idea.

(Walter Badgehot 1826–1877)

Part C

Costing

16. Standard Costing

16:1 Introduction

16:1.1 Origins of Standard Costing

Today's standard costing systems were developed in the early 1900s. It was the scientific management principles advocated by FW Taylor and other engineers who provided the impetus for the development of standard costing systems. Scientific management engineers developed information about standards in order to determine 'the one best way' to use labour and material resources. The standards provided information for planning the flow of work so that the waste of materials and labour was kept to a minimum. According to Solomons (1968) it was G Charter Harrison who, in 1911, designed and installed the first complete standard costing system known to exist. In 1918 Harrison published the first set of equations for the analysis of variances. Much of Harrison's work is contained in today's literature on standard costing.

Since its introduction in the early 1900s standard costing has flourished and is now one of the most widely used management accounting techniques. A survey of 300 UK manufacturing companies by Drury *et al.* (1993) reported that 76% of the responding companies operated a standard costing system. Similar findings were observed in a survey of US companies by Cornick *et al.* (1988). They reported that 86% of the responding companies were using standard costing systems. Despite its widespread use standard costing has recently come under attack for not providing the information that is needed for today's manufacturing and competitive environment and critics are now predicting its demise.

16:1.2 Purposes of Standard Costing

Standard costing is most suited to manufacturing organisations whose activities consist of a series of repetitive operations. It cannot be easily applied to activities of a non-repetitive nature since there is no basis for observing repetitive operations and

Colin Drury

consequently standards cannot be set. Standard costing systems are widely used because they provide cost information for many different purposes such as:

(a) *providing a prediction of future costs that can be used for decision-making purposes;*

(b) *providing a challenging target which individuals are motivated to achieve;*

(c) *assisting in setting budgets and evaluating managerial performance. Standard costs are particularly valuable for budgeting (see **Ch.9**) because a reliable and convenient source of data is provided for converting budgeted production into physical and monetary resource requirements. Budgetary preparation time is considerably reduced if standard costs are available because the standard costs of operations and products can be readily built up into total costs for any budgeted volume and product mix;*

(d) *acting as a control device by highlighting those activities which do not conform with plan and thus alerting managers to those situations that may be 'out of control' and in need of corrective action. With a standard costing system variances are analysed in great detail such as by element of cost, price and quantity. Useful feedback is therefore provided in pinpointing the areas where variances have arisen;*

(e) *simplifying the task of tracing costs to products for profit measurement and inventory valuation purposes. Most organisations prepare monthly internal profit statements and if actual costs are used a considerable amount of time is required in tracking costs so that monthly costs can be allocated between cost of sales and inventories. A data-processing system is required which can track monthly costs in a resource efficient manner. Standard costing systems meet this requirement by maintaining records at standard cost. Inventories and cost of goods sold are recorded at standard cost and a conversion to actual cost is made by writing off all variances arising during the period as a period cost.*

16:2 Variance Analysis

16:2.1 Variable Cost Variance Analysis

Variance analysis is used to determine where, and by how much, an operation's costs deviate from standard. The standard cost for a particular operation is calculated by multiplying standard unit prices (or rates) by the standard quantity allowed for the actual production. The standard cost is compared with the actual cost and the variances are analysed by element of cost, price and quantity. Quantity variances are calculated as follows:

(standard quantity for actual production – actual quantity) × standard price of the resource.

Typical variable cost quantity variances include material usage, labour efficiency and variable overhead efficiency.

Price variances are calculated as follows:

(standard price – actual price) x actual quantity of resources used or purchased.

Typical variable cost price variances include material price, wage rate and variable overhead expenditure (spending). Where different types of materials and grades of labour are used separate price and quantity variances are reported for each resource category.

For cost control variance analysis is most suited to the control of variable costs. For example, the reporting of adverse quantity variances should pinpoint the possible causes of inefficient usage of resources and lead to corrective action to eliminate the efficiency being repeated. Thus, reductions in future resource spending should follow from the reporting of variances that are due to inefficiencies. Alternatively, if the variance is due to a permanent change in input requirements the response should be to change the standard so that more accurate data can be provided for budgeting and decision-making purposes.

16:2.2 Fixed Overhead Variance Analysis

Financial accounting reporting regulations require that, for external reporting, companies should value stocks at full absorption manufacturing cost (*see SSAP9: Stocks and Long-Term Contracts; IAS2: Inventories*). The effect of this is that fixed overheads must be allocated to products and included in closing stock valuations. Predetermined fixed overhead rates must therefore be established for determining standard overhead costs for financial accounting. To compute the standard (predetermined) fixed overhead absorption rates cost centre overheads are divided by a cost centre activity measure (normally units of output, machine hours or direct labour hours) (*see also* **Ch.11**). The cost centre standard overhead cost for a period is computed by multiplying the output by the standard overhead rate. A total fixed overhead variance will arise whenever the actual cost differs from the standard cost of the actual production. The fixed overhead variance can be divided into two subvariances: the volume variance and the expenditure (spending) variance.

The volume variance reflects the fact that fixed overheads do not fluctuate with output in the short term. Whenever actual production differs from budgeted production, the fixed overhead charged to production will differ from the budgeted cost and a volume variance will arise. In addition, an expenditure (spending) variance will be reported if the actual fixed overhead expenditure incurred differs from the budgeted expenditure. In other words, the volume variance is the under or over recovery of fixed overheads arising from actual production differing from budgeted production and the expenditure variance represents the under or over recovery arising from actual expenditure differing from budgeted expenditure. The data in **Table 16:1** is used to illustrate the computation of the variances.

Table 16:1 **Computation of fixed overhead variances**

	Budget	*Actual*
Fixed overheads incurred	£1,000,000	£1,050,000
Output (units)	100,000	90,000
Standard fixed overhead rate per unit of output	£10	

Because the output is 10,000 units less than budget a volume variance of £100,000 (10,000 units × £10) is reported. Thus, £100,000 has not been recorded within the product costs assigned to cost of goods sold or inventories. To rectify this situation a volume variance is extracted and written off as a period expense against the profit and loss statement of the current period. Instead of using units of output many organisations use direct labour hours and machine hours as the allocation bases and recover overheads with output measured in standard direct labour or machine hours.

In **Table 16:1** fixed overheads of £900,000 have been assigned to products within the standard costs. However, actual overheads incurred were £1,050,000. Thus, £150,000 (i.e. the total fixed overhead variance) has not been recorded as an expense for the period within the standard product costs. Besides the volume variance of £100,000 an expenditure variance of £50,000 arises, being the difference between budgeted and actual expenditure. To convert the standard cost to the actual cost the expenditure variance is also written off as a period expense.

Table 16:1 indicates that for standard absorption costing fixed overhead variances must be extracted to convert standard costs to actual costs for meeting financial accounting and monthly internal profit reporting requirements. Evidence also suggests that in many organisations the volume variance is also used for short-term cost control. However, it is questionable whether the volume variance reported in monetary terms, provides useful information for management purposes. Information indicating that actual production is 10,000 units less than budgeted production is useful for management, but to attach a fixed overhead rate to this figure is of little value for control if the fixed costs are sunk costs consisting of facility-sustaining (i.e. infrastructure) costs that are unavoidable for virtually all decisions. Some writers suggest that the volume variance provides a measure of the cost of unused capacity. However, the reported volume variance of £100,000 does not reflect the cost of facilities that remain idle, since the fixed overhead cost will not change if production declines – at least in the short term.

The volume variance is probably only meaningful in monetary terms if an opportunity cost approach is used. For example, a cost of unused capacity has only meaningful significance in the short term if it results in lost output. In this situation the volume variance should be valued in terms of the lost contribution arising from the failure to produce the budgeted output. Where there is no lost output the opportunity cost of the volume variance is zero.

16:3 Criticisms of Standard Costing

16:3.1 A Summary of the Major Criticisms

Standard costing systems were developed to meet the needs of a traditional manufacturing environment which is drastically different from today's manufacturing and competitive environment. The usefulness of standard costing variance analysis in a modern manufacturing environment has been questioned and several writers have predicted its demise because of the following:

  (a) *the changing cost structure;*
  (b) *behaviour is encouraged that is inconsistent with a just-in-time philosophy;*
  (c) *inconsistency with a continuous improvement philosophy;*
  (d) *overemphasises the importance of direct labour;*
  (e) *delay in feedback reporting.*

16:3.2 Impact of the Changing Cost Structure

It is claimed that overhead costs have become the dominant factory costs, direct labour costs have diminished in importance and that most of a firm's costs have become fixed in the short term. Given that standard costing is a mechanism that is most suited to the control of direct and variable costs, but not fixed or indirect costs, its usefulness has been questioned. However, recent surveys in many different countries have reported remarkably similar results in terms of cost structures. They all report that direct costs and overheads averaged approximately 75% and 25% respectively of total manufacturing costs with average direct labour costs varying from 10%–15% of total manufacturing cost.

Clearly the claim by some commentators that overheads are the dominant factory costs is not supported by the survey evidence. Direct materials are the dominant costs in most manufacturing organisations and account for, on average, approximately 60% of total manufacturing costs. Direct labour costs are now of much less importance and tend to be fixed in the short term. Direct materials and variable overheads (e.g. energy costs for running the machines) are now the only short-term variable costs. Thus, standard costing variance analysis for control purposes (*see* **Ch.27**) would appear to be only appropriate for direct materials and variable overheads, the latter being a small proportion of total manufacturing costs. However, the reporting of direct labour variances at periodic intervals is probably justified since efficiencies/inefficiencies in resource consumption are highlighted and provide useful feedback information for redeploying labour or ensuring that in the longer term changes in resource consumption are translated into changes in spending on the supply of direct labour resources.

16:3.3 Inconsistency with a Just-in-time Philosophy

It is claimed that using material price variances to control direct material costs does not support a just-in-time (JIT) purchasing policy. If purchase price variances are used to evaluate the performance of the purchasing department, it is likely that the purchasing management will be motivated to focus entirely on obtaining the materials at the lowest possible prices even if this results in:

(a) *the use of many suppliers (all of them selected on the basis of price);*
(b) *larger quantity purchases, thus resulting in larger inventories;*
(c) *delivery of lower-quality goods;*
(d) *indifference to attaining on-time delivery.*

JIT companies will wish to focus on performance measures, which emphasise all the factors important to the purchasing function, such as quality and reliability of suppliers, and not just price. Nevertheless, material price variances still have an important role to play in JIT companies.

It is also claimed that using the volume variance to measure unutilised capacity motivates managers to expand output and thus increase inventories. This is inconsistent with a JIT philosophy of minimising inventories. Favourable volume variances are reported whenever actual production exceeds budgeted production and therefore profit-centre managers can manipulate monthly profits by expanding output and increasing profits. Attention has already been drawn to the fact that volume variances are inappropriate for short-term cost control and performance measurement purposes. If volume variances are being used for these purposes then the problem arises because of the faulty application, rather than the inadequacies, of standard costing.

Volume variances are required to meet financial accounting requirements. Even if standard costing is abandoned, the under or over recovery of overheads is necessary to meet conventional absorption costing profit measurement requirements. *SSAP9: Stocks and Long-Term Contracts*, for example, requires that the costs of stock 'include all related production overheads'. Furthermore, *IAS2: Inventories* states that 'the cost of inventories should comprise all costs of purchase, costs of conversion and other costs incurred in bringing the inventories to their present location and condition', and that costs of conversion include 'a systematic allocation of fixed and variable production overheads that are incurred in converting materials into finished goods'. It is therefore inappropriate to single out standard costing variance analysis as being responsible for the excess production. The solution is to replace absorption costing with a standard variable costing system for monthly internal reporting.

16:3.4 Motivates Behaviour That Is Inconsistent with a Continuous Improvement Philosophy

It is claimed that the concept of setting standards as targets is not consistent with a philosophy of consistent improvement. When standards are set, a climate is created whereby the standards represent targets to be achieved and maintained, rather than a philosophy of consistent improvement. To be consistent with this philosophy variances should be used to monitor the trend in performance and the focus should be on the rate of change in performance. Standards can also be regularly reviewed and tightened as improvements occur.

16:3.5 Overemphasis on Direct Labour

Some writers have criticised variance analysis on the grounds that it encourages too much attention to be focused on direct labour when direct labour has diminished in importance and is only a small proportion of total factory costs. Surveys, however, indicate that direct labour is the most widely used overhead allocation base. To reduce their allocated costs managers are motivated to reduce direct labour hours since this is the basis on which the overheads are allocated to cost centres. This process overstates the importance of direct labour and directs attention away from controlling escalating overhead costs. This overemphasis on direct labour arises, not from any inadequacies of standard costing, but from the faulty application of standard costing by focusing excessively on volume variances for short-term cost control and performance evaluation. Volume variances should be used primarily for meeting financial accounting requirements.

16:3.6 Delayed Feedback Reporting

A further criticism of variance reporting is that performance reports arrive too late to be of value in controlling production operations. Performance reports are normally prepared weekly or monthly but such a lengthy time lag is not helpful for daily control of operations. For operational control purposes labour and material quantity variances should be reported in physical terms in 'real time'. For example, Puxty and Lyall (1989) in their survey of standard costing practices reported that some companies were using 'online' computers to collect information at the point of manufacture so that variances could be reported and fed into the system instantaneously. Summary variance reports can still be prepared if required, at appropriate periodic intervals if management wishes to monitor deviations from standard and examine the trend in reported variances.

16:4 Variance Analysis in the Context of Activity-based Costing

Mak and Roush (1994) and Kaplan (1994) have examined the role of variance analysis within the context of activity-based costing (ABC) (*see* **Ch.22**). For unit-level activities they advocate that traditional variance analysis should remain unchanged. They define unit-level activities as those activities that are performed each time a unit of product or service is produced. These activities consume resources in proportion to the number of units produced. For example, if a firm produces 10% more units, it will consume 10% more labour cost, 10% more materials, 10% more machine hours and 10% more energy costs. Expenses in this category include direct labour, direct materials, energy costs and expenses that are consumed in proportion to machine processing time (such as machine maintenance). Therefore traditional variance analysis can be applied for direct labour, direct materials and those variable overheads that vary with output, machine hours and direct labour hours.

For non-unit-based activities, which will normally incorporate all the 'so-called' fixed costs, traditional overhead variance analysis needs to be modified to:

(a) *incorporate the different types of cost drivers that are identified with an ABC system;*

(b) *reflect the fact that the focus should be on only those overhead costs that are fixed in the short term but variable in the longer term.*

By creating a greater number of cost pools, and using cost drivers that better reflect the causes of resource consumption, ABC variance analysis provides more meaningful information than traditional overhead variance analysis. **Table 16:2**, adapted from Kaplan (1994), is used to illustrate how variance analysis can be applied to incorporate activity costs and activity cost drivers. The information relates to a set-up activity for a period.

Table 16:2 **Variance analysis to incorporate activity costs and activity cost drivers**

Budget	*Actual*
Activity level: 2,700 set-ups	Total fixed costs: £80,000
Practical capacity supplied: 3,000 set-ups	Total variable costs: £26,000
Total fixed costs: £90,000	
Total variable costs: £27,000	Number of set-ups: 2,500
Cost driver rates (variable): £10 per set-up	
(fixed): £30 per set-up	

It can be seen from **Table 16:2** that budgeted fixed costs of £90,000 provide a practical capacity to perform 3,000 set-ups during the period. Assuming that the number of set-ups has been identified as the appropriate cost driver, a cost of £30 per set-up (£90,000/3,000) will be charged to products. Since budgeted capacity usage is 2,700 set-ups not all of the capacity provided (3,000 set-ups) will be used, and a budgeted cost of unused capacity of £9,000 will be highlighted during the budget process. The actual number of set-ups performed was 2,500 compared with a budget of 2,700 and an unexpected utilisation variance of £6,000 (200 × £30) will be reported at the end of the period. The traditional spending (expenditure) variance is £10,000, being the difference between the budgeted and actual fixed costs incurred. The reconciliation of the fixed set-up expenses charged to products with the expenses incurred that are recorded in the accounts is shown in **Table 16:3**.

Table 16:3 **Reconciliation of fixed set-up expenses with expenses incurred**

	£
Set-up expenses charged to products (2,500 × £30)	75,000
Budgeted unused capacity variance (300 × £30)	9,000A
Capacity utilisation variance (200 × £30)	6,000A
Expenditure variance	10,000F
Total actual expenses	80,000

The capacity variance in **Table 16:3** highlights for management attention the £15,000 unused capacity (£9,000 expected and £6,000 unexpected) and thus signals the opportunity for actions such as reducing the supply of resources or using the surplus resources to generate additional revenues.

In this example it is assumed that the variable set-up costs, such as the cost of supplies used in the set-up activity, varies with the number of set-ups. The variable cost driver rate of £10 per set-up has been calculated by dividing the budgeted variable cost of £27,000 by the budgeted number of set-ups of 2,700. Note that the budgeted variable cost per set-up will be £10 for all activity levels. Thus the estimated set-up costs at the practical capacity of 3,000 set-ups would be £30,000 (3,000 × £10) but the cost per set-up would remain at £10. To calculate the set-up variable cost variance the budget must be flexed. The actual number of set-ups performed were 2,500 and the flexible budget allowance is £25,000 (2,500 × £10). Actual expenditure is £26,000 and therefore an adverse variable cost variance of £1,000 will be reported. The reconciliation between the variable set-up expenses charged to products and the actual expenditure incurred is shown in **Table 16:4**.

Table 16:4 **Reconciliation of variable set-up expenses with expenses incurred**

	£
Variable set-up expenses charged to products (2,500 × £10)	25,000
Variable overhead variance	1,000A
Total actual expenses	26,000

The variable overhead variance of £1,000 is due to either greater usage of supplies (quantity variance) or a greater price being paid for the supplies (price variance). Where cost drivers capture the duration of the activity (e.g. using the number of set-up hours instead of the number of set-ups) Mak and Roush (1994) advocate reporting separate efficiency (quantity) and price variances.

16:5 The Future of Standard Costing

Critics of standard costing question the relevance of traditional variance analysis for cost control and performance appraisal in today's manufacturing and competitive environment. Nevertheless, standard costing systems continue to be widely used. This is because standard costing systems provide cost information for many other purposes besides cost control and performance evaluation (*see* **Chs 48** and **49**). Standard costs and variance analysis would still be required for other purposes even if they were abandoned for cost control and performance evaluation.

Attention should be given to adapting standard costing and reporting variances for those variables that are important to a particular company. Those organisations that face bottleneck/limiting factor constraints, or who have adopted a throughput accounting approach (*see* **Ch.33**), could adapt their variance reporting to price variances at the lost contribution resulting from the lost output arising from the excessive usage of scarce resources. For example, if direct labour or machine hours represent a bottleneck constraint for a particular activity then the resulting labour or machine efficiency variances should be priced at the lost contribution per machine or direct labour hour. For those activities where no bottlenecks occur there is no lost contribution arising from the excessive usage of resources and variances should be priced at the acquisition cost of the resources.

Cheatham and Cheatham (1996) advocate the reporting of quality variances by those organisations that wish to pursue a zero-defects policy and measure the cost of quality (*see* **Ch.18**). They define the quality variance as the standard cost of the output that does not meet specification. In traditional variance analysis this variance is buried in the efficiency variances of the various inputs. To illustrate the computation of the variances direct labour and overhead variances are ignored and it is assumed that the standard usage for the production of a product is 3 kg and the standard price is £5 per kg and the actual usage for an output of 3,000 units (of which 200 were defective) was 8,900 kg. Traditional variance would report an adverse usage variance of £2,500, being the difference between the standard quantity of 8,400 kg for the good output of 2,800 units and the actual usage of 8,900 kg priced at £5 per kg. The variance analysis could be modified to report an adverse quality variance of £3,000 (200 defective units x 3 kg x £5) and a favourable usage variance of £500 reflecting the fact that only 8,900 kg were used to produce 3,000 units with a standard usage of 9,000 kg. The fact that 200 units were defective is reflected in the quality variance.

In recent years there has been a shift from using variances generated from a standard costing system as the foundation for short-term cost control and performance measurement to treating them as one among a broader set of measures. Greater emphasis is now being placed on the frequent reporting of non-financial measures (*see* **Ch.49**) that provide feedback on the key variables required to compete successfully in today's competitive environment. Recognition is also being given to the fact that periodic short-term reporting may be inappropriate for controlling those costs that are fixed in the short run but variable in the longer term. Special cost reduction exercises (i.e. Kaizen costing) for existing products, target costing for future products (*see* **Ch.24**) and activity-based cost management (*see* **Ch.28**) are now being increasingly used to manage future costs.

Nevertheless, variance analysis still has an important role to play. Many organisations have adapted their variance reporting system to report on those variables that are particularly important to them. These variables are company-specific and cannot be found in textbooks. Even though variance reporting is most suited to controlling direct labour and material costs it can also provide meaningful information for managing overhead costs if traditional volume-based cost drivers are replaced with cost drivers that better reflect the causes of resource consumption. Variance analysis, however, cannot be used to manage all overhead costs. It is inappropriate for the control of facility-sustaining (infrastructure) costs but it can be applied to those resources whose costs fluctuate in the longer term according to the demand for the resources. Here, the reporting of variances will be at less frequent intervals and will be based on the approach described in the previous section.

It remains to be seen whether standard costing will decline in importance as a cost control and a performance evaluation mechanism. The survey evidence, however, suggests that practitioners do consider that it is an important mechanism for controlling costs. The survey by Drury *et al.* (1993) reported that 76% of the responding organisations operated a standard costing system. When asked how important standard costing was for cost control and performance evaluation 72% of the respondents whose organisations operated a standard costing system stated that it was 'above average' or of 'vital importance'.

References

Cheatham, C.B. and Cheatham, L.R. (1996) 'Redesigning cost systems: Is standard costing obsolete?', *Accounting Horizons*, December: 23–31.

Cornick, M., Cooper, W. and Wilson, S. (1988) 'How do companies analyze overhead?', *Management Accounting*, June: 41–3.

Drury, C., Braund, S., Osborne, P. and Tayles, M. (1993) *A survey of management accounting practices in UK manufacturing companies*, Chartered Association of Certified Accountants.

Kaplan, R.S. (1994) 'Flexible budgeting in an activity-based costing framework', *Accounting Horizons*, June: 104–9.

Mak, Y.T. and Roush, M.L. (1994) 'Flexible budgeting and variance analysis in an activity-based costing environment', *Accounting Horizons*, June: 93–104.

Puxty, A.G. and Lyall (1989) *Cost control into the 1990's: A survey of standard costing and budgeting practices in the UK*, Chartered Institute of Management Accountants.

Solomons, D. (1968) 'The historical development of costing' , in D. Solomons (Ed.), *Studies in cost analysis*, Sweet and Maxwell.

17. Cost System Design and Profitability Analysis

This chapter contains discussion of the purposes of costing systems and their relationship to profitability analysis. It then highlights areas where there is limited information of current practices. Selected findings of a survey sponsored by CIMA are then outlined. These findings are developed and discussed further in the CIMA publication.

17:1 Purposes of Product Costing

17:1.1 Introduction

During the last decade most organisations have faced dramatic changes in their business environment. Deregulation, increasing levels in global competition and the emergence of integrated enterprise-wide information systems have provided the impetus for companies to review and redesign their costing systems. Recent theoretical developments in cost system design have also provided a further impetus for organisations to re-examine their costing systems. Much has been written about costing systems throughout the 1990s and the ideas underpinning activity-based costing have been conceptualised. This chapter discusses the nature and content of costing systems *currently* used within UK companies, the factors influencing the choice of cost system design, and the information that is extracted from the cost system for different types of decisions.

The conventional wisdom of management accounting, as portrayed in textbooks and reflected in management accounting education, states that product costs are required for two purposes; first, for financial accounting [*cf. Stocks and Long-Term Contracts; IAS2:* Inventories] to allocate the costs incurred during a period between cost of goods sold and inventories; second, to provide information for strategic decision making. For decision making, product costs are required to distinguish between profitable and unprofitable activities, outsourcing and redesigning decisions.[1] Product costs may also be of vital importance in determining selling prices, particularly in thin markets where customised products are provided that do not have readily available market prices.

If the cost system does not capture accurately enough the consumption of resources by products, the reported product costs will be distorted, and there is a danger that managers may drop profitable products or continue to sell unprofitable products. Where product costs are used to determine selling prices the undercosting of products can result in the acceptance of unprofitable business whereas overcosting can result in bids being rejected and the loss of profitable business.

17:1.2   Theory and Practice of Product Costing

In the 1990s a considerable amount of publicity was given to criticisms of product cost measurement and cost systems design. Some notable criticisms were:

1   *Product costs that are computed to meet financial accounting inventory valuation requirements are also used for decision making.*
2   *Over-simplistic allocation methods (such as plant-wide overhead rates) are used to compute product costs and, as a result, distorted product costs are reported.*
3   *Direct labour-based overhead rates are extensively used, despite labour costs declining in importance, and being an inappropriate cost driver for many overhead costs.*
4   *External financial reporting conventions encourage a financial accounting mentality and this has resulted in product costing practices following, and becoming subservient to, financial accounting practices.*

The theory and practice of product costing for decisions has also been discussed. This discussion questions the feasibility of applying the approach advocated by conventional wisdom which states that for decision making only decision-relevant incremental costs that predict the cash flows arising from future decisions should be used.

It is claimed that most organisations produce many products and that in these circumstances it is inappropriate to focus on uniquely relevant costs by ascertaining the avoidable costs for each product related decision. This approach assumes that product decisions are independent. Thus, when a decision is taken relating to a specific product, it is assumed that it will be taken in isolation of decisions made on other products and only those incremental/avoidable costs uniquely attributable to the specific product are included in the analysis. No attempt is made to assign to products a share of the cost of those joint resources which fluctuate in the long term according to the demand for them, but which are not uniquely attributable to specific products.

For those organisations that produce many different products it is likely that product decisions will not be independent. In these circumstances a better approximation of long-term incremental/avoidable cash flows might be obtained by assigning a share of the cost of those joint resources (e.g. support costs but not facility sustaining costs) which will fluctuate in the long term according to the demand for these resources. Thus, where product decisions are not independent, the multiplication of product costs that include the cost of joint resources, by the units lost from ceasing production (or additional units from introducing a new product) may provide a closer approximation of the change in the long term of total company cash flows arising from the decisions. The rationale for this is that the change in resource consumption will ultimately be followed by a change in the cash-flow pattern of the organisation, because organisations make decisions for many products rather than just a single product.

To measure accurately the cost of joint resources, Cooper and Kaplan advocate that activity-based costing (ABC) systems should be used. Thus, ABC evolved to support decisions where the number of products is large and decisions are not independent. Cooper and Kaplan imply that reported activity-based product costs do not provide information that can be used directly for decision making. Instead, they provide attention-directing information that pinpoints those products where losses are reported and which therefore require more detailed special studies to ascertain their long-term viability. Cooper and Kaplan do not specify what cost information should be included in the special studies but presumably such studies would seek to report the impact on organisational long-run incremental cash flows arising from product introduction/ abandonment decisions. The greater overhead visibility provided by ABC, arising from analysing costs by unit, batch and product-sustaining activities should, however, result in better estimates of long-run incremental cash flows.

We conclude that the emergence of ABC systems, or the use of average long-run product costs derived from traditional product costing systems can be viewed as alternative attempts to predict incremental cash flows for complex product-related decisions faced by organisations.

17:1.3   Existing Knowledge of Costing Systems in Organisations

A common feature that emerges from surveys is that full costs are widely used for decision making and that simplistic methods are used to assign overheads to products. It is unclear, however, whether full costs represent a share of all costs, manufacturing cost only, or a share of only those joint resources that fluctuate in the long term according to the demand for them. Direct labour hours and machine hours are reported to be widely used to allocate overheads but it is unclear to what extent other cost drivers are used.

The previous studies have not sought to distinguish between the different purposes (stock valuation, profitability analysis, pricing and product mix decisions) for which cost information is required. The findings do not indicate whether different costs are extracted from a single database to meet different requirements or whether separate databases are maintained for decision making and stock valuation. Also none of the previous studies has gathered information on the explanatory variables or the circumstances facing practitioners. Hence no attempt has been made to analyse the results by the potential explanatory variables. Also little is known of the nature, role and content of product profitability analysis in organisations. It is also apparent from previous studies that profitability analysis is widely used in organisations. A survey of Australian companies reported that product profitability analysis was one of the areas where they would place relatively greater future emphasis.

It has also been pointed out that one of the major roles of ABC is as a resource usage model to develop profitability maps (i.e. periodic profitability analysis by cost objects) for focusing management attention. Despite the increasing interest in profitability analysis little is known about the nature, role and content of profitability analysis in organisations. Finally, previous studies have focused mainly on manufacturing organisations whereas the issue extends to all types of organisations and business categories (e.g. manufacturing, retail, service, financial and commercial).

17:1.4 Missing Information on Costing Systems

Reflecting on the above reveals how little is currently known about current practice in the particular area of product costing and managing products. We have limited information on:

(a) *the nature, content and role of product profitability analysis in managing an organisation's existing product mix. For example:*

  (i) *the extent to which organisations periodically analyse profits by products (or services),*

  (ii) *the level of importance attached to product profitability analysis in signalling the need to make key strategic decisions relating to outsourcing, redesigning or discontinuing products or services,*

(iii) what other mechanisms are used to signal the need to make the key strategic decisions identified in (ii) above,

(iv) the extent to which a hierarchical approach of profitability assessment is used, and if so, the critical profitability measures in the hierarchy that organisations use for decision making,

(v) whether product profitability analysis is used directly for decision making or for attention-directing for signalling the need for a more detailed financial analysis (i.e. special studies).

(b) the nature of the costing systems employed; whether they focus on direct and variable costs only or use some form of full costing involving overhead allocation;

(c) the level of sophistication of the costing system;

(d) the extent to which different explanatory variables influence the design of cost systems currently used by UK organisations. Whether organisations consciously and routinely consider in detail internal organisational factors and external factors when cost systems are designed or reviewed. Whether these factors affect cost accumulation system design and the level of sophistication adopted.

Some of these points are now discussed.

17:2 A Model of Cost Systems Design

Costing systems can vary in terms of what costs are assigned to cost objects and their level of sophistication. Traditionally, costing systems have been classified for inventory valuation purposes [*cf. SSAP9: Stocks and Long-Term Contracts; IAS2: Inventories*] but here we are concerned with costing systems for routine profit reporting for providing attention-directing information for decision making. Typically cost systems are classified as follows:

1. *variable costing systems;*
2. *direct costing systems;*
3. *traditional absorption costing systems;*
4. *activity-based costing systems.*

Variable costing systems assign only variable costs to cost objects and the difference between sales revenues and variable costs is defined as contribution to *fixed costs* and profit. With variable costing systems activities that have negative or low contributions to fixed costs are highlighted for special studies and fixed costs can be taken into account at this stage. Variable costs are interpreted as consisting of only short-term variable costs (normally direct materials and direct labour within manufacturing organisations). The disadvantage of this method is that avoidable fixed costs are not assigned to cost objects.

Direct costing systems only assign direct costs to cost objects. The difference between sales revenues and direct costs represents the contribution to *indirect* costs and profit. They are appropriate where the cost of those joint resources that fluctuate according to the demand for them are insignificant. Using direct costing systems requires that activities that have negative or low contributions to indirect costs are highlighted for special studies. An estimate of those indirect costs that are relevant to the decision should then be incorporated within the special studies. Thus, indirect costs are not accumulated or reported within the routine reporting system. The focus is on contribution to indirect costs for routine reporting and as an attention-directing device. However, an attempt is made to incorporate indirect costs within a more detailed analysis if special studies are undertaken. In contrast, both traditional and ABC systems assign indirect costs to cost objects.

The proponents of ABC argue that traditional product costing systems are obsolete and should be replaced by ABC systems, typically involving the creation of many different activity cost pools and cost drivers. They give the impression that cost system designers must choose between ABC and traditional systems. We argue that it is inappropriate to categorise cost systems as either 'ABC' or 'traditional'. Instead, cost systems should be categorised by two groupings. Firstly, the costs that are assigned to cost objects and secondly, the level of sophistication that is used to assign joint costs to cost objects. We also argue that there is no one ideal costing system and the choice depends on the circumstances.

We have developed a tentative model of the cost accumulation systems, the levels of sophistication and those explanatory variables that ought to influence the design of cost systems (*see* **Fig.17:1**). In column 2 we identify four alternative **cost accumulation systems** that can be used to assign costs to cost objects. Column 3 shows the **level of sophistication** that cost system designers can adopt for assigning indirect costs to cost objects. Those **potential explanatory variables** that, in theory, ought to influence the choice of cost accumulation system and the level of sophistication involved are listed in column 1.

17:2.1   Cost Accumulation Systems

We describe below the four cost accumulation systems we have thus far envisaged (*see* **Fig.17:1, column 2**):

System 1: Only direct short-term variable costs are assigned to products
If these costs are used directly for decision making, avoidable fixed costs will be ignored. Product profitability analysis will only report 'contributions to *all* fixed costs' and there is a danger that low contribution margin products whose avoidable fixed costs exceed the reported contribution will continue to be marketed. However, if the reporting of low contribution margins is used as an attention-director to signal the need for undertaking special studies that incorporate avoidable fixed costs, then direct variable costing systems may be appropriate for product profitability analysis.

System 2: Only direct short-term variable costs and direct fixed costs are assigned to products
With this approach only those incremental costs that are uniquely attributable to specific products are included in the product costs. The cost of those joint resources that fluctuate in the long term according to the demand for them are not assigned to products and are thus excluded from the product profitability analysis. Product decisions are therefore assumed to be independent if product profitability analysis information is used directly for decision making. Alternatively, the contribution to *indirect fixed costs* reported by the product profitability analysis can be used as an attention-directing device for identifying those low contribution products that require a more detailed analysis. At this stage an estimate can be made of the potential savings arising from the reduced consumption of 'joint resources' if the product being investigated was discontinued.

System 3: All direct costs (as in (2) above) plus a share of those joint costs that fluctuate in the long term according to the demand for them are assigned to products
The sophistication of the design of product costing systems for assigning joint resources to products varies. Some organisations have implemented sophisticated ABC systems (using many different cost pools and cost drivers) that seek to measure accurately the share of joint resources consumed by products. Other organisations continue to use simplistic cost systems (using a single cost pool and cost driver) that were designed decades ago to meet financial accounting requirements. If the cost of joint resources is significant then simplistic systems are likely to provide poor estimates of joint resources consumed by products. Distorted product costs will be reported which may encourage managers to drop profitable products or continue to market unprofitable products.

System 4: All costs as identified in (3) above plus a share of facility-sustaining costs are assigned to products

Facility-sustaining costs are defined as the cost of those infrastructure activities that are necessary to stay in business. They are completely independent of business volumes. Examples include depreciation of the plant, property taxes, and lighting and heating of the factory and corporate headquarters. Facility-sustaining costs are common and joint to *all* products marketed by the organisation and are likely to remain unchanged unless there is a dramatic expansion/contraction in the scale or scope of activities. Therefore the assignment of such costs is likely to be inappropriate for product introduction/ abandonment decisions. However, some of the facility-sustaining costs (e.g. plant depreciation) must be assigned to products in order to meet external financial accounting requirements. Furthermore, when making pricing or tendering decisions, managers may demand full cost information as a mechanism for seeking to ensure that products recover the cost of resources consumed, plus a fair share of facility-sustaining costs. Where costs are used as inputs to pricing decisions the cost system should seek to measure accurately the resources consumed by products. Common costs should be allocated according to the benefits received. Empirical evidence, however, suggests that arbitrary allocations are widely used to assign facility-sustaining costs to products.

17:2.1.1 Level of Sophistication

The four categories of cost systems described in the previous section can be further categorised by their level of sophistication. Direct and variable costing are partial costing systems. They accurately assign all direct costs to cost objects but are unsophisticated in the sense that direct costing ignores indirect costs and variable costing ignores fixed costs. The cost systems within the third and fourth categories vary in their level of sophistication in assigning indirect costs to cost objects. Generally the sophistication (and also the accuracy) of a costing system in assigning indirect costs to cost objects is positively related to the number of cost pools and second-stage cost drivers that are used.

Traditional costing systems can vary from a single to many cost pools but their distinguishing feature is that they rely on a small number of second-stage volume-based drivers such as direct labour hours, machine hours, materials cost and units of output. The most simplistic traditional system uses a single cost pool and cost driver to allocate indirect costs to cost objects. In most situations, increasing the number of cost pools increases the accuracy of measuring the indirect costs consumed by cost objects. Organisations may, however, deliberately opt for a simplistic costing system that is easily understandable and which consumes few resources, but ideally the choice should be made on the basis of cost versus benefit.

The level of sophistication (*see* **Fig.17:1, column** 3) can be measured in terms of the number of cost pools and the number and type of cost drivers used by the cost system. The most simplistic system uses a single cost pool and a single cost driver. More sophisticated traditional systems use several cost pools and two volume-based cost drivers (typically labour hours/cost, machine hours or units of output). The most sophisticated traditional systems use many cost pools and more than two volume-based cost drivers. The level of sophistication can be further increased by implementing ABC systems that assign overheads using both volume-based and non-volume-based cost drivers. ABC systems can also vary in their level of sophistication from the use of several cost pools with several volume/non-volume-based cost drivers to the most sophisticated using many cost pools and many cost drivers.

17:2.1.2   Explanatory Variables

We have identified the following potential explanatory variables that, in theory, ought to influence the design of cost systems:

1. *purposes for which the cost information is required;*
2. *cost structure;*
3. *competitive environment;*
4. *product diversity;*
5. *competitive strategy;*
6. *size of the organisation;*
7. *type of organisation.*

We make brief comment on these below.

Organisations can choose to maintain a separate database for each of the major purposes for which cost information is required. Alternatively, they can maintain a single database and extract different information for different purposes. For those organisations that are faced with meeting stock valuation requirements external financial regulations require companies to adopt the fourth cost accumulation system [*cf. SSAP9: Stocks and Long-Term Contracts; IAS2: Inventories*].

Decisions arising from product profitability analysis are unlikely to alter facility-sustaining costs and the fourth cost accumulation system is therefore likely to be inappropriate for profitability analysis. For product pricing decisions where no competitive market price exists and cost-plus pricing is used as a mechanism to determine selling prices, organisations may seek to ensure that all costs are covered and assign most of their costs (including facility-sustaining costs) to products. In other words, the fourth cost accumulation system should be used.

Where the proportion of indirect costs within an organisation's cost structure is high, direct costing systems will trace only a small proportion of costs to cost objects and such systems are likely to be inappropriate for profitability analysis or pricing. Conversely, where the proportion of indirect costs is low, direct costing may be appropriate or, if indirect costs are assigned to cost objects, unsophisticated traditional costing systems using a small number of cost pools and cost drivers may not result in the reporting of seriously distorted costs.

Several studies have examined the relationship between the design and use of management accounting systems and the intensity of competition. It is argued that firms operating in a more competitive environment have a greater need for sophisticated cost systems that more accurately assign costs to products, services and customers because competitors are more likely to take advantage of any errors from managers having to rely on inaccurate cost information to make decisions.

Product diversity applies when products consume activity resources in different proportions. Greater product diversity requires more sophisticated costing systems to capture the variation in resource consumption by different products. The variations in consumption of activity resources can be extended to other cost objects besides products. For example, high customer diversity exists in an organisation which services customers who order high-volume, standard products which require few special demands and other customers who order low-volume, non-standard products requiring large quantities of before and after-sales support.

Competitive strategy describes how a business chooses to compete in its industry and tries to achieve a competitive advantage relative to its competitors. Companies that follow a differentiated strategy and use direct or variable costing systems, or unsophisticated absorption costing systems, will not be able to estimate the incremental costs of achieving differentiation. They need a sophisticated costing system that accurately measures the costs of product and volume diversity that stems from following a differentiation strategy.

Previous studies have noted a positive relationship between company size and management accounting system sophistication. A possible reason for this is that larger organisations have relatively greater access to resources to experiment with the introduction of more sophisticated systems.

Some writers suggest that service companies are ideal candidates for ABC, even more than manufacturing companies. Their justification for this statement is that most costs in service organisations are fixed and indirect. Such costs are treated by simplistic costing systems as fixed and irrelevant for most decisions. This resulted in a situation where profitability analysis was not considered helpful for decision making unless a sophisticated or ABC system was adopted.

Column 1 of **Figure 17:1** lists some potential explanatory variables. Limited further attention will be given to these in this chapter though as they are covered in more detail in our CIMA publication.

Figure 17:1   **A model of cost systems design**

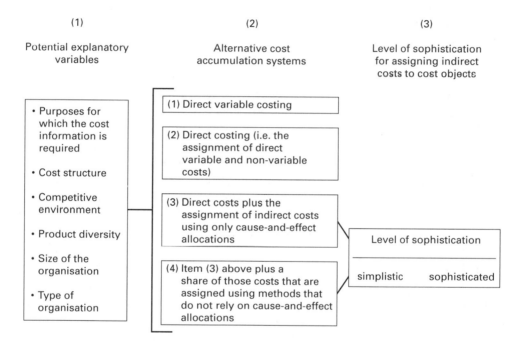

17:3   Survey Findings

17:3.1   Questionnaire

It is against a background of the above that we approached the Chartered Institute of Management Accountants to fund and sponsor research to examine the above issues. In December 1998 a postal survey was undertaken which aimed to gather empirical data on the costing practices of UK companies. Before mailing, eight company visits were undertaken to pilot test the questionnaire and discuss issues relating to the replies. The final version of the questionnaire contained 18 pages and included 72 questions.

The questionnaire was divided into seven sections. The first section contained general questions relating to the organisations' costing systems and the product-costing environment. The second section focused on profitability analysis and decision making, the third on cost accumulation for stock valuation and the fourth on cost information for setting selling prices. The fifth section included questions relating to how activity levels were determined for establishing cost driver rates. Details about the organisational units (e.g. size, business sector, etc.) were collected in the sixth section. The final section collected information about the respondents. For the second, third and fourth sections the respondents were asked to relate their answers only to the purposes specified within the section (i.e. profitability analysis, stock valuation and setting selling prices). Respondents were also asked to confirm whether or not the costs accumulated, or used, for one purpose were the same as those used for other purposes.

The survey was directed towards larger businesses, those utilising 'developed' costing systems and employing a number of accountants. Turnover ranged between £25m to over £300m with most respondents in the larger categories. Replies were received from 187 respondents giving a response rate of 30%. The survey was directed to both manufacturing and service businesses and separate information for these sectors is available. A single database of cost information in companies was the norm. More than 90% of the manufacturing company respondents indicated that a single database was maintained from which appropriate cost information was extracted to provide the required information for both stock valuation and decision making. Respondents were asked the proportion of their company's cost structure accounted for by indirect costs, a wide range was reported from below 10% to above 40% of total costs. Direct costs only were assigned to cost objects by 15% of the responding organisations and the remaining 85% assigned both direct and indirect costs. Over a typical year the majority of organisations (58%) costed over 200 items within their chosen cost object. Periodic profitability analysis is therefore required to monitor the profitability of activities.

17:3.2 Profitability Analysis

Over 90% of the organisations analysed profits at least on an annual basis and monthly profitability analysis (of products, services, components, customers, locations, etc.) was the norm in approximately 80% of the organisations. **Table 17:1** shows the extent and frequency of profitability analysis by the respondent companies. Most of the respondents used profitability analysis as an attention-directing mechanism for identifying potentially unprofitable activities that required more detailed special studies. Other mechanisms, such as a decline in sales volume or the introduction of a superior product by a competitor can also signal the need to undertake special studies but profitability analysis was considered to be the most important.

Table 17:1   **Extent and frequency of profitability analysis (N = 185)**

	Monthly	*Quarterly*	*Six monthly*	*Annually*	*> 1 year*	*Not routinely analysed*
	%	%	%	%	%	%
Products/services	75	9	4	3		9
Components	25	4	3	4		64
Customers/customer categories	47	11	7	9	2	24
Locations	69	4		3		24
Other	7					93

Of those organisations that assigned indirect costs to cost objects virtually all of them separately reported short-term incremental costs and approximately 50% attempted to distinguish between different categories of indirect costs. In particular, they attempted to distinguish between cost assignments using cause-and-effect cost drivers and assignments that do not rely on cause-and-effect allocations. Approximately 80% of the organisations assigned facility-sustaining costs and the norm was to categorise them separately when extracting information for decision making. The evidence suggests that most organisations have the potential to use cost information in a flexible manner. Thus, it is possible that criticisms by various commentators relating to the naïve use of full costs that incorporate arbitrary cost allocations may have been misleading because they may have based their criticisms on what is accumulated within the costing system rather than what is reported or extracted from the system for decision making.

Although most of the organisations traced indirect costs to cost objects they do not necessarily base their decisions on reported costs that involve indirect cost allocations. Because flexibility exists to extract different categories of costs from the database it is possible to report a hierarchy of profitability measures within the profitability analysis. A possible hierarchical approach to profitability analysis is illustrated in **Figure 17:2**. The respondents were asked to indicate the most important profitability measures used by their organisations for decision making. There was approximately a 50/50 split between the use of contribution (sales less direct costs) and a profitability measure that incorporates overhead allocations. **Table 17:2** is extracted from the report showing the companies' preferences for the most important and second most important profitability measure routinely used for decision making. It is clear that tracing of indirect costs to cost objects and the sophistication of this is an issue for many companies.

Table 17:2   **Importance of profitability analysis measures for decision making**

	% indicating most important measure (N = 187)	*% indicating second most important measure (N = 187)*
(1) Revenues less direct costs (Contribution)	50	26
(2) Contribution less indirect costs assigned using cause-and-effect cost drivers	6	7
(3) Row 2 less arbitrary allocations	11	7
(4) Bottom line net profit (sales less all costs)	30	19
(5) Items inserted by respondents	3	3
(6) Only a single measure is used		38 (N = 71)

Most of the organisations grouped individual products, services or customers together and categorised them as product 'lines'. Approximately 60% of these organisations routinely analysed profits only at the product line level. However, most of the organisations could, if required, extract information from the database to analyse product line profitability at the individual product level. Different approaches were reported for dealing with joint costs attributable to a line but not uniquely identifiable to individual products. Approximately 20% did not accumulate costs by individual items and therefore could not analyse profitability by individual items within the line.

Figure 17:2 **An illustration of hierarchical profitability analysis**

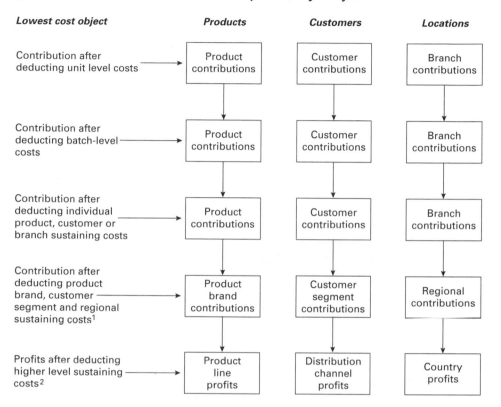

Notes

[1]Consists of expenses dedicated to sustaining specific product brands or customer segments or regions but which cannot be attributed to individual products, customers or branches.

[2]Consists of expenses dedicated to sustaining the product lines or distribution channels or countries but which cannot be attributed to lower items within the hierarchy.

Details were requested on the information that was used in the special studies. Approximately half of the respondents indicated that an attempt was made to isolate incremental (avoidable) costs when undertaking a detailed appraisal and the remaining responses indicated that other qualitative factors, or factors that were specific to their organisations, were taken into account. The responses implied that focusing on profitability measures that include arbitrary allocations of unavoidable costs for attention-directing may not be accompanied by the use of arbitrary allocations within the special studies.

If cost systems fail to capture with sufficient accuracy the resources consumed by cost objects, distorted costs will be reported and there is a danger that potentially unprofitable activities will not be highlighted for special studies. Alternatively, resources may be wasted investigating profitable activities that have been reported as unprofitable within the periodic profitability analysis.

17:3.3   Accuracy of Observed Costing Systems

Within the profitability analysis section of the questionnaire questions were included that focused on the accuracy of assigning indirect costs to cost objects. It was pointed out that these questions related specifically to cost information that is incorporated into the profitability analysis. The findings relating to the number of cost pools and second stage cost drivers used are reported in **Table 17:3** and **Table 17:4**. It can be seen from **Table 17:3** that 3% of the responding organisations used a single cost pool (i.e. a plant-wide or blanket overhead rate), 14% used less than five cost pools and 36% used more than 20 cost pools. The reported findings relating to the use of a single cost pool are much lower than the findings reported in earlier studies in the UK and the USA.

Even if many cost pools are used indirect costs assigned to cost objects can still be inaccurate if a limited number of second stage drivers are used. **Table 17:4** indicates that a single second stage cost driver was used by 35% of the organisations and 69% used fewer than four different cost drivers. More than 10 different types of cost drivers were used by 10% of the organisations.

There appears to be a trend towards the use of an increased number of cost pools compared with the situation in the early 1990s. However, only a small proportion of respondents were using a variety of different costs drivers (or allocation bases) with which to assign the indirect costs of the cost pools. The findings suggest that many organisations are using cost systems that may not accurately assign indirect costs to cost objects. The problem appears to arise because of the use of a limited number of second-stage cost drivers rather than using a limited number of cost pools. However, it is inappropriate to conclude unequivocally that organisations have inaccurate cost systems without considering the impact that more sophisticated systems will have on reported costs. It is possible that the observed unsophisticated systems may be reporting costs that are sufficiently accurate for decision making.

Approximately 25% of all of the respondent organisations were ABC adopters. Generally they claimed in the questionnaire to have adopted ABC and this was confirmed by the number of cost pools and cost drivers they reported. Size and the type of business had a significant impact on the adoption of ABC. The adoption rates were 45% for the largest organisations and 51% for the financial and service organisations. Although the ABC adopters used significantly more cost pools and cost drivers than the non-adopters most adopters used fewer cost pools and drivers compared with what is recommended in the literature.

Table 17:3 **Number of cost pools each having their own individual charge-out rate (analysed by cost objects)**

Number of cost pools	1	2–3	4–5	6–10	11–20	21–30	31–50	Over 50
	%	%	%	%	%	%	%	%
Products/services (N=139)	3	1	6	22	30	12	9	17
Customers (N=8)			25	13	12	25	12	13
Locations (N=14)	7		29	7	29	14	7	7
Other (N=8)		13	12	25	38	12		
Total (N=169)	3	2	9	21	29	13	8	15

Table 17:4 **Number of second-stage cost drivers used to assign overheads to cost objects**

Number of cost drivers	1	2	3	4	5	6	7–10	Over 10
	%	%	%	%	%	%	%	%
Products/services (N=139)	35	25	11	8	6	1	6	8
Customers (N=8)	13	12	13		12	13		37
Locations (N=14)	36	29	7	7	7			14
Other (N=8)	50	25		25				
Total (N=169)	34	25	10	8	6	2	5	10

17:3.4 Stock Valuation, Pricing and Activity Measures

Some questions were directed to organisations for which the use of the cost system for stock valuation was an issue. Only 9% of the organisations that assigned costs for stock valuation purposes used a separate cost accumulation system, one for stock valuation and the other for decision making. Virtually all these organisations used a simplistic system for stock valuation and a more sophisticated system for decision making. Where the same cost accumulation system was used for stock valuation and decision making, the respondents viewed the costing system as being more accurate for stock valuation than for decision-making purposes.

For those organisations that used cost-plus pricing it accounted for over 40% of total sales revenue in 44% of the organisations and less than 10% in 26% of the organisations. For those organisations that used cost-plus pricing extensively (i.e. sales revenues from cost-plus pricing accounted for more than 40% of total sales revenues) no evidence was found to indicate that they used a different number of cost pools or cost drivers. It appears that organisations maintain the same costing system for pricing as for decision making and/or stock valuation. However, they may extract different information from it. The evidence suggests that some form of full costs, involving indirect cost allocations, was used to a greater extent for cost plus pricing compared with profitability analysis information that is used for discontinuation, redesign and outsourcing decisions.

Sixty per cent of the respondents indicated that cost-plus pricing was used to assist in setting selling prices. The discussion that follows relates only to the replies from these respondents. Generally, separate costing systems are not used for cost-plus pricing though different information may be extracted from the database for pricing decisions. The analysis of the responses relating to the cost information that was used for cost-plus pricing indicated that:

1. *15% assigned only direct costs to cost objects for cost-plus pricing (this included 9% that assigned only direct variable costs and a further 6% that assigned both direct variable and non-variable costs);*
2. *7% assigned direct costs plus those indirect costs where cost drivers could be identified that are the causes of the cost varying in the long term;*
3. *78% assigned direct costs plus those indirect costs identified in category (2) above plus a share of those costs (e.g. infrastructure costs) that are assigned using methods that do not rely on cause-and-effect allocations.*

The above results are significantly different from those reported for profitability analysis information that is used for discontinuation, redesign and outsourcing decisions.[2] It suggests a greater usage of a direct costing approach with 50% of the responding organisations identifying contribution (sales revenues less direct costs) as the most important measure for profitability analysis compared with 15%, described above, that assign only direct costs for cost-plus-pricing. It can be seen that 78% used a full cost approach for pricing decisions compared with 41% who indicated that such costs were incorporated within the most important profitability measure for decision making.

Organisations assigning indirect costs to cost objects must decide on the denominator activity level to be used in order to establish cost-centre or activity-centre cost-driver (overhead-absorption) rates. Activity volume levels can be measured in a number of different ways and the actual method selected can have a profound effect on the costs that are assigned to cost objects and unutilised capacity. Three different activity measures are discussed in the literature:

1. *Normal volume based on the anticipated average level of activity over a period of years.*
2. *Budgeted or estimated annual activity.*
3. *Maximum practical annual capacity that is available – this includes both planned utilised and unutilised capacity.*

The most popular measure used was overwhelmingly the budgeted or estimated annual activity, although current literature advocates the use of maximum capacity so that unutilised capacity can be revealed and costed.

17:3.5   Explanatory Variables

A further objective of this study was to examine the extent to which potential explanatory variables influenced the sophistication of the observed costing systems and the information that was extracted from the system. Sophistication was generally measured by the extent of the use of different cost pools and cost drivers. Six potential variables were examined. They were the purposes for which the cost information is required, cost structures, competitive environment, product diversity, size and type of organisation (*see* **Fig.17:1**). Because most organisations used a single cost-accumulation system the findings indicated that the purpose for which the information was required did not influence the choice of the cost-accumulation system. However, different information appeared to be extracted depending on the purpose for which the information was required. The findings also suggest that the competitive environment, size and type of business organisation influenced the sophistication of the cost accumulation system. However, there was no statistical evidence to indicate that product diversity or cost structures were explanatory factors for the sophistication of the costing system. It should be noted that these explanatory variables are notoriously difficult dimensions to capture. However, considerable effort was made to obtain this data and this is explained within the full report.

Other relationships besides those explicitly defined in the research objectives were examined. There was no evidence to indicate that those organisations that extensively used cost-plus pricing adopted more sophisticated costing systems. The responses for those organisations that adopted direct costing were compared with those that did not in terms of size, cost structures and the number of items costed. There was no significant relationship between these items and the type of cost system adopted.

17:4   Conclusion

Our aim was to concentrate on companies with established cost systems. To achieve this objective we selected a sample consisting of all organisations whose objectives were profit making and that employed two or more CIMA qualified members with more than five years' post-qualification experience. This selection process is likely to have resulted in the omission of many small organisations, since they are unlikely to have well-established management accounting systems. Furthermore, many service organisations tend to be relatively small, compared with manufacturing organisations, and many also do not have profit-making objectives (e.g. charities and public sector organisations). Thus our sample contains a lower proportion of service organisations than that which applies for the UK as a whole.

A selection of findings from the study is:

(a) *Most organisations routinely analyse profits by their chosen cost objects at monthly intervals.*

(b) *Profitability analysis is used as an attention-directing mechanism for identifying potential unprofitable activities that require more detailed studies.*

(c) *A single costing system is operated by most organisations.*

(d) *The majority of organisations are using relatively unsophisticated costing systems that may not accurately assign indirect costs to cost objects. Such costs may not be sufficiently accurate for providing attention-directing information or information for pricing decisions.*

(e) *Approximately 80% of the responding firms assigned facility-sustaining (infrastructure costs) and the norm was to categorise them separately when extracting information for decision making.*

(f) *Full costs were used to a greater extent for cost-plus pricing compared with the profitability analysis information that is used as an attention-directing device.*

(g) *Most costing systems separately report short-term indirect costs.*

(h) *Many companies thus have the potential to use cost information in a flexible manner and this was evident from the responses to the information that was included in special studies.*

(i) *A much greater percentage of financial/commercial and service organisations have developed sophisticated costing systems compared with manufacturing organisations.*

(j) *Larger organisations tend to have more sophisticated costing systems.*

(k) *ABC systems coincide with the more sophisticated systems as defined in the study.*

It was also apparent from the survey that the denominator levels used to establish cost driver rates are not consistent with the theoretical approach advocated which is to use practical capacity. If practical capacity is not used to establish cost driver rates then the presumption that modern costing systems represent resource consumption models that distinguish between used and unused resources becomes questionable.

It is also apparent from the research that wide differences exist in the sophistication of the observed costing systems. It has been pointed out that the implementation and development of more sophisticated costing systems is likely to be affected by the extent to which a senior person in an organisation can influence and champion the design and use of the costing system (such as a member of top management, the financial director or the management accountant).

The survey has identified a number of areas that warrant further research. The evidence from the survey suggests that several different categories of costs are separately reported and that the potential exists for cost information to be used in a flexible manner. Future studies should examine in more detail which costs are included within the costing systems, in particular the extent to which manufacturing organisations incorporate non-inventorable costs. The nature, role and content of the cost information that is used, and the role it plays, within special studies is also an area of particular interest for future research.

Finally, it is important to emphasise that this research has concentrated on cost system design and the information generated from the costing system for decisions relating to managing the existing mix of activities, products, services, locations and customers. An important related area for future research is to examine the content of management accounting information, and the role it plays, in managing the cost and mix of future activities.

Notes

1. This chapter will consider cost systems design in both manufacturing and service organisations. In service organisations the 'cost of services' is likely to be the cost object but to simplify the presentation the term 'product cost' is used as the cost object throughout.

2. **Table 17:2** incorporates responses for all organisations, whereas for comparison purposes it should incorporate only organisations that use cost-plus pricing. The results and percentages reported are virtually identical to those reported in **Table 17:2** if only organisations using cost-plus pricing are included in the analysis.

18. **Quality Costing**

This chapter will address the issue of quality, specifically costing of quality. It will not make an evangelistic statement about continuous improvement and the quality journey of total quality management (TQM) but managers and accountants should be aware of the potential for quality measurement, quality management and quality costing.

18:1 Cost Accounting and Quality

18:1.1 What is Quality?

Quality has increased in importance in recent years such that it features in the strategy of most companies in one form or another. A tendency to inspect quality into a product has been replaced by systems which endeavour to build in quality to ensure that quality features in all that a company is engaged in. It has evolved, for instance, to management of the quality of the totality of an organisation. **Figure 18:1** shows the levels in the evolution of quality management. This chapter will use the term 'quality management' to refer to the system to support the pursuit by management of quality objectives for their organisation.

It may be appropriate to start with a definition of quality, however, some writers do not attempt this because it means different things to different people. 'Fitness for purpose' is commonly used but this is very open ended and may make any costing too difficult, for example, if it is not clarified by suitable specifications it may leave the cost collector in doubt as to what parameters will affect the product's suitability. Furthermore what matters is not just quality as measured by conformance to prescribed tolerance levels, but the customers quality rating of the item in question. These issues will be explored later.

Perhaps a more pragmatic definition of quality is that it is concerned with 'enhancing the value of products or services in which a company is in the business of providing to its customers'. This also is some help in focusing the mind of the preparer on a greater scope for accounting support of quality with appropriate costing information.

Figure 18:1 **Levels in the evolution of quality management**
Source: Dale (1994)

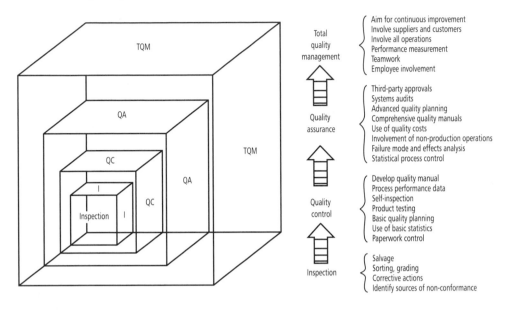

Total quality management	Aim for continuous improvement Involve suppliers and customers Involve all operations Performance measurement Teamwork Employee involvement
Quality assurance	Third-party approvals Systems audits Advanced quality planning Comprehensive quality manuals Use of quality costs Involvement of non-production operations Failure mode and effects analysis Statistical process control
Quality control	Develop quality manual Process performance data Self-inspection Product testing Basic quality planning Use of basic statistics Paperwork control
Inspection	Salvage Sorting, grading Corrective actions Identify sources of non-conformance

18:1.2 Accounting Support of a Quality Strategy

The accounting function has a role to play in regular quality reporting for management control, in evaluating and prioritising quality projects on a financial basis and tracking the ongoing performance of any quality programme (*see* **Ch.49**, particularly **para.49:2.1**). The following model (**Fig.18:2**) illustrates how quality can be tracked from being a part of company strategy, through the selection and implementation of quality projects, into a process which monitors continual quality improvement. Together, the elements of the model define the areas of performance measurement for quality within an organisation and in doing so identify those areas where accounting and costing can play a part.

Figure 18:2 **Accounting support of a quality strategy**

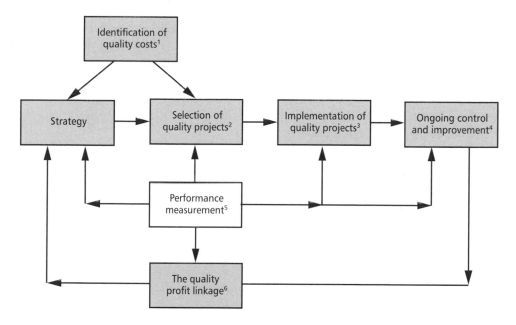

The development of a quality strategy is dependent upon identifying the costs of poor quality (1) through to selecting (2) and implementing quality projects (3) to improve performance. To maintain managerial control these projects must then be controlled and assessed (4). These activities enable continuous performance measurement and assessment throughout the quality implementation (5). This then allows an assessment to be made of the overall effect of the quality strategy on company 'bottom-line' performance (6) by evaluating the overall profit impact of the quality strategy.

In theory the link between profitability and quality seems an easy one to make, however, practical evidence of this link is not as easily illustrated. Quality can be useful in persuading customers to pay a price premium, thereby increasing profit margins or alternatively quality control can be viewed as a form of cost management. Evidence must be sought to verify the existence and strength of this quality-profit linkage in order to maintain momentum and provide management control as quality initiatives cannot be sustained by faith alone.

18:1.3 Quality Costs

'Cost of quality embraces all costs that would be avoided (and incremental revenue that would be earned) if quality was perfect', this is a theoretically appealing definition but has practical limitations for anyone embarking on a cost-of-quality exercise.

For companies which do not have a quality strategy it is claimed that the cost of quality can be typically 15% to 20% of turnover and in service industries this is sometimes more.

Two more pragmatic definitions are:

> Quality costs are those costs which are associated with the achievement of product quality. In broad terms they are considered to be a summation of the costs of preventing errors or product failures, checking whether errors exist, the costs incurred by failure to meet requirements and the investment in quality improvement projects.
>
> (Dale, 1994)

The DTI defines quality costs as 'those costs which are incurred in the design and implementation of quality management systems plus the costs of failure of the systems and products'. The above two definitions can be seen to feature in subsequent discussion categorising quality costs.

18:1.4 Why Measure Quality Costs?

The measurement of costs allows quality-related activities to be expressed in the language of management. It helps to emphasise the importance of quality-related activities and influence management behaviour. It focuses on areas of high expenditure and identifies cost reduction or revenue enhancement opportunities (*see* **Ch.27**). It allows measurement of performance and provides a basis for internal comparison on many levels. It can form the basis for budgets and the control of the whole quality operation. It may reveal quirks in existing costing and measurement, highlight fraud and pinpoint real responsibility for sales or cost performance. Measurement is the first step towards control and improvement.

18:1.5 Prevention, Appraisal and Failure Costs (p-a-f)

Traditionally quality costs have been divided into four categories:

1. *Prevention costs.* The costs of providing systems to prevent defects and service failures. Examples of these might be preventative maintenance, quality inspector training or purchasing of additional equipment to prevent quality problems.
2. *Appraisal costs.* These are the costs of activities that measure and evaluate processes to ensure conformance to specifications. Examples are quality assurance costs, inspection of incoming stock and costs of testing products.
3. *Internal failure costs.* Costs incurred for poor quality of goods or services. Examples are the cost of scrap or reworking or rectifying administration errors or the length of time a service is not available.
4. *External failure costs.* Costs incurred external to the actual organisation such as loss of goodwill; warranty claims and product recalls. Customer complaints are also external failure costs and should be measured along with changes in the customer perception of the standing and quality of the company and its products and services.

Quality costs, can be identified in each of these categories and together create the total cost of quality to the organisation. **Figure 18:3** provides a longer list of the sort of costs that will fall into each category. The p-a-f model is the one enduring approach for tabulating quality costs, it is rational and orderly and it has an appearance of criteria for the inclusion of a cost in a particular quality cost category. It is said to have favour with quality managers in particular because it is in some way equivalent to a set of 'quality accounts', prevention being equivalent to investment, appraisal being like operating costs and failure being equivalent to losses sustained and/or where earning potential could be improved. It is also of value as it provides a general overview for management in order to set policy, such an analysis may be the starting point for a new or renewed quality initiative. It can help senior management formulate the implementation of the company strategy (*see* **Ch.2**) by being able to identify those areas that will benefit most from a quality improvement project. It also allows an evaluation of the current costs being incurred due to poor quality and hence influences the acceptance of quality initiatives.

Figure 18:3 **Typical costs under the p-a-f model**

Examples of prevention costs
1. Part and tool design reviews.
2. Control plan preparation.
3. Quality planning and procedure design.
4. Vendor qualification and quality assessments.
5. Vendor purchase order review and control.
6. Capability study and capability review.
7. Preventive maintenance.
8. In-line statistical process control.
9. Design expenses for inspection equipment.
10. Cost of inspection equipment.
11. Operator and management training.
12. Some quality control administration.
13. Joint planning with vendors.
14. Some prototype trial costs.
15. Customer trial costs.

Examples of appraisal costs
1. Sample preparation.
2. Inspection of sample parts and initiation of tool design changes after the initial sampling.
3. Most testing costs.
4. Vendor product testing.
5. Incoming inspection and testing of materials and components.
6. Initial vendor sample inspection and test.
7. In-process and final inspection and test.
8. Spot inspection.
9. Quality audits.
10. Maintenance and calibration of inspection equipment.
11. Field audit of product usage.
12. Administrative appraisal costs.
13. Original equipment manufacturer (OEM) and supplier audits.
14. Some management information system (MIS) costs.
15. Some production process/environment testing and monitoring.
16. Configuration and reliability engineering on prevention projects.

(cont'd)

(Fig.18:3 *cont'd*)

Examples of internal failure costs
1. Some engineering changes and tool enhancement after sampling.
2. Redesign costs due to deficient planning.
3. Purchase reject reporting and related repurchasing efforts.
4. Cost of processing claims on vendors.
5. Rework of purchased material.
6. Scrap and some inventory shrinkage.
7. Rework.
8. Quality downgrading cost.
9. Quality downtime.
10. Mechanical and electrical downtime.
11. Specification changes.
12. Excess material procurement costs.
13. Cost of safety stock to cushion for quality problems.
14. Administration costs to investigate and follow up failures.

Examples of external failure costs
1. Some engineering changes and tool improvements.
2. Warranty claims on vendors for field failures.
3. Scrap and inventory shrinkage.
4. Rework on returned goods.
5. Reinspection and retest.
6. Pricing errors – lost gross margin.
7. Downgrading cost.
8. Customer return processing and freight.
9. Discounts and allowances.
10. Warranty and liability costs.
11. Investigation of failures.
12. Administrative time spent on follow-up with customers.
13. Loss of existing and future customers.
14. Loss of goodwill.
15. Loss of reputation.

At a general level it may also enable management to monitor a trend of cost over time, say, at monthly intervals once a quality strategy has been adopted. The p-a-f model is, however, of less significance to other functional managers because it does not relate to the specific functional or other activities of the business, other measures of performance (*see* **Chs 48** and **49**) therefore need to be generated to meet this need. This will involve placing financial values on the performance measures in different functional areas and evaluating projects designed to improve quality.

Note that prevention and appraisal costs may increase if quality is to be improved but will be outweighed by the benefits of reduced failure costs. By changing to a system which places more emphasis on prevention of poor quality the costs of appraisal and failure diminish. **Figure 18:4** supports this notion that costs change as quality improves, the reduction of failure costs and the consequent initial investment in prevention and appraisal costs. It is this tendency which has caused some commentators to assert that 'quality is free'.

Figure 18:4 **The cost implications of formal quality assurance**

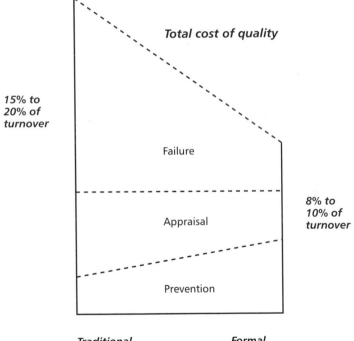

18:1.6 Cost of Conformance/Non-conformance

As an alternative, a broader classification of quality costs is into costs of conformance and those of non-conformance. This is equivalent to identifying the cost of doing things right and the cost of getting them wrong.

Cost of quality = cost of conformance + cost of non-conformance

As the scope of quality management widens the cost of conformance/non-conformance has perhaps more potential for adaptation to the evaluation of economic costs of quality which we shall discuss later. This may therefore be the way forward in categorising quality costs rather than p-a-f, though such a choice may be influenced by particular preferences of the management concerned.

18:1.7 Cost and Market Factors

Evidence from various individual cases suggests that the major cause of increased profitability in the short term is the reduction in the internal costs of quality. These savings are often substantial, for example, companies such as Motorola, Rank Xerox and Hewlett Packard are quoted as having experienced a drop in quality costs of 50% over a three- to five-year period. In the longer term the strategic benefits of quality improvement will result in increased customer satisfaction, improved market standing and increased market share. As a guide, it has been suggested that a 2% increase in customer quality rating of a product or service resulted in a 1% increase in ROI. Therefore measuring short-term benefits on a basis of incremental costs saved may be initially acceptable. But as the quality process develops, methods of assessing the strategic long-term benefits need to be built into the evaluation process if the organisation is to see fully the benefits of its quality strategy. For example, it has been suggested that a 5% retention rate in customers boosts the lifetime profitability of a customer by 50% to 80%. If market benefits are not included it may be that it appears satisfactory to accept a particular level of quality failure (i.e. non-conformance). But on a strategic basis unless the market implications are incorporated this may not be optimal and the costs of this may be greater than anticipated.

We have said therefore that a quality initiative can be argued to be both a way of reducing costs within the process (cost management) and of increasing the 'added value' of a product to the consumer, thereby increasing profit margins.

18:2 Linking Profit and Quality

18:2.1 Balancing Costs and Benefits

The economic quality loss model (EQL) in **Figure 18:5** is one approach to balancing the costs and benefits of quality. This is developed from the prevention–appraisal–failure model of quality costs. It is based on a balance of prevention and appraisal costs with costs of failure to identify an acceptable level of defects or non-conformances. Note that prevention costs will always be positive and therefore other quality costs will also be positive.

Figure 18:5 **The economic quality loss model**

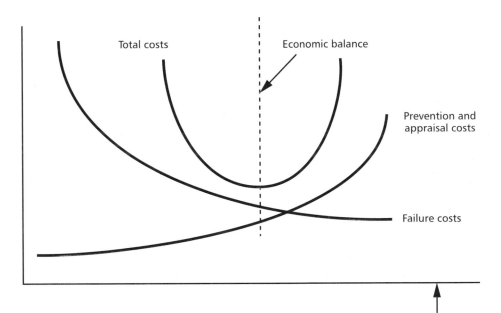

It can be seen that this approach can be linked to the idea of tolerance levels within a standard costing system where a normal amount of wastage is assumed. With this model, when the process is in control, quality costs are also assumed to be minimised with no further scope for improvement. The focus is purely on variances from the average or target value outside the normal spread of data. This is in line with a conventional 'western' approach to the loss function. Once the system is in control then further improvements will be difficult to justify as any other possible quality costs occurring are hidden from the analysis. Within the normal random spread of any process that is 'in control' (say +/– 2 standard deviations) there is assumed to be no quality cost. Quality costs are implied only to occur for products or processes when performance exceeds this spread.

18:2.2 Japanese Approach and Zero Defects

Certain Japanese companies have reported increasing profits and reducing costs in processes with defects as low as one part per million. This is far in excess of any economic balance described by the EQL model above. This is in line with an alternative approach which is to aim for zero defects. The notion of a quadratic loss function (*see* **Fig.18:6**) (called the Taguchi approach, after the Japanese researcher) assumes there are quality costs for processes that are 'in control' because they are not yet optimised. This is illustrated below.

The Taguchi loss function (Dallio *et al.*, 1995) therefore produces a cost for any process that is not achieving its optimum target (say zero defects), regardless of whether the process is within its normal random spread of values. In other words it encourages a striving for still further quality improvements (zero defects) rather than accepting a certain tolerance level.

Figure 18:6 The Taguchi loss function targeting zero defects

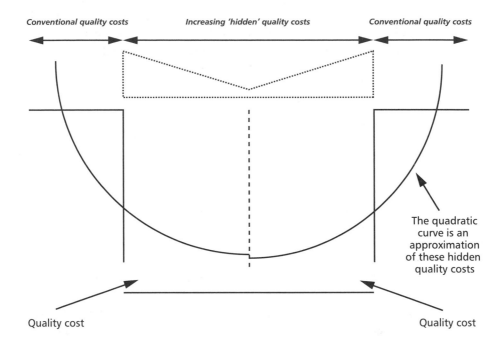

Conventional quality costs   Increasing 'hidden' quality costs   Conventional quality costs

The quadratic curve is an approximation of these hidden quality costs

Quality cost   Quality cost

The cost of conformance (c-o-c) model mentioned earlier allows the zero-defect strategy to be placed within a quality costing system and can be used instead of the p-a-f model. The c-o-c model defines quality costs as the lowest cost of producing a product or service. By avoiding the categorisation of balancing prevention and appraisal with failure (the p-a-f model) it concentrates on attaining the lowest cost possible in a given situation. Using both the Taguchi loss function approach and the cost of conformance model the quality costs are not hidden and the concept of zero defects and continuous quality improvement can perhaps be analysed more effectively.

18:3 Quality Costing in Practice

The following case studies reflect typical situations where quality initiatives have been supported by costing exercises.

18:3.1 Case A

This company is a manufacturing concern, part of an international group, and began its quality improvement programme by developing a quality system suitable for BS 5750 (now superseded by ISO 9000) registration. Management makes no major claims that the calculations of cost savings are absolutely precise, but estimates that the aggregate savings from quality initiatives at just one location are in excess of £3m over the first three years. This is confirmed by the fact that in total the site profit has increased by approximately one-quarter over the three-year period, and this is despite operating in a recessionary market.

18:3.1.1 Integration of Financial and Non-financial Measures
(*See* Chs 48 and 49.)

A trend in the company has been the increasing work by the management accounting section to attach monetary values to non-financial measures. This has created a two-tier system for performance measurement, with figures being expressed in either financial or non-financial terms, as deemed appropriate to the particular readership. For example, production data may be most understandable and useful to plant managers when expressed as daily tonnage, but for general management purposes the sales value or contribution of the output is more useful.

The following is an example of an exercise in the development of measures to convert non-financial values into monetary ones. **Table 18:1** and **Figure 18:7** below are complex documents, to interpret them fully requires detailed knowledge of the company and its operation. The reader is not expected to have this knowledge but they are included to demonstrate the potential of generating financial values (**Fig.18:7**) drawn from non-financial measures which most companies may produce as a matter of routine. The illustration relates to measurement of plant effectiveness. This measure is of key importance to the business owners, as an indicator of the relative efficiency of plant on this particular site. It is thus also useful as a leading indicator of problems with a particular plant, and the potential need for capital investment. From this standpoint of the business unit, the information is of importance in strategic planning.

Table 18:1 illustrates the components of the measure of plant effectiveness.

Overall effectiveness = operation time ratio x operation to performance ratio × quality ratio. That is, columns $T \times L \times H$.

In other words, production can be ineffective due to high levels of loading or downtime, excessive processing time or poor-quality output. Knowing the precise cause of the problem is the first step towards managing it.

Table 18:1 **Non-financial measures of plant effectiveness**

Note: Actual cycle times not specifically recorded, therefore standard times used in order to complete report

		Plant effectiveness		
January to March		Plant A	Plant B	Plant C
A	Running time Hrs	1872	1992	1928
B	Planned downtime Hrs	7040	397.25	159
C	Loading time Hrs (A–B)	1168	1594.75	1769
D	Downtime loss Hrs	25.5	70	29
E	Operating time Hrs (C–D)	1142.5	1524.75	1740
F	Actual processing time Hrs (J × G)	963.722	1608.78	1682.75
T	Operation time ratio (E/C × 100%)	97.8%	95.6%	98.4%
G	**Quantity processed**			
	Output kg (G1)	154.955	348.501	319.415
	Total input kg (G)	166.724	349.736	332.175
H	Quality ratio (G1/G)	0.93	1.00	0.96
I	Standard cycle time per kg	5.78	4.60	5.07
J	Actual cycle time per kg	5.78	4.60	5.07
L	Operation performance ratio (M × N %)	84.4%	105.6%	96.7%
M	Operating process ratio (I/J %)	100.0%	100.0%	100.0%
N	Net processing ratio (F/E %)	84.4%	105.5%	96.7%
	Number of minor stoppages	7	25	11
	Overall plant effectiveness (T × L × H)	76.7%	100.6%	91.5%

In order to show management the opportunity cost of any plant ineffectiveness, the management accountant at the site was given the task of formulating a model to value the cost of quality in each key plant. The idea was to be able to put a £ sign in front of the potential loss created by plant not being used effectively. The figure was viewed as being dependent on the state of demand for the plant's product. If demand exceeded capacity then the lost contribution was obviously far more significant that if the reverse was the case. **Figure 18:7** is an illustration of how the calculation was carried out for one particular plant. Some of the values here were not easy to generate, they cannot be established with the same accuracy or confidence as much of the traditional financial reporting which takes place. Indeed they are based on a number of assumptions which must be understood. However, they are an indication of the sort of values which need to be generated in order to evaluate various quality initiatives. It does require, of course, that executives are comfortable with the assumptions and the detail of the quality-costing data being provided.

Figure 18:7 **Generating financial measures from non-financial measures**

Notes: This document draws data from **Table 18:1** and other company sources
CM – contribution margin

Plant A	COQ calculation *January to March 20XX* *Additional relevant data*	
K	*Average cost of plant operative per hour*	£9.315
O	*Average shift hours*	8
P	*Number of working days in year*	232
Q	*Number of men per shift*	2
R	*Engineering tariff rate*	£19.26
S	*Average cost of materials per minor repair*	£10.54
U	*Overtime multiplier*	1.5
V	*Variable cost/kg*	£1.63
W	*Fixed cost/kg*	£0.95
X	*Disposal cost/kg*	£1.53
Y	*CM cost/kg*	£0.958
Z	*Capacity of plant at 100% operation (kg) 21 shift*	314,500
Z1	*Hours absenteeism*	36
Z2	*Throughput rate kg/hour*	156

		Costs of quality		
	Type of COQ	*Demand/capacity relationship*	*Formula*	*£COQ*
Availability		Demand>Capacity	B × Y × Z2	105,211.39
	Planned	Demand=Capacity	B × ((K × Q)×U)	19,673.28
	Downtime	Demand<Capacity	–	–
	Equipment	Demand>Capacity	D × Y × Z2	3,810.92
	Downtime	Demand<Capacity	D × ((Q × K)+R)+ (S) × No. of stoppages))	2,847.59
Efficiency	Plant Performance Efficiency	Demand>Capacity	(Z–G) × Y	141,569.41
Process Yield	Rate of Good Product ALL		(G–G1) × (V+W+X)	48,370.59
	COQ production plant effectiveness demand>capacity			298,962.31
	COQ production plant effectiveness demand=capacity			68,043.87
	COQ production plant effectiveness demand<capacity			51,218.18
	Absenteeism	Z1 × (K × U)		503.01

The financial controller likened the accounting control and performance measurement to a chain linked by key performance indicators. Following the chain down allows the cause of weak performance to be identified. For example, one of the products made on the site showed a low contribution margin. The reason was that the plant had abnormally high reject levels. At the same time, figures revealed that the maintenance spend versus replacement value of plant was high. In other words the root cause of the low contribution margin was old capital equipment in need of replacement. Before the introduction of detailed quality costing, reject rates by individual plant were not collected and thus the causal chain was incomplete.

18:3.1.2 Cost of Quality/Evaluating the Financial Impact of TQM

In aggregate, the management accounting department has calculated that the quality programme has produced substantial financial benefits by undertaking an evaluation of the costs that have been saved, or the extra revenue generated, by its implementation. An example is summarised in **Table 18:2**. This information was instrumental in generating and maintaining the momentum of the programme. First, it enabled an estimate to be made of the potential benefits if time, money and effort were expended in improving performance. Second, as a cumulative report, it demonstrated to senior management the financial benefits of the initiative. The financial controller clarified their approach: 'Our aim is to identify how much our quality initiative has added to the bottom line. We do this by posing the question, what would results look like if there had been no such initiative?'.

The main saving, as **Table 18:2** shows, is in the form of a reduction in lost time. The reduction shown has an estimated cumulative value of £1.859m, which is valued at the contribution margin per £ of labour cost. This assumes that the lost time represented production time that could have increased the total contribution. The assumption is valid in this instance, but would need to be reappraised if production/demand conditions changed.

A second key area of cost saving is in the reduction in stock levels. A stock-control project led to huge reductions in the overall level of stock, as well as the figures for substandard stock. Over the four-year period the table shows the value of the total stock holding falling to 50% of their original level, and substandard stocks reaching less than 5% of the original figure. In both cases, the financial effect takes the form of an interest saving, assumed in the illustration to be 10%.

Table 18:2 **A summary of company TQM achievements**

Notes:

NR – Net revenue

QDI – Quality defect investigations (i.e. reported non-conformances)

CM – Contribution margin

TQM Achievements to December 20XX

Item	(A) Before TQM	(B) Dec 20XX	(C) Dec 20XX	(D) Dec 20XX	£K effect (A to D)
Substandard stock	£330K	£105K	£16K	£16K	31.4
Total stock less substandard stock	£7.2M	£4.5M	£5.1M	£3.6M	360.0
Stock as % NR	12.3%	8%	9.3%	6.7%	N/A
Lost time	18%	13.4%	9.2%	7.3%	1,859.0
Effluent pass rate	50%	56%	86.2%	95%	*
QDIs received as % of orders	0.6%	0.4%	0.4%	0.4%	6.0 #
Chemical yields (CM effect of increase)	—	£181K	£2K	£106K	289.0
Recycling archival storage files	X	X	£1.2K	£1.2K	2.4
Inventory accuracy	43%	95%	95%	95%	#
					£2,547.8K

The company points out that the cumulative figure for savings does not directly take account of the revenue gains from improved quality, because they take the view that such benefits are too difficult to quantify in their situation of industrial marketing. In other words they have not revealed and reported the 'hidden' cost of quality. Any drop in customer complaints, due to the reduction in the volume of substandard production has not been directly incorporated. But over the longer term that should translate into greater customer loyalty and possibly increased market share, with the associated opportunity to charge higher prices for premium quality. Similarly, the very low stock accuracy levels which existed previously could have caused customer dissatisfaction, and the improvements in this regard will result in better customer relations. These performance improvements will thus create revenue gains, but being conservative the company has decided to omit this. This is an aspect that the company could consider developing if it wishes to take forward, still further, its quality initiative.

18:3.2 Case B

This relates to a financial services company. It is recognised as a leader in the field in which it operates, indeed it was referred to the author as such by another company in the same sector. It categorises its quality management approach as containing a triple focus: quality improvement, customer care, and quality assurance. These capture the aspects of performance which the company believes are 'key to improved profitability', though it was observed that each element cannot be easily separated. In particular it identified areas for potential improvement as:

(a) *error reduction – reducing costs and customer complaints; and*
(b) *improved response speed – to customer requests for services or changing customer circumstances.*

There is perhaps a more market than cost management dimension given the nature of the business.

The quality programme is given high visibility in the company, and support from all levels of the management structure. One key feature of the company's approach is that all quality projects start with a cost audit. This is used to compute the visible costs of errors, poor records, rework, etc. In other words, the failure costs within any single process. This then marks a base point against which to measure performance improvements, in both financial and non-financial terms.

Analysing the effects of the quality programme with reference to the cost elements in the profit equation, the case revealed:

(a) *In one key area of business, a change in the processing system used for financial transactions led to reduced operating costs and productivity increases which yielded £1.1m per year.*
(b) *Rationalisation of the supplier base and tighter management of deliveries led to stock savings of £0.5m over a three-year period and the elimination of overtime working which generated realised savings of a further £26,000 per year.*

18:3.2.1 Market-based Evaluation

Taking a market-based perspective quarterly, surveys of 3,600 customers are used to measure perceived quality of service. The company believes that the increase in customer satisfaction should lead to a large increase in long-term profitability and market share. Long-term customers are generally more profitable, particularly because of cross-selling opportunities, and because they result in reduced costs while retaining market share. This situation created an opportunity for market-orientated quality costing which the company is still developing.

Its approach to evaluating customer-orientated improvements was outlined to the author as follows. **Figure 18:8** shows the market-orientated figures which the company was using in its deliberations to reveal the revenue implications of quality improvement. Dividing the annual income A by the number of customers B reveals the average annual income per customer C. Taking an average number of dissatisfied customers as 10%, and this can be confirmed by surveys, the total of dissatisfied customers is shown at D. Working on the assumption that 50% of dissatisfied customers will switch will reveal a loss of 12,500 customers nationwide, F. The average annual income per customer of £80 can be applied to this number to deduce a total of lost revenue G of £1,000,000.

The above approach can be expanded, for example, if dissatisfied customers spread this 'negative word of mouth' to another 24, the total number aware is now 300,000 in this illustration. If as a result only 1 in 40 buys elsewhere this represents 7,500 lost potential customers, or average lost revenue of £600,000, J.

The figures are indicative only of the thinking of the company, and represent a model only for one part of its business. They suggest that some of the estimates are particularly conservative, for example, one retail chain works on the assumption of negative word of mouth of 1 dissatisfied customer tells 100. Nevertheless they form the basis of justifying investment in staff training and ensuring that appropriate time is spent dealing with the customer. They also place into sharp relief some of the costs of attracting new customers (i.e. customer replacement costs). It is well known within service business that the most cost-efficient way to sell is through retaining existing customers.

Figure 18:8 **Revenue implications of quality improvement**

Lost customer revenue	
A Annual income	£20,000,000
B Total number of customers	250,000
C Average annual income per customer (A/B)	£80
D Number of dissatisfied customers (assume 10%)	25,000
E Percentage of dissatisfied customers likely to switch	50
F Number of dissatisfied customers who will switch (D × E)	12,500
G Revenue lost through 'switching' (C × F)	£1,000,000
Lost opportunity revenue	
H Number of people whom dissatisfied customers will tell (F × 24)	300,000
I Number of potential customers who buy elsewhere owing to negative word of mouth (assume 1:40)	7,500
J Potential lost revenue p.a.	£600,000

The accountant who was proactive in the generation of performance measures and cost of quality reports in this company, observed:

> People don't realise the size of the problem or the potential benefits until they are measured financially. It is putting some concrete evidence behind management hunch – you can be more hard headed – you can prove it. But you have to think beyond the boundaries of much of the accounting you have been doing for the past ten years. Measures and targets have to be developed and you have to think laterally.

It is only with data such as the above that the company feels it can support the notion that satisfied customers will recommend your business and do more business with you, whereas dissatisfied customers will deter new business, and customer defections will undermine your profitability.

18:4 The Accountant's Role in Quality Costing

18:4.1 Involvement

In dealings with some companies it has been apparent that a quality initiative is progressed without the active involvement of accounting personnel. This is unfortunate because there is potential for accounting to be supportive of the initiative with the provision of data related to cost reduction initiatives, analysis of existing and potential product profitability or contribution to fixed costs, the implications of increased plant efficiency, market share improvement or the costs of increased capacity. The above information should be imparted to and requires liaison with the appropriate non-accounting executives who have responsibility for the issue under discussion. The tendency for these executives from other functional areas to generate their own financial information to evaluate and monitor the quality initiative should be discouraged and is inappropriate. It could lead to the use of inappropriate cost data and misinterpretation of the financial impact of decisions.

Having said this, there is also responsibility on the accountant to ensure that the routine costing and reporting systems do reflect the quality or process improvements made. In other words the financial results should not generate distorted messages, the impact of good ideas should be clear. In many areas the accountant is unlikely to lead the whole project because where improvement in say production line layout or with the application of statistical process control are involved others will have a more intimate acquaintance with the system being developed. However, the accountant should be involved to ensure accuracy and appropriateness of the financial data being used in the analysis.

18:4.2 Systems

Costing and accounting systems generally exist to identify costs of products for stock valuation purposes, for pricing and other decisions and for costing of departments within a system of responsibility accounting. It is likely therefore that any cost of quality will be an extraction from the accounts undertaken on an *ad hoc* basis. It is possible to set up a routine for the reporting of the cost of quality and it is desirable that this analysis is reported regularly so management can keep its 'eye on the ball'. But such costs will be extracted from the accounting/costing routine which is established in the company, perhaps for other purposes. By its very nature such analysis involves the extraction of relevant costs and revenues applicable to particular circumstances. Emphasis is therefore placed on collecting data that may not be a part of the normal accounting or (standard) costing system (*see* **Ch.16**, especially **para.16:5**). The use of other data to identify costs of downtime or reworking, errors in documents and customer complaints will all assist in identifying quality costs.

Costs with full overhead absorption [*cf. SSAP9: Stocks and Long-Term Contracts; IAS2: Inventories*] should be treated with care because of the inherent approximation contained in full-cost figures and because they may contain some fixed costs irrelevant to short-term analysis. In such cases the fully absorbed cost may overstate the benefit from a quality improvement. Data drawn from systems established for other purposes inevitably contain approximations which exist within the system and the accountant must not lose sight of this.

A major problem for many companies is the lack of effective identification of the external failure costs as this is often difficult to measure. Assigning the loss of profit per sale and multiplying by a factor that represents the loss of goodwill in the marketplace could be used. This approach evidenced in the example above shows accounting having to recognise a softer side to some data projection and this is an area of work into which accounting may find it is increasingly drawn in the future.

18:4.3 Supporting Strategy
(*See* **Ch.2**.)

One of the reasons for the limited success of some quality initiatives is that they may often be mounted as a programme, separate from any business strategy and hence are not evaluated or controlled on a cost-benefit basis. Some organisations implement quality initiatives as an 'act of faith' and then have trouble continuing such initiatives because any assessment of their success is arbitrary, limited or non-existent. Involvement of accountants in generating appropriate internal and external cost of quality reports and integrating/reconciling these with the periodic financial results is one way in which they can contribute to the quality programme. To do this they need to be more creative and open to new ideas of generating and presenting quality data, to some extent the detail and presentation is limited only by the ingenuity of the accountant and the management involved.

Acknowledgement

Insights for this chapter are drawn from my collaborative work with Margaret Woods and Derek Seary of Loughborough University Business School.

References

Dale, B. (Ed.) (1994) *Managing quality*. Prentice Hall.

Dallio, A., Khan, Z. and Vail, C. (1995) 'Cost of quality in the new manufacturing environment', *Management Accounting (USA)*, August: 20–5.

Tayles, M., Woods, M. and Seary, D.(1996) 'The costing of process quality: Opportunities for new accounting practices' *Management Accounting (UK)*, November: 28–30.

19. Product Life-cycle Costing

19:1 Definition

Management accountants have tended to concentrate on costs during the manufacturing stage of a product's production life cycle and during the maturity phase of its marketing life cycle. Shields and Young (1991) cite references that support the view that life-cycle costing was developed by the Department of Defense in the USA in the early 1960s to improve government purchasing. However, during the past 30 years other organisations have developed product life-cycle costing. Nevertheless, there are still relatively few examples available of product life-cycle costing. The basic idea behind product life-cycle costing is to consider costs throughout a product's life cycle. This raises two basic questions:

1. *What is a product?*
2. *What is the life cycle?*

19:1.1 Products and Product Platforms

Before an organisation can start product life-cycle costing, it must decide how it is going to define a product. In some cases this may be clear cut. However, in some organisations the current trend is not to develop a single product at a time but to attempt to develop a product platform such as a product which will lead to the development of a series of other products (*see* **Ch.8, para.8:5**). It is possible, therefore, to develop the product life-cycle costing for a well-defined series of related products. Generally, of course, this will mean calculating the product platform life-cycle cost over a much longer period than for a single product.

19:1.2 Product Life Cycles

There are different types of product life cycles which need to be distinguished from the life cycle of an industry. Four such product life cycles will be outlined namely:

1. *marketing;*
2. *production;*
3. *customer;*
4. *society.*

19:1.2.1 Marketing Product Life Cycle

This is probably the most widely known of the product life cycles and is often used in product life-cycle costing. The different stages in the marketing product life cycle can be classified as:

- analysis;

- start-up;

- growth;

- maturity;

- decline;

- withdrawal.

This chapter will, as its title suggests, concentrate on the cost aspect of the product life cycle. However, product life-cycle costing can be combined with product life-cycle sales to give a very useful integrated technique which is particularly appropriate when the marketing product life cycle is being used. Marketing is usually the source of estimates of product life-cycle sales but management accountants can play a useful role in integrating product life-cycle sales and costs perhaps as a member of a product life-cycle team.

19:1.2.2 Production Product Life Cycle

From a cost point of view management accountants are familiar with the production product life cycle. The different stages in the product life cycle from a production point of view can be classified as:

- idea;

- planning;

- design;

- development;

- prototype;

- process development;

- manufacturing;

- logistics;

- disposal.

Very often the above nine stages are collapsed into fewer stages with idea, planning, design and development being classified simply as the design stage (*see* **Ch.42**).

However, many stages are included, the basic idea behind this product life cycle is to consider costs throughout a product's life cycle from the idea stage for a new (or updated) product to the final disposal stage for a product. This is a very different way of examining costs. There are already examples where, by considering the possible future costs of the disposal of products by the manufacturer, manufacturers have changed the design and materials for new products.

At present relatively few manufacturers have responsibility for disposing of the products which they manufacture. However, a number of industries can anticipate that in the future they may have a legal responsibility imposed on them to dispose of their products safely and in an environmentally friendly manner. One way of coping with such expected, future changes is to introduce product life-cycle costing. Nevertheless, product life-cycle costing has a much wider application than just considering disposal costs. It is the overall approach of considering costs over the entire life cycle of a product.

19:1.2.3 Customer Product Life Cycle

Many existing product life-cycle costing examples in practice include only the costs which the manufacturer incurs. The costs which customers incur are ignored. However, an all-inclusive view of product life-cycle costing would include the costs incurred both by the manufacturer and the customer. The reason for this is that for some products, a very important factor affecting the purchase decision by customers is the customers's product life-cycle costs which include:

(a) purchase price;
(b) installation costs;
(c) operating costs;
(d) support costs;
(e) maintenance costs;
(f) disposal costs.

For products where the above costs (b) to (f) are significant, it is important that manufacturers include these customers' costs in their product life-cycle costing. For example, for a product (such as a machine) with an expected life of ten years, customers may be willing to pay a higher purchase price for a product which has lower installation, operating, support, maintenance and disposal costs. Manufacturers need to consider such possible trade-offs when designing their products. Concentrating simply on the manufacturer's costs is inadequate for the life-cycle costing of certain products. The manufacturer's and the customers' costs need to be integrated into one product life-cycle cost.

19:1.2.4 Society Product Life Cycle

If relatively few product life-cycle costing examples include the customers' costs as well as the manufacturer's costs, even fewer include the costs which society incurs. The society product life-cycle costs include:

(a) additional environmental costs (such as pollution costs);
(b) additional health costs;
(c) lost time costs;
(d) disposal costs.

Obviously in some instances such society product life-cycle costs can be extremely sensitive.

19:1.2.5 Combination of Product Life Cycle

It is important at the beginning of the product life-cycle costing exercise to define both the product and the product life cycle. It is not, of course, necessary to choose only one of the above product life cycles. Indeed it would be possible to combine the marketing, production, customer and society product life cycles and to attempt an all-inclusive costing of these combined product life cycles. Whatever product life cycle is chosen, it is critical that a great deal of effort is concentrated on the early design stage for new or revised products (*see* **Ch.42**). A theme of this Handbook is that 60% to 90% of costs are committed during the design stage and management accountants need, therefore, to give a great deal of attention to these pre-production stages in the product life cycle both for costing and cost-management purposes (*see* **Ch.27**). The rest of this chapter will concentrate on the production product life-cycle costing for illustrative purposes.

19:1.3 Length of Product Life Cycle

The type of product life cycle is one problem but the above five of marketing, production, customer, society and combination all have one problem in common, namely how to determine the length of the product life cycle. Generally this is a subjective estimate based on experience. It is important that a range of opinions are sought both from different functional managers within the organisation and from a range of different types of customer. Other bases can also be used to estimate the length of product life cycles such as durability calculations. It is also possible to do sensitivity analysis on the length of the product life cycle and this can be combined with the cost estimates associated with different possible product life cycles.

19:2 Costs

19:2.1 Target Costs
(*See* **Ch.24**.)

It can be difficult to estimate costs for one year ahead, but even more difficult to estimate product life-cycle costs over a period of several years. By definition forecast product life-cycle costs will be wrong because we cannot forecast the future accurately. Nevertheless, this does not mean that we should ignore product life-cycle costing. One important advantage of product life-cycle costing is that when unexpected changes occur, an organisation will have a basis on which such changes can be examined. In other words product life costing is dynamic rather than static. During the design stage for a new or revised product, its life-cycle costs will be estimated on the basis of the information available at the point in time. When circumstances change, a product's life-cycle costs need to be revised.

In their examination of nine organisations using product life-cycle costing, Shields and Young (1991) found that existing cost accounting systems are not effective for this purpose. This raises the question of what system would be effective. One possible system is target costing or target cost management (*see* **Ch.24**). The main advantage of target costing is that, instead of starting with an organisation's own costs and building these up to calculate a unit product cost and eventually a product life-cycle cost, target costing begins with the market and works back to a required target cost to be achieved. By using target costing, product life-cycle costing becomes a cost management technique rather than just a costing technique because almost certainly the target cost will be a lower cost than the existing estimated cost for a product and the question is how to achieve the target product life-cycle cost.

19:2.2 Manufacturer's and Customers' Costs

At the very least before calculating only the manufacturer's product life-cycle costs it is important to check that the customers' costs are relatively insignificant. Undoubtedly the best approach is to have a product life-cycle cost which considers both the manufacturer's and the customers' costs. Particularly at the design stage it is necessary to consider trade-offs. For example, customers may be willing to pay a higher selling price for a product which has lower lifetime costs for the customer. The manufacturer needs to consider such a trade-off between increased costs and increased selling price against lower costs for customers.

19:2.3 Development and Design Costs
(*See* **Chs 8** and **42**.)

One advantage of taking a product life-cycle costing view is that it emphasises the critical importance of development and design costs [*cf. SSAP13: Accounting for Research and Development; IAS38; Intangibles*]. There will almost certainly be some development and design (or redesign) costs throughout the production product life cycle but usually most development and design costs are incurred during the planning, design, development, prototype and process development stages. Similarly most development and design costs will be incurred during the analysis, start-up, entry and growth stages of the marketing product life cycle.

Concentrating on the production life cycle, many organisations have found that cutting back on development and design costs has in the end been short-sighted because of the additional costs incurred during later stages in the product life cycle. By taking a product life-cycle view, these development and design costs are more likely to be viewed in terms of an investment decision rather than simply as a revenue expenditure decision.

19:2.3.1 Time to Market

This chapter is concentrating on the cost aspect of the product life cycle but the non-financial aspects of the product life cycle (such as functions of the product required by the customer, quality and time to market) must not be forgotten. One advantage of combining product life-cycle sales and costs is that sometimes this illustrates the crucial factor of time to the market. The first organisation to launch its new product in certain markets may be the one to capture the market. In such a context it is important that a desire to cut development and design costs does not delay the product reaching the market. As usual, top management needs to consider possible trade-offs between costs and non-financial performance measures.

19:2.4 Advertising Costs

By taking a product life-cycle view, it is possible to plan advertising costs over the life of a product. For example, in the example above where being first to the market is critical, the highest advertising costs may be planned for the start-up stage in the marketing product life cycle. In other circumstances, the greatest advertising costs may be planned for the growth stage.

19:2.5 Capital Investment Costs
(*See* Ch.11.)

Again a plan for capital investment should fit with the product life cycle. Usually the start-up and growth stages in the marketing product life cycle will involve the highest level of capital expenditure. Mention of capital investment is also an appropriate time to mention product life-cycle cash flows. Product life-cycle sales, costs and profits are important but so are product life-cycle cash flows. Just as product life-cycle costs need to be managed so do product life-cycle cash flows.

19:2.6 Material, Labour and Overhead Costs

Management accountants will usually have most experience in estimating material, labour and overhead costs. However, the timescale of perhaps many years over the length of a product life cycle may be a new experience. Some organisations have experience of using learning curves but such curves have usually been applied on a relatively short-term basis. As usual management accountants will wish to concentrate their efforts on the areas of greatest expenditure. If labour costs are relatively insignificant, the concentration will be on material and overhead costs.

Continuous improvement of the product and also major redesigns of the product during its life cycle will need to be taken into account. Input from suppliers will be important for materials. A value chain approach (*see* **Ch.40**) may be useful. Similarly will outsourcing or subcontracting (*see* **Ch.38**) be used? If cost tables (*see* **Ch.26**) are available, these should be a very useful tool for product life-cycle costing.

For overhead costs, activity-based budgeting (*see* **Ch.13**) may be helpful. Again major changes in overhead costs can be anticipated during the life cycle of most products. For example, business process re-engineering (*see* **Ch.32**) may be planned either at the beginning of or during the product life cycle.

For all costs benchmarking (*see* **Ch.53**) can be another useful tool in product life-cycle costing. If benchmarking information is available, areas for cost reduction can be highlighted and included in the product life-cycle cost.

19:3 Estimated Costs

In their case studies of nine organisations using target costing Shields and Young (1991) found that product life-cycle costs were estimated by one of the following methods or a combination of these:

(a) *analogy;*
(b) *industrial engineering models;*
(c) *parametric models.*

19:3.1 Analogy Method

This simply involves taking a similar product and using the costs of that similar product as the basis for estimating the product life-cycle costs of the new product. Obviously, adjustments are made for differences between the two products and the comparative basis is very much a starting point. One problem is that old inefficiencies may be perpetuated by this method. One way to overcome such a problem is to combine the analogy method with target costing. The target cost is based on the market and the analogy method gives an internal cost. These two external and internal costs can then be used as a basis for determining the product life-cycle costs.

19:3.2 Industrial Engineering Method

For management accountants this method will probably be the most familiar of the three suggested methods of estimating costs. Estimated material quantities and prices are used to estimate the material costs during a product life cycle. It is, of course, quite possible that during the product life-cycle changes are planned to the material specifications for a product and the product life-cycle costs would take such proposed changes into account.

Estimates will also be made of labour times and rates so that direct labour costs over the product life cycle can be calculated. Aspects such as the short-term learning curve and longer-term proposed changes to the process and level of automation would all be taken into account when arriving at the final labour costs.

Many organisations still use direct labour hours as a basis for calculating overhead costs. If overheads are a relatively small percentage of total costs or if overhead costs are actually driven by volume of output (for which direct labour costs hours are a surrogate), this basis may be adequate for product life-cycle costing purposes. However, some organisations are now using an activity-based approach (*see* **Ch.22**) for estimating their overhead costs. One reason for this is that the activity-based approach usually gives managers a better understanding of what drives their overhead costs and this is useful when estimating product life-cycle costs.

19:3.3 Parametric Models

This method uses non-linear regression models with the dependent variable being the product life-cycle cost. Cost information from current products is used and this may help to determine the other variables which should be included in the models. Examples of such variables include:

- design complexity;

- bulkiness;

- weight;

- performance.

This is a fairly specialist area and, if you are starting from scratch, expert advice would be a good starting point.

19:4 Cost Management
(*See* Ch.27.)

Product life-cycle costing is in the costing section of this Handbook but one reason for calculating product life-cycle costs is for cost management purposes. For example, if a target costing approach is used the really difficult question is how are the product life-cycle costs to be achieved during the various stages of that product life cycle. Even if a target costing approach is not used, one question is how can the costs be reduced during the product life cycle. For many organisations the most significant cost management decisions are taken during the design and development phase. Some possible cost management techniques are discussed in the following section.

19:4.1 Cost Management Techniques

Some of the most successful cost management techniques involve a team composed of individuals from different backgrounds within the organisation such as design, engineering, marketing, production, purchasing and accounting. One such technique is functional cost analysis (*see* Ch.25). For example, once the target cost for a product is set (perhaps for different stages in its life cycle), functional cost analysis is one technique which can be used to achieve that target cost. The basic idea is to segment the product's target cost into a number of target costs to be achieved for each function of a product. This enables different teams to use their creativity to achieve a particular function of a product for a specific target cost.

A related cost management technique to functional cost analysis is design to cost. Again the basic idea is for the teams to design parts or components of a product within a specific cost target at each stage in the product's life cycle. The technique of using standard parts for different products is another technique which can reduce a product's life-cycle costs.

Another design cost management technique is design to manufacture or design to assembly (*see* **Ch.42**). In the past some organisations have found that their designers did not really understand the problems of manufacturing or assembling the product. The designers 'threw the product over the wall to manufacturing'. Design to manufacture or design to assembly try to ensure that designers consider the needs of manufacturing or assembling the product during the design process. This is another example where a cross-functional design team may be useful.

Assuming that product life-cycle costs include the customers' costs in addition to the producer's costs, then cost management techniques such as design for reliability and design for service are important. Additional costs for the producer may increase the reliability of the product and so reduce the customers' costs. Indeed even with the same producer's costs but with a different design it may be possible to improve the product's reliability over its life cycle. Similarly, by considering the problems of maintaining or servicing a product during the design process, it may be possible to reduce the customers' future costs during the life cycle of the product.

Usually the greatest cost management benefits are derived during the design and development stages of a product's life cycle. However, this does not mean that cost management is ignored during the other stages of a product's life cycle (*see* **Ch.27** on cost management). The purchasing of materials, the management of stock, use of production capacity, use of technology, the management of overhead costs (*see* **Ch.28** for activity-based cost management) and the control of quality are some of the cost management aspects during other stages in a product's life cycle.

19:5 Conclusions

Product life-cycle costing is a different way of looking at a product's costs. It is not easy and those organisations with experience of product life-cycle costing are still learning. The most appropriate measure of costs is to include both the manufacturer's and the customers' costs. A major advantage of product life-cycle costing is that it illustrates the influence of the design and development stage on the costs of a product throughout its life cycle.

It is difficult to estimate both the length of the product life cycle and the costs during each stage although techniques are available to assist with such estimates. For cost management purposes, various techniques are useful particularly during the design stage of a product such as target costing, functional cost analysis, design to cost, design to manufacture and design for reliability. Product life-cycle costing is a useful long-term costing and cost-management approach.

Reference

Shields, M.D. and Young, S.M. (1991) 'Managing product life cycle costs: An organizational model', *Journal of Cost Management*, Fall: 39–52.

20. **Contract Costing**

20:1 Principal Features

The Chartered Institute of Management Accountants defines contract costing, in its *Official Terminology* as: 'A form of specific order costing: attribution of costs to individual contracts'. The following characteristics will usually be found with this type of costing as against other methods:

(a) *a formal contract will, or should, be in place between supplier and customer;*

(b) *it is a form of job costing which usually takes much longer than most jobs, so may well cover a number of accounting periods, or even years;*

(c) *specific financial methods will be utilised to account for periodic revenue and profits, which are usually governed by national rules or standards;*

(d) *the work is frequently based on the customer's site, which may include its dedicated management and administrative support;*

(e) *a separate account is normally maintained for each contract, where all direct costs and apportioned overheads are charged. The contract price is credited to the account, so that it effectively becomes an individual profit and loss account;*

(f) *construction and other civil engineering work have traditionally been the main forms to which contract costing relates, but recent years have seen extensions into services, previously provided in-house by organisations (see **Ch.38**), to external providers with innovative contractual needs and thus new contract-costing methods.*

A key to the costing method is therefore the contract, its terms and financial requirements.

Michael Johnson

20:2 The Contract and Concepts of Risk and Reward

20:2.1 Definition

A commercial contract may be defined as 'a mutually binding relationship enforceable by law, stating the mutual assent of two or more parties to do something for a financial consideration'.

The types of contracts that may be found depend very much upon the degree to which cost, time, performance and profit are linked to the nature of the commercial arrangement [*cf. SSAP9: Stocks and Long-Term Contracts; IAS11: Construction Contracts*]. A major element of this is the balancing of risk and reward.

20:2.2 Risk and Reward

The reward to the contractor will be influenced by the amount of perceived risk, that is the higher the risk that the contractor is expected to meet, then the higher the reward that the contractor will expect to receive. In practice, where risk is deemed to be high both for its frequency and impact, the customer normally bears this risk, supporting a standard cost reimbursable (or 'time and materials') type of contract. For low-risk projects, the contractor is more likely to bear the risk with a fixed-cost type of contract preferred. An example of the former may be an innovative oil construction project in a frontier zone, while a standard road development may typify the latter.

A third major category has emerged in recent years, where various concepts of sharing risk and reward have been created, to be known as incentive or target-cost contracts, frequently as part of long-term 'alliancing' relationships.

20:3 Types of Contracts

A wide range of contracts can be found in the modern business environment; three main categories are focused upon in this chapter. These adequately illustrate the various costing issues that may be encountered.

20:3.1 Fixed or Firm-price Contracts

The main features for these types of contracts are as follows:

1. *The prospective purchaser (or engineer on his behalf) prepares a specification, drawings, conditions of contract, etc., stating requirements.*
2. *One or more prospective contractors then tender for the works, accepting the risks inherent in estimating their direct and indirect costs, regardless of later problems that may be encountered. The price is defined for a specific work requirement and will not vary.*
3. *If the work requirement is changed by the customer, within certain specified limits, the supplier is entitled to change the price and probably the time allowed to perform the contract.*
4. *The accuracy of cost estimating and the efficiency of contract performance are crucial to the success of the business. The supplier/contractor is at maximum risk, needing to absorb any cost overruns. It is therefore often the preferred method for clients.*
5. *In these contracts, the customer has usually agreed to pay most of the contract price in a lump sum on completion, less a retention, for payment at a later date. This would be combined with stage or milestone payments for the longer-period contracts.*

20:3.2 Cost Reimbursable Contracts

These contracts, also known as *cost plus* or *time and materials*, are more popular with the contractor, who is guaranteed to have all costs recovered, providing that the contract requirements, as specified, are met:

1. *The customer pays the contractor the costs incurred for the work, plus an additional amount as a fee for profit and general costs of the contract, such as management overheads and business risk.*
2. *The term 'reimbursable costs' means that the cost of performing the work of the contract is received by the contractor as a direct reimbursement. Indirect reimbursement through fixed rates may also be included for items such as contractor's offices, computer costs and reproduction. This distinction is important for costing purposes, both for charging the customer and for internal profitability assessment.*

3. These contracts usually require the contractor to give the customer access to all accounts, so that costs can be verified. Payment is usually made at set intervals (e.g. monthly or quarterly).

4. Where the profit is a predetermined percentage, absolute profit increases as costs increase. Although this type of contract gives full protection to the contractor, there is a distinct disadvantage to the customer in that there is no monetary incentive for the contractor to reduce costs or improve efficiency in any way.

5. Where the profit is a predetermined sum of money, the supplier/contractor's profit is reduced in percentage terms as costs increase. Again, there is no incentive to the contractor for cost and efficiency drives, but at least there is not an incentive to increase costs, unlike the previous method!

20:3.3 Incentive or Target Cost Contracts

There has been an increasing trend in recent years for the contractor to take a significant share of the risks, in return for a potentially improved share of the rewards.

1. The incentive contracts are designed to put pressure on the contractor to strive for an improved performance, by cost, time or quality, while still receiving some protection against uncertainties. This benefit will be shared by the customer and contractor according to the terms of the contract.

2. The most common form of incentive contract relates to cost only, for example, the customer and contractor may agree:

   (a) a target cost for the work;
   (b) how each will share the savings or contribute to overspends;
   (c) to establish a target fee, that which the contractor will earn if actual costs equal target.

The customer therefore agrees to pay the actual costs plus the target fee to the contractor. The fee will be increased or decreased in relation to the cost performance, their respective shares being known as the *share ratio* and agreed in negotiation.

An example of this type of contract is shown in **Figure 20:1**.

Figure 20:1 **Contractor share of profit in an incentive contract**

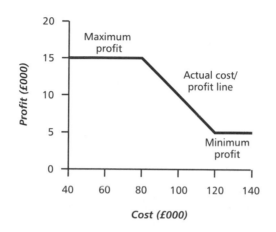

Cost-plus incentive contract

This illustrates the amount of profit that will be gained by the contractor over a range of contract costs. Below £80,000 costs, the profit to the contractor is fixed at £15,000. Between cost levels of £80,000 and £120,000, the contractor's profit is increased by £1,250 for every £5,000 saved. Above the cost level of £120,000, the customer bears the impact of these costs with the contractor maintaining a guaranteed minimum fee of £5,000.

20:4 Revenue and Profit Attribution (Recognition)

20:4.1 Standard Guidelines

Contracts frequently cover a considerable period of time, thus leading to the need for a specific process to attribute or recognise profits for each accounting period. This has been addressed in the UK by the Statement of Standard Accounting Practice for Stocks and Long-term Contracts (SSAP 9), with the following significant points, taken from paragraphs 7 to 11:

(a) **Profit attribution** *should be based on a fair financial view of the activities of the company during the year. If the recording of turnover and taking profit into account is deferred to contract completion, the profit and loss accounts for long-term contracts will, in any year, reflect the results of contracts that have been completed in that year only. It is therefore appropriate to take credit for ascertainable turnover and profit while contracts are in progress.*

(b) **Turnover** *should be ascertained in a manner appropriate to the stage of completion of the contract for the businesses and the industries concerned.*

(c) **Where the outcome for a long-term contract can reasonably be assessed,** *the attributable profit should be calculated on a prudent basis and included in the accounts for the period under review. The profit taken up needs to reflect the proportion of work carried out at the accounting date and to take into account any known inequalities of profitability in the various stages of the contract. The procedure to recognise profit is to include an appropriate proportion of total contract value as turnover in the profit and loss account as the contract activity progresses. The costs incurred in reaching that stage of completion are matched with this turnover, resulting in the reporting of results that can be attributed to the proportion of work completed.*

(d) **Where the outcome of long-term contracts cannot be assessed** *with reasonable certainty before the conclusion of the contract, no profit should be reflected in the profit and loss account in respect of those contracts, although, in such circumstances, if no loss is expected it may be appropriate to show as turnover a proportion of the total contract value using a zero estimate of profit.*

(e) *If it is expected that there will be a* **loss on a contract** *as a whole, all of the loss should be recognised as soon as it is foreseen (in accordance with the prudence concept).*

In summary, the major accounting principles prudence and matching are emphasised. Matching is to the extent of ensuring that reasonable levels of profit are recognised in relation to the work performed, but on a prudent basis.

20:4.2 Revenue and Profit or Loss Calculations

For practical purposes, contracts may be divided into two main categories; construction or other civil engineering with a clearly defined end product, and ongoing service provision contracts.

(a) *Contracts entered into for the design, manufacture or construction of a single asset frequently progress with a degree of uncertainty as to their effectiveness in meeting full contract specification. In their early stages, no profit should be taken in accordance with the prudence principle.*

(b) *Project losses, once recognised should be added to the cost of sales, in the period in which they are incurred. Anticipated losses should also be accounted for and entered into the balance sheet as 'provision or accrual for anticipated losses', that is, dr. project cost account, cr. provision.*

(c) *Where the project is well progressed and the size of the profit is reasonably ascertainable, anticipated profit is usually calculated as:*

$$\frac{cash\ received}{contract\ price} \quad \times \quad estimated\ contract\ profit$$

Taking the cash received basis would be deemed to be more prudent than accepting profit for all work certified, as identified by the contract engineers at any point of time.

(d) *At an intermediate position of the contract, the following formula is often used to determine the attributable profit to date:*

$$2/3 \times notional\ profit \times \frac{cash\ received}{value\ of\ work\ certified}$$

(e) *For ongoing service contracts, revenues and hence profits may be recognised on each part of the contract as it progresses. This is referred to in SSAP 9, paragraph 22. Effectively, work completed will be invoiced periodically and may be included in the profit and loss account. However, any future contract profit-sharing or reward arrangements should not be accounted for, until actually realised. A clearly expected loss, in contrast, should be so recognised, again in line with the prudence principle.*

20:4.3 Progress Payments

Service contracts will effectively be paid by the customer, as incurred, with each month or other period being treated as an activity in its own right. For most construction and engineering work, projects are usually incomplete at any month end, so a progress payment mechanism will be implemented on an ongoing basis:

(a) as required under the terms of the contract;

(b) based on the value of the work done, maybe as a proportion of the contract price;

(c) as certified by the authorised person, such as an architect or surveyor for a building contract or a qualified engineer, as appropriate.

A certificate confirms that work to a certain value has been completed, so that a payment is due. This is usually calculated as:

value of work done and certified by the architect or engineer (at contract price basis),
less a retention (usually 10%)
less payments made to date
equals the payment due.

20:5 Contractor's Costing System

The contracting company will need to maintain its own cost accounting methods to meet the demands of the business. Much of the work is performed on the customer's site, but where work is carried out in the contractor's office, such as in design engineering or some service work, detailed costing systems may be required. This is particularly important for cost plus or incentive contracts, where the client has audit rights.

20:5.1 Direct Contract Costs

Contract costing is notable by its high proportion of direct charges. This may include costs that are normally associated with overheads, such as accountants and clerical staff, who for major contracts may be on site. The details will be discussed later (*see* **para.20:6**), but two specific internal costing features need to be noted for reimbursable and incentive contracts:

1. *Ensure that the contract terms are followed as to what is treated as a direct cost. A person's travel expenses may or may not be allowed to be charged to a reimbursable contract, depending on the purpose of the journey. Clear controls and records are therefore needed.*

2. *Materials and some services may be allowed as a cost plus a percentage uplift to allow for the contractor's administrative effort or superior purchasing power. An example is a computer support services provider, that also acquires equipment for the customer, via a separate agreement. The contractor shares the savings from the purchase (e.g. part of a trade discount), thus needing a specific accounting record. This is in contrast to most construction projects where all such costs are charged directly to the project.*

20:5.2 Internal Services

Modern service companies, with a range of contracts will tend to have a costing structure, along the lines shown in **Figure 20:2**.

Figure 20.2 **Service company cost model**

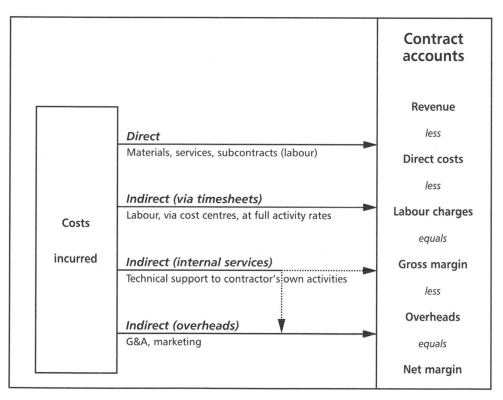

Variations will occur on the model shown in **Figure 20:2**, but the following essential features are usually found:

(a) **Direct costs** *are those described elsewhere (see* **Paras. 20:5.1** *and* **20:6***). Labour will be included in most civil engineering businesses, but may not be in services.*

(b) **Labour costs** *in service companies are often accumulated into a 'home' cost centre to which all salaries and related staff costs will form the basis for a charge out or 'activity' rate for the contracts worked on by the persons concerned, usually via a timesheet. This is the result of each staff group being associated with a number of projects, rather than a single contract.*

(c) **Internal services** *will occur where the contractor's own staff, who normally charge a contract, also support their own company. An organisation providing information technology (IT) services which maintains the IT needs of the rest of its own staff could find this to be a significant part of its business costs.*

20:5.3 Overheads

Overheads tend to be less significant than for most businesses, particularly where large construction projects predominate. The usual head office overheads will still need to be recovered, along with administrative functions that cannot be directly attributed to a particular contract. Rather than the use of subjective apportionment methods, costs such as marketing may be kept separate. Therefore, when contract prices are being negotiated, a contribution to these overheads needs to be considered.

20:6 Contract Cost Accounts

20:6.1 Features of Contract Costs

1. **Materials** *are usually ordered specifically for individual contracts so are costed directly from the supplier's invoices. Any materials required from stores will be obtained in the normal way by means of a stores requisition. (See* **para.20:5.1(2)** *for service company exceptions.)*

2. **Direct labour** *costs are again normally easily chargeable to the contract as most persons concerned are solely involved with that project or activity. All labour benefits and any overtime will usually be related directly to the contract. Therefore,*

all such costs should be straightforward to apply to the work concerned. Exceptions may be found in service industries where multiple contracts may be supported (see para.20:5.2(b)), so that timesheet allocations may be found.

3. **Overheads** *will be relatively low (see para.20:5.3), with the normally recognised production overheads being charged directly to the contract. The term 'direct cost' may be used in a contractual sense, as a contract recoverable item, rather than the strict accounting definition. On-site accountants are direct costs of the contract, and even head office persons may be defined as 'direct' where the contract allows. Both costs will be relatively fixed in relation to the level of activity.*

4. **Subcontract** *work will be treated as a normal contract cost. This is work done by specialist companies, such as plumbers for a building site or navigation experts in a shipyard. This element may form a significant part of the total contract cost. For target or incentive contracts, subcontract work may attract a specific mark-up which is different from that of the main contract work. If so, such costs will need to be separately identified, for profit calculation purposes.*

5. **Plant and machinery** *may be charged to a contract in one of two ways:*

   (a) for short periods of time, a rate per hour, day, etc. is calculated on the basis of usage time. A separate plant account is usually maintained for each category of equipment, debited with costs of maintenance, depreciation (or financing charge) and operating costs. A hire rate is then fixed and charged periodically to the contract, crediting the plant account;

   (b) for long periods of time, the contract is charged with the full plant value on arrival to the contract site and credited with the written-down value on departure. Costs that would be charged to a plant account (as above) would therefore be directed to the contract account;

6. **Incidental income or jobbing work**, *such as minor uses of equipment for additional, local excavation jobs, will be treated as income to the main account.*

20:6.2 Contract Account – Construction Project

Figure 20:3 is an example of a construction project account and the calculation of its attributable profit. The contract was started on 15 August 2005 and the contractor requires the preparation of the contract account for the year ended 31 July 2006, including the profit or loss calculation.

Figure 20:3 **Construction project account example**

	£
Materials purchased	409,440
Direct wages paid	513,000
Direct expenses paid	65,340
Plant and machinery issued to site on 1 September 2005	93,400
Subcontractor work paid	13,800
Overheads apportioned to contract	24,000
The following balances were recorded on the contract at 31 July 2006:	
Materials on site	25,300
Plant and machinery	83,000
Wages accrued	7,300
Amounts owing to subcontractors	2,020

The value of work certified for the year was £1,200,000 and the cost of uncertified work was £61,800. The cash received from the customer was £1,050,000.

	Contract account				
		£			£
Raw materials		409,440	Materials on site	c/f	25,300
Wages	513,000		Plant on site	c/f	83,000
add accrual	7,300	520,300	Cost of uncertified work	c/f	61,800
Direct expenses		65,340	Cost of sales (balance)	c/f	958,200
Plant and machinery		93,400			
Subcontractor	13,800				
add accrual	2,020	15,820			
Overheads		24,000			
		1,128,300			1,128,300
Cost of sales	b/f	958,200	Attributed sales revenue		1,099,250
Profit		141,050			
		1,099,250			1,099,250
Materials on site	b/f	25,300	*(This third section commences with*		
Plant on site	b/f	83,000	*the opening accounts for the next*		
Cost of uncertified work	b/f	61,800	*accounting period.)*		

(cont'd)

(Fig.20:3 *cont'd*)

Notional (or apparent) profit	= Value of work certified – Cost of work certified	
	= £1,200,000 – £958,200	= £241,800
Profit charged	= $\frac{2}{3}$ × $\frac{\text{cash received}}{\text{work certified}}$ × notional profit	
	= $\frac{2}{3}$ × $\frac{£1,050,000}{£1,200,000}$ × £241,800	= £141,050

Note: If the contract is nearing completion, the prudent use of the 2/3 may not be required.

Attributed sales revenue	= Cost of sales + attributed profit	
	= £958,000 + £141,050	= £1,099,250

20:6.3 Contract Account – Service Target Cost Project

Figure 20:4 is an example of a service company which is part way through a long-term contract, on a target cost basis, with quality performance awards.

Figure 20:4 **Service target cost example**

The contract is based on a final (target) cost estimate of £2,000,000 and the revenue to contractor assumes a 12% mark-up, or £240,000. Reimbursable costs are defined and subject to audit by the customer. Any cost savings will be shared between the contractor (60%) and customer (40%), which will not impact the agreed mark-up of £240,000. Performance awards are to be based on a quality-incentive factor, which may range from – 5% to +5%.

At 31 December 2006, costs for the year were £550,000, including a staff bonus element of £10,000 in the labour cost, which is not recoverable through the contract. Forecast costs for end of contract are £1,840,000. It is the contractor's policy that revenues and profit are recognised as services are performed. This is calculated, using a percentage completion method, based on contract costs incurred to date, compared with total estimated costs at completion.

To calculate the attributable profit for the year:

	£
Total cost for the year	550,000
less non-recoverable costs	10,000
Adjusted cost to date	540,000

Forecast cost savings against contract are £2,000,000 – £1,840,000 = £160,000 (8%).

Factor to be applied to recoverable cost to date to calculate revenue (in percentage terms):

$$\frac{(\text{target cost} - \text{forecast savings}) + \text{mark-up} + \text{contractor share of savings}}{\text{target cost} - \text{forecast savings}}$$

$$= \frac{(100\% - 8\%) + 12\% + (60\% \times 8\%)}{100\% - 8\%} = \frac{108.8\%}{92\%} = 1.1826$$

Therefore attributable revenue = £540,000 × 1.1826 = £638,600 and profit = £98,600.

Notes:

(a) *Performance awards should not be anticipated, by using the prudence principle. Actual amounts, on an annual or other agreed time basis, would be incorporated as received.*

(b) *To verify the above factor calculation of 1.1826, it may be applied on a total contractual basis as:*

Target contract cost	£2,000,000
Forecast cost	£1,840,000
Therefore cost savings	£160,000 (£96,000 to contractor, £64,000 to customer)
Mark-up	£240,000

Therefore total profit to contractor	= £96,000 + £240,000 =	£336,000
Total revenue	= £1,840,000 + £336,000 =	£2,176,000
	= £1,840,000 × 1.1826 =	£2,176,000

(c) *In the case of lack of confidence in the full-profit position, the revenue calculation above may be factored down, on a prudent basis.*

(d) *The above gross margin of £98,600 or 15.4%, will be internally assessed with respect to general overheads to evaluate overall contract performance. Some overheads will be contract-specific, such as the staff bonus as above, plus other non-contract reimbursable management costs, to help calculate the net margin position.*

21. Engineered, Committed and Discretionary Costs

21:1 Introduction

Cost classifications are useful when cost behaviour needs to be understood. Terms such as variable costs, fixed costs, indirect costs, direct costs, unit-level costs and so on are quite self-descriptive. Most practitioners are familiar with most of these terms and the difficulty of actually classifying many costs as variable or fixed, direct or indirect. What may not be so well understood are the implications that cost behaviour has for budgeting, control and performance evaluation. In addition, some costing systems are:

(a) *slow to respond to the changing nature of costs; and*
(b) *could adopt better ways of analysing costs to recognise their behaviour.*

21:1.1 Four problem scenarios

There are many situations in which a lack of understanding of the consequences of cost behaviour leads to poor decisions. The term 'unsophisticated investor' is used to describe someone who invests funds but is unable to fully comprehend the information on which sophisticated investors base their decisions. Similarly, we can consider four scenarios in which an unsophisticated decision-maker issues poor directives as a result of an ignorance of the probable outcome of those decisions. Consider these four comments from subordinate managers:

1. I've just come from upstairs. I got the same old story: 'Joe, I like the look of your budget but we need to cut it by 5%. If you take 5% off each item I'll sign off on it'. If I point out that we can't pay 95% of the rates he just says I should take it off somewhere else! As I walked out of his office he called after me: 'And see that you don't have so many machine breakdowns next year, it cost us a bomb this year. It's probably the reason you won't be getting your bonus again!'. And I am supposed to treat him with respect!

2. You think you have problems? Last year we halved production of the TN15 when we introduced the TN16. My boss just hauled me over the coals because we didn't halve the cost of producing the TN15 when we halved production. He simply didn't expect it to cost so much more per unit. Mind you, it isn't as bad as he first thought. He has been doing a bit of reading about costing and a few weeks ago asked for figures on the prime costs and conversion costs. We could have told him not to add the two but he didn't tell us why he wanted them. I should have known he didn't know what he was doing.

3. Did you hear that Rachel, the production manager at the Westover plant, is in trouble for making 20-tonne rolls of material when the customers are asking for two-tonne rolls of material? If she makes what the customers want she can't get her bonus so who can blame her for building up an inventory of what won't sell while having stock-outs of what they want? At least she will get the bonus.

4. My mate at Davidson's down the road does the same job as us but his little unit is treated as a profit centre instead of a cost centre. His bonus is tied to improving his return on investment. Well, apart from not having much influence over the revenue, he has now been told to take on a new project that is only returning 15%. It's higher than their hurdle rate of 12% but below his last ROI of 17%. He has already put off upgrading his equipment for the last few years and can't delay that anymore so the two things together will make his ROI plummet.

A better understanding of cost behaviour, cost categorisation, budgeting for costs and performance evaluation explains these scenarios and how they could have been avoided.

21:2 Revisiting some basic cost categories

Among the most basic of cost categories are direct and indirect costs, conversion costs, prime costs, variable and fixed costs:

Direct costs	have a clear link with the cost object. If the object of a costing exercise is a manufactured product, the components that are input during production can be directly associated with the finished product. Similarly, an amount of labour can often be measured as a direct input required in order to produce the product. This labour is then measured as direct labour.
Indirect costs –	are the costs incurred that either cannot be linked to a particular output or are not included because it is not beneficial to do so. For example, some materials either cannot be directly associated with the product (e.g. machine oil) or the measurement of their consumption costs more than the benefit of doing so (e.g. glue, thread, nails). Supervisory labour and machine-maintenance labour would also be a cost that is indirect to a manufactured product. However, these labour costs are direct costs when their department is the cost object. So costs can be direct to one cost object (such as the department or hospital ward, for example) while indirect to another cost object (such as the product or a patient).
Prime costs –	are all the costs that are considered direct to the cost object.
Conversion costs –	are the costs incurred in converting direct materials into the finished product.
Variable costs –	change in small increments in proportion to a change in micro-level cost drivers. The key is to identify exactly with what they change. The major difference between traditional costing and activity-based costing is that traditional costing methods tend to identify as cost drivers measures that also change with the level of output (e.g. the volume of material, direct labour hours, machine hours, etc.). Activity-based costing argues that many costs change with measures that are linked to output but are not directly variable with output (e.g. set-up costs relate to the number of batches produced, not to the number of units produced).
Fixed costs –	remain unchanged for a wide range of output. For example, the depreciation on a piece of equipment can remain unchanged for a wide range of throughput until capacity is fully utilised. Similarly, the lease charge on computer equipment and the rates on a plant may remain unchanged over a wide range of activity.

From this brief, simplistic overview of direct and indirect, prime, conversion and variable and fixed costs we can see that prime costs can include many that are also components of the conversion costs (*see* **Fig.21:1**). It is possible for costs other than material and labour to be direct to a cost object but the common categories are direct material, direct labour and indirect costs. Two points to note with regard to the production of goods or services are that:

(a) *direct costs will change with output and will be variable; and*
(b) *indirect costs are likely to be a mixture of costs that are variable and fixed with respect to product.*

Figure 21:1 **The relationships between some different cost categories**

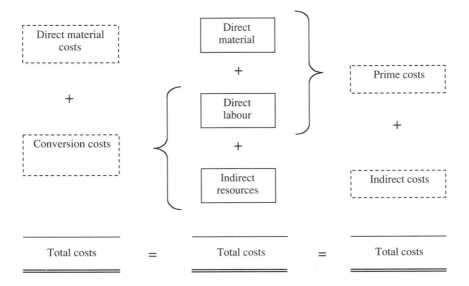

A closer look at how variable 'variable costs' are, and how fixed 'fixed costs' are, can be undertaken by reference to the cost categories; engineered, committed and discretionary costs followed by a brief discussion of cost hierarchies.

21:3 Engineered costs

Engineered costs represent the consumption of resources that have a defined mathematical relationship with the cost object. For example, the making of school dresses would require the consumption of a known amount of material and there would be a good notion of how long it would take a cutter to cut the material and a machinist to sew a dress. The direct materials and direct labour are therefore engineered costs.

21:3.1 Budgeting engineered costs

The determination of engineered costs in the budget relies on knowledge of the following:

(a) *the rate of consumption of the resource is represented by the mathematical relationship between input and output (e.g. three metres of material per school dress); and*

(b) *the rate of payment for the resource (e.g. expected cost of material per metre) should take into consideration anticipated price changes and any discounts related to the size of the order. Within an activity-based management system a premium for the costs caused by dealing with the supplier can also be factored in. This makes allowances for some suppliers causing more costs in dealing with them than with others (e.g. the cost of returns, late deliveries, poor paperwork, re-drilling misaligned holes, the need to chase delayed deliveries, errors in the order delivered and so on). Factoring in the 'cost of dealing' to derive a cost of supplies, rather than the price of supplies, also makes procurement managers responsible for these extraneous costs that are otherwise passed on to managers who have no control over them, since they do not control the source of supplies.*

The sales forecast in the budget indicates the required production of goods in any period and, hence, the consumption of the resources that are represented by the engineered costs. This, in turn, is used to determine the engineered costs that are expected to be incurred in production. For example, if there is a mathematical relationship between production output and labour input, it is possible to derive the expected cost of labour, based on the volume of labour required and the expected cost per hour.

21:3.2 Managerial control of engineered costs

Incurring engineered costs is not a matter of choice for a manager. If there is an output of goods or services, the engineered costs will be incurred, normally in a pattern that is close to expectations. This is the nature of the relationship between an engineered cost and its cost object. If the cost does not follow the predefined pattern of behaviour, analysis of the cost was incorrect in some way, e.g.:

(a) *many costs are treated as if they change with the number of labour hours when there is a tenuous relationship between labour hours and the resource usage that the cost relates to;*

(b) *increasingly, labour cost is not a variable for production due to job and wage security.*

Analysis of engineered costs during performance evaluation can identify how closely they met expectations. Since managers are expected to use the resource at a particular rate and pay for it at a particular rate, the bulk of engineered costs are not subject to control at the point of production. The majority of this cost is determined during the design of the product (whether it is goods or a service). Therefore, managers should only be evaluated on the deviation of the cost from the designed-in engineered cost.

At the product design stage, the choice of processes, materials, labour and so on are made. Hence, a majority of the cost incurred over the life of the product is committed to before production takes place; a fact that has led to the development of life-cycle costing and target-costing techniques. During the production of goods the production manager can only influence:

(a) the level of production; and

(b) how closely the actual costs resemble the forecast pattern for that level of production.

This influence may extend to a small proportion of the total engineered cost incurred unless demand does not match forecast demand, in which case the manager should revise production levels.

21:3.3 Performance evaluation and engineered costs

While the resource cost is derived from the multiple of the amount used and the cost per unit volume of that resource, it is possible to judge the manager's control by separately analysing the difference in cost caused by (a) using a different quantity to expectations and (b) the resource costing more or less per unit volume than expected. **Figure 21:2** presents a simple variance analysis for illustration purposes.

Figure 21:2 **Simple variance analysis of an engineered cost (1)**

	Recorded Data
Expected production in June	600 dresses
Expected usage of material per dress	3m
Expected cost of material per metre	£4
Actual usage of material	1,950m
Actual cost of material	£7,875
The expected (budgeted) material cost is (£600 x 3m x £4)	£7,200
But the actual cost of material is	£7,875

In **Figure 21:2**, we can see that the manager has overspent by £675 and would be penalised by some firms (such as the firm in scenario 3 above). However, if customer demand were underestimated and an extra 80 dresses were needed, we would expect the engineered costs to rise in order to meet the demand for the product. For example, if 680 dresses were produced we would expect material costs to be £(680 x 3m x £4) or £8,160. So the manager now appears to have controlled the cost well. We can even analyse the favourable variance of £285 further, as in **Figure 21:3**.

Figure 21:3 **Simple variance analysis of an engineered cost (2)**

Further analysis	
Expected cost of material for dresses produced	£8,160
Actual cost of material for dresses produced	£7,875
Variance for the resource	£285
Expected cost of 1,950m @ £4 is	£7,800
So the material input cost more than expected by	£75
The expected usage of material for 680 dresses is 2,040m	
90m less than expected was used. At £4 per metre efficient usage saved	£360
An extra cost of £75 and savings of £360 account for the total variance of	£285

Variances such as these are often used for reward and sanction. However, it is dangerous to base bonus payments on variances. The variances should indicate the necessary questions to ask and when to ask them. In instances where the budget has been treated as a spending allowance and bonuses have been tied to meeting costs from the original budget (the static budget), the manager is motivated to meet only the budgeted production, regardless of changing customer demands. This is the way that actual engineered costs can come close to those originally budgeted for.

Performance evaluation therefore needs to evaluate two things:

1. *whether the manager produced enough to meet customer demand but did not over-produce:*
   - *check whether inventory levels are appropriate;*
   - *clarify whether customer demand was met or if stock ran out;*

2. *whether engineered costs were appropriate for the actual level of production:*
   - *base variance analysis on the flexible budget (i.e. expectations for the actual production level (see **Figure 21:3**));*
   - *break the variance for the resource into its component parts.*

The possible causes of these variances include errors in recording data and when predefining how much resource would be used per unit or how much the resource would cost. Taking the four basic engineered cost variances (relating to direct material and direct labour costing more or less than expected and using more or less of the resource than expected), **Figure 21:4** suggests some other causes of variances, including interactions between those variances.

Figure 21:4 **Example causes of some engineered cost variances**

Direct material		Direct labour	
price variance (paying more/less for material than expected)	*usage variance (using more/less of material than expected)*	*rate variance (paying more/less for labour than expected)*	*efficiency variance (using more/less labour than expected)*
Price rise	Inexperienced labour produced more scrap/ rejects	Unanticipated wage rise	Workers not reached the plateau of a learning curve
Buy better quality	Greater yield due to good quality material	Better standard of labour cost more	More rejects or rework require more starts
Buy inferior quality	More scrap due to poor quality material	Cheaper, less experienced and qualified standard of labour	Better or worse standard of labour works at a different pace
Did or did not get discounts	More scrap due to equipment failure	On-costs changed due to government policy	Poor-quality material takes longer to handle

The interaction between the variances, as seen in **Figure 21:4**, demonstrates that bonuses awarded on the basis of unexplored variances can be awarded to the wrong people and the wrong manager can also be chastised for disappointing results. Take, for example, the possible outcomes of the procurement manager achieving a favourable material price variance, and possibly a bonus, by purchasing substandard materials as follows:

- increased scrap means using more material;

- handling difficulties, rejects or rework causes higher labour costs due to longer production times.

In this situation production managers can be penalised for matters outside their control.

21:4 Committed costs

Committed costs are those that cannot be changed during a budget period. Committed costs in a budget cannot represent a spending allowance as there is no choice about these costs being incurred. Indeed, usually they cannot be changed at the time of setting the budget either and usually relate to capacity costs and, sometimes, also to contracted costs.

Examples of these costs include rates, lease costs, depreciation of assets and long-term contracts for security, cleaning and advertising.

21:4.1 Budgeting committed costs

Committed cost is the category of cost that can be regarded as truly fixed. To change them requires actions such as the disposal of assets, breaking contracts and negotiating with governmental bodies for rate concessions.

21:4.2 Managerial control of committed costs

Due to the commitment to these costs, the manager often does not have control over the amount of committed cost that is incurred. The time at which control is exercised over the cost itself is when the asset is purchased, the depreciation policy determined, the long-term contract entered or the lease agreement signed. Those decisions may not be made by the manager who has responsibility for the use of the resource involved. However, it may be appropriate to recognise the manager's responsibility to ensure the efficient usage of the resource, especially where it relates to capacity costs.

The measures that are commonly used in this context are the return on investment (ROI), or return on assets (ROA), and residual value (RI). Senior managers often feel that they understand ROI well and use it freely. However, there are some issues with regard to its use that are frequently overlooked. Its external use to evaluate the performance of the whole organisation, based on published financial statements, should not be confused with its potential use inside the organisation to evaluate the various units in the organisation. For internal use the formula may be represented as:

$$\frac{\text{A measure of profit generation success}}{\text{A measure of the assets used to generate the profit}}$$

$$\text{or} \quad \frac{P}{A}$$

The indicator of success in generating profits may be a contribution margin (revenue less variable costs); controllable margin; divisional contribution (total revenue earned by the division less total costs incurred within the division) or a variety of other measures as appropriate. The measure of the assets used to generate the profit raises the issue of which assets to include and how to value them. The *Statement of Principles for Financial Reporting*, published by the ASB in 1995, defines assets as 'rights or other access to future economic benefits controlled by an entity as a result of past transactions or events'. For our purposes, should leased assets be included, or can managers manipulate the investment base by selling assets and leasing them back? Since credit sales are a feature of the operations of the division, should a proportion of debtors be included even when they are administered by head office? Are depreciating assets to be valued at their original cost or depreciated value? The measurement of fixed assets is covered by *FRS15: Tangible Fixed Assets, SSAP9: Accounting for Investment Properties* and *SSAP13: Accounting for Research and Development*. Relevant international standards include *IAS38: Intangibles* and *IAS16: Property, Plant and Equipment*. The issues with regard to depreciation and asset valuation deserve greater consideration and are listed below.

(a) *If a contribution margin was used as the numerator in the above equation, since depreciation is a fixed cost, it would not affect the measure used in the numerator. Any other profit measure usually includes depreciation, which reduces the numerator. Some depreciation methods reduce the depreciation charge each year, which would automatically increase the ROI.*

(b) *Using the depreciated value of the assets in the denominator means that the denominator would decrease each year. This can gradually improve the ROI regardless of the manager's efficiency in using the assets.*

(c) *If a manager replaces an asset, the depreciation in the numerator will increase substantially, reducing the ROI. The higher asset value in the denominator will also reduce the ROI. The two adjustments together can adversely affect the ROI significantly.*

(d) *The purchase of new assets has a similar effect as the replacement of assets.*

The use of RI is sometimes used to combat the problems associated with ROI. They can be used in tandem or independently. RI seeks to measure the extent to which the division generated a return on the assets in excess of the required return. The formula may be represented as follows:

$$P - A \times R$$

Where: P = measure of profit generated
A = measure of assets used to generate the profit
R = required return on assets

In addition to the decisions about P and A in the formula, as described above, the required return needs to be determined. This can be the firm's hurdle rate for investments, a cost of capital or a variety of other rates. An advantage of RI is that it can use different required rates for different assets or different parts of the organisation. Both ROI and RI suffer from using aggregated figures that do not help managers to make operating decisions as they do not indicate causes for the outcome measured. However, the ROI can be broken down into two measures that reveal the success with which the assets were used to generate revenue, and the proportion of revenue that translated into profits:

$$\text{ROI} = \frac{S}{A} \times \frac{P}{S}$$

Where: S = sales or revenue

21:4.3 Performance evaluation and committed costs

Despite using aggregate figures that are also too late to affect operating decisions, ROI and RI can be useful in the evaluation of a manager's performance and the performance of a division. The greatest problems that occur as a result of the use of ROI and RI relate to the way they are used rather than their basic structure. Some examples are:

(a) *Both ROI and RI depend on a measure of profit generation. However, they are frequently used in performance evaluation when the manager does not have significant influence over revenue. If he or she can only influence profits through tight control of costs, then cost centre evaluation methods should be adopted. Evaluating managers on the basis of measures that are significantly influenced by others (in this case, revenue) normally leads to dysfunctional decision making.*

(b) *A performance measure cannot be identified as good or bad until it is compared with another performance measure. One way of achieving this is to compare the performance of the unit or its manager over time. Hence, the manager has the objective of progressively improving ROI or keeping it stable. This discourages managers from upgrading equipment due to the impact that has on ROI. It also encourages managers to reject projects that would return more than the company's hurdle rate if the expected return on the project is lower than the current ROI. This disadvantage of ROI encourages the use of RI, since the use of the hurdle rate as R (required return on assets) ensures that RI will rise each time a project returning more than R is adopted.*

(c) This trend analysis of ROI also ignores the fact that ROI is subject to fluctuation due to changing environmental conditions, such as economic indicators and government regulation. In such circumstances, the manager is being asked to compensate for these environmental changes. This is not always a viable option, however.

(d) A perceived advantage of ROI is that it allows for the comparison of internal business units and segments of different sizes. These comparisons create an environment of competition that is not conducive to achieving co-operation between them.

(e) The comparison of a division's ROI with that of an external business is also fraught with problems. They often operate in different segments of a market, use equipment of different ages and are at different stages of a product life cycle. When two factors are compared it is vital to assess whether they actually are comparable.

By far the better evaluation of ROI is against the budget. This should take into consideration any changes in the environment, assets and project, to derive the desired ROI in these circumstances. This use of ROI is less likely to motivate dysfunctional decisions.

The use of RI discourages comparisons between segments and units because the absolute figure that is produced does not allow for the different sized units. However, it is sometimes seen to encourage the early transfer of goods between units as the end of the month or financial year approaches. For example, the export manager of a wine producer frequently experienced storage problems at year-end as other managers sent him as much product as possible in order to reduce their asset base, which was used in their RI calculation (this also applies to ROI). Apart from storage problems, the export manager's RI was adversely affected by such action.

ROI and RI apply to managers of profit centres. Variance-analysis issues regarding committed costs in performance evaluation apply to cost centres as well as profit centres.

In contrast to engineered costs that change in volume with the level of output, committed costs do not. Committed costs are always expected to be the same, as long as the level of activity is within what is called the relevant range. For example, for a certain piece of equipment the cost is expected to remain unchanged until the level of production requires the acquisition of more equipment.

The cost remains unchanged, however, the average cost per unit does change. In a situation where the costs of inventory and of goods sold include an amount for fixed-cost recovery in the cost per unit, it needs to be recognised that the average fixed cost per unit changes with production levels. The difference between the budgeted fixed cost and the fixed costs that have been recorded as part of the cost of goods produced is therefore called a production volume (or capacity) variance.

This figure can be manipulated by managers who budget to take transfers of components from other managers. If the receiving manager overstates the amount of transfers in the budget, it is possible (depending on the transfer method used) for the supplying manager to be left with an unfavourable volume variance at the end of the budget period. Two situations in which this can occur deliberately are when, for example, two managers vie for the same promotion or managers receive their bonus from the same bonus pool (so the reward to each is affected by the results of the other managers as well as his or her own). This behaviour can be controlled by better selection of the transfer price method and also the abandonment of bonus pools, which reward managers on the basis of outcomes outside their control.

21:5 Discretionary costs

Discretionary costs are those that can be changed at the discretion of a manager. There may be internal regulations relating to who can authorise a change to costs, however, e.g. maintenance, training, most advertising, research and development.

21:5.1 Budgeting discretionary costs

Discretionary costs can be determined on the basis of what is obtained by the actual expenditure. For example, how much will be spent on advertising in a period can be based on what will be obtained by incurring that expenditure. It is not based on the level of activity or volume of production, nor is it irrevocably preset, however. Planned expenditure may relate to a programme for the maintenance of equipment, a training programme, an advertising campaign or the development of a new product but, by its nature, a discretionary cost can be set at the time of developing the budget and could be changed during that budget period.

21:5.2 Managerial control of discretionary costs

Internal policy may make this a fixed cost for a manager. If tight control is exercised, a manager may not be given the freedom to vary this expenditure. In this circumstance, the cost really becomes a fixed cost to the manager and the line item in the budget is a spending allowance. Alternatively, when a manager is allowed more discretion, the discretionary cost becomes that which they under-spend if other costs become larger than expected. This is sometimes used as a way of achieving the budgeted bottom line (i.e. the actual *total* expenditure equates to the budgeted *total* expenditure). Between the extremes of tight control and absolute discretion over costs, managers may be permitted to vary this expenditure within a range without higher authority (for example by up to 5%). Beyond that range they may be able to vary the expenditure if they present a sound case for doing so.

21:5.3 Performance evaluation and discretionary costs

The difference between budgeted discretionary costs and actual spending in these areas often does not receive the attention it deserves. By their nature these costs can be reduced without appearing to impact on production. However, reducing them to attain short-term results will have long-term repercussions. **Figure 21:5** shows some suggested areas in which spending cuts are sometimes made and the longer-term problems this can create.

Figure 21:5 **Some longer-term problems due to cuts in discretionary spending**

This period's cost cut	*Next period's problems*
Advertising	• Reduced demand for the product
	• Reduced exposure of the company logo
	• Increased confidence in the competitors
Regular equipment maintenance	• Expensive machine breakdowns
	• Increased scrap due to the breakdowns
Training	• Staff do not know how to operate machines or follow procedures
	• Machine breakdowns due to operator error
	• Errors in record keeping
	• Lack of knowledge of new computer systems
Use of outdated IT	• Research and development. New products come along more slowly
	• New products meet launch dates but still have quality problems

21:6 A hierarchy of costs

A useful categorisation of costs was introduced in the literature on activity-based costing. The concept of a hierarchy of costs can be used in any operating environment but it is useful to use a manufacturing environment to illustrate the points that need to be made (*see* **Fig.25:6**). An alternative hierarchy for a particular service environment will then be described.

Figure 21:6 **A hierarchy of costs for manufacturing**

Hierarchy	Description
Unit-level costs	These costs occur each time an extra unit of product is produced. They are the engineered costs that change in volume in proportion to a change in production volume. They have cost drivers that are either the number of units of production or something that itself changes with the number of units produced (e.g. machine hours).
Batch-level costs	These costs are incurred each time another batch of product is made and have cost drivers that relate to batches. For example, set-up costs are incurred each time a batch is produced and the cost driver could be the number of set-ups or the time taken to set up. Similarly, for requisition costs the cost driver equals the number of requisitions. They are variable costs that do not vary directly with production levels.
Product-sustaining costs	These costs can be identified with a particular product but they are not a multiple of the number of products because they can differ from product to product.
Facility-sustaining costs	These costs are incurred in providing facilities for operations but cannot be linked to any particular product.

The issue of the variability of costs can be clearly seen from the description of batch-level and unit-level costs above. Traditionally, unit-level costs are treated as direct costs and batch-level costs are treated as indirect. However, batch-level costs are also traditionally allocated to products by selecting a unit-level cost driver (e.g. machine hours or labour hours), although they do not change at that level. Production managers can reduce their production costs by producing more product in fewer batches, increasing inventory costs for the company. (This is attractive if another manager is responsible for inventory costs.)

The erroneous allocation of batch-level costs is the reason why low-volume products are often undercosted at the expense of high-volume products which have proportionately fewer batches per thousand produced.

Product-sustaining costs can be a collection of discretionary costs (e.g. advertising or research and development) and committed costs (e.g. depreciation of equipment or leased assets). They should be identified and charged to the product. Together with unit-level and batch-level costs, product-sustaining costs can be deducted from product revenue to obtain the product contribution. If market-sustaining costs are included in the hierarchy, it is possible to add the contribution from all products in a market before deducting the market-sustaining costs in order to obtain market contribution.

Facility-sustaining costs are not identifiable with any particular product and their inclusion in product costs often leads to erroneous decisions. They include many head-office costs; landscaping of the grounds and advertising to promote the trademark, for example. They also include many committed costs such as building depreciation. Facility-sustaining costs are unlikely to change if a product is discontinued or another is introduced. Any inclusion of such costs as part of the product cost must necessarily be an arbitrary amount that can mislead decisions.

A similar hierarchy of costs can be identified in most circumstances. For example, a bank's residential training college had difficulty quoting the transfer price for courses provided to the various departments of the bank. Negotiations that centred on how many days a course should run, how many people would attend and whether a course would be specially designed or adapted from an existing course resulted in a complete re-costing of the course for each variation. A hierarchy of costs gave guidance to the college's negotiators so that they could give information in discussions on how any change would affect the costing. The hierarchy classified costs according to:

(a) *course sustaining costs – the costs incurred in the design and preparation of courses;*
(b) *the daily rate – costs that vary according to the number of days courses run (e.g. meals, cleaning of rooms, laundry, etc.);*
(c) *course running costs – the costs that change according to the number of people attending the course (e.g. transport, printed materials, check-in and check-out costs); and*
(d) *conference sustaining costs – the costs associated with letting the facilities for conferences.*

21:7 Blanket budget cut or discretionary suicide

A situation in which a blanket budget cut is applied can be considered in the context of engineered, committed and discretionary costs. As an illustration of this, we can take an example in which one-third of a division's costs are committed (depreciation on equipment, etc.); one third are engineered (direct material and labour, etc.) and one-third are discretionary (research and development, maintenance and training, etc.). In this situation, the manager has been told to reduce the bottom line by 5% by reducing each line item. Taking each category of costs separately, it is possible to forecast what might happen next year if this is done and the manager meets the budget.

(a) The engineered costs can only be reduced by reducing production or by using substandard materials and labour. Assuming the forecast demand is accurate, cutting these costs must mean either: lost sales and long-term lost customers; or high levels of waste, high labour costs (see **Fig.25:4**), poor-quality output and future lost sales. It is therefore in the best interests of the firm if these costs are not cut.

(b) The committed costs cannot be changed unless assets are sold, a number of salaried staff reduced or part of the facilities leased to other units.

(c) Discretionary costs can be changed. Since engineered costs and committed costs are unlikely to be cut, discretionary costs now need to be cut by 15% to achieve the required total budgeted costs. However, these cuts may reduce training, advertising, machine maintenance and research and development. As a consequence, in the next period there is likely to be reduced demand, problems due to untrained staff and poorly maintained equipment and delays to the introduction of new or redesigned products (see **Fig.25:5**).

21:8 Four problem scenarios revisited

The four scenarios described at the beginning of this bulletin are discussed again below.

1. Joe is obviously told each year to make blanket cuts to his budget. Therefore, the only room for manoeuvre is in discretionary costs. It appears that the year before last he reduced maintenance to meet the bottom line of the budget and had extra costs this year because of it. Perhaps this last year he reduced something else that will impact on his results in the coming year.

2. The costs on the TN15 may not reduce even 40% when production is halved. It depends on the committed costs and whether the equipment can be used for anything else. If the deprecation on the equipment was high, the variable costs low and there was not another use for the vacated capacity on the equipment, the cost per unit of the TN15 would increase substantially. The committed cost does not reduce with reduced production so the average cost increases as the committed cost is averaged over fewer units. Of course, adding the prime costs to the conversion costs will include the labour costs twice.

3. This case occurred in a situation where the chief engineer evaluated the performance of the production manager by comparing actual costs incurred against costs in the original budget (the static budget). The only way the manager

could achieve the same costs as in the budget was to make budgeted production. To make more two-tonne rolls of material and fewer 20-tonne rolls of material it would be necessary to incur extra labour costs for changing the roller (a multiple of ten) and the extra wastage incurred when production was stopped, the roll changed and the machines started again. Throughput time would also be down. Evaluation against a flexible budget, based on producing to customer demand, would have solved much of the problem. However, a traditional costing system would still have been incorrect as it would not correctly provide for the massive increase in set-ups.

4. *Adopting a project returning 15% will reduce the current ROI of 17%. The upgrading of equipment has been delayed as this would also have reduced ROI, probably by reducing the profit measure used (increased depreciation) and increasing the asset-base substantially. This would have forced the manager to forfeit his bonus. Adopting the project and upgrading equipment in the same year will give a severely reduced ROI but should provide the manager with a low ROI for steady improvement, and associated bonus rewards, over future years. From the manager's perspective, this is therefore a good year for him to upgrade, even if it were not necessary yet. Evaluation of actual ROI against budgeted ROI could remove these problems.*

21:9 Conclusions

Many errors are made in administering costs and in making cost-related decisions due to an ignorance of the implications of cost behaviour in budgeting, control and performance evaluation. Such a lack of knowledge has often resulted in performance evaluation and reward systems motivating managers to make dysfunctional decisions.

The classification of costs as variable, fixed, direct and indirect is simplistic and a better understanding of cost behaviour can come from other cost classifications. The variability and stability of variable and fixed costs is better understood by classifying costs as engineered, committed or discretionary and by recognising their position in a cost hierarchy. An understanding of costs within these classification schemes assists managers to make better budgeting and control decisions and to promote goal congruence through the performance evaluation system.

Some costing systems have been slow to recognise the changing nature of costs. For example, labour costs that were once truly direct and variable with the production output are now usually fixed. Their classification as a variable cost is justified by their movement from product to product, making the cost variable to the product but not to the firm. There has also been a trend toward machine-operating costs being direct to a product and labour becoming indirect due to its role in supervising more than one piece of equipment at a time.

A revision of costing systems and the use of cost information is overdue for some firms and many firms could adopt better ways of analysing costs to recognise how they actually change.

22. Activity-based Costing

22:1 Unit Product Costing and Overheads

Managers usually wish to know what is the unit product cost for different product lines. An interesting question is why they wish to know such information. The reasons given include for stock valuation, to compare unit price with unit cost, for special pricing decisions and, in some cases, for cost plus pricing decisions. It is important for management accountants to discuss with managers why they wish to know unit product cost information so that the most accurate information possible can be provided.

Nevertheless, despite the best efforts of management accountants, managers must understand that there is no such thing in most organisations as a completely accurate unit product cost. The main reason for this is that most organisations (both manufacturing and service) sell more than one 'product' line and there exists the problem of how to deal with overhead costs. Unlike direct materials, direct labour and direct expenses, most overhead costs are fixed and do not vary with the volume of output. The question then is how to calculate the overhead cost in a unit product cost.

22:1.1 Problems of Traditional Product Costing

Traditionally overhead costs are collected in departments such as purchasing, traced on some basis to production departments and then related to individual product lines by using an overhead absorption basis such as direct labour hours, direct labour cost and machine hours. *SSAP9: Stocks and Long-Term Contracts* states that the costs of stock 'will include all related production overheads'. *IAS2: Inventories* identifies the components of cost as being: cost of purchase; costs of conversion; and other costs incurred in bringing the inventories to their present location and condition. Costs of conversion here include fixed production overheads, which should be allocated to the cost of stock, or inventory, on the basis of normal production capacity. A basic problem with such overhead absorption bases, however, is that they tend to vary with the volume of output and yet

John Innes   425

many overhead costs are relatively fixed and do not vary with the volume of output. Indeed there are relatively few overhead costs (such as electricity for machine power) which do vary with the volume of output.

Given the fact that a completely accurate unit product cost does not exist, does it really matter that overheads are treated traditionally as varying with the volume of output? The answer depends on how the information is being used. If the unit product cost information is used only for the purpose of stock valuation, it probably does not matter too much. It is rather like using first in–first out or average stock valuation methods. The stock valuation does, of course, affect both the assets and the profit figures but basically we are talking about a profit-timing difference.

In contrast if the unit product cost information is used for decision-making purposes for example:

> *(a) to calculate contribution per unit for different product lines to encourage the sales force to push the high-unit contribution product lines; or*
>
> *(b) for subcontracting decisions about which product lines to subcontract (see Ch.38); or*
>
> *(c) for cost-plus pricing decisions (see Ch.35, para.35:5),*

then the treatment of overhead costs is very important and does matter. **Chapter 30** discusses in more detail the use of activity-based information.

Generally managers consider that the traditional method of treating overheads for unit product costing does not reflect the actual situation. One common complaint is that high-volume product lines cross-subsidise low-volume product lines. In other words because a volume-related overhead absorption basis is used such as direct labour hours, high-volume product lines are allocated a disproportionate share of the total overhead costs.

22:1.2 Activity-based Costing

With overheads increasing as a percentage of total costs in many organisations, both in the manufacturing and service sectors (*see* **Ch.13, para.13:1.1** for further details), accountants and managers have begun to question the traditional treatment of overhead costs when calculating unit product costs. With activity-based costing, direct materials, direct labour and direct expenses are treated in the same way as in traditional product costing. The distinguishing feature of activity-based product costing is the way in which overhead costs are treated.

In the mid-1980s Cooper and Kaplan of the Harvard Business School noted in their case studies of organisations such as John Deere that some organisations were treating overheads in a different manner from traditional unit product costing. They called this new method 'activity-based costing' or ABC for short. The basic idea underlying ABC is that activities consume resources and products consume activities. Instead of tracing overhead costs to production departments, activities are identified (*see also* **Ch.13, para.13:1.3**). In a survey of *The Times* Top 1000 companies Innes and Mitchell (1995) found that approximately 20% of responding companies used the activity-based approach. The evidence on the use of the activity-based approach by financial institutions (banks, building societies and insurance companies) is that even more than 20% of financial institutions use ABC (*see*, for example, Innes and Mitchell, 1997).

To implement an ABC system usually a Steering Group is established composed of perhaps two accountants, four managers from different departments such as production, engineering, purchasing and marketing and an information technology specialist. Sometimes consultants are involved. Some organisations use the activity-based approach not only for unit product costing but also for activity-based budgeting (*see* **Ch.13**) or activity-based cost management (*see* **Ch.28**) and therefore very often a manager rather than an accountant leads the Steering Group. In other words some organisations view the activity-based approach as a management technique rather than as a management accounting technique. Indeed ABC is a term often used to include activity-based budgeting and activity-based cost management as well as unit-product costing using an activity-based approach.

22:1.3 Activity-based Unit Product Costing

The Steering Group setting up an activity-based system will go through the following steps:

(a) *interview managers to establish activities such as purchasing or customer services;*

(b) *collect overhead costs by activities into activity cost pools;*

(c) *determine what drives the cost in each activity cost pool (i.e. select appropriate cost drivers);*

(d) *calculate cost driver rate for each activity cost pool being: activity cost pool/cost driver. For example, if the activity of customer liaison costs £10m and the cost driver for the activity cost pool of customer liaison is the number of customers, say 100,000, the cost driver rate for customer liaison is: £10m/100,000 = £100 per customer;*

(e) *for each product line determine the appropriate cost driver usage, for example, if product A has 10,000 customers and product B has 5,000 customers, the customer liaison cost per unit would be:*

Product A   10,000 × £100 = £1,000,000
Product B   5,000 × £100 = £500,000.

The two important differences between activity-based unit product costing and traditional unit product costing are:

1. *collect overhead costs by activity cost pools instead of relating overheads to production departments;*
2. *use activity drivers instead of volume-related overhead absorption bases such as labour hours or machine hours.*

Of course, the total overhead costs remain the same and what is happening is a different analysis of these overhead costs to different product lines under the activity-based approach relative to the traditional unit-product-costing approach.

22:2 Activities

Activities are at the core of activity-based costing but, surprisingly, several different definitions of activities are used. In practice the important point is to listen to the interviewees and select what they deem to be appropriate activities. The activities emerge from questions such as:

(a) *What staff work here?*
(b) *What does each person do?*

In the early activity-based costing case studies which were mainly examples of unit product costing, hundreds of activities were identified. With experience most organisations now begin with many fewer activities – usually well under 100 – and, if necessary, add activities to improve the accuracy of the system. Like much of management accounting, it is a cost-benefit decision, namely what are the benefits of incurring additional costs to identify more activities, select more cost drivers and collect more cost driver information. Further examples of activities are given in **Ch.13, para.13:2.1.**

An important feature of activities, which is one of the major benefits of the wider activity-based approach, is that very often activities cross departmental boundaries. For example, customer liaison may involve not only the customer services department but most other departments in the organisation to a greater or lesser extent. This feature of activities crossing departmental boundaries is even more important for activity-based budgeting (*see* **Ch.13**) and activity-based cost management (*see* **Ch.28**).

22:2.1 Activity Cost Pools

Having identified the relevant activities in an organisation, the next step is to collect the overhead costs into activity cost pools. For the purposes of unit product costing, the basic idea is to collect into the activity cost pool, costs not only relating to that activity but also driven by the same cause, that is, costs which have the same cost driver. If costs, relating to a particular activity have two rather than one cost driver and both sets of costs are significant, one possible solution is to establish two rather than one activity cost pool. For example, the activity of purchasing may have some costs driven by the number of suppliers and some costs driven by the number of purchase orders.

Again it is important to re-emphasise that activity-based unit product costing does not change the total overhead cost. It simply analyses it in a different manner. When you have calculated all the activity cost pools it is important to reconcile this total cost with the total overhead cost to ensure that all overheads have been included in the activity-based costing system.

22:3 Cost Drivers

After the activities and the activity cost pools have been established, the next step is to determine what drives the cost of each activity. The activity-based costing system does not exclude labour hours or machine hours as a possible cost driver but most of the cost drivers will not be related to the volume of output. Examples of activities and their cost drivers are as follows:

Activity	*Cost driver*
Purchasing	Number of purchase orders
	Number of suppliers
Material handling	Number of material movements
Customer services	Number of customer orders

For unit product costing purposes, the cost drivers must reflect not only the amount of work involved in a particular activity (i.e. causing or driving the costs of that activity) but the cost drivers must be related to the individual product lines. Again this can cause problems. For example, if an organisation has 50 product lines, for each of these 50 a link must be made with the cost drivers selected. Using the above four cost drivers as an example, it would have to be established for each product line:

(a) the number of purchase orders;
(b) the number of suppliers;
(c) the number of material movements;
(d) the number of customer orders.

An example of unit product costing using activity-based costing is given in **paragraph 22:4.2** below.

22:4 Cost Layering

The example in **paragraph 22:4** of unit product costing using the activity-based approach assumes that all activity costs are driven at the unit level of production. This was the approach used in the early activity-based costing case studies in the 1980s and is still the approach used today by many organisations. However, Cooper (1992) has introduced a refinement which is called cost layering.

Cost layering assumes that the costs of different activities are driven at different layers or levels of the organisation. A unit product cost can still be calculated, but the presentation of cost layering reminds managers that some overhead costs are driven at different levels. So what are these layers or levels?

22:4.1 Unit, Batch, Product and Facility Levels

Four levels of cost layering can be recognised, namely:

1. *unit level;*
2. *batch level;*
3. *product line level;*
4. *facility level.*

Cost layering suggests that some costs are driven at the unit level, some at the batch level, some at the product line level and some at the facility level. Examples of costs of activities driven at the different levels are:

Level	Example of activity
Unit	Machine power
Batch	Set-up
Product line	Maintenance of product specification
Facility	General management

In other words as volume of output increases, so the cost of machine power will increase, that is, machine power varies with each unit of output. In contrast the set-up costs will vary not with the number of units produced but with the number of batches produced. The costs of other activities vary neither with the number of units nor with the number of batches but with the number of product lines – for example, maintaining and updating the product specification for all the individual product lines. Finally, the costs of some activities are there because the facility exists – such as the cost of general management.

It is important to re-emphasise that a unit product cost can still be calculated using cost layering. However, the presentation to managers reminds them of the arbitrariness of some of the allocations involved. For example, relating the facility level costs such as general management to each unit of product is a very arbitrary exercise and managers need to appreciate this limitation. Cost layering helps to emphasise the 'ball-park figure' aspect of unit product costing even using the activity-based approach. Managers usually accept that activity-based costing gives a more realistic unit product cost than traditional costing but there are still estimates and arbitrary allocations involved in the activity-based costing approach.

22:4.2 Example of ABC with Cost Layering

A simplified example for illustrative purposes is given in **Figure 22:1**.

Figure 22:1 **Example of ABC with cost layering**

Information:

Product X	Annual production of 100,000 units manufactured in batches of 10,000 units
Product Y	Annual production of 100,000 units manufactured in batches of 1,000 units
Product Z	Annual production of 100,000 units manufactured in batches of 100 units

(cont'd)

(Fig.22:1 *cont'd*)

Production costs:

	Product X (£000)	Product Y (£000)	Product Z (£000)
Direct materials	600	600	600
Direct labour	100	100	100
Overhead	300	300	300
	1,000	1,000	1,000

The above production costs assume that production overhead is charged on the traditional basis of 300% of direct labour cost. However, the total production overhead of £900,000 is actually composed of the following four costs:

	£000
Machine power	93
Set-up	333
Maintenance of product specification	204
General management	270
	900

The cost driver information is as follows:

(a) products X, Y and Z all use the same amount of machine power per unit;

(b) set-ups are required for each batch run and the cost per set-up is the same for products X, Y and Z;

(c) the number of product specifications for each product is:
Product X 10
Product Y 20
Product Z 30
60

(d) the time spent by general management on the products is estimated to be in the proportions:
Product X 1
Product Y 2
Product Z 2

(cont'd)

(Fig.22:1 *cont'd*)

Calculation of unit product costs
(a) Traditional costing

	Product X Total £000	Product X Per unit £	Product Y Total £000	Product Y Per unit £	Product Z Total £000	Product Z Per unit £
Direct material	600	6	600	6	600	6
Direct labour	100	1	100	1	100	1
Overhead	300	3	300	3	300	3
Traditional cost	1,000	10	1,000	10	1,000	10

(b) Activity-based costing

	Product X Total £000	Product X Per unit £	Product Y Total £000	Product Y Per unit £	Product Z Total £000	Product Z Per unit £
Direct material	600	6	600	6	600	6
Direct labour	100	1	100	1	100	1
Overhead:						
Unit level:						
Machine power	31	0.31	31	0.31	31	0.31
Batch level:						
Set-up (Note 1)	3	0.03	30	0.30	300	3.00
Product level:						
Product spec. (Note 2)	34	0.34	68	0.68	102	1.02
Facility level:						
General mgt. (Note 3)	54	0.54	108	1.08	108	1.08
ABC cost	822	8.22	937	9.37	1,241	12.41

Note 1:	Number of set-ups
Product X	10
Product Y	100
Product Z	1,000
	1,110

Set-up cost	£333,000
Cost per set-up	£333,000/1,110 = £300
Cost of set-ups for product X is	10 × £300 = £3,000
Cost of set-ups for product Y is	100 × £300 = £30,000
Cost of set-ups for product Z is	1,000 × £300 = £300,000

(cont'd)

(Fig.22:1 *cont'd*)

Note 2:	*Number of product specifications*
Product X	10
Product Y	20
Product Z	<u>30</u>
	<u>60</u>

Total cost of maintaining product specifications: £204,000

Cost of maintaining product specifications for each product:

Product X	1/6 × £204,000 = £34,000
Product Y	1/3 × £204,000 = £68,000
Product Z	1/2 × £204,000 = <u>£102,000</u>
	<u>£204,000</u>

Note 3:	*Proportion of time spent by general management*
Product X	1
Product Y	2
Product Z	<u>2</u>
	<u>5</u>

Cost of general management: £270,000

Cost of general management allocated to each product:

Product X	1/5 × £270,000 = £54,000
Product Y	2/5 × £270,000 = £108,000
Product Z	2/5 × £270,000 = <u>£108,000</u>
	<u>£270,000</u>

The main points to note from this simplified, illustrative example are:

(a) the emphasis of some overheads being driven at the unit, batch, product and facility levels. In reality, of course, many more activities would be included at each of the four levels;

(b) ABC unit costs of £8.22, £9.37 and £12.41 are spuriously accurate but the important point is that from a traditional unit cost of £10 per unit for all three products, the unit costs of the large batch products of X and Y have fallen to just over £8 and £9 respectively and the unit cost of the small batch product Z has increased to over £12 per unit. This is a typical result of applying activity-based costing namely that under traditional unit-product costing large batch products tend to cross-subsidise small batch products. This is because traditional costing uses mainly volume of output overhead absorption bases such as labour hours and machine hours whereas such bases are the exception under the activity-based approach.

22:5 Criticisms of ABC

Activity-based costing is only an alternative technique for dealing with overheads. The chapter has concentrated on the unit-product costing of the activity-based approach and a number of criticisms can be made of this approach.

1. *There are a range of practical problems:*

    (a) *deciding on choice of activities;*
    (b) *selecting an appropriate cost driver for each activity cost pool;*
    (c) *collecting data especially on cost drivers. Many organisations have not collected data previously on cost drivers, such as number of material movements;*
    (d) *selecting appropriate software and having adequate systems support;*
    (e) *costs of designing and implementing ABC system.*

2. *Do activities really cause all costs?*
3. *Does one cost driver really cause or drive all the costs in each activity cost pool?*
4. *How relevant is the activity-based information for decision making? It is often argued that such information raises relevant questions and more information (such as cash-flow information) may need to be collected before a decision can be taken.*
5. *What is the potential economic and behavioural impact of ABC? Many organisations consider the impact to be beneficial but to date the experience of ABC is still limited with few organisations having operated an ABC system for more than five years.*
6. *It is sometimes suggested that ABC can be used as a one-off exercise rather than as a system to replace traditional unit product costing.*

22:6 Benefits of ABC

As with any relatively new management accounting technique, the benefits of ABC are still emerging but those identified to date include the following:

(a) *gives different unit product costings from traditional costing;*
(b) *emphasises that activities cross departmental boundaries (see **Ch.32**);*

(c) *gives a different analysis of overheads;*

(d) *enhances overhead visibility;*

(e) *changes understanding of cost behaviour – particularly with emphasis on cost drivers;*

(f) *raises questions about overheads which can lead to control and reduction of overhead costs.*

The activity-based approach historically began in the 1980s with an emphasis on unit product costing as described in this chapter. However, in the 1990s activity-based budgeting (*see* **Ch.13**) and, in particular, activity-based cost management (*see* **Ch.28**) have become at least as important as activity-based unit product costing. Nowadays it is very much a question of an activity-based approach covering budgeting, cost management and product costing. For example, **Chapter 31** has a case study of implementing ABC in a service-driven business, namely DHL Worldwide Express.

22:7 Use of ABC

In their ABC surveys of 1994 and 1999, Innes *et al.* (2000) found that the use of, and the interest in, ABC showed no increase between 1994 and 1999 with just under 20% of responding companies using ABC and just over 20% of responding companies currently considering the adoption of ABC. In both the 1994 and 1999 surveys a much higher rate of adoption was found in the financial sector. If your organisation is in the financial sector and is not using ABC, it is probably worth the time and effort considering whether or not ABC is appropriate for your business.

In terms of participating in the design of the ABC system, in-house accountants were almost always involved and consultants participated in almost half of the ABC adoptions in the 1999 survey. The responding companies used a variety of software but there was a significant increase in the proportion (58%) in 1999 using specialised commercial ABC packages relative to 1994 (24%). Between 1994 and 1999 the average ABC system had become more complex. Innes *et al.* found that 'in terms of scale, the medium system was designed to cost 40 (1994: 14) cost objects, was based on 52 (1994: 25) activities, which were concentrated into 22 (1994: 10) cost pools and utilised 14 (1994: 10) activity cost drivers' (2000: 352).

Both the 1994 and 1999 survey results suggest that top management support has a strong relationship with explaining the success rating of ABC. This finding of the importance of top management support for ABC is consistent with findings from other studies. Innes *et al.* also found that:

It remains the case that virtually all of those making some use of ABC express very positive views on both its importance and success in general and specific applications within their organisations ... Experience (even if tentative) of ABC does appear to influence perceptions of its worth. While users judged that the financial benefits of ABC outweighed its costs, the opposite concern was common among non-users.

(2000: 360)

Both the 1994 and 1999 surveys found that cost reduction and product or service pricing were the most popular activity-based applications (*see* **Ch.28** for further details of the cost reduction aspect of the activity-based approach).

References

Cooper, R. (1992) 'Activity-based costing for improved product costing' in *Handbook of cost management*, B.J. Brinker, Warren Gorham and Lamont (Eds), pp.B1–1 to B1–50. Boston.

Innes, J. and Mitchell, F. (1995) 'A survey of activity-based costing in the UK's largest companies', *Management Accounting Research*, *6(2)*: 137–53.

Innes, J. and Mitchell, F. (1997) 'The application of activity-based costing in the United Kingdom's largest financial institutions', *The Service Industries Journal*, *17(1)*: 190–203.

Innes, J., Mitchell, F. and Sinclair, D. (2000) 'Activity-based costing in the UK's largest companies: A comparison of 1994 and 1999 survey results', *Management Accounting Research*, *11(3)*: 349–62.

Appendix 22:1 Activity-based Case Studies

Many practitioners are interested in the activity-based approach to overheads but ask about experiences in their own sector. This Appendix lists 50 activity-based case studies arranged by the alphabetical name of the case study but also highlighting the sector such as aerospace, automotive, computer, engineering, finance, glass, healthcare, pharmaceutical, post, printing, software and telecommunications. Even if your specific sector is not included in these 50 activity-based case studies, you can usually find a case study from another sector with similar characteristics to your own sector.

After the listing of these 50 activity-based case studies you will find detailed references listed by the author of each case and, if you are interested, you will be able to find the detailed case study from this list of references. When reading such case studies, it is important to remember that the cases of the late 1980s and early 1990s tended to concentrate on the unit product costing aspect of the activity-based approach rather than on the cost management aspect.

50 Activity-based Cases

Name	*Sector*	*Author and Date*
Advanced Micro	Semiconductor	Cooper *et al.* (1992)
Alfred	University	Acton & Cotton (1997)
Alpha	Electronics	Innes & Mitchell (1990)
American Bank	Finance	Kaplan (1987a)
Arco Alaska	Oil	Cooper *et al.* (1992)
Australian Post	Post	Shanahan (1995)
Auto Lights	Automotive	Datar *et al.* (1991)
Beta	Engineering	Innes & Mitchell (1990)
Braintree	Hospital	Carr (1993)
Brent	Optical	Friedman & Lyne (1995)
Cambourne	Diesel Engines	Friedman & Lyne (1995)
Dell	Computers	Horngren *et al.* (1999)
Douglas	Aerospace	Friedman & Lyne (1995)
E&A	Architects	Chaffman & Talbott (1991)
Farrall	Water	Cooper *et al.* (1992)
Feltham	Aerospace	Friedman & Lyne (1999)
Gamma	Retail	Innes & Mitchell (1990)
Harris	Semiconductors	Dedera (1996)
Henley	Automotive	Friedman & Lyne (1995)

Name	Sector	Author and Date
Hewlett Packard	Circuit Boards	Cooper (1988b)
Ink Creations	Silk Printing	Baxendale & Gupta (1998)
IXXX	Healthcare	Gupta *et al.* (1997)
John Deere	Engineering	Kaplan (1987b)
Lawson	Software	Dub (1998)
Layton	Automotive	Bruesewitz & Talbott (1997)
Lord	Shock Absorbers	Rupp (1995)
Mahany	Welding	Krupnicki & Tyson (1997)
Monarch	Mirror Doors	Cooper *et al.* (1992)
Monarch Paper	Paper	Shank & Govindarajan (1988)
Mueller-Lehmkuhl	Fasteners	Cooper (1986)
Nortel	Telecommunication	Dorey (1998)
Original Bradford	Soap	Gammell & McNair (1994)
Philpot	Credit Cards	Friedman & Lyne (1995)
Richards	Household	Friedman & Lyne (1995)
Rossford	Glass	Colson & MacGuidwin (1989)
Schrader-Bellows	Pneumatic Controls	Cooper (1985)
Siemens	Electrical Engines	Cooper (1988a)
Sisu	Vehicles	Malmi (1997)
Slade	Automotive	Cooper *et al.* (1992)
Spicer	Fasteners	Friedman & Lyne (1995)
Steward	Securities Trader	Cooper *et al.* (1992)
Tektronix	Electronics	Cooper & Turney (1988)
Teva	Pharmaceuticals	Kaplan *et al.* (1997)
Titanic	Motor	Smith & Lekson (1991)
US Postal	Post	Carter *et al.* (1995)
Waltham	Aerospace	Friedman & Lyne (1995)
Wavering	Building	Friedman & Lyne (1995)
Williams Brothers	Metals	Cooper *et al.* (1992)
Winchell	Lighting	Cooper & Kaplan (1987)
Zircan	Chemicals	Friedman & Lyne (1995)

References

Acton, D.D. and Cotton, W.D.J. (1997) 'Activity-based costing in a university setting', *Journal of Cost Management*, 11(2): 32–8.

Baxendale, S.J. and Gupta, M. (1998) 'Aligning TOC & ABC for silk screen printing', *Management Accounting* (US), April: 39–44.

Bruesewitz, S. and Talbott, J. (1997) 'Implementing ABC in a complex organisation', *CMA Magazine*, July–August: 16–19.

Carr, L.P. (1993) 'Unbundling the cost of hospitalisation: ABC can keep health care providers off the critical list', Management Accounting (US), November: 43–8.

Carter, T.L., Sedaghat, A.M. and Williams, T.D. (1995) 'How ABC changed the Post Office', *Management Accounting (US)*, February: 28–36.

Chaffman, B.M. and Talbott, J. (1991) 'Activity based costing in a service organisation', *CMA Magazine, 64(10)*: 15–18.

Colson, R.H. and MacGuidwin, M. (1989) 'The Rossford plant (glass production)', in *Cases from management accounting practice*, M.A. Robinson (Ed.), vol.5, pp.1–8.

Cooper, R. (1985) *Schrader-Bellows*. Harvard Business School cases 1-186-05051 to 055.

Cooper, R. (1986) *Mueller-Lehmkuhl*. Harvard Business School case 9-189-032.

Cooper, R. (1988a) *Siemens Electric Motor Works*. Harvard Business School cases 9-189-089 and 090.

Cooper, R. (1988b) *Hewlett-Packard*. Harvard Business School case 9-198-117.

Cooper, R. and Kaplan, R.S. (1987) *Winchell Lighting*. Harvard Business School cases 9-187-073 to 075.

Cooper, R. and Turney, P.B.B. (1988) *Tektronix*. Harvard Business School cases 9-188-142 to 144.

Cooper, R., Kaplan, R.S., Maisel, L.S., Morrisey, E. and Oehm, R.M. (1992) *Implementing activity based cost management: Moving from analysis to action*. Montvale: Institute of Management Accountants.

Datar, S., Kekre, S., Mukhopadyay, T. and Svaan, E. (1991) 'Overload overheads: Activity-based cost analysis of material handling in cell manufacturing', *Journal of Operations Management, 10(1)*: 119–37.

Dedera, C.R. (1996) 'Harris Semiconductor ABC: Worldwide implementation and total integration', *Journal of Cost Management, 10(1)*: 44–58.

Dorey, C. (1998) 'The ABC's of R&D at Nortel', *CMA Magazine*, March: 19–26.

Dub, S. (1998) 'ABM at Lawson: Putting the technology to work', *Management Accounting (US)*, April: 46–8.

Friedman, A.L. and Lyne, S.R. (1995) *Activity-based techniques: The real life consequences*. Chartered Institute of Management Accountants.

Friedman, A.L. and Lyne, S.R. (1999) *Success and failure of activity-based techniques: A long term perspective*. Chartered Institute of Management Accountants.

Gammell, F. and McNair, C.J. (1994) 'Jumping the growth threshold through activity-based cost management', *Management Accounting (US)*, September: 37–46.

Gupta, M., Baxendale, S. and McNamara, K. (1997) 'Integrating TOC and ABCM in a healthcare company', *Journal of Cost Management, 11(4)*: 23–33.

Horngren, C.T., Sundem, G.L. and Stratton, W.O. (1999) *Cost allocation and activity based costing: Dell Computer Corporation – on location!* A Custom Video Library introduction to management accounting, 11E, Prentice Hall Inc.

Innes, J. and Mitchell, F. (1990) *Activity based costing: A review with case studies.* Chartered Institute of Management Accountants.

Kaplan, R.S. (1987a) *American Bank.* Harvard Business School case 9-187-194.

Kaplan, R.S. (1987b) *John Deere Component Works.* Harvard Business School cases 9-187-197 and 108.

Kaplan, R.S., Weiss, D. and Desheh, E. (1997) 'Transfer pricing with ABC', *Management Accounting (US)*, May: 20–8.

Krupnicki, M. and Tyson, T. (1997) 'Using ABC to determine the cost of servicing customers', *Management Accounting (US)*, December: 40–6.

Malmi, T. (1997) 'Towards explaining activity-based costing failure: Accounting and control in a decentralised organisation', *Management Accounting Research, 8(4)*: 459–80.

Rupp, A.W. (1995) 'ABC: A pilot approach', *Management Accounting (US)*, January: 50–5.

Shanahan, Y.P. (1995) 'Implementing an activity-based costing system: Lessons from the Australian Post', *Journal of Cost Management, 9(2)*: 60–4.

Shank, J.K. and Govindarajan, V. (1988) 'Transaction based costing for the complex product line: A field study', *Journal of Cost Management*, Summer: 31–8.

Smith, K.V. and Lekson, M.P. (1991) 'A manufacturing case study on activity based costing', *Journal of Cost Management, 15(2)*: 45–54.

23. Energy Costing

23:1 Why Energy Matters

Organisations use large amounts of energy for three main purposes – heating, cooling and lighting of buildings; transport; and industrial processes. This consumption is an important business issue for three reasons:

1. *for many organisations it is a substantial cost – which could rise faster than inflation in future – but also one which can often be reduced with relative ease;*
2. *measures to increase energy efficiency can also improve productivity in other areas;*
3. *the production, distribution and consumption of energy has major environmental impacts.*

However, energy consumption and costs are frequently not controlled as closely as costs in other areas since:

(a) *frequently, responsibility for energy consumption is dispersed across an organisation and there is no single, clear line of accountability;*
(b) *because of this, energy costs are often not monitored and controlled so closely through accounting systems as are other costs;*
(c) *accountants and other non-experts may be unaware of the potential to make savings through existing technology, or of the pace of change in energy-related technologies.*

23:1.1 Reducing Costs

(*See* Ch.27.)

Although over-capacity and deregulation have reduced the general level of energy costs over the last decade, they still represent a substantial cost for most organisations.

Martin Bennett and Peter James

There are many cases of organisations which have cost-effectively reduced or stabilised their energy consumption. Manchester Airport, for example, has cut its energy usage consumption from around 750 kWh per square metre of building to around 500 kWh in 1997. This has meant that the airport's rapid expansion has been achieved with very little increase in its absolute energy demand – and has added well over £1m a year to its annual profits. The airport now has a target of reducing its energy budget by 5% a year.

Research has shown that almost all organisations have similar opportunities for cost-effective measures to reduce consumption. ETSU (formerly the Energy Technology Support Unit, and now incorporated into Future Energy Solutions), for example, has estimated that there are sufficient projects meeting normal payback criteria to reduce the current energy demand of industry by 15% (ENDS, 1996). A survey of energy efficiency in small firms also found that half felt that they were taking inadequate precautions to save energy and that only a minority had undertaken such simple – and almost always cost-effective – measures as draught proofing or installing light-sensitive switches (British Chamber of Commerce, 1996).

23:1.2 Increasing Productivity

A number of organisations have also found that actions taken to improve energy efficiency have created further, more intangible, benefits. For example, an energy-efficiency programme at a post office involved lowering a high ceiling to improve heating, cooling and acoustics, and the installation of more efficient and less intense lighting. The expected result was a £30,000 saving in annual energy costs. The unexpected additional result was a 6% improvement in the productivity of letter sorting. Since there had been no other significant changes in operations during this period, this was attributed to the better lighting and improved acoustics. A study co-authored by a US Department of Energy official noted similar examples at Boeing, Pennsylvania Power & Light, Wal-Mart, West Bend Mutual Insurance and other organisations (Romm and Browning, 1994).

23:1.3 Reducing Environmental Impacts

The production, distribution and use of energy creates enormous amounts of pollution and waste materials and, at present, often depletes non-renewable fossil fuels. It is also the principal man-made source of carbon dioxide emissions, which are thought to produce global warming (*see* **Ch.34**).

The UK and other governments have accepted commitments under the Rio and Kyoto accords to reduce their carbon dioxide emissions over the near to medium-term future. In order to meet these commitments they have adopted, or are considering, a range of policy measures including fiscal incentives such as 'green taxes'. Hence, fossil fuels in particular are likely to be more heavily taxed in future in order to discourage their consumption and the consequent generation of carbon dioxide. *The Cadbury Report* (1992) recommended that companies report, in their Operating and Financial Review (OFR), their environmental protection costs and potential environmental liabilities [*cf. FRS12: Provisions, Contingent Liabilities and Contingent Assets*] (*see* **Ch.47, para. 47:2**).

Although with OPEC's loss of influence the oil crises of the 1970s are unlikely to recur in a similar form, supplies of the key fossil fuels – oil and gas – continue to be vulnerable to unpredictable political factors. As a result, cost-effective reductions in consumption not only create environmental benefit but also provide protection against possible long-term increases in price and/or disruptions to supply.

As well as direct business benefits through reduced costs and/or risks, energy improvements by companies also directly assist in reaching the national emissions reductions targets agreed at Rio and Kyoto, and can legitimately be claimed by companies (e.g. in published corporate environmental reports) as part of their contribution to improving the environment.

23:1.4 Dispersion of Responsibility

By its nature, energy consumption is universal across all functions of an organisation. Because of this, responsibility for control over the usage of energy is dispersed. Even if energy costs are allocated against individual managers' budgets based on actual usage (which is frequently not the case – *see* **para.23:1.5**), they may represent only a relatively small proportion of each individual's budget. This may obscure drivers of energy costs which are common across the organisation where clear central direction and guidance could help with control.

Energy costs are usually only a small proportion of turnover and are distributed between a number of departments and budgets. Hence, unless responsibility for energy cost management is clearly identified, control can be dissipated (*see* **para.23:2.2**).

23:1.5 Cost Control

Parallel with this, the experience of the Energy Efficiency Best Practice Programme (EEBPP) of the Department of Environment, Transport and the Regions (DETR) (replaced in June 2001 by the Department for Transport and the Department for Environment, Food and Rural Affairs) has been that in many companies energy costs are initially classified as overheads and then either:

(a) *written off against profits as period costs, without being tracked to processes and products or charged against the budgets of the individual managers whose actions have caused their incurrence in the first place; or*

(b) *where they are tracked to products, processes and individual budgets, this is often not directly based on actual usage but is by general apportionment, for example, on the basis of floor areas of different departments.*

In either situation the link between responsibility and accountability is weakened or lost, since actions by individuals to control their own energy consumption at work are not reflected in their own measured performance. To achieve this would require more detailed direct measurement, for example by installing meters in separate processes and departments.

Even when energy costs are identified they are not always allocated to relevant budgets. In one distribution organisation, for example, the energy costs of its depots were made known to depot managers but were not incorporated into their budgets. Hence, they gained no financial benefit from any reductions in energy consumption so – unsurprisingly – they did not prioritise energy efficiency investments.

23:1.6 Energy-related Technologies

Although many companies still have considerable potential to realise energy savings through relatively simple changes in practice, energy-related technologies can be complex (e.g. combined heat and power (CHP) schemes and 'high-efficiency' motors), and continue to develop fast. Companies need to be able to monitor changes in technologies relevant to their businesses, for example by making use of the literature such as practice guides and other advice available through publicly funded business support programmes (*see* **para.23:4**).

Conversely energy technology specialists can find themselves blocked, in attempting to implement changes, by the organisation's financial processes and their unfamiliarity with these – for example, with the most appropriate way in which to formulate capital investment proposals.

23:1.6.1 Accountants and Energy Management

Accountants can contribute to energy management by:

(a) *ensuring that responsibilities are properly defined and adequate controls are in place;*
(b) *providing necessary data on energy consumption and costs, analysed as appropriate, for planning and decision making;*
(c) *carrying out regular analyses of spending and reporting on significant variances;*
(d) *ensuring that energy costs are properly budgeted, based on realistic cost drivers;*
(e) *identifying and evaluating potential improvements in control, for example through cost-benefit analyses of extended metering systems;*
(f) *participating in any energy teams or task forces which are formed.*

23:2 Energy Management

23:2.1 Key Steps In Energy Management

Energy costing is not something which is done in isolation – to be effective it has to be part of a process of energy management. The flow chart in **Fig.23:1**, which has been developed by BRECSU (formerly known as the Building Research Establishment Energy Conservation Support Unit) for the DETR's Best Practice Programme, shows the seven key steps in this process:

1. *identify clear lines of responsibility;*
2. *establish the facts;*
3. *compare your performance;*
4. *plan and organise;*
5. *pay less for your energy;*
6. *use less energy;*
7. *control and monitor (DETR, 1997).*

Paragraph 23:1.6.1 suggests how accountants in particular can contribute to this proccss.

Figure 23:1 **Step-by-step flow chart**

This Guide sets out seven simple steps to improve the energy efficiency and profitability of your company. These are explained in the diagram below, and described in more detail in the rest of the Guide.

Your best strategy for saving energy will depend on the nature and scale of your business. It is not necessary to complete each of the steps in the flow chart before commencing the next.

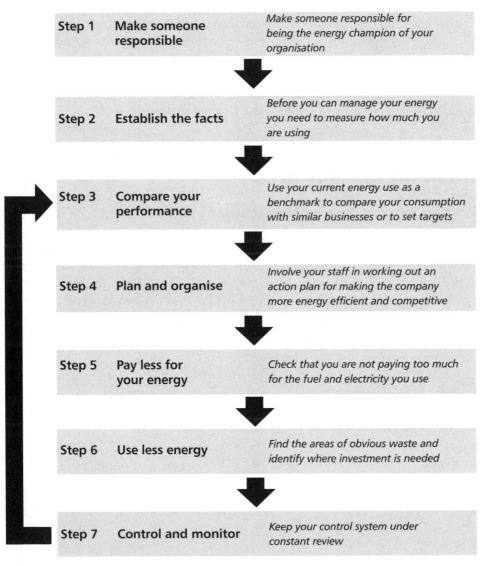

Step 1	**Make someone responsible**	*Make someone responsible for being the energy champion of your organisation*
Step 2	**Establish the facts**	*Before you can manage your energy you need to measure how much you are using*
Step 3	**Compare your performance**	*Use your current energy use as a benchmark to compare your consumption with similar businesses or to set targets*
Step 4	**Plan and organise**	*Involve your staff in working out an action plan for making the company more energy efficient and competitive*
Step 5	**Pay less for your energy**	*Check that you are not paying too much for the fuel and electricity you use*
Step 6	**Use less energy**	*Find the areas of obvious waste and identify where investment is needed*
Step 7	**Control and monitor**	*Keep your control system under constant review*

Reproduced from 'Energy Saving Guide for Small Businesses', Department of the Environment Transport and the Regions, BRESCU, Watford, 1997.

23:2.2 Responsibility

Larger companies will usually have a full-time energy manager (though even here, his or her role will usually be consultative rather than executive, since the actions which cause energy to be consumed may be taken by people at all levels across the organisation). In smaller companies, energy cost control will often be a part-time responsibility, assigned to someone with other responsibilities and with little or no technical expertise (not infrequently a financial controller or equivalent).

23:2.3 Establish the Facts

The key facts for energy management are:

(a) *quantities used, that is, detailed figures for consumption of different kinds of energy (gas, oil, petrol, electricity, etc.), for all significant activities and costs centres within the company;*

(b) *the prices paid, which with deregulation and increased competition in supply have in recent years become far more complex than previously.*

The starting point is to generate aggregate figures for current and historic consumption. In the first place invoice data will be available through the accounting system, but this will usually be in aggregate form which does not help the consuming company to track the total cost incurred to the many energy cost drivers across the organisation. More detailed data will be required which can be obtained only from meter readings. These can then be used to:

(a) *check the accuracy of invoices before approval for payment;*

(b) *understand the broad pattern of consumption and trends over time and highlight any unusual peaks or lows in consumption which can be investigated more thoroughly (e.g. to see if they are connected with equipment malfunctioning);*

(c) *establish whether levels of consumption are sufficient to earn volume discounts, or to be put out for tender among suppliers.*

The next stage is to build disaggregated data for individual processes, cost centres, etc. While much can be done with existing data this will often require collection of new sources such as:

(a) *installation of additional meters;*

(b) *installation of a computerised energy management system;*

(c) *changes in record keeping, for example, to capture fuel consumption, mileage, service and driver data for individual vehicles so that unduly high fuel costs can be identified and analysed.*

Identifying the potential to improve control by increasing the extent of direct measurement, and carrying out cost-benefit analyses of increased metering, etc. is an area where financial managers can make an obvious contribution to energy costing and management.

23:2.4 Comparing Performance

Once the data has been assembled, it can be assessed in order to identify opportunities for improvement. This involves making comparisons:

(a) *over time;*

(b) *between similar buildings, processes, etc. within the organisation;*

(c) *with similar buildings, processes, etc. in other organisations;*

(d) *with 'best practice' benchmarks (see **Ch.51**) (published by the DETR under the Energy Efficiency Best Practice Programme – see **Table 23:1**).*

Table 23:1 **Comparing your building's performance**

Source: Department of Environment, Transport and the Regions – Energy Efficiency Best Practice Programme

Type of building	Good performance less than ($£/m^2$)	Poor performance more than ($£/m^2$)
Offices		
Naturally ventilated/cellular	3.74	6.47
Naturally ventilated/open plan	4.70	7.79
Air-conditioned	8.40	14.92
Factory/warehouse		
General manufacturing	7.80	10.60
Light manufacturing	5.50	9.20
Warehouse/storage	4.00	5.60
High street shops		
Non-food shops	15.00	20.00
Food shops	30.00	37.00
Estate and travel agencies	6.00	8.50
Restaurants	60.00	70.00
Fast food outlets	65.00	75.00
Hotels	*(£/bedroom)*	*(£/bedroom)*
Business/holiday	560	860
Smaller	520	740

Comparisons have to be made with caution for two reasons. One is that trends in consumption and cost do not always correlate – costs can sometimes fall even if consumption levels remain the same or even rise, when good deals have been struck with suppliers. The relative effects of changes in efficiency of usage, and in prices, need to be distinguished in analysing variances so that adverse trends in consumption are not masked by reduced prices paid per unit.

The second reason is that in interpreting the figures, adjustments have to be made for any other significant factors, perhaps uncontrollable by the company, which can affect energy consumption or costs. These might include:

(a) *weather conditions which affect the consumption in buildings of heating or air conditioning. By tracking consumption over time and relating it to the ambient weather conditions through the 'degree-days' method, consumption models can be built which indicate the levels of consumption to be expected at different outside temperature levels. These can be used as benchmarks against which to compare actual consumption, in analysing variances;*

(b) *non-volume-related drivers of energy consumption in production. For example when Baxter International were analysing their total savings achieved through energy efficiency programmes, when preparing their annual environmental financial statement, they were surprised to find in one major facility that despite several improvements which had been implemented, savings in one period appeared to be negative. Further investigation revealed the cause to be that substantial new production capacity had come on stream during the period, but had not reached full utilisation for some time. Since a large part of the energy consumption was determined by the plant merely being on stream, irrespective of the volume of production passing through it, this rather than any real fall in performance explained the apparent – though temporary – deterioration in energy consumption relative to volume.*

23:2.5 Planning and Organising

This stage involves establishment of objectives and targets for reducing energy costs and/or consumption.

An action plan must then be developed to communicate the targets, assign responsibility for achieving them and otherwise support implementation. This may require changes to accounting systems to collect new data, or modify the codings or other aspects of existing categories.

Gaining the commitment of senior management and other staff is vital at this stage. The best means of gaining the former is to make a good business case, with the environmental benefits as an additional benefit – 'icing on the cake'. This can also motivate shop-floor staff. In one project, trades unionists and shop stewards were involved and realised that energy efficiency was a significant competitive issue for their employers and could affect their members' job security. They then encouraged their members to look for areas of potential savings at which, with their close familiarity with operations, they proved very successful.

In many organisations the real barrier to change has been middle management, in part because the energy improvements which they could facilitate are not reflected in their job targets and budgetary responsibilities.

23:2.6 Paying Less for Energy

Deregulation and other factors have made energy markets much more competitive. The situation now is that:

(a) *organisations can purchase from any supplier of gas;*
(b) *organisations with an electricity demand of more than 100 kVA can already purchase from any supplier, and all organisations should be able to do so by late 1998.*

Experts believe that these developments should allow many organisations to reduce their gas and electricity costs in coming years. Cash reductions are more likely to be achieved if organisations have a detailed picture of their current and anticipated consumption. This is particularly important when negotiating for electricity, where a number of factors (many of which also apply to other types of energy consumption) can determine the price and influence the form of contract signed. These include:

(a) *overall volume;*
(b) *pattern of consumption, especially with regard to winter peak periods and off-peak night-time and weekend periods;*
(c) *flexibility of consumption, such as the ability to move demands for energy from peak to non-peak times, and to tolerate temporary cuts in supply;*
(d) *characteristics of the load (e.g. low power factors).*

Often specialist advice will be necessary. One energy consultant (Basford, 1997) has given the following pointers to reducing costs:

(a) *Do not leave renegotiation of your energy contract until the last minute, otherwise you may not have time to get the best deal; you should start at least three months in advance and before your suppliers contact you with their quotations.*
(b) *Do not accept only one quotation, even if it is better than in previous years.*
(c) *Watch out for the basis on which the supplier quotes – is it comparable with quotations provided by other alternative suppliers?*
(d) *Ensure that you get a contract to suit your operations and that if you can reduce consumption at short notice, ensure that you receive adequate compensation for this facility.*

He provides an example of one company spending £60,000 per annum on gas and £30,000 per annum on electricity which saved 35% of the former and 30% of the latter by following this advice.

23:2.7 Use Less Energy

The collection of data should have revealed many areas of potential cost reduction. These can be supplemented by more targeted investigations of particular areas such as lighting, heating or vehicle fuel consumption. Generally speaking, measures can be distinguished between no cost (good housekeeping), low cost or high cost (*see* **Table 23:2**). Obviously, it makes sense to focus on no-cost and low-cost areas first. The sources cited in **paragraph 23:4** give detailed guidance on these areas.

Table 23:2 **Energy-saving measures**

Source: Department of Environment, Transport and the Regions – Energy Efficiency Best Practice Programme

Measures	*Examples*	*Emphasis*
No-cost (*good housekeeping*)	Resetting controls Switch off when not required Repair leaks Reschedule loads/usage	Behaviour of people using existing installed technology
Low-cost	Maintenance Meters M&T monitoring Simple controls Insulation Training end users	A combination of investment in low-cost technology and people involvement
High-cost	Heat recovery systems Combined heat and power Fuel conversion Energy management systems	Investment in high-cost technology with some people involvement

A further option at this stage is to contract with an energy management company. They take day-to-day responsibility for managing energy supply on the basis of taking a share of any cost savings achieved. Such contracts can be very beneficial to companies although care needs to be taken in defining what savings are – for example, actions which would have been taken anyway should be excluded – and in not underestimating potential opportunities for saving.

23:2.8 Monitor and Control

A successful energy management initiative should be not a one-off project but a continuing programme over time. One aspect of this is monitoring the achievement of targets and regularly reviewing progress. The latter also provides an opportunity to consider new information which has come to light since the initial steps were made.

One area where the accounting function can be important is in ensuring that any changes to the accounting system do not conflict with the objectives of energy management (or environmental management – *see* **Ch.34**). This was the case in one company where a business process re-engineering exercise (*see* **Ch.23**) resulted in the condensing of a number of separate energy codes into a single code. This made it more difficult not only to track energy consumption in detail but also to generate data on carbon dioxide emissions from fuel combustion, which will almost certainly be needed for environmental management purposes in future.

23:3 Conclusions

The evidence is that most organisations could do more to reduce or stabilise their energy costs – Example 1 in **paragraph 23:3.1** describes how British Telecom was able to realise substantial savings in energy used in its telephone exchanges, mainly through simple 'good housekeeping' measures. Two frequent barriers in many organisations are lack of information, and a feeling that energy management is too technical a subject for non-experts such as accountants to become involved in. **Paragraph 23:4** provides ways of remedying the former while we hope that this chapter demonstrates that the latter is incorrect. Accountants are key players in the task of understanding and managing energy costs.

23:3.1 Example 1: Energy Costing and Management at BT Telephone Exchanges

BT has reduced its energy consumption substantially in recent years. One factor in this achievement has been benchmarking the energy consumption and costs of telephone exchanges. Energy accounts for around 44% of telephone exchange running costs, so increased efficiency brings considerable financial benefit. A project team of five members was established, with the aim of highlighting the poorest-performing exchanges and identifying ways in which their energy consumption and costs could be reduced.

The first step was to gather data on energy consumption and costs and then to relate these to exchange capacity. This produced a ranking of the energy performance of individual sites. In the first, pilot, stage an audit team was then sent to the three worst performing sites to find the reasons for the poor energy performance. These included powering up of redundant equipment; heating and cooling equipment operating at the same time; and poorly controlled heating and lighting. The result was immediate savings of several thousands of pounds through simple good housekeeping measures, and the potential for further savings through investment. The audit is now being rolled out to all poorly performing sites and should result in annual savings of at least £200,000 per annum just from good housekeeping measures. The benchmarking team is also taking the exercise further by examining the characteristics of the best-performing sites for ideas that can be applied elsewhere.

Some key points which have emerged from the BT initiative were:

(a) *Keep it simple – the more complicated such exercises are, the more costly it will be and the more difficult to persuade people to take action.*

(b) *Focus on easy wins – 20% of sites are likely to have 80% of the potential for energy savings.*

(c) *Build into 'business-as-usual' – otherwise motivation fades after a year or two, as has been the case with some previous energy-efficiency initiatives.*

23:4 Sources of Information in the UK

Local Business Links organisations can provide advice on energy management. The Energy Saving Trust also gives free advice on energy efficiency and grants for improvement to small businesses. Further assistance can be obtained from the Energy Efficiency Best Practice Programme through the Energy Helpline. Hundreds of publicauons on energy efficiency in specific sectors, processes and companies are available from BRECSU, focusing on buildings, and ETSU, focusing on industry and transport.

References

Basford, I. (1997) 'Minimising your energy costs', *Management Accounting*, July/August: 52.

British Chamber of Commerce (1996) *Small firms survey 20: Energy efficiency*. London.

Department of the Environment, Transport and the Regions DETR (1997) *Energy saving guide for small businesses*. Garston: Building Research Establishment.

ENDS Report (1996) 'Low energy prices threaten scope for industrial CO_2 savings', November: 5.

Management Charter Initiative with the Institute of Energy and Gas (1995) *The Good Energy Manager's Guide*. London.

Romm, J. and Browning, W. (1994) *Greening the building and the bottom line*. Snowmass, CO: Rocky Mountain Institute.

The Committee on the Financial Aspects of Corporate Governance (1992) *The Financial Aspects of Corporate Governance* (The Cadbury Report), December.

24. Target Costing

24:1 Definition

The basic idea underlying target costing is to bring the market into the costing system. A target cost can be defined as follows:

Target cost	=	Target selling *less* price	Desired profit

Traditional costing starts with internal costs and builds these up to a total unit cost by adding together:

Unit material cost	+	Unit labour cost	+	Unit direct expenses	+	Unit variable overheads	+	Unit fixed overheads	=	Unit cost

In contrast target costing starts with a unit price set by the market in the future and deducts the required profit margin to find the target unit cost. In summary, target costing begins with the expected future market price for a product and works back to a target cost.

24:1.1 Users' Target Costs

The above is the normal definition of target cost. It is seldom mentioned that, as with much of traditional costing, this definition is a target cost considering only the manufacturer's costs. A wider definition of target costing is to consider not only the target unit cost for the manufacturer but also the target costs for the user. In fact there is very often a trade-off between a manufacturer's target cost and users' target costs because users may well be willing to pay a higher initial price for a product if the future costs of using that product are reduced.

Users' future costs include:

(a) costs of using product;
(b) costs of maintaining product;
(c) costs of disposing of product.

For example, in the case of a large machine with a life of ten years, the buyer may well be more interested in the total costs over the lifetime of that machine rather than the initial purchase price of that machine. Another example is the initial price for a new building against the operating costs of that building during its lifetime. Basically this is the concept of combining the idea of target costing with the idea of product life-cycle costing (*see* **Ch.19** for further details). The rest of this chapter will discuss target costing from the viewpoint of the producer's target cost for illustrative purposes.

24:1.2 Objectives of Target Costing

For most organisations the primary objective, and usually the main reason for introducing a target costing system is to reduce costs. Setting a target cost is only the first step in such a process. Indeed target cost management may be a better term than target costing. However, organisations also introduce target costing for at least three other reasons:

1. *to improve quality (see* **Ch.18***);*
2. *to satisfy customer needs better;*
3. *to introduce new products in a more timely manner.*

For many organisations the actual experience of target costing increases the importance of each of the above objectives of target costing. Obviously target costing can be used in the planning stage for new products. However, target costing can also be applied to existing products during different stages of the product life cycle (*see* **Ch.19**). For example, during the early production stages of a product, a target cost can be set for the mature stage of that product.

24:2 Setting Target Costs

In **paragraph 24:1** above the setting of a target cost seemed to be very clear cut. Conceptually it is but, in practice, there are alternative methods to the subtraction method of future market price less required profit. Two methods used by organisations in Japan are the addition method and the integrated method. Both these methods are called forms of target costing although they do not meet the above strict definition of target costing.

There are two variants of the addition method of setting a target cost. The first variant is based on similar products already manufactured by the organisation and simply sets a cost-reduction objective of 30% to 50% of the cost of a similar product and this is called a target cost. In my opinion this is not really a target cost because it ignores the market. The second variant is when the target cost is based on a cost reduction from existing products of competitors. This variant at least takes some account of the market.

The integrated method of setting a target cost is basically a combination of both the subtraction and addition methods. In other words the target cost becomes a process of negotiation. This is important because the behavioural effects of setting a target cost are absolutely critical. If no one considers that a target cost can be achieved, it will probably not be. There must be a real commitment by everyone involved to achieve the agreed target cost. This is why such a negotiation process can be an integral part of setting a target cost.

The discussion so far has implied that only one target cost is set. This is the case in many organisations but some organisations set tolerance limits of + or − 5% or 10% for their target cost. In other words it is a target cost area. Other organisations set a target cost for different stages in the product life cycle. For example, a target cost of £100 per unit might be set for the planning stage, £80 per unit for the design stage, £70 per unit for the pilot manufacturing stage and £65 per unit for the normal manufacturing stage. The advantage of such a stepped target cost is that managers can monitor that a target cost is going to be achieved. If you have only one target cost of £65 per unit for the normal manufacturing stage it may be only at the manufacturing stage that you realise that you are not going to achieve your target cost and by then it may be too late to take corrective action.

24:2.1 Target Cost Example

A simplified example can illustrate the difference between adopting one target cost or three different target costs and such an example is given in **Figure 24:1**.

Figure 24:1 **Example of setting a target cost**

The projections for a proposed new product A are as follows:

(a) total market life is five years;
(b) forecast sales during the life cycle of product A are:

	Introduction (1st year)	Maturity (2nd & 3rd years)	Decline (4th & 5th years)
Unit price	£30	£25	£20
Sales volume (units)	5,000	36,000	19,000

(c) total investment is £500,000;
(d) required return on investment is 20% per annum.

Alternative of one target cost for product A

		(£)
Sales	5,000 units × £30	150,000
	36,000 units × £25	900,000
	19,000 units × £20	380,000
		1,430,000
Cost of sales		?
Profit being 20% of £500,000 x 5 years		500,000
By deduction cost of sales is		**£930,000**
Target cost = £930,000/60,000 =		**£15.50 per unit**

Alternative of three target costs over life cycle of product A

	Introduction (£)	Maturity (£)	Decline (£)	Total (£)
Sales	150,000	900,000	380,000	1,430,000
Cost of sales	?	?	?	930,000
Profit (Note 1)	52,000	315,000	133,000	500,000
By deduction cost of sales is	98,000	585,000	247,000	
Number of units	5,000	36,000	19,000	
Target cost per unit	19.60	16.25	13.00	

Note 1: Profit as a percentage of sales is £500,000/£1,430,000 which is approximately 35% so that during the introduction phase profit is 35% of £150,000 (i.e. approximately £52,000); during the maturity phase profit is 35% of £900,000 (i.e. £315,000); and during the decline phase profit is 35% of £380,000 (i.e. £133,000).

Figure 24:1 combines the idea of target costing with return on investment and the product life-cycle view (*see also* **Ch.14**). The result is a target cost of £15.50 per unit for product A or a life-cycle view of target costing with a target cost of £19.60 during the introductory stage, £16.25 during the maturity stage and £13.00 during the decline stage of product A. At least £20, £16 and £13 would be the ball-park areas for these three target costs.

24:2.2 Cost Elements within a Target Cost

Having established the target cost starting from a future market price, it might seem that the difficult part is over. In reality this is only the very start of the target costing process. The next step is to ensure that everyone involved in this process of achieving the target cost agrees on the costs to be included in this target. Generally, there is no doubt that the following costs are covered by the target cost:

(a) *direct material costs;*
(b) *direct labour costs;*
(c) *production overhead costs.*

Overhead costs, of course, raise the question of overhead cost per unit. This will involve deciding the level of production. Other costs which are usually included are development costs associated with the product and non-production overheads (*see* **Ch.22**). If some costs are excluded, the target cost needs to be amended accordingly.

24:2.3 Responsibility for Target Costing

In Japan different organisations have different departments responsible for organising and co-ordinating their target costing exercises. For example, the most common department with overall responsibility for target costing is the design department. This is not surprising given the usefulness of the target costing technique in the design of new products and the redesign of existing products.

Other departments which may have overall responsibility in Japan for target costing include the following:

- product planning;

- accounting;

- research and development;

- marketing;

- purchasing;

- manufacturing.

Perhaps the main point which this emphasises is that target costing can be viewed very much as a management technique and not just as an accounting technique.

24:2.4 Target Costing Participants

There may be a target costing team but this will be composed of representatives from various departments (again such as design, product planning, accounting, research and development, marketing, purchasing and manufacturing). Such a team cannot achieve the target cost on its own but will liaise with members of its own department and co-ordinate the overall process to ensure that the target cost is met. Given the importance of materials and subcomponent assemblies for many organisations, such organisations sometimes include their suppliers as participants in the target costing exercise. If an organisation has a long-term relationship with a few suppliers who account for a significant percentage of an organisation's costs, it makes sense to include such suppliers in the target-costing process.

24:3 Target Cost Management

In many respects setting the target cost is the easy part. The difficult part is achieving the target cost set. The usual term is target costing but target cost management describes the technique more accurately. How can organisations manage the costs so that the target cost is achieved?

24:3.1 Segmenting the Target Cost

The first step is to segment the target cost so that different departments or individuals have their own target cost to achieve. Segmental reporting exists in order that users receive the greater level of detail that is required about the results and resources of a business entity, for them to make fully informed decisions. *SSAP25: Segmental Reporting* deals with this in the UK, and *IAS14: Segment Reporting* is the relevant international comparison. Segmenting the target cost is a critical step in the entire process of cost management. How then is the target cost segmented? There are three main bases of segmenting the target cost used in practice:

1. *by part or subcomponent assemblies;*
2. *by function (see Ch.25);*
3. *by department.*

The segmentation by part and by department is fairly self-explanatory. For example, a designer or team of designers would have a target set to design a part or subcomponent assembly for £500. Similarly, a target can be set for a department's costs in relation to a particular product.

A survey of Japanese companies by Yoshikawa (1992) found that assigning the target cost to the functions of a product was the most common method of target cost assignment. **Chapter 25** has a full explanation of functions but, in summary, a product has several functions. These functions can be expressed in terms of a verb and a noun. For example, some functions of a pen could include:

- make mark;

- flow ink;

- store ink;

- prevent stains.

The target cost is then assigned among the various functions of a product. Again, this raises the question of how the target cost is assigned.

24:3.2 Assigning the Target Cost

Whatever way the target cost is segmented, whether it is by part or function or department, the target cost has still to be assigned on some basis. The poorest basis is an arbitrary basis. Another basis is a subjective basis where the target cost team decide on the basis of their experience how the target cost should be assigned. An interesting basis in terms of functions is to ask the customers how important they consider each function to be and assign the target cost to the various functions on the basis of the customers' views. This is another way of bringing external information into the costing system. An example of assigning a target cost of £1,000 for a product to four different functions based on the views of the customers is given in **Table 24:1**. The target cost of the product is £1,000:

Table 24:1 **Example of assigning a target cost**

Function	Customers' views on importance of functions (%)	Target cost assigned (£)
W	40	400
X	20	200
Y	30	300
Z	10	100
	100	1,000

Table 24:1 assigns £400 to function W and this would become the target for the team of designers involved with function W. This is a very useful starting point. The target costing team need to be aware that customers may not put a high weighting on some functions – such as those required by law. However, it is only a question of minor refinements to the customers' views and any such refinements need to be carefully justified.

24:3.3 Achieving the Target Cost

Having set, segmented and assigned the target cost, the designers and others now have the parameters within which they can work. A general guideline is that the earlier you assign the target cost, the easier it is to achieve the target cost. An advantage of assigning the target cost to the functions of a product is that it gives designers and others the maximum flexibility. It allows them to decide how the function should be provided and it allows them to use their creativity to the full. If a target cost is assigned to parts of a product, that implies that some overall design of the product has already been made with specific parts involved. Nevertheless, this more constrained approach in assigning the target cost to parts of a product may be appropriate in certain circumstances.

It is important that everyone is committed to achieving the target cost and that there is an overall co-ordination of the target costing process so that any problem is identified at as early a stage as possible. Target cost management is a cost management technique with the focus very much on the product (*see* **Ch.27**). It is a technique which enables costs to be influenced well before production begins. With 60% to 80% of costs being committed before production begins, such a pre-production cost-management technique is very useful.

24:3.4 Time to Market and Quality

The emphasis in this chapter has been on the cost management aspect of target costing. There are, however, other aspects of target costing. The use of target costing helps to give a structured approach to the design of new products or the redesign of existing products. Some organisations have found that the use of target costing has speeded up the design and redesign process. In some sectors minimising the time to market for new or redesigned products is more important than minimising the cost because of the sales advantages of being first in the market with a new product.

Some organisations have also found that target costing has helped to improve the quality of their new and redesigned products. This, together with the market and customer focus of target costing, has very often improved customers' satisfaction with new and redesigned products. Nevertheless, target costing is only a technique and, as with all techniques, it has its problems and limitations.

24:4 Problems with Target Costing

The first problem usually encountered with target costing is actually setting the target cost. It is obviously very difficult to forecast the future market price at a specific point in time. Almost by definition such a forecast will be wrong but what is sought is not complete accuracy but a ball-park figure.

A second problem is the assumptions to be made about the future market situation including the following:

(a) *existing and new competitors;*
(b) *technological developments;*
(c) *customer preferences.*

Once decisions have been made about such assumptions a third problem is which type of target cost to set? Will it be one fixed target cost or several target costs for different stages in the product's life cycle? (*see* **Ch.19**) Again it is important that everyone understands what type of target cost is involved.

A fourth problem is the exact costs to be included in the target cost. Does the target cost include development costs and non-production overheads? If so, a fifth problem is agreeing the volume of production on which the unit target cost is based. A unit target cost has the same limitations as a traditional unit cost in terms of how overheads are dealt with. Again, if an activity-based approach is used (*see* **Ch.22**), everyone involved in the target costing process needs to understand this.

Having set the target cost, there is then perhaps the most difficult problem of all – how is the target cost to be achieved? This is the really interesting aspect of target costing when, after problems of segmenting and assigning the target cost have been overcome, it is a question of the creativity of all those involved in the target costing process. This is the problem of target cost management which also requires good co-ordination of the process so that problems can be identified at an early stage and solved. Target cost management involves the use of other techniques such as functional costing (*see* **Ch.25**), cost tables (*see* **Ch.26**) and those related to management accounting and design (*see* **Ch.41**).

24:5 Advantages of Target Costing

A very important advantage of target costing is that it integrates some market information into the costing system instead of the costing system being purely internally focused. It seems very sensible to do this and it is perhaps surprising that target costing is not more widespread than it is. A second very important advantage of target costing is that it is a technique which supports the cost reduction process both in the design of new products and the redesign of existing products. It is critical that management accountants contribute to the design and redesign processes during which such a high percentage of costs are committed.

Third, experience has shown that target costing helps to encourage both faster product development and faster redesign because of its structured and co-ordinated approach. Fourth, target costing is one way of linking customer requirements specifically to the design and redesign cost. Fifth, target costing encourages continuous product and process improvements.

24:6 Conclusions

Target costing is a technique well worth considering because it begins with a future market price and works back to a required cost. Setting the target cost is a difficult process but it is a ball-park figure approach. The really difficult part of target costing is actually achieving the target cost. A more descriptive term than 'target costing' is 'target cost management'.

Although a management accountant is usually involved in the target-costing team, in many organisations target costing is viewed as a management rather than simply an accounting technique and the team is often led by a non-accountant. The target-costing team has basically a co-ordinating role because so many departments and individuals are usually involved in the target-costing process. A critical stage for the target-costing team is the segmentation, and assignment of the target cost – for example, using the customers' views to assign the target cost to the individual functions of a product. Other techniques discussed in this Handbook such as functional costing (*see* **Ch.25**), cost tables (*see* **Ch.26**) and management accounting for design (*see* **Ch.42**) can then assist designers and others to achieve the required target cost in the design of a new product or the redesign of an existing product.

References

Yoshikawa, T. (1992) 'Comparative study of cost management in Japan and the UK' *Yokohama Business Review*, *13*, June: 79–106.

25. *Functional Costing*

25:1 Definition

Functional costing was developed by Japanese companies as a means of costing to aid cost management for both existing and new products and services (*see* **Ch.27**). This technique concentrates on the individual functions rather than on the individual parts of a product. For example, the parts of a pen might include the barrel, tip, ink cartridge and top. However, the functions of a pen might include the following:

- make mark;

- add colour;

- hold pen;

- flow ink;

- store ink;

- prevent stains.

As far as possible you try to express the functions in terms of a verb and a noun.

Costing the functions of a product is very different from costing the parts of a product. Basically, functional costing views the product in more abstract terms than traditional costing by costing the functions rather than the parts of a product. Functional costing is a more general approach to costing than traditional costing. It means that if two different products have the same function among their many different functions then that particular function will have the same cost in both products. Functional costing has been included in the costing section of this Handbook but it could also have been included under the decision-making section because functional costing, or more accurately functional cost analysis, is very much a cost management technique. Functional cost analysis is a particularly useful technique for the design of new products or the redesign of existing products (*see* **Ch.42**). The rest of this chapter will discuss functional cost analysis in this context.

John Innes

By concentrating on the functions of a product, it is possible to redesign an existing product so that the new product is very different from the existing product. If you concentrate on the parts of an existing product it is very likely that when you redesign it, the new product is almost the same as the existing product. Functional cost analysis is also one of the techniques which enables management accountants to contribute to the design process of both existing and new products. The chapters on product life-cycle costing (**Ch.19**), target costing (**Ch.24**), cost tables (**Ch.26**), value chain analysis (**Ch.40**) and design (**Ch.42**) discuss some other management accounting techniques which are useful during the design process.

25:1.1 Links to Value Analysis

British Standard 3138 ('Glossary of terms used in work study') defines value analysis as 'a systematic interdisciplinary examination of factors affecting the cost of a product or service in order to devise means of achieving the specified purpose most economically at the required standard of quality and reliability'. Functional cost analysis has similarities with value analysis. The objective is to increase profits and not just reduce costs. Functional cost analysis can help to identify areas or functions of a product where customers wish more to be spent leading to increased profits for the organisation.

Originally value analysis was developed by several American multinational companies and the Japanese have adapted their approach to develop functional cost analysis. Just as Japanese organisations learned from American companies in the past, so today it is worthwhile for western companies to consider some of the Japanese management accounting techniques such as functional cost analysis and cost tables (*see* **Ch.26**) to see whether they can learn and perhaps adapt some of these Japanese techniques. In most current management accounting textbooks there is very little, if anything, about value analysis.

25:2 Functional Cost Analysis

Functional cost analysis is a team activity with from four to seven employees from different areas of the business such as design, engineering, management accounting, marketing, production and purchasing. One of the great strengths of functional cost analysis is that it has a structured approach to achieve a specific objective to which all team members can contribute. This interdisciplinary group activity distinguishes functional cost analysis from much value engineering activity which tends to be dominated by engineers.

Japanese organisations usually run their functional cost analysis exercises with several competing teams considering the same design of a new product or the same redesign of an existing product. When a functional cost analysis exercise was organised in a Scottish organisation, it was considered inappropriate to have competing teams and so the technique was adapted so that the two teams involved co-operated with each other.

25:2.1 Areas of Application

The most common application of functional cost analysis is in relation to products or subassembly components. These can either be entirely new products or existing products to be redesigned. However, functional cost analysis can also be applied to services – leading perhaps to a new way of providing that service. Other areas where the functional cost analysis approach has been used include overheads and even the actual structure of an organisation. Nevertheless, the easiest way to understand functional cost analysis (FCA) is in relation to products and the following discussion is set in the context of physical products.

25:2.2 Selecting Products for FCA

Some Japanese organisations have a functional cost analysis department with perhaps three or four full-time employees who specialise in selecting the topics for functional cost analysis exercises and in co-ordinating these exercises. What criteria are used when selecting products or subassembly components for a functional cost analysis exercise? One criterion is to select completely new products where the functional cost analysis is integrated into the design process for such new products.

For existing products a critical decision is which product to select. For existing products the criteria when selecting products are very complex or very heavy or very bulky with a relatively high cost. The main objective is profit improvement but very often this is expressed in terms of cost reduction. For example, one objective for an existing product is to reduce the cost by 40% without reducing the quality. Very often this objective will be to achieve a target cost (*see* **Ch.24**). For example, for a pen the target cost might be 20 pence.

25:3 Steps in FCA

The basic steps in functional cost analysis are:

(a) select product to be designed or redesigned and decide objectives;
(b) collect information;
(c) decide individual functions of product;
(d) calculate cost of each function;
(e) ask customers to evaluate individual functions;
(f) assign target cost on basis of customers' weightings to each function;
(g) determine problem functions;
(h) brainstorm to generate suggestions for improvement;
(i) decide solution to achieve objectives;
(j) implement solution and audit actual results.

25:3.1 Select Product and Decide Objectives

The first step of selecting the product has already been discussed in **paragraph 25:2.2**. In the examples to date the emphasis has been on a cost reduction objective or meeting a target cost objective. However, depending on the circumstances other objectives can be set for the functional cost analysis exercise. For example, other objectives could include the following:

(a) increase the quality of the product without increasing the cost;
(b) reduce the weight of the product without increasing the cost;
(c) increase the functions of the product without increasing the cost;
(d) develop new patents.

Sometimes functional costing is combined with target costing (*see* **Ch.24**) where the cost is determined from an anticipated future selling price. For example, if the anticipated selling price is £50 per unit and the profit margin is £10 per unit then the target cost is £40 per unit. If the current cost per unit is £70, then the cost per unit needs to be reduced from £70 to £40.

25:3.2 Collect Information

The information collected would include the following:

    (a) existing specifications for product;
    (b) existing designs;
    (c) production process details;
    (d) materials, labour and overhead quantitative and cost data;
    (e) scrap data;
    (f) marketing data about the product.

25:3.3 Decide Individual Functions of Product

This is a brainstorming process and some team members may have difficulty in thinking in terms of functions rather than parts. It is also helpful to relate these functions together. For example, the main function for a pen could be to 'make mark' and if you ask the question *how* do you make a mark? the answer could be by 'adding colour' and if you ask the question *how* do you add the colour? the answer could be by 'flowing the ink'. The technique of pulling these functions together into a functional family tree will be discussed in **paragraph 25:3.11**.

25:3.4 Calculate Cost of Each Function

This is a traditional costing exercise and the results might be:

	pence
add colour	4
hold pen	6
flow ink	6
store ink	10
prevent stains	6
	32

25:3.5 Customers' Values for Each Function

This is a critical step and brings the customers' views into the costing system – something which rarely happens. One way of doing this is by formal market research asking customers to rate all the functions so that they total 100% – for example, the result might be:

	%
add colour	20
hold pen	10
flow ink	30
store ink	10
prevent stains	30
	100

25:3.6 Assign Target Cost to Each Function

The above customer derived percentages can then be applied to assign the target cost of 20 pence on the basis of the customers' weighting to each function as follows:

	pence	
add colour	4	i.e. 20% × 20 pence
hold pen	2	i.e. 10% × 20 pence
flow ink	6	
store ink	2	
prevent stains	6	
	20	

25:3.7 Determine Problem Functions

The costs identified in **Paras.** 25:3.4 and 25:3.6 can then be compared to determine the existing problem functions:

	Existing costs (pence)	Target cost assigned by customers' weightings (pence)
add colour	4	4
hold pen	6	2
flow ink	6	6
store ink	10	2
prevent stains	6	6
	32	20

The above suggests that 'hold pen' and 'store ink' are the two problem functions where the existing cost is much higher than the target cost assigned by the customers.

25:3.8 Brainstorming

This is the really creative part of functional cost analysis where all the team members make suggestions for improvement. This may involve deleting functions, adding functions, combining functions, using new materials, using new production processes or a host of other possibilities limited only by the team's imagination. In this pen example the functional cost analysis team would concentrate on suggesting alternative solutions to the existing 'hold pen' and 'store ink' to try to reduce the cost of these two problem functions identified under **paragraph** 25:3.7 above. Cost tables (*see* **Ch.26**) can be helpful at this stage when calculating the cost implications of different suggestions. No suggestion is rejected outright because what at first seems to be a silly suggestion may, in the end, turn out to be the best solution.

25:3.9 Decide Solution

The team decides the best solution from all the alternatives to achieve the required objectives and target cost. The team members present the findings, the suggested changes and the expected benefits to a small group of top managers in the organisation.

25:3.10 Implement Solution and Audit Results

It is obviously important to implement the chosen solution and ensure that the predicted results are actually achieved in practice.

To prevent overoptimistic assessments of the functional costing results, the team members know that, within a year, an auditor will report to top management on the actual effects of the changes implemented because of the functional costing exercise.

25:3.11 Functional Family Tree

Paragraphs 25:3.1 to **25:3.10** are the steps involved in functional cost analysis. A useful aid in the functional cost analysis process is the functional family tree which is a diagram showing the links between the different functions. For example, the functional family trees for a propelling ballpoint pen and a disposable ballpoint pen are shown in **Figures 25:1** and **25:2**. These functional family trees give an overview of the product and are particularly helpful when deciding the individual functions of the product (**para.25:3.3**).

One way of checking the logic of a functional family tree is to start with the primary function 'make mark' and move to the right asking 'How?'. For example, in both **Figures 25:1** and **25:2** 'How do you make a mark?' the answer is by putting colour. How do you put colour? The answer is by the ink flowing. If you start at the right of the functional family tree and move to the left towards the primary function you can ask the question 'Why?'. For example, why do you store ink? The answer is so that the ink will flow. Why does the ink flow? The answer is to put colour. Why do you put colour? The answer is to make a mark.

Figure 25:1 **Propelling ballpoint pen functional family tree**
Source: Yoshikawa *et al.* (1989) by permission of Warren, Gorham & Lamont

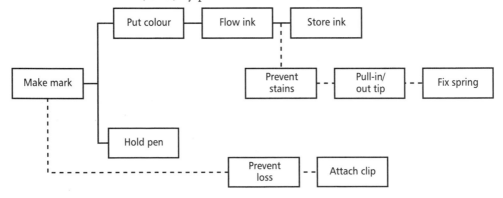

Figure 25:2 **Disposable ballpoint pen functional family tree**

Source: Yoshikawa *et al.* (1989) by permission of Warren, Gorham & Lamont

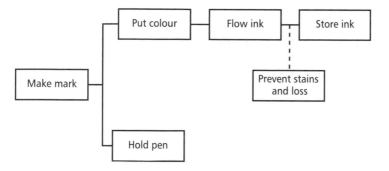

Once the brainstorming step has been finished, it is also useful to take the final solution and draw a new functional family tree to check that no function has been omitted. Again the logic of the new functional family tree can be checked. It may also be helpful to compare the original and new functional family trees to check the similarities and differences in case such a comparison raises questions which the functional cost analysis team have overlooked.

25:4 FCA of Overheads

The functional cost analysis approach can be equally well applied to services or to overheads. One advantage of applying it to an overhead area is that very often the overhead (such as purchasing) is simply a service provided to an *internal* customer. This means that it is even easier to ask the internal customers for their views on the individual functions.

An example of a functional family tree for purchasing is given in **Fig.25.3**. Following a functional cost analysis exercise a modified purchasing functional family tree was developed (*see* **Fig.25.4**) with the major change being closer involvement with a selected number of suppliers. This reduced various costs involved in the purchasing overhead such as:

(a) reduced price negotiations;
(b) simplified documentation;
(c) reduced supplier search;
(d) less supplier vetting.

Figure 25:3 **Procurement functional family tree**

Source: Yoshikawa *et al.* (1994) by permission of Warren, Gorham & Lamont

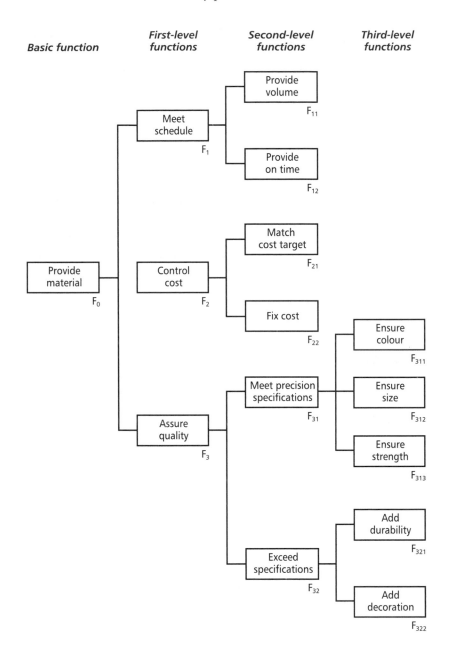

Figure 25:4 **Modified procurement functional family tree**

Source: Yoshikawa *et al.* (1994) by permission of Warren, Gorham & Lamont

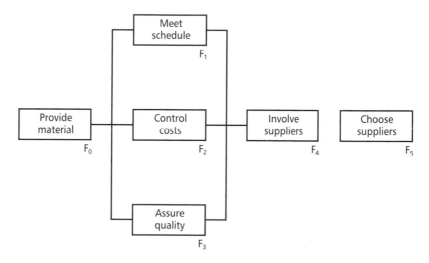

25:5   Functional Costing Case Study

AB is a very large subcontractor in the car industry supplying a range of car parts for some of the major international car companies. One of the strengths of AB is its functional costing that it uses to meet its objective of manufacturing high-quality car parts at a relatively low price. AB devotes more than 10,000 hours (the equivalent of over 60,000 person hours) each year to its functional costing activity.

AB has two types of functional costing training programmes. One programme is for beginners and the other is a more advanced programme. The first programme for new employees is mainly on the job training in functional costing and about 1,500 of AB's employees have been on this programme. The advanced programme is aimed at senior managers who will be team leaders in functional costing exercises. Such senior managers learn functionally oriented product and service improvement. They learn how to define the functions of products and services, how to design new products using functional costing and how to improve existing products and services based on their functionality. More than 100 senior managers a year go through AB's advanced functional costing training programme.

These functional costing training programmes and the functional costing exercises have increased dramatically the number of suggestions for improvements. Last year AB had almost 50,000 such suggestions for improvements. Each year AB sets a cost-savings target from its functional costing activities and during the year monitors the actual cost savings achieved and, if necessary, takes appropriate corrective action.

The diagrammatic representation of the product or service is at the heart of AB's functional costing exercises, namely the functional family tree, but the following questions are asked to enhance, for example, a product's cost effectiveness:

1. *Can a different material be used at a lower cost without any significant impact on customer satisfaction?*
2. *Can a different material be used to reduce the product's weight? It may even be worthwhile using a more expensive material than the existing material if further cost savings can be made later in the production process or if the customer is willing to pay more for a lighter final product.*
3. *Can we reduce the number of components in the product? If so, this would simplify the assembly process and have advantages for supply-chain management.*
4. *Can the design of the function be simplified? This should make the production process easier and should reduce costs.*
5. *Can existing functions be improved or extra functions added such that customers would be willing to pay more for the product?*

The answers to such questions have enabled AB to improve the cost effectiveness of many of its products.

25:6 Limitations of FCA

Functional cost analysis is useful during the design process for new products and for the cost management of existing products but it is only a technique and it has the following limitations:

(a) *Determining customers' values for individual functions can be difficult.*
(b) *It is important to remember that certain functions may be required for safety purposes or by law even although the customers place little value on such functions.*
(c) *There is a danger in the objective having too much emphasis on cost reduction rather than on profit improvement.*

(d) Good cost tables and the use of target costing make it easier to implement functional cost analysis.

25:7 Advantages of FCA

Functional cost analysis can be applied not only to existing and new products but also to services, overheads and even organisation structures. The major advantages of functional cost analysis are as follows:

(a) cost management tool;
(b) new functions can be added to products;
(c) new patents may be developed;
(d) team participants have greater cost consciousness;
(e) useful tool in design process;
(f) competitors' products can be analysed in terms of costs of functions;
(g) better understanding of costs.

25:8 Conclusions

Functional costing could be used simply as a system for costing the functions of a product instead of the parts. However, the real benefits of functional costing derive from functional cost analysis with a multi-disciplinary team using it as a technique to assist with the design of new products or the redesign of existing products. Functional cost analysis can also be applied to services, overheads and even to the actual structure of an organisation.

Functional cost analysis gives a structured approach (including the functional family tree) to the design or redesign process. By using target costing and also incorporating the views of customers on the relative importance of different functions, functional cost analysis enables the team to identify problem functions where the existing costs of such functions are greater than the target cost assigned on the basis of customers' views.

However, the success of the functional cost analysis exercise depends on the creativity of the team in thinking of solutions for the problem functions. This is where the interdisciplinary feature of the team can play a critical role. Indeed it could be argued that important strengths of the functional cost analysis approach are not only the concentration on functions but also the bringing together of team members from different departments with a clear objective to be achieved. The emphasis on functions helps the team to work together to achieve their objective. The use of functions rather than the parts of a product enables the team to take a more abstract view of the product which helps them during their brainstorming phase.

Notes

Material for this chapter was gathered during case study research over several years in Japan with Professor Takeo Yoshikawa of Yokohama National University and Professor Falconer Mitchell of the University of Edinburgh.

References

Yoshikawa, T., Innes, J. and Mitchell, F. (1989) 'Cost management through functional analysis', *Journal of Cost Management*, Spring: 14–19.

Yoshikawa, T., Innes, J. and Mitchell, F. (1994) 'Functional analysis of activity-based cost information', *Journal of Cost Management*, Spring: 40–8.

Yoshikawa, T., Innes, J. and Mitchell, F. (2002) *Strategic Value Analysis*, *Financial Times* Executive Briefings, London.

26. Cost Tables

26:1 Definition

Traditional costing systems have concentrated on costing existing products and services. However, cost tables are designed on the basis that a costing system needs to answer managers' 'what if?' questions. Japanese organisations have developed and used cost tables for many years. Some western organisations have at least partial cost tables even if these may not be as complete as Japanese cost tables.

Cost tables are databases of detailed cost information linked to various drivers. However, these cost drivers relate not only to overhead costs but also to material and labour costs. For example, one driver of the cost of a conveyor belt is its length or a driver of the cost of a motor cycle is the cubic capacity of the engine. These cost tables include not only internal information available within the firm but also external information about, for example, new materials and technological developments. In Japan there are commercial organisations which sell such external information. However, one benefit of the cost tables approach is that it encourages the management accountants who maintain the cost tables to have an external focus and be aware of current developments which are relevant to the organisation. Again this is another example of the costing system having an external focus as well as its more traditional internal focus (*see also* target costing in **Ch.24** and functional costing in **Ch.25**).

Another important feature of cost tables is they are another technique which allows management accountants to contribute during the critical design phase for either new or redesigned products. This is because cost tables allow the cost implications of different design alternatives to be worked out relatively easily. Without such cost tables very often it is a one-off exercise to cost each alternative design. With cost tables it is possible to cost an alternative design during the planning stage of the design process. Obviously the cost is only one factor in the final design decision but cost tables ensure that the cost factor can be considered at the very beginning of the design process. Such cost information may save precious design time by eliminating one or two design alternatives during this planning phase of the design process.

John Innes

26:1.1 Approximate Cost Tables

There are two main types of cost tables namely approximate cost tables and detailed cost tables. If you are starting to develop cost tables from scratch you would choose an approximate cost table. This involves determining a few main cost drivers. Such approximate cost tables are particularly helpful when assessing new product proposals or during the design process (*see* **Ch.42**). An approximate cost table for drilling might be based on the depth of the hole and different types of materials used as in **Figure 26:1**.

Figure 26:1 **Example of approximate cost table**

Source: Yoshikawa *et al.* (1990) by permission of Warren, Gorham & Lamont

Note: This is an illustrative example: the costs are hypothetical.

	Activity: drilling equipment: mark 3 power drill volume: x units per annum											
Depth of hole	**3 inches**				**5 inches**				**7 inches**			
Type of material	**Mat'l ($)**	**Lab. ($)**	**OH ($)**	**Tot. ($)**	**Mat'l ($)**	**Lab. ($)**	**OH ($)**	**Tot. ($)**	**Mat'l ($)**	**Lab. ($)**	**OH ($)**	**Tot. ($)**
Plastic	5	2	3	10	7	5	5	17	8	7	8	23
Steel	9	2	2	13	10	2	2	14	12	4	5	21
Aluminium	10	2	2	14	11	3	3	17	12	3	4	19

Figure 26:1 would obviously give a very simplified view. However, it shows plastic giving the lowest cost of £10 for the three-inch hole, steel having the lowest cost of £14 for the five-inch hole and aluminium having the lowest cost of £19 for the seven-inch hole. In **Figure 26:1** the assumption about the number of units per annum is important particularly for the overhead figures.

Another example of an approximate cost table is for a conveyor belt using different materials (such as rubber, fabric and plastic) with the main cost driver being the length of the conveyor belt. However, more variables could be included such as the thickness or strength of the conveyor belt, the width of the conveyor belt and the number of turns in the conveyor belt. The more variables or cost drivers that are added the more complex the cost table becomes with an increasing number of permutations. Very quickly you move away from an approximate cost table which is useful, for example, at the early design stage or when you need ballpark cost figures. Soon you have developed the other main type of cost table, namely the detailed cost table.

26:1.2 Detailed Cost Tables

Detailed cost tables involve a great deal of work and are used for detailed production costing, purchasing and subcontracting decisions. For example, for purchasing or subcontracting decisions, instead of just relying on competitive tenders it is possible to use detailed cost tables to calculate what the cost should be. Obviously this can be extremely useful during purchasing or subcontracting negotiations. **Figure 26:2** gives an example of a detailed cost table.

Figure 26:2 **Example of detailed cost table**

Source: Yoshikawa *et al.* (1990) by permission of Warren, Gorham & Lamont

Note: This diagram shows one branch of a hypothetical cost table. Additional branches would stem from each of the cost driver alternatives under drilling activity. In addition, similar branches would be prepared for cutting and lathing. At each stage, the table would show unit product cost split into direct material, direct labour and production overhead

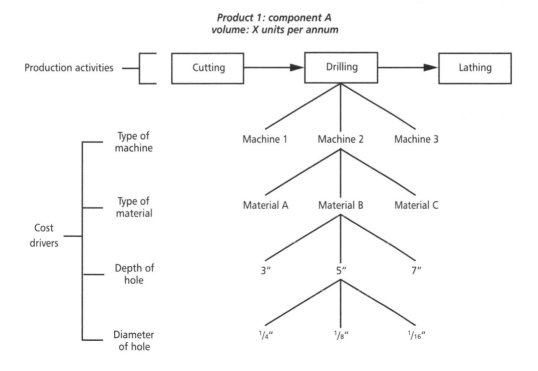

Figure 26:2 expands on the approximate cost table of drilling in **Figure 26:1** which considered only the type of material and the depth of the hole. **Figure 26:2** now includes two more variables namely the type of machine and the diameter of the hole. The cost table data would be held in the form of a database so that 'what if?' questions could be answered about various permutations. For example, the cost table could give the cost of using machine 1 with material A to drill a hole three inches deep and one-quarter of an inch wide or any other permutation involving the four variables of type of machine, type of material, depth and diameter of hole.

Figure 26:2 hints at the amount of data included in detailed cost tables. It must be remembered that Japanese organisations have been developing these detailed cost tables for many years. There is a learning curve about knowing what to include and what to exclude. Updating detailed cost tables also requires a great deal of work. If you were to develop cost tables from scratch, you would probably wish to start with approximate cost tables and, after some experience, you might decide that the extra benefits from detailed cost tables were worth the extra cost of developing these.

26:1.3 Parts or Functions

In addition to the two main types of cost tables, namely approximate and detailed, cost tables can be based either on the parts or the functions (*see* **Ch.25** on functional costing) of a product. Briefly the functions of a product are its features expressed as a verb and a noun. For example, the primary function of a staple remover could be to 'separate paper' and other functions could be to 'remove staples', 'gather staples', 'not tear paper' and 'prevent injury'. Generally, cost tables based on product functions will be more generally applicable than cost tables based on the parts of a product. However, whether parts or functions are used as a basis for the cost tables, there will be considerable start-up costs in setting up such cost tables – particularly detailed cost tables.

26:2 Users of Cost Tables

26:2.1 Design and Redesign
(*See* Ch.42.)

One of the most important uses of cost tables is to assist with the design of new products and the redesign of existing products. One theme of this Handbook is that 60% to 90% of costs are committed during the planning and design stages for new products. Do management accountants in your organisation spend 60% to 90% of their time in relation to the design of new products? The answer in many organisations is that management accountants are not involved at all during the design stage. One reason may be that designers consider that management accountants cannot contribute to the design process.

Cost tables are one technique which enables management accountants to contribute to the design process. Other techniques which are useful during the design process include competitor analysis (*see* Ch.7), management accounting for research and development (*see* Ch.8), target costing (*see* Ch.24), functional costing (*see* Ch.25), value chain analysis (*see* Ch.40) and management accounting for design (*see* Ch.42).

Cost tables mean that the costs of different design alternatives can be compared easily. If the cost tables are based on the functions (rather than the parts) of products, the costs of different designs can be calculated during the planning stage for new products when the functions are known even although the more detailed designs with the parts are not yet available. Some Japanese organisations consider that their cost tables give them a definite competitive advantage during the planning and design stages over some of their western competitors.

Some western organisations have at least partial cost tables although few, if any, of these incorporate external information. Another theme of this Handbook is the increasing focus of management accounting on gathering and reporting to managers information from outside the organisation. Techniques with an external focus include strategic management accounting (*see* Ch.2), the new finance function (*see* Ch.4), strategic financial management (*see* Ch.5), competitor analysis (*see* Ch.7), product life-cycle costing (*see* Ch.19), target costing (*see* Ch.24), environment-related management accounting (*see* Ch.34), outsourcing (*see* Ch.38), value chain analysis (*see* Ch.40), design (*see* Ch.42) and benchmarking (*see* Ch.53). Cost tables are another management accounting technique with an external focus.

In addition to having a role to play in the design of new products, cost tables can also be equally useful when existing products are being redesigned. All the existing cost information will be included in the cost tables but the main advantage will be the other information in the cost tables which will aid the redesign process. Indeed, sometimes it will be the information in the cost tables which stimulates the redesign. For example, the external information may include details about a new material or a new production process from which an existing product would benefit.

26:2.2 Computer-aided Design

Originally the cost tables in Japanese organisations were kept manually. However, the cost tables were soon computerised and are now kept usually in the format of a database. Now some Japanese organisations have integrated their cost tables with their computer-aided design system. This means that designers can see for themselves at the touch of a button the cost implications of different design alternatives without involving the management accountants directly. In such instances a management accountant is still usually a member of the design team to give expert advice and to ensure that the cost information is properly used. Experience has shown that designers sometimes do not understand fully the overhead implications of certain design decisions. Management accountants are also still involved in maintaining and updating the cost tables database.

26:2.3 Capital Investment Decisions

Cost tables can also play a useful role in capital investment decisions (*see* **Ch.11**). For example, the cost tables should include information about new production processes and new machines. Such information can be included in the appraisal of potential capital investment decisions (*see* **Ch.11** for further details). Another use of cost tables stems from their inclusion of such external information. Sometimes the search for such external information can lead to possible capital investment opportunities being identified. This is another example of the cost tables initiating possible action.

26:2.4 Suppliers and Subcontractors

As mentioned in **paragraph 26:1.2** cost tables can be used to estimate what the cost should be for a component or subcomponent assembly to be purchased from a supplier. Similarly if work is to be subcontracted (*see* **Ch.38** for further details), an organisation's cost tables can be used to calculate what the cost should be before the subcontractor quotes for the work. Indeed for some Japanese organisations this was the reason for developing their cost tables in the first place.

If materials and subcontracted items are a significant percentage of an organisation's total costs, it may well be worthwhile considering the costs of developing cost tables. Relying on competitive bids may be fine but how do you ensure that suppliers and subcontractors are using the best possible materials, the newest machines and the best production processes? Cost tables can help you to answer that question by working out what the cost should be before competitive bids are sought. If all the bids are higher than the cost should be per the cost tables, then it is possible to negotiate with the suppliers or subcontractors using the information from your cost tables.

26:2.5 Cost Management

Cost tables have been included in the Costing section of this Handbook but cost management and the above uses of the cost tables mean that cost tables could also have been included in the Decision-making section. For example, **Chapter 27** has further details of cost management. Cost tables give details of what the costs should be and therefore provide a comparison with actual costs which is a basis for cost management and very often for cost reduction.

The external information included in the cost tables can also lead to cost management questions such as:

(a) *Why is a new material not being used?*
(b) *Why is a new production process not being used?*
(c) *Why are the labour costs so high?*

Another cost management aspect of cost tables is the identification of areas where additional expenditure is worthwhile to generate more profit. This is helpful because in some organisations management accountants have a reputation of looking only for cost reduction. Cost management is about increasing profits and not just about cost reduction.

Cost tables also give accountants and managers a better understanding of what drives costs. Volume, of course, is a major cost driver but, just as the activity-based approach (*see* **Ch.28**) has shown that there are a number of drivers of overhead costs, so cost tables have shown that there may also be a number of drivers of material and labour costs. By understanding such cost drivers, it becomes easier for managers to manage such costs.

26:3 Problems of Cost Tables

Although there are great advantages associated with cost tables as illustrated by the above uses and the ability to answer the 'what if?' questions from managers, there are also a number of problems associated with cost tables such as the following.

26:3.1 Time to Construct

It is very time consuming to construct cost tables from scratch. Japanese organisations have developed their cost tables over many years and, in addition to the basic database, they have an expertise in updating their cost tables. It does not take as much time to construct and develop approximate cost tables but it is much more time consuming to develop detailed cost tables because of the greater number of cost drivers included and the additional external information also involved.

26:3.2 External Data

An important feature of the Japanese cost tables is the inclusion of external data. However, it can be difficult to obtain relevant external data. There is also the associated problem of deciding what is relevant data to include for a particular organisation. In Japan, organisations can overcome at least part of this problem by purchasing external data from commercial organisations.

26:3.3 Maintaining Cost Tables

There is a big time investment in terms of constructing cost tables but there is an even bigger long-term time investment in terms of maintaining and updating an organisation's cost tables. For example, a Japanese factory with 1,000 employees had one accountant working full-time on maintaining and updating their cost tables. Maintaining and updating cost tables, so that they continue to be useful, is a never-ending task.

26:3.4 Data to Include

As mentioned in **paragraph 26:3.2** in relation to external data, a difficult problem is to decide what is relevant data to include in the cost tables. For example, developments such as new materials or changes in technology may be excluded from the cost tables because such developments are considered irrelevant. The basic guideline is if in doubt include such data. However, this leads to another problem, namely the level of detail in the cost tables.

26:3.5 How Much Detail?

This is the problem of how much detail to include in the cost tables. In the approximate cost tables decisions have to be made about the most important variables or cost drivers to include. In the detailed cost tables there is also a question of how much detail to include. It is basically a cost-benefit decision as with much of management accounting. Are the benefits of including extra details worth the costs of including such details? Again the circumstances of each organisation will affect such a decision.

26:4 Conclusions

If you were starting to build a cost system from scratch, it seems reasonable to construct a system to answer the 'what if?' questions of managers. This is the basic idea underlying cost tables. Particularly cost tables based on functions are geared to the future rather than the past. Another important feature of the cost tables is their inclusion of external information. In other words, cost tables represent a costing system geared to the future with also an external emphasis.

It would be very difficult to construct detailed cost tables from scratch but much easier to begin with approximate cost tables. Nevertheless, even with approximate cost tables there are various problems including the variables to incorporate into the cost tables, the difficulty of obtaining relevant external data and the cost of updating the cost tables. However, many Japanese organisations consider that cost tables give them a competitive advantage.

The three major benefits of cost tables are in the areas of design, dealing with suppliers or subcontractors and cost management. The question to be answered by an organisation considering introducing cost tables is do such potential benefits exceed the cost of setting up such cost tables? The answer to such a question will depend on the specific circumstances of each organisation.

Notes

Material for this chapter was gathered during case study research in Japan over several years with Professor Takeo Yoshikawa of Yokohama National University and Professor Falconer Mitchell of the University of Edinburgh.

Reference

Yoshikawa, T., Innes, J. and Mitchell, F. (1990) 'Japanese cost tables', *Journal of Cost Management*, Fall: 30–6.

Part D

Decision Making

27. *Cost Management*

27:1 Traditional Cost Management

27:1.1 Budgeting

Perhaps the most traditional cost management techniques are budgeting (*see* **Ch.9**) and standard costing (*see* **Ch.16**). Both techniques are usually applied in terms of a conventional analysis of costs such as materials, labour and overheads. The comparative basis for budgeting is usually internal rather than external and very often the future year against the previous and the current year. For some organisations such traditional cost management may still be appropriate but this chapter also considers the more recent development of strategic cost management.

Whatever method of cost management is used, a critical first question is what costs are involved (*see*, for example, **Ch.23** on energy costs). For example, on a traditional basis what percentage of total costs are materials, labour, production overheads and other overheads? If labour costs are less than 5% of total costs (as in some organisations), you obviously do not wish to spend too much of your total effort on managing such relatively insignificant labour costs. However, if material costs are 40% of total costs, production overheads are 25% and other overheads are 30%, then there are three important areas for cost management. It is surprising how many organisations find that their cost management efforts are poorly directed.

27:1.2 Material Costs

For most manufacturing organisations materials are a significant percentage of total costs and are an important aspect of cost management (*see* **Ch.18** particularly **para.18:1**). Some organisations still continue to build into their standard costs (*see* **Ch.16**) an allowance for wastage and spoilage but other organisations have found that by having no such allowance, managers use their initiative to reduce and even in some cases eliminate such material wastage and spoilage. Even if no standard costing is used it is important to monitor material usage and take appropriate corrective action where necessary.

John Innes   495

Organisations need to monitor the latest developments to assess whether alternative materials might be both better and cheaper. Links with universities can be one way of monitoring such developments. Sometimes the answer can be even nearer to home. One multinational organisation recently discovered that a factory in one country was using a new material but other factories which could have used this new material were unaware of it.

27:1.2.1 Just in time

Traditional organisations have held stocks of raw materials to avoid the possibility of a stock-out which would shut down their manufacturing. The idea of 'just in time' is, of course, much wider than just stocks of materials but 'just in time' has called into question the holding of relatively high material stocks. Why do materials not arrive just in time to be delivered straight to the production line? Very few organisations (including Japanese organisations) operate with zero material stocks but many organisations have used the 'just-in-time' idea to reduce the level of their materials, work in progress and finished goods stocks.

27:1.2.2 Throughput Accounting

Another cost management development closely associated with materials is the idea of throughput accounting (*see* **Ch.33**). The basic idea of throughput accounting is to assume that a number of costs are fixed in the short term and to maximise throughput (sales less material costs) per unit of scarce resource such as per hour of a bottleneck machine. Throughput accounting identifies bottlenecks and constraints and attempts to manage these. Throughput accounting is a useful scheduling technique in circumstances when an organisation can sell all that it can make.

27:1.3 Labour Costs

Historically management accountants have tended to treat the costs of employees working directly on the production line as a variable cost and called this 'labour cost'. The costs associated with other employees have generally been treated as overhead costs (such as production, administration and marketing) and regarded as fixed costs. In some organisations with increased automation such direct labour costs have become a relatively small percentage of total costs. However, in some organisations the control and cost management of such labour continues to receive a disproportionate amount of managerial attention.

Organisations need to decide how variable their labour costs are. Is overtime the really variable element of labour cost which requires close attention from managers? Some organisations have found that treating labour costs as variable is fine in the short run but what has been ignored is the loss of organisational expertise in the longer run. With the increasing international mobility of capital and technology, very often the only long-term sustainable competitive advantage for some organisations is their skilled employees. If this is the case, the cost management of labour needs to recognise this fact.

27:1.4 Overhead Costs

While labour costs have been a reducing percentage of total costs in many organisations, overhead costs have been an increasing percentage of total costs. Of course, many overhead costs are employee-related costs. Traditionally overhead costs are classified into production and other overhead costs (such as research and development, administration and marketing). However, such a classification is not particularly helpful from a cost management point of view.

Zero-base budgeting (*see* **Ch.12**) is one technique which tries to move away from the traditional practice of managing overhead costs by taking the current year's actual overhead costs and adding a percentage to calculate next year's budgeted overhead costs. Instead zero-base budgeting assumes a zero base and requires all overhead costs to be justified. Managers must also decide the minimum level of expenditure necessary for each overhead activity. However, in practice zero-base budgeting has not been very popular and recently two other techniques have been developed which can help in the cost management of overheads, namely activity-based cost management and business process re-engineering.

27:1.4.1 Activity-Based Cost Management

The activity-based cost management approach (*see* **Ch.28**) identifies activities within the overhead area (such as purchasing) and the cost driver for such activities (such as the number of purchase orders). The activity-based approach questions which activities add value for the customer and which are the non-value-added activities where the costs can be reduced or even eliminated. The activity-based approach also gives a different perspective on the overhead costs and, for many managers, this emphasis on activities makes cost management easier.

Another element of the activity-based approach which is helpful for cost management is the fact that activities very often cross departmental boundaries. This encourages managers to manage such overhead costs in terms of activities or processes across the organisation. Very often this may mean identifying for the first time a manager with responsibility for the costs of such an activity or process across the organisation. This can lead to a matrix form of organisation where it is important that cost management responsibilities are clearly defined. A related idea to that of activities or processes crossing departmental boundaries is that of business process re-engineering.

27:1.4.2 Business Process Re-engineering

Business process re-engineering (*see* **Ch.32**) is another cost management technique which aims to achieve major efficiency savings by reorganising business processes in an organisation. Strictly speaking these business processes can be wider than just the overhead costs but many such processes are within the overhead area. In some organisations business process re-engineering, just like the activity-based approach, got a bad name because all that was involved was cost cutting by means of employee redundancies.

Obviously there have been short-term benefits from such policies, but some organisations have found that in the long term they have lost a lot of organisational knowledge and experience which is proving very costly to recreate. In business process re-engineering it is very important to measure the outputs from the process as well as the inputs. The views of both internal and external customers of these business processes are critical when re-engineering such processes.

27:2 Capital Investment Costs

Most organisations have detailed procedures for assessing possible capital investment decisions. Such capital budgeting decisions are discussed in **Chapter 11**. It is perhaps worth emphasising three points.

First, it is a waste of time having sophisticated capital investment appraisal techniques unless there are equally sophisticated search techniques to ensure that the appropriate alternative capital projects are being considered. Some organisations neglect this critical search phase and consider only a very limited range of alternatives. Usually this will result in poor capital investment decisions.

Secondly, during the expenditure phase obviously capital investment costs need to be managed just like other costs. All too often, for example with construction projects [*cf. SSAP9: Stocks and Long-Term Contracts*], there are overruns in relation to the budget. Just as with other costs it is important that such a cost management problem is identified at the earliest possible stage so that managers can decide what, if any, appropriate action needs to be taken.

Thirdly, relatively few organisations conduct post-completion audits of capital projects. Such audits can reveal useful information for future cost management of such projects. For example, have the benefits claimed for capital projects actually been achieved? If not, are there any useful lessons for managers when considering future capital investment decisions?

27:3 Strategic Cost Management

In many ways strategic cost management is complementary to traditional cost management. Many of the management accounting techniques discussed in this Handbook have elements of strategic cost management and this chapter highlights these elements. One theme running throughout this Handbook is the idea of managing the commitment of cost in addition to managing the incurrence of cost.

27:3.1 Cost Commitment During Design

Most costs are committed (but not of course incurred) during the planning and design stages of new products or during the planning and redesign stages of updated or revised products. **Chapter 8** on research and development and **Chapter 42** on design provide further details. The most important point is that, for cost management purposes, management accountants need to be actively involved during the planning and design stages of products. This is when the important decisions are taken affecting almost all costs such as capital investment costs, material costs, labour costs and overhead costs.

By being a team member during the planning and design stages of products (or services) management accountants can ensure that cost is one of the factors taken into consideration. Management accountants can point out the cost implications of different designs during the design process. If an organisation is committing 70% of its costs during the planning and design stages of products, management accountants need to ask themselves if 70% of the total management accounting resource is devoted to these planning and design stages. During this cost commitment of the design stage, management accountants can use various techniques such as product life-cycle costing, cost tables and functional cost analysis. Cost management elements of these techniques will be highlighted in **paragraphs 27:3.2 to 27:3.4.**

27:3.2 Product Life-cycle Costing
(*See* Ch.19.)

Taking a product life-cycle view of costs during the design stage of a product may lead to different design decisions. For example, by taking into account customer costs in operating, maintaining and disposing of a product, an organisation may be able to charge a higher price for its product by designing a product which will reduce customers' future costs.

A related useful technique is environment-related management accounting (*see* **Ch.34**). It seems likely that in the future management accountants will need to pay even more attention to environmental costs. For example, the disposal costs for certain products may become a significant percentage of a product's total life-cycle costs.

27:3.3 Cost Tables
(*See* Ch.26.)

Cost tables are cost databases designed to answer managers' 'what if?' questions. These cost tables include cost information about materials, labour and overheads from both within the organisation and outside the organisation. Such cost information from the external environment (such as cost of new materials or new manufacturing processes) is an important aspect of the strategic element of these cost tables.

Japanese organisations view such cost tables as an important competitive advantage and sometimes their cost tables are integrated with their computer-aided design system. By giving answers to managers' and designers' 'what if?' questions, cost tables can have a major influence in terms of cost management. Instead of being based on the parts of a product, some Japanese cost tables are based on the functions of a product.

27:3.4 Functional Cost Analysis
(*See* Ch.25.)

The primary function of a staple remover might be to separate paper and other functions could include collecting the staples and not damaging the paper. The functions give a more abstract way of thinking about a product than the physical parts of a product. If you try to redesign an existing product by thinking about the parts of that product, the chances are that you are very likely to design a new product which looks very similar to the existing product. However, if you start with the functions of a product, you may finish with a very different design from the existing product.

Again functional cost analysis is another useful cost management technique during the design or redesign stages of products. It is also a team approach with a multi-disciplinary team. A management accountant can contribute as a team member and experience has shown that sometimes the management accountant can provide the best alternative during the brainstorming session which is an integral part of functional cost analysis. In other words once the functions of a product are decided how are we going to achieve these functions?

In addition to acting as a normal team member, a management accountant can also provide costing expertise to help evaluate all the alternatives which the team will generate. This is, of course, where cost tables can be extremely useful and if these are not available, then the management accountant has to cost each alternative from scratch.

The strategic cost management techniques discussed all have a long-term emphasis – for example, cost commitment during the design stage, product life-cycle costing, cost tables and functional cost analysis. All these techniques can play a cost management role during the design stage. Nevertheless, so far in this strategic cost management section, the emphasis has been on an internal perspective although product life-cycle costing does consider customers' costs and cost tables do include information from outside the organisation. However, a number of other techniques such as competitor analysis, benchmarking, value chain analysis, outsourcing and target costing have a much more explicit external emphasis. Again these techniques will be considered briefly in a strategic cost management context.

27:3.5 Competitor Analysis
(*See* Ch.7.)

Analysis of competitors' products is now very common. Usually this will involve a multi-disciplinary team again who will buy and then break down a competitor's product to determine the materials and parts used, how the product was manufactured and assembled and any unusual features. The management accountant in such a team will provide costing expertise so that a cost comparison can be made between an organisation's own product and its competitors' products.

Very often the most difficult cost estimate is that for the overhead costs but usually an organisation will know a lot about its competitors and a reasonable estimate of overheads can be made. Sometimes this comparison of an organisation's own product cost with a competitor's product cost raises questions which can lead to cost management improvements. One main advantage of competitor analysis is that it gives an external point of comparison rather than simply a comparison with what an organisation did in the past.

27:3.6 Benchmarking
(*See* Ch.53.)

Another method of external comparison is benchmarking. An organisation can benchmark its various processes against other organisations usually in different industrial or commercial sectors. All organisations can improve and benchmarking provides a means of identifying areas of the business where improvements can be made.

Benchmarking raises questions why other organisations can perform certain activities more efficiently, and such questions are usually the starting point of a process leading to better cost management. The advantage of benchmarking across different industries is that very often (and sometimes because of competitive analysis) organisations in the same industry do things in a very similar way. In contrast, organisations in different industries may adopt a very different approach and this can provide very useful cost management information.

27:3.7 Value Chain Analysis
(*See* Ch.40.)

Another technique which looks beyond an organisation's boundary is value chain analysis. An examination of the chain back to suppliers and forward to customers can sometimes lead to cost management suggestions. A simple example is where suppliers are providing goods in packages which then have to be split by the next organisation in the chain. It is surprising how often such examples arise during value chain analysis.

Value chain analysis also concentrates on where value is being created. It is very easy to become obsessed with cost management or even cost reduction and forget that the objective is actually profit improvement. Value chain analysis is one of the techniques which reminds managers that sometimes the basic problem is too little cost. It may be that by spending more, even more sales and profits can be generated.

27:3.8 Outsourcing
(*See* **Chs 38 and 39.**)

Some organisations have been deciding what their core competencies are and have outsourced or subcontracted some or all of their other activities. For example, some organisations have become design only organisations and have subcontracted everything else including the manufacturing of products. This is an extreme case and much more common is to attempt to manage costs by outsourcing a limited range of processes or activities.

For cost management purposes the contract in outsourcing is critical. Again this contract needs to include not only current costs but also future costs and outputs (including quality of service). However, if an organisation has chosen the correct activities to outsource and a good supplier or subcontractor, then in some cases this may be the best way to manage such costs. Nevertheless, it is important to consider the long-term view when outsourcing because an outsourcing decision may mean that an organisation loses certain skills which it will find very expensive to replace in the future.

27:3.9 Target Costing
(*See* **Ch.24.**)

Another strategic cost management technique which has an external emphasis is target costing. Historically management accountants have built up a unit product cost from internal information on materials, labour and overheads. Target costing starts from the market and estimates a future unit selling price for a product and deducts the required profit margin to calculate a target cost which has to be achieved. This is a very useful cost management technique during the design process.

It may be difficult to calculate such a target cost because obviously the future is uncertain. However, the most important aspect of target costing is deciding how such a target cost can actually be achieved. 'Target cost management' is a better name than 'target costing'. Techniques such as cost tables and functional cost analysis are helpful during this target cost management process.

27:4 Conclusions

Perhaps the most important step in cost management is deciding which costs you need to manage. For example, a cost which is seldom, if ever, mentioned in the management accounting literature is that of foreign exchange losses. For multinational companies this can sometimes be the most important cost to manage and this is usually done by the treasury department. This example of foreign exchange exposure is mentioned to illustrate the point that each organisation must consider carefully where to concentrate its cost management efforts.

Another general point is that cost management itself has costs associated with it and these costs need to be assessed in relation to the benefits from such cost management. What has been termed in this chapter 'traditional cost management' is still extremely useful and relevant for most organisations. In recent years the management of overhead costs has received a great deal of attention and rightly so but it is important to remember that for many organisations material costs remain the most important cost.

Strategic cost management is very often complementary to 'traditional cost management' by taking a longer-term and external view. It cannot be emphasised enough that management accountants need to be involved in the design team when most cost commitment decisions are actually made. Management accountants can contribute to the design process with techniques such as product life-cycle costing, cost tables, functional cost analysis and target costing.

Management accountants can try to ensure that managers have external points of comparison by using techniques such as not only target costing but also benchmarking, competitor analysis and value chain analysis. It is unlikely that any one technique will give all the cost management answers for any one organisation. However, what such management accounting techniques have in common is that they give managers a slightly different view of their organisation's costs and this often leads to new questions, further investigations and better cost management. For any profit-making organisation, the real test of any cost management is the end result in terms of profit improvement.

28. Activity-based Cost Management

28:1 ABC, ABCM, ABM and ABB

As detailed in **Chapter 22**, activity-based costing (ABC) was highlighted by Cooper and Kaplan of the Harvard Business School in the 1980s from case studies such as those of John Deere. The early ABC cases highlighted the objective of unit product costing which is discussed in detail in **Chapter 22**. However, as experience with the ABC system grew it became clear that the cost management objective was at least as important as the unit product-costing objective. This became known as activity-based cost management (ABCM) or activity-based management (ABM). One specific aspect of ABCM is activity-based budgeting which is discussed in **Chapter 22**. **Chapter 30** also expands on using activity-based information.

The details of the activity-based approach are discussed in **Chapter 13** (*see* **paras 13:1.3, 13:2** and **13:3**) and **Chapter 22** (*see* **paras 22:1.2, 22:2** and **22:3**). The activity-based approach is concerned only with overhead costs (both production and non-production overheads) and does not deal with direct materials, direct labour or direct expenses. The essence of the activity-based approach is that, first, activities (such as purchasing, material handling and customer services) are identified. Secondly, overhead costs are collected in relation to these activities to form activity cost pools. Thirdly, for each cost pool, a cost driver is selected and this cost driver should drive or cause the costs in that particular cost pool. For example, the cost drivers for the activity cost pools of purchasing, material handling and customer services might be number of purchase orders, number of material movements and number of customers.

In summary, the three main features of the activity-based approach are:

1. *activities;*
2. *activity cost pools;*
3. *cost drivers.*

How then can the activity-based approach be used for cost management purposes?

John Innes

28:1.1 Managing Activities

The traditional way of reporting overheads is in terms of expenses usually by overhead department such as salaries, travel and depreciation on equipment. The two main reporting differences for the activity-based cost management approach are:

1. the reporting is by activities (not departments) and very often activities cross departmental boundaries (see **Ch.13, para.13:2.2** for details);
2. the activity-based reporting is not by expenses but by subactivities.

For example, the traditional analysis of the overhead department of purchasing might be as shown in **Table 28:1**.

Table 28:1 **Traditional analysis of overhead department of purchasing**

	£000
Salaries	300
Travel	100
Depreciation on equipment	50
Other expenses	50
	500

In contrast the activity-based analysis of purchasing might include more expenses incurred in departments other than purchasing such as production departments (placing purchase orders), finance department (vetting potential suppliers), stores (receiving goods ordered) and accounts payable (checking and paying invoices). So, the total cost of the activity of purchasing might be £800,000. Obviously this is an important piece of information on its own because it may change the way in which managers view the activity of purchasing. Managers may give more attention to the cost management of the activity of purchasing.

The second difference is the detailed analysis of the activity of purchasing. Instead of an expense analysis as under traditional overhead costing, the activity-based approach gives an analysis such as in **Table 28:2** (reconciled to the above £500,000 for purposes of comparative illustration).

Table 28.2 **Analysis of purchasing – activity-based approach**

	£000
Vetting suppliers	40
Requesting competitive bids	100
Agreeing contracts	60
Placing purchase orders	150
Liaising with suppliers	50
Resolving problems	100
	500

The activity-based analysis in **Table 28:2** gives a very different perspective on the overheads from the traditional overhead analysis even in the above analysis where the total figure of £500,000 remains the same. Of course, the total overhead cost figure remains the same under both the traditional and activity-based analyses. The activity-based approach is simply a different way of analysing the overheads.

Most managers consider that the activities-based analysis gives them a more useful breakdown of the overhead figure. It gives more visibility to the activities underlying the overheads and may raise different questions from a traditional overhead analysis. For example, in the activity-based analysis of the £500,000 of the purchasing activity why is £100,000 spent on resolving problems? This is the first step to beginning to manage the overhead cost of the purchasing activity.

The activity-based approach also encourages managers to consider how best to manage the activities. There are various possibilities for managers to consider for example:

(a) *Can the number of activities or subactivities be reduced?*
(b) *Can the cost level be reduced for any activity?*
(c) *Can some activities be combined?*
(d) *Can the functions of any activity be achieved in a different way?*

Again such questions can be the starting point for cost management. Two other approaches which are used extensively are to classify activities into:

1. *core, support and diversionary activities; or*
2. *value-added and non-value-added activities.*

These two activity-based cost management approaches will now be considered in more detail.

28:1.2 Core, Support and Diversionary Activities

Some organisations consider it helpful to classify activities into core, support and diversionary activities. Perhaps the best way to understand this classification is with an example. For a travelling salesperson the following classification of activities would apply:

(a) *core activity is making the sale with the customer;*
(b) *support activity is driving to the customer;*
(c) *diversionary activity is sitting listening to the customer complaining about all the problems associated with the previous order.*

Again such an analysis of activities is a different way of looking at overhead costs. A typical breakdown of costs in a well-run organisation is as follows:

core activities	30%
support activities	30%
diversionary activities	40%

Obviously, the objective is to examine these diversionary activities to reduce the time spent on such activities. The experience of most organisations is that they are unable to eliminate diversionary activities but they can reduce substantially the amount of time spent on such activities. This means that more time can be spent on core and support activities.

28:1.3 Value-added and Non-value-added Activities

An alternative analysis of activities to that of core, support and diversionary is that of value-added and non-value-added activities. The question is which activities add value for the customer. Many activities may add value for the organisation but not for the customer.

For example, in the purchasing activity analysis in **Table 28:2** the activity of resolving problems does not add any value to the customer. The problems should not arise in the first place as far as the customer is concerned. Similarly, many of the activities associated with the raw materials store are non-value added from the customer's point of view. For instance, unpacking materials, storing materials, checking materials and disposing of slow-moving materials are all activities which do not add any value for the customer.

Again, having classified activities into value-added and non-value-added categories, the objective is to eliminate or at least reduce the amount of resources spent on non-value-added activities. Usually the fact of highlighting some activities as non-value added will have an effect in itself. However, one problem with such a classification is that no individual likes to think that they are performing non-value-added activities. The behavioural effects of this value-added and non-value-added classification have therefore to be considered. Nevertheless, this value-added and non-value-added classification is a powerful cost management tool.

28:2 Use of ABCM

In a survey of *The Times* Top 1000 companies Innes and Mitchell (1995) found that approximately 20% of the respondents (251 in total) were using the activity-based approach and 27% were in the process of considering it. The detailed applications are given in **Table 28:3**.

Table 28:3 **Activity-based applications**

	Percentage of companies using activity-based approach (%)
Stock valuation	29
Product/service pricing	65
Output decisions	47
Cost reduction	88
Budgeting	59
New product/service design	31
Customer profitability analysis	51
Performance measurement	67
Cost modelling	61

In their 1999 survey of activity-based applications, Innes *et al.* found that 'cost reduction, pricing, performance measurement/improvement and cost modelling remain the most common applications with over 60% use by the adopters' (2000: 353). Pricing is closely related to unit product costing that is discussed in the activity-based costing chapter (*see* **Ch.22**). This 1999 survey also showed that over 60% of activity-based adopters used customer profitability analysis. Therefore, cost reduction, customer profitability analysis, performance measurement and cost modelling will be considered in more detail in **para.28:3**.

28:2.1 ABCM in Financial Institutions

As the surveys by Innes and Mitchell (1995 and 1997) have shown, there are a number of different aspects of activity-based cost management. Activity-based budgeting is discussed in **Chapter 13** and will not be discussed again in this chapter. However, four further aspects of activity-based cost management will be discussed further namely:

1. *cost reduction;*
2. *customer profitability;*
3. *performance measurement;*
4. *cost modelling.*

The only other aspect of the activity-based approach used by more than 50% of the companies in the survey reported in **Table 28:3** was product/service pricing (*see* **Ch.35**) which relates more specifically to the unit product costing of the activity-based approach (*see* **Ch.22**).

28:3 Applications of ABCM

28:3.1 Cost Reduction

The Innes and Mitchell (1995) survey revealed a number of different approaches to analysing activity-based costs. Accountants often get a bad reputation for always looking for cost reduction. It is important to emphasise therefore that the analysis of activity-based costs can also reveal areas where more expenditure might be beneficial to an organisation. For example, activities which are identified as core or value added may be considered for additional expenditure especially if such activities are also bottleneck activities, that is, capacity of activity cannot meet the customer demand.

Accepting this important point of identifying areas for additional expenditure, the remainder of the discussion in this section will be framed in the context of cost reduction. The Innes and Mitchell (1995) survey found five different methods of analysing activity-based costs which were all used by approximately half of the activity-based respondents. These five methods of analysing activity-based costs were:

1. *value-added and non-value-added categories;*
2. *subactivities or task listing;*
3. *relative activity cost size profile;*

4. *activity flowcharts or maps;*
5. *core, support and diversionary categories.*

The first and last of these methods, namely value-added/non-value-added and core/support/diversionary activities, have already been discussed in **Paras. 28:1.2** and **28:1.3**. The subactivities or tasks listing recognises that in some cases for cost management purposes a more detailed analysis of activities may be required. Indeed some organisations have a hierarchy with:

(a) *processes across the whole organisation leading in some cases to business process re-engineering (BPR – see Ch.32). Indeed in some organisations BPR has developed out of the activity-based approach;*
(b) *activities which may cross a number of departmental boundaries;*
(c) *subactivities or tasks which tend to be concentrated in one department.*

The value-added/non-value-added or core/support/diversionary analysis can also be applied to these subactivities. This analysis of subactivities can be a useful method of driving cost out of an overall activity.

The relative activity cost-size profile is basically a listing showing the activities with the highest cost. Again this can be a useful starting point for cost reduction. This relative activity cost-size profile can be combined with a value-added/non-value-added or core/support/diversionary activity analysis. Such a combined approach helps to avoid the danger of using the relative activity cost-size profile on its own and concentrating on cost reduction for core or value-added activities.

Some organisations use the activity flowcharts or maps not only for purposes of cost reduction but also to help to identify the activities. One point to be careful about with the activity maps is to avoid the mistake of restricting activities to a single department. The activity flowcharts or maps can be useful in highlighting how many activities cross departmental boundaries. Activity maps can show clearly the number of departments involved in any one activity. Activity maps may reveal that some activities have become increasingly complex and it may be possible to simplify them. Activity flowcharts or maps can also show that certain subactivities are being duplicated unnecessarily in two different departments.

28:3.2 Customer Profitability

Strictly speaking customer profitability can also be used with traditional costing with overheads. However, the fact that managers generally accept that the activity-based approach to overheads is closer to reality than traditional costing has encouraged the use of customer profitability as one aspect of activity-based cost management. Activity-based information has encouraged almost a database approach to overheads. In other words, the basic information is available on activities, activity cost pools and cost drivers, and this information can be accessed to give overhead details related to cost objects such as product lines, divisions, distribution channels and customers.

Most organisations already have sales by customers although some multinational organisations found that they did not even have this information. For example, some banks organised their data on a transactions basis and did not gather together all the transactions for their multinational customers. However, assuming that sales information by customer is available, the activity-based system can be used to complete the cost information by customer by including the overhead costs.

Some organisations have used the resulting customer profitability information not only for cost management purposes but also as an input to their strategic decision making. Customer profitability information using the activity-based approach has revealed in some organisations that only 20% of the customers account for 100% of the profit with many customers being loss making.

One organisation found that previously 'profitable' customers using only production overhead costs became unprofitable when non-production overhead costs were also included. The problem is how.to manage such 'unprofitable' customers but, at least, by recognising some customers as unprofitable managers can begin to try to take action to improve the situation. One supplier to a large supermarket chain actually showed the activity-based customer profitability information to the supermarket chain to emphasise the costs caused by all its special requests. In this particular case the supplier managed to renegotiate the contract with the supermarket chain so that this particular supermarket chain actually became a profitable customer for this supplier.

28:3.3 Performance Measurement
(*See* Chs 48 and 49.)

Some organisations have found that, following their experience with the activity-based cost management system, cost drivers are used as the basis of a performance measurement system. Very often the performance measure is expressed as follows:

Cost of activity/Volume of cost driver.

For example, the cost of the activity of purchasing might be £1m, the cost driver for the purchasing activity might be the number of purchase orders and if there are 100,000 purchase orders so the cost per purchase order of £10 is used as a performance measure.

Using cost drivers as performance measures for overhead activities may be fine but, as with all performance measures, the behavioural implications must be kept in mind. For example, using the above performance measure of cost per purchase order, one simple way to reduce this cost per purchase order is simply to halve each purchase order, that is, to have 200,000 instead of 100,000 purchase orders which might increase the cost of the purchasing activity from £1m to £1.2m. However, the effect on the performance measure is to reduce the cost per purchase order from £10 to £1.2m divided by 200,000 (i.e. £6).

Stated in this way, this illustrates how silly the above is. The performance measure of cost per purchase order has actually encouraged employees to increase the cost of the purchasing activity from £1m to £1.2m with no corresponding benefit to the organisation. When designing and using activity-based performance measures, perhaps the most important factor to consider is how will this particular performance measure influence employees' behaviour.

Furthermore, activity-based performance measures should be used not only to control the performance of overhead activities, but also to encourage problem solving and improvement in performance. Some organisations have found that concentrating on the non-financial aspect (i.e. the volume aspect) of the cost driver such as the volume of purchase orders has been beneficial for improving performance.

Another important point to remember when using activity-based performance measures (both financial and non-financial) is that some activities cross departmental boundaries. This means that it is important to establish who is responsible for achieving different performance measures. Some organisations have retained their departmental structure but turned it into a matrix structure by also having someone responsible for processes (or activities) across the organisation.

28:3.4 Cost Modelling

By giving a different perspective on overhead costs, the activity-based approach has also encouraged organisations to use the activity-based database for modelling purposes. This enables accountants to answer 'what if?' questions from managers. For example, activity-based information can be helpful in managing the customisation costs of products. Some organisations found that their sales force was promoting very heavily certain optional extras on their basic product. However, the activity-based modelling revealed that these options were in fact very costly and the organisation was selling these options at a large loss.

Similarly, the activity-based modelling of sales, marketing and distribution costs has been useful for some organisations. For example, in one organisation it revealed previously hidden cost problems with certain distribution channels. Corrective management action was taken to overcome these problems.

28:4 Conclusions

The survey and case study evidence suggests that there is now considerable experience with activity-based cost management in both the manufacturing and service sectors. The importance and success ratings in the surveys by Innes and Mitchell (1995 and 1997) and Innes *et al.* (2000) were consistently high for the following aspects of activity-based cost management:

(a) *cost reduction;*
(b) *budgeting;*
(c) *customer profitability analysis;*
(d) *performance measurement;*
(e) *cost modelling.*

Although there is a wide range of applications within activity-based cost management, the most popular is that of cost reduction. Within the cost reduction application, a number of methods are used to analyse activity-based costs including classification into value-added/non-value-added activities and core/support/diversionary activities. However, even without such detailed analysis, a very important advantage of the activity-based approach is that it gives a new visibility to overhead costs from the traditional reporting of overheads. Such visibility from the activity-based approach makes it easier to manage the overhead costs. If overheads are a significant cost element in your organisation, it is certainly worth considering activity-based cost management. For example, see **Chapter 31** which has a case study of implementing ABC in a service-driven business, namely DHL Worldwide Express.

References

Innes, J. and Mitchell, F. (1995) 'A survey of activity-based costing in the UK's largest companies', *Management Accounting Research, 6(2)*: 137–53.

Innes, J. and Mitchell, F. (1997) 'The application of activity-based costing in the United Kingdom's largest financial institutions', *The Service Industries Journal, 17(1)*: 190–203.

Innes, J., Mitchell, F. and Sinclair, D. (2000) 'Activity-based costing in the UK's largest companies: A comparison of 1994 and 1999 survey results', *Management Accounting Research, 11(3)*: 349–62.

29. ABM in Practice – A Case Study

This case is based on research in an actual organisation, though key details have been amended for the purposes of this publication. Background information is presented first, followed by details of activity-based management (ABM) in practice in this organisation.

29:1 Background Information

The Crimton (Teesside) site is a small part of a US-based group. Its activities relate to production, there is no marketing or sales function.

29:1.1 Size

Turnover – Crimton $200m, Group $4.7bn
Employees – Crimton approx. 550, Group 25,600

29:1.2 Nature of Business/Industry

Crimton is a manufacturer of mid-range machine tools, 170 produced per day. Manufacturing is to order and customers collect. The Crimton site also 'hosts' the central UK groups responsible for purchasing, finance, human resources and manufacturing support.

29:1.3 Key Product Groups

There are two product groups: 'X' and 'Y' machines. Crimton also operates a kitting facility, providing machine tool-kits for export. This last is a growing activity.

Karen Johnston, Jane Gibbon,
Jan Loughran and John Robinson

29:1.4 Customers

There are 125 customers.

29:1.5 Countries of Operation

World-wide group. Crimton serves markets in the 'central area' of the world, stretching from the west coast of Ireland to the east coast of Russia.

29:1.6 Relationship with Head Office

The US-based President and Chairman have been with the group for many years. There is a history of long-term vision shown at senior levels, resulting in a belief among employees in the group's continuing commitment towards growth and development.

Local functional managers have dual reporting relationships, within the plant hierarchy and within a functional hierarchy.

29:1.7 External Change – Competitive Environment

The major driver for change is regulation which leads to a need for significant research and development to meet increasingly stringent standards.

29:1.8 Internal Change

(a) *Organisation – This is relatively stable.*
(b) *Key management – This is stable at senior levels and locally new appointments to plant manager and UK manufacturing director have not resulted in major changes.*
(c) *IT – There have been no major changes to management information systems during the last five years. Accounting information is produced using bespoke mainframe systems.*
(d) *Production methods – The manufacturer process system (MPS) is a synthesis of the management techniques and philosophies which have been adopted by the group in pursuit of 'customer-led quality'. In the production area a Kaizen approach has led to significant change in work practices and continues to be applied at all levels. Output has increased from 100 to 170 machine tools per day.*

(e) *Capital investment – Advanced manufacturing technology incorporating mixed model scheduling has been established on the shop floor for a number of years. While some activities have been upgraded recently, the majority of tasks have remained stable.*

(f) *Employment issues – Within the past five years the company has responded to short lead times, JIT and oscillating volumes by introducing fixed-term contracts for approximately 15% of the manufacturing staff. The company has thus been able to deliver continuous employment to its core workforce avoiding the necessity for redundancies.*

The company is in the process of building self-directed teams. Seven steps towards this goal have been identified and step five has been achieved.

Union membership is significant among shop floor workers and staff.

29:1.9 Major Management Initiatives

The major initiatives affecting the plant have originated in the US group head office. Over the past five years these have centred on the introduction of MPS (*see* **para.29:1.8**). The plant operates TQM, JIT and Kaizen practices in the production area. All of these have been in place for some time and continue in use. There has not been a formal review of the outcomes of these initiatives. Productivity and profit have improved since their introduction, however, and there are no plans to scale down their use. Workers accepted the initiatives, which were introduced with the commitment that they would not result in redundancies. Widespread publicity and training has accompanied the introduction of these initiatives.

29:2 Management Accounting

29:2.1 Performance Measures Used

The overriding goal of customer-led quality is sought through five key objectives as described in the group's annual report:

1. *comparative advantage for customers (product performance, economic value to the customer, customer support);*
2. *return on equity;*

3. *profitable growth;*
4. *responsible citizenship;*
5. *outstanding people.*

Monthly reports to the group focus on 14 measures. Of these there are three which are viewed as most important, PBIT, first-time OK (quality) and cost per unit. This last measure includes overheads.

Quarterly income statements compare performance with annual operating plans, and provide revised forecasts for the remainder of the year.

Additional performance measures are used to promote 'functional excellence' in supporting functions; the finance function, for example, monitors indicators such as speed of report production and training received.

29:2.2 Control Culture

Operating units make decisions based on the framework described in **paragraph 29:1**. The annual operating plan is developed jointly with group and local management. It includes the following elements: capital, marketing, technical, financial and MPS.

29:2.3 Cost Analysis for Key Product Groups

The major element of cost for both machine tool types is direct materials, 79% for X series, 77% for Y series. Overhead is 17% of X series cost and 15% of Y series cost. Standard costing is used to manage direct materials and direct labour costs. Overheads are identified as materials, labour or unit related and allocated to products accordingly. Allocation of material-related costs are based on value, which in turn is seen as a measure of complexity.

29:2.4 Use of Cost Information

(a) *Operational management – As mentioned in **paragraph 29:2.1**, one of the three key measures of performance.*
(b) *Pricing – Not currently used, but marketing function wants to use activity-based costs in future.*
(c) *Business processes – Increasingly used in this area.*
(d) *Strategic decisions – At plant level, main decisions of this type are sourcing issues, make or buy.*

29:3 ABM at the Outset

29:3.1 Why ABM?

Initial interest in ABM arose with respect to product costing. The focus now, is on process improvement and the elimination of waste.

The initial ABC work carried out in the late 1980s was found to be difficult to carry out. In the Crimton environment refined overhead allocation information was not felt to be worth pursuing, given the low proportion of product cost it represents, and the relatively undifferentiated product range (in terms of overhead consumption).

The company then began to look at activities within a functional framework. This then developed into the cross-functional perspective which is taken at present.

29:3.2 The ABM Project

The project has developed into an examination of 18 support processes carried out at the plant. Support activity was targeted since it was felt that Kaizen initiatives had already addressed the issue of waste in the production areas.

A finance-based team facilitates the ABM process which begins with the identification of a sponsor who will take ownership of a particular process. The team then documents the process, involving all those taking part in the process. Non-value-added activities and improvement opportunities within the process are identified and discussed at a feedback meeting. A report is produced, detailing the findings and measuring indicative financial implications of the improvement opportunities.

The sponsor then becomes responsible for progressing the improvements, possibly by including them in the annual operating plan.

29:3.3 ABM Objectives

The ABM objectives to eliminate waste and promote improvement are emphasised during the training process. The use of ABM is promoted by the group Vice-President of Finance.

29:3.4 Project Structure

The UK ABM co-ordinator reports on ABM issues to the corporate co-ordinator. Each UK plant has dedicated ABM staff, usually part time. These teams meet regularly to review progress and share experiences. By contrast the US has a central team which travels from location to location.

29:3.5 Project Planning – Feasibility

Local effort is led by the plant controller and the ABM team leader. The plant operating committee was consulted and involved in the introduction of ABM. No formal cost-benefit analysis was undertaken, and consultants were not involved.

29:4 Project Implementation Experience

29:4.1 Structure

The ABM team consists of five members of the accounting staff, one of whom leads the team and reports to the plant controller. Their commitment to the project is part time. They are assisted by an undergraduate placement student who is assigned to the project full time.

Finance staff assigned to the project include those responsible for product costing and budgeting.

29:4.2 Timescale

ABC for product costing was examined in the late 1980s. After this was rejected the company began activity analysis by function, moving to cross-functional activity analysis in mid-1994; this continued and was completed.

29:4.3 Meetings/Decisions

The progress of the project is managed principally through:

(a) the finance function management hierarchy;

(b) the plant operating committee, on the agenda approximately monthly;

(c) the UK ABM steering group (chaired by the UK ABM co-ordinator) quarterly.

29:4.4 Training

The core finance team have attended group conferences, CIMA seminars and have undertaken self-study using a range of books. Cascade training on the broad principles of ABM is given to all staff.

29:4.5 Use of IT

Specialist software has been used, supplemented by a spreadsheet package.

29:4.6 Formal Procedures

The ABM activity proceeds as follows:

1. *Identify a process sponsor, sufficiently authoritative to procure the co-operation of the necessary staff.*

2. *Establish a contract between the sponsor and the ABM team identifying key players, timescales, tasks, roles and responsibilities.*

3. *The ABM team leads an introductory meeting with key players at which a high-level flowchart of the process is developed.*

4. *A series of interviews with individual actors in the process is conducted by the ABM team. During these interviews ideas and opportunities for waste elimination are sought.*

5. *The process is documented and presented to all those participating at a closing feedback meeting. The feedback includes an indicative financial measure of the improvement opportunities identified.*

6. *Responsibility for progress with regard to process improvement is left with the sponsor.*

29:4.7 Starting Point/Progress to Date of Writing

The ABM project is confined to 18 support processes. This is because the production processes within the plant have addressed waste and improvement through Kaizen initiatives. The order in which the processes were analysed was determined by operational constraints of participating functions. All are completed.

29:5 Implementation Problems/Solutions

The following covers problems the team have faced, and any remedial actions taken.

29:5.1 Initial Direction

The team struggled at first in the face of changing guidance from the US. As mentioned previously, the first efforts were focused on ABC, followed by functional ABM. This did not gain support outside the finance function, and was followed by the cross-functional approach which is the perspective of the current project.

29:5.2 Resource

The project began with only part-time staff. This level of resource was insufficient and an undergraduate placement student was assigned to the project. Administration and progress chasing were improved but other members of the team continue to manage their commitment to the ABM project alongside other commitments, which creates problems when deadlines coincide. The progress of the ABM project is one of the finance function's performance indicators, but the level of priority assigned to ABM work is below that of other tasks.

29:5.3 Team Membership

All the members of the ABM team are from the finance function. This was a source of concern for the plant controller, who would have preferred to involve other functional specialists. The approach taken has sought to counter the effect of the single function team by involving all key individuals in the process being examined, at every stage. An operational manager (sponsor of the first process to be examined) considered the finance-based team a positive advantage since 'we needed someone to ask the stupid questions'.

29:5.4 Senior Management Support

Acceptance and support by the plant operating committee was not initially forthcoming. Increased awareness training was necessary for this group, since their role was critical in delivering the wide-ranging involvement necessary to the project. It is clear that team members continue to perceive a need for top-level support in terms of publicity and training.

29:5.5 Project Team Skills

A review carried out by a member of the team records a number of concerns felt by members of the team relating to the conduct of the ABM process. Many of these relate to activities which would have been unfamiliar to team members prior to this project, with the result that they have had difficulty in performing them. These activities include project management, communication skills, interviewing and team working.

29:6 Benefits/Successes

Project team members identify the following aspects of the approach taken at Crimton as having produced positive results.

29:6.1 Process Orientation

Analysis of activities has been undertaken from a process perspective, involving cross-functional analysis and communication. This had led to increased co-operation, since individuals are less concerned to justify their own role. It has also led to greater opportunities for process improvement by ignoring functional boundaries. Other UK sites within the group have undertaken their analysis within functional areas, and must then use the data to build process views. They have thus avoided the necessity of involving individual staff in multiple interviews. It was considered that the price of a number of multiple interviews was worth paying for the benefits gained.

29:6.2 Involvement of Top-level Sponsors

This has assisted in gaining the co-operation of staff at more junior levels. It has also resulted in increased commitment among the senior management team as they gain experience of ABM.

The role of the sponsor has developed in the light of experience to become the visible leader in each process with finance staff acting as facilitators.

29:6.3 Presentation/Publicity

The ABM team invested in materials carrying a logo to identify and publicise their work. They publish progress to date, including indicative cost savings.

29:6.4 Reflective Team/Self-critical

The team seeks to learn by experience, and has applied its techniques to itself. As the ABM work continues, the approach taken is constantly being refined, the lessons learned in one process are applied in the next.

29:6.5 Involvement of Key Finance Staff

The involvement of staff whose operational responsibilities include costing and budgeting is creating a platform of knowledge and skills for future developments in these areas.

29:7 Key Outcomes

The key outcomes which have occurred so far as a result of the project are:

1. *Wasted effort within processes has been identified and communicated to those involved in the processes. Improvement opportunities identified so far have been measured at about £500,000.*
2. *There is a more visible accounting function, more clearly aligned with the operational effort of the plant, associated with a more positive view of the finance team as partners.*

3. *The project has been a catalyst for change, and facilitated process improvements.*
4. *Communication has improved among all participants in the ABM work, across cross-functional and hierarchical boundaries. The documentation which is created was identified as valuable by operational managers.*
5. *Information about the costs of processes, and an indication of the cost consequences of improvements provides a means of prioritising change efforts. It is noted that operational managers did not share this view, the financial measurements were seen as irrelevant by them.*
6. *Information for ad hoc decision making has improved; there is a more imaginative perspective on cost identification for such decisions as make or buy.*

Are these the intended outcomes? – These outcomes were not identified at the outset of the project.

There has been no effect on information systems, nor, as yet, on reported information although this is intended in the future. The nature of decisions using information is referred to in the points set out above, and has been affected by the project.

29:8 Operational Problems and Solutions Applied

Operational problems in some respects echo those described in **paragraph 29:5** within implementation. The efforts made to avoid potential problems are also set out below:

1. *Recruiting top-level support. The scepticism of some members of the plant operating committee remains an issue. Significant effort by the finance team, in particular the financial controller, was expended in promoting ABM to this group. The publicity given to the output from the project, in respect to savings identified, has also been helpful.*
2. *Quantifying and delivering the benefits. The measurement of improvement opportunities has been undertaken as an indicative exercise only. To date the subsequent delivery of those benefits is not measured or controlled. The process sponsor is responsible for progressing them. It is intended that this step will be monitored through a plant steering committee, and form part of the annual operating plan for the plant.*
3. *UK savings not comparable with US. The ABM exercise in the US plants has generated higher savings opportunities due to the lack of a preceding Kaizen initiative.*

29:9 Human Issues

These issues have been touched on elsewhere, but the following draws them together.

29:9.1 Conflict

The ABM project has been carried out as an open process, inputs and outputs visible to all participants. Conflict among those taking part has occurred and resolution was not easy. Within the ABM team conflict has arisen and the operation of the team is under self-review as mentioned in **paragraph 29:6.4**.

29:9.2 Resistance to Change

This has not been experienced as a problem because of the prior experience with Kaizen. There were full discussions of the project with union representatives, which also served to minimise any such resistance.

How has the planning and control system been affected?
As yet it has not been affected. It is intended at some future stage to introduce activity-based budgeting, but this is a significant way ahead.

Have the cost-benefits been realised/achieved?
The measurement of improvement opportunities has been undertaken as an indicative exercise only. To date the subsequent delivery of those benefits is not measured or controlled. The process sponsor is responsible for progressing them. It is intended that this step will be monitored through the plant steering committee, and form part of the annual operating plan for the plant.

29:10 Conclusion

How successful?
The group's positive view is reflected in its continuing commitment to the project. Those interviewed shared the opinion at the time of writing that ABM is a worthwhile undertaking.

Next step?

After the completion of the mapping of all the processes, data will be provided to the group which will be recorded in a database and used to undertake benchmarking. The group then intends to revisit activity-based costing, primarily driven by the marketing function.

There is also an intention to move towards activity-based budgeting – a development which would be welcomed by operational managers, whose budget reports do not currently assist in the management of operational activities.

29:10.1 Benefits

1. *A more visible accounting function, more clearly aligned with the operational effort of the plant, associated with a more positive view of the finance team as partners.*
2. *The project has been a catalyst for change.*
3. *Communication has improved among all participants in the ABM work, across cross-functional and hierarchical boundaries.*
4. *Information about the costs of processes, and an indication of the cost consequences of improvements provides a means of prioritising change efforts.*
5. *Information for ad hoc decision making has improved and there is a more imaginative perspective on cost identification for such decisions as make or buy.*

29:10.2 Interaction with Other Initiatives

ABM is presented as a management approach which supports other management initiatives such as JIT and TQM, all of which require an understanding of the processes supporting them.

Extensive training has been given on the other initiatives. The ABM project has been assisted by the environment created by these other initiatives, and by the positive experience associated with the period of their introduction, i.e. no job losses and improved performance.

30. Using Activity-based Information

30:1 Activity-based Information

Many organisations have now implemented activity-based costing (ABC) or activity-based management (ABM) systems. Typically, managers in these organisations are introduced to the information from the systems in the context of it resolving a particular problem they have or of it meeting a particular need. Frequently these managers do not understand the other ways in which they could use information from the same system for other purposes.

In addition, due to this lack of appreciation of the different uses to which information from an ABC or ABM database can be put, a number of organisations do not adopt activity-based methods. When the one system can improve the information used for a wide variety of decisions, the cost and inconvenience of implementing and maintaining it can be more adequately justified.

This chapter presents a range of uses to which activity-based information (ABI) can be put. A knowledge of the principles of ABC (**Ch.22**) and activity-based cost management (ABCM) (**Ch.28**) are assumed. **Chapter 31** also has a case study on implementing ABC in a service-driven business, namely DHL Worldwide Express.

30:2 Costing and Pricing

A prime focus of ABC is to trace costs to a cost object for the purpose of profitability analysis. The cost objects are most likely to be either products (i.e. either goods or services) or customers.

30:2.1 Bidding

ABC provides incremental costs more easily than traditional costing methods because of its hierarchical classification of costs. Preparing bids is facilitated by the ready availability of cost driver rates and variations to the project can be costed quickly because it is easy to focus on cost elements that will change. For example, a residential educational course that is reduced from five days to three may not affect administrative costs or course material costs. The prime change will be in per diem costs such as meals and accommodation.

30:2.2 Customised Pricing

The costs of customised products are also easy to obtain once the required activities are identified. Job specifications may be costed by reference to the cost driver rates.

30:2.3 Customer Negotiations and Service

A detailed knowledge of what causes costs, as provided by the ABC model, is of enormous benefit in the negotiation of contracts with customers. Rather than recosting the entire contract, ABC enables the negotiator to adjust costs in the relevant category of costs (e.g. engineering changes). Conventional costing systems typically include such costs in an overhead cost pool and do not explain their behaviour.

A similar situation exists with regard to the provision of after-care services to customers. For example, conventional cost systems often treat such customer service costs as overhead costs and allocate them over total production. If the organisation does not regard after-care service as a discrete product it is unlikely to be separately costed. However, some products may require far more service calls than others, and some customers may expect more service calls than others. Costing support services separately highlights such disparities and provides guidance in the management of these costs.

30:2.4 Transfer Costing

Transfer charging has increased significantly during the last decade, especially in units that provide services to other units in the organisation. These charges are often based on the costs of the goods or services supplied (the main alternative is a market-based transfer price). In some cases this transfer costing has identified the need for a more sophisticated costing system than the conventional system already in place. Such a need tends to become apparent when the unit receiving the service questions the charge being made. Such charges usually cannot be justified on the basis of information coming from traditional cost systems. The inequities of the allocations made by broad-based blanket rates lead to many arguments followed by requests to outsource.

The use of ABC to cost these services appears to reduce tensions due to the ability of the unit providing the service to justify the charge and, consequently, the perceived equity of the system. ABC also makes it easy for the units involved in the transfer to negotiate changes in the transaction. As one internal consultant explained: 'When that manager realised the cost of the Rolls Royce report he was asking for we started analysing the cost of various changes that would still ensure his needs were met'.

30:2.5 Customer Profitability

Traditionally the production costs of products supplied to customers have been the only costs directly identified with the customers. However, there has been a growing realisation that many other costs are incurred in dealing with customers, and that customers often cause excess costs by their behaviour. Examples of suffering heavy penalties by dealing with 'awkward' customers include dealing with frequent telephone calls, frequent engineering changes, receiving and filling many small orders from JIT customers, irregular ordering and filling orders for non-stock items.

As related in **Chapter 28, paragraph 28:3.2**, many customers can be found to cause losses when non-inventoriable costs, or non-production costs, are identified with them. In addition, the large customers (in volume or revenue size) have the greater capacity to cause greater losses and also tend to expect favoured treatment.

The information that can be extracted from an activity-based information system can be used to associate costs with the customers for whom the costs were incurred. It can also be used to decide how to resolve the problems highlighted. For example:

(a) *Once it is known how much extra cost is incurred in dealing with a JIT customer (due to either holding inventory for them or producing in frequent short runs) the method of charging that customer can be adjusted to allow for these costs. The result can be a change in the customer changing the requested delivery pattern or paying adequate compensation for special treatment. Either way, the customer can be turned from a loss producer to a profitable customer to deal with.*

(b) *It has been found that irregular ordering can cause extra costs as production schedules need frequent adjustment and overtime may be required. A discount can be offered for regular orders, especially if detailed well in advance.*

(c) *The number of orders placed by customers affects costs. When the cost of handling an order is known (administration, scheduling, dispatch) it is possible to make a charge for each order placed. Again, this may modify the behaviour of customers. Some costs can be reduced by arranging for large customers to be able to key orders through from their own computer terminal.*

(d) *It may be surprising how much costs increase due to customers ordering items that are not normally held in stock. Solutions include reducing product range, but this may not be desirable if customers are thought to be attracted by the availability of a full range of products. One method of dealing with the situation is to deal through franchised outlets that specialise in these items. An alternative is to give a discount on items held in stock, so that a premium is paid for those that are not normally in stock.*

(e) *It is possible to take the data concerning customer-generated costs to those customers to negotiate ways in which transactions with them can become profitable.*

These are a few examples of ways that customers may be persuaded to modify behaviour or compensate for their demands. When fewer than half of your customers are profitable to deal with (this is not uncommon), the need for action and/or negotiation with them becomes paramount.

30:2.6 Target Costing
(*See* **Ch.13**.)

The use of activity-based information for costing products that are in the design stage helps to achieve the target cost since each component and activity is separately costed. Ways to redesign the product and/or the production process to reach target cost are guided by the activity-costing data. Firms that adopt this approach to target costing estimate that the target cost can be attained in a fraction of the time that their previous methods took.

30:2.7 Product Range

The selection of product mix can be assisted by ABC since the contribution of each product towards covering common (facility sustaining) costs and generating a profit are often more accurately identifiable.

Product contribution = Revenue earned by the product – Product-related costs

For decisions based on product profitability analyses, this ABC contribution approach is more relevant than the full costing methods that cloud the issue by misrepresenting facility-sustaining costs as product costs. By incorporating these irrelevant data in the product cost, informed decision making is impaired. Rather than relating facility-sustaining costs to the cost of the product, they should be recognised as extra costs that must be covered before a profit can be recorded.

Total contributions from all products – Facility-sustaining costs = Profit

This formula is still too simplistic for more complex organisations. However, it can easily be refined to allow for different levels of sustaining costs. For example, an organisation may operate in several markets, with a range of products in each. In these circumstances there will be market-level costs that can be identified with a market but not with individual products. The contribution from each product within a market, less the market-sustaining costs, will provide market contribution.

Similarly, a manufacturing plant may produce a range of products. Plant contribution to covering head office costs may be derived by deducting plant-sustaining costs from the total product contribution from the plant. Contributions may therefore be derived for business segments [*cf. SSAP25: Segmental Reporting, IAS14: Segment Reporting*], markets, particular industries, geographical areas and so on.

This analysis of contributions at different levels also illustrates the way that the cost hierarchies may be determined. Any level at which a report of performance is desired may be identified as a cost level to which relevant costs may be traced. For example, if 'State contribution' is considered useful information, there will be 'State operations-sustaining costs'. If there are not 'State operations-sustaining costs', or they are difficult to identify, then it is not appropriate to find 'State contribution' or, what may be known as profitability by State. Perhaps the operational structure uses broader regional areas such as 'north-west region'?

30:3 Cost Management

Whereas ABC accounts for costs, ABM is used to manage costs. Costing methods may highlight areas of concern but costs are incurred because resources are used up and, usually, costs are controlled by controlling the resource usage. Some of the ways in which costs can be managed were described in the preceding section in which costing and profitability calculations highlighted opportunities for cost management. Other ways to manage costs follow.

30:3.1 Overhead Reduction

With the separation of overheads into groups of costs that behave in a similar way, certain excesses are highlighted and unnecessary activities identified. Excesses draw attention to the need to take action with regard to the cost incurrence, such as scrapped work, a high number of movements of work in progress and distance components travel during conversion from initial input to finished goods inventory. The distance components travel between successive processes (a total during production of two kilometres is not unusual) often highlights the need for workplace re-engineering. The whole floor plan of a factory can be redesigned to minimise movement distance.

When it found how expensive movements were, one firm cut holes in the wall down one side of the factory to build on several delivery bays so that all deliveries could be made to a point beside the start of processing for the particular component being delivered.

30:3.2 Minimise Non-value Activities

The previous subsection illustrated some ways of reducing non-value-adding costs. The initial act when introducing ABM is usually to classify all activities as value adding and non-value adding and then minimise non-value-adding costs.

Some unusual responses to information on non-value-adding activities have been recorded. For example, one firm relocated a fax machine from an equipment room to the centre of an open-plan office to reduce the number of times office staff would walk to the fax machine only to find a queue for its use or an incoming fax prevented their immediate use of the machine. The time saving that resulted was costed and found to be significant.

At the suggestion of the shop-floor workers (who had helped collect the activity data), another firm had a washroom installed beside a factory workroom.

30:3.3 Continuous Improvement

Once improvements have been implemented in an attempt to contain costs it is necessary to continue to monitor the costs and the activities. Not only does this assist management to ensure that cost management does not deteriorate again, it can be used to encourage further, iterative improvements. In particular they can be highlighted in a balanced business scorecard (BBS).

The BBS has four quadrants that encompass the main influences on the welfare of the organisation. For example, there may be a quadrant for: the financial perspective; the customer perspective; the internal business perspective; and innovation. So that they can be easily digested, each quadrant should have three to five measures that relate to the aspect of the business in that quadrant. The measures in the different quadrants of the BBS interact and the scorecard acts like the dashboard of a car, showing the current situation at a glance.

The interaction of these measures is more easily identified when they are based on ABI and their use to promote continuous improvement is becoming more widespread.

30:3.4 Supplier Evaluation

Vendor appraisal programmes are becoming a necessary part of total quality management (TQM) programmes as the guaranteed quality of deliveries significantly reduces appraisal costs and the effort to achieve a high standard of supplies is part of the prevention initiative of the TQM programme.

The use of ABI to evaluate the performance of suppliers is the inverse of the customer profitability assessment discussed in **paragraph 30:2.4**. Suppliers cause unnecessary costs by supplying goods at the wrong time, in the wrong amounts, by getting paperwork wrong, and by supplying substandard goods. These and other causes of costs for which suppliers are responsible can be identified with the suppliers that cause them. The cost of the items purchased from the suppliers may be far greater than the price paid for them.

Once a supplier has been assessed, the prices quoted by that supplier can be increased by a suitable percentage to estimate the cost of the items supplied by that supplier. For example, Supplier A may have a margin of 3% added to its quoted prices, while Supplier B has a margin of 5% added to its quoted prices. This written-up figure (representing the cost of the item rather than the price of it) should be used by purchasing officers to select the source of purchases. If these written-up prices/costs are used for purchase variances, disputes between purchasing managers and production managers often reduce dramatically. The likelihood of purchasing managers buying substandard materials at cut prices is virtually eliminated.

All suppliers assessed under these schemes should be reassessed at six-month intervals. Further, it may be necessary to assess different supplies from individual firms separately. The ABI and ABC information on the supplier can be used in discussions with the supplier when indicating what aspects of their performance need to be improved. Suppliers that achieve a high standard of assessment in the appraisal scheme can even be given a reward in the form of a plaque, indicating that they are a favoured vendor.

30:3.5 Product Design
(*See* Ch.41.)

Activity-based information may be used in product design even when target costing is not undertaken. For example, a choice between alternative designs that are aesthetically and functionally equally pleasing may be based on cost information. Furthermore, since the activities involved in production of the product are detailed it is often possible to design products and processes to minimise the likelihood of defects. Complicated processes and complex products provide greater scope for errors to occur. ABI can help simplify both processes and products.

30:3.6 Productivity

Productivity measures are activity measures. Many firms utilise ABI to monitor productivity in more detail. When productivity requires investigation ABI is likely to provide more useful information about the sources/causes of variances.

30:4 Resource Allocation

There are a variety of techniques that assist in decisions about resource allocation. This is an important function of management as it determines what can be done during the financial year and, if funds are unlimited, imposes constraints through deciding what will not be done. Such decisions must be consistent with the strategic direction adopted by the organisation. Complying with the strategic plan should prevent myopia (or short-termism) from hindering long-term preparations.

30:4.1 Activity-based Budgets

Basing budgets on ABC is called activity-based budgeting (ABB). Activity-based costing systems make it easier to have devolved budgets. Each budget is prepared on the basis of the activities to be undertaken during the coming budget period. As the unit that will be responsible for performing activities is known the budget can be broken down into individual unit budgets. Each unit manager should have influence in preparing the budget (creating a feeling of ownership of the budget) and be held responsible for meeting the budget or explaining variances.

This budgeting method facilitates responsibility accounting (holding individual managers accountable for activities and financial results over which they have control), and is consistent with zero-base budgeting (ZBB) principles.

ZBB requires the justification for every item in the budget as well as the amount entered for each item. This contrasts with the incremental approach to budgeting in which budget amounts are based on prior period allocations and results, making adjustments such as a percentage increase to allow for inflation. The incremental approach leads to a 'use it or lose it' mentality. It may lead to the funding of activities that are no longer undertaken or that may be undertaken but are no longer required.

30:4.2 Capital Expenditure

As illustrated in **paragraphs 30:2.1** and **30:2.3**, incremental costs are easier to identify through the use of ABC than under the traditional costing approaches. Since incremental cash flows are the cornerstone of good capital project analysis, relevant information can be provided by an ABC system very quickly.

30:4.3 Transfer Charging

Transfer charging was discussed in **paragraph 30:2.4** in terms of costing the product being transferred. However, transfer charging is a means of reallocating (transferring) resources. It ensures that funds get transferred to units whose products are in demand. ABC makes transfer charging easier and often results in more appropriate transfers of resources.

30:4.4 Staffing

A major resource in some organisations, especially service organisations, is human resources. The utilisation of staff can be managed by reference to activity analyses. With an analysis of what activity is being performed and at what times, it is easy to determine suitable staffing levels.

In bank retail outlets the information can help to meet customer demands at peak times. The same is true of clerical staff dealing with claims in an insurance company. Since claims are often closely forecast three months ahead, staffing requirements for handling claims can be equally well forecast. As a further example, in hospitals, the distribution of nursing staff through the hospital could be justified by reference to activity analyses.

30:4.5 Outsourcing
(*See* Ch.38.)

Previously called 'make-buy' decisions, outsourcing decisions determine whether goods or services will be obtained from outside the organisation or from within. Outsourcing is becoming particularly prevalent in the public sector.

The costing of the internal provision of the product is obviously very important in making decisions with regard to which products to outsource, and ABC can assist in this regard. Hence, this is a cost-management issue.

It cannot be assumed that a decision made in one part of the organisation will be equally valid in another part of the organisation. For example, a producer of plastic sheeting found it to be cost-effective to recycle scrap plastic (i.e. use it to produce plastic beads that could be used in its products that used a lower-standard material input) at one plant, but to be cheaper to have this recycling process outsourced at another plant (due to low volume).

Apart from the costing and cost management issues, outsourcing decisions have important resource implications. Many outsourcing decisions determine the existence or discontinuance of whole units or subunits of an organisation. It is therefore very important to accurately identify the costs that will discontinue if the outsourcing option is selected. This decision must therefore include consideration of the change of activities and whether these changes will really reduce resource requirements. For example, saving the time of half of one operative may not produce any cost savings, and reducing the use of floor space (which is often used to allocate costs to departments) may not save occupancy costs.

30:5 Other

30:5.1 Introduce Cost Culture

Some organisations purposely adopt ABC methods, and circulate the information from it, to make managers cost-conscious. If this is done appropriately, by making it necessary for the managers to constantly monitor the costs that relate to decisions, a cost culture soon develops. In organisations where this cost information is distributed to workers, they also become cost-conscious and often begin to make cost-saving suggestions.

30:5.2 Validation/Vindication

ABI may be used to validate proposals as the database makes a detailed cost analysis of most proposals relatively easy. Traditional methods are far less accurate with regard to activity inputs than material inputs, leaving much room for the validity of proposals to be challenged.

When ABI is first made available this validation process is often undertaken in retrospect. Many managers find that the ABI vindicates past statements or decisions that were based on 'gut feelings', increasing their confidence in the decision and in their abilities, and gaining the respect of others.

30:5.3 Prioritise Action

Due to the detail available from an ABI system it can be used to prioritise action. For example, costs are broken down into activity pools that highlight the size of problems in monetary terms. The activity analysis also highlights problems in volumes (i.e. in physical terms) such as time spent on reworking individual products. Naturally the greater problems should be prioritised for immediate attention. Spreading one's attention too widely creates the lack of focus that hinders real progress.

30:5.4 Accountability

As indicated in **paragraph 30:4.1** on ABB, ABC helps with the devolvement of responsibility, and hence of accountability. Similarly, ABM helps when holding managers accountable for the activity undertaken within their departments. In the trend towards greater accountability, both internally and externally, ABI can therefore be used to focus attention (through the activity analysis), identify key performance indicators and monitor those measures.

30:5.5 Assess Competitiveness

Some segments of firms have been forced to justify their existence by demonstrating their competitiveness against external suppliers. The profitability of individual segments is often obscured by inappropriate overhead allocation methods. The external supplier may be a small firm that, consequently, has clearer knowledge of the profitability of its few (or only) products. In the process of using ABC for this purpose, the segment will typically discover ways to become even more competitive, as the ABI reveals opportunities for better cost management and improved customer services.

30:5.6 Restructuring

ABC may redefine suitable activity groupings (for example, include the packaging of each product within the unit in which production takes place instead of having all products packaged in one unit, or reversing this situation). ABI may cause job descriptions to be rewritten to reduce overlap of responsibilities and to better consolidate related decision making. In these and other ways, restructuring of the organisation may be indicated by the ABI. Further, the ABI can assist in the decisions with regard to the new structure.

Examples of such decisions include the following:

(a) *Two adjacent plants for one firm decided that one larger maintenance unit would be more efficient than having one maintenance unit on each plant. Human resources were not decreased but peaks and troughs on the two plants rarely coincided so the workers, as well as plant operations, were advantaged by better equating the supply and demand of these human resources.*

(b) *ABI on a marketing unit in an international bank found that less than 30% of the time of its managers was spent on marketing and sales effort. The data revealed how much time was spent on administrative support tasks that could be performed by administration staff, leaving the highly-paid marketing specialists with time to perform to their job descriptions. A marketing business support unit was introduced and marketing results increased dramatically.*

(c) *A training college segregated its conferencing business from its management training business, providing clarity of purpose and responsibilities while encouraging transfers of services for resources.*

(d) *A large international organisation, whose main businesses mined and converted natural resources, redefined the profit centres and cost centres in its IT division when the ABI clarified which centres could influence revenue generation and which could not.*

30:6 Conclusions

This chapter has sought to make managers more aware of the wide range of uses to which activity-based information can be put. It is not exhaustive and the suggested uses can each be adopted and adapted in a variety of ways.

Many managers feel that it would be of benefit to have 'brainstorming' sessions and group presentations so that they can learn from each other's experience. The frequent feedback from managers in organisations that have ABI available, usually through the adoption of ABC or ABM methods, is that they would like to understand the potential uses of the data better.

The typical experience of firms that do implement an activity-based technique is that benefits derived are greater than expected, the uses wider than expected. However, this chapter does not claim to produce an index of the benefits of adopting activity-based techniques. The benefits are much broader than the uses to which the ABI can be put and the insights that emerge. The greater benefits are often found to be behavioural and personal. For example, communication patterns between managers change, formal communication becomes more effective (related to the understandability of information requests and responses), the ease of 'managing' improves and job satisfaction increases. In fact, the reported benefits of adopting methods that generate activity-based information require their own chapter.

Three factors must be recognised with regard to the successful use of ABI:

1. *the firms in which the benefits of adoption are identified have implemented ABTs after careful consideration and their experiences are not necessarily replicable in a firm that does not have the scope to experience such benefits;*
2. *the literature on ABC often promotes the use of ABC in firms in which overhead costs are a large proportion of total costs. However, very successful use of ABC and ABM has been found in other firms in which overhead costs were a large proportion of profit but a very small proportion of total costs (e.g. an insurance company in which claims represent 50% of costs);*
3. *the changes suggested by ABI are not restricted to lower-level management. Higher-level managers tend to believe that change applies to 'others'. They believe that, by definition, everything they do or require to be done is value adding. However, they need to be responsive to the findings of the activity analyses if both they and ABI are to maintain credibility.*

31. Implementing ABC in a Service-driven Business – DHL Worldwide Express

31:1 Introduction

This chapter describes how we, at DHL Worldwide Express, one of the world's leading air express companies, have designed and implemented an activity-based costing system to help us understand and manage the costs of our key processes and improve customer profitability. It should not be seen as an academic guide on how to implement ABC, but rather as a practical example of how we did it at DHL. I have included not just what worked well, but also what did not work well at all. I believe this is important as we can learn just as much from failure as we can from success.

I have structured this case study in four sections:

1. *The reason – DHL's big problem. Why did we decide we needed ABC in the first place, and how could it help us solve our big problem?*
2. *Building the ABC model – first attempt. How we built our first model designed to cost products, and what its shortcomings were.*
3. *Building the ABC model – second generation. How we built a more sophisticated model, this time with the emphasis on costing customers.*
4. *Using the model to manage profitability. Actually putting the costing system to work and using it to improve profitability.*

Other relevant chapters are **Chapter 22** with the principles of ABC, **Chapter 28** with activity-based cost management, **Chapter 13** with activity-based budgeting and **Chapter 30** on using activity-based information.

Martin Holton

31:2 The Reason – DHL's Big Problem

DHL, as an air express company, sells a service which is fairly easy to understand. We pick up shipments from customers' premises, typically towards the end of the business day. We fly them to a hub, where the shipments are sorted overnight. They are then flown to the destination country where the import procedures are carried out, and the shipments are then delivered to their consignees.

But what made us develop an ABC system?

To understand why DHL felt the need to develop an ABC system I first need to explain the context of DHL's big problem, and the best way I can do that is by giving a few facts and figures.

DHL started up in the US in 1969. By 1972 we had spread to the Far East and South Pacific, by 1975 we had opened in the UK and Western Europe, followed by Canada and the Middle East in 1976 and 1977. Africa in 1979 was followed by Eastern Europe and China and now the DHL network covers the world.

By the end of 1973 DHL had 400 employees. By 1983 this had grown to 11,300 and by 1993, 29,000. We now have well over 60,000 employees worldwide.

The number of flights per day used by DHL has grown from 14 in 1973 to nearly 800 by 1983, and now stands at more than 2,000. The number of aircraft owned and operated by DHL has grown from five in 1978 to more than 220 today. The number of service centres has grown from 73 in 1973 to more than 2,300, the number of hubs has grown from – well perhaps I will stop here as I think I have made the point.

DHL's big problem is growth!

I do not expect much sympathy as I realise this is not the worst problem a company could have, but it can be a problem none the less. While growth in revenue is certainly good news, growth in costs is not. The challenge, of course, is to manage that growth in such a way that it improves profitability.

In the mid-1980s DHL was going through a period where profitability was not growing at the rate we would have expected. When we tried to analyse the results of the business to understand how we could improve our management of all this growth, we found that the only measures available were the traditional finance reports, i.e. the profit and loss statements and the balance sheets.

We certainly had excellent information on such critical business parameters as the short-term portion of the long-term debt, the VAT recoverable, the guarantees and utility deposits and, of course, my favourite, the unamortised goodwill on the trademark.

I, personally, do not have a financial background and had great difficulty understanding what all of this meant, so I decided to take a pile of these reports to our financial controller and, dumping them on his desk, I asked: 'Can you explain in simple language what all this is?'. 'Yes' he replied, 'this is the s**t we collect every month!'.

I felt pleased that he had found a way to explain it all in terms that I could indeed understand, in spite of the fact that I warned him I was looking for something I could use as a quote.

Of course what I suspect he was trying to say was that this was information which he had to produce, but which he recognised was probably of limited use for managing the business. What he would probably have added was that if you ask the accountants to do all the reporting, do not be surprised if they only report on things that are important to accountants.

As a manager with a background in marketing and with responsibility to devise a system to improve profitability, I was particularly struck by what we did not report on, and consequently what we did not know about our business. We did not know the cost of our products. Therefore we did not know the cost of serving our customers, and consequently we did not know where we were making profit, by product, by customer, by industry group, by sales territory, etc. Without knowing which parts of our business were profitable and which parts were not, it was going to be pretty difficult to know where growth was improving profitability, and where it was making the situation worse.

Another burning question we could not answer was how the growth in direct costs compared to the growth in overhead costs. We carried out a quick exercise in one of our major countries dividing costs into three groups. The first group was direct operations, the second was sales and customer service and the third group included IT accounting, management and administration. It was a sort of mini ABC exercise, tracking the growth in average cost per shipment in each of these groups of costs over a four-year period.

The results showed that while operations costs per shipment had only grown by 4%, sales and customer services had grown by 25%, and IT accounting, management and administration had grown by a massive 67%.

Before this study we had always concentrated on managing operations costs, often putting pressure on the couriers to be more productive, whereas we now realised that we should have been concentrating far more on controlling our overhead costs. Of course, putting pressure on the couriers may have been keeping them fit and healthy, but it was clearly not the answer to our profitability problems.

What I am trying to say is that we were most definitely in urgent need of a good activity-based costing system.

31:3 Building the ABC Model – First Attempt

In 1987 DHL enlisted the help of a rather expensive, but very fashionable consulting company and started to design an ABC system. Although the system may have been a little simplistic, it was not a bad first attempt. We expressed DHL's business in terms of 30 activities, and identified five cost drivers for those activities, but unfortunately absorbed overheads by product.

The absorption of overheads was driven by the concern expressed by the finance and accounting managers that if there were any 'left-over' costs not included in products, then we could not trust the sales and marketing people to make sure these were recovered in pricing.

Why absorb by products? At the time it just seemed the easiest solution. DHL markets a service transporting shipments, but sees these shipments as different products. The main products are Dox, international document shipments, WPX, (Worldwide Parcel eXpress), for international dutiable goods, ECX, European Community eXpress, DOM, domestic shipments, etc.

So the cost model was built. Costs from the general ledger were allocated across the activities according to the proportion of each cost line that was thought to be consumed by each activity. These activities were then allocated to products by means of the five cost drivers: shipments, courier stops, customer accounts, etc.

The essence of ABC is cause and effect, it must be shown that each cost driver is the cause of the level of the activity for which it is the driver. For example, the activity of picking up shipments was driven by the number of courier stops, the activity of sorting packages was driven by the number of shipments, etc.

However, where the methodology started to look weak was on activities like providing IT support, which was supposedly driven by products (shipment types), or worse still, the activity 'other administration', (if this is not overhead then I do not know what is), which was also deemed to be driven by shipments.

Anyway, this was the way we built our first ABC model, and we began to use it to calculate the profitability of the business. The results gave us many new insights into our profitability, but one of the most striking, was that it told us customers in the heavy manufacturing industries tended to be profitable whereas banks were invariably unprofitable.

As a major proportion of our customers were in the banking sector, and we had made very little headway in penetrating the heavy-industry sector, this was generally seen as rather bad news. (I would not want to give the impression that it created total panic!)

With hindsight, it is quite obvious why the model produced these results. Much of the cost being allocated to shipments was not actually driven by those shipments, i.e. there was no clear cause and effect relationship established. Instead shipments were just being used as an arbitrary means to absorb overhead costs. This cost might work out to be around $5 per shipment in a given country.

If we now imagine a customer in the heavy-manufacturing sector sending, for example a 1 tonne shipment to Hong Kong, that customer would be allocated $5 worth of overhead, over and above the costs that were actually being driven by that customer. Now imagine a bank also sending 1 tonne to Hong Kong. The vast majority of shipments that banks send by DHL are light-weight documents, say, half a kilo per shipment on average. This means that the 1 tonne of bank documents could well be made up of 2,000 shipments each receiving $5 worth of overhead. In other words the customer in heavy manufacturing would get an arbitrary allocation of $5 overhead and the bank would be hit with $10,000.

I know it looks ridiculous when I describe it like that, but at the time because of the way we were trying to force all costs into our products, it was not obvious to us at first. There was a general feeling of uneasiness about the ABC system in the finance community, although we were not quite sure what was wrong.

You can imagine the disastrous effect this could have had on our business, but fortunately our sales people knew exactly what to do with the profitability information that finance was giving them. They ignored it!

Whether this was good judgement on the part of our sales force, or just their natural instinct to ignore anything coming from finance is hard to say, but this time they were right. They knew how DHL prices compared with market rates, they knew which customers the competition were targeting, they had a feel for what ought to be good business and what ought not. They were convinced that they knew how to price and when to discount, and if the ABC information clashed so fundamentally with their perceptions then it must be wrong.

To cut a long story short, we ended up with an ABC system which had lost credibility and was not achieving the purpose for which it was designed. As our understanding improved we found ways to adjust the output of the model to produce more accurate results, but it was too late. The credibility had gone and nobody was prepared to base any decisions on a discredited costing system.

31:4 Building the ABC Model – Second Generation

We were still convinced that ABC would provide the answer to our problem, but this time we knew we had to get it right. We set up a cross-functional project team representing various potential users of ABC information and retained the support of a smaller consulting organisation whose people had a demonstrable track record of successful ABC implementation, and set about designing a new, second generation, costing system.

We began slowly, often having heated debates about how we should measure activities and drivers until it finally became obvious to us that the only answer to the question: 'what is the cost?' is: 'it depends what you want it for'. Were we building a system for product costing or cost management? Some members of the project team were expecting the cost model to be used for product costing, while others were thinking more along the lines of customer costing. Others clearly wanted the model to support process management, and then there were always the accountants worrying about whether or not the model was going to reconcile.

Of course the model has to reconcile in the sense that we have to be able to show that it is neither missing out nor double-counting any costs. What we had to resist was the temptation to absorb arbitrarily all the costs just to make sure there was nothing left over. We had already made that mistake with our first model and we were not going to let it happen again. I will come back to this issue of overhead costs later, but for the moment let us deal with this question of what the model is to be used for.

One of the most fundamental choices that this question will drive is the level of detail to be used in defining activities. We eventually decided to fix a standard for DHL, at a level of detail suitable for product and customer costing. After piloting the methodology we thought that 80 to 90 activities seemed to be about right. As the methodology developed and as we received more feedback from different countries building their cost models the number of activities was updated and finally settled at 106 primary activities. Although that may sound like a lot, in practice it is rare for any given country to use every available activity when building its cost model.

These standard 106 primary activities are documented in our 'Chart of Activities' and are coded in such a way that they can be easily consolidated into 15 activity categories. We believe that this is an appropriate level of detail for regional reporting to our head offices where these activity categories can be reviewed for the purpose of strategic cost management. The coding system also allows each of the 106 primary activities to be split into up to 100 secondary activities, as and when this is required for process costing or other local cost management initiatives. As an example, one of our countries carried out a process improvement initiative on their billing and collection process and created over 400 subactivities in order to arrive at a level of detail where they felt they could identify which activities were adding value and which ones were not.

We have a requirement for our countries to build cost models using the standard 106 primary activities which consolidate into 15 activity categories. There is no standard below that level, but the flexibility exists for any country to create subactivities as required for local cost-management purposes.

Apart from this question of levels of detail we also needed to sort out the issue of product costing versus customer costing. You may wonder why a service-driven business like DHL thinks in terms of products. I have a suspicion that it may simply be that many of our sales and marketing people went to business schools, and that is what they teach in business schools. While I fully accept that the concept of products can be very helpful in marketing strategy, we found that from a costing point of view, products were not a significant driver of cost.

When trying to understand what drives product costs we came to the conclusion that if we ask the question: 'what is the cost of a 10kg ECX shipment from London to Frankfurt?', the only answer is: 'it depends who sends it'. (Actually, it depends on who receives it as well.) What we found was that it was the customer characteristics that made the overwhelming difference in cost. Our cost model defines front-line activities which are driven by such things as courier stops, shipments, kilos, invoices, phone calls, sales visits, etc. All these cost drivers can be linked directly to customers and the cost of any given customer can be calculated according to its consumption of these drivers. Although we can calculate the average cost per product, costing products as a means to costing customers would add nothing to our methodology, and would simply cause an unacceptable degree of averaging.

Having mentioned front-line activities, the ones driven directly by customers, I should now mention that our cost model also recognises that some activities are support activities. These support activities are not driven directly by customers, but are there to support other activities. You could think of the front-line activities as being driven by external customers and the support activities as being driven by internal customers. So instead of being linked to customers through cost drivers, the support activities are reallocated over the activities that they support according to how those activities drive the support activities. I may have made that sound more complicated than it really is so let me give an example.

Let us take salary administration. It is a support activity which is clearly not driven directly by customers. However it is driven by the number of DHL staff who have their salaries administered. Therefore the front-line activity of picking up shipments will not only include the personnel costs, the vehicle costs, etc., coming directly from the general ledger, but it will also be loaded with the reallocated cost of salary administration based on the number of heads involved in the pick-up activity.

So is it really that straightforward? Well, not quite, because we also have to reallocate salary administration over other support activities like IT support to PC users. Now the problem is that you do not know the full cost of salary administration until you have loaded it with the reallocated cost of IT support (based on the number of PCs used by salary administration), and you cannot do that until you have loaded the cost of salary administration onto IT support (based on the number of heads in IT support). You can see the trap we are heading into, but what is the solution? My suggestion is to buy one of the off-the-shelf ABC software packages that will do this for you, this is what we did in DHL. The alternative would be for me to explain the mathematics behind this, and the very idea is already giving me a headache.

When we were evaluating ABC software packages, one of my team who is an engineering graduate and is a gifted mathematician assured me that the software did the job adequately (that is the only part of the explanation I really understood), so that is good enough for me.

Having discussed front-line and support activities we come to the third and final type of activity, the unattributable (or overhead), activities. These are activities which are neither driven directly by customers nor are they support activities which find their way to customers by being reallocated over front-line activities. They are activities which are not in any way (directly or indirectly) driven by customers. As the underlying principle of ABC is cause and effect, where there is none, these activities cannot be attributed to customers.

Examples of these unattributable activities are the costs of business infrastructure such as accounting, auditing, consolidation, the cost of the board of directors, legal and statutory costs, etc. They are simply the costs of existing as a company. Also included are such business-sustaining costs as strategic advertising, prospecting for new business, research and development – in fact all the costs necessary to ensure future business continuity and growth.

None of these costs is driven by existing customers, therefore they should not be attributed to those customers. Unfortunately, somebody will have to pay for these costs and, of course, that can only be the people who pay for everything in the business – our customers.

We considered the possibility of simply leaving out the unattributable costs but were concerned that they should be included in the results of our cost model as a reminder that they do have to be recovered. However we were certainly not going to repeat the mistake of our previous cost model, by arbitrarily absorbing these costs on the basis of shipments.

Driven by our intention to give the users of our costing system the best information possible to support decision making, we decided to show two results. First, the profitability of a customer based solely on the costs actually driven by that customer, i.e. the front-line costs loaded with the appropriate support costs. Then a second result showing the profitability with the unattributable cost spread back as a percentage mark-up on the costs actually driven by the customer.

We found that it was important to use this method of spreading back the unattributable costs, as any other method of absorbing this cost (e.g. shipments, kilos revenue, etc.) would have given a distorted view of profitability and would have artificially favoured one type of customer over another. In practice what our costing system says is: This customer's consumption of cost drivers will drive our costs by a given amount. If the revenue exceeds that amount, the customer is making a contribution to overheads and profit. However, do not forget that on average each customer will have to contribute another 'X' percent to cover the overhead before it starts to generate profit.

The problem I am now faced with is when I am told by a sales manager that he can see how much the average unattributable overhead is, but how much does an individual customer have to contribute? If that customer's revenue covers the front-line and support costs, but is not enough to cover the unattributable costs, is this good business?

I believe this is a question of marketing strategy and not a question of costing. Unattributable cost should simply be recovered the same way that profit targets are recovered. When preparing next year's budget we know that the revenue must be equal to the total of front-line costs, support costs, unattributable costs and profit. Clearly we do not expect to make the same profit on every customer. We will make more on some customers and less on others, we may even accept to make a loss on some (it can be very entertaining listening to a sales representative trying to explain why). The recovery of unattributable overhead costs is treated in exactly the same way. If we recover less than the average on some customers, then we have to recover more on others.

DHL's ABC system will not tell sales and marketing people how much overhead they should recover, or how much profit they should make on each customer, but it does give them the information they need to be able to make those judgements themselves.

This leads me on to the last part of this case study. Once we had completed piloting the methodology, documented it, trained it and rolled it out to all our major countries how did we actually use it?

31:5 Using the Model to Manage Profitability

Having designed and implemented an ABC methodology we were keen to get the maximum benefit from it. I have a firm belief that ABC is not meant to be an accounting system. It is a management tool providing support for profitable decision making.

The original idea behind building our ABC system was to provide us with customer profitability data to support marketing decisions such as pricing, discounting, customer targeting, etc. We used it extensively to evaluate the potential profitability of new business, identifying which business we should take at what price and which business we should avoid. However, when we discovered that in some cases our existing customers were unprofitable and that simply hitting them with a price increase was not an option, we were faced with the question of what we could do to reduce the cost of serving these customers.

If we were to identify opportunities for reducing customer costs we needed to improve our understanding of how our costs were being driven through the interface with our customers.

While piloting our costing methodology we had become increasingly aware of how important it was for us, as a service-driven business, to understand and manage our customer interface. For many of our front-line activities, involving direct interaction with the customer, we found that there were enormous differences in the way that some customers drove our costs compared to others. Let me explain this by using the example of the activity: picking up shipments.

We were convinced that the time, and therefore the cost, in picking up shipments was simply driven by the number of shipments that were picked up from any one customer. Consequently my team and I spent much of our time, armed with stop watches, driving around with couriers and collecting data. The consultant in our team was responsible for this part of the study, and after a couple of weeks he presented the data he had collected back to the steering committee.

Instead of seeing a nice neat graph showing that the more shipments a courier picked up from a customer, the longer that pick-up took, we saw wild variations in pick-up times irrespective of the number of shipments per customer. It was obvious to me that the consultant had a poor understanding of our business and had probably misinterpreted his data, so he was sent back to think again.

The consultant checked over his data and decided that it was probably weight rather than shipments, i.e. kilos per customer, that was driving our courier pick-up times. However, when he came back to present his findings there was still no correlation between pick-up times and either shipments per customer or kilos per customer. He had even tried shipments multiplied by weight, and in his desperation to find a correlation he tried out a series of complicated mathematical formulae, and even resorted to using logarithmic scales on his graphs but without success. Still puzzled by the mystery of what was driving pick-up costs, I set about reviewing the data myself.

While I had my nose buried in data, our consultant had a brilliant idea (who says you do not get value for money from consultants?). He simply asked a courier why it took longer to pick up from one customer than it did from another, irrespective of shipments or kilos. (With hindsight this was the obvious thing to do. I cannot understand why I did not think of that!)

The courier told him:

> Well this customer, for example, is a real pain. I have to get a security pass to enter the premises, then there is never any space to park the van. The shipper's office is on the sixth floor and there's no lift. When I get there, the shipper is always wandering about somewhere else in the building and even

when I find him the shipments are never ready, so I have to help pack the shipments and prepare his paperwork for him. The pick-up usually takes about half an hour. Now this other customer is no trouble. I just reverse up to their loading bay and they normally have the shipments in the back of my van before I even have time to get out of the cab. It never takes more than two or three minutes. That is why some customers take longer than others, but then everybody knows that, don't they?

The conclusion we came to was that for those front-line activities involving direct interaction with the customer, the key cost driver was the customer. To be more accurate I should say that it was the efficiency of the interaction between DHL and the customer. With some customers that interaction works well, they consume very little of our time and are cheap and easy to serve. With other customers that interaction works badly, the customer consumes a large amount of our resources and is expensive to serve. Therefore for activities such as courier pick-up, delivery, sales, customer service, credit control, etc., we calculate the cost of interface time and then grade our customers according to how much they consume.

Of course, managing this customer interface opens up many opportunities to reduce costs. One example of this is the case of the Cambridge courier. While collecting customer grading data during one of our ABC pilot studies (in Cambridge), we asked the relevant front-line staff to grade their major customers according to their consumption of DHL's time. One of our couriers sent back his grading form on which he had graded one of his customers as taking an average of 40 minutes per pick-up. Thinking that this was abnormally long and that something should be done about it he wrote 'See note attached' on the form, and attached a log he had kept for a week, documenting what happened each time he made a pick-up from this customer.

Each day there was a description of the difficulties of dealing with this customer, with the courier noting how he was sent backwards and forwards between different departments, trying to find lost Customs documentation, then being sent back to pick up new shipments that had arrived while he was looking for the paperwork for the original shipments, then finding there was no paperwork for the new shipments, etc. The log included such gems as: 'Wednesday: another 13 minutes wasted looking for a shipment which shipping finally discovered they had already sent two days previously. This problem occurs frequently'. And so it went on day by day, telling the story of a messy, disorganised customer and of a customer interface that was not working as it should. The courier ended his log with a suggestion to his station manager that something should be done to help the customer get organised.

I enquired whether there had been any follow-up to the courier's suggestion. I was told that the station manager had been to see the customer to help them introduce a system for recording their shipments and had encouraged them to organise their shipping department around agreed cut-off times for the courier pick-up. As a consequence, things were now running more smoothly.

A quick calculation of the time saved gave the impression that we had immediately reduced the cost of serving this customer by around $250 in the first month alone. However, if we take into account the fact that we had to buy lunch for the shipping manager to achieve this, then we actually only saved around $200!

I realise this is not a lot of money, but this was only one customer in one month. What counts is that we had found a technique for identifying inefficiencies in our customer interface, and correcting them. Of course this technique does not just save DHL money, it also saves the customer money and improves the quality of service we can provide.

This saving will not be seen as an immediate reduction in the costs shown in our general ledger, as we still have to pay the courier even if he has less work to do. However, in a business with the level of growth that DHL has, we see the benefit in the form of not having to hire the next courier as soon as we would have otherwise expected. In other words, there is a slowing down in the rate of cost growth compared to revenue growth.

Using the ABC model to improve profitability is all about balancing price, cost and service level. If we add service, how much cost does it add? If this service is of value to the customer, we would expect it to add more revenue than cost. If we cannot add more revenue then the customer obviously does not value the service, so what can we do to reduce the cost? We can use margin management techniques to target our growth to profitable customers, while using cost management techniques to identify and eliminate costs that are not adding value.

Since we first started using ABC there has been a change in focus. It started, originally, as a methodology for costing products. Then we moved to costing customers, then as a basis for cost management, and more recently, as a means of facilitating business process improvement.

Different countries in the DHL network have seen how well ABC fits in with other modern management techniques, although this can lead to confusion about what it should be called. Some suggest that we should call it ABM rather than ABC or even ABCM. One of our countries believes that ABC, BPI and TQM are all part of the same technique, others argue about whether ABC should be a part of TQM, while others say it is all really BPI (while others call this BPR) and where does ABM end and BPI and TQM start?

As I find this discussion somewhat pointless, I have tried to end this confusion by finding a suitable name for the techniques that we are now using. My suggestion is that we simply call it CSTQABPRI. For those who have not yet come across this terminology, that is continuous strategic total quality activity-based process re-engineering improvement. I am sure all the leading consultants will be selling this very soon.

32. Business Process Re-engineering

32:1 Principles of BPR

32:1.1 Controversial Origins and Application

32:1.1.1 Original Doubts

Business Process Re-engineering (BPR) has generated controversy ever since it was first proposed by Hammer (1990), a former professor of computer science at the Massachusetts Institute of Technology, and subsequently popularised by Hammer and Champy (1993). The initial controversy was over whether such a concept even existed. When protagonists of BPR described successful exercises, it seemed these exercises involved different approaches: there was no single theme. Moreover, when others sought to emulate previous success by embarking on a 'BPR exercise', there seemed to be a high rate of failure. Common statistics such as 'seven out of ten BPR projects fail' had little meaning because there was no clear definition of what constituted either BPR or a failure. However systematic studies (e.g. by Hall *et al.* (1993)) did indicate BPR-type projects rarely delivered benefits in business terms.

32:1.1.2 Long-term Damage

Even when an exercise termed BPR had been applied successfully, its wisdom was later called into question. In the United States, when companies spoke of 're-engineering' it was as a synonym for widespread cost cutting. The favoured targets in these exercises were middle managers and, in retrospect, the removal of these staff led to the loss of much of the knowledge and intelligence of the company. Indeed, the current interest in knowledge management can be viewed as an attempt to undo the damage caused previously by BPR. For this reason, 're-engineering' is a loaded term, sometimes avoided since it is equated with indiscriminate job cuts. Conversely, others have coined the term to add a little excitement to an otherwise dull exercise – 're-engineering the finance function' sounds so much more significant than 'making the accounts department more efficient' but usually means the same thing.

32:1.1.3 Established Approach

While even Hammer (1996) has now moved onto the 'beyond re-engineering' theme, there has been left behind a set of characteristics which underpin most systematic BPR efforts and can now be called an established approach to BPR.

32:1.2 Common Characteristics

32:1.2.1 Scope of Change

An entire process, defined as a set of activities linked to satisfy a customer's requirement, is subject to change, as opposed to an individual department within a process (*see* **Ch.28, para.28:3.1**). BPR considers the cross-departmental, horizontal perspective of the company rather than the vertical, departmental perspective, as shown in **Figure 32:1**, which also lists some of the key attributes of a process.

Figure 32:1 **Process view**

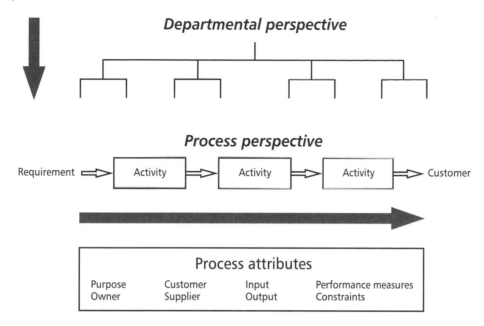

32:1.2.2 Scale of Improvement

BPR projects are expected to deliver order-of-magnitude (i.e. factors of ten or more) changes to key parameters, for example, cost, time or quality. The necessity for such improvement is dictated by the competitive environment, either through the availability of new supply-side factors (e.g. new technology, or new customer demands).

32:1.2.3 Radicalism

The objective is to sweep away the previous methods which resulted from gradual evolution as opposed to optimal design. To do this a fresh start is needed and this implies that a radical as opposed to an incremental approach to change is required. The relationship between radical change and continuous improvement is shown in **Figure 32:2**.

Figure 32:2 **Radical and continuous change**

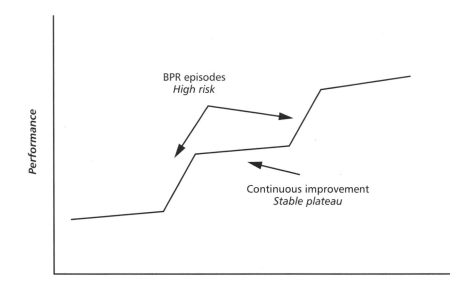

32:1.2.4 Multiple Aspects to Change

BPR principally address three aspects of the organisation simultaneously: operational process (i.e. organisation of work); technology (especially information technology); and the people (e.g. cultural change), as amplified below.

32:1.2.5 Process

Corporate hierarchies have evolved into functional departments that encourage functional excellence but which do not work well together in meeting customers' requirements; in particular, they incur excess cost, are too slow and create quality problems by creating inter-departmental hand-overs of work. The preference is to replace these with organisational structures which span whole processes.

32:1.2.6 Technology

Advancing technology offers the chance to radically reorganise work, either performing work more efficiently or enabling an entirely different approach be taken, for example, by the removal of intermediaries.

32:1.2.7 People

Staff roles have become specialised with the result that staff are only responsible for a small part of an overall task. This can result in loss of accountability for a finished task, deskilling of work and the need for highly complex scheduling systems. BPR emphasises the need to empower staff through technology and delegated authority and thereby reduce this fragmentation.

32:1.3 A Typical Approach

In a detailed exposition of BPR, Davenport (1993) has suggested a five-step approach: identifying processes for innovation; identifying change levers; developing process visions; understanding existing processes; designing and prototyping new processes. This approach focuses on the BPR exercise itself, though there is also a need for a prior examination of strategy and a subsequent implementation plan.

   Furthermore, those who undertake BPR projects face a tension between, on the one hand, conceiving genuinely new ideas and, on the other, ensuring that proposals can be translated into realistic project plans for change to the organisation. Booth (1995) proposes one approach to resolving this tension:

(a) *Review the external factors, for example, the relation between the firm, including the operation of the top-level current (that is the 'As-Is' processes), and its environment, for example, competitors, customers and standards.*
(b) *Undertake a bottom–up activity analysis of the organisation (see **Ch.13, para.13:2**) and fit this detailed view to the top-level mapping of the As-Is processes obtained in the first step. The activity analysis can also be used to allocate the costs to activities and hence calculate the current profitability of business segments (e.g. products or customers).*

(c) *Generate radical ideas for change and define the new 'To-Be' processes. The number of change initiatives to achieve this transition needs to be limited, perhaps to no more than five of these otherwise the company is likely to be overloaded, though naturally the upper limit will depend on circumstances. Special teams need to be set up to push these changes through.*

(d) *Sweep up the more numerous smaller, focused ideas for change. These can be implemented in parallel within the existing departmental structure.*

(e) *Ensure that the improvement is sustainable by setting up the programme management systems and initiatives for training and cultural change.*

Within this general approach, however, there still remains much scope for diversity.

32:1.4 Differences in Approach

Comparisons of re-engineering approaches as practised by the major consulting firms are published by the Gartner Group (an independent assessment company). They highlight differences in:

(a) *method content, for example:*
  (i) *variety of analytical modelling methods;*
  (ii) *recognition of motivation issues and managing the resistance change;*
  (iii) *links between BPR and the implementation of associated software solutions;*
  (iv) *inclusion of knowledge management or information engineering methods;*
(b) *the support tools, or 'delivery mechanism' for both process and project management;*
(c) *technology transfer between consultant and client.*

32:2 BPR in Practice

32:2.1 Common Processes

32:2.1.1 Order Fulfilment

The supply-chain processes span the receipt of order (often with a commitment to delivery date) to physical delivery of the good and service. Typical processes might include:

(a) *define customers' product or service requirements;*
(b) *agree delivery and schedule operations;*
(c) *manage operations capacity;*
(d) *procure supplies;*
(e) *supervise inventory.*

32:2.1.2 Customer Development

Some customer-facing processes are not directed towards satisfying an existing requirement. To develop new business, other important processes include:

(a) *support existing customers;*
(b) *identify current or potential customers' future requirements;*
(c) *acquire new customers.*

32:2.1.3 Business Development

Not all new business development is concerned with the specific requirements of specific customers. There may be the need to develop general solutions (i.e. products) or deal with general groups of customers (i.e. markets). Relevant processes include:

- product development;

- product planning;

- brand management.

In practice there can be a tension between the development of brands for general consumer markets and the development of specific customers; this is most keenly felt in fast-moving consumer goods companies which have to combine substantial marketing to consumers directly with 'trade marketing' to powerful intermediaries (i.e. retailers).

32:2.1.4 Business Maintenance

The main business maintenance processes include:

- human resource management;

- financial management;

- infrastructure maintenance;

- corporate governance.

32:2.2 Process Improvements

Analysing an organisation on process lines does not, in itself, lead to improvements. It may, however, prompt a recognition where process simplifications are possible. In summary, some the main types of improvement are:

(a) *eliminating duplicated or redundant activities. If the process is complicated, duplication and the retention of non-value-added activity becomes possible;*
(b) *avoiding unnecessary data collection. There can be inertia in changing data-collection procedures, with the result that data may be collected to support a procedure which is no longer carried out;*
(c) *avoiding unnecessary decision points. If there are unnecessary decisions, this offers the chance for simplifications of the subsequent conditional paths;*
(d) *moving from a serial process to a parallel process. The direct benefit is lead-time reduction but there are ancillary benefits (e.g. avoidance of lengthy iterations);*
(e) *combining or separating process flows. In some cases similar processes exist side by side and it would be possible to combine these, perhaps with the addition of some conditional tests, to achieve economies of scale. In other cases, separation of process*

is called for; this is particularly the case where the same process is being used to support both high-volume/low-variety and low-volume/high-variety flows;

(f) *removing intermediaries. New technology may permit the removal of whole parties from a process, that is, 'cutting out the middle man';*

(g) *avoiding unnecessary movement. Sometimes this is physical movement; in other cases it involves data crossing departmental boundaries.*

Very commonly process modelling is used to detect these opportunities for improvement to the As-Is processes or to define a new set of To-Be processes from scratch.

32:2.3 Process Modelling

Process modelling has evolved from its flowcharting origins to cover four types:

1. *behavioural, showing how activities interact in a process;*
2. *activity-based, showing what activities are being undertaken in a process (see* **Chs 13, 22** *and* **28**) *and the information that flows between activities;*
3. *organisational, showing where in the organisation the activities are performed;*
4. *informational, showing the data entities involved in a process and their interrelationships.*

The first two types are most relevant to business process redesign (organisational structure and information systems typically follow after the business processes are defined, though can sometimes be a determinant).

Behavioural models can be built using role activity diagrams, which illustrate the roles that are taken in a process (which are indirectly related to the people, positions or departments involved), the activities they undertake and the decisions that are taken to control the process. While in some ways this form of modelling is the most sophisticated it is not necessarily the best for the organisational design because:

(a) *much of the detailed knowledge in the precise interaction of roles may not be necessary to identify opportunities for improvement;*
(b) *behaviour within a process can vary according to the interpretation by individuals. Given this, it is less easy to model a 'moving target'.*

To avoid these problems one approach is to fall back to functional (or activity-based) modelling. This requires, first, the identification of the top-level processes and, second, the decomposition of these into activities. One technique that has been used to good effect in this area is the IDEF$_0$ method. As background, IDEF originated in a United States Air Force Program for Integrated Computer Aided Manufacturing ('ICAM') and stands for ICAM Definition; IDEF$_0$ (the most common) models functions and activities (IDEF$_1$ models information flows and IDEF$_2$ models systems dynamics).

Figure 32:3 shows how activity models can be built up in successive levels of detail.

Figure 32:3 **IDEF$_0$ diagram**

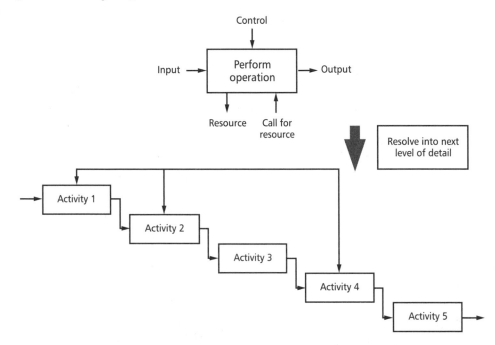

The highest level, Level 0, is the process name. The top-level process is then successively broken down into lower levels of activity per level, with three to six activities per level. Therefore more than a hundred activities can be modelled with three levels of decomposition. The use of IDEF$_0$ for process modelling of systems is widespread, though it does have its critics. Some claim that the decomposition can obscure as much as it clarifies, others claim that it is insufficiently precise (e.g. it does not show conditional paths), though this lack of precision can be an advantage, allowing the model to skate over areas of marginal interest.

The use of mechanistic techniques such as process modelling can, however, obscure a fundamental point: BPR must find new ways of doing things, that is, it must be creative.

32:2.4 Innovation

Successful BPR cannot be done by rote because original thought can never be a drill – but this does not mean process redesign has to be disorganised; indeed, with a little preparation the chances of producing new ideas for process re-engineering are excellent. The key is to understand that *process design is a design process itself* and therefore the well-established techniques used for successful product design can be applied to process design. A very simple design process is outlined below, which is a vast improvement on the more usual unstructured 'workshop'.

The first step in obtaining new ideas is to recognise that most of them will be other people's and to spread the net widely. The sources of new ideas include:

(a) *employees. Staff may be harbouring years of dissatisfaction with the way the company's operations make their life difficult;*
(b) *customers. These can be a very useful source of ideas since they bear the brunt of any problems;*
(c) *suppliers. These can offer useful ideas on how better to integrate their operations with those of the organisation;*
(d) *the press. Regular reading of the business press reveals reports on how other companies have achieved success or of new systems and technologies that are becoming available;*
(e) *competitors. If all your new ideas are being lifted off competitors you have a problem, since you can only be a me-too player. However, there is no harm in adapting a good idea when you see it, perhaps using a former employee of a competitor.*

The next step is to employ 'brainstorming' sessions to combine and multiply the ideas. At this stage it is essential to avoid criticising or assessing the ideas because this will discourage creativity, as people can become reticent if they see the ideas of others being knocked down. The level of documentation also needs to be kept to the minimum necessary to assure the quality of the work. Most of the best ideas will arise from informal meeting of minds and this can be suppressed by cumbersome bureaucracy.

The ideas can then be developed individually after the meeting and the less promising ones dropped; a brief cost-benefit analysis of the remaining ideas should be also undertaken. Eventually, an independent assessment of the ideas is essential. To be useful, this assessment needs to develop the ideas further as opposed to merely finding fault. One technique that has been developed in software design is a peer group review, which employs:

(a) the individuals who have now collated their proposals for change;

(b) a review team whose purpose is to comment on the proposals;

(c) a chairman, who steers the discussion in a constructive direction to enhance the original proposals.

The meetings should last no more than a few hours, with the conclusions formally summarised and a follow-up meeting scheduled within a few days, when individuals can present their modified proposals. In this way the iterative process of developing the ideas can operate as rapidly as possible.

32:2.5 Technology Push Versus Business Pull

When developing the ideas a choice will have to be made between either pursuing the ideal business solution and designing the tools to support that solution (i.e. 'business pull') or researching the market for the tools which are available and moulding the business processes to use them ('technology push'). The first course of action may seem the natural course, however, this may not always be the case.

There will be occasions when supply-side factors, such as information technology, completely change the way business can be undertaken. Henderson and Venkatramann (1993) highlight a fault of many strategic planning methods, in that they focus too heavily on the demand side and then outline an information systems planning method which can consider both the supply and the demand factors. More mundanely, 'technology push' often prevails because of the high cost of customised information and physical systems needed to support an unusual process design. Therefore any process re-engineering has to take account of the standard solutions which are on the market.

32:2.6 Useful Tools

32:2.6.1 Process Value Analysis

Process value analysis is an advance on classifying activities as value-added activities or non-value-added activities (*see* **Ch.28, para.28:1.3**). *An activity only derives value from its role in a process.* Process maps are drawn and the causes of the underlying process failure are identified and possible process improvements identified. These proposed solutions and improvements are then discussed with those involved.

An understanding of the underlying activity costs within the process is essential but the old adage 'relevance over precision' applies here: the activity map need not be detailed and the allocation of costs to activities need not be especially accurate – an allocation accuracy of some 10% will suffice. Focus is also important: remember the Willie Sutton rule, named after a bank-robber who achieved fame by being attributed (incorrectly) with the remark that he robbed banks 'because that's where the money is' – so focus on the big numbers.

Once costs have been established, it is necessary to consider the value of the output of the process, that is, to ask the customers the importance attached to the output's characteristics (e.g. its price, timeliness or quality). This should be done separately for individual market segments.

The simplest method is to ask customers to score the importance of various characteristics and compare this profile with that which the process is actually delivering. A more complex approach is conjoint analysis.

32:2.6.2 Conjoint Analysis

This customer research method enables potential customers to choose between combinations of characteristics (including price) and a monetary value for each characteristic is inferred from a series of these choices. Once the monetary values have been quantified it then becomes possible to strike the best compromise between increased service and increased cost.

At first sight the rigour of this method is attractive but one disadvantage is the effort involved in conducting the conjoint analysis; furthermore the method loses the qualitative comment from the research samples which can be illuminating when trying to analyse a market segment's value framework.

32:2.6.3 Challenge Groups

One approach to obtaining qualitative comment on the value is to set up challenge groups between users and providers. The principle is simple: the providers of products and services (i.e. the output of processes) and their recipients are brought together in meetings to discuss the ways in which costs may be reduced. The two sides often have radically different views on the cost, quality and timeliness of the outputs provided. It is often quite feasible to eliminate some high-cost/low-value outputs or to increase quality and timeliness with minimal expenditure. A useful chart for assisting in this process is shown in **Figure 32:4**.

Figure 32:4 **Classification by value and cost**

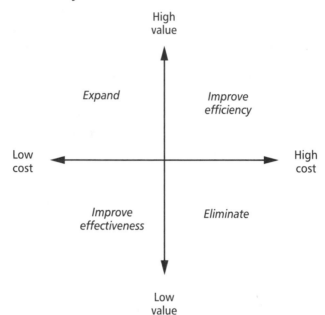

These meetings need to be properly facilitated. Obviously the person who chairs them must not be partisan and must be able to guide any conflict to a useful conclusion. Where cost reduction is the objective, the options for cuts can be ranked in order of priority (indeed this exercise can be used as part of a priority-based budgeting exercise). The use of the challenge groups will have brought together the internal view of cost and the external view of value: we now consider an alternative, more analytical method, of achieving the same goal.

32:2.6.4 Quality Function Deployment

In product design a perennial problem is the relating of the internal characteristics of a product, which concern the engineers and designers, to the parameters which concern customers. The same applies to the design of a process. Quality function deployment is a means of achieving this correlation. It is sometimes known under a particular variant, the 'House of Quality', proposed by Hauser and Clausing (1988).

The basis is a matrix, the rows of which describe the customer requirements, for individually identified parameters, and the columns describe the various internal characteristics. The rows can be further annotated with the performance of the company in each of the parameters that concern customers, compared with competition. The columns can be annotated with measures of the internal characteristics. Where the external parameters and internal characteristics are connected, this is marked by a cross.

While very simple, the advantage of the matrix is that it permits the external and internal views to be combined in a single sheet where mismatches of effort can be identified. In the 'House of Quality', the matrix is taken to represent a house and a roof is added to the matrix, showing correlation between the various internal characteristics themselves.

32:2.6.5 Other Tools and Techniques

There are many other tools and techniques available to improve processes, Booth (1995). Tools include cause and effect analysis (to get to the root of quality problems) and life-cycle costing (*see* **Ch.19**) (to identify when costs become committed as opposed to incurred). Techniques include applying just-in-time principles to clerical operations (to avoid unnecessary backlogs) and introducing market-base mechanisms (to avoid the central allocation and control of resource).

The wide variety of tools and techniques is potentially distracting, especially for a project team that enjoys applying them (they are generally quite intellectually stimulating). It is therefore crucial to identify the main priorities of the business and ensure these are addressed, rather than latching onto a particular area and applying tools and techniques for their own sake.

32:2.7 Causes for Failure

Some articles offer advice on how to succeed with BPR. An alternative approach (Kotter, 1995) offered a checklist on eight common causes of failure:

1. *not establishing a great enough sense of urgency;*
2. *not creating a powerful enough guiding coalition;*
3. *lacking a vision;*
4. *undercommunicating the vision by a factor of ten;*
5. *not removing obstacles to the new vision;*
6. *not systematically planning for and creating short-term wins;*
7. *declaring victory too soon;*
8. *not anchoring changes in the corporation's culture.*

32:3 BPR in Context

32:3.1 Change Management

There are three elements to BPR: the analysis of the situation, the synthesis of new approaches and implementation. Of these it is the last that is the most challenging and this is the province of change management.

Bringing about change in organisations is immensely difficult. To most engaged in a business, it is not primarily a profit-making institution, but rather a social fabric and a context for political manoeuvring. This may even have its positive effects, for example, the level of commitment towards an organisation may be greater than if a purely economic view was taken. However, it does mean that creating change is difficult: it is inadequate to advance rational arguments concerning the economic benefit of the proposed change because employees also have emotional and political interests in the organisation.

Machiavelli (1514) provided a succinct and perceptive view on the hazards of change and the need for strong leadership:

> It should be borne in mind that there is nothing more difficult to handle, more doubtful of success, and more dangerous to carry through than initiating changes ... The innovator makes enemies of all who prospered under the old order, and only lukewarm support is forthcoming from those who would prosper under the new ... But to discuss this subject more thoroughly, we must distinguish between innovators who stand alone and those who depend on others, that is between those who to achieve their purposes can force the issue and those who must use persuasion. In the second case, they always come to grief, having achieved nothing.

He goes on to offer to advice to the would-be leader that is refreshingly realistic, compared to the platitudes that make up most modern change management advice:

> From this arises the following question: whether it is better to be loved than feared or the reverse. The answer is that one would like to be both the one and the other; but because it is difficult to combine them, it is far better to be feared than loved ... men love as they please but fear when the prince pleases, a wise prince should rely on what he controls, not on what he cannot control. He must only endeavour ... to escape being hated.

A more contemporary account of the application of change management is the turnaround of General Electric by Jack Welch, provided by Tichy and Sherman (1993).

32:3.2 Programme Management

Programme management differs from project management, which is concerned with the management of a single set of tasks to specification, in terms of cost, quality and timeliness. Programme management is concerned with the management of a group of projects so that the overall effect enables the company to achieve its range of targets. The two tasks are quite different: project management is deterministic, quantifying resources and dependencies, or deals with risk and uncertainty in numerical, probabilistic terms. Programme management considers less precise but equally important factors, such as the effectiveness and relevance of the project to the organisation and its strategy. Programme management avoids the outcome of 'the operation was a success but the patient died', that is, a project being successful in its own terms but not contributing to the business goals, which is a potential problem with BPR, as noted by Hall *et al.* (1993).

While it might appear that no one could possibly object to programme management it can fall foul of organisational politics. Often senior managers hitch their careers to a particular project and the last thing they want is an overarching programme to prioritise projects according to business need.

32:3.3 Performance Measures
(*See* **Chs 48** and **49**.)

Performance measures are too often neglected in BPR exercises. Substantial improvements in performance can be obtained simply through a change in measures (with no process redesign) and if processes are redesigned but the measures remain the same, then no change may occur.

It is necessary to design a performance management framework that acts as a link between the goals, objectives and strategies of a company and its plans and its programmes and actions, as shown in **Figure 32:5**.

Figure 32:5 **Performance management framework**

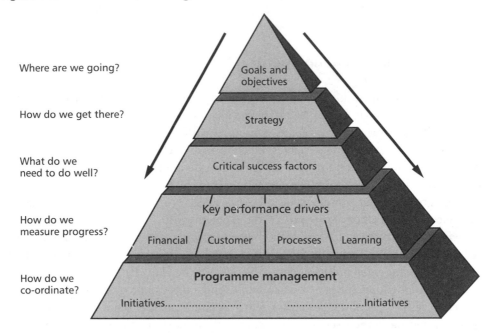

Where are we going?

How do we get there?

What do we
need to do well?

How do we
measure progress?

How do we
co-ordinate?

Goals and
objectives

Strategy

Critical success factors

Key performance drivers

Financial | Customer | Processes | Learning

Programme management

Initiatives............................ ....Initiatives

Furthermore the measurement framework must be balanced between the financial, customer, internal, employee and other perspectives and the relations between the different types of measures must be understood.

32:4 Common Blind-spots of BPR Exercises

32:4.1 Strategic Direction

The starting point for a BPR exercise is usually an inspirational vision. This needs to be checked for consistency with the strategic direction of the company. Processes are simply the means by which strategy is translated into action; prior to aiming for process excellence, there has to be confirmation that this will help realise the strategy. An example of an inappropriate BPR exercise, was one multinational's re-engineering of the accounts payable function, the success of which led to a dramatic worsening in the company's working capital position!

32:4.2 Continuous Improvement

The links between BPR and continuous improvement approaches is often unclear. One way of integrating the two is through the performance measurement framework which should form part of any BPR exercise. The performance measurement framework provides a means for steering the direction of the improvement. Some frameworks also encourage the enabling of continuous improvement and benchmarking, for example, the Business Excellence Model of the European Foundation for Quality Management.

32:4.3 Risk Management

Those undertaking BPR exercises often take a positive relish in the fact they 'are betting the farm', that is, risking the company. This is a remarkably immature attitude to risk management. In the real world, risks are analysed, avoided and hedged.

A formal risk-management element, assessing risk against return, is an important part of any BPR exercise.

32:4.4 Demand Side

Those engaged in BPR exercises are usually engineers, IT professionals or accountants, that is those engaged in the supply, operations or control aspects of the company. Perhaps for this reason, they tend to neglect the demand creation, or marketing, aspects of the company.

Incorporating this perspective is not simple, because marketing can seem to depend on flair not process. However, other creative activities, such as research and development, are susceptible to process analysis (to quantify the likely rates of innovation given the commitment of particular resource) and the same applies to marketing. A recent example of an attempt to integrate the supply and demand perspectives of the value chain is the efficient consumer response, an initiative in the grocery and consumer goods industries to improve the performance of the entire value chain by encouraging closer co-operation between manufacturers and retailers in both logistics and marketing activities.

32:5 BPR in the Future

32:5.1 Sources of Information on Development of BPR

There are hundreds of relevant internet sites but two are always worth a visit:

- *www.sequena.com*

- *www2.warwick.ac.uk/fac/soc/ier/publications/bulletins/ier53.pdf*

Otherwise, an internet search engine will produce reams of references.

32:5.2 Business Transformation

Some regard the re-engineering of a single process as insufficient. The true objective is to transform an entire company from one state to another (i.e. business transformation). While this may appear even less likely to succeed, given the difficulties experienced in re-engineering even a single process, it does recognise that many of the factors that require transformation within a process, are common to all processes. These factors are often called 'levers of change': one comprehensive set of levers is the 'McKinsey Seven Ss': skills; strategy; structure; shared values; style; staff; systems. This, however, is simply one division and others can be developed; for example, the pentapartite classification of finance/capital, markets/strategy, people, processes/operations and technology covers most aspects of an organisation and the potential to change it.

32:5.3 Knowledge Management

A company does not consist of processes alone. In particular, there is the ambience in which the processes operate. Some of these were listed above as 'levers of change' but one aspect is more in the nature of an intangible asset – knowledge.

Knowledge allows processes to operate. Some knowledge is codified but much is tacit, that is, residing in people's heads in an unclassified form. Modern BPR methods address this aspect directly and seek to ensure that the mechanisms for knowledge accumulation and transfer exist with the company. Although technological solutions are readily available, in practice the biggest barriers to the sharing of knowledge are motivational and political.

32:5.4 Biological Paradigm

Finally, it seems that BPR is, as the name suggests, an inherently engineering-orientated approach: an ideal performance is identified and a process designed to deliver that performance. In conditions of uncertainty such approaches are not always robust, for example, the proposed solution may work perfectly under the specified conditions but fail totally under slightly different ones.

A biological approach may offer greater adaptability. Rather than attempt to design the optimal solution an alternative approach might be to ensure the organisation has the necessary competencies to adapt to the unforeseen and is flexible enough to do so. New ideas are continually spawned and the more successful ones allowed to flourish under the principles of natural selection.

Others would argue it is the capitalist system that should provide the mechanism for natural selection. This economic Darwinism is the ultimate riposte to BPR and business transformation. Given the difficulty in creating change, why bother? Let the leviathans perish and their carrion be consumed by their successors.

32:6 Future Developments

Although BPR is now a well-established approach to company reorganisation, there is a particular, recent technical innovation that is changing its form of implementation. This is web technology that may be classified by scope, for example:

(a) *intranets, that use browsers to allow information exchange within companies, across a range of platforms;*

(b) *the internet, to allow open information exchange between companies;*

(c) *extranets, to support closed communication between suppliers and customers.*

Alternative classifications consider the impact of the technology on relationships. Common classifications consider the impact on:

• the sell-side, i.e. e-Sales;

• the buy-side, i.e. e-Procurement;

• employees, i.e. e-Workforce.

An appreciation of the potential impact of these technologies can be gained from considering their most complex manifestation in the form of electronic marketplaces for the exchange of goods and information between companies.

Business-to-Business ('B2B') trading exchanges are electronic markets, not based in a physical location, e.g. a stock exchange or a merger square. They are a development beyond 'hub and spoke' arrangements, which have operated on the buy-side (where a company arranges to purchase electronically from its suppliers) and on the sell-side (where a company sells to customers via a portal). Diagrammatically (*see* **Fig.32:6**) they resemble a butterfly, hence the colloquial term 'fat butterfly' that is sometimes applied to trading exchanges.

Figure 32:6 **The fat butterfly**

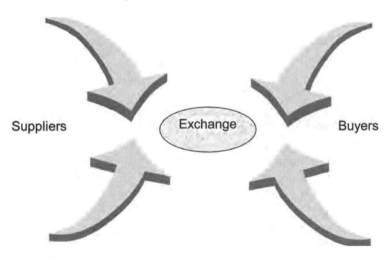

B2B exchanges are set to deliver large savings, even to lean value chains. The major benefits include:

(a) *Purchasing process efficiency. A manual purchasing process is complex and labour intensive. Using an automated means of research, qualification, tendering and ordering yields substantial savings.*

(b) *Low-cost supplies. Even with substantial procurement effort it is still possible to miss potential suppliers with inherent cost advantages, perhaps because of distance or lack of awareness of the suitability of the product.*

(c) *Lead-time. In time-critical applications, e.g. project orientated work, then procurement activity can lie on the critical path. Reduction in duration of the project equates to a saving in time-related overhead costs.*

(d) *Capacity utilisation. If capacity is under-utilised, this represents an opportunity cost in lost contribution; if capacity is over-utilised, maintenance may be compromised and overtime costs incurred. The availability of exchanges to even out supply and demand leads to higher supply-chain efficiencies.*

(e) *Volume. There may also be an increase in volume for exchange participants, either at the expense of those who do not participate or through a general increase in economic activity as buyers and sellers are brought into contact and lower prices stimulate demand. The increased volume has an immediate effect in providing amortisation of fixed costs over higher volume with possible economies of scale and an indirect benefit of learning curve advantages.*

(f) *Consolidation. A widespread trend is to consolidate the number of suppliers that a company uses, in order to gain the benefits of supplier partnerships and lower prices in return for higher volumes. The use of B2B exchanges can expedite this process.*

(g) *Inventory. Cheaper and more rapid procurement makes it economic to hold less inventory. Inventory holding costs can be substantial (estimates range up to 25% of the inventory value) because of the cost of capital, storage, tracking, issue, waste and obsolescence.*

(h) *Quality. High inventory levels give rise to high quality-related costs, since quality issues take longer to emerge and the backlog has to be rectified. A reduction in scrap and rework cost will follow from lower inventory, and, in some cases, a reduction in warranty costs if the quality problems reach the customer.*

(i) *Productivity and customer service. Despite holding inventory, stock-outs can still occur with consequent down-time and customer service failures. Streamlined procurement reduces the incidence and duration of stock-outs.*

(j) *Resale. In project environments, it is common to over-order material, to allow for potential wastage. If the wastage does not arise, then surplus material may have to be written off. Trading exchanges can offer a convenient means of resale.*

(k) *Align specifications. Finally, an important indirect benefit arises from the rationalisation of specifications within a company. In the manufacturing industry, activity-based costing studies have shown that a major cost driver for a company is the number of parts that it must handle. Therefore, there are major benefits through the reduction in complexity that follows a rationalisation of specifications. Electronic exchanges assist in this process by enforcing a clear categorisation on products so that unnecessary duplications of specification within a category become more apparent. This is especially valuable to companies that have grown by merger and acquisition and there is a retention of the original specifications, giving rise to unnecessary complexity.*

While these benefits will accrue to value chains that adopt B2B exchange trading, in practice they arise in three forms:

1. *Strategic sourcing, namely a rational examination of the sourcing of material and services by all parties within the value chain.*
2. *E-trading, that is the use of electronic technologies to make trading more efficient. Electronic Data Interchange, which is well established but has only proved economic where a large volume of orders is placed with a particular supplier. However, the internet offers more flexibility through the use of standard interfaces.*
3. *Exchange trading, where an interactive trading forum is created in 'e-space'.*

In practice it is difficult to separate the origins of the savings. An intention to commence exchange trading generally leads to a re-examination of suppliers, not least on the basis of their willingness to invest in e-trading (or, on the sell-side, an approach to a few key customers). Once a few trading partners have been selected to commence a pilot, then limited electronic ordering is undertaken over the internet. Finally, a move can be made to full exchange trading, which yields additional benefit over bilateral electronic trading in terms of:

(a) *Economies in the creation and maintenance of electronic catalogues (obviously maintaining a separate catalogue for every customer is a major undertaking).*
(b) *Standardisation of interfaces, especially user interfaces, so that those placing orders with different suppliers do not need to learn different procedures.*
(c) *The access to value-added services through the exchange. The provision of information content on exchanges or the provision of chargeable services is a further feature of an exchange, to create a 'community of interest'.*
(d) *The benefits of equity participation in a liquid exchange. The benefits of exchanges can flow three ways, to the buyers, the sellers or to the exchange itself. The income from the exchange, factored by significant price/earnings ratings, can make it a valuable item.*
(e) *Improved access to a supply base for electronic tendering and auctioning. Whereas catalogue purchasing is feasible with bilateral arrangements, alternative trading arrangements such as tendering and auctioning need multiple (and sometimes simultaneous) participation. Auctioning can take various forms: price-up or price-down, open or sealed.*

Exchanges may either be vertical, focusing on the supply chain for a particular industry, or horizontal, where goods and services required by all industries are traded, e.g. office supplies.

For a company choosing to participate in, or create, a B2B exchange, it is not sufficient to have identified a long list of potential benefits. It also needs to quantify the benefits, identify an implementation path and anticipate the obstacles.

Quantification can be either top-down or bottom-up. An example of a top-down approach was produced by Goldman Sachs for the automotive industry (Lapidus, 2000). The automotive supply chain is notoriously lean and therefore it was surprising that even in the back-end of the supply chain, supply-chain costs could be reduced by 6%. Once online direct sales and the ability to make-to-order were accounted for, the potential for the total system cost reduction rose to a remarkable 14%. Given that most other industries do not have current efficiencies approaching that of the automotive supply chain, the scope of the potential savings can be seen to be enormous. Many of these savings will flow through to the customer, but the participants in the supply chain will also benefit from higher volumes spurred on by lower prices.

Bottom-up quantification requires process mapping to determine the current processes and the future processes, after electronic trading has been adopted. The cost of the current processes can be readily ascertained by an activity-based costing exercise. The cost of the future processes can be estimated using benchmark information on electronic transaction costs. A by-product of this analysis will be a more complete understanding of cost behaviour and the relative profitability of different market segments and channels to market.

Creating an exchange is of course a major undertaking; however, even adopting trading on an existing exchange requires careful preparation. There are five areas that require attention (*see* **Fig.32:7**):

1. *project management, to co-ordinate actions in diverse functions, such as finance, purchasing and information systems;*
2. *process and skills, to define new processes and train employees to use them;*
3. *IT liaison, to ensure that the information systems infrastructure can support electronic trading;*
4. *supplier (or customer) liaison, to ensure that the items, process and terms of business conform to that agreed between the parties;*
5. *culture and communication, to convince staff of the benefits of the new ways of working.*

Figure 32:7 **Exchange adoption approach**

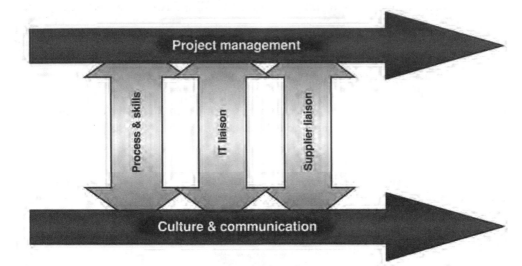

The most neglected area is the last. It is often not appreciated that adopting exchange trading causes shifts in influence within a company; in particular it can restrict the latitude to choose suppliers (to those on the exchange) and it also provides central visibility on purchasing activity and performance. In companies where individuals value their latitude to 'do deals' with favoured suppliers this may cause suspicion or resentment. One approach to overcoming this is to begin exchange trading with a few selected partners from a few locations within the company where support is strong. Once the benefits have been demonstrated (e.g. in allowing purchasing staff to concentrate on higher-value activity), the new practices can then be rolled out to more suppliers and more locations. Generally, companies begin trading using electronic catalogues and then progress onto tendering and auctioning.

32:6.1 Conclusion

In the years since it was first proposed, BPR has changed in nature. Originally the emphasis was on imposing a uniform engineered solution in order to maximise efficiency. The implementation costs and the risks of failure were high.

We are now seeing a less black-and-white approach where a degree of diversity in technologies and processes can be tolerated, in order to reduce risks and implementation costs. This has been made possible by the emergence of web technologies that allow for efficient co-ordination between differing entities, without the need for complete uniformity.

References

Booth, R. (1995) *Conquer the cost service compromise*. Burr Ridge, IL: Irwin.

Davenport, T. (1993) *Process innovation*. Boston, MA: HBS Press.

Hall, G., Rosenthal, J. and Wade, J. (1993) 'How to make re-engineering really work', *Harvard Business Review*, November–December.

Hammer, M. (1990) 'Reengineering work: Don't automate: Obliterate', *Harvard Business Review*, July–August: 104–12.

Hammer, M. (1996) *Beyond reengineering: How the process-centered organization is changing our work and our lives*. Harper Business.

Hammer, M. and Champy, J. (1993) *Reengineering the corporation*. New York: Harper Business.

Hauser, J. and Clausing, D. (1988) 'The house of quality', *Harvard Business Review*, May–June.

Henderson, J. and Venkatramann, N. (1993) 'Strategic alignment: Leveraging information technology for transforming organisations', *IBM System J., 32*: 4–16.

Kotter, J. (1995) 'Leading change: Why transformation efforts fail', *Harvard Business Review*, March–April.

Lapidus, G. (2000) 'eAutomotive: Gentlemen, start your search engines', Goldman Sachs Investment Research, January.

Machiavelli, N. (1961) *The Prince*. London: Penguin Books (originally published as *Il Principe*, 1514).

Tichy, N. and Sherman, S. (1993) *Control your destiny or someone else will*. New York: Doubleday.

33. Throughput Accounting

33:1 Definition

Throughput accounting is a method of performance measurement which seeks to identify the rate at which the organisation generates profit from sales through analysis of constraints and bottlenecks.

Throughput accounting grew in response to the theory of constraints (TOC). The fundamental idea of this theory developed by Eliyahu Goldratt and Jeff Cox originally in their book 'The Goal' was that every commercial organisation must have a constraint otherwise they would achieve infinite amounts of what they desire, that is, profits.

As a constraint is a factor which limits the organisation from achieving its desired goal of making more profits then managers should strive to manage real or potential constraints. There really is no choice, either you manage the constraints or they manage you. Constraints will determine the outputs of the organisation.

From an accounting point of view TOC demands a different approach. Efforts are very focused on constraint or bottleneck alleviation whereas traditional management accounting emphasis focuses on unit cost and its reduction.

33:2 Key Features

There are a number of key features which differentiate a throughput accounting approach.

1. ***Throughput contribution** – sales less total variable costs (often material costs only in the case of manufacturing companies). This is the rate at which the system generates money.*

2. **Investments** – *these are the same as assets in conventional financial accounting except for inventories. In throughput accounting inventory is valued at its bought-out cost alone. It includes no allocations of labour variable or fixed cost.*
3. **Operating expenses** – *these consist of all expenses the organisation incurs which are not deducted at arriving at the throughput calculation.*

The order that these features are listed, that is, throughput then investment and finally operating expenses represent a conscious emphasis in throughput accounting.

Throughput is the most important feature of a commercial organisation in its attempt to generate more profits. Next comes investment and finally operating expenses.

It is particularly important to note that operating expenses are seen as subordinate to expanding the throughput potential of the organisation. If throughput is noted as T and operating expenses as OE and investments as I, then:

$$T - OE = \text{net profit}$$

and

$$\frac{T - OE}{I} = \text{return on investment}$$

As can be seen from the above formulae a throughput accounting system retains many of the features available in conventional accounting systems with just a few key differences of emphasis.

It has many similarities to a marginal contribution or super variable cost approach. One major difference lies in its treatment of direct labour. Throughput is defined as sales revenue less material cost only, whereas in many marginal costing systems direct labour is also assumed to vary proportionately with changes in production volumes.

Figure 33:1 illustrates the differences between conventional absorption costing, marginal costing and throughput accounting.

Figure 33:1 **Differences between conventional absorption costing, marginal costing and throughput accounting**

Note: ᵃ variable overhead, both production and non-production

Conventional variable costing	Variable costing with direct labour classified as fixed	Throughput accounting	Simplified throughput accounting
Revenue	Revenue	Revenue	Revenue
– direct materials	– direct materials	– totally variable costs	– direct materials
– direct labour			
– variable overhead[a]	– variable overhead[a]		
= contrib. margin	= contrib. margin	= throughput	= throughput
– fixed expenses	– fixed expenses	– oper. expenses	– oper. expenses
= profit	= profit	= profit	= profit

Certainly the treatment of variable costs and direct labour in particular has been a key discussion point in debating the usefulness of throughput accounting.

It should be understood that the convention of developing the calculation of throughput as sales less material cost implies that all other costs are fixed. This contrasts starkly with conventional fully absorbed standard costing and activity-based costing (*see* **Ch.22**) which suggests that overhead changes uniformly due to volume and 'cost drivers' (*see* **Ch.22, para.22:3**).

In fact it is quite permissible under throughput accounting for fixed overhead to be added to the organisation (suggesting variability) **but only** if some fixed cost resource has itself become the constraint or bottleneck to the organisation. The implicit assumption is that no new resources should be added until a constraint reveals itself.

By keeping the assumption of no automatic resource addition with additional volumes or mix, throughput accounting pressurises the system to reveal the limiting factor or constraint and then deals with it as described in the five steps of focusing. If the constraint is a machine or labour an engineering expense or material planning cost then it is added when appropriate. In other words, the relevant costs are taken into account which may mean adding fixed overhead.

33:3 Getting Started – The Five Steps of Focusing

There are five steps of focusing in the theory of constraints used to deal with a constraint or bottleneck.

1. *Identify the systems constraint.*
2. *Exploit what resource is available to reduce the effects of the constraint.*
3. *Subordinate everything else to the constraint.*
4. *Elevate. In the event of steps 1 through 3 not breaking the constraint then it must be elevated, that is, broken by adding additional resource.*
5. *Go back to step 1 in order to reveal the next constraint to the organisational goal.*

In many respects it is the first step which is the most important. Operationally identifying the constraint may not be so easy because in modern businesses there are differences of sales mix and volume variances with changing tastes of consumers adding to ever-decreasing product life cycles and common production processes.

In throughput accounting terms the starting point is an analysis or verification of the factors which will prove most crucial in determining the success of the organisation in achieving its goal. This may be completed by producing a sensitivity analysis as shown in **Figure 33:2**.

Figure 33:2 **Sensitivity analysis**

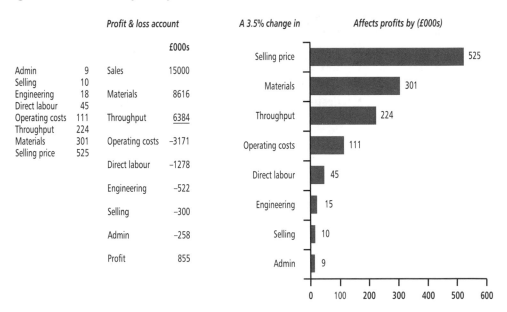

33:4 Sensitivity Analysis

It can be seen from **Figure 33:2** that when the sensitivity factor of 3.5% is applied to the summary revenue and cost headings then each contributes less and less to the bottom line if one were to be successful and improve each one. The descending contributions highlight that it is sales, material cost and throughput which are the most wealth-producing aspects in the business. It is therefore essential that these factors are seen as most important in the company.

We have identified the system's major constraint. That is, the company makes more profit fastest when it generates more sales. If the company wants to generate more sales it will **have** to purchase more raw materials. If the company wants to generate throughput it will have to be able to convert the raw material into products and to do that it must have a clear understanding of its real or potential bottlenecks.

In fact there are two additional observations which need recording about the sensitivity analysis. First, it makes no difference if the proportions of material cost to sales revenue change, the largest wealth-generating part of the business continues to be elements or throughput. As one might expect because it includes sales. Secondly, if in identifying a product cost as opposed to this 'overview' of the company one were to show two products, one with low and one with high throughput, it is very unlikely that the allocation of operating expenses would reverse their ranking. Again this general statement is supported from the view that product profitability is often determined at the design stage and if this is done badly there is only so much one can expect from operational improvements in making the product to retrieve the position. That is, if a product is badly designed and takes an age to manufacture; or if the concept was poor and the sale price is limited then the throughput is likely to be low.

33:5 Constraints and Bottlenecks in Production

As throughput accounting has its roots in production we need to establish some production principles to appreciate the relevance of the throughput accounting approach.

Figure 33:3 **Typical production environment**

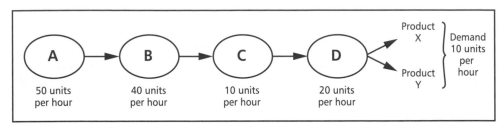

Figure 33:3 illustrates a fairly typical production environment in which two products are produced, X and Y. To make the products there are four stages of manufacture A, B, C and D and we will assume for simplicity that these represent four different machines. The demand for product X plus the demand for product Y is 10 per hour in total. Machines A, B and D have more than enough capacity to be able to fulfil that demand. Machine C also has enough capacity although it can only produce 10 per hour.

Machine C is **not** a bottleneck. We define a bottleneck precisely as any resource for which the demands are greater than its ability to supply. However Machine C is a constraint. In the event of there being a surge in demand or a failure in the supply chain, say by a breakdown of machine A, then machine C will find it very difficult to respond and recover.

A throughput approach here would make the following observations regarding production before any improvement programmes were initiated:

1. *No more than 10 per hour is required from the line because of demand and C's ability to produce and so to make any more by the additions of overtime, shifts etc. would be to encourage waste.*
2. *Machines A and B should reduce their output to the pace of C's consumption.*
3. *D will not be able to work faster than C and therefore we should not expect greater output.*
4. *If A and B work to their own potential a large amount of inventory will start to accumulate in front of C.*
5. *There is not much room to manoeuvre if anything jeopardises the output of C therefore we should allow the development of a Kanban or protective inventory buffer to develop in front of machine C to a well-defined limit.*
6. *We would put an additional quality check in front of C to make sure the constraint resource is not working on a part that has already become scrap at an earlier stage. Quality is often cited at the end of a line and this is too late to stop our constraint resource using its precious time on a part doomed from a prior process.*

33:6 Contrasting Throughput Accounting and Conventional Approaches

How does a throughput approach to accounting in this environment differ to a more conventional cost accounting approach? First, we must attach some revenue and cost data to the production environment.

Table 33:1 shows how a conventional approach would record the information.

Table 33:1 **Conventional approach**

	Product X	*Product Y*
Sell price	£100	£80
Material cost	£50	£48
Labour and overhead		
Process A	£10	£10
Process B	£8	£6
Process C	£4	£3
Process D	£2	£3
Total unit cost	£74	£70
Unit profit	£26	£10
Volume	50	80
Total profit	£1300	£800

When information is displayed by the finance department like this it is reasonable to assume the following.

(a) *product X will be favoured compared with product Y in profitability ranking;*
(b) *the focus of the sales force will be to sell more of product X;*
(c) *the focus of the operations in the factory will be around the reduction of the cost of components produced on process A, as it has the highest unit cost.*

In throughput accounting the starting point is different. It commences with analysis of the throughput contribution of each product as in **Table 33:2**.

Table 33:2 **Throughput approach**

	Product X (£)	Product Y (£)
Sell price	100	80
Material cost	50	48
Throughput	50	32

At this point, having identified the throughput contribution of each product, the throughput accounting system seeks out the constraint process rather than highest unit cost.

In this instance we can see from **Figure 33:3** that the constraint process is C. The next question to be answered is how much of resource C do products X and Y consume.

Let us suppose that we find that product X requires six minutes of processing by resource C and product Y requires three minutes of processing. **Table 33:2** can now be added to in order to see the product contributions in the light of consumption of a limited resource, which in this instance is a machine C. **Table 33:3** illustrates this.

Table 33:3 **Throughput per constraint**

	Product X	Product Y
Sell price	£100	£80
Material cost	£50	£48
Throughput	£50	£32
Consumption of resource C	6 mins per part	3 mins per part
Throughput per constraint minute	£8.33/constraint minute	£10.66/constraint minute

This indicates a completely different profitability ranking than a more conventional cost-allocation approach.

The fact is, however, that resource C is not a true bottleneck only a constraint and therefore in throughput accounting both products would be seen in a favourable light. The emphasis, however, would be to encourage the sale of more of product Y than product X where there was a choice.

From an operational point of view the cost of resource A would be ignored in favour of seeking out methods of increasing the capacity of resource C in anticipation of more sales opportunities. The second and third steps of focusing demand that the focus is on constraint exploitation and alleviation.

33:7 Throughput Accounting and Sales Mix

In a cost allocation system labour and overhead may be assigned to products in a number of ways.

In a conventional standard costing accounting labour hours or machine hours are the two most commonly used methods of allocation (*see* **Ch.16**, particularly **para.16:5**). *SSAP9: Stocks and Long-Term Contracts* gives some guidance on the matter, stating that overheads should be allocated on the basis of the company's normal level of activity, and should be applied by reference to the most significant direct cost; in practice, normally direct labour hours or direct machine hours. *IAS2: Inventories* states that fixed production overheads should be allocated using a measure based on 'normal capacity'. These conventional methods have been heavily criticised by a variety of sources as being no longer relevant since the change in pay systems meant that people were no longer paid by the 'piece' and the change to greater amounts of fixed cost meant that allocations using labour and machine hours were outdated.

In activity-based costing (ABC) systems (*see* **Ch.22**) it is assumed that all costs vary with volume or mix, that is, activity. If one were to change from conventional accounting to ABC it is most likely that more labour and overhead would be assigned to low-volume products from higher-volume ones.

In a throughput accounting application the profitability of products is likely to be seen as higher than in an ABC environment as no attempt is made to assign operating costs onto individual products. Thus throughput accounting is more tolerant of higher mix and may actually encourage it whereas ABC may seek it out to drop the lower-volume products and concentrate on the higher-volume ones.

For the throughput approach to be comfortable that more small batches, that is, greater mix can be a desirable possibility, it relies upon the finance function to understand and encourage certain principles regarding capacity by measurements.

Table 33:4 contrasts the primary differences in measurements between a product cost-based system and a throughput accounting system.

Table 33:4 **Primary differences in measurements – throughput accounting versus product cost-based system**

Conventional product cost basis	*Throughput basis*
Value added ... each time I make something	Value added ... each time I sell something
Local efficiency	Schedule adherence
Utilisation	Activation and availability
Product cost	Cost of producing a certain schedule of orders

Inventory valuation:
  material
  labour
  overhead
	Inventory valuation:
	  material

Ranking by prod. prof.	Ranking by throughput/constr. minute
Capital expenditure Focus expansion and cost reduction	Capital expenditure Focus constraint alleviation Flow improvement
Subcontract – allocated to prod. cost and contained in profitability calculation Make versus buy	Subcontract – short of time not allocated to a product Subcon/constraint minute

33:8 Rationale of Throughput Emphasis

33:8.1 Value Added

In throughput accounting the value adding practice of crediting the profit and loss account with making a product is removed. This is to make sure that capacity is not used up in the waste of overproduction. Value is only added by making a sale.

33:8.2 Schedule Adherence

Particularly relevant in a machining and assembly environment, it is a measurement which not only removes the idea that making a lot is good but also encourages the manufacturing to be synchronised. That is, even if we are capable of making 6,000 parts over a period of time, if our schedule asks for only 4,500 parts we will investigate variances of over as well as underproduction.

33:8.3 Activation and Availability

These two measurements can easily be incorporated into the reporting system. By reporting them separately we are recognising that utilisation of a resource is really made up of two factors, activation and availability. When a resource like a machine is needed it should always be available in good working order. It is right to record its 'uptime'. However a machine should not be activated just to keep it busy, that is a waste which may leave downstream operations idle and is certainly again a waste of overproduction.

33:8.4 Cost of Producing a Schedule

Instead of focusing on the product cost certain throughput accounting environments can use simulation techniques to assess the cost of producing a certain schedule of orders. This requires the sell price and material cost files to be linked with production. It also requires very rapid 'what ifs?' to be run so that, for instance, the assumption about batch sizes and set-ups can be varied and their implications for throughput assessed.

33:8.5 Product Profitability

As described above ranking of products is seen as conditional on their consumption of limited resources.

33:8.6 Make Versus Buy
(*See* Ch.11.)

As in other accounting systems the decision to make or buy can be viewed as a strategic one regarding core competencies which the company may wish to retain or not. In this respect throughput accounting differs very little from other approaches. Where a decision is required to subcontract because a bottleneck situation has arisen then the throughput accounting approach is different. Throughout accounting recognises that it is short of time on a bottleneck or constraint resource and therefore the actual product to offload onto a subcontract or should not be allowed to influence the product profitability ranking. For the purposes of ranking, the variable cost of the subcontract work is therefore excluded.

Which product to have subcontracted in these circumstances is determined by calculating the subcontract cost per constraint minute.

33:8.7 Capital Expenditure
(*See* Ch.11.)

The focus is on improved flow characteristics through the plant and bottleneck or constraint alleviation. This is designed to reduce the waste of unnecessary movement and delays within the organisation.

33:8.8 Batch Sizes

In throughput accounting there is an understanding that flow characteristics are best served by reducing work in progress and finished inventories. These in turn are helped by distinguishing between the process batch and the transfer batch. Poor batching policies often induced by a reliance on MRP planning systems are largely responsible for wandering bottlenecks.

33:8.9 One-piece flow

Figure 33:4 illustrates the advantages of achieving one-piece flow. It shows two factories that produce the same products and are in competition with each other. They are also in close proximity so that their labour and overhead costs are the same. Further, they have over a period of time developed the same vendor base for raw materials and machinery. Both factories have a three-stage sequential process as shown using machines A, B and C, with A taking 10 mins, B taking 20 mins and C taking 10 mins. There is a one-minute transfer between machines.

The only difference between the factories is that Factory 1 transfers batches through its plant in the process batch quantity or order quantity and Factory 2's transfer batch policy is for it to be in units of one.

There is a significant advantage to reducing the process batch size as shown in the time Factory 2 takes to process 1,000 units – the total elapsed time is almost halved. This is a huge advantage for Factory 2 over Factory 1.

Figure 33:4 **One-piece flow**

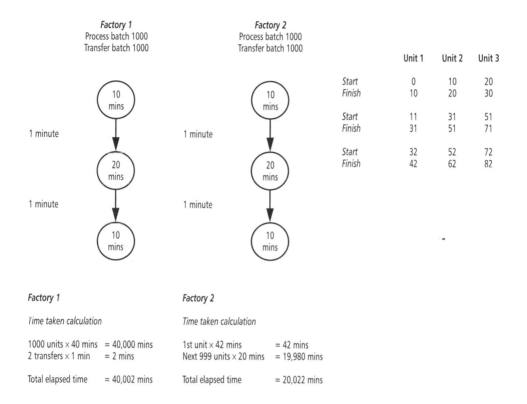

		Unit 1	Unit 2	Unit 3
	Start	0	10	20
	Finish	10	20	30
	Start	11	31	51
	Finish	31	51	71
	Start	32	52	72
	Finish	42	62	82

Factory 1

Time taken calculation

1000 units × 40 mins	= 40,000 mins
2 transfers × 1 min	= 2 mins
Total elapsed time	= 40,002 mins

Factory 2

Time taken calculation

1st unit × 42 mins	= 42 mins
Next 999 units × 20 mins	= 19,980 mins
Total elapsed time	= 20,022 mins

Factory 2 can cope with almost double the volume that Factory 1 could process over the same time period. This would give it a much reduced unit cost despite the similar total-cost profiles.

Alternatively, the improved capacity could be turned into a competitive advantage in the market place by creating different product features which could be achieved at significantly less cost in Factory 2 than Factory 1.

Furthermore, on average there is less inventory held in Factory 2, which means better cash flow. Of course there are hurdles to overcome in the achievement of one-piece material flow but the rewards are potentially enormous. The principle that the transfer batch need not equal the process is one of the revolutionary concepts of synchronised production and lean thinking. The innovation centres on the exploitation of the constraining resource B which is the slowest operation. As B is kept constantly busy in Factory 2 the result is significantly better than the way it is activated in Factory 1.

33:9 Conclusions

There are some clear advantages to a company developing a throughput approach to accounting, rather than a cost allocation approach.

1. *It is simpler to understand and portray.*
2. *It may be considered as an approach more likely to unify an organisation, as operator or staff reduction is actively discouraged.*
3. *It develops confidence that an improvement, which reduces the need for labour in a particular process, will be seen by management as an opportunity and challenge to increase throughput elsewhere.*
4. *It places emphasis on total performance, rather than individual product or work-centre performance and thus is particularly unforgiving of the 'muda' of over-production.*

34. Environment-related Management Accounting

34:1 Introduction

34:1.1 The Need for Environment-related Management Accounting

Business is faced with increasing pressure from environmental issues, and business success is increasingly affected by the capability to respond appropriately. Accountants and financial managers in business are in a position to support these responses. To date, the limited work which has been done in the field has focused on what might be termed financial accounting issues, that is, the provision of data on environmental performance, environment-related financial liabilities, etc. to external stakeholders through financial and environmental reports. The Operating and Financial Review (OFR), for example, should discuss relevant environmental protection costs and potential environmental liabilities. *FRS12: Provisions, Contingent Liabilities and Contingent Assets* requires that (environmental) liabilities be recognised as soon as the obligation exists. However, there is growing interest in the topic of environment-related management accounting, that is, the development and use of information to support internal decision making on environmental issues.

34:1.2 Financial Impacts of Environmental Issues

The development of environment-related management accounting is driven by the evidence that the environment can create significant financial costs and benefits for organisations. Some recent examples include:

Martin Bennett and Peter James

(a) *The Kyoto treaty to restrict emissions of greenhouse gases will inevitably create increases in the price of fossil fuels.*

(b) *10-20% of the capital cost of many new projects in the chemical, oil and other industries are being devoted to environmental protection.*

(c) *The UK's landfill tax has introduced a new cost pressure for large generators of waste.*

(d) *Exxon's final bill for fines, compensation and clean-up costs for the Exxon Valdez oil spill in Alaska is not yet finalised but already stands at around $10bn.*

(e) *New regulations or public opposition can often require scrapping of equipment and raise operating and disposal costs – as with Shell and the Brent Spar oil storage platform.*

(f) *Some products and technologies can be 'sunsetted' as a result of environmental legislation – as when concern about depletion of stratospheric ozone led to action to phase out CFCs in the 1980s and other chemicals in the 1990s.*

(g) *Conversely, legislation and other environmental initiatives can force demand for new products such as solar energy.*

34:1.3 Future Importance of Financial Issues

These are all consequences of the growing changes to, and pressures on, habitats, the atmosphere, air quality and other natural resources which are vital to our well-being, due to two key drivers:

1. *Growing population – forecast to rise from five to eight billion over the next 40 years and not susceptible to attempts to reduce this, because of the high proportion of the world's population currently of, or approaching, child-bearing age.*

2. *Rising living standards – with current trends suggesting that global per capita income will rise by at least its historic rate of 3–4% per annum for the foreseeable future.*

Increasing wealth and living standards have also historically tended to generate environmentally intensive activities – such as switching from walking, cycling or public transport to cars, or from holidaying in Blackpool to vacations in Benidorm or Brazil.

It is clear that these drivers can be reconciled with environmental and social well-being only through a combination of more efficient technologies, redefinitions of consumer well-being and/or slower increases in living standards (with much debate as to the precise balance which will be required). Even mainstream business sources such as the World Business Council for Sustainable Development are accepting estimates that a 'factor 4' (i.e. 300%) average reduction in the environmental impacts of the chains delivering products and services to customers will be required in coming decades. Companies like Dow Chemical are responding by introducing proactive 'eco-innovation' programmes in their businesses (Fussler with James, 1996).

Most experts agree that achieving changes of this kind will be possible only with new financial penalties and incentives to prompt business action. The penalties will include increasing the costs of environmental 'bads' such as pollution, waste and resource consumption through taxes and other means. The incentives will include financial and other incentives to improve performance, such as creating tradable pollution permits which can be sold if a company reduces its emissions.

The growing need to understand the impacts of these penalties and incentives on a business – and to use the information to guide and monitor consequent actions – will be the fundamental driver of environment-related management accounting in coming years. This is not to say that other management-accounting type activities – such as helping to develop better non-financial data for internal environmental management or external reporting – are not important (*see* **para.34:4.5**). But financial costs and benefits will be the basic raw material of the discipline for the foreseeable future.

34:2 What Are Environmental Costs and Benefits?

34:2.1 Definition

The first question is what is an 'environmental cost' (or benefit)? The management accounting maxim 'different costs for different purposes' is based on a recognition that cost and benefit data is context-dependent and that consistency of definition is therefore impractical. This maxim is equally valid for the field of environment-related management accounting. However, it is clear that there are some areas – such as corporate reporting of environmental expenditures – where consistency is important and some action is needed.

A pragmatic definition is that environmental costs and benefits should be defined as those, in any organisation, for which environment-related factors (e.g. current or likely future environmental legislation) are a significant driver (not necessarily the only driver). This is not a water-tight definition and would be inadequate for external reporting [*cf. FRS12: Provisions, Contingent Liabilities and Contingent Assets*], but can be sufficient to guide management internally. One working definition that the AT&T Green Accounting Team (*see* **para.34:5.1**) adopted was that an environmental cost is any cost for which an environmental manager or professional, through his or her expertise and experience, is best equipped to help to identify the cost driver(s) and therefore to identify methods of managing that cost.

34:2.1.1   Example 1: Glaxo Wellcome

Glaxo Wellcome was commended in the judges' report on the 1997 Association of Chartered Certified Accountants' Environmental Reporting Award Scheme for its work on identifying environmental costs. The company has developed a standard definition with which all of its sites are required to conform. This includes costs for waste management and minimisation, environmental staff, installation and running costs of pollution control equipment, installation of bunds, monitoring exercises, consultancy fees, process or product changes to reduce environmental burdens, energy conservation projects and training. However, the company notes that some areas – such as the CFC propellant replacement programme – remain to be addressed and there is clearly scope for more work in the area.

34:2.2 Environmental Costs

These can potentially include at least seven different elements:

1. *expenses which are wholly and exclusively required for purposes of environmental protection. This is the definition adopted by most national statistical bodies. The common element in all their definitions is the capital cost of equipment; some also include its operating costs. However, most exclude other wholly environment-related expenditures such as the labour costs involved in environmental management. Some companies such as Philips have found that these definitions are too narrow to encompass all the environmental costs which are relevant to their businesses;*
2. *expenses of remediating environmental problems created by past actions (the 'present costs of past sins'), for example, contamination of soil and groundwater (these are included in the first category in some countries but not all);*
3. *expenses which are largely related to purposes of environmental protection, that is, including those incurred used for both environmental and non-environmental purposes using, where necessary, some form of apportionment of actual expenditures;*
4. *the costs of inefficiency, that is, suboptimal utilisation of environmental resources such as energy or water. The amount of environmental cost is the difference between actual consumption and an ideal level. The German textile producer Kunert estimated that its costs of inefficiency were approximately 10% of its turnover;*

5. *intangible costs, such as damage to reputation, which are difficult to quantify;*
6. *opportunity costs, that is, foregone benefits as a result of environmental actions. An example would be failure to be included on a tender list and win business, as a result of failing to meet the purchaser's environmental criteria;*
7. *external costs to society which are not reflected in the company's own transactions or accounts but, some would argue, should be.*

34:2.3 Environmental Benefits

Similarly, environmental benefits could encompass any or all of:

(a) *additional revenues arising from environmental action (e.g. the sale of materials recovered as a result of recycling);*
(b) *intangible benefits arising from environmental actions, such as the enhanced value of a consumer brand;*
(c) *reduction of environment-related risks;*
(d) *avoided costs as a result of environmental action, for example, through better utilisation of energy and materials (see **Ch.23**), or by preventing the need for pollution control expenditures through waste minimisation schemes.*

34:3 Current Initiatives in Environment-related Management Accounting

The growing scale of environment-related costs such as pollution control in many organisations means that they are already highlighted by normal costing, budgeting and other accounting processes. One recent study to which the present authors made a contribution (Tuppen, 1996) concluded that most actions being taken at present are mainly relatively simple ones such as identifying and allocating energy and waste disposal costs (*see* **Ch.23**) which either did arise, or could well have arisen, for non-environmental reasons. However, it – and other studies – have identified additional initiatives which could be worthwhile in many companies, particularly:

(a) *development of energy and materials balances;*
(b) *development of aggregate estimates of environment-related costs;*
(c) *identification, tracking and allocation of specific environment-related costs;*
(d) *incorporation of environment into investment or product appraisal.*

34:3.1 Development of Energy and Mass Balances

Consumption of energy, materials, water and other resources is of great economic and environmental importance. They form an important cost element for many organisations, some of which is potentially avoidable. Resource consumption is of great environmental importance for many reasons, but principally because a large proportion of pollution of air, water and land is related to the extraction, processing, distribution, use and disposal of natural resources. Most experts also agree that current resource prices do not fully reflect their environmental costs, but will increasingly do so in future as they are gradually internalised through taxes and other means.

A number of studies and initiatives have found that many organisations do not fully understand their resource throughputs and costs. Hence, the starting point for any energy efficiency, waste minimisation or other environment-related management accounting initiative is to develop such an understanding through a mass and/or energy balance, that is, a detailed tracking of all inputs, internal flows and transformations and outputs of energy and physical substances. This is important not only to reveal the scale of potential savings and environmental improvement through action but also to help to prioritise between alternative options.

The calculation of mass balances, or 'eco-balances', has been particularly well developed in Germany and Austria as a holistic input-output model of manufacturing processes, which has enabled companies to identify potential cost savings that would otherwise have been missed (Bennett and James, 1999). In the UK, the Energy Efficiency Best Practice Programme (EEBPP) of the Department of Environment, Transport and the Regions (DETR) has produced a large number of publications on the general principles of understanding and managing energy flows and costs (*see* **Ch.23**). The UK Environmental Technology Best Practice Programme is doing the same for other areas such as waste and water costs and for specific sectors such as foundries and metal finishing.

34:3.2 Development of Aggregate Estimates of Environment-related Costs and Benefits

These can be valuable for internal decision makers in developing awareness of the magnitude and nature of environment-related financial impacts, suggesting priority areas for any initiatives, and tracking progress over time. There is growing evidence that the environment can have significant impacts on expenses, revenues, assets and liabilities and that these impacts are often underestimated (*see* Example 2 in **para.34:3.2.1**) on a study in the US). A survey of European industry (Bartolomeo *et al.*, 1999) similarly reported that when environment-related costs that would otherwise be 'hidden' in overheads were revealed, this strengthened the case for proactive measure which would prevent or at least reduce pollution at source. This could for example be through product or process re-design resulting in waste minimisation at source, in preference to 'end-of-pipe' controls which have an effect only after a potential problem has already been created. However, it also found that the mere identification of costs was not necessarily sufficient on its own – it was also necessary that these costs then be allocated to appropriate cost objects or budgets in order to provide the necessary motivation to take action.

34:3.2.1 Example 2: Potential Scope for Reducing Environmental Costs

Pilot studies of six US sites by the World Resources Institute found that by their definition, environmental costs comprised almost 22% of non-feedstock operating costs at Amoco's Yorktown refinery and 19% of the manufacturing costs of a Du Pont agricultural pesticide (Ditz *et al.*, 1995). In the first phase of the Aire and Calder Valley study (Johnston, 1994) potential improvements worth £2m p.a. were identified across the 11 industrial sites studied, with more longer-term possibilities in prospect when the project had run longer. Seventy-two per cent of the proposals stimulated by the project had pay-back periods of less than 12 months (in many cases, zero since they required no initial investment). In addition, these and other initiatives such as product redesign can sometimes increase product quality and therefore sales revenues. The British drug company Zeneca has also saved several million pounds per annum from waste minimisation exercises at its Huddersfield plant.

Of course, once the 'low-hanging fruit' has been gathered there may be a point at which further cost reductions are not available. However, if increasing regulatory and social demands continue to increase and to create new potential costs for business, this point may be delayed for some time. Even after many years of waste minimisation initiatives Dow, for example, is expecting to find a large number of waste minimisation and similar projects which can provide annual returns on capital of at least 30% to 40% over the coming decade.

As with a 'cost of quality' approach, making such financial impacts apparent can make it easier to take, and win support for, further environmental initiatives. This has been a major motivation behind Baxter International's 'Environmental Financial Statement' (*see* Example 3 in **para.34:3.2.2**).

34:3.2.2 Example 3: Baxter International

Since 1990 the American multinational health care products company Baxter International has produced an annual 'Environmental Financial Statement' (EFS). It has been published in summary form in their annual Corporate Environmental Report since 1992, though the main target audience is internal – senior and operational managers.

The EFS is a one-page summary of the costs and benefits arising from environment-related actions and programmes across the corporation. Costs are primarily for staff and production equipment. The main benefits have been savings achieved in environment-related costs which would otherwise have been incurred, for example on the disposal of wastes and the purchase of resources such as ozone-depleting substances and packaging. These savings were largely prompted by programmes initiated by Baxter's environmental management function and implemented by operational management. The effect has been to demonstrate that, over time, good environmental management has been not merely a 'hygiene factor' cost incurred only in order to comply with the law, but a positive financial benefit for the company which can be measured financially.

Designing the EFS required some creative ingenuity in measurement. In particular, many of the costs reported in the EFS are incurred only once, but generate lasting benefits. However it is not possible to measure these long-term benefits directly from the accounting information since the figures collected and reported there are influenced also by other factors, in particular business growth and external prices. To capture these long-term benefits, the concept of 'cost avoidance' was devised, so that the EFS calculates both:

(a) *'savings' – the difference between the actual spend on a cost item in the current year, less the actual spend in the previous year;*
(b) *'cost avoidance' – the difference between the actual spend in the current year, and the hypothetical amount which would have been incurred if there had been no improvement in environmental performance (and allowing for the actual increases in business volumes and prices, which would otherwise mean a significantly higher total cost). This calculation therefore uses a hypothetical, calculated benchmark against which to measure performance, similar to the procedure of 'flexing the budget' in conventional variance analysis.*

The total benefit is then measured by the sum of both 'savings' and 'cost avoidance'. To measure 'savings' alone, in the context of an expanding business and general inflation, would under-reflect the real contribution to profit made by the environmental improvement.

Preparing this statement requires that some definition of environmental costs and benefits is applied. Baxter's approach is deliberately pragmatic – the costs and benefits arising from environment-related actions across the organisation, including those originating outside the environmental management function. This is clearly imprecise, but sufficient for Baxter's purpose which is to use the EFS not primarily for external reporting or even as a problem-solving tool within the business, but as an attention-directing signal to attract attention to the potential value of environmental actions for the business, by providing a basis for discussion in management meetings.

As their vice-president for environment, health and safety, Bill Blackburn, puts it:

> When Baxter adopted its strong upgraded environmental policy in 1990, we were concerned that it not be a 'trophy policy' – one that hangs in the lobby like a moose-head merely to impress visitors. We wanted a living animal. Goal setting and measurement, in helping with quality principles, has helped bring our policy to life. Our balance sheet is one area of measurement that has strengthened our program by bringing together our environmental and business professionals. It enables these professionals to focus on common opportunities using a common language – the language of business – money. It has been the ultimate tool for integrating our environmental program into our business.[1]

34:3.3 Identification, Tracking and Allocation of Specific Environment-related Costs

Conventional management accounting is criticised by environmental management accountants for failing to make visible to management not only the full scale of environmental costs, but also the reasons for the incurrence of those costs, that is, their 'cost drivers' – the particular products and/or processes which generate wastes, emissions and effluents which subsequently cause costs for the company. Research has found that:

(a) *a high proportion of environment-related costs such as for waste disposal and licensing are allocated in accounting systems to overhead accounts;*
(b) *these are then either not tracked to processes and/or products but written off as period costs, or if they are tracked, then frequently on general apportionment bases which obscure the underlying causal cost drivers.*

In this respect, much environment-related management accounting is simply a particular application of activity-based costing (ABC) (*see* **Ch.22**) which seeks to demonstrate the importance of the environment as a cost driver and to achieve a better allocation of costs to relevant budgets so that they influence behaviour (in this case to reduce environmental costs by improving environmental performance).

Producers also need to consider the lifetime costs of their products – for example, by requiring end-of-life disposal routes. Gaining a better understanding of these costs, as companies like Philips have developed models to achieve, allows timely action to be taken to minimise or avoid them through redesign and/or to put more cost-effective disposal routes in place (*see* **para.34:4.1**).

Sometimes companies which operate similar activities at multiple geographically dispersed sites can generate worthwhile benefits by carrying out pilot studies to identify opportunities which may be relatively small in their own right, but which can be significant when more widely applied across the rest of the corporation (*see* Example 4 in **para.34:3.3.1**).

34:3.3.1 Example 4: Pacific Gas and Electric

After identifying and realising substantial environmental and business benefits in the high profile areas of generation and transmission and largely resolving their current challenges in these areas, the American West Coast utility Pacific Gas and Electric is now examining other areas of its business such as offices and servicing. In 1996, for example, it commissioned a consultancy, Decision Focus, to identify those of its service centres which represented 'best practice' in respect of materials and wastes management. As part of this task the consultancy developed a 'mass balance' analysis for one of these service centres. This highlighted the fluid in switches, transformers and capacitors, and the oil wastes produced as a result of vehicle fleet operations, as being the most hazardous. It also highlighted several relatively simple changes which could create both environmental and business benefit. Two examples which have been implemented have been to amend maintenance schedules so that servicing intervals are determined by usage (e.g. by mileage driven, for vehicles) rather than at fixed time intervals, and to change storage procedures for equipment such as transformers.

Follow-on projects have included life-cycle cost evaluations of individual hazardous waste streams. In 1997 these were conducted for printer cartridges; vehicle parts cleaning solvents; aerosol container wastes; nickel cadmium batteries and parts-washer wastes. Improved procedures were identified for four of these, with potential reductions of 6.5 tons of waste and savings of up to $350,000. As a result of the exercise the company has now introduced a nickel-cadmium battery rejuvenation scheme which is expected to save $82,000 per year in disposal costs and new procurement.

34:3.4 Incorporation of Environment into Investment Appraisal
(*See* Ch.11.)

Environmental factors can be significant in determining the ultimate returns from new investment. It is therefore important that they are identified and considered during the early stages of investment decision making. This not only allows major problems to be avoided but also provides an opportunity for remedial action at a stage when the costs of doing so can be relatively low.

Many companies are currently bringing environment into capital budgeting by requiring qualitative assessments of impacts arising from major investments. This can be extended in two main ways:

1. *by widening the range of costs and benefits which are taken into account, for example, by using the methodology of total cost assessment (TCA) developed for the US Environmental Protection Agency (EPA) by the Tellus Institute (see para.34:3.4.2);*
2. *by adopting appraisal techniques to take account of the long-term benefits of environmental actions and/or the specific risks of investments with serious environmental impacts.*

Example 5 in **paragraph 34:3.4.1** provides a checklist of environment-related factors to be taken into consideration when making decisions on capital investments and new product introductions.

34:3.4.1 Example 5: Future Proofing Investment and Product Appraisal Decisions

(a) *Have all business cases been scrutinised/signed off by environmental staff?*
(b) *Have the end-of-life costs of equipment and products been calculated/considered?*
(c) *Have all pollution control and environmental management costs been included?*
(d) *Have possible increases in the costs of pollution control, energy, water and transport and the effects of these on the business case been considered?*
(e) *Do the approvals involve the use of hazardous or controversial substances? What would be the effect of bans, more stringent regulations and/or higher costs for such substances?*
(f) *Do or could environmental groups or other external stakeholders have objections to the decisions and might these influence the costs, payback periods etc.?*

(g) *Will the decisions make use of existing pollution control, take-back or other forms of environmental infrastructure, and could the costs of these increase in future?*

(h) *Could the equipment or products generate long-term liabilities and, if so, have these been assessed?*

(i) *Are the investments or new products achieving substantial improvements in environmental performance compared to those they are replacing or alternatives? If not, can this be achieved?*

(j) *Will the decisions still be valid in a world where much greater attention is paid to environmental issues?*

34:3.4.2 Total Cost Assessment (TCA)

The Tellus Institute examined how environmental factors could be brought into the appraisal of capital investment proposals, in particular the breadth of the 'cost inventory' of costs and benefits which could be brought into the analysis. They developed a framework of a number of 'tiers' of costs and benefits; the tiers become increasingly comprehensive as one moves up the framework:

Tier 0 direct costs only
Tier 1 direct costs, and also indirect costs (overheads)
Tier 2 tiers 0 and 1, plus legal liability costs
Tier 3 tiers 0 to 2, plus intangible costs and benefits

Tier 0 includes direct and visible costs only – those which in conventional accounting and costing systems are already being tracked to the products and processes which cause them, and which management are therefore already well aware of and understand.

Tier 1 are the indirect costs – real and environment-related costs but which are not allocated to the processes etc. which create them, because they are posted to overhead accounts and subsequently either:

(a) *written off as period costs; or*

(b) *if they are tracked to processes etc., this is by apportionment on general bases which conceal the real underlying cause-and-effect cost drivers.*

In many systems these can include costs such as energy (*see* **Ch.23**), waste management and disposal, and permitting and licensing costs for effluents and emissions. These are referred to as 'hidden costs' since the effect of this costing treatment is that their scale and causes may not be apparent.

Tiers 0 and 1 deal only with actual costs which are already being incurred currently. However, current operations may give rise at some future time to fines and penalties for non-compliance under criminal law, and claims on companies from third parties under civil law, which Tier 2 captures. These are more uncertain than Tier 0 and 1 costs, and probabilistic and future rather than definite and current.

Tier 3 is concerned with the potential benefits of environmentally responsible business policies, such as an enhanced image among customers and other stakeholders, improved staff morale and improved staff health and safety. These are intangible and even more difficult and subjective to assess, but as with other 'soft assets' such as consumer brands, some assessment of their value may be essential in order to develop a full picture.

Most of the experiments carried out to apply the TCA have concentrated on extending investment appraisal exercises to include a greater proportion of Tier 1 costs in addition to the Tier 0 costs which are already included, and are similar in principle and purpose to activity-based cost analyses. In one study, two business decisions from a paper company were taken and evaluated both by the company's normal method, and also by a TCA analysis which brought in several Tier 1 costs which would normally be excluded such as energy, water, insurance and the treatment, management and disposal of wastes. The effect was to demonstrate that these projects which would normally have been evaluated to be unprofitable were in fact commercially acceptable – for one of the projects the payback period was reduced from 11 to two years, and the internal rate of return increased from zero to 36%.

34:3.4.3 Excessive Discount Rates

There are two aspects to this:

1. *rates applied which are generally higher than would be rationally justified, for example by reference to capital market-based risk models such as the Capital Asset Pricing Model (see **Ch.11, para.11:2.4.1**);*
2. *failure to adjust discount rates used to appraise specific projects to reflect differing levels of project risk.*

This would have a distorting effect on projects with lower-than-average risks, which is likely to include many potential investments in clean technology, or 'pollution prevention at source' (P2). Compared with (say) alternative investments in new products, markets or technologies, P2 investments (to replace 'end-of-pipe' techniques which deal with pollution and waste only *after* it has been created) are likely to carry lower-than-average risks since their success is less dependent on uncontrollable external variables.

34:3.4.4 Truncated Time Horizons

Any evaluation of a project with a life several years into the future is subject to the increasing uncertainty which is inevitable in estimating future cash flows as the analysis extends further into the future. In order to compensate for this, one crude but straightforward technique sometimes adopted is to impose an arbitrary future point in time (say, five or ten years) beyond which future costs and benefits (usually benefits more than costs) will not be brought into the analysis.

The effect of arbitrarily shortened future time-horizons combined with excessive discount rates is to build into the analysis a bias against more fundamental and strategic projects, which may take several years to justify their initial investment. This has been identified as a significant factor in the (alleged) short-termism of much of western industry.

34:4 Future Opportunities

All the above areas are likely to be developed further in future. They will probably be joined by five others which are currently in the early stages of development within management accounting, but which have the potential to reduce environmental impacts considerably as well as to generate business benefit:

1. *life-cycle costing;*
2. *full cost accounting;*
3. *shareholder value;*
4. *sustainability accounting;*
5. *environment-related performance measurement.*

34:4.1 Life-cycle Costing
(*See* **Ch.19.**)

This identifies all the costs incurred during the whole life of a particular product (or system). Environmental costs can be a significant element in the total cost of buying, using and disposing of a product. It can therefore be sensible to identify and calculate these at the time of purchase. Two particular areas which a number of organisations have started to examine are:

1. *the costs of dealing with emissions or wastes from equipment operation;*
2. *the costs of disposing of products at the end of their lives.*

Life-cycle costing provides the framework to consider costs not only within the organisation itself, but also along the product chain, by including as well as internal costs also costs incurred upstream (by suppliers) and downstream (by customers and consumers). This can help to identify opportunities where modest extra spending by the company may increase value for the customer disproportionately, which can be reflected in an increased selling price and/or increased sales volume.

Baxter International has generated substantial savings in materials costs for itself through packaging redesign. As well as this benefit, reducing the quantity of packaging which the final user has to dispose of is becoming an increasingly significant selling point in countries such as Germany with strict legislative controls.

The American chemicals company Monsanto found that net savings could be realised over the product chain by reformulating some of its products from a liquid to a solid form (e.g. granules). Although usually this meant higher costs in production and transport (since liquids are usually more compact), the environmental consequences of spills are less with solids since they can be recaptured more quickly and completely than can liquids. Some of their customers, particularly smaller US companies, were sufficiently concerned about their ability to avoid all spillages – and the potential legal and financial consequences if these occurred – to justify Monsanto reformulating some product lines and reflecting this in their selling prices.

In a slightly different context, Xerox's 'totes' project provides an example of a life-cycle cost analysis in practice, across the company's European logistics chain (*see* Example 6 in **para.34:4.1.1**).

34:4.1.1   Example 6: Xerox Plc's 'Totes' Project [2]

In Europe, Xerox manufactures products such as copiers at two sites, in the UK and the Netherlands respectively; transports them in bulk to their European Logistics Centre, in the Netherlands; and from there tranships across Europe to customers and distributors. Xerox has always accepted the return of old copiers from customers at the end of their lives, even in advance of any prospect of 'take-back' legislation, so that products also move in the reverse direction. Because of the need to protect products through their logistic chain, substantial quantities of packaging have been needed, with each of the company's main product lines (23, at the time of this project) having its own customised design of packaging.

Although all involved recognised that logistics was a major cost for the business, there was no consensus on the amount, with estimates of the total cost varying by a factor of up to six. The problem was that the company's regular accounting systems, like those of most companies, followed conventional responsibility accounting principles and were therefore based on the company's organisation structure. Since logistics costs follow the process of the company's distribution pattern and are incurred across several different responsibility centres, they were not identified and reported separately.

A logistics financial reporting system was set up specifically to deal with this, collecting data from across the whole of the organisation. Although Xerox aims wherever possible to devolve responsibility to operating companies, this necessarily had to be done from the centre. Economies of scale in logistics depend on being able to look at the supply chain holistically – the ability to achieve this is one way in which the corporate centre is able to add value to the business's operations. This system reported that the total costs of logistics were towards the top end of the previous range of expectations, which prompted a search for potential cost savings. This was reinforced by reports from the sales force of increasing concern among customers and distributors about the quantities of packaging wastes which Xerox's delivery system imposed on them, particularly in countries where tough 'take-back' legislation was expected.

One solution proposed was to rationalise the current range of different types of packaging, which were generally designed to be disposable, into a more limited number of reusable containers, or 'totes'. The final decision was to standardise on two tote designs (large and small), which would cater for not only all the current product range but also possible future designs which were currently being planned, and also discontinued products which might still have to be taken back from customers. Standardising on two instead of 23 packaging designs necessarily meant that packaging was now being overspecified for some products, so a series of detailed cost analyses were carried out to assess whether this was justified. A total of over 400 combinations of products and destinations were analysed, each with up to 17 different cost items, at different stages in the logistics chain. These showed that overall, the savings comfortably exceeded the additional costs, although this was not even across the whole of the chain: the new totes system meant that some responsibility centres faced increased costs. Implementing the new system required adjusting individual centres' budgets accordingly, or renegotiating supplier contracts for those activities which had been outsourced.

Xerox's totes project provides an example of process-based costing in an environment-related context, following an approach similar to product life-cycle costing – here, costing across the life cycle of a package. It also demonstrates the combination of management tools: the overall measure of the total costs involved through the logistics financial reporting system to illustrate their scale and to direct attention, and the detailed cost analysis needed to evaluate and prove the case for the specific proposal.

34:4.2 Full Cost Accounting

Projecting future costs is an important part of investment appraisal and is also valuable for other purposes. The environment can be an important determinant of these future costs. This is highly visible with new legislative or regulatory demands. However, forward-looking companies will also be considering the potential costs of possible future legislation or other environmental action. One indication that this may happen is when costs in one country are much lower than in others. Another is when there are large external damage costs created by environmental impacts which are not yet reflected in the company's internal financial calculations.

Although the methodology of calculating and applying external costs is controversial and any estimate is inevitably subjective to some extent, as the 'Polluter Pays' principle is reflected in more stringent environmental legislation, current external costs may provide at least an approximate indicator of possible future internal costs for a business. One possible application could be as one of a variety of methods of evaluating the future whole-life environmental performance of new products at the product design stage (Bennett and James, 1998b). They can also be used as an indicator of environmental performance for its own sake.

Companies making capital investment and other decisions with long-term financial consequences might be wise at least to consider the implications of these. Ontario Hydro is one of the few companies to have examined how this can be done in practice.

34:4.3 Shareholder Value

In recent years there has been an increasing interest in measuring shareholder value (*see* **Ch.48, para.48:6**). This is usually defined as the present value of the company's future cash flows, discounted at an appropriate rate. As environment can affect all of the main parameters in this equation – future expenses, revenues and cost of capital – it is therefore an important element to be considered in any calculations.

The revenue implications of environmental actions may be particularly important in this respect. There are many who believe that opportunities for volume growth and/or the higher pricing of eco-efficient products provides much greater opportunities than do saving or avoiding expenses by waste minimisation or other measures. However, it is difficult to devise satisfactory techniques to generate quantitative data on this topic.

34:4.4 Sustainability Accounting

There is ever more pressure for business – and therefore environment-related management accounting – to pay greater attention to the environmental and social sustainability of its operations.

One way in which this can be achieved is through the development of measures to relate environmental impacts to an economic parameter, for example, sulphur dioxide emissions per unit of value added. This will allow the most eco-efficient companies or operations to be identified and, ultimately, may allow comparison with some benchmark measure determined by government or regulatory bodies.

However, knowing that an organisation is using resources efficiently says little about whether their use is sustainable. Sustainability implies limited 'eco-capacity', that is, a finite availability of physical resources such as fossil fuels and biological materials and of environmental 'sinks' such as the atmosphere. The costs of exceeding this eco-capacity can, in principle, be calculated by governments and then disaggregated to company-level through taxes – for example, a carbon tax – or other means. The relationship between these 'costs of unsustainability' and value added can therefore be a crude measure of an enterprise's sustainability.

In a world where all such costs were internalised through taxes and other measures, sustainable value added will be the equivalent of economic value added, but this is far from the case at present. Hence, approximations to sustainable value added can be produced by taking estimates of damage costs. This has been done by the Dutch software company, BSO Origin (Tuppen, 1996). Figures are available for many impacts although there is limited consensus about the best basis of calculation or their accuracy. However, this may change in future.

34:4.5 Environment-related Performance Measurement

Non-financial performance measurement, to supplement conventional financial measures, has become topical in recent years. Its recent growth is largely attributable to quality programmes, but it has developed from these into models such as the 'balanced scorecard' (*see* **Ch.49, para.49:2.2**) which position performance measurement as a key support tool to achieve strategic objectives. The principle behind these models is that, even if a company's ultimate goal is to maximise the financial targets of profits and shareholder value, these are outcomes rather than causes, and lagging rather than leading indicators. In order to achieve these financial objectives, businesses should focus on leading, controllable areas such as process and product quality, customer service, and organisational learning and innovation, and should develop and use regular performance measures in each of these areas.

A distinct but complementary driver in environmental management is the policy voluntarily adopted by many companies, to recognise their accountability to a broad range of stakeholders extending beyond their own investors and to discharge this responsibility through regular external reporting. This usually takes the form of annual corporate environmental performance reports, modelled on the external financial reporting process, but requiring performance measures which by their nature are necessarily non-financial.

Although financial accounting and performance measurement is almost invariably the domain of accountants and financial managers, in many organisations the lead has been taken by others such as the operational managers involved, and the IT managers who provide the capability to collect, process and report on the large quantities of data involved.

Many companies have developed advanced systems to measure and report on their environmental performance, both in order to report externally and to support internal management (Bennett and James, 1998a and 1999). However these have been widely criticised as:

(a) *unreliable, since based on non-systematic and ad hoc data collection procedures;*
(b) *not always reflecting the environmental issues which should be of primary concern to the particular organisation;*
(c) *often not linked to other business objectives;*
(d) *tending to measure efforts and inputs (e.g. number of environmental audits carried out, or environmental management systems installed) rather than outcomes (reductions in emissions and wastes and resulting financial savings).*

As with non-financial performance measurement in other areas, environmental performance measurement is not usually the responsibility of the accounting and finance function. However it has been argued that accounting and finance skills are as necessary with non-financial as with financial measures, and that there is potential for accountants to extend their activities into this area.

34:5 The Role of Accountants

34:5.1 Processes to Integrate Accounting with Environmental Management

Researchers have found that the process of developing mutual understanding and awareness between accountants and environmental managers can be as important as any specific outcomes. Yet there have been few instances in practice of accountants working with environmental colleagues in these areas. When this does occur, it tends mainly to be confined to capital expenditure decisions about pollution control investments, or assessing the level of environmental liabilities. This finding corresponds with research in other areas which also has found that management accounting practice can be slow to adapt (Drury et al., 1993), and that initiatives in new or developing areas such as non-financial performance measurement is often taken by functions other than accounting.

Gray *et al.* (1993) have identified three main areas of relevance:

1. *providing data captured within accounting systems to environmental managers and others;*
2. *bringing financial sophistication to environmental decision making, particularly through the development of financial indicators;*
3. *introducing expertise in financial data collection, integration, verification and communication into the area of environment-related management accounting.*

More needs to be done to develop processes which bring accountants and environmental staff together. A research project into the links between management accounting and environmental management in European industry (Bartolomeo *et al.*, 1999) found that these were weak in most companies but that there was considerable potential for closer links, for example by applying accounting skills to ensure the reliability of data used in environmental performance measurement. A study by CIMA (1997) suggested that management accountants have a key role to play in environmental management, in particular as a key element of this is the sustainable use of resources, and a fundamental function of management accountants is to provide information to enable others to manage resources with maximum effectiveness.

Specific measures which can be taken to improve links include:

(a) *making relevant environmental training available to accountants;*
(b) *nominating one or more environmental champions among accounting staff;*
(c) *training environmental managers in basic accounting and financial management;*

(d) *including environmental managers in investment appraisal and other business case processes;*

(e) *including environmental managers in accounting change activities such as activity-based costing or business process re-engineering.*

34:5.2 Links with Other Management Accounting Developments

One study (Tuppen, 1996) noted that many of the developments in environment-related management accounting are closely related to other current developments in management accounting. Some examples are:

(a) *product life costing (see Ch.19);*

(b) *strategic management accounting (see Chs 2 and 3);*

(c) *activity-based costing (see Ch.22).*

34:5.2.1 Product Life Costing

The term 'product life costing' is used with two different meanings, in different contexts. In environment-related management accounting it refers to the calculation of total costs over the whole life of an individual product, from extraction of raw materials to final end-of-life disposal ('cradle-to-grave'). Its more usual use in management accounting has been not to refer to an individual product but to a product line, from original design through to withdrawal from the market. Although the use of the term is different, both uses reflect a realisation that it is necessary to measure costs beyond the traditional costing focus of only those incurred within the company during the production phase.

34:5.2.2 Strategic Management Accounting

Positive environment-related management accounting aims not only to respond to but to anticipate the effects on business of what is likely to be an increasingly important factor in the business context in the future. Advocates of a strategic approach to management accounting argue that past practice has tended to be focused too narrowly on matters internal to the business such as controlling and reporting on production processes. They argue for a more ambitious and outward-looking perspective which aims to predict and plan for likely changes in markets and technologies.

34:5.2.3 Activity-based Costing

One of the most widely discussed recent developments in management accounting has been activity-based costing (ABC). The initial objective of ABC (from which there have been several extensions) was to identify improved ways to understand overhead costs and identify their cost drivers (*see* **Ch.22, para.22:3**), in order to allocate costs more accurately to products and processes than do traditional apportionment methods.

As noted in **paragraph 34:3.3**, several environment-related management accounting projects have aimed to take the same approach with environmental costs. In some cases this has been explicit (e.g. AT&T), in others implicit (e.g. the Tellus Institute's TCA framework). The basic premise is the same, that:

    (a) *a high proportion of environment-related costs are 'hidden' in overheads;*

    (b) *these are either not tracked to processes and/or products, or if they are, then usually on general apportionment bases which obscure the underlying causal cost drivers.*

From an ABC perspective, the defining feature of 'environmental costs', as expressed by AT&T's Green Accounting Team, is that these are the costs for which environmental professionals, through their expertise and experience, are best equipped to help to identify the cost driver(s) and therefore to identify methods of managing those costs (*see* **para.34:2.1**).

34:6 Conclusions

The growing cost and revenue implications of environmental issues are making environment-related management accounting increasingly important. Many of these costs and revenues will be addressed by normal management accounting processes, but the evidence is that many will not – and that companies will suffer as a result.

In many ways, environment-related management accounting is merely the application of many of the ideas of advanced management accounting to a particular area. For example:

    (a) *it can be seen as an application of ABC that focuses on environment as a key cost driver;*

    (b) *its emphasis on end-of-life and other downstream and upstream costs from the organisation itself relates to broader debates on the topic of product life costing;*

(c) its emphasis on future threats and opportunities supports those who argue that *management accounting in general must become more strategic and less focused on short-term controlling and reporting;*

(d) *the environmental critique that conventional investment appraisal has difficulties in dealing with uncertainty and long-term strategic benefits links into more general discussions on these topics;*

(e) *it forms one element of the 'balanced-scorecard' approach advocated by Kaplan and others.*

Environment-related management accounting can also contribute to management accounting more generally since the rapid development and pan-organisational nature of environmental issues also means that it provides useful experience in dealing with some of the key generic challenges of management accounting. These include:

(a) *how far it is essentially about the collection and manipulation of quantitative data or also has a qualitative, 'process' dimension;*

(b) *the trade-offs between simple measures which can easily be understood and used but may not capture a complete picture of performance, and more complex ones with the opposite characteristics;*

(c) *the primary objective in any situation, for example, whether control, analysis to support decision making, developing awareness or motivating continuous improvement.*

Finally, environment-related management accounting has several unusual characteristics which may ultimately spread to other areas of management accounting. One of these is the need to evaluate different kinds of data – the 'apples and pears' problem. Another is the high degree of external interest in the area – sometimes resulting in a requirement to disclose certain data – and the consequent emphasis on effective communication and verification. As similar requirements for disclosure are being, or could be, adopted in other areas such as the performance of regulated utilities, experience in the environmental area of 'management accounting in a goldfish bowl' also has a wider significance.

Notes

[1.] A full case study on Baxter's EFS, by the authors of this chapter, is available as an Appendix to Tuppen (1996), and an abbreviated version is included in Bennett and James (1998b).

[2.] A full case study, by the authors of this chapter, on Xerox's totes project and the financial analysis which supported it is available in Bennett and James (1998b).

References

Bartolomeo, M., Bennett, M., Bouma, J., Heydkamp, P., James, P., de Walle, F., Wolters, T. (1999) *Eco-Management Accounting.* Dordrecht, NL: Kluwer Academic Publishing.

Bennett, M. and James, P. (1998a) *Environment under the spotlight – current practice and future trends in environment-related performance measurement for business.* London: Association of Chartered Certified Accountants (ACCA).

Bennett, M. and James, P. (Eds) (1998b) *The green bottom line: Environmental accounting for management – current practice and future trends.* Sheffield: Greenleaf Publishing.

Bennett, M. & James, P. (Eds) (1999) *Sustainable measures: Evaluating and reporting on environmental and social performance.* Sheffield: Greenleaf Publishing.

Chartered Institute of Management Accountants (UK) (1997) *Environmental management: The role of the management accountant.* London: Chartered Institute of Management Accountants (CIMA).

Ditz, D., Ranganathan, J. and Banks, D. (Eds) (1995) *Green ledgers: Case studies in corporate environmental accounting.* Washington, DC: World Resources Institute.

Fussler, C. with James, P. (1996) *Driving eco-innovation.* London: Pitman Publishing.

Gray, R., Bebbington J. and Walters, D. (1993) *Accounting for the environment.* London: Paul Chapman and Association of Certified Accountants.

Johnston, N. (1994) *Waste minimisation: A route to profit and cleaner production.* London: Centre for Exploitation of Science and Technology.

Tuppen, C. (Ed.) (1996) *Environmental accounting in industry: A practical review.* London: British Telecom.

35. **Pricing**

35:1 Introduction

Product pricing is one of the most delicate and important business decisions that managers have to make. A lot of the daily activities of a company are determined by the prices of input factors and the prices of output. In today's fiercely competitive globalised markets prices greatly influence purchasing behaviour and some consumers base purchasing decisions on price alone, thus inevitably determining the success of a company's products. Prices lead to 'wars' between rival companies such as those witnessed recently between newspaper publishers, telephone companies and supermarket chains. To protect the consumer, governments intervene in pricing policies through their regulatory bodies or 'watchdogs' who enforce existing competition law or enact new legislation if necessary. As changes in prices affect inflation, governments also intervene in pricing policies through adjustments of interest rates and public spending levels. This chapter addresses the pricing decision by looking at all the important variables that affect it and makes suggestions for better pricing.

35:1.1 Definitions

Prices can be defined as the monetary values attached to products exchanged between the buyers and sellers of those products in their respective markets. Name variants of price include fees, rents and charges, depending on the nature of the product involved in the transaction. Examples of products include raw materials, a manufactured good, building a manufacturing plant, drilling an oil well, a software package, a pathology test, an outpatient attendance in a hospital, a consultancy service, a share, a financial service and a management training programme.

35:1.2   Pricing as a Process

Pricing is the process through which product prices are established using internal cost and other information and external or market-related information. Therefore the pricing decision is not a simple cost accounting or marketing exercise. It is a decision that impinges on many other decisions such as the output decision, the investment decision (*see* **Ch.11**) and the financing decision. Setting and changing prices incurs costs and this requires managing the whole pricing process and the people involved in it. The more efficient this process, the better the management of the entire organisation and the better the financial and non-financial results.

35:1.3   Internal Versus External Pricing

The exchange of a product at an agreed price, or the commercial transaction, can take place within an organisation or outside it. When the transaction is internal, the product is exchanged or 'transferred' between two sections of the same organisation at a 'transfer price'. This special form of pricing is dealt with in **Chapter 36**. The remainder of this chapter deals with pricing decisions which involve external transactions between independent organisations, in particular manufacturing companies.

35:2 The Accounting Role of Price

Accounting is essentially about producing and supplying financial information to internal and external users of the information. Although accountants may not be too influential in price setting, prices are information which permeates all branches of the accounting function for both sellers and buyers. In the accounting equation, the price to be paid for a product has opposite signs in the cost and revenue functions of the buyer and the seller, being a cost for the former and a revenue for the latter. Therefore prices affect costs, contribution margins, profits, assets and liabilities and, consequently, can be pivotal in strategy formulation and decision making.

35:2.1 Prices in Financial Accounting

Financial reporting regulations require the financial accountant to apply the *matching principle* in preparing financial statements which form a key part of the published annual accounts of companies.

In the specified accounting period, usually the commercial year, purchase prices of input factors are key determinants of the costs to be matched to the revenues of the same accounting period, with product selling prices as the key determinant of revenues. Without the price information the matching of the costs and revenues of the goods sold would not be possible and the accountant would not be able to produce the main accounts, namely the profit and loss statement and the balance sheet. Since prices affect costs and revenues in opposite ways, buying or selling at the wrong price affects the profit or loss figure, the retained earnings and dividends figures and the inventory figure reported by the financial accountant in the audited annual accounts.

Between accounting periods, revenues and costs are also expected to translate into cash inflows and outflows (*see* **Ch.10**) as reported in the cash-flow statement, hence price is also a key determinant of cash flow. Charging high prices may force buyers into liquidity problems. While unpaid suppliers increase the current liabilities in the balance sheet, customer accounts still outstanding increase the debtors, both having financing and cash-flow implications. Cash flow is a key determinant of capital investment decisions. Finally, if price turns customers away, unsold stock will go to 'swell' inventories in the balance sheet which in turn will entail financing costs. More cash tied up in inventories means less cash for investment opportunities and wealth creation.

35:2.2 Prices in Management Accounting

Management accountants are instrumental in preparing relevant accounting information for internal users, including financial accountants and managers. Knowledge of, or the calculation of, prices is essential for the management accountant in the preparation and internal provision of the information to assist managers in planning, decision making and control as follows.

To translate the company's goals and objectives into budgets, prices of input factors are used to calculate standard costs of the resources to be consumed (*see* **Ch.16**) and prepare various budgets (*see* **Ch.9**), while product selling prices are used to set sales budgets. Cash budgets (*see* **Ch.10**) and pro forma financial statements are then derived. Expected break-even points are also determined, especially for short-term decisions. Prices, costs, production volume, sales and revenues are therefore inextricably linked in the planning and budgetary process.

Since budgets are widely used for control, prices affect the budgetary control process in many ways, depending on how difficult the budget target is to attain, the flexibility of the performance evaluation system, the incentive scheme, the experience and entrepreneurial skills of the budgetee, as well as competition and general economic conditions. The relationship between pricing and behaviour is discussed below.

A common 'headache' for senior managers is detecting and eliminating slack built into budgets by subordinates. For instance, building slack in the budgets to secure favourable price, sales and profit variances and earn rewards for meeting or exceeding the budget misleads the performance evaluation exercise into praising and rewarding actions which may undermine value creation. An example of this is buying substandard raw materials at a cheaper price which may secure a favourable variance from the budget price and probably earn an undeserved reward. However the damaging effect of such action will become manifest on the production line because of wastage and machine stoppages, and from customer complaints about product quality. If budgetees are suspected of or found to build slack through price manipulation, this could only lengthen the iterative budgetary cycle as submitted budgets would bounce back on budgetees and senior managers would not grant approval until after a series of resource consuming revisions of those budgets suspected of carrying slack. Therefore, budgeting without price information is not possible and the less accurate this information the less reliable the management accounts and the budgetary control process. Price can thus play a key role in shaping managerial behaviour.

35:3 Pricing Decisions

We have established above that price is an important business factor with serious financial and other implications. Hence, it can be said that pricing decisions are probably the most important and challenging decisions that (marketing) managers have to take. In strategic terms, because pricing is a product-related decision, price is a key but complex variable in the marketing mix beside product attributes, markets, sales promotion and advertising. Strategy formulation involves analysis of environmental factors which include customers and competitors. Even when prices are based on costs, the reactions of the company's customers and competitors cannot be ignored. When and where applicable, knowledge of competitors' price tactics is essential for formulating operational strategies. In this strategic choice, the perceptions, objectives and the constituent elements of price must be considered as outlined below. This puts the pricing decision in a proper context and enables the choice of the appropriate pricing formula, be it cost or market-based.

35:3.1 Varying Perceptions and Objectives of Price

As prices bind together buyers and sellers with diverging and probably conflicting objectives and expectations, their perceptions of price and their behaviour should naturally diverge. While one company in the industry may be strapped for cash and, therefore, its pricing strategy is geared towards immediate cash flow, its competitors might be driven more by improving product quality while ensuring price stability, maintaining or increasing market share, environmental responsibility and higher long-term returns. Thus, in addition to being a monetary value, a price is also:

(a) *a means to an end in facilitating commercial activity and resource allocation for both customers and sellers;*

(b) *a cost or cash outflow that the buyer would like to minimise;*

(c) *a revenue or cash inflow that the seller would like to maximise;*

(d) *a bargaining card for the buyer (what does the customer want?);*

(e) *a measure of product quality and quantification of value;*

(f) *a means to recover costs and earn desired returns on investments for the seller;*

(g) *a 'cheaper' alternative to debt for the seller to raise much-needed funds;*

(h) *a competitive tool for the seller (e.g. market share, ability to continue trading, reputation, social responsibility).*

35:3.2 Practical Elements of Price

Prices are generally based on production costs or determined by market forces with the marketing department usually playing a leading role (see for instance the 1997 survey by the Professional Pricing Society, USA). Thus the monetary value that a price embodies is affected by one or more of a host of internal and external factors, some of a strategic nature as the following list shows:

(a) *the nature and quality of the product exchanged (i.e. differentiating features);*

(b) *the seller's ability to accurately forecast demand (including the effect of demographic trends, advertising, and health and ecology awareness campaigns on changing tastes);*

(c) *the size and the frequency of the transaction (e.g. bulk purchase versus just-in-time delivery and responsibility for defects);*

(d) *the discounts and other concessions offered or obtained (if varying the price is a more profitable strategy and does not contravene current price competition law with regard to discrimination and predation);*

(e) *credit terms (in particular when the price is cost-based and the company has cash-flow problems);*

(f) *the company's after sales service (quality service and reliability versus low prices);*

(g) the general relationship between the buyer and the supplier (e.g. brand loyalty, mutual trust, current level of debtors and bad debts and past factoring experience);

(h) the nature of market competition (e.g. monopoly, oligopoly, niche markets, barriers to entry, new entrants with low-priced imitation products such as computer software packages);

(i) the existence of product substitutes (e.g. aluminium versus steel for aircraft construction);

(j) the existence of complementary products;

(k) the position of the product on its life-cycle curve (new versus mature or dying products) (see **Ch.19**);

(l) negotiation skills of buyers and sellers (including 'equality of information' and 'variation of price' clauses when contracting with the Ministry of Defence);

(m) price elasticity of demand (how sensitive is demand to small changes in price, i.e. price expectations of customers);

(n) the degree of vertical integration and the existence of 'middle men' or intermediaries between buyers and sellers;

(o) production and transaction costs (in the long run all costs must be recovered);

(p) availability of cheaper substitute input factors (e.g. raw materials);

(q) production process efficiency and ability to pass on cost savings to customers through reductions in price;

(r) the level of the profit mark-up in a cost-based price;

(s) the use of 'cause-related' marketing (where customers are told how much of the price they pay goes to a good cause or charity);

(t) availability and feasibility of subcontracting options (cost of making versus buying in);

(u) general economic climate and inflation levels;

(v) government intervention through industry regulation and price watchdogs (e.g. the forthcoming EU-wide tobacco advertising ban – to be phased in between 2001 and 2006 might force companies to compete on price. However lower prices could fuel overall tobacco consumption and lead to more health problems);

(w) tax regimes (for example net car prices are lower in countries where tax is paid on car purchases; see for instance the European Commission report IP/98/154 on car prices differentials in the European Union).

After identifying and assessing the set of relevant internal and external factors that influence the pricing decision at hand, the manager's task then is to set or choose the 'correct' or 'optimum' price for the product. Depending on the set of influential factors admitted to the pricing decision, the price can either follow market trends, be entirely based on current production costs or combine the two sets of information.

35:4 Economics, Markets and Regulation

Pricing is central to microeconomics theory in its discussions of supply-demand relationships, resource allocation and economic efficiency and welfare, especially when conditions of perfect competition can be assumed.

35:4.1 The Economist's Model

In simple terms, the economist's optimal price-output combination that ensures efficient allocation of resources and maximises profits is where marginal cost equates marginal revenue, that is, price equals marginal cost. In practice, however, the manager is likely to find the economist's pricing framework theoretically elegant but rather inoperable because of its assumptions of:

(a) *complete knowledge of customer preferences, demand curves and the product's price elasticity;*
(b) *complete knowledge of marginal cost and marginal revenue curves;*
(c) *perfect or near-perfect competition, with a large number of well-informed buyers and sellers.*

While managers may have control over costs and supply, their partial or incomplete knowledge of customers, competitors and markets makes demand curves difficult to estimate. Moreover, other factors beside price affect demand (e.g. product design and manufacturability, product quality, advertising, company reputation, competitors' actions, takeovers and mergers, demographic trends and fashion). Marginal cost and revenue functions are also difficult to construct from internal cost accounting data, especially for joint products and companies with many products. Opportunity costs of using resources and fixed costs cannot always be ignored in setting prices if these costs are related to product decisions. Finally, market imperfections are more the norm than the exception, for example because of concentration and monopolistic competition.

35:4.2 Market-based Pricing

Through pricing research a company can establish what the general market trends are and what the competitors are up to. Research does show that market conditions, especially competitors' pricing tend to be a very difficult barrier for a company's pricing strategy. Many of the external factors listed in **paragraph 35:3.2** affect the relationship between a company and its suppliers and customers because of their influence on the pricing and output decisions. When a company chooses to bypass existing market prices and uses cost to determine price levels, such a strategy can only be successful if the company builds a cost leadership profile for itself. It can do this by identifying and remedying the many deficiencies that characterise costing models. This is discussed in **paragraph 35:5**. In addition, the company cannot ignore competition law when this is applicable as explained below.

35:4.3 The Role of Regulatory Bodies

Pricing decisions are subject to both national and international laws and regulations. Pricing decisions in the new global market are affected by the North American Free Trade Agreement (NAFTA) 1992, the General Agreement on Tariffs and Trade (GATT) 1994 and the creation of the World Trade Organisation (WTO) 1994 to implement GATT. Of direct relevance to pricing decisions are the elimination of import duties, the intricate agreements on trade in products, services, intellectual property as well as 'the rules of origin' and the rules on anti-dumping. The rules of origin classify materials and goods in terms of their country of origin for the purpose of preferential tariff treatment. Anti-dumping measures prevent multinational companies from using unfairly low prices to 'dump' their products in and depress foreign markets. For example, Asian steel manufacturers have been accused of deliberate dumping practices in the US to escape the current Asian economic crisis. Their selling prices to the US are sometimes lower than their cost to make in the home country and certainly much lower than those of US producers at home. Related to anti-dumping measures is the extensive legislation on international transfer pricing which is discussed in **Chapter 26**.

EU competition law is underlain by Article 86 of the EC Treaty of Rome which prohibits price fixing arrangements, especially by companies dominating 40% or more of relevant markets and capable of abusing their dominant position. The enforcement of EU competition law can result in severe sanctions imposed on contravening companies such as Tetra Pak which was fined Ecu 70 million in 1994 for discriminatory and predatory pricing. Deliberately selling at unreasonably low or loss-making prices disadvantages rivals, destroys competition and denies consumers choice. British Sugar and Tate & Lyle, who between them controlled 90% of the white sugar trade in the UK, were recently fined £28 million and £5 million respectively by the European Commission for forming a cartel during 1986–90 and practising horizontal price fixing which forced abnormally high prices on consumers.

National governments intervene in pricing policies to protect consumers, maintain price stability, promote economic growth and efficiency and achieve financial, social and environmental goals. Maintaining price stability is central to a country's monetary policy as this is clearly stated in the Bank of England Act 1998. UK competition law that pertains to pricing has so far been embodied in various Acts of Parliament which are likely to be harmonised and superseded by the current Competition Bill which draws on the EC Treaty. The law aims at protecting the consumer from anti-competitive practices by, for example, preventing minimum price agreements, predatory pricing and price discrimination or, in the case of the utilities, by setting maximum prices, limiting price increases or requiring price reductions. The Department of Trade and Industry (DTI), the Competition Commission and the Office of Fair Trading (OFT) play an important law-enforcing role. Recent examples include:

(a) *The report by the MMC on the retail market for electric goods which triggered the Government's decision to abolish the recommended retail price system as from September 1998. This is similar to the abolition of resale price maintenance in the US in 1975 by the Consumer Goods Pricing Act.*

(b) *The report by OFT on the main British supermarkets which it challenged for avoiding price competition and not offering customers the best deals. While controlling two-thirds of the retail market, the main supermarkets were found not to pass price discounts from their suppliers to their customers, resulting in profits three times higher than those of their European counterparts.*

Dedicated price control in the UK is effected through various regulators who are independent of ministerial control such as OFFER for electricity, OFGAS for gas, OFTEL for telecommunications, OFWAT for water and ORR for rail services. Similar regulatory bodies can be found in other countries, for example, the Independent Pricing and Regulatory Tribunal of New South Wales which was set up in 1992 to regulate the prices of government monopoly services. Notable developments in the UK include:

(a) *OFWAT's recent guidelines setting fixed price limits for a number of years for water and sewerage services to provide incentive for water companies to become more efficient and improve services to customers. Regular price adjustments will be made to reflect efficiency and achieve the Government's 10% target reduction in water bills.*

(b) *To prevent unfair pricing as well as other uncompetitive practices, OFTEL introduced in 1996 a Fair Trading Condition into the licences of telecoms operators. Taking into account UK and EU competition law, the Condition focuses on price abuse by dominant operators and outlines measures for dealing with unfair pricing, especially predatory pricing. On the other hand, price discrimination whereby 'different units of the same good or service are sold at prices not directly corresponding to differences in the cost of supplying them' is not seen as unfair unless proven uncompetitive.*

35:5 Cost-based Pricing

Although companies take different views for setting and changing prices, cost-based (or accounting-based) pricing is common practice in business and can be justified as follows:

(a) cost information is 'readily available' from the accounting information system;

(b) a cost formula is 'quick' and 'simple' to understand and apply;

(c) costs represent a starting point or 'a rule of thumb' for price calculation and stability (in market-based pricing, the first company to set the trend must have used product costs to calculate selling prices);

(d) in the long-run all costs, including capacity and financing costs, must be recovered and doing this through pricing provides a 'protection floor' against costs and ensures the company's survival. In fact these costs are resultant from product decisions;

(e) idiosyncratic or speciality products are difficult to price otherwise as useful external price information does not usually exist for these types of product.

There are two variants of cost-based pricing: the contribution margin or variable costing approach and the absorption or full costing approach. In either case, a profit mark-up is normally added to the cost to arrive at the selling price. The mark-up is usually a positive figure that can be calculated in a variety of ways, unless the price is equal to cost in which case the mark-up is equal to zero as is the case in health care contract pricing in the National Health Service (*see* **para.35:5.3**).

35:5.1 Variable Costing Approach

Price = all variable costs + profit mark-up

where

mark-up = allowance for all fixed costs + profit margin (or return on assets)

i.e. $\text{mark-up} = \dfrac{\text{Fixed costs} + \text{profit margin (expected return)}}{\text{Production volume} \times \text{unit variable cost}} \times 100\%$

For simplicity assume a desired return of 20% on an investment of £5m, giving a total return of £1m for both products SYS01 and SYS02 in the example below.

Table 35:1 **Cost information for Systematik Ltd**

	Product	
	SYS01 *(complex design)*	*SYS02* *(standard design)*
Total annual budgeted output	50,000 units	200,000 units
Variable costs per unit:		
Direct materials	£50	£30
Direct labour @ £10 per hour	£25	£15
Variable overheads	£15	£15
Total	£90	£60
Total allocated fixed costs	£500,000	£1,200,000

Total fixed costs are absorbed into unit product cost on the basis of direct labour hours.

Applying the variable cost formula to the cost information in **Table 35:1** above we get:

$$\text{SYS01: mark-up} = \frac{£500,000 + 1,000,000}{50,000 \times £90} \times 100\% = 33.34\%$$

$$\text{SYS02: mark-up} = \frac{£1,200,000 + 1,000,000}{200,000 \times £60} \times 100\% = 18.34\%$$

Table 35:2 **Variable cost-based pricing at Systematik Ltd**

	Product	
	SYS01 *(£)*	*SYS02* *(£)*
Unit variable cost	90	60
Profit mark-up	30	11
Selling price	120	71

For short-term decisions such as accepting a special order when Systematik Ltd has spare production capacity, the prices calculated above are not very useful as they include irrelevant fixed cost items. Instead, minimum prices could be set equal to the incremental costs of £90 and £60 for additional units of SYS01 and SYS02 respectively.

35:5.2 Absorption Costing Approach

Price = all costs + profit mark-up

i.e.   mark-up = $\dfrac{\text{profit margin}}{\text{Output} \times \text{unit full cost}} \times 100\%$

Using the cost information in **Table 35:1** above we can calculate the following:

Total labour hours: (2.5 hours x 50,000) + (1.5 hours x 200,000) = 425,000 hours

Fixed overhead cost absorption rate = $\dfrac{£1,700,000}{425,000}$ = £4 per direct labour hour

Fixed overheads for: SYS01 = £4 x (2.5 x 50,000) = £500,000
SYS02 = £4 x (1.5 x 200,000) = £1,200,000

Assuming no other fixed costs, the profit mark-ups are:

SYS01: mark-up = $\dfrac{1,000,000}{50,000 \times £100} \times 100\% = 20\%$

SYS02: mark-up = $\dfrac{1,000,000}{200,000 \times £66} \times 100\% = 7.58\%$

Table 35:3 **Absorption cost-based pricing at Systematik Ltd**

	Product	
	SYS01	SYS02
	(£)	(£)
Unit variable cost	90	60
Unit fixed cost	10	6
Total cost	100	66
Profit mark-up	20	5
Selling price	120	71

35:5.3 Absorption Costing in Pricing Health Care Services

A special application of absorption costing is the 'top-down' method of pricing health care packages in the National Health Service (NHS) introduced with the creation of the internal quasi market in 1991 which requires that:

(a) *in charging fund-holding purchasers, providers (hospitals) must equate price to full cost. Full cost consists of direct costs (e.g. labour and materials), indirect costs (e.g. recharges) and overhead costs (e.g. support services). The guidelines further require analysing costs into variable, fixed and semi-fixed categories at specialty level and if possible at subspecialty or procedure level;*

(b) *costs include depreciation at current cost and a notional 6% return on assets;*

(c) *indirect and overhead costs are apportioned using the most appropriate bases;*

(d) *no planned cross-subsidisation is allowed between services.*

Under the top-down costing approach, total budget costs are 'cascaded down' to specialties, using the 'most appropriate' bases of apportionment or measures of activity. Specialty costs are then charged to procedures. This is illustrated in **Figure 35:1** where:

(a) *overhead department costs (e.g. salary of chief executive, maintenance costs, energy costs, building depreciation) are allocated to diagnostic services and patient care departments (boxes 2 and 3);*

(b) *the costs of diagnostics and patient care services are then apportioned to specialties (boxes 4, 5 and 6). Ideally diagnostic service costs should be allocated to patient care services first to have more cost traceability and accuracy;*

(c) *finally specialty costs are then split to give a cost per procedure.*

Relevant legislation is found in the National Health Service and Community Act 1990 and the National Health Service Regulations (1992 on Pharmaceutical Services and 1997 on Indicative Amounts). Under the auspices of the relevant Prescription Pricing Authority, the regulations indicate how basic prices of drugs, medicines and listed appliances should be calculated. The sale of branded pharmaceutical products to the NHS is regulated by the Pharmaceutical Price Regulation Scheme (PPRS) 1993. Under PPRS, pharmaceutical companies negotiate prices which guarantee them target levels of return on capital employed, taking into account research and development costs which are usually high.

Figure 35:1 **Top-down costing at Somewhere NHS Trust**

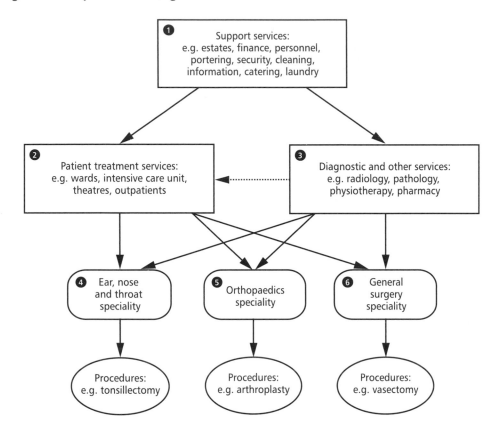

35:6 Key Problems with Cost-based Pricing and Possible Remedies

Despite the fact that product costs are widely used in product pricing by manufacturing companies and are compulsory for health care contracts and for some contracts with the Ministry of Defence, selling prices determined in this way may be very inaccurate and devoid of any theoretical justification. Because they may ignore demand and competition, cost-based prices may result in lost sales if they are set too high, or lost profits if set too low. Maybe one argument that speaks loudly in favour of market-based prices is that, while cost information is usually anchored in the past, useful as it is for financial reporting, pricing decisions are forward-looking and need information of the same nature. Economic efficiency is central to good pricing as is exemplified by the new regime of non-military spectrum pricing in the UK. The Wireless Telegraphy Act 1998 has abolished the previous cost recovery system based on administrative costs which encouraged hoarding and inefficient use of spectrum by large users and disadvantaged small licensees. By using derived market values to determine spectrum prices, the new pricing system aims at achieving allocative efficiency of a finite resource. Specific problems that taint the usefulness of product cost information for pricing are highlighted below.

35:6.1 Product Design Problems
(*See* **Ch.42.**)

The more unnecessarily complex the design of a product, the more consumption of resources, the longer the production cycle time, the more the cost and the higher the cost-based price. Design simplification with positive effects on product quality and functionality can reduce resource consumption and cost, add value and increase demand. In some cases, this may not be possible without investing in state-of-the-art technology.

For health care services, the equivalent to product design is clinical practice. For example, allowing minor operations to be performed by qualified GPs in their practices can shorten waiting lists and change cost profiles. The reduction of cost and price is also possible by switching certain types of surgery (e.g. cataract and varicose veins operations) to a day case basis. This reduces hospital stay and frees resources and such savings can then be passed on to the purchaser through reduced contract prices. The number of clinical procedures involved in outpatient and inpatient services affect treatment cost, and changing clinical procedure by adopting advances in medical research and technology can simplify treatment, reduce costs and contract prices. However, cost reduction through technological change may not be an option given the current financing arrangements and uncertainties about how to manage the NHS. In the main, better cost-based pricing is possible through cost management where the adage 'the way we do things here' is questioned and alternative ways for positive change are continually sought and tried. Some NHS Trusts have undertaken process re-engineering projects to enable them to reduce costs and create a climate of continuous improvement in patient care. Embedded practices, as explained below, are not always the best.

35:6.2 Normalised Process Inefficiencies

The 'normalisation' of process inefficiencies is done through setting standard costs during the budgetary process. It is not uncommon to find that organisations operate with 'acceptable' levels of wastage and defects which they factor into budget standards of cost such as raw materials and labour. Such inefficiencies are non-value-added activities which consume scarce resources and add to the product cost, but the irony is that attaining those standards becomes commendable performance which may bestow rewards. More ironic is that not only are the inefficiencies also factored into the cost-based selling price and passed on to the customer, but the company allows itself to earn a profit margin on them. Thus not only externalities are created, but the artificiality of the profit mark-ups and related incentives also creates social costs and raises ethical questions. The simple example in **Table 35:4** below illustrates the above points, assuming a process with 10% 'normalised' wastage of direct materials and labour.

Table 35:4 **True value-added pricing**

	Product X	
Cost information	*Cost and price inclusive of 10% wastage*	*Cost and price net of wastage*
	(£)	*(£)*
Direct materials	8.00	7.20
Direct labour	4.00	3.60
Overheads @ 200% of direct labour cost	8.00	7.20
Total cost per unit	20.00	18.00
50% profit mark-up	10.00	9.00
Selling price	30.00	27.00

Eliminating the inefficiencies reduces product cost by 10% and allows the company to be more price competitive by passing on savings to the customer through a reduced price of £27. Additional savings are possible as the company will need less quantities of input, less storage space and, therefore, less financing costs of balance sheet items. Allocative and productive efficiencies are possible by implementing some of the 'novel' cost management techniques described in this Handbook such as value chain analysis (*see* **Ch.40**), activity-based management (*see* **Ch.28**), quality management (*see* **Ch.18**), business process re-engineering (*see* **Ch.32**) and target costing (*see* **Ch.24**).

35:6.3 Squeezed Profit Margins

Profit mark-ups do not necessarily reflect market realities as they may be very arbitrarily set and changed. For example empirical research has consistently shown that managers in the UK tend to overestimate the cost of capital (i.e. the desired return on capital investments) because of ignorance of capital structure and financing costs, being naturally too averse to risk and less entrepreneurial, and wanting to satisfy a rigid performance evaluation system. If the desired profit margin included in the selling price is based on an exaggerated desired return, the selling price is unjustifiably high.

One way of overcoming this is by relating profit mark-ups to demand conditions for different products and markets. By analysing data on price-demand relationships for a particular product, a marketing manager can establish whether demand is inelastic and then calculate higher profit mark-ups when this is the case.

35:6.4 Cost Misclassifications

As product costing involves subjective assessment of cost behaviour, prices may be altered by artificial relabelling of costs into variable, fixed, direct or indirect. For example, a manager under pressure to increase capacity usage, sales and profits, may only be able to do so by selling additional output at a reduced price, say variable cost plus mark-up. Relabelling some costs as variable allows a better than normal contribution margin. Disparities observed between NHS Trusts in costing health-care products may be more indicative of choice of accounting method and costing assumptions therein rather than differences in clinical activity and quality. Some progress in costing health provision has however been achieved since the introduction of the internal market. Health-care providers must disclose costs in the various categories of variable, fixed, direct, indirect, overhead, pay and non-pay.

A possible way forward is the introduction of compulsory cost accounting standards (e.g. Statement 4: Managerial Cost Accounting Concepts and Standards for the Federal Government. 31 July 1995, FASB, USA). In contracting with the US Government, companies are required to demonstrate uniformity and consistency in measuring, assigning and allocating of costs to contracts. For this purpose, the Cost Accounting Standards Board (CASB) was established within the Office of Federal Procurement Policy. CASB reports annually to Congress and has the exclusive authority to make, enforce, amend and repeal cost accounting standards. Once promulgated, the standards become mandatory for use by all government executive agencies and by contractors and subcontractors 'in estimating, accumulating, and reporting costs in connection with pricing and administration of, and settlement of disputes concerning, all negotiated prime contract and subcontract procurement with the US in excess of $500,000'. Moreover, contractors and subcontractors 'must disclose in writing their cost accounting practices, including methods of distinguishing direct costs from indirect costs and the basis used for allocating indirect costs'. They must also 'agree to a contract price adjustment, with interest, for any increased costs paid to such contractor or subcontractor by the US by reason of a change in the contractor's or subcontractor's cost accounting practices or by reason of a failure by the contractor or subcontractor to comply with applicable cost accounting standards'.

35:6.5 Arbitrary cost allocations

Full costs, and by the same token selling prices, carry arbitrarily allocated indirect or overhead costs. In modern, less labour-intensive manufacturing companies, a high proportion of product costs come from cost allocation rather than direct cost elements. Prices derived from fully allocated costs do not necessarily reflect efficient operating conditions. The problem is more serious in companies with diverse products with differing claims on the activities that incur the indirect costs. The problem of arbitrary cost allocations is the major deficiency of traditional cost accounting systems. The inclusion of 'sunk costs' such as depreciation charges of already acquired fixed assets in the calculation of prices is also questionable. Moreover, the subjectivity inherent in assessing cost behaviour can result in wrongly classifying costs into variable, fixed, direct or indirect categories. Poor cost information leads to setting poor selling prices and making poor cost-based decisions such as subcontracting or discontinuing apparently costly products. Plausible alternatives include:

(a) *Activity-based costing or ABC (see **Ch.22**) which, to some extent, does alleviate the arbitrariness problem through multiple cost allocation bases. By simply changing the assumptions about overhead cost incidence and the use of multiple cost drivers, ABC exposes product complexity and shifts overhead cost from the standard high-volume product to the more complex low-volume product, resulting in more overhead costs per unit for the latter. Cost-based prices need to be adjusted accordingly, with more room for manoeuvre for pricing standard high-volume products.*

(b) *A possible improvement in pricing health care contracts is by using a 'bottom–up' approach which builds cost profiles up from the various activities within a specialty. This has been refined further by the recent development of nationally agreed Health Resource Groups (HRGs) in the UK. HRGs group together clinically similar procedures which consume resources in similar amounts. Examples of HRG text labels for orthopaedics are 'congenital hip dislocation', 'hand procedures', 'tendon and muscle procedures', and 'primary knee replacements'. HRGs may be likened to cost tables (see Ch.26) and, once fully developed for all specialties, they should result in more accurate costs and prices.*

(c) *Long-run average incremental cost of output based on current valuation of assets plus appropriate mark-ups for common costs. OFTEL recommends this approach for interconnection charging by British Telecom and for pricing of telecoms services in general. Being based on current asset values, prices derived in this way have the advantage of informing future investment decisions. They can also be used, in line with EU guidelines, to determine whether an operator is practising predatory pricing to eliminate competitors. Prices below average variable costs are generally presumed predatory.*

35:6.6 Customers' Perceptions of Product Value

As product cost can be fraught with imperfections, cost-based pricing should include some measurement of the customer's perception of value. Functional cost analysis and cost tables can facilitate conjoint measurement of the functions of the product with respect to the utility the customer perceives in using the product to satisfy needs. In the conjoint measurement exercise values are attached to functions. These values can then be used, in addition to cost information, to set the selling price that would please all parties to the transaction.

To create customer value, cost-based pricing can also benefit from supplier development programmes whereby customers intervene in the supplier's operations to provoke process change which eventually leads to cost reductions. Not only do these programmes act as a catalyst of change, they also help narrow the gap between varying perceptions and reduce product cost. The company cannot afford to ignore constructive views from its customers to overcome complacency and inefficient practices and legitimise positive change. Supplier development programmes usually identify areas for improvement to better current product quality, delivery performance and reduce costs by a set percentage at a time.

35:7 Conclusions

The foregoing analyses have shown that pricing decisions are critical and complex for both manufacturing and non-manufacturing organisations. Pricing decisions can determine the success or failure of products and affect profits and cash flows. Managing product prices is managing an entire process which involves inextricable internal and external factors. The complexity of the pricing decision transcends single rules of thumb or cost plus formulae and requires a balanced approach which combines cost and market information, including the customer's perception of value and finding the right trade-off between the various internal and external variables involved in the pricing process.

36. Transfer Pricing

36:1 Introduction

Transfer pricing is one of the most emotionally and politically charged contemporary business concerns and has proven elusive and intractable to both academics and practitioners, especially when it involves cross-border intra-firm trade. It remains elusive because of its business sensitivity and the fact that little is known about company practice, in particular what determines the pricing policies for specific transactions. Many products in many companies are made in different international locations and this results in substantial cross-border intra-firm activity currently estimated at one-third of world trade, making transfer pricing the most significant international tax issue for multinational companies. This chapter examines the main issues involved in intra-firm trade and pricing in the light of the most recent theoretical and empirical developments.

36:1.1 Definitions

Transfer prices can be defined as the prices charged for products exchanged in internal transactions between sellers (or transferors) and buyers (or transferees) who belong to the same organisation, usually a decentralised company. Prices can be cost or market-based (*see* **Ch.35, paras 35:4.2** and **35:5**). Name variants include internal prices, internal charges, recharges, and charge-backs. Transfer prices come also in the disguise of management fees, royalties and finance costs. Examples of transferred products include raw materials and primary products such as ore and plastic granules, components and subassemblies, as well as finished manufactured products, data processing, a funds transfer in a bank and a pathology test in a hospital. A transfer-pricing system (henceforth TPS) consists of the set of transfer prices, tacit agreements and written policies that regulate internal transactions.

An early exposure draft (*ED45: Segmental Reporting*) which preceded the standard *SSAP Segmental Reporting*, proposed that the basis of transfer pricing be disclosed. The subsequent standard dropped this requirement as it was thought that this could be prejudicial, or generally unhelpful. However, *IAS14: Segment Reporting* lists, as a required disclosure, the basis of pricing inter-segment transfers and any change therein.

Messaoud Mehafdi

36:1.2 Domestic Versus Multinational Internal Markets

Transfer pricing can only exist if a company 'sells to' and 'buys from' itself. Depending on the geographical location of a company's business activities, internal transactions can be 'domestic' or 'international'. Domestic transfer pricing takes place within an organisation in its home country, whereas international transfer pricing is more contentious because it involves at least two different countries and tax jurisdictions. Recent evidence shows that a substantial share of the activities of multinational companies consists of cross-border intra-firm transfers of tangible and intangible products.

36:1.3 The Transfer-pricing Process

Similar to the external pricing discussed in **Chapter 35**, transfer pricing is an integrated and complex process through which internal prices are set, requiring informed judgements based on internal and external information. Price is only one element in this process. The Inland Revenue defines transfer pricing as 'the process by which members of a group set the prices at which they pass goods, services, finance, and intangible assets between each other' (*Modernisation of the Transfer Pricing Legislation: Outcome of Consultations,* 17 March 1998, Inland Revenue). Because transfer pricing has been and is expected to remain a complex and contentious management and tax problem, it requires managers to address the entire process through which prices are established, starting with plausible justifications (strategic or otherwise) for internalising trade. In the transfer-pricing process, cost and market-based prices apply to both types of market, but with different sets of factors affecting the intra-firm transaction and its pricing.

36:2 Contextual Variables

The results of existing empirical research so far show that there is no one universal transfer-pricing formula and there is no need to search for one. Companies use a variety of cost and market-based transfer prices and the international 'arm's length' principle recognises the impossibility and impracticality of confining the pricing of international intra-firm transactions to any one formula. The transfer-pricing problem is context-bound and the search for 'correct' transfer policies depends on the specificities of the context within which the internal transaction takes place and requires a multi-disciplinary approach. Although the transaction, the seller and the buyer are all internal to the organisation, the variables involved in the transfer-pricing activity are both internal and external as explained below.

36:2.1 Endogenous Variables

Modern transfer pricing is identified with companies with decentralised managerial structures and internalised markets such as the one depicted in **Figure 36:1**. In their strategic pursuit of better efficiency and the circumvention of uncertainty, large manufacturing companies throughout this century adopted the multi-divisional structure combined with varying degrees of decentralised management and, in many cases, vertical integration. Ideally, divisions should be distinguishable autonomous economic entities with clear organisational demarcation lines, homogenous activities, allocated resources and separable responsibilities for outcomes. However such an ideal is nowadays difficult to find as internal markets are more the norm than the exception in large companies, especially multinationals, and it is the selling and buying activities to and from divisions that create the transfer-pricing problem which blurs divisional demarcation lines.

The degree of autonomy a divisional manager has on all aspects of the transfer-pricing transaction is therefore crucial in the conduct of intra-firm trade. Hence, for the management of the hypothetical company Metalik International plc (henceforth MIP), the following elements of structure and strategy are central to the transfer-pricing process:

(a) *organisational structure and managerial hierarchy (real versus pseudo decentralised divisions A, B, C & D; degree of divisional autonomy and accountability);*

(b) *leadership style (authoritarian versus participatory; praise versus blame culture);*

(c) *desirable degree of vertical integration or disintegration (magnitude of intra-firm trade for MIP and each of the four divisions; sequence of production flow);*

(d) *make or buy decisions (product and market diversification, core versus non-core activities, outsourcing advantages, strategic internalisation and competitive position);*

(e) *output, productivity, economic growth objectives and resource allocations policies (MIP and each division);*

(f) *type of transferred product (raw material, intermediate, final, intangible);*

(g) *nature and importance of the transferred product (e.g. new, mature, standard, idiosyncratic, technologically and commercially sensitive);*

(h) *capital investment requirements (see Ch.11) of intra-firm trade (risk sharing and transferor's ability to recoup investment through TPS);*

(i) *process efficiency (technology, production norms, delivery time, spare capacity);*

(j) *final product considerations (price and quality of Division C's products);*

(k) *conflicting objectives of the TPS (financial and non-financial, divisional versus corporate; short versus long term; conflict resolution procedures);*

Figure 36:1 **Transfer-pricing linkages for a multinational aluminium company**

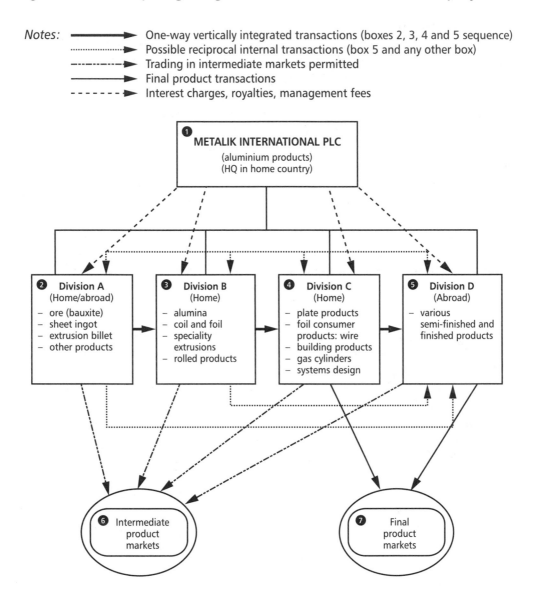

Notes:
⟶ One-way vertically integrated transactions (boxes 2, 3, 4 and 5 sequence)
┈┈┈▶ Possible reciprocal internal transactions (box 5 and any other box)
┈┈─┈▶ Trading in intermediate markets permitted
⟶ Final product transactions
┈┈┈┈▶ Interest charges, royalties, management fees

❶ **METALIK INTERNATIONAL PLC**
(aluminium products)
(HQ in home country)

❷ **Division A**
(Home/abroad)
– ore (bauxite)
– sheet ingot
– extrusion billet
– other products

❸ **Division B**
(Home)
– alumina
– coil and foil
– speciality
  extrusions
– rolled products

❹ **Division C**
(Home)
– plate products
– foil consumer
  products: wire
– building products
– gas cylinders
– systems design

❺ **Division D**
(Abroad)
– various
  semi-finished and
  finished products

❻ Intermediate
product
markets

❼ Final
product
markets

(l) divisional managers (previous experience with intra-firm transactions; entrepreneurial and negotiation skills; availability and manipulation of asymmetrical information; performance management system; results sharing);

(m) intermediate product costing system (information accuracy, reliability and timeliness; activity-based costs).

36:2.2 Exogenous Variables

A manufacturing company such as MIP may justify intra-firm trade on the basis that it has special skills at organising the production and marketing of certain products. Intra-firm trade is now recognised as a key determinant of multinational business activity and is valued at billions of US dollars. In addition to the internal variables listed above, external factors need also to be admitted to the transfer-pricing equation, especially when intra-firm trade crosses national frontiers. These include:

(a) the existence of reliable intermediate product markets (for both buying and selling divisions A, B, C & D);

(b) degree of (imperfect) competition in the intermediate markets;

(c) policies on and incentives for foreign direct investment (relationship with host governments, joint-venture opportunities, tax advantages, wage negotiation);

(d) company's earnings management strategy and global profit positioning;

(e) international fiscal regimes (tax rates, rules on profit repatriation, double taxation);

(f) international transfer-pricing legislation (e.g. IRS, OECD, Inland Revenue, EU);

(g) environmental (see Ch.34) and ethical considerations (dumping, tax evasion and earnings management, corporate governance, moral and social responsibility);

(h) European Monetary Union as the euro is expected to have a direct effect on TPS by eliminating currency differences, making prices more comparable, and facilitating tax audits;

(i) special rules when contracting with governments (e.g. the costing and pricing rules of the Cost Accounting Standards Board in the US cover the 'transfer of commercial items between divisions, subsidiaries, or affiliates of a contractor or subcontractor' as part of 'the standards governing measurement, assignment and allocation of costs to contracts with the United States' (Office of Federal Procurement Policy, Public Contracts Chapter 7, Sec. 422).

36:3 Accounting Aspects of Transfer Pricing
(*See* **Ch.48, para.48:5.3.**)

In contrast to a cost allocation system which makes users of a service share its costs, a TPS is an internal market mechanism used for sharing costs, revenues and profits. In this respect, various internal trade combinations can be envisaged in a divisionalised company, depending on the organisational definition of the selling unit (or transferor) and the buying unit (or transferee):

(a) a cost centre selling to a cost centre (e.g. IT to maintenance);
(b) a cost centre selling to a revenue centre (e.g. maintenance to distribution division);
(c) a cost centre selling to a profit/investment centre (e.g. IT to operating division);
(d) a profit centre selling to a cost centre (e.g. IT to maintenance);
(e) a profit centre selling to a revenue centre (e.g. operating division to distribution);
(f) a profit centre selling to a profit/investment centre (e.g. two operating divisions).

In any of the combinations outlined above, a transfer price is a revenue for the transferor and a cost for the transferee, thus affecting their financial results in opposite ways but not necessarily in the same financial amount (*see* **Ch.40, para.40:2.3**). Naturally, an 'autonomous' and financially accountable transferor would want the highest price to maximise revenue and profit, whereas the transferee would want the lowest price to minimise costs. Transfer pricing involving profit and investment centres is the most delicate of the combinations because transfer prices would figure in divisional accounts and be part and parcel of the profit performance evaluation package (*see* **Chs 48** and **49**).

36:3.1 Transfer-pricing Formulae

Many formulae have been suggested for pricing internal transactions but, similar to external prices, transfer prices are either cost-based or market-based, the latter being more theoretically justified than the former. Existing empirical evidence from across the globe shows that companies use a multitude of cost and market-based prices but it is still not clear why a particular method prevails. When the intermediate product does not have a market outside the company, a pricing formula can only be based on product costs. In this case, the transfer price is not externally verifiable and can create all sorts of problems if:

(a) the transfer price is imposed on the transferee division (i.e. no negotiation allowed);

(b) the volume of transfers is significant and the transaction is repetitive (sometimes a division is set up solely to make and sell intermediate products to sister divisions);

(c) the transfer price is not high enough to recover the transferor's investment in specific assets, especially when the transferor is charged by the company the cost of capital used;

(d) the transferee is aware of the transferor's process inefficiencies which are factored into the transfer price and the transferee is not permitted to offset these against a higher final product price; and

(e) the transfer price is included in the financial performance evaluation of divisions.

Existing research has consistently revealed that companies throughout the world widely use full cost-based transfer prices even when market prices exist. In this case an unhappy transferor or transferee can always 'fight' for a fairer deal if a market price is perceived as such. Fairness also depends on whether trading in the intermediate market is fettered or not and whether the terms of the internal transaction (price, volume, etc.) can be negotiated. The deficiencies of cost-based pricing discussed in **Chapter 35, paragraph 35:6** also apply to transfer prices if these are based on cost, except that in this case the buying division, as an internal customer, may not be able to switch to cheaper external suppliers if the internal trade is controlled by central management or an intermediate market does not exist. Equally applicable here also are the suggestions made in **Chapter 35** to alleviate the deficiencies of traditional costing, namely through improved product design and better cost-management systems.

36:3.2 Financial Reporting

While the transfer-pricing information may be included in divisional performance reports as part of the management control system, it is uncommon for published consolidated financial statements of companies to divulge transfer-pricing information. At best, an audited profit and loss statement mentions that '*turnover is net of intra-group sales at arm's length prices*' but will probably end up catching the suspicious eye of the tax man despite the auditor's 'true-and-fair-view' seal of approval.

Transfer pricing has always been regarded as belonging to the domain of management accounting which, unlike financial accounting, is generally not regulated. Neither SSAP 25 (*Segmental reporting*, ASB, June 1990) in the UK nor FAS 131 (*Disclosures about segments of an enterprise and related information*, FASB, June 1997) in the US compelled companies to reveal their inter-segment pricing policies. The ASB's consultations with businesses resulted in no desired wish from the latter to change or replace SSAP 25 in a way that would make it compulsory on companies to disclose transfer-pricing information. It will be interesting to see how long this will remain so now that the Inland Revenue's overhaul of the UK transfer-pricing rules has been completed and the new legislation enforced. In the US, FAS 131 does not require companies to disclose transfer-pricing information, although disclosure is required on resource allocation to, and performance evaluation of, a company's constituent segments; and, as we have seen, *IAS14* has now made disclosure a requirement for those adopting international standards (*see* **para.36:1.1**). Resource allocation and performance evaluation are almost inseparable from the functions and workings of a company's TPS.

In its *Guidelines for Multinational Enterprises* the Organisation for Economic Cooperation and Development (OECD, 1976, revised 1991) provided only a voluntary code of conduct which states that companies should publish 'the policies followed in respect of intra-group pricing' and should refrain from using transfer pricing 'which does not conform to an arm's length standard, for modifying in ways contrary to national laws the tax base on which members of the group are assessed'. In compiling balance-of-payments statistics, countries are now required by the International Monetary Fund (IMF, Balance of Payments Manual, 5th edition, 1993) to show the amounts of intra-firm transactions and reinvested earnings. Of particular relevance to transfer pricing are paragraphs 91–106 of Chapter V 'Valuation of transactions' (pp. 26–28 of the Manual) which sets out arm's length guidelines for internal pricing. According to recent research by the World Trade Organisation (WTO) and a joint IMF/OECD 1997 survey, neither intra-firm trade nor reinvested earnings are reported by some countries, including G7 countries, despite the new IMF international guidelines.

The absence of stringent financial reporting regulation does not, however, prevent the careful analyst from closely scrutinising the published accounts of multinational companies to detect anomalies which might indicate heavy misuse of transfer prices to minimise taxable profits in host countries. The typical 'window dressing' in the segmental reports is a high turnover figure but little or no taxable profit in the host country and the reverse in the home country. High transfer prices offset the high turnover in the host country, and the profit is 'repatriated' to the home country where it is taxed. Many multinational companies have been in the spotlight in the US, the UK and elsewhere because of such reporting anomalies, some ending up paying huge sums in back taxes and hefty fines for tax evasion. Details of pending court cases in the US, including the names of the companies involved, are published by the Bureau of National Affairs (BNA) in its bi-weekly *Tax Management: Transfer Pricing*.

36:4 Transfer-pricing Manipulations

The main reason why transfer pricing has become the most significant international tax issue for transnational corporations (TNCs) is easy to gauge. Fiscal authorities have learnt not to put too much faith in the financial statements of foreign-controlled subsidiaries which, in many cases, they justifiably suspect of deliberate misuse of their TPS to avoid and evade taxation. By manipulating transfer prices, for example by misrepresenting the costs of imported inputs such as intermediate products, TNCs reduce their global tax bills by reducing the tax revenues of their host countries. In the wake of intensified international legislation, many TNCs have set up their own 'transfer-pricing teams' or enlisted the services of experts from leading accountancy firms to tackle the problem, map out tax plans, produce required documentation, ensure compliance with legislation, assess all possible outcomes of current TPS, and avoid becoming a soft target of expensive, intrusive and tedious tax audits. Transfer-pricing job adverts have now started to appear in leading newspapers (e.g. *The Financial Times*).

36:4.1 Foreign Direct Investment and Intra-firm Trade

The international significance of transfer pricing is determined by the rapidly growing size of intra-firm trade. In the borderless world being shaped by globalisation TNCs account for around 70% of world trade and play a significant part in the economies of both host and home countries through foreign direct investment (FDI). The United Nations Conference on Trade and Development (UNCTAD), the WTO, the IMF and the OECD estimate that $1.6 trillion, or about one-third of current world trade in goods and services, takes place within TNCs. Intra-firm royalty payments and management fees exceed 70% (*The Financial Times*, October 1997). Short and long-term borrowing and lending of funds between TNCs and their affiliates is also increasingly recognised as a main category of FDI. The increasing significance of intra-firm trade is considered by the WTO as a strong indicator of the growing inseparability between global trade and investment with FDI reaching the unprecedented figures of $350 billion (annual flow) and $3.2 trillion (total existing amount or stock). Such is the importance of FDI that it has led to suggesting a new framework, the Multilateral Agreement on Investment (MAI) under the aegis of the OECD. Moreover, as OECD member countries account for around 85% of FDI outflows and 60% of inflows, statistics on intra-firm imports and exports are regularly compiled in the OECD's Activities of Foreign Affiliates database.

The amount of intra-firm trade for individual countries is also significant, with an IMF estimate of 50% of total trade for the UK and accounting for 40% of the US trade deficit. It is interesting to note that more than 40% of US imports were intra-firm in the early 1990s (*The Financial Times*, 1 October 1997). For industrial sectors, OECD 1996 statistics show that intra-firm trade as a percent of total trade is 70% for pharmaceuticals and semi-conductors, between 50–80% for computers and motor vehicles and 30–50% for consumer electronics and non-ferrous metals. Percentages are also high for individual companies. For example, two-thirds of Nissan's sales in Europe are sourced from Nissan's European production plants, mainly UK and Spain. In Singapore, more than 80% of Compaq Computers' output goes to sister plants in other countries (*Singapore Business Times*, 18 November 1997).

36:4.2 Forms of Transfer-pricing Manipulation

An MNC can manipulate transfer pricing for tax advantages by:

(a) *manipulating the cost of imported inputs by setting higher than market transfer prices for intermediate products;*

(b) *charging higher than market interest charges for inter-corporate debt to take advantage of differential tax treatments of debt finance. This is known as 'thin' capitalisation when the internally borrowed funds are disproportionately higher than the equity base. As debt finance brings tax relief, companies can shift tax liabilities from high- to low-tax countries by manipulating the transfer pricing of loans to and from countries with different corporate income tax rates such as EU countries. Interest-free loans between a UK resident company to a non-resident associated company are not immune from tax audits. The ruling of the Inland Revenue Special Commissioners is that corporation tax assessments may be raised after imputing interest;*

(c) *charging higher-than-market royalty fees for the use of the company's technological know-how and intellectual property (e.g. patents, formulae, licences, etc.);*

(d) *charging 'management fees' over and above market rates.*

Some managers the author has spoken to in the UK and France see these transfer-pricing activities as 'legitimate business opportunities' in a free market economy, rather than objectionable and unethical practices that should attract the wrath of the tax man.

36:4:3 Reasons for and Extent of Transfer-pricing Manipulations

A multinational company may try, but not necessarily succeed, to use transfer pricing to:

(a) *reduce its global tax bill;*
(b) *maximise flexibility of funds movement and avoid limits on profit remittances;*
(c) *get the lion's share in a joint venture (proportionate share ownership of profits);*
(d) *disguise an 'imperialist exploitation' image;*
(e) *protect knowledge advantage.*

Tax authorities become concerned and suspicious when only a few of the many successful companies operating in their fiscal territory file taxable profits. The extent of transfer-pricing litigations can be gleaned from the following statistics.

(a) *The total amount of transfer-pricing taxes and penalties currently at issue in the US Tax Court alone exceeds $4 billion (Houston Business Journal, 3 February 1997).*
(b) *An estimated $4.4 billion was 'repatriated' from India to the US during 1993 through under-invoiced exports and over-invoiced imports in a total trade worth $7.3 billion (a Florida International University study).*
(c) *In the Houston area alone the investigation of 25 companies in 1996 resulted in $427 million in additional taxes and penalties (Houston Business Journal, 3 February 1997).*
(d) *A $1 million fine was imposed on Morgan Stanley & Co. by the Market Regulation Committee of the National Association of Securities Dealers (NASD, 13 April 1998) for manipulating the price of ten securities that underlie the NASDAQ 100 Index. The price manipulation involved intra-firm dealings between the company's OTC Desk and its Program Trading Desk to lock and cross markets.*
(e) *The Financial Times (24 September 1998) reported that an unidentified company settled a £1 billion transfer-pricing adjustment in a one-off payment to the Inland Revenue.*

36:4.4 International Transfer-pricing Legislation

The purpose of the unabating international efforts, led by the US tax authority - the Internal Revenue Service (IRS), the Committee for Fiscal Affairs of the Paris-based

Organisation for Economic Co-operation and Development (OECD) and more recently the European Union, is to provide a world-wide consensus on the pricing of international intra-firm transactions and create maximum transparency. The OECD guidelines contained in Transfer pricing guidelines for multinational enterprises and tax administrations (OECD, Paris, 1995) have prompted fiscal authorities in many countries to follow suit in their attempt to prevent and curtail transfer-pricing abuses. These guidelines are seen by some as an attempt to soften the rather tough stance taken by the US and to bring about a desirable compromise.

In the UK, the following Acts of Parliament deal with international transfer-pricing issues:

(a) *the Income and Corporation Taxes Act 1988, Schedule 28AA: Transfer Pricing (para.6), sections 770–773: Transfer Pricing Provisions;*
(b) *the Finance Act 1998, Ch.36. Schedule 16: Transfer Pricing, etc.: New Regime. Schedule 17: Controlled Foreign Companies.* This has now been superseded by the Finance (No.2) Act 2005 where, in Section 40 and Schedule 8, changes were made to the transfer pricing rules and certain loan relationship rules.

The adoption of the OECD model in the UK has coincided with the introduction of the self-assessment tax framework for companies. Following Budget announcements by the Chancellor of the Exchequer, the Inland Revenue published a comprehensive consultative document or Condoc (Modernisation of the Transfer Pricing Legislation, 9 October 1997) which drew profusely on the OECD guidelines to formulate the proposed changes to the existing legislation. Except for specific queries and some reservations (e.g. by finance directors from the 100 Group on compliance costs and the timing of implementation with the new millennium), the new legislation has generally been hailed as a positive move by members of the business community who participated in the consultation rounds and responded to the Condoc.

There is general acceptance on four key points:

1. *aligning UK transfer-pricing legislation with the OECD guidelines;*
2. *bringing the new transfer-pricing legislation within the new self-assessment framework for accounting periods ending on or after 1 July 1999 (see the latest Finance (No.2) Act 2005 for detail);*
3. *introducing refinements to minimise compliance costs;*
4. *continuing with the Inland Revenue's central monitoring of transfer-pricing enquiries.*

In sum, the search for international legislative consensus in transfer-pricing regulation aims at protecting national tax revenue and revolves around:

(a) *the arm's length principle which is the agreed international standard governing related party cross-border transactions, using one of three primary methods:*
 1. *comparable uncontrolled price method (which uses externally verified prices of similar transactions involving unrelated parties);*
 2. *the resale price method (which deducts a certain percentage from the selling price of the final product to allow for profit);*
 3. *the cost plus method (which marks up the producer's cost to find the price);*
(b) *cost contribution arrangements (CCAs): CCAs provide for the sharing of costs and risks involved in developing, making or obtaining services and manufactured products;*
(c) *advance pricing agreements (APAs) which have originated in the US as an alternative to 'intrusive' and expensive tax audits by fiscal authorities. An APA enables a multinational company, particularly if it operates in the US, to negotiate an agreement with one tax jurisdiction (unilateral APA) or more tax jurisdictions (multilateral APA), in advance of cross-border internal transactions, about transfer prices over a specified period. Although the respondents to the Inland Revenue's Condoc expressed a lot of interest in and support for unilateral APAs, the new legislation does not make APAs obligatory and further consultations are needed ahead of the next Finance Bill for developing acceptable APA procedures. One reservation about APAs is that they may trigger undesirable audits of prior years by ever-suspecting and scrutinising tax authorities;*
(d) *enforcement of the above rules through transfer price adjustments and fines when it is established that there is failure to conform with the regulations and there is tax evasion;*
(e) *double taxation. In the European Union this is now dealt with in the EU's unprecedented transfer-pricing arbitration convention which went into effect between many member states in January 1995 and is expected to remain in force until the end of 1999. As no cases have been reported since the convention took effect, the UN's Group of Experts on International Co-operation in Tax Matters backed off from a suggestion to set up a multinational arbitration framework for resolving transfer-pricing issues (UN E/1998/57, 26 May).*

In any case, keeping contemporaneous documentation detailing and supporting transfer-pricing policies in use and comparables with competitors is essential to prove there is compliance with the requirements of the tax jurisdiction in case a fiscal probe is instigated. Compliance with documentation requirements reduces the risk of intrusive tax audits and hefty penalties. Even with such documentation made available, there is no limit to how far back into time an enquiry is taken by doubting fiscal authorities. For example, Glaxo-Wellcome lost in the High Court when it tried to challenge the Inland Revenue over investigation procedures concerning transfer pricing. The court upheld the Inland Revenue's legal power to examine the company's tax affairs before June 1986. Landmark cases in the US where the arm's length methods listed in (a) and (b) above have been enforced and adjustments made to the taxable profits of the companies investigated are now accessible on the *Transfer Pricing Network* on the internet.

36:5 An Integrated Illustrative Example: Metalik International Plc (MIP)

Figure 36:1 depicts possible transfer-pricing linkages in a hypothetical multinational aluminium company which operates in a highly concentrated and competitive industrial sector. This example encapsulates the complexities of the transfer-pricing problem and demonstrates why it is not a simple exercise in accounting and pricing.

36:5.1 MIP's Domestic Transfer-pricing Issues

Internal transfers in this highly vertically integrated company include mined and refined bauxite (Division A to Division B); refined hydrated aluminium oxide or alumina (Division B to Division C), various semi-finished and finished aluminium products (Division C to Division D). Division A extracts the ore from a mine situated in another country and does the smelting and refining in its home country. The strategy of vertical integration dictates the flow of production from one division to another, with Division A's primary output transferred at a price to Division B which, after further processing, transfers to Division C, again at a price. Division C's various finished products are partly sold in the domestic markets. Therefore the main issues involved in the domestic scene are:

(a) *the organisational definition of each division (e.g. cost versus profit centre);*
(b) *the amount of Division A's investments to enable intra-firm trade to other divisions;*

(c) the mining, transportation, refining and smelting costs to Division A;

(d) the proportion of Division A's output that must be 'pushed' to Division B to comply with the company's strategy of vertical integration;

(e) whether Division A can satisfy all the requirements of Division B and whether the latter can buy from the intermediate markets (both domestic and international);

(f) the transfer price from Division A to Division B (cost versus market; concessions);

(g) how much of Division A's inefficiency costs are factored into the transfer price;

(h) other terms of the transaction, in addition to price, between Division A to Division B;

(i) whether Division B perceives real value created by Division A, paid for by the transfer price;

(j) how the transfer price affects the financial performance of each division;

(k) whether the company can resolve disagreements between Division A and Division B (does the company have arbitration procedures?);

(l) all the above points apply to internal transactions involving Divisions B, C and D.

36:5.2 MIP's International Transfer-pricing Issues

MIP's international transfer-pricing activity is mainly between Divisions C and D. Division D sells the transferred products to many important overseas customers. The main issues involved here are:

(a) extent of intra-firm trade between Division C and Division D;

(b) Division D operates in a foreign country and is subject to its tax laws;

(c) import-export regulations; foreign exchange controls and political risk;

(d) customs duties; freight and insurance costs;

(e) Division D's relationship with the host government;

(f) Division D's competitive position;

(g) management incentives and subsidiary performance evaluation;

(h) funds positioning and Division D's profit repatriation through the transfer price;

(i) legal and ethical issues.

Let us assume that a typical transfer-pricing activity from the parent company, MIP, to its overseas subsidiary, Division D, involves a semi-finished product which costs Division C £230 per unit to make and the arm's length or market price for similar products is £280. Division D resells the product for £450 per unit after minor customising work and repackaging costing £50. Assuming a corporate tax rate of 50% in the host country and 30% in the home country, we can envisage the following four scenarios to illustrate the international tax effects of transfer pricing.

Table 36:1 **Scenario 1: Metalik plc charges Division D a 'give and take' transfer price of £330**

	Division C (£)	Division D (£)	Metalik plc (£)
Selling price	330	450	450
Less – production cost	−230	−50	−280
– transferred cost		−330	
Taxable profit	100	70	170
Tax rate	0.3	0.5	
Tax to pay	−30	−35	−65
Net profit	70	35	105

If the company charged Division D a transfer price equal to the £280 market price, it would have to pay tax of £60 per unit sold which is £25 more than the £35 declared. The £25 differential is the additional profit denied the host government and repatriated home instead through the higher than market transfer price $(330–280) \times 0.5 = £25$ per unit.

Table 36:2 **Scenario 2: Metalik plc charges Division D a 'lion's share' transfer price of £380**

	Division C (£)	Division D (£)	Metalik plc (£)
Selling price	380	450	450
Less – production cost	−230	−50	−280
– transferred cost		−380	
Taxable profit	150	20	170
Tax rate	0.3	0.5	
Tax to pay	−45	−10	−55
Net profit	105	10	115

Although the company pays some tax on its income, it evades tax equal to the profit repatriated of $(380–280) \times 0.5 = £50$ per unit.

Table 36:3 **Scenario 3: Metalik plc charges Division D a 'profits come home' transfer price of £400**

	Division C	Division D	Metalik plc
	(£)	(£)	(£)
Selling price	400	450	450
Less – cost	–230	–50	–280
– transferred cost		–400	
Taxable profit	170	0	170
Tax rate	0.3	0.5	
Tax to pay	–51	–0	–51
Net profit	119	0	119

With a high transfer price of £400, the company pays no tax on its profitable activities in the host country, thus evading a total tax bill equal to the profit repatriated of (400–280) × 0.5 = £60 per unit.

Table 36:4 **Scenario 4: Metalik plc charges Division D a 'tax allowance' transfer price of £500**

	Division C	Division D	Metalik plc
	(£)	(£)	(£)
Selling price	500	450	450
Less – production cost	–230	–50	–280
– transferred cost		–500	
Taxable profit	270	–100	170
Tax rate	0.3	0.5	
Taxable pay refund	–81	50	–31
Net profit/(loss)	189	–50	139

In this extreme but not unusual case, not only does the company not file any taxable profit in the host country but it also claims a rebate as it reports losses. The total tax evaded is equal to the total profit repatriated = (500–280) × 0.5 = £110 per unit, that is, the sum of the rebate + original tax = £50 + £60 = £110 per unit.

36:6 Other Aspects of Intra-firm Trade and Transfer Pricing

Most of the extant theoretical and empirical research has so far focused on manufacturing companies, in particular their cross-border internal trade and the tax implications of transfer-pricing policies. Equally important areas that call for serious consideration are briefly outlined below.

36:6.1 Transfer Pricing in Service Organisations

Little is known about transfer pricing in the service industries, despite the fact that MNCs engage in intra-firm trade of services and intangibles. Transfer pricing is found in:

(a) *commercial banks and building societies where deposit-taking units trade funds with lending or mortgage units. Next to nothing is known here about the relationship between TPS, performance of deposit accounts and lending terms to borrowers;*

(b) *the National Health Service in the form of recharges since the introduction of the internal market and financial accountability. Little is known here about the TPS (recharges) and the cost of health care provision and contract pricing.*

36:6.2 Transfer Pricing and Value Creation

Companies need to examine their TPS not only in terms of international fiscal legislation, but also in terms of their effect on value creation, especially when the typical internal trade is materially significant (*see* **Ch.46, para.46:4.1**). This can help determine whether internal trade is at all justified in some cases and whether alternatives, such as discontinuing a product or outsourcing intermediate products and services should be pursued instead.

36:6.3 The Ethical and Environmental Dimensions

In addition to their obsession with tax issues, companies need to seriously consider the ethics as well as the environmental impact of their transfer-pricing activities. To this end, an ethical and environmental code of conduct is needed. As it did with the pricing guidelines since 1979, the OECD may spearhead such a global project in which tax authorities, MNCs and accounting firms could take an active part.

36:7 Conclusions

Transfer pricing is a topical business issue that continues to attract the attention of tax authorities throughout the world. This will gradually make transfer-pricing manipulation by MNCs difficult if not impossible, thus thwarting tax evasion plans. At best transfer pricing is a 'necessary evil' that serves conflicting objectives whether for domestic or international intra-firm transactions. Formulating adequate transfer-pricing policies depends on many contextual variables, some financial and quantitative, others strategic, qualitative, managerial and behavioural. No one 'cure-all' magical formula exists to fit all situations and companies can at best formulate imperfect solutions to a complex and intractable problem.

37. **Shareholder Value in Practice**

How can the principles of value creation be incorporated into a methodology for running a business? Although the title 'shareholder value' implies a technique for FTSE plcs, the principles of managing for value are equally relevant in private companies. The approach to managing is also known as value-based management.

37:1 Overview – What Is Shareholder Value?

Is shareholder value just another fad that management will have to adopt and then discard five years later? The short answer to this is no: shareholder value is founded on the facts of economic life as they confront corporations today. If they are to be successful, companies cannot ignore these facts.

Shareholder value is a proposal to change the fundamental basis on which businesses are managed. It starts with a long-established cultural assumption that the providers of capital, individuals or collective funds, have a free choice about where they invest their money. This choice means that they have to make a calculation each time they invest about risk and reward. The higher the risk, the greater the reward that they will want. Since risk-free options are available, it is important to estimate and consider the risk to reward ratios that make it worthwhile investing in anything with a higher risk than zero. Therefore, since any commercial exercise contains some element of risk, the level of expected reward, in the form of returns, can be assessed in relation to the degree of risk incurred by investing.

The value of a business now to shareholders is related to its ability to generate future cash flows from their invested capital, measured by the net present value (NPV) (*see* **Fig.37:1**).

Figure 37:1 **Future cash flows**

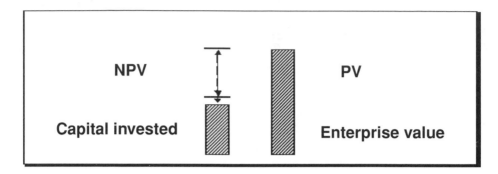

Shareholder value is an approach that relates an operating manager's potential to influence financial performance with the market's view of his or her company's performance.

Maximising shareholder value entails maximising the spread between the capital invested in a business and the enterprise market value (MV) of the business. In the capital markets this spread is known as the market value added (MVA). It is important to note that maximising shareholders' wealth is not the same as maximising the enterprise market value of the business. This is because the enterprise market value can simply be increased by investing ever-increasing amounts of capital (*see* **Fig.37:2**).

Figure 37:2 **Enterprise market value**

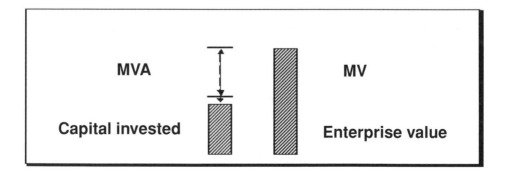

Shareholder value-based measurement of financial performance is therefore different to the typical short-termist approaches of conventional thinking. Shareholder value is forcing the measurement of financial performance to be taken more seriously due to the acknowledged link between cash flow and share price performance.

37:1.1 Background

In 1981 the influential US *Financial Analysts Journal* ran an editorial which is credited with first championing the maximising of shareholder value.

> Those who criticise the goal of share value maximisation are forgetting that stockholders are not merely the beneficiaries of the corporation's financial success, but also the referees who determine management's financial power ... any management, no matter how powerful or independent, that flouts the financial objective of maximising share value does so at its own peril.
>
> (Treynor, 1981)

Professor Alfred Rappaport of Northwestern University, Illinois, after much early work in the late 1970s and early 1980s published in 1986 the book which became the seminal work *Creating shareholder value – the new standard for business performance.*

At a theoretical level, the 1980s saw a growing body of academic opinion which challenged the value of accounting-based measures such as EPS as the best way to judge a business. Much has been written on the ease with which such measures can be manipulated. While it suited few people's interests to change, this growing attack gradually eroded the previously sublime confidence in financial accounts as the most appropriate measure of corporate success.

The greatest impact, however, came at the practical level. Throughout the 1980s an aggressive takeover climate prevailed in both the UK and the US as large corporate boards ignored Treynor's warning. Corporate raiders stalked the markets claiming to be the shareholders' friend with promises to release new shareholder value. Threatened boards turned to their consultants for help and they in turn developed new ways of judging shareholder value with new tools to help their clients enhance such value. Corporate raiders are notorious cost cutters and business history suggests that many acquired businesses are able to prosper with diminished cost structures. The question then becomes; why can corporate managers not make the same kind of decisions that raiders make? The answer, of course, is multifaceted, having to do with differences in corporate culture and the need to make 'difficult' decisions.

Shareholder value encourages executives to think in value-based terms and to make bold decisions that result in growing shareholders' wealth. What is particularly attractive about shareholder value is that it provides a framework within which the trade-offs of investment can be viewed holistically to allow strategic planning, e.g. short-term cash flows relating to long-term investment can be weighed up against longer-term cash flows.

37:1.2 A New Financial Standard

Increasingly, investors and analysts are turning their attention to shareholder value, i.e. to the capacity of a business to generate long-term cash flows in excess of its cost of capital.

Using this means ignoring many conventional accounting numbers. Earnings measures in particular, once the basis of most share performance analysis, are being superseded by cash-flow measures as the determinant of share price performance.

37:1.3 The Competitive Landscape Is Changing

It has become something of a cliché that the world is getting smaller and that every country's economy is being affected by globalisation, but it is no less true. In the past decade, most companies have seen rapid transformation of their businesses. This trend is set to continue, more than likely at an ever-increasing rate. New strategies will have to be adopted to survive in the globalised, market-driven years ahead. Management will have to evaluate the potential impact of the growing number of strategic options and will need to rethink key strategies concerning products, markets, customers, employees and assets. Successful organisations will determine how to deploy resources more effectively and adopt accurate performance measures to achieve their new objectives. Rewards linked to the implementation of these new strategies will help to reinforce the messages.

Companies must also look inward to launch restructuring and management initiatives: business process re-engineering, activity-based management, compensation management, benchmarking, focusing on core competencies and outsourcing non-core activities. Many internal approaches, however, may fall short due to poor or obsolete performance measures. Even senior managers frequently lack the time and ability to cut through the plethora of data supplied by various management 'tools'. As a result they do not know if they are applying the correct strategies or optimising resource allocation, or if implementation is on target.

Companies need new tools to manage change and to guide the organisation in the right direction. The right tools, properly aligned with a shareholder value focus, will enable managers to rise to the challenges of new environments.

37:2 Managing for Shareholder Value

Managing for shareholder value is a methodology that involves measuring and, more importantly, managing all aspects of a business in accordance with the desire to create, and ultimately to maximise, wealth for shareholders that satisfies both the capital and product markets. The underlying philosophy is to encourage managers to act like owners. This requires managers to understand how value is created and then to use that understanding as the basis for decisions and actions at all levels and covering all areas of the business.

Most large companies consist of a number of business units whose objectives should be to create shareholder value. But, for many of the managers who run these businesses, creating shareholder value is so remote and conceptual that to tell them to go forth and create it is tantamount to telling them to go out and do their own thing.

Shareholder value analysis can however, often be seen as an inspirational influence by showing such management teams a clear focus for their efforts.

A process for planning and managing the creation of shareholder value is possible, if the company is logical, systematic and determined. The key aspect of shareholder value is its integrated nature, allowing a consistent approach to strategy selection, resource allocation, performance measurement and reward systems.

37:2.1 Shareholder Value Analysis

In undertaking a shareholder value analysis, managers need to ask themselves the following questions:

- What shareholder return do we need to achieve to satisfy investors? [*cf. FRS14: Earnings Per Share*, whose objective is 'to improve the comparison of the performance in the same period and of the same entity in different accounting periods by prescribing methods for determining the number of shares to be included in the calculations of earnings per share and other amounts per share and by specifying their presentation'. See also *IAS33: Earnings Per Share*].

- Which business units are contributing to shareholder value and which are destroying value?

- What new strategies or initiatives are required to increase shareholder value?

- How much value will be created by these new strategies and initiatives?

- How will managers be rewarded for implementing these strategies and initiatives?

Before embarking on an implementation plan however it is wise to note that shareholder value is not just a technical accounting exercise and if it is regarded as such then its effects will be minimised and perhaps negated entirely.

37:3 Shareholder Value Implementation Plan

There are five stages in a typical implementation plan:

1. *Making shareholder value the mission.*
2. *Value modelling the business.*
3. *Developing value-creating strategies.*
4. *Defining value-based and performance measures.*
5. *Aligning compensation with value creation.*

There are also two crucial parallel streams of activity:

1. *Develop a shareholder value competency.*
2. *Build a value infrastructure.*

37:3.1 Making Shareholder Value the Mission

This phase is concerned with establishing a goal for the organisation that reflects the capital market's expectations. This imperative for value can only be created by top management and their commitment is essential before it is communicated throughout the organisation.

All corporate performance measures must serve one ultimate objective. If, for example, a business unit has the objective of doubling earnings during a five-year period, then measuring annual earnings and comparing the actual performance to the objective provides an important signal about how well the objective is being met. Similarly, if improving customer satisfaction is an important objective, then measures taken from customer surveys can be used to gauge progress. These kinds of measures are useful tools however, they often conflict with each other, e.g. doubling earnings may not go hand-in-hand with improving customer satisfaction. For this reason, management needs a governing objective, capable of evaluating trade-offs throughout the organisation. *The value imperative* provides the definitive guide: 'The purpose of the strategic process should be stated explicitly: It is to identify, develop and select the highest value strategies for each business unit in the portfolio and for the corporate centre' (McTaggart *et al.*, 1994).

The classic example of this philosophy in practice is captured in the following quotation from Robert Goizueta, former chief executive of shareholder value champions Coca Cola: 'I get paid to make the owners of the Coca Cola Company increasingly wealthy with each passing day. Everything else is just fluff'.

A good UK example is Lloyds TSB whose mission statement reads: 'to achieve a total return for our shareholders which is the best in the financial services industry'.

Defining success as merely increasing earnings, for example, can lead to destruction, rather than creation of shareholder value. A business's success must be measured by the net present value of its current and future free cash flows.

The value imperative must be communicated through goals that are tailored to the level of the organisation. For the head of a business unit, this may mean explicit value creation measured in financial terms. For a functional manager, it may mean some combination of customer service, market share, product quality or productivity. The key however is that they are all linked to the governing objective.

37:3.2 Value Modelling the Business

This phase is concerned with establishing if the company is creating value and determining what features of both its internal and external environments give it this competitive advantage.

In any shareholder value analysis most of the value drivers can be flexed to see how a company's economic value can be improved. The starting point for analysis is to determine the current shareholder value at the corporate level and then attempt to decompose it through business units to product markets and then set a rate at which that value should improve to satisfy shareholders in the future.

There are six steps involved in value modelling:

1. *Get hold of the last full year's accounts.*
2. *Establish the current business plan.*
3. *Determine the company's cost of capital and disaggregate to business units and product sectors.*
4. *Calculate shareholder value at total company and business unit level.*
5. *Decompose the business plans into key value drivers and their impact.*
6. *Allocate central resources to units and drive down the value drivers.*

Steps one and two require no further comment here.

37:3.2.1 Cost of Capital

The cost of capital is the opportunity cost of funds to an organisation, which seen from the perspective of the providers of those funds represents their required rate of return.

Companies may have more than one source of financing, in which case the cost of capital has to reflect in some way the breadth of different interests.

37:3.2.1.1 Calculating the Cost of Capital

A business with 60% equity and 40% debt and with a cost of equity of 12% and a cost of debt of 8% would have a weighted average cost of capital (WACC) of 10.4%.

37:3.2.1.2 Cost of Debt

The cost associated with any debt is usually calculated by estimating the yield on the cash flows paid out by way of interest after tax and any redemption payment on maturity. The calculation is:

$$\text{Cost of debt} = \text{interest rate} \times (1 - \text{tax rate})$$
$$= 11.4 \times (1.0 - 0.3)$$
$$= 8.0$$

37:3.2.1.3 Cost of Equity

The cost associated with equity relates the required return to the level of risk attached to an investment. This assumes that a risk-free investment is the starting point for any investment. Thus, anyone contemplating investing in the UK would require at least the return available from government securities. For any level of risk above this some compensation would be required. The most popular method for calculating the cost of equity under this principal is the capital asset pricing model (CAPM).

$$\text{Cost of equity} = \text{Risk-free rate} + (\text{Beta} \times \text{Equity market risk premium})$$

37:3.2.1.4 Risk-free Rate

This represents the most secure return that can be achieved. A good proxy for this is the average yield on index-linked gilts which can be found daily in the *Financial Times*.

37:3.2.1.5 Beta

This measures the risk premium by comparing a share's volatility with market volatility. The source for UK company betas is the Risk Measurement Service from the London

Business School, published quarterly. The service lists all UK public companies and an industrial sector analysis. If your company is not listed use a similar company or sector as a proxy.

37:3.2.1.6 Equity Risk Premium

This represents the excess return over and above the risk-free rate that investors demand for holding risky securities. The definitive research appears annually in the Equity Gilt Study produced by Barclays Capital and the historic answer is around 8%. There is much debate over what the expected value of this premium will be in future with the only consensus being that it will be lower than 8%.

A typical calculation will be:

Cost of equity   = 4.8 + (0.9 x 8.0)

                     = 12

This shows a cost of equity of 12% given a risk-free rate of 4.8%, a beta of 0.9 and an equity risk premium of 8%.

Business units WACC can be calculated using proxies from the wider corporate market or by disaggregating the company WACC using business unit weightings such as assets employed.

37:3.3 Calculating Shareholder Value

Calculating corporate shareholder value added (SVA) is quite straightforward and requires only modest adjustments to standard reported measures such as profits and capital employed. SVA is the residual income remaining after deducting the cost of all capital from the net profit after tax.

The basic, single year formula is:

SVA   =   NOPAT − (k x capital)

where

NOPAT is net operating profit after tax

k is the after tax weighted average cost of capital (WACC)

capital is the capital employed; fixed assets plus working capital.

Adjustments to profits are typically made to refine NOPAT to a cash equivalent, e.g. by adding back movements on deferred tax and provisions. Each organisation will have its own requirements for such adjustments that need to be consistent throughout the period of the plan, the real key is honesty: there is no point in managers trying to fool themselves.

By performing this calculation for each year in the business plan and adding a perpetuity assumption, the present value of future shareholder value added can be calculated using the WACC as the discount rate.

So the full formula is:

$$\text{Shareholder value} = \sum_{t=0}^{n} \frac{(SVA)^t}{(1+k)^t}$$

If the present value is positive value is being created. For a public company this shareholder value measure equates to MVA.

> Market value = Shareholder value plus capital

This value can be related to the market value of the equity of a quoted company by subtracting the market value of any debt from the above result.

This calculation of shareholder value provides a powerful link from corporate planning to the capital markets to be used for both internal communication and investor relations. From a management point of view, the simplest and most important link is:

> Shareholder value or MVA = Present value of future SVAs

The primary task of management is to maximise shareholder value. However because this is by nature a long-term measure, it can be a poor measure of short-term and operational performance. Using the SVA calculation allows value to be managed in the shorter term and across the business while maintaining consistency with the long-term objective.

The next step is to attempt to find the source of the value created and identify sources of value destruction. There are two steps that facilitate the move to a shorter time frame and allow the value to be managed:

1. *Calculate the SVA for business units.*
2. *Consider the components that make up shareholder value, these are called value drivers.*

37:3.4 Value Drivers

Value drivers are variables that affect the value of the organisation. Alfred Rappaport identified seven value drivers which although adopted as the 'standard' by many practitioners and serve as a sound starting point for any shareholder value analysis, need not be prescriptive and are certainly not comprehensive:

Three relate to NOPAT:

- Sales growth rate.

- Operating profit margin.

- Cash tax rate.

Two relate to capital:

- Fixed asset investment.

- Working capital investment.

Two relate to the time that a business is expected to create value and the discount rate:

- Growth duration period/planning period, being the number of years' data, including the competitive advantage period.

- Weighted average cost of capital (WACC).

These value drivers serve as a common planning and analysis tool for business units, product lines and market segments. Using the historical performance of the value drivers to compute the company's performance can determine where value has been created or destroyed in the past. To reach a true understanding of value creation however, it is vital to focus on expectations of future changes to the value drivers.

It is important to recognise the relationship between the value drivers representing both cash inflows and cash outflows. The ability to achieve targets for one driver may be dependent on another, e.g. to achieve sales growth may require additional working capital. Without adequate fixed assets and working capital it may be impossible to achieve a certain growth rate, let alone sustain it.

An understanding of the value drivers will provide the basis for strategic decision making and for evaluating the business performance.

37:3.5 Developing Shareholder Value-creating Strategies

This phase is concerned with sustaining or creating competitive advantage in the future and builds on the understanding of the performance variables, identified above, that drive the value of the business. This involves the systematic analysis of the business, the market in which it operates and its strengths and weaknesses as well as those of its competitors.

An organisation cannot act directly on value; it has to act on the things that it can influence, such as customer satisfaction, operating costs and capital expenditure, with shareholder value serving as the focal point. This focus provides the single direction for all management action.

Strategies for creating value can be grouped into four categories. Those that:

1. *increase the return derived from capital already employed;*
2. *grow through investing in projects where the returns exceed the cost of capital;*
3. *curtail investment in, and divert capital from, uneconomic activities;*
4. *reduce the cost of capital.*

Management can look internally at corporate restructuring, sales issues such as product profitability and marketing to improve margins. Managers can also look outside the company at strategic acquisitions to improve value through synergy or a better product package or a better distribution channel. These strategies focus on the leverage points where the operational managers and staff actions provide a direct, measurable impact on share price. These alternative strategies for producing changes to competitive performance should be quantified using the key value drivers. Rigorous evaluation of strategic options against the drivers is a key element of shareholder value analysis.

Very few companies go through the process of valuing their strategic plan. Yet, unless the management knows the value of their plans they are flying blind. Putting a value on the strategy in this way helps management to understand the value that they intend to create and how this matches up to their investor's expectations.

Once the right strategy is in place, the company is faced with the challenge of implementing it and measuring the progress to achieving the strategy. The link between financial planning, strategy development and strategy implementation should be further reinforced by mapping the value drivers on to business specific performance measures that drive the success with customers, markets and operations.

37:3.6 Defining Shareholder Value-based Performance Measures

This phase is concerned with the key link between corporate strategy implementation and business unit management, namely performance measurement. Business unit strategies, critical success factors, decision-making processes and key performance indicators should all contribute to increasing value.

Value-based performance measurement provides assurance that managers throughout the organisation focus on value creation and the drivers of value. By understanding where value is created and where the leverage points are, performance is measured by the results of processes and activities that impact shareholder value.

Companies create business units and performance management systems to identify clearly where value is created. For many business units it will be appropriate to express their objectives and performance in terms of the underlying value drivers, rather than the summary metric as the value drivers are shorter term in nature but at the same time consistent with the long-term measure of shareholder value creation.

Managers should feel that they own their businesses and be held accountable for enhancing value. For example, under the stewardship of Percy Barnevik, ABB consisted of over 5,000 profit centres and more than 1,300 business units which had to meet a market test to survive.

Performance measurement that is based on the production of shareholder value provides a strong linkage from the executive suite through the organisation to operations management. Each level is held accountable for a meaningful contribution; from the chief executive who is responsible for total shareholder value, to operations management, which may be accountable for some aspects of expense control, stock management and various aspects of time and quality. Performance measurement focuses on value creation for interim periods and features two components:

1. *Planning – the setting of goals and the commitment of resources.*
2. *Performance reporting – the provision of feedback on performance compared to plan.*

Performance measures should do more than merely reflect financial results, for example, according to *FRS3: Reporting Financial Performance*, or *IAS1: Presentation of Financial Statements* they should help managers to make decisions. Managers are faced with apparent conflicting objectives on a daily basis. By using value as the objective for decision making through the use of integrated performance measures, managers can more easily balance multiple perspectives and think through the trade-offs that they are expected to make.

37:3.7 Align Compensation Schemes with Shareholder Value Creation

A natural follow-on from performance measurement is the link to remuneration. This involves adjusting the compensation system to measure individual managers' performance based on value creation. Many shareholder value consultants argue that changing incentives to encourage managers to act like owners is vital to completing the value 'journey'.

Their reasoning is that if rewards are not based on the creation of shareholder value, most of the potential benefit could be lost. If, however, rewards for managers are securely tied to this process, so that managers know that if value is created, their own wealth will be increased, then success is far more likely.

An effective shareholder value-based compensation scheme should reward managers for acting in a way that the shareholders would most approve. For senior executives this requires a scheme that rewards them when the company as a whole is creating value for shareholders. For business unit managers it means rewarding them for maximising the value creation of their business unit. The aim of any compensation link should be to incentivise staff on the basis of decisions that they can influence.

A link to compensation is also important to establish shareholder value as an integral part of the management process and avoid it being seen as another 'initiative'.

37:3.8 Developing Shareholder Value Competency

Before a business can effectively manage for shareholder value, a clear understanding is required of how value is actually created. Implementing shareholder value is a 'journey' and a programme of education and communication is critical to success.

An implementation team should strive to achieve a critical mass of knowledge by building value skills in a wide cross-section of the company. In doing so they should employ strategic issue analyses that are tailored to each business unit rather than a canned or generic approach to communicate concepts. Staged training programmes should be conducted to introduce new processes and requirements.

Shareholder value techniques, when properly employed, should create an organisational culture in which all goals, objectives, decisions, strategies, achievements and responsibilities are based around the value added to the organisation. Sufficient understanding should be achieved to provide a base from which to communicate confidently with investors about the positive changes that have come about as a result of the shareholder value focus.

A shareholder value competency should facilitate all levels of decisions to be managed for value creation.

- Directors – strategic planning decisions and external communication to manage investor perception.

- Business heads – resource allocation decisions.

- Operational managers – planning, budgeting and operational decisions.

The aim is to produce a mind-set whereby managers gain an insight into the value of the trade-offs that they regularly make and help to generate a broader set of alternatives to improve the information that is available for decision making.

Shareholder value in practice effectively means imposing on existing businesses the same type of rigorous discipline that is applied to new project approval.

37:3.9 Build a Shareholder Value Infrastructure

Management processes need to be aligned behind value. Typically processes in companies are out of balance; they may use payback to evaluate projects, determine compensation on revenue or earnings and Finance and Planning functions are divorced from operating decisions. A value focus will help to align these processes.

A value-based infrastructure is concerned with ensuring that there is a logical coherence to the key planning and control systems used within the business. The company will need to create the appropriate data and communication infrastructure to integrate the planning, budgeting, target setting, managerial reporting and compensation systems.

Standardised, easy-to-use valuation templates and report formats to facilitate the submission of management reports should be developed. The IT system, in particular, will have to be adjusted to generate data appropriate to the new management requirements. The availability of crucial data, e.g. business unit balance sheets is essential, as is an understanding of the concept of activity-based costing to allow the assignment of shared revenues, costs and assets between product markets and customer segments.

Activity-based management can be a powerful precursor to managing for shareholder value as the principles of segmentation (*cf. SSAP25: Segmental Reporting, IAS14: Segment Reporting*), customer and product profitability and cost drivers can all play an important part in understanding the drivers of value. Allocating capital to marketing channels, market segments or products should be a logical next step for companies that have embraced activity-based management.

A value-based infrastructure will set shareholder value maximisation as the clear, unambiguous objective for corporate and business unit strategic planning. It should provide a clear, consistent quantitative framework within which to formulate and evaluate those strategies. Resource allocation decisions should be derived directly from strategic decisions; business unit strategies that create value should be funded and business units that prepare strategic plans that fail to create value should be asked to review their options and submit a revised plan.

Targets and performance measures are required to track the progress of the value maximising strategy and to promote value maximising operational decision making. Link objectives with strategy, strategy with measures and link incentives to measures. If managerial commitment is to be secured, it is important that lower-level managerial bonuses as well as higher-level share options are triggered by effectively the same measures as those related to subsidiary performances.

Shareholder value should not be allowed to be regarded as a one-off initiative. There is a need to follow up the initial implementation with ongoing reinforcement of the principles and concepts involved. The need for active reinforcement should diminish once value-based systems are in place to support the structure and culture.

37:4 Why Is Shareholder Value Not More Widely Adopted?

(a) *Lack of awareness of the practical implementation measures.*
(b) *Reluctance amongst management accountants to buy in to the concept.*
(c) *Genuine technical problems, particularly at divisional level.*
(d) *Perceived difficulty in establishing the cost of capital.*
(e) *Difficulty in valuing the capital employed at a point in time.*
(f) *Dealing with synergies and transfer pricing between divisions.*
(g) *Organisational problems such as a perceived stakeholder culture clash.*

The most common reason for failure is underinvestment in the training and development required to enhance the capabilities of the organisation.

The approach is rarely used at all in private companies, where managers perceive the technique to be applicable only to companies listed on a stock market. However the concept of managing for value creation is relevant to all organisations, large or small. If a company is not covering its cost of capital, then the logical conclusion is that it would have been better if investors' or owners' money had been placed elsewhere.

37:5 Keys to Successful Shareholder Value Implementation

(a) *Establish visible top management support.*
(b) *Focus on better decision making among operating (not just financial) personnel.*
(c) *Achieve critical mass by building skills in a wide cross-section of the company.*
(d) *Tightly integrate the shareholder value approach with all elements of planning.*
(e) *Under-emphasise methodological issues and focus on practical application.*
(f) *Use strategic issue analyses that are tailored to each business unit rather than a generic approach.*
(g) *Ensure the availability of crucial data (e.g. business unit balance sheets).*
(h) *Provide standardised, easy-to-use valuation templates and report formats to facilitate the submission of management reports.*
(i) *Tie incentives to value creation.*
(j) *Require that capital and human resources requests are value based.*

37:6 Illustration of Successfully Managing for Shareholder Value

Lloyds TSB provides a good example of a successful company managing for shareholder value. Their mission is: 'to achieve a total return for our shareholders which is the best in the financial services industry'.

Brian Pitman, former chief executive was committed to the philosophy and is on record as saying:

> we are not interested in chasing growth or size for their own sake, but in creating value for our shareholders.

> over time, maximising shareholder value will produce the highest level of benefits for all stakeholders.

Managing for shareholder value has manifested in the implementation of strategies to increase the return derived from capital already employed, grow through investing in projects where the returns exceeded the cost of capital and curtail investment in, and divert capital from, uneconomic activities.

Lloyds' focus on shareholder value reaped impressive results in terms of an exponential rising spread between the market value of the company and the capital invested in the business over the last 10 to 15 years. Shareholder value doubled every three years from 1984 to 1996. This performance it should be noted was achieved in a market where there is over-capacity, commoditisation, increasing risks and growing consumerism. With an example like this, it is no wonder that the concept of shareholder value is proving popular with both managers and investors.

37:7 Conclusion

Managing for shareholder value integrates the management cycle of strategy formulation, resource allocation and performance measurement and provides a common language for planning, reporting, incentives and compensation as well as investor communications.

Shareholder value in practice is as much a management philosophy as a strategic management process: a decision-making framework as well as a means of rigorous fact-based analysis. The major benefit that a company adopting this philosophy would get is likely to be a higher market value. Why? Because as Stewart points out, investors recognise and reward integrated decision making that is shareholder value focused.

> 'To satisfy astute investors... a company must earn a rate of return that exceeds its cost of capital. Those that do so will add value to the capital they employ and will sell for premium stock prices. Those that do not will have misallocated or mismanaged capital and will sell for stock market values that discount their capital employed.'

The beauty of shareholder value is that it returns businesses to the basics. Their *raison d'être* is there for all to see and informs every decision made in the organisation. Owners, naturally, like managers who act like owners.

As a management philosophy shareholder value provides the overriding objective of maximising shareholder wealth. It focuses managers' attention on cash flow and operating value, improves understanding of the market and a business's place within it, emphasises the long-term as well as the short-term view and provides comparable business plans and project evaluations for all businesses in a group.

The emphasis on cash flow is one easily appreciated by owners and managers in small and medium-size businesses. To them shareholder value is easily understood. For those in large organisations, cash flow can be seen as peripheral to the 'big issues', such as corporate strategy.

If in doubt with your implementation, focus on the underlying philosophy rather than the detailed techniques. Do not get stuck on technical issues, if necessary, compromise the technique and provide a link to incentives to secure successful implementation.

References

McTaggart, Kontes and Mankins (1994) *The value imperative*. Free Press.

Rappaport, Alfred (1994) *Creating shareholder value*. Free Press.

Stewart, G.B. (1991) *The quest for value*. Harper Collins.

Treynor, Jack (Ed.) (1981) *Financial Analysts Journal. The Journal of the Association for Investment Management and Research.*

38. Outsourcing or Subcontracting

38:1 Introduction

Subcontracting or, to use the more fashionable term, outsourcing, is a method of operation that is becoming increasingly popular. So what exactly is it, and what role should management accountants play in its implementation and operation? These are just some of the questions that this chapter seeks to answer. The following chapter (39) gives evidence from a case study of outsourcing in practice.

38:2 What is Outsourcing?

Outsourcing is a contractual relationship with an outside supplier to assume responsibility for an operation that a company is currently supplying internally (*see* **Chapter 20** for contract costing). It is no longer the refuge of the financially weak or technically deficient enterprise, but has become an accepted strategic tool of many companies.

38:2.1 Historical View

What to outsource has historically been decided as shown in **Fig.38:1**.

Figure 38:1 **What to outsource?**

Is this operation strategic to my business? ·············· NO ············· = Outsource

YES

=

Keep it

38:2.2 Current View

However, today companies are asking a different question, as shown in **Figure 38:2**.

Figure 38:2 **Outsourcing – a current view**

Is this operation a core competency, whether strategic or not? ······· NO ······· = Outsource

YES

=

Keep it

Perhaps the most common operation that is being outsourced today is the data-processing or IT operation, which is very strategic to all companies, but not necessarily a core competency for many.

38:3 Examples of Outsourcing

38:3.1 Business Services

- Reprographics and copying/publishing.

- Records management.

- Real-estate maintenance.

- Machinery and equipment management.

- Procurement operations.

38:3.2 Logistics

- Import and export services.

- Transport selection, carrier monitoring, etc.

- Warehousing.

38:3.3 Information Technology

- Data-processing operations.

- Hardware maintenance and leasing.

- Software development and application.

38:3.4 Human Resources

- Pension management.

- Payroll operations.

- Communications and public relations.

38:3.5 Finance

- Tax administration.

- Accounts payable.

- Accounts receivable and debt management.

- Treasury operations.

38:3.6 Manufacturing and Development

- Parts and component supply.

- Assembly operations.

- Complete branded product, including development.

38:3.7 Customer Care

- Call-centre operations for post-sale support.

- Warranty services.

- Product repair.

38:3.8 Marketing

- Advertising and promotion.

- Pre-sales administration.

38:4 Selected Industry Studies

Many studies have been conducted on outsourcing, but perhaps some of the most pertinent findings are as follows.

38:4.1 Business Services

Of the firms surveyed:

(a) *77% had efforts underway to outsource some aspect of their business support services;*
(b) *39% outsourced some or all of their electronic imaging;*
(c) *7% outsourced records management.*

Source: Pitney Bowes Management Services, 1994 study of 100 of the FORTUNE 500 Companies

38:4.2 Logistics

Of the companies surveyed:

(a) *66% outsourced import/export services;*
(b) *63% employed freight-brokers for transport selection, carrier monitoring, insurance, tariff and customs compliance;*
(c) *48% outsourced warehousing.*

Source: KPMG-Peat Marwick, 1994 study of 309 FORTUNE 1000 Companies

38:4.3 Information Technology

Of the companies surveyed:

(a) *50% of companies with IT budgets in excess of $5m outsource IT;*

(b) *85% of banking and finance companies with IT budgets of $5m outsource IT.*

Source: Frost and Sullivan Market Intelligence, 1992 Survey of 1200 Companies

38:4.4 Human Resources and Finance

Of the executives surveyed:

(a) *45% stated that they outsource payroll management;*

(b) *38% stated that they outsource tax administration;*

(c) *35% stated that they outsource benefits management;*

(d) *34% stated that they outsource employees compensation;*

(e) *the number of HR executives using outsourcing as part of a flexible staffing strategy increased from 18% to 30% in just one year.*

Source: Olsten Corporation, 1994 study of 400 Companies

38:4.5 Health Care

Of the hospitals surveyed:

(a) *67% use outsourcing providers for at least one operational department;*

(b) *90% of these hospitals use outsourcing providers for support services; 77% for clinical services; and 51% for business services.*

Source: Hospitals and Health Network, 1995 Annual Survey

38:5 Why Outsource?

(*See* **Ch.39, para.39:2.**)

The drive behind an outsourcing project can be wide and varied, can be for short-term benefits, and can be implemented for longer-term strategic reasons. Very often, if the reasons are for short-term gain, an outsourcing project can prove unsuccessful. The pitfalls of outsourcing will be detailed later, (*see* **para.38:6**) but the reasons for outsourcing can usually be categorised as either longer-term reasons, or shorter-term drivers.

38:5.1 Longer-term Reasons

38:5.1.1 Improving Customer Focus and Accelerating Growth

Outsourcing lets a company focus its energies or areas of growth, while having operational details assumed by an outside expert. If outsourcing is used properly it can result in an organisation-shaping management tool which can lead to a clearer and more effective focus on meeting customer needs.

Outsourcing can also enable an organisation to accelerate its growth and success through expanded investment in areas which offer greater competitive advantage.

38:5.1.2 Access to Better Capabilities

Outsourcing providers can bring extensive capabilities, in many cases world-class and worldwide expertise. Very often, such suppliers can bring access to new technologies that a company does not currently possess.

38:5.1.3 Re-engineering Benefits

Outsourcing allows an organisation to immediately realise the anticipated benefits of re-engineering (*see* **Ch.32**) by having an outside organisation – one that is already re-engineered – take over the process.

Re-engineering is the fundamental rethinking of business processes with the aim of seeing dramatic improvements in critical measures of performance such as cost, quality, service and speed.

38:5.1.4 Shared Risks

Outsourcing is a vehicle for sharing risks across many companies. Outsourcing providers make investment not just on behalf of one company, but on behalf of many clients. By sharing these investments, the risks borne by a single company are significantly reduced.

38:5.1.5 Releasing Resources for Other Purposes

Outsourcing can allow an organisation to redirect it resources from non-core activities towards activities which have provided the greater return in serving the customer.

Usually these resources are people resources, and people whose energies are currently focused internally can then be focused externally – on the real customers.

38:5.2 Short-term Drivers

38:5.2.1 Making Capital Funds Available

Outsourcing can be a way to reduce the need to invest capital funds in a non-core business function, or indeed, divert capital funds available for core activities. For example, when a company outsources its vehicles, buildings or computers, these no longer compete for the company's capital. Often, these types of investments have been difficult to justify when compared to areas more directly related to producing product or serving the customer.

It can also improve certain measurements of the company by eliminating the need to show return on equity from capital investments (*see* **Ch.11**) in non-core areas.

38:5.2.2 Cash Generation

Outsourcing often involves the transfer of assets from the company to the outsourcing provider. Depending on the value of the assets involved, the sale may result in a significant cash injection to the company (*see* **Ch.10**).

Very often, such assets are sold at net book value, which, in some instances, may be higher than the market value (*see FRS15: Tangible Fixed Assets* or *FRS11: Impairment of Fixed Assets and Goodwill,* for detail on valuations). In those cases, the difference between the two values actually represents a loan from the provider to the company, which is repaid in the price of future services or products. Part of the cash generation is income from the sale of the assets, and part is a loan to be repaid over time.

38:5.2.3 Reducing and Controlling Operating Costs

The single most important tactical reason for outsourcing is to reduce and control operating costs. Access to an outsourcing provider's lower cost structure, which may be the result of economies of scale or some advantage based on specialisation, is clearly and simply one of the most compelling tactical reasons for outsourcing.

38:5.2.4 Lack of Available Resources

Companies very often outsource because they do not have access to the required resources and skills within their own organisation. For example, if a company is expanding its operations into a new field of activity, or a new location, outsourcing may be a viable and important alternative to building the required capability from the start.

Rapid growth or expansion of operations is a strong indicator that outsourcing may be the proper decision for a company.

38:5.2.5 Function Difficult to Manage or Out of Control

Outsourcing is an option for addressing the problem of a particular activity being difficult to manage, or being out of control (*see* **Ch.45**). However, outsourcing does not mean an abdication of management responsibility, nor does it work well as a knee-jerk reaction by companies in trouble.

If the root cause of a poorly managed or out-of-control organisation is that it does not understand its requirements, then it certainly will not be able to communicate them to an outside provider either.

38:5.3 Reasons for Outsourcing – Summary

The reasons for outsourcing can be many, but can be crystallised by the model shown in **Fig.38:3**.

Figure 38:3 **Reasons for outsourcing**

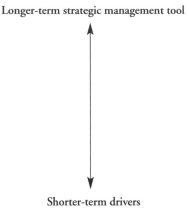

Motives

Customer focus and accelerating growth

Access to better capabilities

Re-engineering benefits

Shared risks

Releasing resources for other purposes

Making capital funds available

Cash generation

Reducing and controlling operating costs

Lack of available resources

Function difficult to manage or out of control

Longer-term strategic management tool

Shorter-term drivers

38:6 The Pitfalls of Outsourcing

There are many pitfalls in outsourcing a particular project or activity, and it is essential that the wrong attitude and approach to outsourcing is not taken, that is, 'this is no longer our business, under our control, and it is someone else's responsibility'.

While this at first glance may appear true, it is vitally important that each company realises that a strong relationship needs to be built between the organisation which is outsourcing and the outsourcing provider.

So what are the common pitfalls?

38:6.1 Cost Savings Are Not Always Realised

Very often, companies think that outsourcing providers, with their economies of scale can perform operations 30% to 50% cheaper than current in-house operations. In reality, such savings are rare.

In addition, many contracts do not reflect the changing market pricing, for example, market costs for hardware, software and personnel may dip over time in an IT outsource, but contracts could specify a fixed price.

38:6.2 Outsourcing Providers Can Outsource Themselves

Companies that outsource are sometimes unpleasantly surprised to find that their service provider is not working on their projects – somebody else is! This may occur because the outsourcing provider does not have all the resources it needs to provide the full service.

One safeguard is to build subcontractor approval rights into contracts, and to specify that critical projects or systems be handled by the primary outsourcing provider.

38:6.3 The Scope of Service Changes
(*See* Ch.39, para.39:3.1.)

Business need change from year to year, and it can be difficult to anticipate needs several years out, when negotiating a contract.

Companies can sometimes find themselves butting heads with their provider a few years into the deal, wishing they had defined change management procedures or built flexibility amendments into the contract.

38:6.4 Poor Communication

Very often, poor communication can result from the company focusing its energy and time managing the remaining parts of its business, and assuming the outsourcing provider will deliver the goods or service.

There can be natural barriers and distrust which may arise from the clash of two different corporate cultures.

Both parties must co-ordinate standards, policies, times of work, and clearly identify responsibilities. Both parties need to be held accountable for their respective responsibilities.

38:6.5 The Pitfalls of Outsourcing – Summary

While these pitfalls can be overcome, perhaps the best summary of avoiding these pitfalls is to ensure that the company who is outsourcing does not catch 'tunnel vision'. In other words, outsourcing requires re-engineering of business processes. If a company simply outsources, without re-engineering, then complications will arise, and performance will not be optimised.

38:7 The Management Accountant's Role in Outsourcing
(*See* Ch.39, para.39:4.)

38:7.1 The Traditional Role

Outsourcing can allow a company to lower its costs, turn a fixed cost into a variable cost, release capital investments for use in other areas, avoid future investments and generally refocus management on the bottom line.

These are key areas in which the management accountant can exert influence and bring appropriate information and analysis to the decision-making table. For example, if the key driver is to match costs with revenue, then a related benefit which outsourcing can bring is the variable nature of unit-priced outsourcing, which in effect translates a fixed-cost infrastructure into a pay-as-you-use variable-cost structure. This, in turn, may have an effect on a company's pricing methodology.

These, however, are traditional areas of management accounting focus.

38:7.2 Additional Roles of the Management Accountant

There are two fundamental and additional roles that the management accountant can bring to the table.

38:7.2.1 Bring All Costs to the Decision-Making Table
(*See* Ch.39, para.39:3.3.)

Very often, outsourcing deals can initially look favourable, but after a few years of operation, additional costs can filter through which eliminate the initial forecasted advantages. For example, a company may outsource the manufacturing of a product primarily because the forecasted costs from the supplier are lower than the current in-house costs.

However, due to supply/demand fluctuations, or changes in freight and duty parameters, or other business dynamics, additional costs are passed on to the company who outsourced.

The management accountant can provide invaluable financial information based on experience, or benchmarking the experience of other companies.

38:7.2.2 Monitor the Costs of Outsourcing
(*See* Ch.39, para.39:3.2.)

The management accountant should monitor the total costs of any new outsourced activity, including the remaining in-house costs of maintaining the relationship with the service provider.

Many companies can dream up the proper business case to outsource, but the management accountant should monitor the actual performance against the projected business case. This may involve gathering information outwith the traditional business systems, or adding an activity-based cost approach to a particular outsourced project.

38:8 Conclusions

Outsourcing, or subcontracting, has been a fashionable trend in the late 1980s and 1990s, and some activities have been highly successful, while others have failed miserably.

The motives for outsourcing should be carefully examined and the pitfalls avoided. The management accountant has a key role to play in both influencing the decision to outsource, and monitoring the business and cost effects of such a project.

But, perhaps the best overall approach to outsourcing is to ask yourself the question: 'What will be the effect on our customers if we outsource?'.

39. Case Study of Outsourcing and Management Accounting

39:1 Introduction

The previous chapter (*see* **Ch.38**) discussed the implications of outsourcing on management accounting. This chapter considers the case of a large UK supermarket chain, which has introduced outsourcing for a number of activities. It is based on an interview with the Director of the Finance Service Centre. The agenda included: the decision to outsource; managing suppliers; and accounting implications of outsourcing.

39:1.1 Background to the Company

The company is a large UK supermarket retailer, which offers a diversified range of products. The mode of sales delivery has diversified over time, with home (internet) shopping worth approximately £500 million turnover per annum. The company also has several hundred stores throughout the UK.

39:1.2 Organisational Change

Changes to the supply chain, and accounting, are driven from Board level. The company aims to be the outstanding company in its sector for customer service, and aims to raise quality, while retailing products at, or below, the price of its main competitor. This strategy is predicated upon increased customer sophistication and changing customer demands.

39:1.3 The Company's Supply Chain

The supply chain within this organisation has undergone significant changes. New innovations include: a programme of 'continuous replenishment', with store managers reporting twice a day on sales information; and supply chain management systems to assist in warehouse automation.

39:1.4 Accounting Measures

Accounting measures used to assess the performance of sub-contracted services include a target return on investment of 15% or more, a measure of pay-back, and additional qualitative measures. Each piece of outsourced work is measured as a separate cost centre, with certain functions monitored frequently (e.g. hauliers) and others annually.

The management accounting function uses a 'balanced scorecard' approach (*see* **Ch.3, para.3.1**), with emphasis on customer focus. This is represented pictorially as a wheel, divided into four quadrants: Customer, Operations, Finance and People. Information is gathered, controlled and fed into a five-year rolling plan, directed by the Board.

The function of management accounting within this organisation is to provide clarity for meeting business aims. Accounting metrics are revised in order to measure particular aspects of performance and service provisions more transparently.

39:1.5 Information for Reporting

The majority of the information required for reporting is generated by standardised systems which co-ordinate stock and sales. These include an activity based costing approach (*see* **Chs 28, 29, 30, 31, and Ch.38, para.38:7.2.2**), rather than a more conventional resource-based approach; a change introduced to relate more accurately financial costs, such as overheads, and 'hidden costs', in distribution and warehousing, to the processes that generate such costs.

39:2 The Decision to Outsource

Outsourcing is an arrangement whereby a third party provider assumes responsibility for performing functions at a pre-determined price and according to predetermined performance criteria. The respondent has to consider the rationale behind outsourcing their organisation's functions.

39:2.1 Extent of Outsourcing

Chapter 38, para.38.3, lists the types of activities that an organisation might choose to outsource. In this organisation, a certain amount of IT support is outsourced. The nature of activities that are outsourced extensively are the sort of things that numerous businesses outsource. This includes, for example, facilities management, transport services, catering, cleaning, and so on.

39:2.2 Effect on Costs

As we saw earlier (*see* **Ch.38, para.38:5.2.3**), an important reason for outsourcing is to reduce and control operating costs. In this company, the decision to outsource is principally a cost-driven decision. For example, how much would they expect to save? The Director of the company explained as follows:

> I guess to make a decision to outsource worthwhile, and to make it worth taking the risks you take on when you cede control of the corporation to somebody else, I think you should aim to be saving about 15%.

39:2.3 Desire to Free Up Time

Sometimes, the decision to outsource may be influenced by a company's desire to free up more time for concentrating on its core business (*see* **Ch.38, para.38:5.1.1**). For this company, the Director said the following:

> On the IT side, it's influenced quite heavily by the desire for free time. The reason why it's a big driver in IT is because we're constrained by lack of good people. So the good people that we have, we want to focus on strategic goals. We don't really want those people hung up on day-to-day IT operations support. For finance it's a little bit different, because we don't have the same scarcity of resources, so for most of the core finance functions, which are run out of the main building, the sort of staff that we need for support are far more readily available. I guess with IT there's an element of freeing up strategic people to work on more business critical issues, because they're a limiting factor. In finance it would be more about cost, because we could get the people ourselves. We could get as good people as anyone else could - perhaps even better, because of the strength of our brand name.

39:2.4 Access to Skills

It can be important to the organisation considering outsourcing that the newly outsourced activities provide the business with enhanced or additional skills or capabilities (*see* **Ch.38, para.38:5.1.2**). For this company, the Director thought that it would 'depend on the scarcity of those skills'. For example, when outsourcing their IT services, scarcity of skills was 'key', because of 'a real constraint on the number of good IT people that are available in the marketplace'. However, for other disciplines, where there was more availability, he thought that this was a less important issue.

39:2.5 Increase in Flexibility

We might expect benefits from outsourcing to include the release of resources for other purposes (**see Ch.38, para.38:5.1.5**), thus leading to increased flexibility. Within this company, the Director thought the opposite:

> My expectation and experience is that we'd probably get less flexibility. My experience is in having run an accounting centre like this in-house for the company, but also having worked as an outsource service provider, where I provided outsourced services to another organisation along a similar model to this. Flexibility always sounds like a real plus when you start to talk about outsourcing. But what inevitably happens with outsourced services is that any change becomes the focus of a contractual discussion, and so a lot of changes get put on hold while the outsourcer and the recipient of the services negotiate over who's going to provide the services, and at what cost. I think, if flexibility is key, that for me is a reason to keep things in-house, rather than to outsource them.

39:2.6 Accountability

We saw in **Ch.38** that poor communication could lead to problems, and that both parties to an outsourcing contract need to be held accountable for their respective responsibilities (*see* **Ch.38, para.38:6.4**). But this director did not think that outsourcing should affect accountability in any way:

I don't think it should affect accountability at all. If we were to outsource everything that happened in this building, I would expect to retain the accountability for it, even though it was being done by the outside service provider. I would still be accountable, but I don't think I'd be responsible. If it all broke down and went wrong, I'd be the person who got fired, still, even though I wasn't actually doing the work. One of the things that is really important for outsourcing to work is to have someone within the organisation who really feels that they are accountable for making that relationship work well. If you don't have that … if everyone within the company were to stand back and abdicate their responsibility and say 'well, that's all been outsourced', then it doesn't work. So I think the accountability for making it work still has to stay very clearly within the organisation. But the responsibility for the actual doing could be placed with any number of external service providers.

39:3 Managing Suppliers

The process by which the company manages its supply chain should give some insight into how outsourcing might influence factors such as accounting and accountability.

39:3.1 Contractual Agreement

Given the difficulty in anticipating the organisations' needs for years to come (*see* **Ch.38, para.38:6.3**), how might it decide on the size and duration of the contract with specific suppliers?

I think our traditional model would give us the greatest value, so I think we'd model the number of alternatives economically, and drive towards the one that would give us the biggest value for our organisation. In some instances that might mean a supplier would like us to commit for a long time and is prepared to give us a very good rate to do that. In other situations it might mean that we would want to minimise our own commitment and maybe just do a one-year rolling contract with a chance to renegotiate each time. But the decision would principally be an economic one.

We've tended to try to avoid actually having big contractual documents and commitments. We try to structure arrangements in such a way that the shared interests of the two parties is so strong that it doesn't need a formal contract. So there's a tendency within our business to try to avoid getting into big contractual bureaucracy, and to just manage things in a very informal, but a very open and direct way. I think if we were to outsource a major part of the finance function we'd have to go for a much more disciplined contractual approach, and we would certainly need to have some sort of back-out clause. But having said that, I think when you outsource something, the magnitude of the change that you create is so great, you have to make it very hard to back out of it. The harder it is to make the change, the harder it has to be to unmake it, because otherwise, as soon as things start to get tough, everyone starts to look at the contract for ways to back out. And outsourcing your key services is so important, you've got to take the decision for the right reasons, and then you've got to make it work. The onus has got to be on everybody to make it work.

39:3.2 Supervision and Monitoring

Communication needs to be good, so that each party understands his or her role (*see* **Ch.38, para.38:6.4**). The supervision and monitoring of contracts should be made explicit and clear from the start. In this organisation, it worked as follows:

In the examples that we have at the moment, there have got to be very transparent service agreements in place. So both sides have got to be very clear about what's expected. If targets are not being met, there's got to be a real focus around having plans in place to improve processes. And there's got to be, I think, ongoing and very frequent dialogues at senior levels between both organisations. It's really around creating a very, very clear and measurable set of expectations; and then having processes in place to capture real data to measure how well those things are happening. And of course having targets, so that everyone knows what it is we should be heading towards.

39:3.3 Hidden Costs

Chapter 38 (**para.38:7.2.1**) showed us that it was important to bring all costs to the decision-making table. It is therefore essential to try to identify any 'hidden' costs that might occur through outsourcing. This director could not think of any specific examples that had arisen in his organisation. He did, however, elaborate on the issue:

> I think the biggest hidden cost is that you go into a contract expecting that everyone will deliver what the contract requires them to deliver. The real costs start to arise when people don't deliver what's expected, and I think there can be a real drain on resources, just in terms of managing that situation. If we had a team of people internally, who weren't delivering on their targets, then we could address that very easily. But if we've got a team of people externally, who aren't delivering on their targets, it's much harder to fix that, and a lot more energy gets drawn in to what can sometimes be quite a negative discussion. Whereas if it was something we're struggling with internally, the discussion would be very positive: 'how can we fix this?' So I think a lot of energy can get diverted into each side defending its position, rather than focusing on getting things sorted out.

39.3.4 Dealing with Problems

Continual monitoring is important, so that actual performance can be compared to projected target performance (*see* **Ch.38, para.38:7.2.2**).

> I think the difficulty is that the onus is very much on them, then, to fix that problem, and this is a problem with outsourcing things which are critical to the business – you do lose control. You can have all sorts of contractual conditions and service level agreements and key performance targets in place, but if the people delivering the service are fundamentally failing to deliver, there's very little that we can then do about it, except to go to the service provider and say '(y)ou are not delivering on these following five things. We want to know by the end of tomorrow what you're going to do to change that'. But at the end of the day you have actually transferred responsibility for that service, so fixing it if it goes wrong is very difficult. Ultimately, you have to resort back to the contract, you have to consider putting it out to other suppliers, you have to consider putting it back in-house.

39:3.5 Control

What measures might be put in place to maintain control over the companies that provide outsourcing services for an organisation? In this organisation, the Director was very clear about what might be done:

> The one that's key to me is a purchase audit group that we have. With the group, we have a very clear budget, and they have targets that they have agreed. They know the level of activity that we expect from them. They know the results we expect them to give in terms of converting activity into pound notes. But what we've done with that function is we've set up our own team to work alongside theirs, so we've actually got some people who are working on delivering the service, but who are still our employees. Because of this question of letting go of the skills, we actually want our people to get more skills out of the arrangement, not less. Having people within our organisation who have the accountability, and who are actually involved in the service delivery, is absolutely key.

39:3.6 Impact of Outsourcing

It might be thought that outsourcing could have a negative impact on existing staff, who feel undervalued, and overlooked. Therefore, introducing outsourced activities should be done with tact and diplomacy.

> I think we've used it very sensitively, simply because there is this potential negative impact on staff. I think the case for doing it has got to be so clear cut that staff can understand why we've done it. It's either got to be that these people have skills that we simply do not have and can't acquire, or it's got to be that these people can do this in a way which is so much more efficient than we can do it. And even then it's got to be done in a way that says, this is right for our own staff because it then frees them up to work on other things that are important to our company.

39:3.7 Privacy

In terms of the potential loss of privacy that might arise having decided to outsource, this Director said:

> 'I don't think we have really; I don't think it's a problem for me. We've obviously got confidentiality arrangements in place with anybody who's got access to any of the company's data. Yes, I think we open up the organisation to external third parties, but in return, I think we also get a lot of insight from third parties. I think we're balanced.'

39:4 Accounting Implications

(*see* Ch.38, para.38:7)

Finally, we consider the influence that an organisation's decision to outsource might have on accounting information systems.

39:4.1 Assessing Suitability of Contracts

(*see* Ch. 38, para.38:7.2.1)

In making the decision to outsource, and in choosing between alternative suppliers, an organisation might use a number of possible accounting calculations, such as NPV, DCF, Breakeven, Cost/Benefit analysis. This company used, primarily, a return on investment calculation, along with payback periods. Furthermore, as the Director explained:

> 'if the money was right, then we'd get on to qualitative measures. There's no point getting something cheap if it's flawed. But the principal measure that we use for any business case is a cash return on investment'.

39:4.2 Change in Accounting Information

We might believe that the use of accounting information should change once a company begins to outsource. In fact, in this organisation, little had changed. Partly, this was due to the fact that more information would require more assimilation and interpretation, and would cut down on any cost savings made through outsourcing. Furthermore, this company had a 'well-developed management information suite of reports', which worked adequately as they stood.

39:4.3 Identifying Core Activities

The identification of which functions are 'core' activities, and which should or could be outsourced, was not considered to be an accounting decision in this company. Rather, it was a business decision. If it were an accounting activity, then the accountants would decide. But if it were, for example, a logistics decision, or a supply chain decision, then the manager of that department or activity would take that decision. They would not have accountants tell them, but it would be a business decision, based on their intuition about the costs. Then, they would use the accountants to help them build the business case. In this sense, the accountants would be facilitators.

39:4.4 Control over Outsourcing Companies

When outsourcing core activities, the organisation might wish to retain control over an aspect of the outsourced company's accounting system. This director said:

> 'we would research their organisation and their financial strength before committing to any sort of agreement with them, but thereafter I'm not sure that we would continue to monitor. I think we would do a lot of due diligence upfront, before selecting an organisation. It would probably just depend on the organisation'.

39:4.5 Accounting for Outsourcing

In terms of accounting for outsourced work, what impact might this have on a company's management accounts? In this organisation, it was dealt with as follows:

We treat each function as a separate cost centre. We expect the benefits of the outsourcing deal to cover all the costs, and generate a certain amount of revenue on top of that. And that revenue we will then offset against our costs, and treat it as a cost saving. So we'll try and keep it very transparent. We'll say, '(W)e did this arrangement ... that's the financial benefit from doing it, that's the financial cost of running it. Here is the cost saving compared to when we were doing it ourselves, or if we weren't doing it at all'. And that we will offset against our costs.

On the work that we're doing to recover value from our supplier relationships, there's an expectation that we will make claims on suppliers of around £10m a year. And of that £10m there is then an expectation of a certain percentage of that, that will be enhancement for profit, and all the costs will have to be covered out of the balance. So the budget for that activity looks like '...here's the value of the claims we expect to make', then there's a recovery rate where we expect x% of those actions to be turned into cash, because some of those actions will be successfully defended by the suppliers. Then out of those claims recovered, there is this amount of money we expect to spend on the cost of the activity. So the bottom line is, out of these claims, we expect this percentage to turn into cash each year. And that has its own cost centre, and its own budget, and what we expect to see drop out at the end of the year is that amount of money.

39:4.6 Evaluating Outsourcing

How might a company evaluate the financial cost or benefit of its outsourced activities? In this company, each was treated on an individual basis:

Every one is a one-off, looked at individually. It should be monitored continually. It would depend on the nature of the provision of the service. I'm sure with things like our cleaning contract, we'll monitor the quality on an ongoing basis, but we'd only fundamentally review the contractual relationship maybe once a year. With something that was a little bit more critical to the business, then we would be reviewing it on a far more regular basis than that. So I'm sure for things like hauliers, which are absolutely key for getting goods from distribution to our stores, then there would be far more regular monitoring, and far more frequent dialogue.

39:4.7 Breakdown of Relations

In any situation where a contract is made between the organisation and a third party, there is the possibility that the contract might break down. In the case of an outsourcing contract breaking down, what might be the role of management accountants in evaluating the costs of failure to the company? Our respondent suggested the following:

> I suppose there will always be a cost of breaking a contract. There will always be a cost of putting something else in its place. I think we would evaluate that decision on the same basis that we would evaluate any contractual arrangement, which is around the cash return on investment, and the payback period. We probably tend to make it a forward looking decision. So if you cancel a contract, you've got to do something else instead. Either you've got to go and recruit people to do it yourself, or you've got to commit to another service organisation to do it for you instead. So I think we would tend to look at it by saying, 'in future we're going to do this instead of that. To put this future strategy in place, there are things we need to do, one of which might be the cost of breaking the previous contract or the cost of dismantling that'. So that would go into the cost of this new way forward. I think, generally, it would be reactive.

39:5 Conclusions

This case study of a particularly successful retail organisation, with several different supply-chains and a substantial amount of outsourcing, provides some illuminating insight into how outsourced suppliers might be integrated into the system. Rather than see this as requiring ground-breaking and new methods of accounting for activities, the director of this organisation thought that the benefits to be obtained from outsourcing should not be overtaken by the costs involved; whether these be in terms of time and effort, or of the financial variety. Therefore, simplicity seemed to rule, but this should be matched with close monitoring and clear accountability of everyone involved. The role of the management accountant, in this case, was therefore primarily of a facilitator, rather than as a leader of change.

40. Value Chain Analysis

40:1 Introduction

40:1.1 Value Activities and Competitive Advantage

A successful firm is one which creates and retains value for its customers in excess of the costs it incurs in creating that value (Ohmae, 1982; Porter, 1985). To create value, a firm needs to perform value activities in designing, producing, marketing, delivering and supporting its products. Each value activity can contribute to the firm's cost position and create a basis for differentiation. A firm which performs the value activities more cheaply and better than its rivals, throughout the phases of the industry's evolution, gains sustainable competitive advantage over those rivals. Therefore, to understand the sources of competitive advantage, it is necessary to systematically analyse how the value activities are performed and how they interact with each other. The value chain concept is useful for this analysis. It is a means by which a firm can be disaggregated 'into its strategically relevant activities in order to understand the behaviour of costs and the existing and potential sources of differentiation' (Porter, 1985: 33). Sector or industry value chains are often too broad and can obscure important sources of competitive advantage. The relevant level for constructing a value chain is the firm's activities in a particular industry. In a diversified firm the relevant level is the business unit.

40:1.2 The Value Chain

A firm's value chain (*see* **Fig.40:1**) shows the total value it creates and consists of value activities and margin. The margin is the difference between total value and the collective costs of performing the value activities. Total value is defined as the amount buyers are willing to pay for the firm's product.

Noel Tagoe

Figure 40:1 **The generic value chain**
Source: Porter (1985:37)

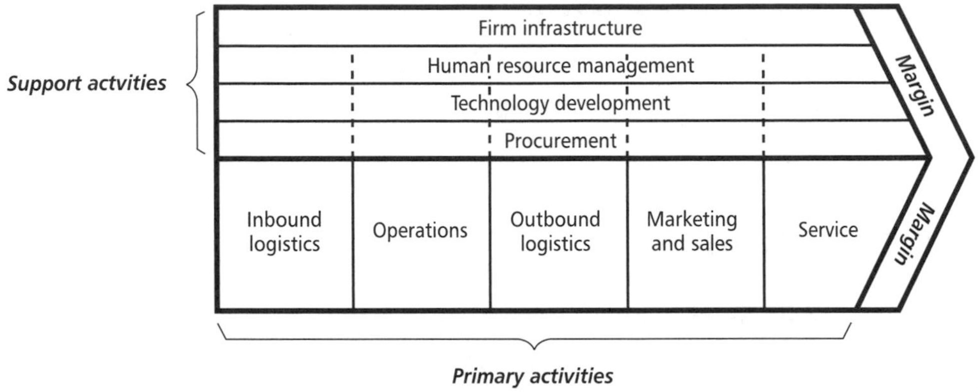

40:1.2.1 Primary Activities and Support Activities

Value activities could be primary activities or support activities. Primary activities are those activities performed in the physical creation of the product, its sale and transfer to the customer and after sales assistance. Support activities support the primary activities and each other by providing purchased inputs, technology, human resources and other firm-wide functions (Porter, 1985: 38). Primary activities comprise the following:

(a) *inbound logistics: activities related to receiving, storing and disseminating inputs to the product, such as material handling and warehousing;*
(b) *operations: activities associated with transforming inputs into the final product, such as machining, packaging, assembly and equipment maintenance;*
(c) *outbound logistics: activities relating to collecting, storing and physically distributing the product to customers, such as finished goods warehousing, order processing and delivery vehicle operations;*
(d) *marketing and sales: activities associated with providing a means by which customers can purchase the product and inducing them to do so, such as advertising, promotion, sales force and pricing; and*
(e) *service: activities associated with providing service to enhance or maintain the value of the product, such as installation, repair, training and parts supply.*

Support activities consist of the following:

(a) *procurement: the function of purchasing inputs used in the value chain. It is present in every value activity and therefore tends to be spread throughout the firm. Consequently, its total magnitude is often obscured;*

(b) *technology development: all the activities that can be grouped as efforts to improve the product and the process. It does not apply only to technologies directly linked to the end product. For example, office automation for the accounting department falls under technology as does process or product-related research and development (R&D) activities;*

(c) *human resource management: activities involved in the recruiting, hiring, training, development and compensation of all types of personnel. It occurs in different parts of the firm and can therefore lead to inconsistent policies. It affects competitive advantage through its role in determining the skills and motivation of employees and the cost of hiring and training. However its cumulative cost and the trade-offs in the costs of its different components are rarely understood; and*

(d) *firm infrastructure: a number of activities including general management, planning, finance, accounting and legal, which support the entire chain. It is often viewed only as an overhead but can be a powerful source of competitive advantage. For example, a good management information system can contribute significantly to a firm's cost position.*

40:1.2.2 Interdependencies and Linkages

Value activities are not just a collection of independent activities but rather a system of interdependent activities in which the performance of one activity affects the performance and cost of another. Competitive advantage does not only derive from the individual activities but also from the complex linkages between them. Though the linkages are crucial for competitive advantage they often go unrecognised because they are subtle. Three forms of interdependence can arise. First, internal linkages within the same value chain which reflect the impact of one activity on another. For example, by reducing the number of parts in a product, the product development activity could reduce the cost of production. Secondly, linkages between the value chains of business units within the same firm can occur when a value activity is shared by the business units. Sharing can increase throughput, reduce unit costs and improve the pattern of capacity utilisation. Finally, vertical linkages exist between a firm's value chain and those of its suppliers and customers. These can provide benefits for both the firm and its suppliers and customers. Just-in-time (JIT) production practices exploit such vertical linkages. All three forms of interdependence provide opportunities for joint optimisation and raise problems of co-ordination (Porter, 1985; Hergert and Morris, 1989).

40:2 Value Chain Analysis

Value chain analysis is an iterative process which involves the following tasks:

(a) *divide the firm into strategic business units (SBUs);*
(b) *identify the value-creating activities in each SBU;*
(c) *assign costs, assets and value (i.e. revenue) to each value activity;*
(d) *use cost drivers to investigate the cost behaviour of each value activity and how it relates to other value activities in its value chain, in those of other SBUs in the same firm, and in those of its suppliers and customers; and*
(e) *repeat the process for competitors (see **Ch.7**).*

40:2.1 Strategic Business Unit (SBU)

A diversified firm manufactures many products often using different production processes and technologies. It might also operate in several markets and industries each with different underlying structures. The products, processes, technologies, markets and industries which the firm produces, uses or operates in, or some combinations of them, constitute different subunits of the firm. Each subunit or group of subunits may provide different sources of competitive advantage and should, therefore, be analysed and managed separately. The SBU concept provides a means for such analysis. It groups different subunits of a firm based on some important strategic elements common to each.

Defining SBUs is not easy. The guiding principle is to determine what subunits of the firm can be considered autonomous such that decisions about one group of sub-units can be made in relative (but not total) isolation from decisions about another group (Hergert and Morris, 1989: 179). Two main steps are involved. First, the analyst should look for shared or common characteristics between units. In practice the analyst looks inside the firm for shared costs and technologies, and outside the firm for shared markets, distribution channels and customers. The internal and external perspectives might not yield the same results. In that event, the second step is to identify the *most critical* shared resources and form the SBUs along those dimensions. Different SBUs will still share important resources thus creating linkages between them. These linkages can be significant sources of competitive advantage and should therefore be analysed, understood and exploited.

A useful source of advice on this issue is contained in *SSAP25: Segmental Reporting* which, although accepting that no single set of factors may be universally applied to help us define a reportable segment, does at least offer some basic guidance for segmenting information by business or geographically. See also *IAS14: Segment Reporting*, which defines a business segment as 'a distinguishable component of an entity that is engaged in providing an individual product or service, or a group of related products or services and that is subject to risks and returns that are different from those of other business segments'.

The SBU concept has been criticised by Prahalad and Hamel (1990). They noted that at the root of the concept of SBUs lies the notion that a firm is a portfolio of business. In their opinion, a firm should rather be viewed as a portfolio of competencies which span SBUs. In this way shared resources across businesses can be identified and effectively utilised. The need to identify how resources can be effectively shared across business units is a defining feature of value chain analysis. Therefore, when applied in the value chain analysis, the SBU concept overcomes the weakness identified by Prahalad and Hamel.

40:2.2 Value-creating Activities

Identifying the firm's value-creating activities starts with the generic value chain (**Fig.40:1**). It is then disaggregated into individual value-creating activities which are technologically and strategically distinct. The disaggregation is guided by three principles. First, the activities must represent a significant or rapidly growing percentage of operating costs or assets. Though most firms can easily identify activities that represent a large proportion of costs they often overlook smaller but growing value activities.

Secondly, value activities must be disaggregated if they have different cost drivers (*see* **Ch.22, para.22:3**). Thus advertising and promotion should belong to separate value activities because advertising cost is sensitive to scale while promotional costs are mostly variable (Porter, 1985). Also, since both internal and external linkages can influence overall costs, any activity which is linked with another activity, or is shared across SBUs or with customers or suppliers, should be separated. Therefore, in order to identify value activities one must know the behaviour of costs. However, this rarely happens in practice. To start with, the disaggregation of the generic value chain is often based on the best guess about important differences in cost behaviour. Subsequently, the analyst systematically examines the cost behaviour of the disaggregated value activities, puts together those whose perceived cost behaviour differences are minor and further separates activities which still reveal crucial differences in cost behaviour. This task requires several iterations of analysing cost behaviour, aggregating and/or disaggregating activities as the cost analysis proceeds.

Thirdly, and finally, value-creating activities should be separated if key competitors perform them differently (such as when a competitor shares that activity with a related SBU and the firm does not). Sometimes differences among competitors might indicate that an activity is the source of a cost advantage or a basis for differentiation.

40:2.3 Costs, Assets and Values of Value Activities

Operating costs are assigned to the activities in which they are incurred. In principle, this is straightforward though it can be time consuming. Often, accounting records are reworked to match costs with value activities rather than with accounting classifications especially for purchased inputs and overheads. The cost of a shared activity is initially allocated to one business unit and later shared out on the basis of some allocation formula. The allocation formula is based on an understanding of the cost behaviour of that activity.

Assigning assets to value activities is more complex. The analyst assigns assets to the activities that employ, control or most influence their use (Porter, 1985: 65). Asset accounts are often regrouped to correspond to activities and valued in a consistent manner. The assets 'may be assigned at their book or replacement value and compared to operating costs in this form, or [their] book or replacement value may be translated into operating costs via capital charges' (Porter, 1985: 66).

In assigning value to a value activity it is important to remember that value chain analysis is based on the notion that a product gains value as it passes through the stream of primary activities. Since value is defined as the willingness of the buyer to pay for the product at each processing stage, it can be difficult for the analyst to know the value to the buyer of an intermediate activity. Where the intermediate products are sold on the external market, their prices can be used as proxies for value of the activities performed on them. If no external markets exist for the intermediate products transfer prices (*see* **Ch.36**) can be used. Porter also advises that costs can be useful surrogates for the value of such intermediate activities.

The precision of financial reporting is not required for the purposes of assigning costs, assets and value to value activities. Broad estimates are often adequate to highlight strategic issues especially where the costs of generating accurate figures are prohibitive. However, where particular activities are revealed to be important to cost advantage, the analyst can make a greater effort at precision.

40:2.4 Cost Behaviour and Cost Drivers

The analyst must investigate the cost behaviour of each value activity and how it relates to the other value activities in its value chain and in those of its related SBUs, suppliers and customers. The rationale for this investigation is to understand the underlying cost structure of each activity with the view to controlling or reconfiguring it in the value chain to achieve sustainable competitive advantage. Porter refers to the determinants of cost as *cost drivers* and identified the following ten:

1. *economies and diseconomies of scale;*
2. *learning and spillover;*
3. *pattern of capacity utilisation;*
4. *linkages;*
5. *interrelationships;*
6. *integration;*
7. *timing;*
8. *discretionary policies;*
9. *location; and*
10. *institutional factors.*

Detailed definitions of these cost drivers are provided in **Table 40:1**.

Identifying cost drivers is not always easy. Sometimes the cost driver of an activity can be intuitively clear from examining its basic economics. For example, the costs of the sales force is determined by local market share because high local share reduces travel time (Porter, 1985: 87–8). Where this is not the case the firm can employ at least two approaches to identifying cost drivers. First, it can examine its own internal experience using past cost data and adjusting for inflation, changes in policies and other confounding events. Second, the analyst can interview individuals with extensive knowledge of value activities such as production managers. Such individuals may be asked 'what if?' questions regarding the effect of changing various production parameters.

Table 40:1 **Cost drivers and their definitions**

Source: Hergert and Morris (1989: 184)

		Definition
1	Economies and diseconomies of scale	Impact of scale on the costs of performing an activity. Increasing complexity can lead to diseconomies.
2	Learning and spillover	Reduction in cost of performing an activity due to experience. Learning from the experience of others is called spillover.

(cont'd)

(Table 40:1 *cont'd*)

		Definition
3	Pattern of capacity utilisation	High fixed costs and high change over costs provide opportunities for joint optimisation of production logistics and marketing.
4	Linkages	The cost of an activity is related to how other activities are performed within the same value chain and in the chains of suppliers and buyers.
5	Interrelationships	An SBU may be able to benefit from sharing scarce resources with another SBU within the same firm.
6	Integration	Vertical integration may reduce transaction costs, but at the expense of flexibility and scale. Buying goods or services that were sourced in-house is particularly difficult.
7	Timing	There are circumstances in which it pays to be the first mover. In others it is better to be a follower.
8	Discretionary policies	Decisions by the firm, not related to the other cost drivers, influence the cost of an activity (e.g. product specification).
9	Location	The skills of the labour force, access to transportation, etc., all affect costs.
10	Institutional factors	Government incentives, union power, regulations of all sorts, have a major impact on costs.

40:2.5 Competitor Value Chain
(*See* **Ch.7.**)

Analysing the value chain of competitors can be very difficult. The main difficulty lies with identifying the value-creating activities and their underlying cost structure without privileged access to internal information. Although it is not an impossible task, the difficulties in obtaining such information must not be underestimated. A list of sources of information for competitor analysis is given in **Chapter 7, paragraph 7:3.1.** Again, it must be stressed that the figures should only be estimates and not precise ones.

40:3 Accounting and Value Chain Analysis

The suitability of accounting data for strategic analysis (including value chain analysis) has been questioned by some strategy writers. For example, in Porter's opinion, though 'accounting systems ... contain useful data for cost analysis, they often get in the way of strategic cost analysis' (Porter, 1985: 63). This criticism relates primarily to the 'traditional' accounting systems of the 1980s. Since then new accounting and cost systems have been identified, some of which are capable of providing useful information for strategic analysis. This section presents some of the difficulties and problems inherent in using data from 'traditional' accounting systems for value chain analysis. It concludes with some thoughts on how some more recent accounting and costing methods, such as activity-based costing (ABC), overcome some of the difficulties.

40:3.1 Difficulties and Problems

Hergert and Morris (1989) identify five main obstacles to using accounting data for value chain analysis. These obstacles are:

1. *the accounting system will not recognise SBUs as a dimension for data accumulation where a firm is not organised around SBUs (p.180);*
2. *there is no obvious correspondence between value activities as defined by the value chain and the responsibility centres of accounting systems, therefore assigning costs to activities is well nigh impossible (p.181);*
3. *because traditional accounting systems collect costs around products they offer very little help if the physical product does not create buyer value. Even if the physical product is important cost accounting systems run into trouble because they distinguish between product costs and period costs (p.182);*
4. *accounting systems assume independence of subunits and thus rarely collect information for co-ordinating and optimising different activities. When this is not the case, they use rudimentary tools for modelling interdependencies (p.183); and*
5. *cost-centre budgets are a poor reflection of the economics of performing an activity. This is due to the inability of accounting systems to diagnose cost drivers and their behaviour (p.185).*

According to Hergert and Morris, very little can be done to resolve these difficulties because they are inherent in the design and operation of traditional costing systems. Possible exceptions include building a product costing system for period costs (to deal with part of the third obstacle) and ensuring that the chart of accounts and cost-centre budgets are compatible with value chain analysis (to deal with the fifth obstacle).

40:3.2 Overcoming the Difficulties

The first obstacle puts together two issues, namely organisational design and the dimensions along which costs are accumulated. The first issue is mainly the responsibility of top management and Porter advises that firms intending to use value chain analysis should structure themselves along SBU lines. The problems presented by the second issue appear insuperable because Hergert and Morris assume that the dimensions along which the accounting system accumulates costs are not compatible with the SBU notion. This assumption might not be true for the more recent systems. For example, ABC systems (*see* **Ch.22**) collect costs of activities and allocate them to products or distribution channels (Cooper and Kaplan, 1991; Yoshikawa *et al.*, 1993). Since SBUs are often defined in relation to products or distribution channels (i.e. the cost objects of ABC), among others, it is possible to organise ABC systems to give SBU information even if the firm is not formally structured around SBUs. Further, because ABC systems can allocate activity costs to cost objects other than products they can overcome the third obstacle of Hergert and Morris (1989). Finally, rigorous cost driver analysis is an integral part of the ABC methodology. As a result cost centre budgets of firms using an ABC system might not be poor reflections of the economics of performing an activity as Hergert and Morris allege (i.e. the fifth obstacle).

The lack of correspondence between value activities and accounting responsibility centres – Hergert and Morris's second obstacle – presents some challenges. This obstacle might reflect at least three differences which exist between cost centres and value activities. First, some value activities may not be recognised as such and they may be performed by different functions. Therefore, they may have no organisational counterparts. Secondly, a function might contain more than one value activity but the cost centres into which that function has been subdivided do not recognise this fact. Thirdly, the definition of different functions does not distinguish between primary and support activities (Hergert and Morris, 1989: 181). These challenges are, however, not insurmountable. Responsibility centres can be redefined so that they map to value activities. It might be easier to make such modifications with more recent systems, such as ABC systems, than with traditional systems.

Whereas traditional accounting systems rarely model interdependencies and linkages, more recent systems are explicitly taking these issues on board. Accounting systems are now modelling and/or managing interdependencies to support supply-chain management (SCM). For example, accountants in purchasing firms are now required to understand the cost structure of suppliers in order to embark upon joint cost-reduction efforts. This understanding is derived through open book accounting and other means of observing or enquiring about the supplier's costs. Open book accounting involves the supplier and purchaser sharing their cost information with each other, including cost drivers with the view to identifying areas were cost could be more effectively managed. Nissan subsidiaries in the UK used this approach to good effect (Carr and Ng, 1995). Supermarkets use electronic point of sale (EPOS) – part of the accounting system – and electronic data interchange (EDI) systems to link up with suppliers. This linkage enables the alignment of order processing, forecasting and the monitoring and management of goods from source to check-out. Tagoe and Innes (1998) also provide evidence of changes in accounting performance measures relating to the accounts payable system of a major electronic company in order to ensure effective and on-time delivery of components to its manufacturing facility. A team (including accountants) from the same electronic company is working closely with distribution channels to improve their stock turn. The accounting system is an integral part of this effort.

This section has sought to demonstrate that the problems of using accounting data for value chain analysis are not insuperable (*see* Shank and Govindarajan, 1989). More recent methods of accounting for and managing costs, such as target costing, functional analysis (often using value engineering and market research) and Kaizen costing are being identified, refined and disseminated (e.g. Cooper, 1995). Nevertheless there can be considerable difficulty in overcoming them. Consequently it might be useful for firms intending to use value chain analysis regularly to create an accounting system for that purpose. This system can be linked to existing financial reporting and management accounting systems such that transaction data can be captured once for all three systems. This arrangement would make it possible to perform value chain analysis without recruiting an army of analysts to rework management accounting data.

References

Carr, C. and Ng, J. (1995) 'Total cost control: Nissan and its UK supplier relationships', *Management Accounting Research, 6*: 347–65.

Cooper, R. (1995) *When lean enterprises collide: Competing through confrontation.* Boston, MA: Harvard Business School Press.

Cooper, R. and Kaplan, R. (1991) *The design of cost management systems.* Englewood Cliffs, NJ: Prentice-Hall.

Hergert, M. and Morris, D. (1989) 'Accounting data for value chain analysis', *Strategic Management Journal, 10*: 175–88.

Ohmae, K. (1982) *The mind of the strategist: The art of Japanese business.* McGraw-Hill.

Porter, M.E. (1985) *Competitive advantage: Creating and sustaining superior performance.* New York: Free Press.

Prahalad, C.K. and Hamel, G. (1990) 'The core competence of the corporation', *Harvard Business Review*, May–June: 79–93.

Shank, J.K. and Govindarajan, V. (1989) Strategic cost analysis: *The evolution from managerial to strategic accounting.* Homewood, IL: Irwin.

Tagoe, N. and Innes, J. (1998) 'Accounting and supply chain management: A case study of trust', paper presented at the 1998 European Accounting Association Congress in Antwerp, Belgium, April.

Yoshikawa, T., Innes, J., Mitchell, F. and Tanaka, M. (1993) *Contemporary cost management.* London: Chapman and Hall.

41. Supply Chain and Management Accounting

41:1 Supply-chain Management

It has been argued that traditional management accounting techniques do not readily support supply-chain management perspectives. In order to identify a role for management accountants and management accounting in this important strategic area, this chapter looks at recent developments in management accounting that can be used to provide positive support to supply-chain initiatives.

A familiar definition of the term 'supply-chain management' is:

> The strategic management process, unifying the systematic planning and control of all technologies, materials and services, from identification of need by the ultimate customer. It encompasses planning, designing, purchasing, production, logistics and quality. The objectives are to optimise performance in meeting agreed customer service requirements, minimising cost, whilst optimising the use of all resources throughout the entire supply chain.

(DTI, 1997)

Inter-firm supply chains involve the organisation working actively beyond its own legal and organisational boundaries to encompass relationships with suppliers and customers along the value chain (*see* **Ch.40**). This philosophy runs in contrast to the internal focus prescribed in traditional management accounting that does not recognise the potential for exploiting linkages with the firm's suppliers and customers. Practising management accountants have to develop new techniques which will facilitate the management of new organisational forms (for example, strategic alliances, partnerships, networks, virtual organisations), the growth of which has been a significant feature of supply-chain management developments aimed at securing competitive advantage in a dynamic market place. In essence, management accounting systems must be capable of identifying costs and value adding processes across traditional organisational boundaries and be focused on supporting and influencing the successful transition towards more co-operative ventures between organisations.

41:2   Limitations of Traditional Systems

Before discussing recent developments aimed at supporting supply-chain initiatives, it is worth first listing the limitations of traditional management accounting systems. The limitations of traditional management accounting systems in terms of supply-chain management developments are as follows:

(a) *Traditional management accounting systems tend to focus on the internal operation of the organisation and fail to provide information on external relationships in the supply chain.*

(b) *Traditional management accounting systems tend to focus on functions rather than processes. The basic nature of a supply chain demands information on processes.*

(c) *Traditional management accounting systems tend to be based on a culture of adversarial relationships with suppliers and customers rather than on collaborative relationships.*

(d) *Traditional management accounting systems tend to be focused, in terms of performance measurement, on financial measures of performance rather than on a balanced approach incorporating both financial and non-financial measures. The fundamentals of supply-chain management demand measurement of non-financial indicators such as quality, speed, delivery, reliability and service as well as financial measures (see **Chs 48** and **49**).*

(e) *Traditional management accounting systems tend to be focused on the short term rather than looking at longer-term development issues. Developing strong supply-chain relationships takes time and involves an investment in time for the future. The benefits associated with this investment in time need to be evaluated in the long term.*

(f) *From the perspective of many non-financial managers, management accountants are still regarded as working in an 'ivory-tower' environment rather than as members of a management team.*

(g) *These limitations need to be addressed in order to enable management accounting and management accountants to play an important role in future supply-chain management developments.*

The potential for management accounting to contribute significantly in this area was highlighted in a couple of surveys published in late 1999 (A.D. Little, 1999; ISCAN, 1999). The surveys identified areas for future development and significant mention was made of accounting issues. Specific mention was given to the following:

(a) *The need to develop effective systems to measure the benefits of supply-chain relationships.*
(b) *The need to identify and achieve effective cost reduction and price targets.*
(c) *The need to focus on cost effective processes providing compelling value to the customer.*

The industrialists involved in the surveys were on the whole non-financial people who identified an opportunity for accountants to be involved in developing supply-chain relationships. However, this involvement would need to come through the use of relevant techniques and through the involvement of management accountants as members of supply chain management teams.

41:3 Management Accounting for Supply Chains

A review of the previous literature on the impact of supply chain management reveals the following major potential implications and opportunities for management accounting:

(a) *Strategic management accounting techniques (see **Ch.2**) need to be employed which ensure that management accounting focuses on information outside the organisation as well as internal information. Information about a supply chain involves knowledge of the costs of suppliers and customers and the cost of competitors' supply chains.*
(b) *Lean production models and applications demand the identification of value-adding and non-value-adding processes and the costs associated with these (see **Ch.28, para.28:1.1** and **Ch.32**). Activities in the supply chain need to be assessed with regard to both costs and their contribution to the creation of value. Linked to this is the concept of horizontal information systems, which are based on processes rather than functions.*

(c) *Benchmarking (see **Ch.53**) has been advocated as a useful framework for measuring and assessing the performance of supply chains. Benchmarking may take place against other organisations or other supply chains.*

(d) *Strategic opportunities of information technology in the supply chain – developments such as Electronic Data Interchange and Enterprise Resource Planning models (see **Ch.52**). Information technology will act as an enabler for future developments in supply chains.*

(e) *Identification of cost drivers and analysing costs through the supply chain are essential components in the search for competitive advantage. Activity-based information (see **Chs 13, 22, 28, 29, 30** and **31**) can provide relevant information about activities across the entire chain of value adding activities (both internal and external to the organisation).*

(f) *The need to identify total costs throughout the supply chain and the various linkages together with the associated use of target costing (see **Ch.24**).*

(g) *The need to support active collaboration and partnership with open book accounting. Cost transparency and the sharing of cost information can help to develop trusting relationships.*

(h) *Performance measures need to recognise and identify benefits associated with relationships through the supply chain. This necessitates the use of a balanced approach to performance measurement (see **Ch.54**).*

(i) *Management accountants need to develop their commercial and business understanding as well as forming closer working relationships with their fellow managers.*

In simple terms, there is an opportunity for management accounting to play an active positive role in the management and development of supply chains. The competitive impact of supply-chain developments such as strategic alliances and collaborative ventures can be enhanced by the use of appropriate management accounting techniques and systems.

41:4   Some Evidence from Practice

Having identified some of the problems of traditional management accounting systems in this area and some of the suggestions for ways in which management accounting can be changed to accommodate supply-chain management thinking, we will now go on to look at some actual examples of developments in management accounting which are recognised as contributing to successful supply-chain management initiatives. These examples come from a study carried out by Berry *et al.* (2000) on the implications of inter-firm supply chains for management accounting. The techniques and issues we will consider are as follows:

(a) *open book accounting and shared budgets;*
(b) *target costing;*
(c) *horizontal information systems based on processes;*
(d) *identification of non-value adding activities through the supply chain;*
(e) *balanced scorecard approach to performance measurement across the supply chain;*
(f) *accountants as members of multi-functional teams.*

These new developments will be explained through the use of three small case studies, which illustrate the practical application of these techniques.

41:4.1   Case Study – Dextron

Dextron designs, assembles and builds electronic machines for business use in an intensely competitive market. A 'Cost Management Group' (CMG) was set up within Dextron as part of a strategic response to competitive pressures and the need to improve all aspects of the supply chain.

The CMG was given considerable freedom to take and propose initiatives. Initially the group just consisted of two people – a project accountant and a project engineer. However, over time this group has expanded and other functional areas have joined the team for *ad hoc* projects. The group is free to operate across boundaries both inside and outside the organisation. Among the projects that have been undertaken to gain significant cost reductions are:

(a) *reduction in the number of suppliers;*
(b) *make-or-buy decisions;*
(c) *reduction in lead time given to suppliers for part or component orders;*
(d) *benchmarking suppliers;*
(e) *development of suppliers suggestion schemes;*
(f) *supplier management programmes;*
(g) *exercises on cost of quality;*
(h) *benchmarking and tear-down analysis in order to understand competitors' products and processes.*

These projects focused attention on processes and each project led to others. A monthly report is prepared by the group that highlights key cost, activity and supplier issues. It has been estimated that the CMG has generated savings of between 8 and 10 million dollars over two years. An important feature is that the CMG has been freed from the normal monthly and annual time cycles of the accounting and reporting structures in the company. This ability not to be bound by artificial time boundaries has enabled the group to have both a short-term project focus and a longer-term development focus. The role of the accountants in the CMG has been central to its effectiveness as they have become immersed in production, commercial, organisational, managerial, catalytic and change management issues while not losing the substantive accounting contribution they were making.

41:4.2   Case Study – Alliance

This case is based around a business relationship involving two companies in the manufacture and supply of a customised component in the automotive industry. The assembler, a subsidiary of a large American multinational, was developing a strategic partnership with a supplier which itself was a subsidiary of a large UK multinational. The companies had been doing business for about 25 years but until recently their relationship had been a traditional arm's-length relationship.

The concept of a strategic partnership started with the formation of a draft alliance agreement based on a document drawn up by the assembler, which stressed the principle of an open and trusting relationship that 'delivers tangible and measurable benefits to both sides over a long period, and allows for the sharing of ideas and information'. The agreement specified:

(a) *Cost reduction targets – specific mention was made of a 6% cost reduction, which was interpreted as an 'all-in cost'.*

(b) *Areas for continuous improvement – both companies to work together to develop a culture which searches for waste, and actively eliminates waste everywhere. Specific reference made to issues such as pull systems, scheduling, people networking and Electronic Data Interchange.*

(c) *A management review process – three-monthly review process.*

(d) *A grievance procedure – to deal with situations where either organisation was having difficulty meeting its commitments under the partnership arrangements.*

(e) *The nature of cross-company teams whose brief was to seek out and design mutually beneficial technological projects. Accountants from both organisations were included in this multifunctional team.*

The concept of open book accounting was part of the relationship. Here, open book accounting was not perceived as a mechanism whereby only the supplier opened its books to the customer. It was recognised, in this relationship, that the need to share information must be two-way and that there was also a need for the customer to open its books to the supplier, sharing data (including cost and value-added calculations) with the supplier. An important part of the relationship was therefore a willingness to look across company boundaries and allow open book analysis within pre-agreed limits. It is interesting to note, however, that the sharing of management accounting information was made more difficult by the idiosyncrasies in the individual firm's management accounting systems.

Specific use was made of several management accounting techniques in order to gain benefits out of the newly developed collaborative arrangements:

(a) *Discussions concentrated on operational processes rather than functions. For example, a particular process was identified where 'all-in cost' could be reduced if a procedure, which was currently carried out by the assembler, was in fact completed by the supplier. Such a cost reduction was only possible by looking across organisational boundaries. A non-value adding process was eliminated through this change in responsibility.*

(b) *The technique of target costing was also used to enable managers to think 'outside the box'. Target costing was linked to the total cost concept to initiate cost reduction activities. Linked with the use of target costing, it was agreed that cross-company teams would be established to design new products at the concept stage.*

(c) *Discussions also took place with regard to the use of a balanced scorecard performance measurement and reporting system – customer perspective, internal business perspective, innovation and learning perspective, financial perspective – across organisational boundaries. This was perceived as a means of measuring the benefits of partnership to both organisations. The relationship between financial and non-financial indicators to be identified and communicated widely within the organisations.*

41:4.3   Case Study – Morrison Construction

The momentum for change in the construction sector came from government commissioned reports that promoted the concept of partnering between supplier and client and the concept of total cost improvement. The benefits of such partnering would be seen through improvements in quality, quicker completion times and a reduction in costs. Morrison Construction enthusiastically took on board these ideas and produced operating margins that far exceeded the average in the industry.

The following are some examples of the management accounting practices used to support these partnership arrangements:

(a) *In the construction of a large supermarket, Morrison has a partnership arrangement with a large retail organisation and the retail client would give a budget (linked to the concept of target cost) to Morrison Construction which would aim to work within that budget. If they complete the project at a cost less than the original budget, then the profit is shared between the two parties on an agreed basis. In order for this to work, there is a necessity for open book accounting. Similar arrangements also exist with utility organisations in the water supply sector.*

(b) *For performance measurement, Morrison uses the concept of the balanced scorecard. They adopt a system, which uses the imagery of a golf course and 18 holes with par scores identified for each hole. The actual performance against par is subject to both internal and external perceptions of what has happened. A documented relationship between Morrison and Thames Water provided some interesting insights into the extended use of the balanced scorecard, which measured the relationship in terms of innovation, customer service, quality and cost issues.*

41:4.4   Key Issues from the Three Cases

The three case studies illustrate ways in which management accounting helped managers dealing with supply-chain management issues. In terms of evaluation, the cases can also be identified as being at three different stages of supply-chain development:

(a) *Dextron – can be described as serial dependence where Dextron is the dominant organisation and most of the management accounting initiatives involve improved understanding and control over suppliers' costs. Accountants were involved, in association with the purchasing department, in the selection of suppliers and associated benchmarking exercises. Detailed discussions took place with suppliers about the level of their costs and their willingness to reduce them. This led to a reduction in the number of suppliers.*

(b) *Alliance – can be described as reciprocal dependence where both parties in the arrangement were seeking improvements through open negotiation and sharing of information. The management accounting initiatives here concentrated on open book accounting, target costing and understanding the costs of processes both inside and between the organisations. Performance measurement was concerned with identifying the benefits of the new arrangements for both organisations. Management accounting played a constitutional role in the establishment and management of trusting and collaborative business relationships. The Procurement Director at the assembler organisation was particularly keen for management accountants to be active participants in these supply-chain developments.*

(c) *Morrison Construction – can be described as mutual dependence where complete collaboration is the key driving force of the relationship. The management accounting initiatives here continued to include open book accounting and target costing but extended these by including agreed formulas for sharing profits and losses. Developments in the construction sector are particularly interesting because the sector is moving from a culture where adversarial relationships dominated to one where partnership and collaboration is now seen to be potentially more productive and financially rewarding.*

(d) *A common theme in these cases is the involvement of management accountants (Quantity Surveyors in construction) in multifunctional teams. These teams were designed to work on understanding processes along the chain that crossed functional and organisational boundaries. Management accountants are therefore developing their broader managerial and personal skills, and commercial capability, as well as their financial knowledge. Much of this work was being done through ad hoc projects alongside the normal accounting systems, which remained unchanged.*

41:4.5   Additional Findings from Other Companies

As well as the three organisations already covered, Berry *et al.* (2000) also reported on results from 14 other briefer studies of firms in supply chains, five of which were based on intra-firm evidence. The organisations came from a wide range of different industries – engineering, manufacturing, electronics, telecommunications, retail, pharmaceuticals, logistics and publishing. Brief summary additional findings from these organisations are as follows:

(a) *Most of the organisations were managing supply-chain relationships link by link, rather than across the complete supply chain. This meant that management accounting developments tended to concentrate on a supplier and immediate customer. This limits some of the benefits that can be attained through further understanding of costs throughout the supply chain. In the A.D. Little (1999) survey on European Supply Chains, it is suggested that there is a danger of suboptimisation if the performance of supply chains are measured link by link rather than measuring the performance of the entire chain.*

(b) There was evidence of the development of process-driven integrated information systems. This links in to the continued development of Enterprise Resource Planning models (see Ch.52).

(c) The driving force for most of the developments in supply-chain management was the notion of world class performance. We did find evidence, in different organisations, of horizontal information systems, Kaizen costing, benchmarking (see Ch.53), open book accounting, value engineering (see Ch.25) and target costing (see Ch.24). These techniques were being used sparingly in inter-firm and richly in intra-firm contexts. Opportunities exist for these techniques to be used further in inter-firm contexts.

(d) Consistent increasing involvement of management accountants in multifunctional teams and supply-chain issues (see Ch.4). The appointment of management accountants to jobs carrying the title of 'supply-chain accountant' or 'continuous improvement manager' suggests that the contribution of management accountants in this area is now being recognised.

Having looked at some of the evidence from practice, we will now make brief reference to the important role of information technology in supply-chain developments.

41:5   Information Technology

Reference has already briefly been made to Electronic Data Interchange (EDI) and Enterprise Resource Planning (ERP) (*see* **Ch.50**). Developments in information technology have enabled strategic information systems to be utilised across organisational boundaries. It has enabled increased information sharing, a better quality of information being distributed, and the utilisation of software to enable key members of the supply chain to be linked. It is important to recognise, however, that information technology acts as an enabler, but that it is only management action on aspects such as re-engineering processes that will actually eliminate those processes that do not add value.

Future developments in e-business involve ERP models developed by software companies (for example SAP) which provides opportunities for e-commerce and e-partnering. The future development of concepts such as virtual organisations, which involve co-operation between several independent partners who share their resources, skills and knowledge to produce a best customer solution, will be enabled through developing information technology. Importantly, the development of the virtual organisation takes concepts such as strategic alliances further and will require further changes in the way management accounting systems operate. Some of the ideas already discussed will need to be developed further to maintain a positive role for management accounting and management accountants in these new hybrid forms of organisations.

41:6 Conclusions

The material presented in the chapter suggests that management accountants and management accounting have a significant role to play in the management of supply chains. In order to take advantage of these new opportunities, management accountants need to develop their skills in terms of personal relationships and business acumen as well as the continued maintenance of their financial and analytical skills.

A significant feature of supply-chain management developments has been the growth of new organisational forms aimed at securing competitive advantage in a dynamic market place. Management accounting information will need to adapt to these new forms as relationships move from independence to mutuality and partnership through closer collaboration. New techniques, identified in this chapter, are required in order to take full advantage of the opportunities that exist through supply-chain management developments.

References

A.D. Little (1999) *A European supply chain survey*. Brussels: Arthur D. Little Consultants.

Berry, A.J., Cullen, J., Seal, W.B., Ahmed, M. and Dunlop, A:. (2000) *The consequences of inter-firm supply chains for management accounting*. London: CIMA.

DTI/Supply Chain Networks Group (1997) *Supply chain management attitude survey*. Report of the Supply Chain Working Group, April. Sheffield: ISCAN.

ISCAN (1999) *Supply chain management attitude survey report*. Sheffield: ISCAN.

42. Management Accounting for New Product Design and Development

42:1 Economic Significance of Design and Development

It is difficult to assess the contribution of good product design and development to corporate performance. Certainly poor design was one cause that was frequently advanced to explain the decline of the British manufacturing industry in the 1960s and 1970s. More positively, and recently, a 1997 survey for the Design Council, London, showed that 92% of British businesses now agree that design helps to produce a competitive advantage, and 87% believe that it can increase profits and help diversification into new markets. Another 1997 survey by Sentance and Clarke of the London Business School found that managers ranked the new product development (NPD) activity as the primary source of competitiveness, ahead of traditional growth paths like investment in new plant capacity, skills and retraining, acquisitions and diversification. A reflection of the pivotal role of product design and development in competitiveness is the fact that the British manufacturing industry spent an estimated £10bn on the activity in 1995.

42:2 Some Reasons for Cross-functional Collaboration

The importance of product innovation to competitiveness has generated a substantive amount of empirical evidence which suggests that companies that innovate successfully

Bill Nixon

have much in common. The ability to manage multi-disciplinary teams is widely acknowledged as one of the features most closely associated with effective product innovation. Although historically the accounting role in NPD has been mostly a minor, and usually belated, one that is frequently characterised as a tension between accountants, who argue numbers, and product managers, who argue taste and instinct; nevertheless there are several strong reasons for closer links between the functions. These reasons include:

(a) *The high percentage of a product's life-cycle costs (see **Ch.19**) that are locked in once a design is frozen. For example, the General Motors' calculation that 70% of the cost of manufacturing truck transmissions is committed in the design stage is consistent with the recent experience of the Ford Motor Company. Faced with aggressive, price-based, Japanese competition, Ford undertook a comprehensive exercise to cut costs on its 1997 Taurus. The cost cutting was meant to be invisible to Taurus customers; for example, the Ford engineers redesigned a pin for the Taurus's door hinges which saved $2 per vehicle, and they borrowed a part from the Lincoln Continental to reinforce sheet metal underneath the seats which saved $1.50. The total cost reductions achieved by a thorough search amounted to just $180 on a car whose retail price starts at $17,995.*

(b) *Competitive pressures (see **Ch.7**), fuelled partly by the accelerating rate of technological diffusion and the increasing difficulty of protecting intellectual property, are forcing companies to anticipate and design to market-determined target prices rather than simply add a margin to costs. The difficulty of sustaining for very long competitive advantage through product functions and characteristics means that price-based competition must be anticipated and impounded in the concept definition and design stages.*

(c) *Speed-to-market pressures have caused a move from designing and developing products on a one-by-one basis to developing technology platforms for an entire family of products. Thus, for example, Jaguar cars notes in its brochure for the new V8XJ series that:*

> When Jaguar launched the award-winning XJ series three years ago, our sights were already set on the future with the challenging task of designing its replacement. Once again the brief was simple: 'Develop the most powerful refined and attractive range of luxury saloon'.

The management practices and literature relating to time-based competition and platform-based product development are largely isolated from developments in quality and profit management. Although all of these practices are of value in appropriate situations their 'bottom-line' contribution is synergistic when an integrative approach is adopted.

(d) *The task of integrating the many dimensions of the product design and development activity has become more complex; developing platforms for a product family, that may in turn spawn several generations, requires management accounting information at an early stage in order to focus ideas quickly and to align them with product portfolio, technology, competitive and corporate strategies. Management accounting information can also help the NPD team to define design parameters relating to a product's function, form and ergonomics; customers' quality, performance, price and life-cycle cost requirements need to be balanced with the company's profitability requirements. Even when a concept is precisely defined, account must be taken of the fact that the relative importance of customers' requirements change over the product life cycle. Management accounting information is required for early design decisions relating to, for example, the cost and value of maintaining design flexibility to accommodate quick and economic redesign over the product's life cycle (see **Ch.19**), as well as the degree of modularity, which has implications for outsourcing, maintenance and module interface arrangements. Price-based competition compels early evaluation of the profit impact of different designs and scenarios; for example, the effect on profit of a development expense overrun, a schedule delay, a unit cost overrun or a price reduction.*

42:3 The New Product Development Team

The role of management accounting and management accountants in NPD teams depends in large part on:

(a) *The relative importance of different design parameters to the competitiveness of the company. For example, if product development is premised on the view that 'quality remains after the price is forgotten' (Henry Royce of RR) then it is likely that accounting will play a minor role in development. Conversely, if price and/or life-cycle costs to customers are central to competitive advantage then management accountants are more likely to be members of the core product development team.*

(b) *The culture of the organisation. For example, the structure, systems and management style of a company may encourage job rotation and the acquisition by individuals of multiple perspectives of the business; they may also encourage functional mindsets and a bunker mentality that constrains cross-functional communication and collaboration. Management accountants, for example, are more likely to play a central role in the NPD process if they have a good appreciation of the design and development process, the constraints and opportunities that exist and of the techniques that are used to manage the many dimensions of design and development. Similarly, designers with an appreciation of price-driven competition and of management accounting techniques are more likely to understand the value of accounting information and profit management in the early stages of design. Empirical evidence suggests that the role and focus of management accounting changes over the development life cycle; from strategic and risk evaluation in the idea generation (see **Chs 2** and **4**) and concept definition stages to achieving cost targets in the prototype and pre-manufacture stages (see **Chs 14** and **18**).*

42:4 Management Accounting Support for New Product Development

Management accounting can assist both the evaluation of NPD expenditure proposals and the detailed design and development process (*see* **Ch.8**). However, effective accounting support for NPD requires a good understanding of the management process in all stages of the design and development process operated by each company; indeed, the development process may vary within a company depending, for example, on the cost that the development entails, the degree of innovation and risk involved, and on the product's sponsor or champion.

A prelude to designing a management accounting information system to support NPD is to establish the extent to which the existing NPD process needs to change, perhaps because of time-based competitive pressures, a trend towards greater modularity in design, greater reliance on platforms or, simply, perceived weaknesses in the process. For example, most companies have had in the last decade to adopt simultaneous development methods and so-called 'lean-product development' approaches to replace time-consuming and expensive linear, relay-team techniques (Cooper, 1995). Once some consensus view on the existing and the optimum NPD processes has been reached management can decide where on this continuum the accounting system should focus.

Many of the techniques discussed in this Handbook can support the NPD process, for example, Competitor Analysis (**Ch.7**), Quality Costing (**Ch.18**), Product Life-cycle Costing (**Ch.19**), Target Costing (**Ch.24**), Functional Costing (**Ch.25**) and Cost Tables (**Ch.26**). These methods are not mutually exclusive and indeed have considerable synergy when used simultaneously. However, possibly the greatest scope for management accounting development is through a further fusion of extant management accounting concepts and techniques with those already employed to manage the NPD process; techniques such as quality function deployment (QFD), design for manufacture and assembly (DFMA), failure mode effect analysis (FMEA), value engineering and others that aim to determine the optimum design for performance, quality and cost (*see* **Fig.42:1**). Indeed, management accounting methods like target cost, Kaizen costing and functional cost analysis evolved from, and are supported by, techniques pioneered by engineers and mathematicians like Taguchi and Deming.

Figure 42:1 **Some new product development techniques**

- Quality function deployment (QFD).

- Functional analysis system technique (FAST).

- Product, technology and industry life cycles.

- Benchmarking.

- Critical parameter management (CPM).

- Computer-aided design (CAD).

- Rapid prototyping.

- Design for manufacture and assembly (DFMA).

- Manufacture and design evaluation (MADE).

- Design-for-cost including target costing and Kaizen costing.

- Design-to-cost.

- Value engineering.

- Value analysis.

- Taguchi methods.

42:4.1 Establishing an Agreed Understanding of the New Product Development Process

The task of ascertaining the NPD process is far from straightforward. In part, this is because the process involves every function as well as suppliers and customers; the difficulty is also attributable to the fact that companies do not always make explicit the criteria for the major stage-gate decisions. The protracted, circuitous discussions that are a feature of the early 'fuzzy front end' of NPD reflect, in many instances, organisational characteristics just as much as the innate technological and commercial uncertainty. Notwithstanding the more recent emphasis on multi-disciplinary teams working in parallel on development, the experience of attempts to model the process suggests that different views prevail in the same organisation on both the strategic significance of NPD projects and on the development process itself depending, for the most part, on the organisational level and functional background of individuals. Even within the design function in the same company industrial designers and design engineers often exhibit very different perceptions of the nature, purpose and value of design in that company; the different views are partly attributable to the fact that responsibility for the design function is often split between the engineering and marketing functions.

The views of NPD team participants frequently differ on:

(a) *when stage-gate, go/terminate decisions are required and on the criteria at each stage;*
(b) *the company's risk management policy;*
(c) *the relative importance and implications of three related cost categories, namely:*
  (i) *the cost of developing a product, or range of products;*
  (ii) *the cost of producing the product or product family; and*
  (iii) *the life-cycle costs of the product for the customer.*

It can also be difficult to establish a consensus within an organisation on how and when designs are frozen and the links between the concept definition, design and development stages. If the company's policy is to keep the design open as long as possible (which can reduce the risk of expensive post-launch change requirements) and to deliberately overlap the concept definition, design and development stages then that policy requires a level of communication, collaboration and co-ordination, as well as a product architecture, that can accommodate changes quickly and economically. In some circumstances, for example, if expensive equipment with long lead times is required, it may be necessary to create a stable target, to define the concept clearly before undertaking development. Management accounting information that is tailored to the early concept definition and design stages can help to optimise the solution to meet performance, quality, cost and profit requirements and to expedite decisions on design choices.

42:4.2 Design and Development Techniques

Effective management accounting support for the design and development activity requires not only an understanding of the process but also of the techniques employed, several of which require financial data and all of which have implications for costs, cash flows and profit margins.

42:4.2.1 Quality Function Deployment (QFD)

It is almost a cliché that successful product innovation begins with a clear understanding of the customers' immediate and latent needs. QFD is a comprehensive design and development technique that aims to identify customer needs precisely so that they can be translated into design targets and major quality assurance points to be used throughout the production phase. Toyota began using the QFD system in 1977 and attributes significant reductions in both development times and start-up costs to its use.

The integrative power of QFD stems from two key features of the technique. First, the focus on the needs of the end customer in the market place is extended to every supplier and intermediate customer in the value chain. Thus, for example, when drawings are supplied to manufacturing by design, manufacturing is regarded as the customer of the designers. Second, the QFD technique goes beyond definition of needs and examines the relationship between these requirements and how they will be met. A simple example of a first stage, general, definition of customer requirements for a car in a particular segment might be: low price, good handling in wet and icy conditions, long service interval and low internal noise level. The initial, general, response to the needs in terms of suppliers' specifications might be: standard engine and suspension, front-wheel drive, new technology oil filter material and oil cooler, vibration-free engine mounting and extra sound insulation around the passenger compartment. Some of these specifications may support more than one of the customers' requirements. Proposed solutions may satisfy one requirement while creating conflict with another; for example, a new oil filter and cooler may meet the requirement for long service intervals but conflict with the low capital cost requirement. QFD helps to highlight these relationships in a graphic, visual way as illustrated in **Figure 42:2.**

Figure 42:2 **Relationship between customer requirements and proposed solution**

Source: Adapted from Fox (1993: 75)

Notes: W = Weak

M = Medium

S = Strong

N = Negative relationship

SN = Strong negative relationship

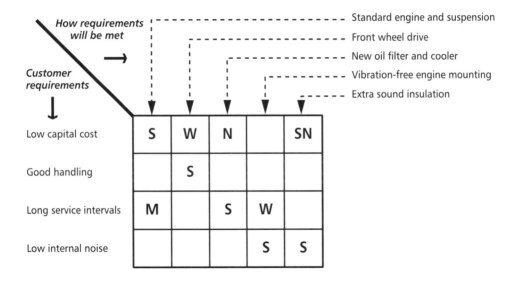

In principle, the broad, market-oriented perspective of QFD provides a powerful framework for balancing quality and function requirements so as to achieve target profit margins; lean-product development management practices using an array of design (*see* **Fig.42:1**) and cost management techniques can help to enhance quality and functionality and to reduce cost and time-to-market. In practice, this synthesis has in the past occurred mainly in Japan partly, it seems, because many Japanese managers' perspectives transcend narrow functional boundaries and are more strategic and integrative.

42:4.2.2 Function Analysis System Technique (FAST)

FAST is the primary tool used in QFD to decompose the overall functional requirements of a product so that the network of higher and lower-level functional relationships can be identified and charted. A systematic examination of why each function exists and how it occurs provides a good basis for evaluating the relative efficiency and effectiveness of different possible solutions as well as their costs (*see* Ch.25). Functional analysis is also necessary for decisions relating to the location of functions within modules.

42:4.2.3 Value Engineering (VE) and Value Analysis (VA)

VE complements FAST; it aims to find ways to achieve the specified functionality at the required standards of quality and performance and at the target cost. Like target costing, VE is applied during the product design and development stages in an endeavour to manage the costs and benefits of a product's basic and secondary functions.

Once production commences VA continues the search for the lowest overall cost consistent with product attributes; VA therefore supports Kaizen costing that also supersedes target costing in the production phase of NPD. Because of the broad technical, commercial and financial scope of VE and VA these activities are usually the responsibility of multi-disciplinary teams.

42:4.2.4 Design for Manufacturing and Assembly (DFMA)

DFMA focuses on the transition from the design and development phase to full-volume manufacture. The many processes that DFMA encompasses, including FAST and VE, aim to reduce cost, increase quality and reduce time-to-market by making it easier to manufacture and assemble parts and components. A smooth transition from design to manufacture needs early participation by manufacturing and component suppliers in the design evolution together with support from properly integrated systems to assist in managing the process.

42:4.2.5 Manufacture and Design Evaluation (MADE)

MADE software packages evolved, mostly in the aerospace industry, to deal with the complex interactions that exist among R&D, design, production and operation costs. The models, which contain data on hundreds of thousands of parts, simulate the impact of design changes on the respective cost categories.

42:4.3 Evaluation of Expenditure

In the last decade a broad consensus has emerged among managers, economists and accountants that conventional capital investment appraisal techniques (*see* **Ch.11**), like discounted cash flow (DCF) and payback, have many limitations that discriminate against investment in innovative development projects.

The most common criticisms of the DCF method are that:

(a) *its preference for cash now rather than later gives it a short-term bias;*
(b) *it fails to take account of the consequences of* not *investing – the opportunity cost concept; if, for example, a company's expenditure to keep abreast of relevant emergent technologies is inadequate to support its core technologies then it is likely to quickly lose technology-based competitive advantage;*
(c) *it attributes no value to the options that expenditure on projects like development of a technology platform can create; and*
(d) *its implicit assumption that decisions are now or never is inconsistent with the incremental, risk-reduction process that managers adopt to cope with the uncertainty inherent in innovative projects.*

The perceived limitations of DCF have caused many of its critics to advocate the option pricing theory (OPT) approach for those decisions that entail a great deal of uncertainty and the primary purpose of expenditure is to maintain discretion and to defer commitment. Case-study research by the author suggests that the OPT and DCF approaches are complementary rather than mutually exclusive. In the concept definition, design and development stages when uncertainty is still high, opportunity cost and OPT concepts are more appropriate methods for quantifying and evaluating estimated costs and benefits. However, in the near-market, pre-manufacturing stage, when many technological and commercial uncertainties have been reduced and commitment is greater, cash-flow projections are more reliable and DCF calculations are both relevant and important. This blend of OPT and DCF is more likely than either method used alone to balance the tension between the control necessary for financial strength and the freedom needed for creativity and innovation. An understanding of the design and development aims, parameters and processes permits the use of evaluation techniques and management accounting information so as to balance all of the many dimensions and perspectives that NPD decisions entail: a balance between customer and corporate needs, strategy and operations, core and emergent technologies and between qualitative and quantitative dimensions.

Acknowledgements

The author is grateful to the Design Council, London, for funding the research on which this chapter is based. Sincere thanks are also due to my co-researcher, John Innes, who provided an invaluable contribution at every stage.

References

Cooper, R. (1995) *When lean enterprises collide: Competing through confrontation.* Boston, MA: Harvard Business School Press.

Design Council (1997) *Annual review.* London: Design Council.

Dixit, A.R. and Pindyck, R.S. (1995) 'The options approach to capital investment', *Harvard Business Review*, May-June: 105–115.

Economist, The (1996) 'Optional investing', 4 January, p.4.

Fox, J. (1993) *Quality through design: The key to successful product delivery.* London: McGraw Hill.

Sentance, A. and Clarke, J. (1997) *The contribution of design to the UK economy.* Design Council research: Short programmes working paper. London: Design Council.

Tatikonda, L.U. and Tatikonda, M.V. (1996) 'Tools for cost effective product design and development', in B.J. Brinker (Ed.), *Emerging practices in cost management*, pp. B3.1–B3.8. Boston, MA: Warren, Goreham & Lamont.

43. Management Accounting and Human Resource Management

43:1 Competitive Advantage

For many organisations today one of the main competitive advantages is their employees. Other sources of competitive advantage include research and development, brands or product design. Historically accountants (both financial and management accountants) have not been very good at providing information on such sources of competitive advantage. For example, financial accountants have tended to ignore intangible assets and in takeover situations have classed any premium as goodwill. There is seldom any detailed analysis of the reasons underlying such goodwill figures (*see FRS10: Goodwill and Intangible Assets* or *IAS38: Intangible Assets*).

Management accountants – particularly with the development of strategic management accounting (*see* **Ch.2**) – have begun to turn their attention to various sources of competitive advantage. For example, there is research and development performance measurement (*see* **Ch.8**) and management accounting for new product design (*see* **Ch.42**). This chapter considers the contribution of management accountants in relation to human resource management.

43:2 Human Resource Management

Studies have shown that competitive advantage can be gained through effective human resource management. Bratton has defined human resource management as:

> That part of the management process that specialises in the management of people in work organisations. Human Resource Management emphasises that employees are the primary resource for gaining sustainable competitive advantage, that human resource activities need to be integrated with corporate strategy, and that human resource specialists help organisational controllers to meet both efficiency and equity objectives.

(1994: 5)

In a study examining the management of change, Ezzamel *et al.* (1995: 55) found that 'virtually all interviews indicated that human resource management policies and practices form a key part of the new approach to management and organisation'.

Recently human resource management has been more closely linked to an organisation's strategy. Strategic human resource management has been developed integrating human resource management practices with strategies such as cost/efficiency or product differentiation. Armstrong (1995) suggests that in order to improve performance, human resource managers must be able to understand the language of management accounting. Armstrong also supports the performance of human resource management activities being expressed in management accounting terms.

43:3 Management Accounting Contribution

In some organisations management accountants provide little or no specific information for human resource managers. For example, some organisations do not even report on a monthly basis the costs of recruitment, selection, training and development of employees. However, management accountants can provide information for human resource managers in the following areas:

- planning;

- costing;

- performance measurement.

43:3.1 Planning

In a few organisations some management accountants are now working in a partnership or consultant relationship with human resource managers and different accountants are fulfilling the control function. It is difficult for the same accountant to perform these very different consulting and controlling roles. One critical aspect of the partnership or consulting role for the management accountant is during the planning stage. Human resource managers and management accountants can work together during the planning stage – for example in relation to budgeted employee costs.

Management accountants also have a role to play in helping human resource managers set their financial targets. It is also important to ensure that the human resource strategy integrates into the organisation's overall strategy. Again management accountants can assist human resource managers with their measurement experience.

Schuler and Macmillan (1984) provided case examples of 20 companies that had successfully pursued two specific strategic thrusts, namely cost/efficiency or product differentiation using human resource management practices. Schuler and Macmillan then illustrated how resource planning, staffing, appraising, compensating, training, employee development and union-managerial relations were directed towards the 'target' to achieve the cost-efficiency or product differentiation strategic objectives. This is one area where management accountants can provide essential information.

Another area where management accountants are assisting human resource managers in some organisations is financial appraisal of projects. For example, one organisation found that it was losing more than 50% of its new recruits during their first year of employment with the organisation. It was easy for the management accountant to assist the human resource manager in preparing a case for more than trebling expenditure on recruitment and selection with the objective of employing the best people who would stay with the organisation. This project was an outstanding success.

43:3.2 Costing

Some, but by no means all, organisations collect and report the costs of recruitment, selection, training, employee development and employee costs. This is a basic contribution from the management accountants. However, most human resource managers appreciate some analysis and interpretation of such costs from the management accountant. In a few organisations there is very much a dialogue between human resource managers and management accountants.

With current developments such as benchmarking (*see* **Ch.53**) and outsourcing (*see* **Ch.38**), it is critical that managers and accountants have a very detailed understanding of costs. If not, incorrect decisions can be made. Such mistakes can usually be avoided if human resource managers and management accountants are working closely together.

A related area to human resource costing is the external financial reporting of human asset accounting. Over 20 years ago Flamholtz (1974) suggested the need for information on accounting for people as organisational resources. The primary purpose of human resource accounting is to help management plan and control the use of human resources effectively and efficiently and to report the financial effects. However, although Flamholtz emphasised the internal reporting aspect of human resource accounting, the actual developments to date have been mainly in the area of external reporting. Management accountants could play a very important role in the internal reporting of human resource accounting (both financial and non-financial).

43:3.3 Performance Measurement

Performance measurement can be a very fruitful area for discussion between human resource managers and management accountants. Monthly reports can include the following:

(a) detailed analysis of employees' remuneration;
(b) detailed analysis of employees' associated costs;
(c) productivity information;
(d) absence information in financial terms;
(e) cost of overtime and overtime hours as percentage of gross hours worked;
(f) cost of training and training hours as percentage of gross hours worked;
(g) employee turnover.

The above suggests comparing actual performance over time. However, targets or budgets can also be set and compared with the actual results so that variances from budget can be reported and analysed with action being taken where necessary. Another form of comparison is to use a benchmarking approach against other organisations. For example, one benchmarking scheme involves 20 organisations with a mixture of financial and non-financial performance measures such as:

(a) cost per employee;
(b) profit per employee;
(c) average remuneration;
(d) average cost per hire;
(e) training hours per employee;
(f) resignation rate.

Management accountants can also assist human resource managers with an analysis of the links between financial and non-financial performance measures. For example, some organisations now conduct an employee satisfaction survey. One organisation pays particular attention to changes over time in this staff satisfaction index on measures of:

- staff satisfaction;

- level of information;

- empowerment;

- commitment.

In this organisation the management accountants are now working with the human resource managers to examine the relationship movements in the organisation's profit. Obviously this is not a one-to-one relationship but early investigations have already revealed some interesting information.

43:4 Survey Results

A 1998 survey funded by CIMA of companies in the Times Top 1000 companies showed that some management accountants are already working closely with human resource managers. The main components in the human resource management strategy are given in **Table 43.1**.

Table 43:1 **Human resource management strategy components**

	% of Respondents
Training and development	67
Performance measurement	61
Change management	45
Team work	44
Variable pay	32
Flexibility	31
Total quality management	25
Outsourcing	11

In relation to management accountants providing information for human resource managers on performance indicators the results were as in **Table 43:2**.

Table 43:2 **Contribution of management accountants**

		% of Respondents
Full contribution by management accountants	1	13
	2	30
	3	21
	4	15
	5	19
	6	2
No contribution by management accountants	7	____
		100

This suggests that management accountants are making an important contribution to providing information for human resource managers.

The two areas where management accountants have the highest level of involvement with human resource managers are:

1. *providing information for decision making;*
2. *measuring performance.*

Three other areas where management accountants assist human resource managers are:

1. *setting targets;*
2. *monitoring activities;*
3. *reporting.*

Management accountants also report information on:

- recruitment;

- training and development;

- outsourcing;

- employee turnover,

but they provide very little information on selection.

Human resource and finance directors' views on the future role of management accounting are also interesting. The Human Resource Strategy and Planning Manager of one company suggested:

> Management accountants should have a key role in helping determine performance indicators, providing measurable data and in helping link human resource outcomes to target and productivity results. Management accountants should play a key role in providing a better fix on the possible impact of the developing human resource strategy on the bottom line.

The Finance Director of another company stated:

> The future competitive advantage must lie in a stronger strategic alliance between management accounting and human resource management. The management accountants need to become more aware of the people factor in relation to financial performance and the human resource people need to become more financially literate.

Another Finance Director expressed his views on non-financial indicators as a role of management accounting:

> A truly integrated management accounting function could assist by providing data which enables sensitive monitoring of the return on human resources. However, greater sensitivity to non-financial perspectives is essential.

43:5 Conclusions

Management accountants have an important role to play in providing information for human resource managers in the following areas:

(a) *setting of strategy and targets;*
(b) *costing information on:*
    (i) *recruitment;*
    (ii) *training;*
    (iii) *employee development;*
    (iv) *employee costs;*

(c) *non-financial information;*

(d) *performance measurement;*

(e) *benchmarking against other organisations;*

(f) *relationships between movements in employee satisfaction surveys and movements in profit.*

Management accountants cannot ignore the fact that for many organisations one of their main competitive advantages is their employees. Management accountants need to provide information to assist human resource managers.

Acknowledgement

The authors are extremely grateful for the research funding from CIMA for our project into the role of management accounting in strategic human resource management.

References

Armstrong, P. (1995) 'Accounting and human resource management' in J. Storey (Ed.), *Human resource management: A critical test*, Routledge.

Bratton, J. (1994) 'Human resource management in transition' in J. Bratton and J. Gold (Eds), *Human resource management – theory and practice*, Macmillan, pp. 3–31.

Ezzamel, M., Green, C., Lilley, S. and Willmott, H. (1995) *Changing managers and managing change*. Chartered Institute of Management Accountants.

Flamholtz, E.G. (1974) *Human resource accounting*. Dickenson.

Schuler, R.S. and Macmillan, I.C. (1984) 'Gaining competitive advantage through human resource management practices', *Human Resource Management*, 23(3), Fall: 241–55.

Part E

Control

44. Financial Control

44:1 Introduction

Financial controls have evolved significantly over the past century with an increasing emphasis in line with the pace of business change, diversification to match the changing structure of commercial organisations and even adaptations that have found their way into non-profit making organisations. Their impact has probably been most dramatic in the electronic world of the so called new economy businesses. The spectacular rise of internet-based organisations in the late 1990s was followed by reported equally spectacular falls of many during 2000. The common link frequently appeared to be a significant lack of financial control, or as the financial press would note, the new economy failing to accommodate old economy realities.

This chapter reviews the traditional measures, more associated with the large industrial, capital intensive organisations, though with updated versions of these measures, along with the control needs of the modern 'people-oriented' businesses. This is followed by an analysis of financial controls that are associated with the life cycle of products, the product portfolio, with a final brief discussion on non-profit-making organisations.

44:2 Finance and Cost: Review of Definitions

In order to develop an understanding of the control aspects of finance and cost, the meaning of each term will be reviewed, followed by the principles of control in order to construct the meanings of financial and cost control. Various useful techniques and practices then follow.

Finance is usually defined as the science or management of economic resources. This covers both the receipt and expenditure of those resources, expressed in monetary terms.

Michael Johnson   751

The monetary requirements emerged historically as a common form of measurement, thus providing a basis for controlling trade in goods and services.

Cost can be defined as the monetary measurement of the use of economic resources to produce a specified item or activity. It is therefore the price to be paid for a benefit, though its make-up will frequently be a complex matter to determine, so that the method of costing should be clarified, for example, 'standard' costing (*see* **Ch.16**).

By **comparing** the two terms, the boundaries of which are not clear cut, 'cost' is a specific, though major, part of finance. However, finance is usually considered to be much broader based as the financial manager is responsible for all aspects of economic resources, both long and short term (*see* **Ch.5**). The cost accountant tends to be more focused on the technical aspects of assessing data of what has been consumed in the production of goods and services and in providing management information for decision-making purposes. A simple example would be that finance looks at both costs and revenues of a business, with its focus on optimising the difference, that is, profit, while costs and their controls tend to be one sided, that is, their reduction.

44:3 Control

44:3.1 Control Concepts in a Financial Environment

The concept of control may be defined as including the following features:

(a) *An objective is established for the activity being controlled, such as a planned level of profit, or cost savings from an agreed level, in a production process.*

(b) *A model of the process, activity or system is designed to achieve the objective described in (a) above. A project development plan would fit into this category, with progress milestones and associated costs incorporated into the approval process.*

(c) *Progress and final results are measured for the activity being controlled. A monthly cost status report is an example, particularly to report at the milestone points in the project as in (b) above.*

(d) *Progress in (c) is compared against the standard expected and variances reported.*

(e) *Control is only effective when the facility for corrective action is taken, so that alternatives must be available to an appropriate decision-maker.*

Financial control tends to be relatively broad based, to inform management how well the business is doing. The format and timing of the information will be structured to meet its needs, largely on the tactical and strategic levels. Education is often needed for management to gain full benefits of the availability of financial control information that modern systems can produce.

Cost control tends to be more operational, that is, to meet short-term needs. A consistent approach is more likely to be applied in its presentation. The functionality of modern computerised systems with their large databases and means of access has given recent improved opportunities for more detailed, online, cost-control facilities.

44:3.2 Feedback and Feedforward Controls

(*See* **Ch.44, para.44:1.3**.)

Feedback control is the term for monitoring activities on a historical basis against that desired, in order to take corrective action. This action will be to avoid a repeat of a similar situation, such as underestimating the complexity of opening up a new office, should a further one be planned, or to modify the input of raw materials into a process.

Feedforward control uses the predictive part of the cost model to anticipate certain results as a basis to take corrective action, where required. It therefore introduces a forecasting feature, requiring the judgement and expertise of the forecaster to aid management. In a costing exercise, the accountant needs an intimate knowledge of the business, suitably aided by communications with the relevant technical experts, to prepare relevant and timely reports.

44:4 Financial Control Methods Overview

Controls emanate from the delegation of decision rights by the owners of the business to employees over the use of company resources; the principles of agency. To help compensate for the lack of incentives that employees may possess in the proper management of these resources, a controls system must be installed. Economic controls are therefore essentially required to support the credibility of information for decision-making purposes, or to protect the creditors or owners of the business. They are designed to influence people's behaviour in order to meet the desired objectives and strategies of the organisation in which they operate, so that they act in the organisation's best interests. A number of methods that are commonly found are explained below.

As Anthony and Govindarajan (1998) have observed, business unit managers usually have two performance objectives: 'First, they should generate adequate profits from the resources at their disposal (subject, of course, to legal and ethical considerations). Secondly, they should invest in additional resources only when such as investment will produce an adequate return'. It is therefore critical to ensure that the most appropriate financial control methods are selected.

44:5 Financial Control of Assets Employed

Assets are created in a business for the prime purpose of generating profits. A relationship is therefore expected between these assets and profits as a measure of:

(a) *the success of the business as an economic entity;*
(b) *support to management in its decision-making process.*

Before moving onto the generally accepted methods of relating profits to assets, the term 'assets' needs to be clarified. Consider **Figure 44:1** which illustrates, in outline, the financial structure of a selection of recently published annual reports of UK quoted companies. Three industrial sectors are included, with the average reported results of two companies in each sector, where their main balance sheet categories are shown in proportion to net assets or shareholder funds. For example, the fixed assets of the oil and gas companies are 186% and sales revenues are 136% of net assets.

Figure 44:1 **Financial statements to show the relative significance of main balance-sheet categories**

Balance sheets as at 31 December 20XX					
Industrial group	Oil and Gas		Computer Services	Construction & Engineering	
Fixed assets		186	63		136
Current assets	55		161	594	
less current liabilities	-47		-119	-435	
Net current assets		8	42		159
less other creditors/provisions		-94	- 5		-195
Net assets/shareholder funds		100	100		100
Sales revenue		136	401		1,252

Care is required not to read too much in this small sample, e.g. a high long-term debt situation in the engineering company tends to reduce the net asset base of the third group and thus inflate the remaining balance sheet categories, but some obvious conclusions can be drawn. Oil and gas companies are clearly capital intensive, therefore financial controls in such an industry will focus on the decision-making processes in capital investments and ensure that their expected outcomes are subsequently monitored and met. A profit/capital investment relationship is therefore crucial. Much of the manufacturing industry will be similarly represented.

Computer services businesses are people oriented; assets that are not (normally) found in a balance sheet. The appropriate financial controls therefore tend to be more related to staff costs and the revenues that they can create, more a case of managing working capital. Construction and other engineering businesses fall in between, so that controls may be both in managing working capital, particularly their contracts with customers, and in capital investments, such as opening up a new construction yard. For further guidance on the definition of assets, see, for example, *FRS15: Tangible Fixed Assets, FRS10: Goodwill and Intangible Assets, IAS16: Property, Plant and Equipment* and *IAS38: Intangibles.*

Focusing initially on long-term capital investments, two main methods are frequently found to facilitate their financial control, namely:

1. *return on investment (ROI), or return on capital employed (ROCE) where profit is shown as a percentage of the assets deemed to have generated it;*
2. *residual income (RI), or economic value added (EVA) where income or added value is calculated as excess funds over the cost of capital return on assets.*

The simplified financial statements in **Figure 44:2** are presented as a basis to illustrate their calculations.

Figure 44:2 **Financial statements example**

	Balance sheet as at 31 December 20XX		
			£000s
Fixed Assets			
Cost	3,000		
less depreciation	1,600		1,400
Current assets	200		
less current liabilities	100		
Net current assets			100
Net assets			1,500
	Profit and loss account for 20XX		
Sales			900
less expenses			650
Profit before tax			250

44:5.1 Return on Investment (ROI)

Assets are funded externally by persons or institutions, or internally by profits that have been created by assets already in place. The price of external sources is based on:

(a) *loans with a specific rate of interest; or*
(b) *share capital with an expectation level by the shareholders in the form or dividends or capital growth.*

The combination of these sources is known as the weighted average cost of capital (WACC), which is the cost of finance, weighted according to the proportion that each element bears to the total pool of capital (*see* **Ch.5, para.5:4.3** and **Ch.11, para.11:2.4.3.2**). The 'actual' return from assets therefore needs to be measured as feedback to the managers of the business and on to the financial providers.

The summary accounts in **Figure 44:2** produce a ROI of 250 ÷ 1,500 = 16.7%, when using 'investment' or 'capital employed' to equal fixed assets plus net current assets. A clear definition of the base is critical for its appropriate use:

(a) *for any comparison with a similar set of figures produced by a comparable business unit in the company or with another entity – the 'benchmarking' concept;*
(b) *for investors to ascertain the return on their investments.*

Two main investment bases may be found, as follows:

1. **Net assets**, as in **Figure 44:2**. Here, the fixed assets used in the calculation are gross less depreciation to give a net book value basis.
2. **Gross assets** which use fixed assets at cost only. The example in **Figure 44:2** would result in an asset base of £3,000,000 (fixed assets) plus £100,000 (net current assets), or £3,100,000. Similarly, profits should be adjusted to add back depreciation. Let us assume that the fixed assets are depreciated on the straight-line method over 15 years to give £200,000 per annum and therefore an adjusted profit of £450,000 (£250,000 + £200,000). The ROI becomes 14.5%. The argument for this approach is that £3,100,000 represents the actual investment that has been made in the business.

The results in this example of 16.7% and 14.5% are not far apart, but the net assets' basis can vary considerably over time. For example, using the above data with an annual profit of £250,000 and assuming a single fixed asset only, end of years 1, 6 and 11 will record as in **Table 44:1**.

Table 44:1 Financial statement example – year-end results

Year	Fixed assets (£000s)	Depreciation (£000s)	Net book value (£000s)	Total investment (£000s)	Net profit (£000s)	ROI (%)
1	3,000	200	2,800	2,900	250	8.6
6	3,000	1,200	1,800	1,900	250	13.2
11	3,000	2,200	800	900	250	27.8

In practice, the use of net assets is the most commonly used approach for overall reporting purposes, despite its acknowledged failings. The main reason appears to be its ease of availability through published annual reports and accounts, which make it the natural favourite for stock market analysts and others in intercompany comparisons.

44:5.2 Residual Income (RI)
(*See* **Ch.46, para.46:4.2.**)

The RI method incorporates the cost of capital to the business, which ideally is the WACC. This cost is applied to the assets employed and subtracted from the net profits to determine the effective 'return' on the business. Should the rate be 10%, this would be calculated as in **Table 44:2**.

Table 44:2 **Financial statement example – the RI method**

	£000s
Profit before tax	250
less capital charge (£1,500 x 10%)	150
Residual income	100

44:5.3 ROI and RI Compared

Both methods are used in practice, each with its own supportive features.

(a) *ROI is a control tool that comprehensively covers key elements of the two main financial statements, namely the profit and loss account and the balance sheet.*

(b) *ROI is easy to calculate and understand, being based on the overall accounts, or a particular part, of the business. RI produces a specific value, which in itself may not be very meaningful. ROI is commonly used for company and divisional performance evaluation purposes, such as a comparison against a specific target. As such, it is probably the most regularly used financial control tool.*

(c) *ROI data is readily available to all interested stakeholders, so can be used for intercompany comparisons, as is often found in the financial press.*

(d) *RI is frequently more appropriate for internal investment controls, particularly where a company is looking for consistency over its business units. Any project achieving a return in excess of the cost of capital will also motivate managers to support the company in achieving this return. The ROI method could result in a rejection of a such a project proposal, where the project return is less than the existing average ROI.*

For example, using the above accounts, a company with a cost of capital of 10%, has a project proposal of £600,000 investment which produces an annual net profit of £70,000, after depreciation (£40,000) *see* **Table 44:3**.

Table 44:3 **Financial statement example – ROI and RI comparison**

	ROI – net asset basis (£000s)	*Residual income (£000s)*
Existing investment	1,500	1,500
Proposed project (end of first year)	560	560
Proposed asset base	2,060	2,060
Profit first year (250 + 70)	320	320
less *capital charge (2,060 x 10%)*		206
Proposed residual income (RI)		114
Proposed return on investment (ROI)	15.5%	
Existing position	16.7%	100

On an RI basis, the new project improves the overall return (from 100 to 114), so should be selected; the ROI interpretation shows a decline (from 16.7% to 15.5%), so would be a disincentive to managers rewarded on this criterion.

It is this situation that shows the strength of RI over ROI. Any positive RI indicates a financial benefit to the investment organisation, in that value will be added and management can be motivated by appropriate rewards by such added value, the essence of EVA described in **paragraph 44:5.4**. ROI, however, may show added value of an investment by exceeding the cost of capital, but incentives to invest may be hindered by the returns being below existing levels.

44:5.4 Economic Value Added (EVA)

This term is of increasing modern usage, following its trademark registration and promotion by Stern Stewart & Co., for performance measurement and control. Its calculation is similar to residual income, that is, earnings in excess of the cost of capital as a measure of managing that capital. Its proponents tend to emphasise the following two points, (each of which are equally appropriate to RI):

1. *EVA (see **Ch.48, para.48:6.3**) is a useful annual control mechanism, to verify the ongoing results of an investment that has been justified by net present value (NPV) calculations. As the NPV project appraisal tool is the discounting of future cash flows at the cost of capital rate to present values, it is mathematically similar to EVA. EVA then can measure the actual return on an ongoing basis against the original NPV-based project assumptions.*

2. *The cost of capital (see **Ch.5, para.5:4.3**) is analysed into its constituent parts, mainly the costs of debt and equity. Debt financing is an aggregate of the rates payable to the various financial institutions and the equity rate is that expected by shareholders. The cost of capital to be applied should be the weighted average of the two.*

EVA has attracted considerable attention as a valuation and incentive tool, with major corporations, such as Coca-Cola, AT&T and LucasVarity incorporating its features. Stern Stewart & Co. has successfully promoted this variation on residual income, by detailed attention to the components of the factors that make up the EVA calculation (such as Biddle *et al.*, 1999), often customised to the industry or organisation concerned.

44:5.5 Other Control Indicators

The return on assets' concept has obvious appeal to all providers of finance, in that a reward measurement tool is provided for the economic resources that these providers have made. The managers of the investments, whether by loan or equity, are therefore encouraged to use the ROI and RI tools in some format. However, in businesses where the provision of long-term investments to acquire fixed assets is relatively minor, other factors may need to be considered. Service companies, such as providers of information technology development and support facilities, often present balance sheets where the assets are dominated by short-term debtors and the liabilities by trade creditors and short-term loans, as seen in **Figure 44:1**. An important control area is therefore to manage working capital and to ensure that sufficient profit is made on its trading position.

The simplified financial statements in **Figure 44:3** are taken from the average of three European IT service providers, to illustrate these points.

Figure 44:3 **Financial statements of European IT service providers**

Balance Sheet as at 31 December 20XX		
		£millions
Fixed assets		53
Current assets	185	
less current liabilities	155	
Net current assets		30
Total assets less current liabilities		83
less long-term creditors and provisions		23
Net assets		60
Profit and Loss Account for 20XX		
Sales revenue		432
less expenses		407
Profit before tax		25

A simple net-assets-based ROI on the figures in **Figure 44:3** would produce 40% (25/60); an effective return to most investors. Further analysis shows, however, that relatively small changes in operating costs, or even the payment practices of the trade debtors, could readily eliminate this positive result.

44:5.6 Gross and Net Margins

The **gross margin** percentage is the gross profit as a percentage of revenue which helps to verify the degree of success of the entity's trading position. It is often used as a trend analysis for a comparison with prior periods. Service industries, which tend to be dominated by labour costs with relatively low fixed overheads, in contrast to modern industrial organisations, frequently use this measure. Direct costs are often readily understood, so that a margin is added to this total to cover overheads, other costs and the projected profit, for simple price-fixing purposes.

The **net margin** percentage is the net profit as a percentage of revenue. In the accounts above (**Fig.44:3**), this is calculated as:

$$\frac{\text{Net profit before tax}}{\text{Sales revenue}} = \frac{25}{432} = 5.8\%$$

The net margin is often a key internal control measure for a service company to impose on its business units.

In practice, these margin controls should not be used in isolation, but adopted in conjunction with other measures. They focus on a limited range of the financial resources, namely working capital (net current assets) which are consumed by the business on an ongoing basis. The return on total investments still should be considered, such as provided by ROI and RI, as well as any non-financially quantified assets that are critical to the entity, such as a skills' shortage.

44:6 Financial Controls for the Product Portfolio

Products and business units will usually experience a life cycle from inception, through growth, maturity and to final decline. Timescales and their features will vary, including cash and profit profiles, but certain basic principles can frequently be found. By using the following well-known life-cycle strategic planning model matrix by the Boston Consulting Group (BCG) in **Figure 44:4**, with its four distinct stages, we can see that the appropriate financial controls will change with each development stage of the product.

Figure 44:4 **BCG product life-cycle matrix**

Note: FCM – financial control measure

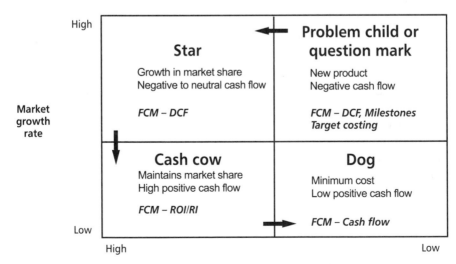

44:6.1 Product Development – 'Question Mark'

The development and launch phase of a product requires innovative management at a time of high business risk. The initial financial aspect for project approval will be one of evaluation, rather than control, usually by the use of discounted cash flow (DCF) techniques (*see* **Ch.11, para.11:1.3.5**). This, however, should set the initial control mechanism, such as targets for cash flows. Milestones should then be established for the stages of the product research and development work (*see* **Ch.8**) and actual costs monitored against the targets set for those forecast for the stage concerned. Anticipated future costs will need to be updated, to ensure that the project continues to be financially viable. Target costing concepts may be introduced, as briefly reviewed in **paragraph 44:6.6** and in detail in **Chapter 24**.

44:6.2 Growth Stage – 'Stars'

Once the product is launched, and cash flows clearer than previously considered, a negative cash flow will be a critical factor to monitor with various cash management techniques in play, such as to ensure that funds are available to cover maximum cash exposure. Financial evaluation techniques, such as DCF, will justify the launch into the market and any major investment decisions. The long-term impact of current decisions will be needed, including the possible use of further DCF calculations to compare against prior year figures, as a control basis and to focus on long-term strategies. Avoid the use of the short-term ROI at this stage.

44:6.3 Product Maturity – 'Cash Cows'

The business now is making a profit on the product with maximum cash inflows taking place. In the overall business, this stage will help to finance the next 'problem child'.

(a) Short-term financial measures, such as ROI may be used for any investments and general progress, but the long-term view must not be overlooked.

(b) Market support is needed to ensure that market position is held and profits are optimised in the long term, rather than following a short-term profit maximisation exercise.

(c) Production capacity should be monitored and the real cost of any replacement plant and equipment considered. Some products remain at the maturity stage for many years, thus requiring long-term evaluation techniques.

44:6.4 Product Decline and Termination – 'Dogs'

Products or businesses in terminal decline will show little or no profit, but cash flow may still be positive. This is particularly true in capital-intensive industries where high depreciation may significantly reduce reported profits (e.g. mining or the oil extraction industries), but revenues may well exceed ongoing operating costs. Financial controls are to:

(a) *minimise investments, unless payback is within the lifetime of the overall project;*
(b) *implement cost-reduction methods to maximise cash flow;*
(c) *revalue assets on a realistic basis, rather than on the normal 'going concern' accounting concept;*
(d) *determine product termination or disposal.*

44:6.5 Business Acquisitions

The financial controls stated above will equally apply to entities that are acquiring businesses with different life-cycle activities. For example, those that concentrate on a specific business phase, such as conglomerates with an emphasis on mature cash-generating businesses, may find that their controls are totally inappropriate should they take over a research-focused activity.

44:6.6 Target Costing
(*See* **Ch.24.**)

Target costing is used to describe the reduction of life-cycle costs (*see* **Ch.19**) of new products or services, while ensuring that all customer required specifications are met, in order to be able to market the product or service on a long-term profit basis. This is usually applied following market research to obtain the required selling price for market penetration; anticipated profit is then deducted to leave a target cost to be achieved. If this target is less than planned costs, cost cutting techniques are implemented in order to reach this number as part of a comprehensive cost management system. Attention will be made to all aspects, such as the associated supply chain. Recognition is also given to the reality that most life-cycle costs are designed into the product, so that real attention is required at the pre-production phase, not after manufacturing has begun. For further details of this costing method *see* **Chapter 24.**

44:7 Non-profit-making Organisations

The commercial world's emphasis on profitability as a control measure is not going to have the same significance to an organisation that is not designed to generate profit. Financial performance must now be viewed in the context of the overall objectives of the organisation. Many of these objectives will not readily be expressed in financial terms, but may still be connected to financial inputs. For example, hospitals may have constraints in bedspace, patient waiting times or technical specialists. In financial terms, these can be considered as limiting factors, so that once identified, resources can be directed to these factors to help optimise their contribution. Any significant decision should state the expected outcomes of that decision, such as the results of purchasing specialised equipment and those outcomes can then form the criteria for the control measures for subsequent performance measurements.

Effectiveness, not just financial efficiency, is a key focus area, which is getting the best possible combination of services from the least resources. The linkage of financial and non-financial controls to the objectives of the organisation may well be helped by the use of the balanced scorecard (*see* **Ch.49, para.49:2.3** and **Ch.15, para.15:4.1.4**). For example, recent work by Kaplan and Norton (2001) points out that, in private-sector transactions, the customer both pays for and receives the service, whilst in non-profit making organisations, donors provide the financial resources and other people, constituents, receive the services. The balanced scorecard is then illustrated as the ideal method to place both the donor and recipient perspectives at the top and then identify the internal processes that will deliver desired value to both groups of 'customers'.

References

Anthony, R.N. and Govindarajan, V. (1998) *Management control systems*. Irwin McGraw-Hill: USA.

Biddle, G.C., Bowen, R.M. and Wallace, J.S. (1999) 'Evidence on EVA', *Journal of Applied Corporate Finance, 12(2)*: 69–79.

Kaplan, R.S. and Norton, D.P. (2001) 'Balance without profit', *Financial Management*, CIMA, January.

45. Financial Control in a Rapidly Changing Business Environment

45:1   Managerial Megatrends

For the majority of the 20th century, a style of management which had been dubbed 'scientific' when it was articulated by Frederick Winslow Taylor, dominated the business scene. Significantly, however, it relied on a presumption of stability and was developed in and for a national context.

Today's conditions, however, could not be more different. It is now almost a cliché to say that we are living through turbulent times thanks to the massive changes emanating from all the spheres of influence on business enterprises: scientific, technological, social, political and economic. Moreover, these influences have become more intertwined as the context has become global.

For managers, the most obvious consequence of this turbulence has been an increase in the frequency and speed with which decisions have to be made and, hence, an overwhelming feeling of discontinuity. No longer can it be assumed that tomorrow will be very much like yesterday: the safest starting point is with the assumption that tomorrow will be different. This increased uncertainty has ushered in new techniques under the 'risk management' umbrella.

In particular, the definition of an enterprise in terms of what it has always done – the facilities it has used, the products it has offered and the markets it has served – is now seen as a constraint. New technologies facilitate the introduction of new products and the tapping of new markets but they also engender competition from new quarters. Consequently, a much higher proportion of decisions are strategic in nature; concerned with *what* the enterprise does. This is in sharp contrast to the old model's preoccupation with tactics; concerned with *how* to do what it has always done.

David Allen   767

There was a time when answering the question 'How well did we do what we chose to do?', dominated the management accountant's agenda. Rigid annual budgets, keyed into long-range plans, were seen as good practice. Nowadays, however, two other questions have become pre-eminent: 'How well did we choose what to do?' and 'What should we do next?'. In answer to these questions, rolling budgets keyed into regular strategic reviews are needed.

The old model was developed in an era of shortages, which led to a supply-side orientation, with a focus on the products that were offered. Now, customer orientation is the order of the day: the starting point for any strategic review is with the twofold question 'What characterises the customers we wish to delight and what are their needs?'. Whereas the role of the sales force used to be to sell what the business could make now their task is to find out what it is that would delight the customers. In turn, whereas the primary focus of management accounts used to be on product profitability, customer profitability is now seen as being at least as important.

The search for functional excellence which reinforced, and was reinforced by, this preoccupation with tactics – epitomised by the desire to minimise unit costs – is now seen to lead to serious sub-optimisation. Strategic decisions demand a generalist approach, involving trade-offs across functions. Something more than minimum cost may be preferable, for example, if functional excellence is associated with tailoring the product to the customer's needs so that he is delighted to the point of coming back for more.

Significantly, these trade-offs between functions are almost invariably also trade-offs between time frames, e.g. an opportunity to reduce costs now against an opportunity to increase volume in the future. The old model spawned cost and works accounting but, by contrast, the new model requires management accountants to use the concept of net present value much more than they did formerly.

In this rapidly changing environment, it is noticeable that people at the centre of organisations are finding it impossible to keep up with the changes at the periphery and are forced to push authority out to those closest to the action. In some cases, this leads to disposals but, more frequently, it means devolution to business units.

It is here that we can now see the old model for what it was. Namely one based on command and compliance: 'Do this because I am telling you to and because I will be checking to see that you conform'. The new model, in contrast, is based on trust and commitment: 'I trust you to make the right decision in the prevailing circumstances because you are closest to the action and I know that you are committed to achieving our objective'.

In a management accountancy context, budgetary control became so closely associated with the command and compliance approach that its reputation plummeted in contemporary management thinking. In order to pave the way for more devolved and adaptable controls, which enable those closest to the action to decide what is right in the circumstances, extremists have argued that the word 'budget' should be expunged from the terminology.

Alongside this, we have seen the confrontation of the old model being superseded by a more co-operative approach based on teamwork, partnership and loyalty. For example, notice should be taken of the relentless increase in the perceived importance of corporate governance, aimed at balancing the interests of the various groups of stakeholders as follows:

- on the financing side, the lenders, taxers and owners;

- on the business side, customers, suppliers, employees and Customs and Excise.

In particular, the requirement for quoted companies to include in their annual reports a statement highlighting the uncertainties they face, the risks that are thereby opened up and the control systems they have put in place, should be noted.

This chapter looks at the impact these megatrends have had on the approach to control in general, and to financial control, in particular. Specifically, the trends from tangibles to intangibles, measurement to assessment and analysis to synthesis will be analysed.

Permeating all of this, however, is the recognition that the accounting model, which used to be seen as providing the information necessary to control an organisation, is now seen as not only inappropriate but seriously misleading. Seeking to maximise profits will almost always have the effect of weakening the long-term financial health of an organisation.

The reason for this is rooted in the fact that the accounting model, which existed around for hundreds of years, was designed for stewardship reporting: explaining to investors what had been done with their money. Accounts have now come to be used in a regulatory context, e.g. for the determination of distributable profits and as inputs to taxation computations. Confidence is engendered by having accounts prepared (or, at least audited) by people who are seen to be passive and impartial. Inevitably, perhaps, this has led to the bases on which accounts are prepared becoming increasingly standardised, ostensibly to facilitate comparisons between enterprises.

It is important to appreciate, however, that one does not control events by reporting on them after they have happened. As the accounting subset of accountancy shrinks (thanks to cookbook standards, the application of computers and the arrival of accounting technicians) the financial management subset has been expanding. Significantly, financial managers are not passive and impartial; they are proactively involved in the teams that make decisions and therefore shape events. Moreover, the information they provide to their colleagues is customised to their (increasingly frequent, as we have seen) decision-making needs.

Needless to say, this has had an enormous impact on the work of management accountants and the skills they need to hone; a point to which we will discuss in **paragraph 45:3**.

45:2   From Tangibles to Intangibles

In those far-off days of scarcity and rationing and, hence, of supply-side orientation, there was a reasonable degree of correlation between the value of a business (essentially its capacity to generate cash for its financing stakeholders, discounted back to a present value) and its net assets as shown on the balance sheet (essentially the aggregate of costs carried forward to be charged against future revenues).

In a rapidly changing environment, however, what the accounting model treats as an asset can be a strategic liability. Property can be in the wrong place, machinery can be obsolescent and stock is an embarrassment in a just-in-time environment. Consequently, there is no longer any correlation between the value of a business and the carrying costs of its assets, rather the primary sources of a business's competitive advantage and, hence, of value, include its:

- pace of innovation, in the form of product and process development;

- reputation in the marketplace for quality and service, enabling it to roll out new products;

- ability to recruit and retain the best people and motivate them to seek to delight customers;

- flexibility of response to changing customer needs, arising in particular from its information and control systems.

In turn, such 'intangible' assets are nurtured by the investments required by the accounting model to be treated as costs charged against current profits: research, development, marketing, training and information. The easiest way to improve performance as measured by traditional methods, therefore, is to skimp on the very investments that are vital to the enhancement of the organisation's awareness of, anticipation of and adaptation to, its changing environment.

A number of vested interests (including the consultancy arms of accountancy practices) have argued that accountants should 'measure the true value' of these intangible assets and add them into their balance sheets. Unfortunately for them, the expression 'measuring value' turns out to be an oxymoron, since value cannot be objectively verified or, therefore, audited. Like beauty, it is in the eye of the beholder and can be quantified only by way of a subjective assessment of the impact on future cash flows and, hence, the value of the business.

At this point, it is worth recalling that the accounting model was designed by and for the outsider looking in and therefore capable of objectivity. As Peter Drucker pointed out many years ago, however, if you look into a business, all you will see are costs. Despite using words like assets, book value and net worth, they do not have everyday meanings but simply refer to costs which have not yet been charged against revenue. The fundamental concept is that of capital maintenance, with profit being defined as 'what an enterprise could afford to distribute and still be well off as it was'.

Meanwhile, financial managers and their colleagues are insiders looking outwards. The judgements they and their colleagues make are subjective; what they think will be the outcome of the particular action they are considering. They put values on the expected outcome and the fundamental concept is the adequacy of the return.

Take, for example, an investment in advertising. In arriving at a decision as to the level of investment, the impact on demand of the various feasible options needs to be quantified. In doing so, such questions as 'What do we think will be the response of our competitors, our immediate customers, and the ultimate consumers?' should be considered.

This usually amounts to the compilation of a diminishing returns curve. In practical terms, it is useful to have a general purpose chart available and to invite the manager concerned to suggest the scale. The financial manager's role is to relate that curve to other pieces of information (notably unit contributions and customer loyalty) so as to be able to put values on the potential outcomes and, by comparing them with the respective outlays, identify the optimum level of investment, i.e. the level that maximises the beneficial effect on the value of the business.

It is important to note, and for it to be seen, that the financial manager is not second-guessing the sales manager. Rather, by calling up all relevant information, the point is reached where it can be shown that: 'If your assessment of the investment/impact relationship is correct, this is the optimum level of investment'.

Meanwhile, on a macro level, arguments that balance sheets must include intangibles, so as to get closer to the value of the business, can be excused only by a total ignorance of the purpose of accounting statements. They are designed not to show how much wealth has been created but how much has been realised in the form of tangible assets. Indeed, if it were possible to measure such value accurately (as with costs that have been incurred), it would mean that future cash flows were predetermined, which would mean that future decisions were pre-empted: once measured, value could be neither created nor destroyed, which is clearly nonsense.

In this context, it is important to distinguish between potential (which may or may not be realised) and value. Monitoring involves comparing a current assessment of value with a benchmark based on the preceding assessment plus the cost of capital and minus the cash generation. Some people would describe a shortfall as a 'destruction of shareholder value' but, seeing it as a dissipation of potential, offers far more insight.

In the real world, however, a large part of the work of financial managers is to provide information on alternative options so that managers can reach a decision. There cannot be one measurable value; rather, there are many possible values, depending on the action taken.

The problem is that these areas are seen as soft assessments, as opposed to the hard measurements which are the focus of accounting reports, which leads us to 'assessment'.

45:3　From Measurement to Assessment

The literature of the old model was peppered with references to measurement. Typical mantras were 'if you can't measure it, you can't control it' and 'you get what you measure'. There were, fundamentally, two main reasons for this.

The first reason was the presumption of stability: believing that tomorrow would be like yesterday and then understanding that yesterday was a crucial step in preparing to manage tomorrow. If interest rates were expected to be stable, for example, and the enterprise was expected to stay within a defined range of businesses, then it was possible for theorists to argue that, by looking backwards (at past small lot share-price fluctuations) one could measure the 'risk adjusted cost of capital' applicable to all time frames.

The second reason was the prevalence of the command and compliance approach to control: bosses needing to check that their underlings had done what they had been told to do. Performance had to be measured at departmental, divisional and even total enterprise levels by comparing what actually happened with what ought to have happened according to a rigid 'once a year, for a year' budget. If actual results were worse than budget, someone must have underperformed.

Accounting statements, being totally backward-looking, were seen as the natural way to measure performance and one particular derivative thereof, the ratio of profits to assets (subdivided into constituents in what was known as the Du Pont chart) came to be seen as the pinnacle of a comprehensive structure of control. Management accounting techniques were developed to analyse results so as to show the reasons for any underperformance, e.g. lower volume, selling prices, efficiency or utilisation. The language, such as the classification of variances from standard or budget as favourable or adverse (that is, in terms of their effect on reported profits), said it all.

Today, however, it is recognised that:

(a) *if you can measure it, so can the competition. The most powerful elements of any strategy now are likely to be the ones which are difficult (or even impossible) to measure, such as design, image, reputation and skill. Giving priority to what can be measured, therefore, is likely to weaken the competitive position of a business;*

(b) *if you can measure something, it has already happened and, therefore, cannot be changed. Conversely, some of the most important things in life cannot be measured because they have not happened, as with a problem that has been avoided;*

(c) *others cannot be measured because they have not happened yet, as with the outcomes of decisions currently being made. Anyone who insists on waiting for the measurement of outcomes before making a decision will never make a decision;*

(d) *you cannot measure something without distorting it. Accounting numbers like earnings per share were useful indicators of progress, e.g. until they were adopted as measures of performance;*

(e) *some things cannot be measured even after the event. Despite consultants' claims to the contrary, it is not possible to measure the impact of advertising, as opposed to other aspects of the marketing mix, e.g. because nobody knows what the sales would have been without it.*

Gradually, the limitations of the return on assets as an indicator of progress have become obvious to practitioners. In particular, as it ignores any change in potential, the easiest way to improve reported performance measured in that way, is to slow down the rate of expansion because the increase in tangible assets precedes the related return and revenue investment reduces profits, meaning that expansion will always have an adverse effect on the return on assets.

Decision making is a completely forward-looking activity and, although it is possible to seek the one objectively verifiable truth about the past, there are no facts about the future: nobody *knows* what is going to happen. Therefore, the key input to the decision-making process is a set of forecast relationships, asking, for example, what effect do we think:

- a change in selling prices would have on demand?

- advertising would have on demand?

- a change in volume would have on costs?

- a more flexible manufacturing process would have on lead times and the variety that could be offered?

- shorter lead times or greater variety would have on demand?

By definition, the accounting model is backward looking since one cannot account for something which has not happened. This means that the figures contained in accounts are verifiable by an independent outsider (the auditor) who must inevitably focus, therefore, on the profits that have been realised and the assets that are tangible. The accounting model makes no claim to quantify the value created by an enterprise, only how much has been realised in the form of tangible assets.

In sharp contrast, decision making and hence financial management are forward-looking activities. Since there are no facts about the future, decisions are based on judgements as to what might happen. The focus is on potential which is, of course, intangible.

The link with the previous section is compelling in the sense that the whole of the future is intangible. The financial manager's role is to help colleagues put a value on something that has not yet happened. Subjectivity is par for the course: remember that, in the advertising example, the question was 'What do *we* think the competitors, the customers and the consumers will do?'.

Accountants whose experience has been concentrated on the backward-looking accounting task find this revelation quite alarming. If there are no facts about the future, then forecasts cannot be accurate: why associate ourselves with them? Why should we profess to be able to evaluate proposals, strategies and even entire businesses on the basis of projected cash flows?

The answer to this question is bound up with the concept of shared information, a vital ingredient in the team-based management we saw as being typical of the new model. Take, for example, that most common of decisions, the setting of selling prices. The key inputs are the first two relationships mentioned above, price-volume (which will be input by the sales manager) and volume-cost (which will be input by the production manager), and the optimum can then be identified by way of calculus or a spreadsheet.

The forecast outcome of the decision needs to be logged, not least in order for other members of the team to share the perception and the likely consequences. The production manager, for example, needs a forecast of demand in order to ensure that the required plant, people and materials will be available.

On a more complex level, a decision to invest in a more flexible production process will call for the production manager to quantify the improvements (to lead times and variety, etc.) to be expected at different levels of investment. It is the sales manager, however, who will say what impact those benefits will have on demand and the financial manager who will put those two scales together and identify the optimum point, i.e. the level of investment expected to have the most beneficial effect on the value of the business.

The finance function has the opportunity to have the master franchise for information and therefore be the modern equivalent of the Oracle at Delphi: collecting forecasts from those in the best position to make them and consolidating them in a business-wide model which is made available to colleagues in a form relevant to the decision making in their area.

This is not to say that looking backwards is to be avoided. Within a comprehensive structure of control, it serves two purposes. One is as an aid to understanding the dynamics of particular situations. Keeping track of the cost of capital, for example, prompts thoughts as to the components – interest rates, uncertainty and risk aversion – and is therefore a good introduction to thinking about what it might be in the future. The other is as a context in which progress is monitored and in which those responsible are required to explain why actual outcomes differed from the forecasts on which the related decision was made. Comparing what the cost of capital has been with what it was expected to be, provides a basis for the accountability of the treasurer; comparing actual sales with forecast ensures the accountability of the sales manager.

The main message here is that measurement is only one subset of quantification and is applicable only when something has already happened or exists. Assessment is another subset, appropriate to what has not yet happened and what does not yet exist. Given the absence of facts, we need to be as comfortable with the subjectively judgemental as we are with the objectively verifiable.

Moreover, as the above examples imply, there has to be considerable interaction between the various functions and decisions, which leads us on to the topic of analysis.

45:4   From Analysis to Synthesis

The literature of the old model was also peppered with references to analysis. If we believe that tomorrow is going to be very much like yesterday then, by analysing the past, managers will improve their chances of successfully managing tomorrow.

Analysis is a reductionist concept: it involves breaking things down and calls for the skills associated with the left side of the brain. This thrives on repetition, experience and knowledge. If tomorrow is going to be different, however, managers need to synthesise their judgements as to the possible futures. Synthesis is a holistic concept: it involves building things up and calls for the skills associated with the right side of the brain. This thrives on novelty, innovation and imagination.

The key to general management is to see it as a collection, not of separate modules, but of interdependencies. At the top level, this means linking people, finance, strategy and information. A business is unlikely to delight its customers if it does not have people who are motivated to do so and the requisite information and finance. Equally, those who guard the financial resources are unlikely to release funds unless they have confidence in the people and can access the information that justifies the investment.

Knowledge is only one subset of information and, like measurements, can only refer to something which has happened or exists. Managers' beliefs as to such things as what would delight customers or what impact advertising might have on the demand curve are vital pieces of information but are beyond knowledge. As Albert Einstein himself observed, knowledge only takes you so far: all major developments have sprung from the application of imagination.

The left side of the brain is appropriate to the identification and resolution of problems (which it was assumed in the old model, would persist unless action were taken to eradicate them) and is seen as being the masculine side (linking with the confrontation of the old model). The right side, in contrast, is appropriate to the identification and pursuit of opportunities (which may or may not be grasped) and is seen as the feminine side (linking with the co-operative feature of the new model).

The old style of management was very operationally focused. At that level, repetition was paramount until a problem was met which then prompted managers to progress to the tactical level so as to think about *how* it might be overcome. The strategic level was rarely visited, the presumption being that the business would carry on doing what it had always done – using the same facilities to produce the same goods or services for the same customers – as enshrined in the long-range plan; hence, the natural tendency toward left brain thinking which thrives on repetition and is geared to problem solving.

The new style starts with the strategic level, which looks outwards and forwards in search of opportunities to use different facilities, to produce different goods and services for supplying to new markets. Having identified the combination of such dimensions of strategy that appears to maximise the value of the business, managers move on to the tactical level to consider such questions as how high a price to charge, before actually doing things. In this environment, it is right brain thinking that is called for, given its association with novelty and opportunity grasping.

Again, accounting, with its emphasis on analysis, is supportive of the old model; because it is essentially a technique based on adding up and taking away, any figures it contains can be analysed. The net operating assets figure, for example, is the sum of the fixed assets, stock and net monetary assets (debtors minus creditors) figures. The value of the business, however, is the product of the interaction of the various dimensions of strategy being pursued.

Take two related items, namely investments in product development and advertising. If we were to invest in product development, so that our product was the best on the market, but for some reason we were not prepared to invest in communicating that to the customers, it is likely that we would not sell many, and the value we would put on the proposal would be negative. Likewise, if we invested in advertising but, on trying the product, the customers discovered that it was not the best available, they would not come back for more and again it is likely that the value we would put on this proposal would be negative.

If the two are put together, however, and investment is made into improving the product and in advertising to communicate its attributes, it is likely that the sustained increase in volume would mean that the proposal showed positive value. In other words, these two dimensions of strategy are interdependent: the value of an investment in product development depends on the level of investment in advertising and vice versa.

In a similar way, other investments have knock-on effects, e.g. an investment in training might lower the variable costs which means that increased volume arising from product development or advertising brings greater benefits. It would be foolish to try to put a value on each individual dimension and hope that the sum would indicate the value of the business. The value of a business is holistic, not additive: the whole is worth more than the sum of the parts.

Some commentators have accepted the point that controls based on backward-looking accounting numbers are at best inadequate but go on to argue that the problem is one of not measuring enough and to advocate the 'balanced scorecard'. All such systems in existence, however, are no more than multiple scorecards, since they lack a crucial component: a balancing mechanism.

In any event, for people in real businesses, the idea of balancing past measures is irrelevant. What must be balanced, or optimised, are the various possible futures and our efforts to pursue the chosen one; a task for which the concept of net present value is eminently suitable. Where that concept was used in the old model, it tended to be positioned as indicating whether a particular proposal had positive net present value or not. In the new model, however, the question is which combination of feasible alternatives has the greatest favourable impact on the net present value of the business as a whole.

In place of the long-range plan and rigid 'once a year for a year' budgets, there is an attachment to business models. These show the basic relationships (such as the elasticity of demand) and the higher-level relationships (such as the impact of advertising on the elasticity of demand) linked so as to culminate in the value of the business.

45:5   From Accounting to Financial Management

In exploring the various trends, it becomes clear that the old accounting model, characteristically backward looking and inward looking, so as to report on what has happened, is inappropriate as a basis for financial control in a rapidly changing environment.

This should not be surprising, since the accounting model represents the static branch of the science. It seeks to apportion transactions between short, discrete periods of time, primarily by separating outlays into two categories: 'capital' (to be carried forward on the balance sheet) or 'revenue' (to be charged in arriving at current profits). In this way, it facilitates the calculation of the profit, albeit weeks or months in arrears, for the period and the assets at the end thereof.

Financial management, on the other hand, is dynamic. It is concerned with the long-term continuum and its strength is that it avoids the necessity of stating whether a proposed outlay should be treated as capital or revenue in order to discuss whether it appears to be worthwhile. What matters is cash flow and specifically the adequacy of the excess of inflows over outflows.

Whereas it used to be a matter of pride to say that management information was fully integrated with the accounts, today the reverse now applies and the best systems of management information are insulated from the rigidities of the accounting model. The fact is that, although accounting numbers might provide 'attention directing' information, they do not provide 'decision support' information.

It is important to understand that the above comments are not meant to denigrate the accounting model which has an important role in corporate governance. Neither are they to be associated with calls to tamper with the accounting model (e.g. the advocacy of current costs or the capitalisation and depreciation of revenue investments) which destroy its objective verifiability. However, it is necessary in order to make the point that there is another side to management accountancy; namely, financial management.

Indeed, the skills required for the two jobs are very different. Accounting uses the left brain skills to analyse what exists, financial management uses the right brain skill of synthesis to imagine what does not yet exist.

Increasingly, companies are separating the two tasks: if you want the objectively verifiable truth about a certain past, look to accounting but if you want help making a subjective judgement about an uncertain future, look to financial management. What is not acceptable is to employ people who spend the first three and a half weeks on accounting and are available for financial management duties in only the last two or three days of every month.

In that situation, it is often found that organisations have a surplus of accountants, who are good at looking backwards and inwards, and a shortage of those who are good at looking forwards and outwards. Careful management of the surplus of accounting specialists is needed if motivation is not to be damaged. Experience shows, however, that the shortage of financial managers tends to persist: most of them display the characteristics which mark them out for promotion to general managers!

The wane of accounting and the waxing of financial management amounts to a shift from 'hard' to 'soft' concepts and is consistent with other identified trends from:

- confrontation to co-operation;

- command and compliance to trust and commitment;

- tangibles to intangibles;

- measurement to assessment; and

- analysis to synthesis.

Many accountants find it hard to make the transition. 'If there are no facts about the future', as one accountant commented, 'can you blame me for spending all my time looking backwards?'. The answer to this question is that our quantitative skills are just as applicable (and currently in greater demand) to judgements about the future, as to facts about the past.

46. Management Control

46:1 Defining Management Control

Management control is a process for detecting and correcting unintentional performance errors and intentional irregularities, such as theft or misuse of resources. It is also a process for motivating and inspiring people to perform organisational activities that will further an organisation's goals. The challenge for management control is to persuade and ensure that organisation members pursue organisationally desirable activities.

CIMA (1996) define management control as:

> The final stage in the management process, in which assurance is sought that organisational goals are being achieved and procedures adhered to, or alternatively that appropriate remedial action is taken. Control may be focused on results, on actions or on personnel.

There are a number of dimensions to the topic, for example, its interface with strategy, human behaviour and how it is operated in divisionalised companies, this chapter will explore and develop each of these. We shall see that some of the exercise of management control takes place around the construction and use of budgets. The chapter will conclude by discussing a recent tendency of some companies to dispense with some of the detail of budgeting (the so-called 'beyond budgeting' approach).

46:1.1 Management Control in Context

A good starting point is to place management control within an overall organisational planning and control framework. A common subdivision of the planning and control framework in organisations is *strategic planning, management control* and *operational* or *task control.*

Mike Tayles

The following three descriptions of the three types of control are brief but adequate to differentiate them:

1. Strategic planning *(see **Ch.2, para.2:2**) is the process of deciding on the goals of the organisation and the formulation of the broad strategies to be used in attaining these goals. This process uses methods quite different from management control or task control.*
2. Management control *is the process by which management assures that the organisation carries out its strategies.*
3. Operational or task control *is the process of assuring that specific tasks are carried out effectively and efficiently (see **Ch.38, para.38:5.2.5**).*

Although accountants and management are involved in all aspects it is clear where the emphasis of the chapter will lie. Most readers will have an appreciation of what is involved in these three management processes, however, they have distinct features as the **Table 46:1** will show.

Table 46:1 **Distinctions among strategic planning, management control and operational control**

Characteristic	*Strategic planning*	*Management control*	*Operational control*
Focus	One aspect at a time	Whole organisation	Single task or transaction
Structure	Unstructured and irregular	Rhythmic, prescribed procedures	Rational, relies on rules
Nature of information	External and predictive, less accurate	Internal and some historical, more accurate	Tailored to the operation, often non-financial
Persons involved	Few top management	Many top and middle management	Junior managers/ supervisors or none
Mental activity	Creative, analytical	Administrative, persuasive	Follow direction or none
Source discipline	Economics	Social psychology	Physical sciences
Time horizon	Long term	Short term	Day-to-day or real time

It will be clear from the foregoing that the three processes within planning and control are undertaken in line with different levels of the organisation hierarchy, that is, senior management, middle managers and junior managers/supervisors.

46:1.2 Outline of a Management Control System

Any system consists of a structure and a process. The formal *management control structure* is built around responsibility centres which emphasise performance related particularly to cost, revenue, profit and investment. Centres established on the above lines attempt to tailor the (internal reporting) management control system to the organisation structure and the consequent delegation of authority within the organisation. This is in line with the controllability principle reporting to a manager about those things over which he or she has most influence or control.

The *management control process* involves both informal and formal communication and interaction. The diagram shown below (**Fig.46:1**) is used to depict the phases of this process in a typical organisation.

Figure 46:1 **Phases of management control**

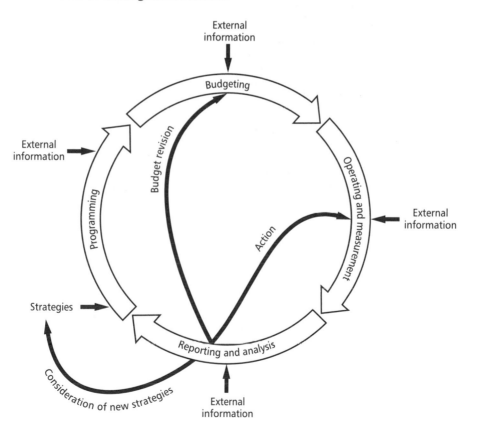

To elaborate on the features of this, *programming* is the link with strategic planning (*see* **Ch.2, para.2:2**). It identifies the products a company intends to develop, projects which management intend to pursue to meet the organisation's overall goals. *Budgets* (*see* **Ch.7**) are derived from these and are specified in terms of a manager's responsibility. *Operating and measurement* is the collecting of actual costs and outcomes identified to both programmes and responsibility centres. Finally, *reporting and analysis* take place as a basis for control to the budget, for the co-ordination of activities and as a basis for future decisions perhaps to change the original plan.

46:1.3 Feedback and Feedforward

Models of control can be based on feedback or feedforward. A feedback style is carried out after the event and is essentially error-based. That is, the detection of a deviation between actual results and an objective is what causes a control action to occur. In contrast, feedforward control consists of a prediction being made of anticipated future outputs. If the expected outputs differ from what outputs are desired control actions are implemented to minimise these differences. Control is therefore achieved, if the control actions are effective, before any deviation from the objective output occurs. *See* **Figs. 46:2** and **46:3** for examples of feedback and feedforward systems.

Figure 46:2 **A feedback control system**

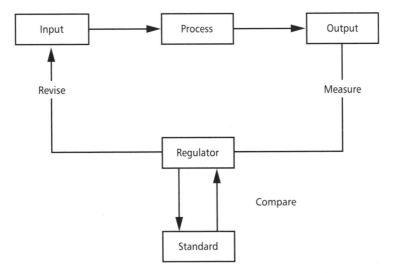

Figure 46:3 **A feedforward control system**

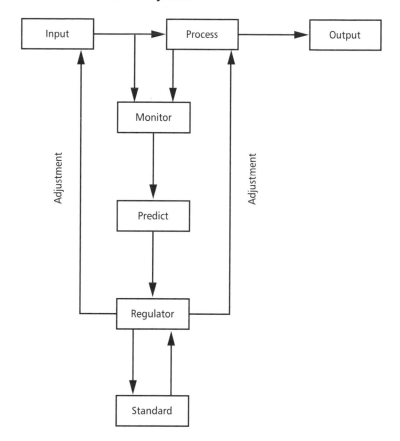

Traditional budgetary control (*see* **Ch.9**) is an example of feedback where actual outcomes are compared to budgets. The budgetary process is one of feedforward, in that expected outcomes are compared with desired outcomes (e.g. spending levels, ROI, market share etc.). These are revised in successive iterations until a desired outcome is identified. In practice it may be observed that many companies do not simply adopt a feedback approach, that is, comparison of actual to budget. They operate processes which require periodic reforecasting of likely outcomes in order to better manage their planning and control activity. They are adapting the principles of feedforward and feedback to meet their management control needs.

46:1.4 Programmed and Non-programmed Decisions

It follows from the above, however, that in theory at least, to operate an anticipatory (feedforward) control system requires a well-developed predictive model. A barrier to more effective control, in some circumstances, may be the lack of this predictive ability. It will be appreciated that some decisions exist where the situation is sufficiently understood that a reliable prediction of the outcome can be made, called programmed decisions. Conversely, others will have no formal mechanism for predicting likely outcomes and will therefore rely more on the judgement of managers, called non-programmed decisions.

This insight has implications for the control information used by management. In the case of the former (programmed decisions) the model is explicit and known, it is possible to instruct subordinates what to do, how and when to do it, giving and requiring little scope for judgement. Subordinates can be responsible for doing what they are told. By contrast where predictive models are not well formed (non-programmed decisions) it is more appropriate for the subordinate to be told of and work towards the desired outcome as a control measure. How such an outcome is obtained is left to the discretion of the subordinate.

The distinction between these two types of situation is that they have implications for the type of information appropriate for control. One may be quite closely pre-specified in terms of inputs (detailed costs) to achieve an output – programmed decision, or the other may be broadly specified, for example, a total budget or target ROI being identified so that a manager may use his or her discretion/judgement in how the money may be spent to achieve the desired outcome.

It has been suggested that management accounting systems have often been designed on the basis that decisions are programmed, whereas in practice they are used in some non-programmed situations, that is, conditions with a high level of uncertainty. In practice therefore the management control system needs to be used with greater flexibility than the original design may suggest.

46:2 Management Behaviour and Management Control

Central to management control within organisations is the construction and use of budgets. The technical issues within planning and budget preparation are fairly straightforward though they may result in voluminous records in a large organisation. Some would argue that the problem arises out of how managers use the information provided by the budget system and how such use affects the information that is entered into the budget (*see* **Ch.9, para.9:6**). These can have implications when:

(a) *budgets are seen as forecasts;*
(b) *budgets are used as targets; and*
(c) *budgets are compared with actuals to evaluate both the manager and business unit performance.*

46:2.1 Budget as Forecasts

General observations and academic experiments have suggested that managers behave conservatively when required to make budgets which are to be used as forecasts for future achievement. That is, they underestimate sales and overestimate costs. They see it as in their interests to incorporate 'slack' into the budget. Managers also engage in games of building up slack in good years and converting it to reported profit in poor years. Conversely, there are observations from other studies that some managers, after a run of mediocre results, deliberately overstate revenues and understate cost estimates. They no doubt feel the need to make an immediate favourable impact by promising better performance in the future. It may be, of course, that this merely delays the problem for which these managers are subsequently censured when they fail to hit these optimistic targets.

46:2.2 Budgets as Targets

From many psychological studies it is pointed out that better performance is achieved when targets exist than when this is not the case. Furthermore, demanding targets extract better performance than weak ones. This is up to a point, totally unattainable targets tend to be counterproductive. The precision which is applied to a target is seen to be important because if targets are not accepted by an individual, then poorer performance may result from that person's 'withdrawal' from the task than would apply if a less demanding target had been set. It is also important that managers achieve their targets frequently enough to ensure giving a positive reinforcement in their efforts. A practical consequence of this is that a budget which might get the best performance out of a manager, a demanding target, is unlikely to be achieved most of the time. It is not therefore a useful forecast of actual out-turn. Conversely a budget that is an accurate forecast of what is likely to be achieved will only motivate a modest level of performance.

46:2.3 Budgets in Performance Evaluation

A further use of budgets is as a basis for setting performance standards and rewards, for example, bonus, status or enhanced promotion prospects are often linked to budget attainment. Organisations are complex, tasks interdependent, there are many dimensions of performance and these are not all easily quantified and certainly not in financial terms. Problems can occur here because the budgets are quite narrow specifications of what are desired or organisational outcomes. Placing emphasis on budget achievement can have repercussions on other, perhaps long-term, aspects of organisational performance. Stressing the need to achieve these budget results may result in the budget being met but this may be as a result of manipulation by managers of both the budget and actual results.

46:3 Coping with Conflicts in Management Control

It will be apparent from the foregoing that budgets serve various purposes and in some cases these purposes may be in conflict. There can be tensions and conflicts between budgets used for different purposes and management needs to have some strategy and methods of dealing with this. We shall look particularly at tensions between three major functions of budgets: budgets as forecasts; budgets as targets; and budgets in performance evaluation.

46:3.1 Forecasts or Targets

As a forecast the budget seeks to be the best assessment of the likely outcome of the interaction of the organisation with its environment. The most effective planning budget is that which is most probable. The budget level set for this purpose will not necessarily get the best performance out of managers: it will not create optimum motivation. Generally it is believed for budgets to motivate, higher objectives should be set – stretching targets, that is to say, possible but not probable results. Budgets set for motivation purposes run the risk of not being likely to be met most of the time. So if this sort of budget is used for planning there is a risk that it will not be attained, furthermore it will not help to identify optimal use of resources for the organisation.

If the original budgets are to be used as targets involving motivation then they are likely to be difficult to achieve. As they are consolidated into an overall picture, say for the whole business unit, they may need to be reviewed to be more in line with the requirements of financial planning. In other words, as the budgets are aggregated upwards through the hands of senior managers it may be necessary for these managers to reduce the target to levels that are reasonable and consistent for planning purposes. If a senior manager has typically six middle managers reporting to him or her, all with stretching targets, the likelihood of all the budgets, and by implication the target of the senior managers, being met is low. A major concern here, however, is that it may be perceived that in effect two budgets are being operated. One to manage most of junior and middle management and one (an easier one) for senior managers. It would be necessary to break down this perception before it had adverse repercussions on morale.

An alternative approach is to operate within a culture of difficult targets, and to consolidate based on these difficult targets, but to ensure that systems are in place for managers to signal early when they are unlikely to be met by:

(a) *advance warning being given by the appropriate responsible manager; and*
(b) *the company having some contingency plans for coping with various eventualities of budget non-attainment.*

One thing can be certain is that the consolidated budget will be unlikely to be met and hence the tight budget approach may be unhelpful for planning. Indeed it would be appropriate to have contingency plans for various degrees of budget underachievement and these would have to be in detail.

46:3.2 Targets or Performance Evaluation
(*See* **Chs 48** and **49**.)

The potential for conflict here relies on the fact that budgets are often viewed by managers as fixed standards of performance against which they will be judged. In other words once objectives are set they are fixed and failure to achieve them will be seen as unsatisfactory performance and will have repercussions. There is certainly something to be said for setting targets and not deviating from them, it focuses the mind of the budgetee.

On the other hand in evaluating managers it is often considered appropriate to remove uncontrollable expenses. Indeed it may often be deemed desirable to adjust for uncontrollable and unforeseeable environmental influences that have occurred during the planning period. The latter view is taking a perspective of 'if I knew then what I know now' what budget would I have set. But what is the likely effect on motivation of an opportunity to change the budget during or at the end of the planning period? Motivation may be impaired by the fact that it is anticipated that performance standards may change or be changeable, though equally they are not helped by the rigid application of clearly inappropriate fixed budgets.

This conflict can be dealt with to an extent by differentiating the levels of management for whom the uncontrollable/unforeseeable factors apply. The ability to foresee and respond to, that is, control for, unforeseeable and unforeseen events is reduced for lower-level managers anyway. Whereas at most senior levels greater responsibility should apply. After all senior managers in large organisations are often employed specifically for their ability to anticipate and deal with uncertain economic and environmental situations and influences. Making this sort of differentiation can help to retain commitment and motivation.

A variation on the above is to generate some preagreed sets of circumstances, external environmental measures which will trigger budget adjustment. A range of agreed factors could be known to all and apart from these causing some revision to occur, the budget as originally set would be retained as a requirement and commitment.

46:3.3 Forecasts or Performance Evaluation

Any conflict that may occur here is partially alleviated by the fact that planning and evaluation are separated by the time element, therefore the conflict is less pronounced. If, at the end of the budget period, or appropriate subdivision of it, adjustment can be made to the budget for uncontrollable or unforeseeable environmental factors, as mentioned above, the budget can function as both a forecasting/planning and an evaluation tool. If we ignore the motivation role this is possible though care should be taken to ensure that it does not look as if it just involves a moving of the goal posts.

Some of the above approaches can be incorporated into a system of periodic reforecasting or rolling budgets. These often occur on a quarterly basis. Commitment is often maintained because a manager knows that once finally agreed for a quarter (some three or six months before the budget period actually commences) the budget will not be modified again, for planning or evaluation. Yet because the budget period has been significantly shortened, the individual manager finds the impact of any failure easier to tolerate. Also the budget undergoes two revisions before it is final and so it can be adjusted for what might be termed unforeseeable events in a more current timescale than under conventional budget systems.

Some companies using this approach adopt a system which requires on the one hand reporting of actual results, but also forecasting of the anticipated operating results for the remainder of the budget period. These revised forecasts become input to the budget process so that a manager's performance in planning is examined in addition to executing established plans (*see* **Fig.46:4**).

Figure 46:4 **Types of control comparison**

Budget versus actual	How are we doing? Are we on track towards our objectives?
Budget versus forecast	Will we remain on track towards our objectives? What will happen if no action is taken? Do we need to take action?
Budget versus revised forecast	Will proposed action put us back on track?
Latest forecast versus previous forecast	Why has the forecast changed? Is the situation improving/deteriorating?
Actual versus past forecast	Did thing turn out as expected? If not, why not? Are we being too optimistic/pessimistic in our forecasting?

46:4 Management Control of Divisions

Much of business, not just in the UK, is carried out in a highly aggregated industry structure consisting of very large enterprises. It is an observable fact that many organisations currently operate within divisionalised organisation structures. That is they are wholly or partly owned by another company. A division can be defined as:

> a segment within the organisation where the divisional chief executive has responsibility for both the production and marketing activities of the segment. The division may be a unit of a parent company or it may be a wholly or partially owned subsidiary (*see SSAP25: Segmental Reporting or IAS14: Segment Reporting*).

The extent to which senior management in head office is involved in the planning of strategy for each division varies depending on the nature of, and variability among, the industries within the group. For example, some companies which operate within a closely integrated structure require central planning. Other conglomerates with investment in a wide range of diverse businesses leave most strategic planning to be undertaken within the business units. Notwithstanding this different degree of emphasis, management control within divisionalised undertakings is sufficiently important to require specific comment. This will be illustrated selectively with findings from a survey of manufacturing companies on which the author collaborated (Drury *et al.*, 1993).

46:4.1 Divisional Autonomy
(*See* Ch.36.)

Divisionalisation involves dividing a company into separate self-contained segments or divisions that allow divisional managers to operate with a greater degree of independence than if they were operating departments. However, central management cannot grant total freedom to their divisional managers. Certain responsibilities will be delegated together with the necessary authority to take appropriate decisions, but only within centrally determined guidelines. The restrictions that such guidelines can place on divisional managers can have a significant impact on divisional autonomy. Some restriction on divisional autonomy is inevitable as central management must exercise control over divisional operations in order to integrate the activities of the organisation as a whole.

From the survey of practice it was apparent that the greatest degree of decision-making autonomy given to divisional managers is in the area of operating policy (setting selling prices, levels of output and stocks). Central management exerted close control over capital expenditure (*see* Ch.11) although divisions had some discretion in choosing capital projects within certain limits, generally close control over capital expenditure was maintained by central management. Respondents indicated that these long-term decisions and the funding of them through borrowing were so important for the whole organisation as to require central control.

46:4.2 Methods Used to Evaluate Divisional Managerial Performance
(*See* Ch.48, para.48:5.)

The most commonly used measure to evaluate divisional performance is return on investment (ROI). Various surveys have indicated a strong preference for ROI. It has been suggested that firms prefer to use ROI because, being a ratio, it can be used for inter-division and interfirm comparisons. ROI for a division can be compared with the return from other divisions within the group or with other companies outside the group whereas absolute monetary measures such as profit, cash flow or residual income may not be so meaningful. A second possible reason for the preference for ROI is that 'outsiders' tend to use ROI as a measure of a company's overall performance. Corporate managers therefore want their divisional managers to focus on ROI so that their performance measure is congruent with 'outsiders' measure of company overall economic performance.

ROI is not the only financial performance measure that is used, others include a target profit before interest, target cash flow and target profit after charging interest on capital employed by the division, usually called residual income (RI). The findings suggest that corporate management does not rely exclusively on a single accounting measure; instead a range of available techniques is used to give a general picture of divisional performance.

The management control theory suggests that divisional performance ought to be evaluated using residual income (RI) (*see* **Ch.44, para.44:4.2**) rather than return on investment (ROI). ROI, being a ratio rather than an absolute measure of divisional profitability, can encourage managers to make suboptimal decisions. For example, a manager who is currently earning a 30% return might be reluctant to accept a project earning only a 25% return as this would dilute the division's rate of return. However, if the company (and the division's) cost of capital is 15%, the project is profitable and ought to be accepted. The residual income method would encourage the 'correct' decision by showing that the profits earned by the division would exceed the interest charge computed on its capital employed. A project with a 25% return would be acceptable to the divisional manager if performance is evaluated on the basis of residual income since 25% return could be added to profits while deducting only a 15% cost of capital.

In spite of this shortcoming, ROI is still preferred in practice, perhaps because the head office is usually intimately involved in capital investment decisions. Furthermore, if ROI is used flexibly as an evaluation tool, it can be adapted to cope operationally with projects whose returns are in excess of the cost of capital but less than the division's current return.

46:4.3 Allocation of Corporate Costs

In theory it is appropriate to distinguish between the economic performance of a division, which would be established periodically, when an investment or disposal decision is faced, and the performance of its manager(s) which may be developed routinely. Following earlier comments it is advocated that costs should not be allocated when evaluating the division's *managerial* performance, because they represent uncontrollable costs, but full allocations may be appropriate for evaluating the division's *economic* performance. It would appear that in practice this distinction is not always followed.

In line with the principles of responsibility accounting and controllability, it could be advocated that divisional managers should be evaluated strictly on the basis of costs and revenues directly traceable to them. Thus all allocations of indirect costs, such as central service and central administration costs which are not controllable by divisional managers, ought not to be allocated to divisions for *managerial* performance evaluation purposes. Such costs can only be controlled where they are incurred, which means that they can be controlled only by central service managers and central management. In other words the performance measure should be controllable profit or controllable ROI, not using the net profit.

Despite the many theoretical arguments against allocations for cost control and managerial performance evaluation the evidence indicates that allocations are quite widely used for these purposes. The survey responses indicated that 51% of the organisations measure divisional managerial performance after (and 49% before) allocating corporate costs. The most important performance evaluation reasons were 'to remind profit centre managers that indirect costs exist and that profit centre earnings must be adequate to cover some share of these costs' and 'it encourages divisional managers to put pressure on service department managers or general managers to do a better job of controlling central costs'. It was also suggested that the allocation of central costs can lead general management to question whether it would be better if an existing central service were to be supplied (wholly or partially) either from outside the company or within each division. It would presumably act as a signal that further detailed investigation of this issue should take place.

46:4.4 Defining the Investment Base

Companies using either ROI or residual income must decide which assets should be used in the investment base. When evaluating divisional managerial performance the logic previously developed would state that only those assets that can be directly traced to the division and controlled by the divisional manager should be included in the asset base. Assets managed by central headquarters should not be included. For example, if debtors and cash are administered centrally, they should not be included as part of the asset base. On the other hand, if a divisional manager can influence these amounts, they should be included in the asset base. Virtually all of the respondents indicated that fixed assets, inventories and debtors are included in the assets base.

46:4.5 Valuation of Assets

Asset valuation has an important impact on ROI and residual income calculations. External analysts might refer to the net book value of assets to calculate financial performance (*see FRS15: Tangible Fixed Assets or IAS16: Property, Plant and Equipment*), but for internal management control purposes this is not essential. The major limitation arising from using net book values is that, other things being equal, ROI and residual income will increase solely with the passage of time as depreciation reduces the asset base. Hence there is a danger that managers will postpone investments in new assets and continue to operate older assets with low written-down values, because it enhances their reported ROI.

Some companies calculate ROI and residual income based on the gross book value of the assets. This eliminates the incentive to avoid investment in new assets but creates a new incentive to replace existing assets with new assets. This is because the increase in the asset base is only the difference between the original cost of the old asset and the purchase cost of the new asset. This difference is likely to be significantly less than the incremental cash flow of purchasing the new asset.

Valuing assets at replacement cost is conceptually superior to historical cost and provides a reasonable approximation of an asset's economic value. This was considered by an ICAS discussion document called 'Making Corporate Reports Valuable'. The Committee compiling the report expressed a preference for net realisable value over current replacement cost 'principally because it is value-based whereas replacement cost is cost-based … [and] value rather than cost is important in assessing financial wealth'. However the vast majority of organisations use the net book values to compute ROI and residual income. Only a small proportion use the alternatives of gross book value, current value, replacement cost or some other departure from historical cost. The general impression is that the rules and procedures established for external financial reporting strongly influence the methods adopted for evaluating the performance of divisional managers.

46:5 Non-financial Measures
(*See* Ch.49.)

The accountant preparing financial information in the context of management control must be aware of the increasing role of non-financial information in strategic planning, managerial and operational control. It has long been the case that operational control has been supported by non-financial measures. For reasons of both relevance and timeliness it has been common to use performance measures to evaluate efficiency, material waste, throughput and many other operational aspects using quantitative but non-financial measures. Initial impact is made with a non-financial perspective though this could subsequently be reported with financial values attached.

For the last decade in particular greater publicity has been given to the formalising of non-financial measures at the strategic planning level. Although executives have perhaps always considered the need for non-financial measures at this level, recent initiatives have been to encourage a more structured approach to their development. These would ensure that executives gave equal emphasis to all important areas of an organisation's strategy and performance, not just the immediate cost and revenue factors. These would therefore cover other aspects such as customer-orientated performance, operational measures and innovation. Consultants have been active in marketing this approach using appropriate buzzwords such as 'balanced scorecard', 'performance pyramid' and 'performance measurement matrix' to name only a few. While the use of non-financial measures is not new this is an encouragement to undertake a more formal consideration of it in relation to key result areas and critical success factors of the business.

The benefit of the development of non-financial measures related to strategic plans flows logically into management control. To ensure that strategic plans are operationalised at the management control level the measures developed in the former can be cascaded down to middle management to develop targets and generate plans appropriate to each functional area. So that broad strategic statements about customer orientation can be supported by targets for defect reduction and reduction in customer complaints, on time delivery and price competitiveness. In the area of innovation, measures can be developed about the number of new products, the success of continuous improvement processes and milestones for new product introduction. When considering the efficiency of manufacturing processes, cycle time and process yield are typical measures which may be developed.

While they will not replace the use of financial information they provide a useful complement and an opportunity to generate a balanced perspective of organisational performance. This development can be seen as both an opportunity and a threat to accountants. It could be claimed that as the accountant is a specialist in periodic reporting that all measures should be reported through the accounting reporting system and this would enhance the profile of the accounting function. However, the choice of the accountant for this role is not automatic, for example others, such as IT specialists, take over this responsibility. Alternatively, the generation and evaluation of these measures could be undertaken by the executives to whom they specifically relate. In which case each functional area may tend to take on its own responsibilities for management accounting information.

46:6 Budgeting and Beyond

We have discussed that budgets serve as a means of planning and control. It is often the case that many organisations have budgets as integral components of their management control systems. They are also a means for communication of short-term goals to members of the organisations as well as a means of motivation. Unit and division managers will hopefully prepare their budgets to be congruent to the organisation's goals. Budgeting has become so much an integral part of firms' management systems that some managers think that they cannot operate without it.

Budgeting requires several important skills, including forecasting, knowledge of how activities affect costs and the ability to see how the organisation's different activities fit together. Budgeting is normally done by a budget team, which is co-ordinated by the financial controller and the team reports to a budget committee that includes senior management. Managers are often strongly motivated to find ways of improving the process of budgetary planning and control in order to improve competitiveness.

46:6.1 Limitations of Traditional Budgeting

Budgeting is not without its critics however; it has been pointed out that in some organisations the process is inefficient, lengthy and not giving good value for the management time devoted to it. Some problems with and criticisms of the planning and control process have already been mentioned (*see* **para.46:2**). A summary of some of the objectives of budgets and some of the problems that a traditional approach to budgeting leads to is shown in **Table 46:2**.

Typical problems with budgets are:

(a) *the inefficient budget process;*
(b) *the focus is mainly on financial outputs;*
(c) *the difficulty of sometimes relating budgets to strategy and goals;*
(d) *the rigid annual cycle of budgets may not fit with the business cycle;*
(e) *managers tend to behave in their own best interest not that of the organisation;*
(f) *departments and divisions of a single organisation may use somewhat different formats and data sources in which to compile their budget information.*

Thus the criticisms are that the mechanics of the process are confused and inefficient, the level of commonality and aggregation being sought is excessive, often counterproductive and the technology used in the processes is unsuitable.

Table 46:2 **Limitations of traditional budgeting**

Objective	Practice	Problem
Strategy coherence	Last year plus	Not linked to strategy
	Across-the-board cuts	Wrong services cut
Resource management	Functional organisation	Suboptimal performance possible
	Cost element focus	Outputs not visible
Continuous improvement	Incremental improvement	Internally driven targets
Manager behaviour	Command and control	Lack of commitment
	Financial emphasis	Dysfunctional behaviour
Added value	After-event reporting	Variances not prevented
	Bureaucratic	Wasted opportunities

46:6.2 Overcoming Limitations

One way to address these limitations, and some companies have tried, is to develop more rules and closer co-ordination of activities. The standardising of documents and processes, the common treatment of particular operations and allocations, clearer definitions of responsibilities are also adopted to deal with some of the shortcomings. Improved budget manuals and more guidelines, more extensive training of managers have been undertaken.

Some businesses seem to think that adopting a standardised process of budget preparation and uniform documentation, for example, is an appropriate and positive way forward. It is also possible to observe that there is scope for greater support from the rapid development of technology in large organisations. The spreadsheet is a frequently used basis of schedule preparation, but increasingly budgets are supported through particular accounting packages or ERP systems. Additionally, companies can use web-based approaches to collect and collate the various budgets of subunits of their organisation.

46:6.3 Further Budget Innovations

Over recent decades some other 'innovations' have been suggested, for example zero-based budgeting, priority-based budgeting and activity-based budgeting (ZBB, PBB, ABB), these are mentioned briefly in **Chapter 9**, and ZBB and ABB are discussed in **Chapters 12** and **13**. Further possible approaches to be adopted by companies are rolling budgets or more radically the significant de-emphasis of budgets.

A rolling budget is a variation and extension of the annual budget system, in that it seeks to ensure that planning and budgeting are a continuous process and as up to date as possible. It makes budgets and budgeting an ongoing operation rather than a once-a-year process. Say a company divides its annual budget into four quarters, then as Year One Quarter 1 progresses, so Quarter 2 is reviewed and revised in some detail in the light of the latest information. At the same time the budget for the other quarters 3 and 4, which were previously in less detailed form, are reviewed and updated. Additionally, Year Two Quarter 1 is added so that a full budget year is always in view.

Benefits of this approach are that management can always have in front of it plans for a full year. This will emphasise the longer-term focus of the organisation. It also ensures that managers are constantly thinking about planning for the future and the validity of these plans. It keeps planning at the front of the manager's mind all of the year not just at the annual budget round. As a result of this it is likely that the actual performance is being compared with a more realistic target than if the budget was prepared only once a year. In terms of control comparison there is some similarity between rolling budgets and the reforecasting approach mentioned earlier (*see* **para.46:3.3**).

46:6.4 Beyond Budgeting

A more radical approach is the significant de-emphasis of budgets in the organisation, that is, moving 'beyond budgeting'. Even though there have been innovations in the budget process such as ZBB, PBB, ABB, mentioned earlier, there are some authors who call for the discarding of budgets. They suggest that because of their limitations and problems budgets are not a good use of resources.

This suggestion takes the view that the traditional budgeting approaches are based on business developed in the 20th century, the so-called 'Industrial Age'. Budgets originated in organisations that generally follow a functional and hierarchical structure, the multi-divisional form. The multi-divisional (M-form model) structure, as illustrated in **Figure 46:5**, was suitable and effective for the Industrial Age. In this M-form structure (the 'Control' model), senior management is the main source of knowledge and experience.

Figure 46:5 **M-form model of management structure**

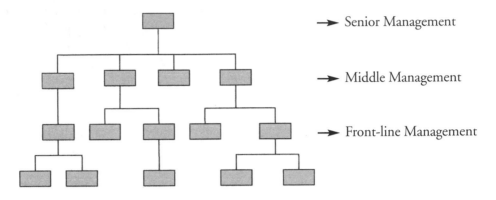

Its major role is to formulate strategy and allocate resources. Middle management maintains organisation control and front-line managers are supposed to be the implementers.

The M-form model is argued to be 'too bureaucratic, rigid and unresponsive, and it creates a culture that is risk-averse and gives a false sense of security'. The M-form model is claimed to be not 'in tune' with today's fast-changing competitive age.

Modern organisations do not necessarily function with tall hierarchies and narrowly defined functional areas. They often have very flat structures, managers often working in project teams. The company functions through the operation of networks. Thus, a new structure, the N-form model (the 'Enterprise' model) as illustrated in **Figure 46:6** is recommended for the emerging 'Information Age'. The front-line managers are considered the entrepreneurs, strategists as well as decision makers who constantly create and respond to new opportunities for the business. The middle managers are the horizontal integrators building competencies internally and externally, while the top managers are supposed to motivate and provide the sense of purpose while frequently challenging the organisation's ongoing ideas and processes. This model is based on trust, between managers, workers, customers and partners. The N-form company needs a different approach to budgeting from the organisation used to the M form of structure.

The above views are put forward by the 'Beyond Budgeting Round Table' (BBRT), this is a research body run by CAM-I, a US-based organisation. BBRT has studied several organisations that have abandoned traditional budgeting and used the findings to formulate a new model that is applicable to the modern organisation, in the Information Age.

Figure 46.6 N-form model of management structure
Source: Adapted from Hope and Fraser (1997)

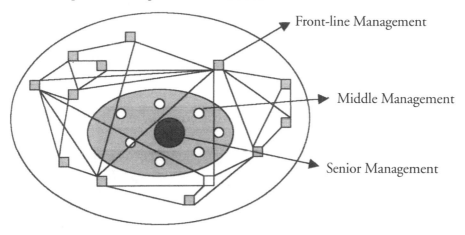

BBRT's main purpose is to move from the 'Industrial Age' where the economic model is the 'Control' model to one based on enterprise, innovation and empowerment, the 'Enterprise' model.

The beyond budgeting model consists of:

(a) *divorcing target-setting from financial planning, a reduced financial emphasis at lower organisational levels and more non-financial measures;*
(b) *more frequent financial forecasting, usually quarterly at a higher level only;*
(c) *cultural change in the way the organisation deals with planning and control.*

So far the 'beyond-budgeting' approach has been adopted by relatively few organisations; they are reporting significant improvements, but incontrovertible proof is difficult to establish. A typical scenario of control in a 'beyond-budget' company is shown below:

• A high-level summary financial planning undertaken by the Head Office staff to ensure overall financials are acceptable and liquidity is maintained. These are probably in quarterly rolling budget form. But these are not relayed in detail to individual operating units.

- Targets are developed and cascaded down the organisation in appropriate form. These will tend to be predominantly non-financial and are composed of both leading and lagging indicators. There are a number of performance measure scorecard approaches, which can be followed in this regard.

- Control of fixed costs by a reporting of cost trends and the use of activity-based systems.

- Resource allocation decisions based more on project appraisal methods than on annual budget allocations.

Figure 46:7 **Culture change from traditional budgeting**

Source: Adapted from Hope and Fraser (1997)

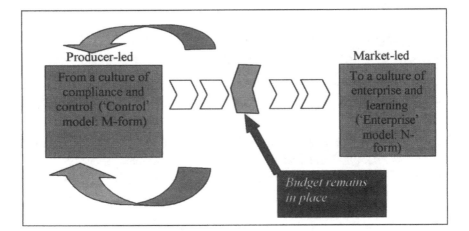

It is further suggested that persisting with the 'traditional budgeting' model can be a barrier for the organisation to moving from the M form to the N form. It is pointed out that many organisations have adopted the new 'Enterprise' model such as total quality management, business process re-engineering, decentralisation, empowerment, economic value added and balanced scorecard, but studies show that they fail to attain the intended benefits because they still attempt to comply with the requirement of the traditional 'Control' model budgeting system. As long as budgeting remains in place, the organisation tends to return to its old culture (*see* **Fig.46:7**).

It is possible to be critical of some of the above ideas in that they could represent a list of consultants' recommendations. However, the resources spent on the whole budget process are considerable and companies are justified in asking whether this represents value for money in their operations. Given the rapid and radical change experienced in many business sectors and economies throughout the world and the significant developments in IT, companies would be recommended to consider evaluating alternative approaches. That said, they should be aware that such a culture change would need serious investment and training, benefits would be unlikely to be achieved in the short term.

46:7 Conclusions

The content of this chapter reflects the culmination of current thought and practice about accounting systems of management control – persuading the members of companies to pursue organisationally desirable activities. Though much of it is topical, it is fair to say that it has been practised for many years and we are still learning how to operationalise management control systems, how to make them most effective. Management control within large, often divisionalised organisations, is complex, time consuming and expensive. Management should regularly ask whether the management control process is in fact adding value.

Companies are always searching for ways to improve systems of management control. This could include greater emphasis on control, more controls, or control in different ways. An increase in the use of non-financial measures is one such way. Accountants have at times been criticised for giving more attention to developing controls than understanding the true nature of control. Learning from this, however, some companies report placing reduced emphasis on formal controls relying more on social control and self-control of employees, so reducing the emphasis on formal planning and control systems. This is in line with modern management practices and the current vogue for employee empowerment, resulting in reduced formal systems of control and more management by direct observation, management by walking about (MBWA).

From some of the earlier discussion it is quite feasible, for example, for a division to be given a broad target for achievement, say ROI, and for the management of the division to be left to decide how that target is to be achieved and in what detail it is planned for, making them more 'bottom-line' profit accountable only. This would reduce the detail of budgeting and reporting back to senior management and would be fully in line with delegating responsibility to lower levels of the management hierarchy within the flatter structures and leaner organisations currently being developed. In this regard the ideas of the 'beyond budgeting' approach are worthy of consideration. The proposals of the Beyond Budgeting Round Table have been outlined in **paragraph 46:6.4**.

The establishment of financial values as overall measures of performance and management control is useful, it ensures that the organisation is broadly on track for its overall financial objectives. But managers are becoming increasingly aware that they are only one aspect of control and company practices are tending to fall in line with this.

References

Anthony, R.N., Dearden, J. and Govindarajan, V. (1992) *Management control systems.* Irwin.

CIMA (1996) *Management accounting official terminology.*

Drury, C., Braund, S., Osborne, P. and Tayles, M. (1993) 'A survey of management accounting practices in UK manufacturing companies', ACCA Research Report No. 32.

Hope, J. and Fraser, R. (1997) 'Beyond budgeting', *Management Accounting*, CIMA, UK.

47. Corporate Governance

47:1 Introduction

Despite the fact that issues of corporate governance now attract considerable amounts of public attention, there is no agreement as to what the term corporate governance means. The OECD in its *Principles of Corporate Governance*, for example, writes that:

> 'Corporate governance is one key element in improving economic efficiency and growth as well as enhancing investor confidence. Corporate governance involves a set of relationships between a company's management, its board, its shareholders and other stakeholders. Corporate governance also provides the structure through which the objectives of the company are set, and the means of attaining those objectives and monitoring performance are determined.' (OECD 2004, p.11)

This is a fairly broad definition of corporate governance that includes reference to both shareholders and other stakeholder groups. It also recognises that corporate governance is about the relationships between management, the board and shareholder and stakeholder groups, and also about the internal functioning of the company.

Other definitions of corporate governance are more restrictive. For example, Shleifer and Vishny (1997), in their review of the literature, write that:

> 'Corporate governance deals with the ways in which suppliers of finance to corporations assure themselves of getting a return on their investment. How do suppliers of finance get managers to return some of their profits to them? How do they make sure managers do not steal the capital they supply or invest in bad projects? How do suppliers of finance control managers?' (p. 737).

This approach to defining corporate governance, which focuses on the relationship between managers and the suppliers of capital, usually the equity investors, is often referred to as the agency approach. It excludes other stakeholder groups and does not make reference to the internal workings of the company.

A perspective on corporate governance that is more directed to the company performance, rather than just the relationship between managers and the suppliers of finance, is provided by O'Sullivan (2000) who writes that:

> 'Corporate governance is concerned with the institutions that influence how business corporations allocate resources and returns. Specifically, a system of corporate governance shapes who makes investment decisions in corporations, what types of investment they make, and how the returns from investment are distributed. (p. 1).

This places corporate governance in the context of social, economic, organisational and institutional conditions that may vary from one industry to another, and from one country to another.

Although the term corporate governance can be understood in different ways, codes of best practice, such as the *Combined Code* in the UK and the OECD *Principles of Corporate Governance*, focus on shareholder rights, board composition and structure, executive compensation and relations with shareholders. There is also emphasis on the quality of the disclosure of information, principally through the financial statements, and on internal control.

While financial reporting is at the heart of corporate governance codes, there are implications for management accounting. Specifically:

(a) *Information to the board of directors, including non-executive directors.*
(b) *Performance measurement.*
(c) *Risk management.*

These areas will be considered in the context of the provisions of the *Combined Code*. UK companies that are listed in the US are also affected by the provisions of the Sarbanes-Oxley Act of 2002 and so, where relevant, the provisions of this Act will be considered.

47:2 The Combined Code and the Sarbanes-Oxley Act of 2002

The development of corporate governance in the UK has its origins in a series of corporate collapses and scandals in the late 1980s and early 1990s. In particular, the collapse of BCCI and the Maxwell scandal increased public concern about the quality of financial reports and corporate governance. The *Committee on the Financial Aspects of Corporate Governance*, chaired by Sir Adrian Cadbury, was set up in 1991 by the business community in order to improve the quality of corporate governance of UK companies.

The *Report of the Committee on the Financial Aspects of Corporate Governance* (the Cadbury Report) was published in 1992. The Committee defined corporate governance as '... the system by which companies are directed and controlled' (para. 2.5). Within this context, the governance of companies is seen to be the responsibility of the board of directors who set the company's strategy, supervise managers and report to shareholders on their stewardship. The Report contains a code of best practice that includes consideration of the separate roles of the chairman and chief executive, the balance between executive and non-executive directors, and reporting on the company's position and the effectiveness of its system of internal controls.

Concerns about executive pay in the mid 1990s, in particular the size of the increases in basic pay, the gains from share options, and the amount of compensation for loss of office, led the CBI to set up *The Study Group on Directors' Remuneration* under the chairmanship of Sir Richard Greenbury. The report of the Study Group, usually referred to as the Greenbury Report, contains a code of best practice that includes recommendations on remuneration committees, the determinants of the remuneration policies, and the disclosure of details of the remuneration policy.

The recommendations contained in the Cadbury and Greenbury Reports were brought together and updated in 1998 in the *Combined Code*. At the time the *Combined Code* was published, it was agreed that the Institute of Chartered Accountants in England & Wales (ICAEW) would provide guidance on the provisions relating to internal control. This guidance, *Internal Control: Guidance for Directors on the Combined Code*, usually referred to as the Turnbull Report after the chairman of the committee responsible for the report, was published in 1999.

Corporate scandals, this time in the US, led to the changes in the Combined Code. Following the collapse of Enron and Wordcom, in 2002 the UK Government appointed a Derek Higgs to lead a committee to review the role and effectiveness of non-executives. The report of this committee, *Review of the Role and Effectiveness of Non-executive Directors* (the Higgs Report), was published in January 2003 and contained recommendations, some of which were suggestions for a revision of the Combined Code. Also in 2002, the Financial Reporting Council, which is responsible for the maintenance and publication of the *Combined Code*, set up a group under the chairmanship of Sir Robert Smith to clarify the role and responsibilities of audit committees and to develop the guidance on audit committees contained within the *Code*. The report *Audit Committees: Combined Code Guidance* (the Smith Report) was also published in January 2003. Later that year, the Combined Code was amended to incorporate the recommendations contained in the Higgs and Smith Reports. The *Combined Code* was revised again in 2006, although this time the changes were somewhat limited.

The corporate scandals in the US also led to US Congress to enact the Sarbanes-Oxley Act of 2002. The purpose of the act is to protect investors by improving the accuracy and reliability of corporate disclosures by both US listed companies and non-US companies with a presence in the US. Its provisions would, for example, affect a UK listed company which is also listed in the US.

47:3 The Board of Directors

Codes of corporate governance devote considerable attention to the board of directors. There are cross-national differences in the way in which boards are structured. It is common in some countries for companies to use a *two-tier* board structure in which there is both a management board and a supervisory board. Companies in other countries invariably adopt a *unitary* board structure in which, in the case of large companies, there is usually a mixture of executive directors and non-executive directors. Most, if not all, the non-executive directors of listed companies are likely to be independent.

In the UK, the *Combined Code* sets out as principles that: (1) every company should be headed by an effective board; (2) there should be a clear division between the responsibilities of chairman and chief executive; and (3) there should be a balance between executive and non-executive directors. There are also principles relating to appointment to the board and re-election of directors, information to the board and the personal development of directors, and the evaluation of the performance of the board, its committees and individual directors.

Management accountants have a role in enabling the board to implement the principles of the *Code*. To understand this it is important to first consider the role of the board, and the role of non-executive directors, and the information that directors require in order to meet their responsibilities.

47:3.1 The Role of the Board

The Combined Code sets out, as supporting principles, the roles of both the board and non-executive directors within unitary boards. The board is seen as responsible for:

(a) *Providing the company within entrepreneurial leadership. Such leadership should be provided within the context of prudent and effective controls so that the risks can be effectively assessed and managed.*

(b) *Setting the strategic aims of the company.*

(c) *Ensuring that there are the appropriate resources in place, both financial and human, in order that the company's objectives can be met.*

(d) *Reviewing the performance of management.*

(e) *Setting the values and standards for the company.*

(f) *Ensuring that the company's obligations to shareholders and others are understood and met.*

47:3.2 Non-executive Directors

Within this context, the role of non-executive directors is to 'constructively challenge and help develop proposals on strategy', to monitor the performance of management in meeting objectives, and the reporting of performance. They also have responsibility for ensuring that the company has a robust system of financial control and risk management, and for the integrity of financial information. Finally, non-executive directors have responsibilities in relation to executive directors, specifically in determining their pay, appointing and removing executive directors, and in succession planning.

47:3.3 Information

The Combined Code contains the principle that:

'The board should be supplied in a timely manner with information in a form and of a quality appropriate to enable it to discharge its duties. All directors should receive induction on joining the board and should regularly update and refresh their skills and knowledge.'

As a supporting principle, the chairman is responsible for ensuring that the directors receive accurate, timely and clear information. The responsibility for providing this information is seen to lie with management, although directors should seek clarification or amplification where necessary.

47:3.4 Board of Directors and Management Accounting

The *Combined Code* indicates that the board should receive information in a timely manner that is of appropriate quality to enable directors to carry out their responsibilities. These responsibilities include setting the company's strategic aims, ensuring that there are appropriate resources available to meet these aims, and reviewing the performance of management.

In a CIMA report, Starovic (2003) suggests that reports to the board should facilitate decision making. In particular, the reports should lead directors to ask the appropriate questions and take decisions that will enable the company to achieve its objectives, both short- and long-term, so as to create sustainable shareholder value. The CIMA report also identifies the qualities that make information useful. These are:

(a) *Relevance*. *The information contained in the reports to the board should be focused so as to reflect the company's objectives and strategy.*

(b) *Integrated*. *The system of data collection should be capable of being used for both internal and external reporting purposes.*

(c) *In perspective*. *The information contained within reports to the board should be presented in the context of the relevant time period - past, current or projected.*

(d) *Timely*. *Although there is usually a trade-off between accuracy and timeliness, it is considered better to present information in a timely fashion even if the information is not completely accurate.*

(e) *Reliable*. *The information contained in reports to the board should be of 'good enough' quality in order to ensure that directors have confidence in the information.*

(f) *Clear*. *Reports to the board should be written clearly and simply.*

Non-executive directors have particular information needs as they are not involved in the company's day-to-day operations. The Higgs Report comments that non-executive directors should have 'adequate information' of the right kind in order for them to carry out their role effectively. Some non-executive directors comment upon the danger of information overload which could lead to issues being overlooked. Non-executive directors should also be provided with information well in advance of board meetings in order that they can thoroughly consider issues. The responsibility for ensuring that the directors receive accurate, timely and clear information lies, according to the *Combined Code,* with the chairman.

Performance measurement is important to the role of the board in setting the strategic aims of the company and in reviewing the performance of management (*see* **Ch.54** and **Ch.24, para.21:4.3**). The CIMA Report (Starovic, 2003) suggests that the board should agree with management the high level key performance indicators (KPIs). These KPIs may be financial and non-financial and they should reflect the company's strategic performance.

47:4 Internal Control and Risk Management

Like corporate governance, the term *internal control* is used in a variety of ways. In order to appreciate the different uses of the term, it is useful to begin with the definition provided by the Treadway Commission in the US. The Commission adopts a broad definition of internal control that refers to the processes by which the board of directors, management and others provide reasonable assurance that objectives are met in relation to: (1) the effectiveness and efficiency of operations, including business performance and safeguarding the entity's resources (*see* **Chs 46 and 53**); (2) the reliability of financial reporting (*see* **Chs 45 and 48**); and (3) compliance with applicable laws and regulations. Within this context, the Commission identifies five inter-related components of an internal control system:

(a) **The control environment** *which is seen as the integrity and ethical values of the personnel, together with the philosophy and operating styles of management.*
(b) **Risk assessment** *which includes the identification and analysis of the risks, arising from both within and outside the entity, associated with meeting management's objectives.*
(c) **Control activities** *which include the policies and procedures that are put in place in order to ensure compliance with the directions of management.*
(d) **Information and communication** *which include the identification, capture and communication of pertinent information that enables personnel to meet their responsibilities.*
(e) **Monitoring** *the operation of the internal control system.*

This approach to the definition of internal controls can be used to examine the way the term is used within the Combined Code in the UK and the Sarbanes-Oxley Act in the US.

In its guidance for directors on implementing the provisions of the Combined Code that relate to internal control, the Turnbull Report takes the broad approach to defining internal control as seen in the report of the Treadway Commission. It defines an internal control system as '... encompassing the policies, processes, tasks, behaviours and other aspects of a company that, taken together:

(a) *facilitate its effective and efficient operation by enabling it to respond appropriately to significant business, operational, financial, compliance and other risks to achieving the company's objectives;.*
(b) *help ensure the quality of internal and external reporting; and*
(c) *help ensure compliance with applicable laws and regulations, and also with internal policies with respect to the conduct of the business'* (para. 20).

In looking at the effectiveness of a company's risk and control system, the report considers four areas: (1) risk assessment; (2) control environment and control activities; (3) information and communication; and (4) monitoring. It therefore closely follows the approach taken by the Treadway Commission.

By contrast, the Sarbanes-Oxley Act adopts a narrow definition of internal control. The Act refers to *internal control over financial reporting* and, for the purposes of the Act, the Securities and Exchange Commission defines this as the processes that 'provide reasonable assurance regarding the reliability of financial reporting and preparation of financial statements for external purposes in accordance with generally accepted accounting principles...'. These processes include the maintenance of records reflecting the transactions of the company in a form suitable for the preparation of financial statements in accordance with generally accepted accounting principles. Further, the system should include the requirement that receipts and payments are made in accordance with authorisations of management and the directors. Finally, the system should provide reasonable assurance that prevent, or allow timely detection of, any unauthorised use of the company's assets that could have a material effect on its financial statements.

47:4.1 Internal Control and Management Accounting

In the context of a broader definition of internal control, as adopted by Turnbull and the Treadway Commission, management accountants have an important role to play, especially in the *information and communication* and *risk assessment* components of an internal control system.

Management accounting addresses a significant element of the *information and communication* component of an internal control system. For example, an appendix to the Turnbull Report contains a set of questions which directors can consider when following the guidance provided in the report. The first question under *information and communication* is:

> 'Do management and the board receive timely, relevant and reliable reports on progress against business objectives and the related risks that provide them with the information, from inside and outside the company, needed for decision-making and management review purposes? This could include performance reports and indicators of change, together with qualitative information such as on customer satisfaction, employee attitudes etc.' (p. 14)

Management accountants have an important contribution to ensuring that the directors and managers receive 'timely, relevant and reliable reports on progress against objectives'.

Management accounting may also address significant elements of the *risk assessment* component of an internal control system. For example, the appendix to the Turnbull Report also contains a set of questions relating to risk assessment that are relevant to management accounting:

> 'Does the company have clear objectives and have they been communicated so as to provide effective direction to employees on risk assessment and control issues? For example, do objectives and related plans include measurable performance targets and indicators?'
>
> 'Are the significant internal and external operational, financial, compliance and other risks identified and assessed on an ongoing basis?' (p. 13)

As indicated previously, management accountants can make an important contribution to the design of measurable performance targets and indicators. In addition, both performance measurement and the identification, quantification, and analysis of business risks are key elements within Strategic Enterprise Management (SEM).

47:5 Conclusion

Corporate governance issues have attracted considerable public interest in recent years, and yet there is an absence of consensus about what the term means. Despite this lack of agreement, codes and principles of good corporate governance have been developed in several countries and by international organisations such as the OECD. Good quality financial reporting by companies is an important feature of most of these codes, and here the financial accountant has a key role. Management accountants also are important to the effective governance of companies, particularly in enabling directors to carry out their various roles and in supporting the system of internal controls.

References

Committee on the Financial Aspects of Corporate Governance (1992) *Report of the Committee on the Financial Aspects of Corporate Governance*. London: Gee.

Financial Reporting Council (2006) *The Combined Code on Corporate Governance*. London: FRC.

FRC-appointed group chaired by Sir Robert Smith (2003) *Audit Committees: Combined Code Guidance*. London: FRC.

Higgs, D. (2003) *Review of the role and effectiveness of non-executive directors*. London: DTI.

Internal Control Working Party of the Institute of Chartered Accountants in England & Wales (1999) *Internal Control: Guidance for Directors on the Combined Code*. London: ICAEW.

Organisation for Economic Co-operation and Development (2004) *OECD Principles of Corporate Governance*. Paris: OECD.

O'Sullivan, M.A. (2000) *Contests for corporate control: Corporate governance and economic performance in the United States and Germany*. Oxford: Oxford University Press.

Shleifer, A. and Vishny, R.W. (1997) A survey of corporate governance. *The Journal of Finance*, 52, 2, 737 - 783.

Starovic, D. (2003) *Performance Reporting to Boards: A Guide to Good Practice*. London: CIMA.

The Committee of Sponsoring Organisations of the Treadway Commission (1992) *Internal Control - Integrated Framework*. New York: AICPA.

The Study Group on Directors' Remuneration (1995) *Directors' Remuneration: Report of a Study Group Chaired by Sir Richard Greenbury*. London: Gee.

48. Financial Performance Measurement

48:1 Why Measure Financial Performance?

48:1.1 Influencing Behaviour to Achieve Results

It is said that 'you get what you measure'; conversely, what you do not measure you do not get. The measurement of financial performance is thus intended to ensure the attainment of an organisation's financial objectives: the focus of budgetary control.

Budgetary control links strategic objectives (*see* **Ch.2**) to day-by-day operations using a mix of feedforward and feedback controls, *see* **Fig.48:1**:

(a) *the feedforward:feedback control model shown in **Fig.48:1** has two halves;*

(b) *the feedforward half begins with a vision of a desired future, leading to the formulation of alternative strategies for realising it;*

(c) *the chosen strategy has goals or objectives attached to it;*

(d) *plans are then made to attain them;*

(e) *these are then realised via annual budgets (see **Ch.9**), standards (see **Ch.16**) and targets;*

(f) *the feedback half of the control model (see **Chs 44 and 46**) involves the comparison of actual performance with the budgets, standards and targets;*

(g) *such comparisons are the start of a process where significant variances are explored leading to appropriate action and organisational learning at the right organisational level and stage of the decision-making process;*

(h) *some variances may require actions at the operational level; others the revision of plans, the modification of objectives or the adoption of a new strategy or vision.*

Stan Brignall   815

Figure 48:1 **Feedforward:feedback control model**

Source: adapted from Fitzgerald *et al.* (1991)

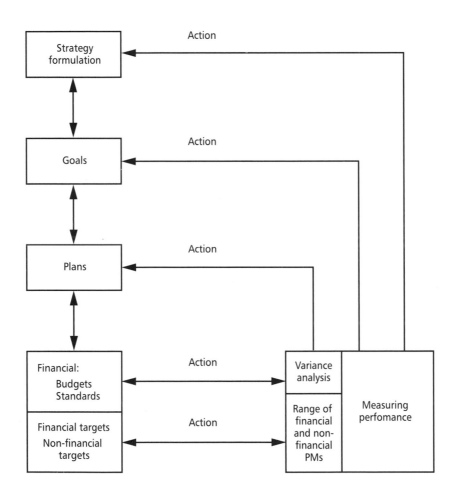

48:1.2 The Differing Objects of Performance Measurement

From the point of view of the firm, the object may be:

(a) *Internal: traditional focus of management accounting; may be the firm as a whole, or a part of the firm such as a division, strategic business unit (SBU), department, process, product or an individual manager.*

(b) *External: a competitor (see **Ch.7**); a supplier; a customer; or the 'best in class', as in some types of external (as opposed to internal) benchmarking (see **Ch.32**).*

From the point of view of an outsider (such as an investment analyst or a bank manager), the object may be at corporate level, or perhaps at divisional level, and so on.

Differing levels of organisational focus and whether performance is being measured from the inside or the outside will obviously affect the type of information which is available and the degree of detail required: there is no one best way of measuring performance as it depends on why performance is being measured. **Chapter 54** discusses implementing a balanced performance measurement system.

48:1.3 The Influence of Different Stakeholders

It is not just why performance is being measured and at what organisational level of analysis that matter, but from whose point of view. Traditional financial performance measurement focuses on the needs of shareholders, but there are many other stakeholders with differing interests who are interested in organisational performance, as **Figure 48:2** makes clear.

Figure 48:2 **Stakeholders and their expectations**

Stakeholders	*Expectations*
Internal stakeholders	
Employees	Job security, job satisfaction, compensation
Shareholders	Dividends, capital gains
Managers and directors	Compensation, job security, promotion prospects, power, prestige
External stakeholders	
Trading partners	
Customers	Product quality, service, value, product/service choice (including green products)

(Fig.48:2 *cont'd*)

Stakeholders	Expectations
Trade suppliers	Assurance of payment, continuity of business
Suppliers of non-equity finance	Secure and adequate returns
External groups	
Local communities	Employment, responsibility for environment
Regulatory bodies	Compliance with legislation
Environmental groups	Responsibility for environment, compliance with environmental legislation
Public	Responsibility for environment, employment

Traditional financial performance measurement within for-profit organisations assumes that managers try to maximise shareholders' wealth. Obviously, the needs of all stakeholders cannot be met if management focuses solely on meeting the needs of shareholders, although some other stakeholders may have overlapping information needs. For example, credit suppliers will be as concerned as shareholders with the liquidity of the firm.

With multiple stakeholders, managers may not always act to maximise shareholder wealth, but try to satisfy all major stakeholders.

48:2 Three Key Questions in Performance Measurement

48:2.1 What Has Happened?

When comparing actual with budgeted performance, the first step is to find out what has happened and decide which areas require investigation. This may be a matter of experience, intuition, simple rules of thumb (e.g. all variances in excess of 10% or £500) or sophisticated diagnostic techniques.

48:2.2 Why Has it Happened?

The second step is to find out why actual performance deviated from expectations, which may involve discussions with those concerned.

48:2.3 What Are We Going to Do About It?

The third step involves taking corrective action at the right organisational level and stage of the decision making process. This should involve appropriate organisational learning, which may be single loop or double loop. Double loop learning goes beyond single loop in questioning the continued relevance of the organisation's strategy.

48:3 The Use of Ratios in Financial Performance Measurement

48:3.1 Introduction

For financial ratios to be a valid basis for comparison:

(a) *over many time periods within the same firm (a 'time-series' analysis); or*
(b) *at any point in time across a sample of firms ('cross-sectional'); or*
(c) *over multiple time periods across a sample of firms ('cross-sectional time-series' analyses),*

certain problems have to be overcome.

Re (a): (a) *Have consistent accounting policies been followed?*
(b) *Has inflation distorted comparability over multiple time periods?*

Re (b): (a) *Are the accounting policies followed comparable between companies?*
(b) *Have they been followed consistently?*
(c) *Have the ratios been defined consistently?*

Re (c): (a) *Do any of the above cause problems?*
(b) *Has inflation affected different companies differently?*

The comparison of ratios to some industry average is often done to find 'good' or 'bad' performers. This should be done carefully, because the ratios of companies in the sector may not conform to the properties of the normal distribution.

We will use a numerical example to look at some ratios.

48:3.1.1 Example

Companies A and B manufacture similar products. Extracted information from their most recent accounts is shown in **Figure 48:3**.

Figure 48:3 **Accounts for companies A and B**

| | *Income statement for the year ended 31 December 20XX* | | | |
| | *Company A* | | *Company B* | |
	(£k)	*(£k)*	*(£k)*	*(£k)*
Revenue		1500		1100
Cost of sales		<u>1110</u>		<u>653</u>
Gross profit		390		447
Expenses:				
– selling and distribution	129		211	
– administration	135		150	
– loan stock/debenture int.	<u>24</u>		<u>9</u>	
		<u>288</u>		<u>370</u>
Net profit for the year		102		77
Dividend paid:				
– preference	8		–	
– ordinary	<u>29</u>		<u>35</u>	
		<u>37</u>		<u>35</u>
Net profit retained for the year		65		42

(cont'd)

(Fig.48:3 *cont'd*)

Balance sheets as at 31 December 20XX

	Company A		Company B	
	(£k)	(£k)	(£k)	(£k)
Non-current assets (NBV)				
Tangible assets				
– freehold property		345		350
– plant and equipment		270		310
		615		660
Current assets				
– inventories (stock)	570		290	
– amounts receivable (debtors)	220		280	
– cash in hand	10		25	
	800		595	
Less current liabilities				
– amounts payable (creditors)	390		320	
– bank overdraft	115		55	
Net current assets		295		220
		910		880
Capital and Reserves				
share capital: £1 ordinary shares		300		500
8% £1 preference shares		100		–
		400		500
Reserves: share premium	50		30	
revaluation	150		100	
retained profits	110		150	
		310		280
Shareholders' funds		710		780
Loan capital: 12% debentures		200		–
9% loan stock		–		100
		910		880

48:3.2 Profitability Ratios

Profitability ratios attempt to measure the ability of the organisation to generate profit. There are two basic types:

1. *those which relate profit to sales;*
2. *those which relate profit to some measure of the 'total' asset base.*

Other things being equal, the higher both ratios are the better. The link between them is the 'total' asset turnover, an activity ratio (*see* **Fig.48:4**).

Figure 48:4 **Total asset turnover**

Note: [a] capital here defined as long-term capital, or net assets

	Company A	Company B
Profit to sales:	126/1500 = 8.4%	86/1100 = 7.8%
Asset turnover:	1500/910 = 1.65	1100/880 = 1.25
Return on capital[a]	126/910 = 13.8%	86/880 = 9.8%

Comparing Company A with Company B, the former's higher ROC is mainly due to its higher asset turnover (8.4% × 1.65 = 13.8%, but 8.4% × 1.25 = 10.5%): this may or may not mean that Company A is more efficient than Company B.

The return on investment/capital is the primary financial performance measure, but this may be of doubtful use when prepared from historical cost accounts (HCA), where the NBV of fixed assets may be far below their market value, for example.

A good profit measure is the profit available for appropriation, that is, after deduction of all expenses but before paying dividends and tax.

'Total' assets may be defined in different ways:

(a) *Shareholders funds (i.e. net assets), where both short and long-term liabilities have been deducted from total assets. Here the numerator should be after deduction of interest payments on debt:*

Company A   *Company B*
102/710 = 14.4%   *77/780 = 9.9%*

(b) *Total long-term capital (i.e. shareholders' funds plus long-term liabilities). Here the numerator should be before deduction of long-term interest payments:*

Company A   *Company B*
126/910 = 13.8%   *86/880 = 9.8%*

(c) *Total capital (i.e. total assets). Here the numerator should be before deduction of any interest payments:*

Company A   *Company B*
126/1415 = 8.9%   *86/1255 = 6.9%*

Note that as well as calculating the net margin on sales, it will also be useful to check the gross margin on trading:

Company A
390/1500 = 26%

Company B
447/1100 = 40.6%

This information confuses our story, as:

(a) *A has a similar net margin on sales to B;*
(b) *A has a higher ROC than B, because it has a higher asset turnover;*
(c) *however, B has a higher gross margin on sales than A.*

Therefore, B must have a higher ratio of expenses to sales than A – evidence that it may not be as efficient at controlling non-production expenses as A, though its control of manufacturing costs appears to be better – or is it charging higher prices?

48:3.3 Activity Ratios

Activity ratios measure how efficiently the organisation's resources have been used. There are three primary activity ratios:

1. *stock turnover;*
2. *debtors' collection period;*
3. *'total' asset turnover (where this has at least three alternative definitions, as above).*

Stock turnover shows the number of times the year-end or 'average' inventory [*cf.* SSAP9: *Stocks and Long-Term Contracts, IAS2: Inventories*] is 'turned over': the higher this is the better. As stock will usually be valued at cost but turnover at selling price, it is better to relate stock to cost of goods sold. Stock turnover is a primitive measure of trading activity.

Company A
1110/570 = 1.95 times

Company B
653/290 = 2.25 times p.a.

Debtors' collection period relates average or year-end debtors to turnover, and may be multiplied by 365 to give 'debtor days'. It may be complemented by similar calculations for creditors; they both affect the firm's liquidity.

Company A
debtor days (220/1500) × 365 = 53.5 days
creditor days (390/1110) × 365 = 128.2 days

Company B
(280/1100) × 365 = 92.9 days
(320/653) × 365 = 178.9 days

Company A's better asset turnover (*see above*) is not due to better stock turnover, but it does have better debtor and creditor days; however, the major source of the difference is A's higher fixed-asset turnover.

48:3.4 Liquidity Ratios and the Du Pont Pyramid of Ratios

Liquidity ratios help assess whether the organisation can pay its short-term debts. There are two primary liquidity ratios:

1. the current ratio;
2. the 'acid test'.

Current ratio (sometimes called the working capital ratio) is current assets over current liabilities:

Company A
800/505 = 1.58

Company B
595/375 = 1.59

The acid test (sometimes known as the liquid or quick ratio) excludes stocks from the current assets as in a crisis the B/S value of stocks might not be realisable:

Company A
230/505 = 0.46

Company B
305/375 = 0.81

While the current ratios are similar, B's acid test is higher and hence more satisfactory.

Another measure of liquidity is the 'defensive interval', which is current assets less stocks divided by average daily expenditures on operations:

Company A

$$\frac{230}{(1110 + 264)/365} = 61 \text{ days}$$

Company B

$$\frac{305}{(653 + 361)/365} = 110 \text{ days}$$

Again, B looks better than A.

Profitability, activity and liquidity ratios are interconnected via a 'pyramid' of ratios, first used by the Du Pont Corporation (US) in the 1920s, the peak of which is ROI/ROC.

48:3.5 Capital Structure (or Gearing) Ratios

Gearing ratios look at the implications of the organisation's capital structure, the level of shareholders' equity versus long-term debt, as the two classes have different claims over the organisation's resources.

Equity are the 'residual claimants': in the event of the company being wound up they will be paid last. Their returns (dividends) are variable/avoidable depending on the organisation's competitive success and need to retain profits for investment; dividends are also taxed.

The suppliers of loan capital, on the other hand, lend on the basis of a fixed/unavoidable periodic return (interest), which may vary with some market rate. Interest payments are tax-deductible.

These differences have two consequences:

1. *loans are cheaper than equity because of the tax benefit, their lower variability of returns and their comparative unavoidability; but*
2. *they have a risk effect called 'financial gearing', which is similar to the 'operational gearing' caused by the presence of fixed as well as variable operating costs in a company's cost structure. As rational investors are risk averse, the cost of equity capital rises as financial gearing rises, cancelling out the effect of more cheap debt capital. Firms with high levels of financial and operating gearing may be vulnerable to downturns in trading.*

There are three basic measures of 'financial gearing':

1. *the ratio of debt to equity (D/E);*
2. *the ratio of debt to debt plus equity (D/D+E);*
3. *the number of times interest on long-term capital is covered by profit.*

	Company A	Company B
D/E	*200/710 = 0.28*	*100/780 = 0.13*
D/D + E	*200/910 = 0.22*	*100/880 = 0.11*
times interest covered*	*126/24 = 5.25*	*86/9 = 9.6*

* where depreciation has been deducted from profit, as a non-cash expense it may be added back for the purposes of this ratio.

B is not only more liquid than A in the short term, but also has less financial gearing. Note that many analysts would treat preference shares as debt when calculating gearing: this would further worsen A's relative position.

48:3.6 Stock Market Ratios

Stock Market ratios (for PLCs only) relate the share price and various measures of returns. The three most important stock market ratios are:

1. *the dividend yield;*
2. *the earnings per share (EPS);*
3. *the price:earnings (P/E) ratio.*

We will take the P/E ratios of the two companies as 'given', enabling us to work out the Share Price (SP) and the other ratios:

	Company A	Company B
P/E (given)	*15*	*10*
EPS	*94/300 = 31.3p*	*77/500 = 15.4p*
SP = P/E × EPS	*15 × 31.3p = 469.5p*	*10 × 15.4p = 154p*
dividend yield	*29/300 = 0.0206*	*35/500 = 0.0455*
	4.695	*1.54*
	or about 2%	*or about 4.5%*

where the dividend yield is the expected dividend as a proportion of the stock price.

The higher a firm's P/E ratio the more it is expected to grow. A has the higher P/E ratio and share price hence would appear to have better growth prospects: this is supported by its lower dividend yield, which indicates that its directors wish to retain more cash for reinvestment.

48:4 Cash-flow Statements

48:4.1 The Objectives of Cash-flow Statements

(a) FRS1 Cash Flow Statements requires reporting entities within its scope to prepare a cash flow statement in the manner set out in the FRS.

(b) Cash flows are increases or decreases in amounts of cash.

(c) Cash flows should be listed under the following headings: operating activities; returns on investments and servicing of finance; taxation, capital expenditure and financial investment; acquisitions and disposals; equity dividends paid; management of liquid resources; financing.

48:4.2 Definitions of Cash

1. Cash in hand

2. Deposits repayable on demand of any qualifying institution less overdrafts from any qualifying institution repayable on demand.

48:4.3 FRS 1 and its Revision

Issued in July 1990, ED54 was the forerunner of FRS 1. It proposed that funds statements be prepared on a *cash* basis only, and that flows of cash be classified under three main activity headings: operating, investing, financing. A new version of FRS 1 was published at the end of October 1996 which came into force for accounting periods ending after 23 March 1997. The new FRS 1 headings for the disclosure of cash flows are:

* operating;

* returns on investment and servicing of finance;

* taxation;

* capital expenditure and financial investment;

* acquisitions and disposals;

- equity dividends paid;

- management of liquid resources;

- financing.

48:5 Divisional Performance Measurement (DPM)
(*See* Ch.46, para.46:4.2.)

48:5.1 Reasons for Divisionalisation

Certain factors cause control problems in organisations:

- size;

- diversity;

- uncertainty;

- span of control.

The result is that managers delegate responsibility from the corporate centre by setting up responsibility centres of four types: cost, revenue, profit and investment centres. Managers are held accountable for the costs, revenues or assets under their control.

Divisionalisation (*see* **Ch.27**) is the most common form of decentralisation, defined as:

> The assignment of profit responsibility to divisional managers; the establishment of a central headquarters mainly concerned with strategic planning and control; and the commitment of corporate managers to organisational performance rather than the performance of any specific division.

Note Goold and Campbell's (1987) identification of four '*styles*' of corporate: SBU relations, which imply differing degrees of *divisional autonomy*. An SBU may be defined as 'an operating unit which sells a distinct set of services or products to an identifiable group of customers in competition with a defined set of organisations' (Fitzgerald *et al.* 1991: 21).

For *SBU (and divisional) managers* the line of business is 'given' and their task is to select a strategy to beat the competition while satisfying organisational performance requirements.

The task of *corporate managers* is to monitor the performance of their portfolio of businesses, change it when needed, raise finance and allocate resources.

There are four potential benefits of decentralisation:

1. *it optimises decision making;*
2. *closer monitoring of operations;*
3. *improved status, motivation and training of middle managers;*
4. *it separates responsibility for suggesting and implementing projects (SBUs/ divisions) from responsibility for sanctioning and monitoring them (corporate).*

There are three potential problems:

1. *local optimisation but corporate suboptimisation;*
2. *monitoring costs (asymmetric information);*
3. *duplication of activities in separate SBUs/divisions.*

How should we measure divisional/SBU performance? It depends on what the SBU/division is/should be trying to achieve [*cf. SSAP25: Segmental Reporting, IAS14:Segment Reporting*].

In accounting and finance our usual assumption is that managers of for-profit businesses are trying to maximise their shareholders' wealth. This implies that they are trying to invest in positive NPV projects (projects that offer the prospect of an economic rent).

Given the above, we have some choices when deciding how to measure financial performance:

(a) *absolute measures: various definitions of 'profit';*
(b) *ratio measures: for example, return on sales (ROS); return on investment (ROI);*
(c) *residual income (RI; profit less a cost of capital charge).*

48:5.1.1 Profit Measures

Figure 48:5 **Example: Division A**

Sales revenue of Division A		£100k
Direct costs:	variable operating costs	£45k
	controllable fixed costs	£25k
	non-controllable fixed costs	£10k
Indirect costs:	apportioned head office cost	£15k

This data may be summarised as follows:

	Division A (£s k)				
	Contribution margin	*Controllable profit*	*Direct profit*	*Net profit*	
Sales revenue	100	100	100	100	
Direct costs: var.	45	45	45	45	
Contribution margin	55				a
fixed controllable		25	25	25	
Controllable profit		30			b
fixed non-controllable			10	10	
Direct profit			20		c
Indirect costs				15	
Net profit				5	d

[a] Contribution margin is useful for S/T decision making, but excludes all non-variable costs so it is poor for control.

[b] Controllable profit is useful for measuring the divisional manager's performance.

[c] Direct profit is a good measure of the division's performance.

[d] Net profit measures the division's full cost performance, but is this a good control measure at managerial or divisional level?

Division A is profitable, but is it profitable enough?

48:5.2 Return on Investment Versus Residual Income (ROI v RI) Debate

48:5.2.1 Ratio Measures: ROS and ROI

$$\text{ROI} = \text{ROS} \times \text{asset turnover} = \frac{\text{npbit}}{\text{assets}} = \frac{\text{npbit}}{\text{t/o}} \times \frac{\text{turnover}}{\text{assets}}$$

Many Japanese firms prefer to combine ROS with the use of JIT to keep stocks to a minimum, believing the other assets are 'fixed' hence the use of ROI causes dysfunctional behaviour, such as delaying asset replacement; but most divisions/SBUs are *investment* centres so ROI seems an appropriate PM.

ROI is a ratio: ? numerator   (is either of these manipulable?)
                     ? denominator

Same ROI may be earned by different strategy choices, even within the same group of companies:

	Conventional store	*Discount store*
Sales	£2m	£2.4m
Divisional profit	£240k	£192k
Divisional investment	£1m	£800k

The ROI computations are:

Conventional store: $\dfrac{240}{2000} \times \dfrac{2000}{1000} = 12\% \times 2 = 24\%$

Discount store: $\dfrac{192}{2400} \times \dfrac{2400}{800} = 8\% \times 3 = 24\%$

Two divisions operating in different sectors may have the same ROI target (if they have the same systematic risk - beta), but how they attain it may vary; different targets could thus be set for the two subcomponents of ROI.

   Noting that ROI is often called the accounting rate of return (ARR): ROI/ARR similar to IRR/cost of capital, so intuitively appealing, *but* actions that increase divisional ROI may make the group worse off, and vice versa.

48:5.2.2 Example

A division with assets £90k and npbt £20k: ROI = 22.2% > required ROI (given) of 15%: this excess return is the accounting equivalent of an economic rent = a +ve NPV = an IRR > risk-adjusted cost of capital. *Suppose* an opportunity for the division to invest £15k which should earn £3k p.a.: a return of 20% > required return (15%), but less than the current return (22.2%); will the divisional manager make the investment?

New ROI = new npbt = £23k = 21.9% < current 22.2%
          new assets   £105k

Also, *suppose* the division has an asset/activity/product returning 18%: it might be tempted to dispose of it even though it is earning > 15%.

Suppose a second division: assets £50k and profits £12.5k: ROI 25%. This division seems to be doing better than Division 1...but is it? Division 1 has an extra £40k assets (90 − 50) on which it earns £7.5k (20 − 12.5): a *marginal* ROI of 18.75% > 15%, so Division 1 is more valuable.

Any profit-based system is open to manipulation and may lead to dysfunctional actions, for example, delaying asset replacement reduces ROI denominator and so increases ROI.

48:5.2.3 Residual Income (RI)

This is the operating profit of a division less a cost of capital charge, calculated by multiplying the division's controllable asset base by its risk-adjusted cost of capital. RI is similar to the notion of economic income (where interest is deducted as a payment to capital for a factor input). A project with a zero NPV – its IRR = cost of capital – would make an accounting profit before deducting interest, and would break even after interest. Such a project would have a zero RI and would be marginally acceptable to a profit-maximising organisation.

Let us return to our previous example with two divisions of differing sizes: what are their respective RIs?

	Division 1	*Division 2*
Invested capital	£90k	£50k
Profit	£20k	£12.5k
15% cost of capital charge	£13.5k	£7.5k
Residual income	£6.5k	£5.0k

Division 1 is more profitable as its RI is higher by £1.5k, even though its overall ROI is lower (22.5% versus 25%). The RI difference = excess return on incremental investment (18.75% − 15%) × incremental investment £40k (£90k − £50k) in Division 1.

Also, if Division 1 takes its 20% project opportunity (£15k investment, £3k p.a. return) its RI will increase, whereas if it disposes of the £20k asset earning £3.6k p.a. its RI will decrease:

| | *Options for Division 1* | |
	New investment	*Disposal*
Invested capital	£105k	£70k
Profit	£23k	£16.4k
Capital charge (15%)	£15.75k	£10.5k
RI	£7.25k	£5.9k

In conclusion:

(a) The RI measure will always increase when we add investments earning above the cost of capital or dispose of investments earning below the cost of capital, so RI is always consistent with NPV and IRR investment rules – unlike ROI. The organisation as a whole will <u>always</u> prefer a higher divisional RI to a lower, whereas one may increase divisional ROI (e.g. by unfair transfer pricing) yet make the organisation as a whole worse off.

(b) RI easily allows for differing divisional risk, by varying the cost of capital charge.

(c) But surveys of practice show that ROI is far more popular than RI, see **Table 48:1**.

(d) One reason for ROI's popularity is that it is more easily understood than RI, which is an absolute number not directly related to the size of the division.

Table 48:1 **ROI versus RI**

Source: survey of UK Manufacturers by Drury *et al.* 1993

	%
Target ROI set by group	55
Target RI	20
Target profit before interest	61
Target cash flow	43
Ability to stay within budget	57

48:5.2.4 Example

Two divisions, P & Q; common cost of capital 15%; P has £1m assets, Q £10m; both set target RI £100k:

	P (£k)	Q (£k)
Assets	1,000	10,000
npbit	250	1,600
Cost of capital 15%	150	1,500
npaibt (RI)	100	100
ROI before interest	25%	16%

In conclusion, the target RIs need to reflect a division's asset structure.

There are three RI implementation problems:

1. *What interest rate? – depends on the division's business risk and the firm's financial risk.*
2. *When should it be changed? – when the risk free rate, the market risk premium or the expected inflation rate change.*
3. *Same rate in each division? – should vary with beta.*

There are four conclusions about ROI versus RI:

1. *RI is better at promoting goal congruence than ROI: it is consistent with NPV (and IRR where this is consistent with NPV). However, RI can be difficult to implement (interest rate!).*
2. *Divisional targets should vary according to a variety of factors. One way of approaching this could be to categorise/classify divisions, for example, use Boston Consulting Group matrix/life cycle/mission.*
3. *Which is better: RI or ROI? Solomons's (1965) two cases:*
   (i) if divisional managers have little control over asset investment, ROI is all right <u>provided</u> interest is not deducted in the numerator (i.e. use npbit);
   (ii) if divisional managers have a significant say in asset investment it is all right to deduct interest and RI is better.
4. *surveys show that ROI is by far the commonest: is case 3) (i) the norm?*

48:5.3 Potentially Distorting Effects of Transfer Prices and Overhead Allocations
(*See* Ch.36.)

Where transfer prices cannot be based on an external competitive market for the goods to be transferred, the general rule for pricing transfers should be applied:

standard variable cost + lost contribution margin from not selling outside

Where transfers are made at a price other than either of the two above, the financial performances of the buying and selling divisions will be distorted.

Where divisional profit is measured after deducting allocated costs which the divisional manager cannot control, the division's financial performance may be distorted.

48:5.3.1 Behavioural Considerations

(a) *Need to make divisional performance measures (dpms) consistent with npv.*

(b) *Need to make dpms avoid short-termism, especially short-term profit: dpms should be situation-contingent.*

(c) *Need to avoid manipulation of dpms while allowing participation in setting them.*

(d) *Need to avoid or allow for the problems associated with transfer prices and overhead allocations.*

(e) *Need to involve people at all organisational levels (e.g. interdisciplinary teams; bottom–up empowerment).*

48:5.4 Financial Performance Measurement Versus Capital Investment Appraisal
(*See* Ch.11.)

The Fisher:Hirshleifer model of investment decision making shows that the use of the NPV decision rule is consistent with the maximisation of shareholder wealth, and that NPV will always give the right investment decision whereas IRR will not. If capital projects are selected on the basis of NPV or IRR, why are divisions and their managers appraised on the basis of RI or ROI?

48:6 Shareholder Value Approaches
(*See* **Ch.34, para.34:4.3.**)

48:6.1 Introduction

In recent years various forms of managing for shareholder value have been proposed as alternatives to traditional accounting-based financial performance measures. These measures are usually based on cash not accounting flows and may be used for both strategic planning and performance measurement.

48:6.2 Shareholder Value Analysis (SVA)

$$SVA = NPV - MV_{debt}$$

Shareholder value analysis is an NPV-based technique where expected net cash flows from operations are discounted using the weighted average cost of capital; deduct the market value of debt and the result is shareholder value.

48:6.3 Economic Value Added (EVA) vs Residual Income (RI)

EVA = capitalised value of all future RIs, where

RI = residual income for a period = $NOPAT - WCCC$

where $NOPAT$ = net operating profit after tax
$\quad\quad WCCC$ = weighted cost of capital charge

48:6.4 Market Value Added (MVA)

$$MVA = MV_{D,E} - BV \text{ (including capitalised R\&D)}$$

where $MV_{D,E}$ = market value of debt and equity
$\quad\quad BV$ = book value

48:6.5 Bonbright's Deprival Value System and Tobin's Q

Deprival value is the lower of replacement cost (RC) and economic value (EV), where EV is the higher of present value (PV) and net realisable value (NRV); deprival value is the valuation principle underlying current cost accounting (CCA); the usual deprival value (or value to the owner) is RC.

Tobin's Q is the ratio of MV/RC; where Q >1, there is an incentive to invest in assets.

48:7 Problems with Financial PMs
(*See* Ch.9, para.9:6.3.)

48:7.1 Defects of the Historical Cost Accounting Convention

(a) *Not based on cash flows.*
(b) *Does not accurately allow for the distorting effects of inflation.*
(c) *The performance of organisational subunits (e.g. SBUs) may be distorted by transfer prices and cost allocations.*
(d) *ROIs are often poor proxies for IRRs.*

48:7.2 Based on Outdated Notions of the Typical Firm

(a) *Assumes a hierarchical structure but many firms today have flat structures.*
(b) *Focuses on the problems of manufacturers but services now provide a greater proportion of GDP and employment.*
(c) *Assumes stable, predictable and relatively uncompetitive markets.*

48:7.3 Inward Looking

Focus is on internal efficiency not external effectiveness, so discourages comparisons with competitors and customers as alternative sources of performance information.

48:7.4 Backward Looking

The focus is often on comparisons with past performance using historical cost numbers rather than on forecasting and managing future performance. The information is often too aggregated and untimely.

48:7.5 Leads to Short-termism and 'Managing by the Numbers'

The use of a 'budget constrained' rather than a 'profit conscious' or 'non-accounting' budgetary control style (Hopwood, 1972) may lead to the manipulation of operations to ensure the budget is attained.

48:7.6 Focus on Just One Set of Stakeholders: Shareholders

An over focus on meeting the financial desires of shareholders may lead to a failure to satisfy other key stakeholders such as employees and customers.

48:7.7 Neglect of Non-financial Aspects of Performance But a Continued Need to Measure Financial Performance: Need for Multi-dimensional PM

Companies do not compete solely on cost and price so information is needed on non-financial dimensions of performance as well (*see* **Chs 49** and **18, paras 18:3.1.1** and **18:3.2**).

References

Drury, C., Braund, S., Osborne, P. and Tayles, M. (1993) *A survey of management accounting practices in UK manufacturing companies*, ACCA Research Paper.

Fitzgerald, L., Johnston, R., Brignall, T.J., Silvestro, R. and Voss, C. (1991) *Performance measurement in service businesses.* CIMA.

Goold, M. and Campbell, A. (1987) *Strategies and styles: The role of the centre in managing diversified corporations.* Basil Blackwell.

Hopwood, A.G. (1972) 'An empirical study of the role of accounting data in performance evaluation', empirical research in accounting: selected studies, supplement to *Journal of Accounting Research, 10*: 156-82.

Solomons, D. (1965) *Divisional performance: Measurement and control.* R.D. Irwin.

49. Multi-dimensional Performance Measurement

49:1 Strategic Management Accounting (SMA): A First Attempt

(*See* Chs 2 and 3.)

49:1.1 Simmonds's Ideas (1983)

(a) Recommended modelling and monitoring the strategies of competitors as well as your own.
(b) Recommended supplementing comparative unit price and unit cost information over time with market information such as relative market share and sales volume.

49:1.2 Two Criticisms of Simmonds: No Mention of Customers or the Non-financial Determinants of Competitive Success

(a) A focus on competitors' neglects, another major source of external performance information: customers.
(b) Market information such as trends in market share is an aspect of measuring the results of implementing one's chosen strategy: it tells one nothing about what has determined those results.

49:2 Multi-dimensional Performance Measurement (MDPM) Models

(*See* Ch.54.)

49:2.1 The Results and Determinants Framework (RDF)

The RDF emanated from CIMA-funded research into PM in services by Fitzgerald *et al.* (1991). It has three main elements:

1. *It places PM within a feedforward:feedback control model (see* **Ch.48, Fig.48:1**).
2. *It proposes the SBU as the primary unit/level of organisational analysis.*
3. *It proposes six dimensions of performance measurement (see* **Chs 8 and 18**), *split between two which measure the success of an SBU's competitive strategy and four which determine that strategy's success: see* **Fig.49:1**.

Figure 49:1 **The results and determinants framework**

Source: Fitzgerald *et al.* (1991)

Dimensions of performance	Types of measures
Financial Performance	Profitability
R	Liquidity
E	Capital structure
S	Market ratios
U	
L Competitiveness	Relative market share and position
T	Sales growth
S	Measures of the customer base
D Quality of service	Reliability
E	Responsiveness
T	Aesthetics/appearance
E	Cleanliness/tidiness
R	Comfort
M	Friendliness
I	Communication
N	Courtesy
A	Competence
N	Access
T	Availability
S	Security
Flexibility	Volume flexibility
	Delivery speed flexibility
	Specification flexibility
Resource utilisation	Productivity
	Efficiency
Innovation	Performance of the innovation process
	Performance of individual innovations

With six dimensions of performance, interactions and trade-offs among them are inevitable and tracing the chains of cause and effect will be hard. These interactions and trade-offs may have short-term versus long-term considerations: for example, a decision to increase quality may require investment which may initially hit cash flow, then unit costs and so short-term profit; subsequently quality may improve which may cause sales and market share to rise; eventually unit costs should fall and profits rise.

An input–process–output model gives ideas about *where* to measure PM: at the input stage, during the process, at the output stage or using a combination: for example, measures of resource utilisation often take the form of ratios of outputs to inputs. Fitzgerald *et al.* (1991) identify three service delivery process types, which primarily affect *how* to measure performance and appropriate costing systems: *see* **Figure 49:2.**

Figure 49:2 **Service classification scheme**

Source: Fitzgerald *et al.* (1991)

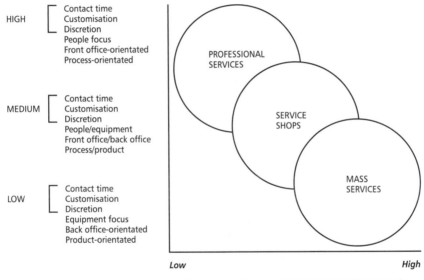

Number of customers processed by a typical unit per day

In this classification scheme the volume of demand placed on a service SBU is shown on the horizontal axis, with professional services (e.g. accountants) processing some tens of clients per day and mass services (such as Heathrow airport) some thousands per day, service shops being the intermediate category, processing some hundreds of customers per day. On the vertical axis, aspects of the way in which the SBU responds to the demand placed on it are shown, which have implications for cost traceability (which declines as one moves down the diagonal from professional to mass) and PM.

Five unique characteristics of services make it harder to measure and control performance:

1. *the customer is present in the service delivery process;*
2. *many aspects of service performance are intangible;*
3. *heterogeneity of staff performance and customer expectations;*
4. *simultaneity of production and consumption of most services;*
5. *perishability of most services.*

Fitzgerald *et al.* call for a balanced basket of measures:

(a) *financial and non-financial;*
(b) *quantitative and qualitative;*
(c) *internal and external;*
(d) *customer and competitor-based.*

The mix and weighting of the measures in the basket will be determined by the SBU's strategy (which may change as it moves through its life cycle): an SBU competing via cost leadership would emphasise financial and resource utilisation measures; one competing via service quality differentiation would be weighted towards quality measures.

The choice of measurement *mechanism* will be determined by service process type; for example, service quality would be measured for all clients in a professional service by face-to-face discussion; in a mass service it would be done via a questionnaire applied to a sample of customers.

Some key issues in PM will straddle process types; others will be unique or will require different mechanisms: *see* **Figure 49:3**.

Figure 49:3 **Key issues in PM**

Dimension	Professional		Mass
Competitiveness		repeat business market share	
Financial performance		cost traceability	
Quality of service	customer:staff unique to job every customer		customer:organization standard service sample
Flexibility	job flexibility customised		peak charges standardised
Resource utilisation	focus on staff		staff and facilities
Innovation		shows up in measures on other dimensions	

We now give two RDF case studies: Arthur Andersen Consultants and BAA.

49:2.1.1 Case Study: Arthur Andersen Management Consultancy

Arthur Andersen is an example of a professional service organisation.

Performance Dimension	*Mechanism or Measure*
Competitiveness	% repeat business
	success/failure in tendering
Financial	profit
	value of WIP
	fee adjustments
Quality	customer satisfaction
Flexibility	job scheduling
Resource utilisation	staff rotation and transfers
	chargeable ratio
Innovation	No. of new proposals
	'networking'

49:2.1.2 Case Study: British Airports Authority (BAA)

BAA is an example of a mass service organisation.

Performance Dimension	*Mechanism or Measure*
Competitiveness	number of passengers
	cargo tonnage
	air traffic movements
Financial	return on net assets
	profit
Quality	equipment faults
	trolley availability
	cleanliness
	catering
	uniformed staff
Flexibility	part-time staff
Resource utilisation	costs per employee
	costs per passenger
	income per employee

The RDF may be linked to performance-related pay. In the BAA example: competing on a strategy of service quality differentiation; senior airport managers eligible for a sizable bonus if profit targets are met or exceeded, but for every one of five quality targets unmet, 20% of the bonus is removed.

The need to get employees and managers motivated and understanding others' problems, for example, at Holiday Inns the finance director presents the marketing results and the marketing director the financial results.

Three interacting, contingent variables should affect the design of appropriate PMSs:

1. *External environment:*

    (a) *What is the state of the macroeconomy?*
    (b) *What are the regulatory effects on performance?*
    (c) *How is our sector doing?*
    (d) *How volatile, uncertain and competitive is our sector?*

    With regard to the latter, Simons (1991) has argued that in an uncertain and competitive environment one should use an 'interactive system'; in a certain and uncompetitive environment, use 'management by exception'.

2. *Internal environment: organisational structure and culture; process type.*
3. *Business mission and strategy: the literature identifies four business missions (build, hold, harvest, divest) and two generic strategies (cost leadership and differentiation).*

Where there are three contingent variables there is a possibility of *misfits* between mission, strategy and environment, for example, to build via low cost and price or to harvest via differentiation.

These interactions among contingent variables may also affect and be affected by the style of corporate:SBU relations.

Goold and Campbell's (1987) 'four styles' of corporate:SBU relations (*see* **Fig.49:3**) are as follows:

1. *centralised control (e.g. Sainsbury's);*
2. *financial control (e.g. BTR);*
3. *strategic control (e.g. Courtaulds);*
4. *strategic planning (e.g. Shell).*

Figure 49:4 **Pros and cons of the generic head office control**

Source: Adapted from Goold and Campbell (1987) and Goold and Quinn (1990)

Styles and features	Pros	Cons	Suitable conditions
Centralised - Business unit strategy developed at the centre - Tight operational control	- Controls over business unit activity and direction - Maximises synergies between business units - Ensures cohesion of strategy at corporate level	- Reduced ability to respond to local or specific market needs - Reduced ownership of business unit plans - Reduced potential to develop business management skills	- Close interrelationships between business units - Narrow market/product spread - Organisation which is not empowered
Strategic planning - Centre closely involved in the development of business unit strategy and has 'final say' - More flexible strategic controls	- Builds checks and balances into business unit strategy development - Ensures integration of strategies across business units and at an aggregate level - Encourages creation of ambitious plans	- Potential demotivation of business unit management - Reduced ownership of business unit plans - Reduced flexibility and responsiveness through more bureaucratic planning process	- Organisation requiring broad integrated strategy - Focus on long-term competitive advantage - Narrow market product spread
Strategic control - Strategies developed by business units but challenged and approved by centre - Control exercised through strategic milestones and financial budgets	- Accommodates need for both long-term strategy and short-term financial performance - Addresses synergies between business units - Motivates management through increased business unit autonomy	- Hardest form of control to implement - Can create ambiguity in planning and at business unit level - Strategic and financial plans may conflict	- Diversified organisation with variety of businesses some of which are interrelated - Need to balance variety of stakeholders - Need for management of mature businesses and development of new income streams
Financial control - Strategic plans developed by business unit - Tight financial control by centre through short-term budgets	- Motivation of management to improve financial performance quickly - Clear targets - Good means of developing business management skills	- Biased against long-term or innovative strategies - Reduced ability to exploit synergies between business units - Reduced flexibility and creativity through rigid bureaucratic control systems	- Diversified organisation with variety of disparate markets/products - Unintegrated corporate strategy - Strong short-termist financial orientation

49:2.2 The Performance Pyramid

The performance pyramid of Lynch and Cross (1991) focuses on PM at different levels within the organisation: *see* **Figure 49:5.**

Figure 49:5 **The performance pyramid**
Source: Lynch and Cross (1991)

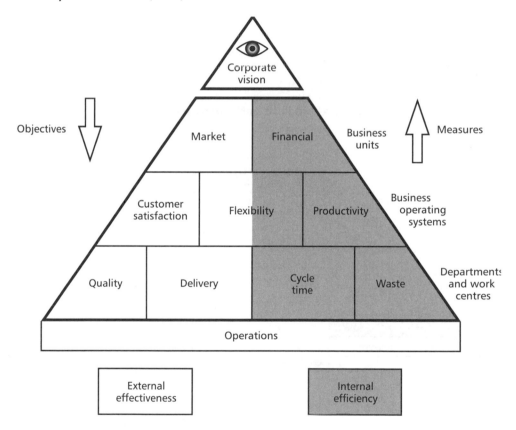

This MDPM model has many similarities with the RDF, but advocates the measurement of different aspects of the determinants of competitive success at different levels within an SBU, while discussions at senior SBU level with corporate managers should focus on measures of market and financial results. The model also stresses the need for both vertical *and* horizontal flows of information.

49:2.3 The Balanced Scorecard

Kaplan and Norton's 'balanced scorecard' (1992) is the best known MDPM model. It advocates measuring performance from four perspectives:

1. *financial;*
2. *customer;*
3. *internal business;*
4. *innovation and learning,*

and recommends the adoption of a 'balanced scorecard' of measures across the four: *see* **Figure 49:6**.

Figure 49:6 **The balanced scorecard links performance measurement**

Source: Kaplan and Norton (1992: 72)

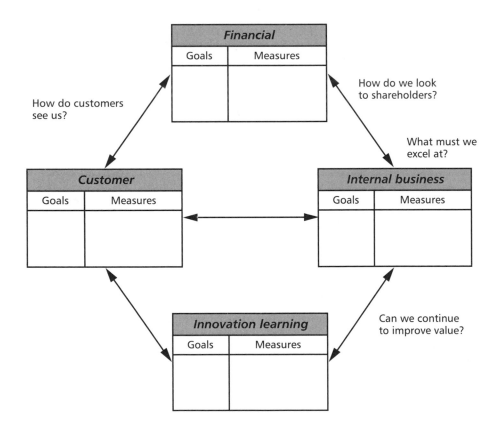

Figure 49:7 summarises the commonalities among the three models, which should be applicable within any organisation, including MNCs.

Figure 49:7 **Comparative performance dimensions across three models**

Stakeholder interests	Fitzgerald et al.	Lynch and Cross	Kaplan and Norton
Shareholders	Financial	Financial	Financial
	Resource utilisation	Productivity	Internal business
	Efficiency	Cycle time	Efficiency
	productivity	waste	
Customers	Competitiveness	Market	Customer
		Customer satisfaction	
	Quality	quality	
	12 Factors	delivery	
	Flexibility	Flexibility	
	delivery	delivery	
	volume	cycle time	
	customisation		
Employees	Innovation	N/A	Innovation and learning

49:2.4 Core, Non-core and Contingent Factors in MDPM

Brignall and Ballantine (1996) have argued that there are three core elements to the design of any MDPM system:

1. *a control model (feedforward, feedback or a mix);*
2. *a level/unit of organisational analysis (e.g. corporate, SBU, product);*
3. *multiple dimensions of performance (e.g. as in the balanced scorecard or the RDF).*

Examples of elements relevant to PMS design but which will not always be present in all firms ('non-core') are management techniques to aid performance such as ABC, TQM, BPR or JIT.

The design of any firm's PMS will need to take into account three interacting contingent variables:

1. *the external environment;*
2. *the internal environment; and*
3. *business mission and strategy.*

49:2.5 A Contingent Approach to Performance Measurement System (PMS) Design

There is no one best PMS as its design should be situation-contingent.

49:3 From Performance Measurement to Performance Management

49:3.1 A Dimensions, Standards and Rewards Framework: Making MDPM Work

Fitzgerald and Moon (1996) advocated the use of a *dimensions, standards and rewards* framework when trying to implement any system of MDPM. The framework is founded on answering three questions:

1. *What should be measured?*
2. *How should standards/targets be set for the measures?*
3. *What should be the rewards for meeting the targets/standards?*

What measures? A balanced set of measures across the six RDF dimensions (or across the balanced scorecard's four perspectives, or any other set of dimensions).

What targets? These should be set by ensuring they are *owned* by those held accountable; that they are *achievable*; that they are *equitable* between units.

What rewards? The bases for these should be *clear*; they should *motivate* those concerned; they should related to matters *controllable* by those affected.

49:3.2 Interactions and Trade-offs among Dimensions: Tracing the Chains of Cause and Effect in MDPM

Kaplan and Norton (1997) discussed chains of cause and effect among performance measures within their four perspectives, but this line of thinking was greatly advanced in their concept of 'strategy mapping' (2000, 2001). Strategy maps show how an organisation plans to convert its various assets (including intangible assets) into desired outcomes. Companies can use the template to develop their own strategy maps, that are based on the balanced scorecard.

At far left, from bottom to top, the template shows how employees need certain knowledge, skills and systems (**learning & growth perspective**) to innovate and build the right strategic capabilities and efficiencies (**internal process perspective**) so that they can deliver specific value to the market (**customer perspective**) that will lead to higher shareholder value (**financial perspective**). For the customer perspective, companies typically select one of three strategies: operational excellence; customer intimacy; or product leadership.

Strategy maps show the cause-and-effect links by which specific improvements create desired outcomes – for example, how faster process-cycle times and enhanced employee capabilities will increase retention of customers and so increase a company's revenues and profits to increase shareholder value. Kaplan and Norton argue that the best way to build strategy maps is from the top down, starting with the destination and then charting the routes that will lead there.

Some criticisms of strategy mapping are:

* Balanced scorecard (BSC) assumptions and the logic of strategy maps:

  effective learning & growth by employees → efficient internal business processes → satisfied customers → good financial results for shareholders

* An assumed one-way *linear cause and effect* relationship, always culminating in financial outcomes for shareholders.

* Similar to other MDPM models, such as the Results and Determinants Framework – but are relationships that simple?

* The reality: according to Norreklit (2000) PMs in a balanced scorecard are 'interdependent'; Kaplan and Norton have confused logical relationships with causal ones.

- But, per Davis (1971), multiple phenomena may be co-related (or not); may co-exist (or not); may co-vary (or not), whether positively or negatively, whether incrementally or discretely; may be similar or opposite phenomena; and (finally) may be independent or dependent phenomena in a causal relationship.

- Drivers may drive drivers; outcomes drive outcomes; outcomes drive drivers; drivers drive outcomes – or there may be no relationship at all.

- Many of these interrelationships are possible among the performance variables and their measures in the four perspectives of a balanced scorecard. Therefore, *pace* Norreklit (2000), it is reasonable to conclude that many performance variables may not be interdependent, still less causally or even logically related.

- This may help to explain the weak and conflicting results from tests of causal relations among claimed performance drivers and their outcomes reported in empirical research to date (Ittner and Larcker, 1998a, 1998b).

Unfortunately, similar 'chains of cause and effect' are implicit within other MDPM models, such as the RDF and the Performance Pyramid. However, the flaws in such causal chains would facilitate the incorporation of social and environmental aspects of organisational performance, that are of concern not just to activists and members of the public but to many ethical investors as well. Accordingly, Brignall (2002) puts forward a case for including social and environmental performance indicators in mainstream MDPM models such as the balanced scorecard.

We may conclude that a knowledge of likely chains of cause and effect across performance dimensions which will result from certain actions is key to the management of performance, but these studies are in their infancy, and while various techniques are available for studying past causal relationships, this may not be helpful when discussing the rival merits of alternative future strategies.

49:3.3 The Relationships Between MDPM and Other Management Techniques, such as TQM and BPR

(*See* **Chs 18** and **32**.)

These studies are also in their infancy. One example is the study by Brignall et al. (1999) which examined the implications for PM and target setting of choosing incremental versus step-change process improvement (using case studies and surveys).

Some companies in the four service sectors studied use both strategies, which in the survey sample of 40 service companies across four sectors established that continuous incremental and periodic step change-type approaches to process change differ simply by degree and have similar drivers of change. Under both approaches, targets were predominantly related to past (financial) performance, imposed by management, with little difference in the use of rewards.

Two basic types of accountants were found:

1. *entrenched (do not want to be involved in organisational change);*
2. *team players (use their skills to complement those of other team members),*

but accountants were largely uninvolved in either form of process change!

In six case studies where accountants were fully involved in process change, six prerequisites to such involvement were found:

1. *accountants needed to have sound accounting systems to free their time so they could act as*
2. *team players in cross-functional change management teams*
3. *using their extensive business and process knowledge*
4. *with a flexible view of their role*
5. *and good interpersonal and communication skills*
6. *to meet challenge and change in the organisation.*

These hands-on accountants played five key roles to further their involvement in organisational change programmes. They were:

1. *generalists acting as part of the senior management team but taking commercial responsibility for decisions;*
2. *non-traditional accountants who spent much of their time out of the office interacting with people from other functions;*

3. *the linchpins of the organisation, linking up, down and across the organisation using accounting and other information as the 'glue';*
4. *the facilitators of change decisions, not only circulating information but explaining its significance and ensuring a focus on relevant information;*
5. *not just functional specialists but turned data into information for others to use.*

Brignall *et al.* (1999) argue that the management accounting profession is bifurcating, with some active accountants getting involved with the change programmes that at other organisations are threatening their counterparts' role and status.

49:3.4 The Design of a Performance Measurement System

Per Brignall (2000), the design and implementation of a multi-dimensional performance measurement system (MDPMS) for an organisation requires:

1. *Identification of key stakeholders/institutions:*

individuals	institutions
shareholder	institutional shareholder or public sector funder
employee	union or professional association
customer	industrial customer or institutional purchaser
etc.	etc.

2. *Identification of stakeholders' information needs.*
3. *Given the insights of institutional theory (Brignall and Modell, 2000), will the PMS be balanced and integrated, or decoupled? Whose interests will dominate?*
4. *What is the primary level of organisational analysis for performance measurement (PM) (e.g. product, customer, department, function, process, SBU, division, corporate)?*
5. *What are the organisation's strategic typology; business mission and strategic position? And do they change with the business/product life cycle?*
6. *What is the nature of the internal environment?*
7. *What is the nature of the external environment?*
8. *Adaptation of a suitable MDPM model (e.g. balanced scorecard, performance pyramid, results and determinants framework), to meet the requirements above.*
9. *Application of the Fitzgerald and Moon (1996) 'dimensions, standards and rewards' framework to smooth the implementation process.*

49:3.5 From Performance Measurement to Performance Management

To move from performance measurement to performance management requires:

1. *The estimation of inter- and intradimensional interactions and trade-offs through time across the many dimensions of performance (Kaplan and Norton's (1996, 1997) 'chains of cause and effect') – this might be effected by 'strategy mapping' (Kaplan and Norton, 2000). Brignall and Ballantine (1996a) suggest this might be done using shareholder value analysis, value based planning, soft systems methodologies, the RDF and financial modelling.*

2. *What are the components of the organisational change/performance improvement programme (e.g. new leadership, new HR management practices, TQM, BPR, revised organisational structure and so on)? These will affect what must be measured and managed as they are determinants of performance.*

3. *What are the 'complementarities' (Milgrom and Roberts, 1995) among the chosen MDPMSs and the various elements of the organisational change programme,* which together are the *determinants of organisational performance?*

4. *Future research into the determinants of organisational performance might employ a dual strategy: large-scale surveys using multivariate statistical analyses to test for the 'complementarities' (the 'what' or 'content') of performance determinants in different organisations in different sectors; longitudinal case studies to describe the 'why' and 'how' (context and process) of performance determinants in successful and unsuccessful organisations.*

49:3.6 Summary

Current best practice in PMS *design* is to use a multi-dimensional framework to measure and manage performance, within a feedforward:feedback control model, which has a balanced set of financial and non-financial measures, quantitative and qualitative measures, internal and external (competitor- and customer-focused) measures which link strategy to operations in a balanced and integrated PMS.

The needs of key stakeholders should be tied to specific indicators, e.g. *shareholders/funders of services*: financial PM such as ROI; *customers/purchasers of services*: competitiveness results, customer satisfaction with service quality (18 factors) and flexibility (3 types); *employees*: staff turnover, sickness rates, training days, etc.

We need to know more about how MDPMS are used and who benefits (Brignall and Modell, 2000), about the determinants of performance and their links to MDPMSs, and the complementarities among PMs, performance determinants and performance management systems (Brignall, 2000). Finally, MDPM models such as the balanced scorecard are now being integrated into advanced IT systems for managing performance strategically, such as strategic enterprise management systems. When experience of implementing such systems is sufficient they will be reported here, but for ideas as to likely problems in implementing them see Brignall and Ballantine (2001).

References

Ballantine, J. and Brignall, T.J. (1996) 'Performance measurement frameworks: Critique, synthesis and research issues', WBS working paper.

Ballantine, J., Brignall, T.J. and Modell, S. (1998) 'Performance measurement and management in public health services: Some UK and Swedish experience', *Management Accounting Research*, *9*, March: 71–94.

Bates, K. and Brignall, T.J. (1993) 'Rationality, politics and healthcare costing', *Financial Accountability and Management*, February: 27–44.

Brignall, T.J. (1993) 'Performance measurement and change in local government: A general case and a childcare application', *Public Money and Management*, October–December: 23–30.

Brignall, T.J. (1997) 'A contingent rationale for cost system design in services', *Management Accounting Research*, *8(3)*: 325–46.

Brignall, T.J. (2000) 'From performance measurement to performance management: The determinants of performance', paper presented at the EAA Annual Congress, Munich, March.

Brignall, T.J. (2002) 'The unbalanced scorecard: A social and environmental critique', in A. Neely, A. Walters and R. Austin (Eds), *Performance Measurement and Management: Research and action*, pp. 85–92. Boston, MA: Performance Measurement Association.

Brignall, T.J. and Ballantine, J. (1996a) 'Performance measurement in service businesses revisited', *International Journal of Service Industry Management*, *7(1)*: 6–31.

Brignall, T.J. and Ballantine, J. (1996b) 'Interactions and trade-offs in multi-dimensional performance management', paper presented at a conference on Strategic Management Accounting, University of Alberta, Edmonton, Canada, 10–11 May; available as WBS Working Paper no. 247, October 1996.

Brignall, T.J. and Ballantine, J. (2001) 'Strategic enterprise management systems: A partial solution to performance improvement', presented at the 24th Annual Congress of the EAA, Athens, 18–20 April.

Brignall, T.J. and Modell, S. (2000) 'An institutional perspective on performance measurement and management in the new public sector', *Management Accounting Research*, September: 281–306.

Brignall, T.J., Fitzgerald, L., Johnston, R. and Markou, E. (2000) *Improving service performance: A study of step-change versus continual improvement*. London: CIMA.

Brignall, T.J., Fitzgerald, L., Johnston, R. and Silvestro, R. (1991) 'Product costing in service organisations', *Management Accounting Research*, *2(3)*: 227–48.

Coates, J.B., Davis, E.W., Longden, S.G., Stacey, R.J. and Emmanuel, C. (1993) *Corporate performance evaluation in multinationals*. London: CIMA.

Davis, M. (1971) 'That's interesting! Towards a phenomenology of sociology and a sociology of phenomenology', *Philosophy of the Social Sciences*, *1*: 309–44.

Emmanuel, C., Otley, D. and Merchant, K. (1990) *Accounting for management control*. Van Nostrand Rheinhold.

Fitzgerald, L. and Moon, P. (1996) *Performance measurement in service businesses: Making it work*. London: CIMA.

Fitzgerald, L., Johnston, R., Brignall, T.J., Silvestro, R. and Voss, C. (1991) *Performance measurement in service businesses*. London: CIMA.

Goold, M. and Campbell, A. (1987) *Strategies and styles: The role of the centre in managing diversified corporations*. Basil Blackwell.

Goold, M. and Quinn, J.J. (1990) *Strategic control: Milestones for long-term performance*. The Economist Books.

Govindarajan, V. and Shank, J. (1992) 'Strategic cost management: Tailoring controls to strategies', *Journal of Cost Management*, Fall.

Ittner, C.D. and Larcker, D.F. (1998a) 'Innovations in performance measurement: Trends and research implications', *Journal of Management Accounting Research*, *10*: 205–38.

Ittner, C.D. and Larcker, D.F. (1998b) 'Are nonfinancial measures leading indicators of financial performance? An analysis of customer satisfaction', *Journal of Accounting Research*, *36*(Supplement): 1–35.

Kaplan, R.S. and Norton, D.P. (1992) 'The balanced scorecard – Measures that drive performance', *Harvard Business Review*, January–February: 71–9.

Kaplan, R.S. and Norton, D.P. (1993) 'Putting the balanced scorecard to work', *Harvard Business Review*, September–October: 134–47.

Kaplan, R.S. and Norton, D.P. (1996) 'Using the balanced scorecard as a strategic management system', *Harvard Business Review*, January–February: 75–85.

Kaplan, R.S. and Norton, D.P. (1997) 'Why does business need a balanced scorecard?', *Journal of Cost Management*, May–June: 5–10.

Kaplan, R.S. and Norton, D.P. (2000) 'Having trouble with your strategy? Then map it', *Harvard Business Review*, September–October: 167–76.

Kaplan, R.S. and Norton, D.P. (2001) *The strategy-focused organization*. Harvard Business School Press.

Langfield-Smith, K. (1997) 'Management control systems and strategy: A critical review', *Accounting, Organizations and Society, 22(2)*: 207–32.

Lynch, R.L. and Cross, K.F. (1991) *Measure up! Yardsticks for continuous improvement.* (2nd edition published 1995) Basil Blackwell.

Miles, R.E. and Snow, C.C. (1978) *Organizational strategy, structure and process.* New York: McGraw-Hill.

Milgrom, P. and Roberts, J. (1995) 'Complementarities and fit: Strategy, structure and organisational change in manufacturing', *Journal of Accounting and Economics, 19(2)*: 179–208.

Norreklit, H. (2000) 'The balance on the balanced scorecard – a critical analysis of some of its assumptions', *Management Accounting Research, 11*: 65–88.

Otley, D.T. (1980) 'The contingency theory of management accounting: Achievement and prognosis', *Accounting, Organizations and Society, 5*: 413–28.

Porter, M. (1980) *Competitive strategy.* Free Press.

Silvestro, R., Fitzgerald, L. and Johnston, R. (1992) 'Towards a classification of service processes', *International Journal of Service Industry Management, 3(3)*: 62–75.

Simmonds, K. (1983) 'Strategic management accounting', in D. Fanning (Ed.), *Handbook of management accounting*, pp. 25–48. Gower.

Simons, R. (1991) 'Strategic orientation and top management attention to control systems', *Strategic Management Journal, 12*: 49–62.

50. Case Study: Development of a Non-financial Performance Measurement System

50:1 Background

This company is a large hotel company established in the 1960s to construct and market first-class hotel developments both in its domestic market in the Middle East and internationally. In the late 1980s the company was restructured and top management decided to concentrate on the management of resorts and hotels. A national government controls this hotel company and owns approximately 75% of its shares.

In the early 1990s the high turnover of senior managers was a cause for concern for this company. During the past six years there have been three restructurings initiated by the Board of Directors. Currently, this company manages approximately 50 hotels throughout the world.

50:2 Management Strategy

Current management strategy has been developed with the aims of improving guest services and guest satisfaction. A comprehensive marketing campaign is planned for each location. The company is pursuing the following strategies to compete effectively in the face of the current domestic and international competition:

(a) *In-depth pre-planning to determine the most strategically advantageous services and facilities.*

(b) *Integrated marketing with the aim of increasing the profitability of each hotel.*

(c) *Establishing a well-known brand name and corporate identity.*

(d) *Setting up standard operating practices and procedures in all hotels and monitoring such practices and procedures.*

(e) *Employee training and development including:*
   (i) *customer-care skills;*
   (ii) *management skills;*
   (iii) *sales management;*
   (iv) *recruitment, assessment, selection and retention;*
   (v) *team building;*
   (vi) *appraisal skills for managers and supervisors.*

50:3 Non-financial Performance Measures

Top management recognised the need for a standard performance evaluation model because in the 1990s each hotel evaluated, analysed and reported on its own non-financial performance. In the late 1990s therefore, the company introduced a standard system of non-financial performance measurement for all hotels to assess and evaluate the quality of service. These non-financial performance measures (NFPMs) included the following:

(a) *occupancy rate;*

(b) *time taken for guests to complete their bookings;*

(c) *responsiveness of receptionists;*

(d) *friendliness of staff;*

(e) *responsiveness to customer needs;*

(f) *knowledge and competence of staff;*

(g) *availability of hotel facilities;*

(h) *design of hotel;*
(i)   *appropriateness of front desk;*
(j)   *tidiness and cleanliness of hotel;*
(k) *degree of receptionists' recognition of each customer;*
(l)   *number of repeat guests to total number of guests;*
(m) *time taken to respond to guest telephone calls;*
(n) *number of disagreements with guests;*
(o) *guest evaluation of room preparation;*
(p) *guest evaluation of restaurant.*

50:3.1 Reasons for Adopting NFPMs

A major reason for increasing the use of NFPMs was the competition from other hotel companies both in the domestic and international markets. This company was involved in the upper end of the hotel market and was dealing with business guests and high-income tourists expecting special service. Such demanding customers were another reason for adopting NFPMs in order to try to improve the service offered to guests.

Another reason for this company adopting NFPMS was that managers recognised the limitations of their financial performance measurement system. One manager stated:

> These financial performance measures make assessments using mainly financial considerations that are directed at lowering expenses and increasing revenue. This thinking sidelines the company's survival and long-term success. The financial performance measures are short term and affect adversely guest satisfaction and also the company's reputation.

Financial performance measures neglect non-financial critical success factors such as quality of service and customer satisfaction.

By its very nature the hotel sector is service orientated and very dependent therefore on all employees. This company is using NFPMs to help to measure and improve quality of service and customer satisfaction. The General Manager commented:

> One of the stimuli for using NFPMs is the nature of this industry. The hospitality industry is reliant on the service that is provided mainly by its employees and this is the main determinant for success or failure. This industry depends on a high degree of customer loyalty which cannot be realised without loyal, highly focused and competent employees.

50:3.2 Organisational Influences on NFPMs

This company had developed an aggressively offensive marketing strategy and managers believed that this change in marketing strategy had encouraged greater use of NFPMs. For example, the Marketing Director stated:

> Our adoption of an aggressive marketing strategy has encouraged us to adopt more focused practices such as higher quality and improved customer satisfaction – especially with the nature of competition in this industry being of a non-financial nature. This in turn encourages more use of NFPMs.

Several managers mentioned that the extent of managers' operational experience affected the use of NFPMs. Usually operational experience in the hotel industry gave managers a better understanding of the industry and more confidence to use NFPMs. However, a lack of such operational experience encouraged managers to rely solely on financial performance measures. A General Manager of one of the hotels suggested:

> Corporate managers' level of knowledge of operational procedures and the effectiveness of their monitoring and control of units has a direct effect on their use of NFPMs. The more operational experience that corporate management has, the more unit managers will use NFPMs, because corporate managers will focus more on the quality of service that units provide.

50:3.3 Environmental Conditions Affecting Use of NFPMs

The General Manager of one of the hotels considered that the shareholders over-emphasised financial aspects of the company. He described the company as being between two contradictory forces namely the shareholders with their strong financial emphasis and the nature of the hotel industry with its emphasis on service. This shareholder emphasis on financial aspects discouraged the use of NFPMs. The Vice-President of the company suggested:

> The use of the NFPM system is not as fully developed as it could be because of the conservative attitude of the shareholders which is excessively financially oriented and which encourages the use of financial performance measures.

In this particular company the Government owned approximately /5% of its shares and, therefore, government officials influenced the selection of both the Directors and top executive managers. One of these Directors mentioned that the government officials were excessively finance dominated which meant the appointment of Directors and top managers with financial expertise. This Director considered that this government influence had a negative effect on the use of NFPMs by both the Board of Directors and top managers. However, in recent years the Board and top managers had begun to realise the limitations of financial performance measures and this had led to increased use of NFPMs.

50:3.4 Management Strategies Affecting the Use of NFPMs

This company adopted a number of management strategies which encouraged the use of NFPMs. First, the company benchmarked itself against a number of other international hotel chains and benchmarked itself against their best practices. For example, on a monthly basis several managers visited competitor hotels as guests and evaluated their services and facilities. Furthermore, there was also reasonable employee mobility between different hotel chains. Such benchmarking encouraged the use of NFPMs.

Secondly, employees are one of the most important critical success factors in the hotel industry. This company had made great efforts to develop and train its employees and to implement leading-edge human resource policies. The aim was to be best in its class of hotels. The Director of Training stated:

> The training department provides intensive courses to develop employees' skills and abilities. These courses include acting, filming and role-playing in real-life situations that may occur. The objective is to help employees to become more sensitive to the needs of guests.

Top management also used the results of employee satisfaction surveys. The General Manager of one of the hotels considered a successful HR strategy to be a critical factor when implementing NFPMs. This was one of the reasons for reducing the number of short-term contracts.

One strategy which discouraged the use of NFPMs was that in the past top management did not have an integrated model of performance evaluation. Operational divisions and individual hotels had developed their own NFPMs. One of the Directors argued:

> A standard integrated performance evaluation model strengthens the ability of top management to evaluate the performance of different units and make the most appropriate decision at the right time.

A Senior Financial Adviser stated:

> The management of the company is implementing the Balanced Scorecard as a performance evaluation model to assess the company's critical success factors. Historically, the operational divisions and the individual hotels developed their own NFPMs to assess their operational progress.

Another strategy which discouraged the use of NFPMs was that the current reward system was inconsistent with the management objective of increasing the use of NFPMs. The current reward system was basically financially orientated and it neglected NFPMs. The Director of New Projects considered that there was a need to develop an integrated reward system (related to both financial and non-financial performance measurements). This integrated reward system is based on specific proportions of financial and non-financial performance measurements. Furthermore, if the positive feedback from guest comment cards, 'shopper' guest assessments and other operational measurements was less than 90%, the staff concerned would not qualify for a bonus even if the financial performance measurements were outstanding.

50:3.5 Consequences of Using NFPMs

Several managers were convinced that using NFPMs had helped to improve long-term bottom-line profit. The Director of New Projects argued that the use of NFPMs had resulted in an improvement in quality of service, customer satisfaction and flexibility and this was now being reflected in improved profit figures. A General Manager of one hotel suggested:

> Revenue determinants are customer satisfaction, quality of service and flexibility which ensure long-term profitability. As an operational manager in a hotel, I have and am seeing such a relationship clearly. Customer loyalty will ensure the continuity and the consistency of revenue in the long term.

A General Manager of another hotel elaborated further:

> The effective use of NFPMs will generate better bottom-line profit. In my
> experience, the failure to use such measures or neglecting the application of
> these operational measures will negatively affect customer satisfaction. This in
> return affects customer loyalty which negatively impacts on future profits.

Several managers mentioned that the use of NFPMs required substantial capital expenditure by companies in the short term. One of the Directors explained that the use of NFPMs led to capital expenditure on replacements and improvements. A General Manager of one of the hotels suggested:

> Making effective use of NFPMs needs a steady flow of capital expenditure,
> particularly in the short term. This affects negatively short-term bottom-line
> profit and pressurises hotel managers to balance long-term bottom-line profit
> and capital expenditure in the short term.

Similarly, the use of NFPMs encourages increased investment in training programmes – particularly for supervisory and managerial levels. Again such increased training expenditure can have an adverse effect on profit in the short term with the benefits from some of these training programmes coming through in the medium – or longer term.

A General Manager of one of the hotels suggested that the use of NFPMs also encouraged the adoption of new technologies to improve the quality of hotel service. A General Manager of another hotel argued that the international reservation system, new computer programs and improved management information system were developed mainly because of the use of NFPMs. The Marketing Director mentioned that the most recent computer programs were designed to improve the service offered to guests. For example, one program opens a file for each new guest and retains details of the preferences of each guest. The Personnel Director stated:

> One of the most important results of using NFPMs is the importing of the
> latest and the most advanced international technological developments which
> would not have been adopted if the company had not used the results of
> quality of service and customer satisfaction measurements.

This company used its NFPMs as a guide in setting its annual budget. The Financial Controller suggested that NFPMs were the best system for monitoring and controlling quality and customer satisfaction. A Financial Controller of one of the hotels suggested:

> In the last few years the budget has been very accurate and represents the real needs of the operational divisions and departments. This can be seen from the similarity between the budget numbers and the annual financial statements. This comes from using NFPM results as guidelines for budget preparation.

50:4 Conclusions

This hotel company has developed a NFPM system over a number of years using a bottom-up approach. It realises that further changes are still required such as a more integrated performance measurement system (combining NFPMs and financial performance measures), less use of short-term contracts and closer links between the NFPM system and the executive reward system.

The reasons for this company adopting NFPMs included the following:

(a) competition;
(b) limitations of financial performance measurement system;
(c) improvement of quality of service and customer satisfaction;
(d) aggressive marketing strategy;
(e) operational experience of managers.

The following management strategies encouraged the use of NFPMs:

(a) benchmarking against best practices of international hotel chains;
(b) HR strategy encouraging employee training;
(c) employee satisfaction surveys.

The consequences of using NFPMs were:

(a) improved bottom-line profit in the long term;
(b) increased capital expenditure – particularly in the short term;
(c) increased training for supervisory and managerial levels;
(d) adoption of new technologies;
(e) improved annual budget setting.

51. *Tableau de Bord*

51:1 The French System

Historically British management accountants have tended to look towards the US rather than Europe for new developments in management accounting practices. Obviously the English language has been an important factor influencing this perspective. However, recently increasing attention is being paid to developments in Japanese management accounting practices such as target costing (**Ch.24**), functional costing (**Ch.25**) and cost tables (**Ch.26**). In contrast relatively little attention continues to be paid to developments in French or German management accounting practices.

One distinctive characteristic of French management accounting practices is their *'tableau de bord'* system which most French organisations have been operating for many years. The very fact that such a system has survived suggests that it provides useful information for French managers and makes it worthy of consideration. So, what exactly is the French *'tableau de bord'* system?

51:1.1 What Is *'Tableau de Bord'*?

The French *'tableau de bord'* is basically a performance measurement system (*see* **Chs 48** and **49**) built up from a subdepartmental basis. However, its foundation is a self-reporting and self-control basis with managers in a subdepartment choosing their own performance measures and then monitoring the actual outcomes for these performance measures selected. Each subdepartment develops its own *'tableau de bord'*.

This might seem to be a rather chaotic system with each subdepartment having its own performance measures. However, these performance measures should be related to the critical success factors of each subdepartment such as quality or delivery time. The managers in each subdepartment should be well placed to determine such critical success factors. Very often the resulting performance measures will be non-financial (*see* **Ch.49**). For example, one critical success factor for the distribution subdepartment of the export department might be delivery on time. The related non-financial

John Innes 867

performance measure might be the number of late deliveries to export customers perhaps reported as a percentage of all export deliveries.

Another constraint on the system is that the managers in each subdepartment need to consider their links with other subdepartments and departments. The organisation's overall objectives cannot be ignored. The result is that links are formed between the *'tableaux de bord'* in different subdepartments and departments. Of course, there may not be links between all the performance measures but at least a few performance measures will be linked together.

51:1.2 Homogeneous Cost Pools

The above has discussed the *'tableau de bord'* being based on subdepartments. The French talk about 'sections homogènes' within departments which can be translated in terms of homogeneous cost pools and these are the equivalent of the above subdepartments. An example of such a subdepartment or homogeneous cost pool for an overhead department is the export distribution section of the export department. An example of a subdepartment or homogeneous cost pool for a production department is the grinding section. Managers within each subdepartment then develop their own *'tableau de bord'* for their homogeneous cost pool. Lebas has defined the *'tableau de bord'* as:

> the managerial system that supports the achievement of performance just like the dashboard on a car allows the driver to reach his destination ... These indicators are not all expressed in the same unit, their coherence comes from a model of the car operating system.
>
> (Lebas, 1993: 6–7)

This quotation emphasises that the essence of the *'tableau de bord'* is as a performance measurement and control system. However, it is very much a bottom-up self-control system rather than the top-down, imposed control system which is the norm in many British organisations.

51:2 Performance Measurement System

The essence of the *'tableau de bord'* is that each subdepartment (such as the vehicle maintenance subdepartment) selects its own performance measures. For example, for the vehicle maintenance subdepartment the number of vehicle breakdowns expressed as a percentage of the total number of vehicles or the total hours that vehicles are off the road expressed as a percentage of total vehicle hours driven could be two possible performance measures.

Greif (1993) has shown how managers in French factories actually use the *'tableau de bord'*. The key performance measures selected by managers in a subdepartment are usually non-financial performance measures which are related to the critical success factors within that particular part of the organisation. For example, for the materials receiving subdepartment in the stores the non-financial performance measures might include the weight of materials received and the number of material deliveries received.

51:2.1 Self-control System

This chapter on *'tableau de bord'* has been included in a handbook of management accounting but, strictly speaking, the *'tableau de bord'* is not part of the formal management accounting system. The *'tableaux de bord'* are constructed by managers and operated by the subdepartments themselves in terms of both reporting the results for the chosen performance measures and controlling the future results. The *'tableaux de bord'* are very much a management technique based on a decentralised style of management and their essence is a self-reporting and self-control system. The responsibility for monitoring the performance measures in a *'tableau de bord'* and for taking appropriate, corrective action rests with the managers in the subdepartment itself rather than with higher level managers outside the subdepartment.

51:3 Development of *'Tableau de Bord'*

One advantage of the self-reporting and self-control aspect of the *'tableau de bord'* is that as circumstances change either in the external environment or within the subdepartment, managers can easily adapt the performance measures in relation to the changed circumstances. Experience has shown that developing a *'tableau de bord'* for a subdepartment requires a great deal of time and effort. The starting point is for managers to consider how their subdepartment fits into the overall organisation and how it relates to the organisation's objectives.

Experiences with *'tableaux de bord'* vary from organisation to organisation and from subdepartment to subdepartment. In one organisation which recently implemented a *'tableaux de bord'* system, managers spent their time as follows:

(a) *50% of the time involved in setting up the 'tableaux de bord' was spent on discussing, clarifying and agreeing the objectives of their subdepartment;*

(b) *20% on discussing and agreeing the critical success factors for their subdepartment;*

(c) *30% on discussing and agreeing the performance measures for their subdepartment.*

In addition to being a performance measurement system, the *'tableau de bord'* system also operates as a channel of communication - particularly within subdepartments.

51:3.1 Financial and Non-financial Performance Measures

The managers within each subdepartment choose their own performance measures and most of these are usually quantitative, that is, non-financial (*see* **Ch.49**). However, one or two financial performance measures (*see* **Ch.48**) may also be included in the subdepartment's *'tableau de bord'*. Of course, even the non-financial performance measures may be related to other financial performance measures. Nevertheless, one weakness in the *'tableau de bord'* system is very often a lack of understanding by managers about the relationships between financial and non-financial performance measures. Many managers are happier dealing with non-financial performance measures and many neglect financial measures.

A feature of the *'tableau de bord'* system is that usually multiple performance measures are used within each subdepartment. With most subdepartments having more than one critical success factor, it means that managers need more than one performance measure. Indeed very often managers suggest more than one performance measure for each critical success factor.

The targets and actual results for these performance measures are very often displayed on charts within the subdepartment so that all employees can see how the subdepartment is performing. Such open communication means that there is a very good chance that corrective action will be taken as soon as a problem arises with any performance measure. In addition to the performance measurement and communication aspects of the *'tableaux de bord'*, there is also a motivational aspect. The *'tableaux de bord'* work best not only in a decentralised management system but also where there is a participative management style.

51:4 Vertical Integration

Most of the discussion so far has centred on the subdepartment aspect of the *'tableaux de bord'*. However, the links of each subdepartment's *'tableau de bord'* with other subdepartments and with the organisation's overall strategy have already been pointed out. This means that the *'tableaux de bord'* of different subdepartments become linked together by certain common performance measures. In particular, there are very strong links between subdepartments within the same department. In other words the *'tableaux de bord'* are linked together vertically both within departments and between departments by means of a few common performance measures.

There is an important vertical integration aspect of the *'tableau de bord'* system which gives it an overall coherence instead of just being a performance measurement system for individual subdepartments. Nevertheless, despite such vertical integration the distinguishing features of the *'tableau de bord'* system remain:

(a) *bottom-up performance measurement system (in contrast to more common top-down system);*

(b) *subdepartment managers choose their own performance measures;*

(c) *self-reporting and self-control in relation to chosen performance measures.*

51:5 Responsibility Accounting

Gray and Pesqueux (1993) compared responsibility accounting in American organisations with the 'tableaux de bord' in French organisations. They found some similarities but the most important differences were:

(a) *much more use by French organisations showing the results of their performance measures (and particularly their non-financial measures) on charts so that everyone in the subdepartment can see at a glance how the subdepartment is doing;*

(b) in the American organisations the information reporting for the responsibility accounting system was very centralised whereas, in contrast, in the French organisations the information reporting system for the 'tableau de bord' was very decentralised, that is, located within each subdepartment.

51:6 Links with Activity-based Approach

The activity-based approach to overheads (*see* **Chs 13, 22** and **28**) has been slower to develop in France than in the US or the UK. Nevertheless, a number of French organisations are now introducing an activity-based approach. Such organisations are finding that this activity-based approach to overhead costs complements their existing *'tableau de bord'* system. Basically the activity-based approach examines activities or processes across the organisation – it is very much a horizontal approach. In contrast, as discussed in **paragraph 51:4** the *'tableau de bord'* system provides a vertically integrated approach. The combination of the activity-based approach and the *'tableau de bord'* system gives a matrix approach to performance measurement for the organisation for its overhead areas. Of course, the *'tableau de bord'* system applies not only to overhead subdepartments but also to production subdepartments and in this respect it has a much wider application than the activity-based approach.

51:7 Conclusions

Just as we can learn from American and Japanese management accounting practices, so we can learn from French management accounting practices. One such French practice is the *'tableau de bord'* system with its bottom–up approach based on subdepartments and homogeneous cost pools. The distinguishing features of the *'tableau de bord'* system are as follows:

(a) subdepartment managers select their own performance measures taking into consideration:

    (i)   links with other subdepartments;

    (ii) organisation's overall objectives;

    (iii) subdepartment's critical success factors;

(b) mostly non-financial performance measures;

(c) self-reporting system for actual results of performance measures;

(d) self-control system for taking corrective action in relation to performance measures;

(e) communication and motivational aspects;

(f) vertical integration of 'tableau de bord' system both within and between departments on the basis of a few common performance measures.

If your organisation operates a decentralised system with a participative management style, it is certainly worth considering whether a version of the French *'tableau de board'* system might be appropriate. It is certainly a different approach from the top-down performance measurement and control system used in many organisations.

References

Gray, L. and Pesqueux, S. (1993) 'Evolutions actuelles de systèmes de tableaux de bord', *Revue Francaise de Comptabilité*, February: 30–2.

Greif, M. (1993) *'Le déploiement du tableau de bord dans les ateliers'*, *Revue Francaise de Comptabilité*, March: 15–18.

Lebas, M. (1993) '*Tableau de bord* and performance measurement', paper presented at MARG Conference at the LSE on 22 April.

52. Information Management Delivering Business Intelligence

This chapter is an extract reproduced by kind permission of the publisher Pearson from *Transforming the finance function, adding company-wide value in a technology-driven environment* by Margaret May, published in 2002 in the *FT Executive Briefing Series*.

52:1 Introduction

During the last part of the 20th century, finance, aided in part by separate computer systems, managed to adopt an insular approach to its function within the business. Located at head office, concentrating on its financial, control and statutory obligations, it had far too frequently lost sight of the need to produce relevant, timely, meaningful information for the business. This had been, in part, a consequence of the drive in the 1970s to merge costing, management and financial accounting systems into one super, integrated system. Management information became the financial accounts, slightly modified, compared to budgets and then issued as the monthly management accounts pack. This information had little relevance to the operational managers of the business. This inevitably resulted in the growth of informal information systems all over the organisation, with each department having its own dedicated team producing the management information that it needed to run the business.

In the 21st century, the role of the information manager is pivotal within the organisation. The latest technological advances mean that it is now possible to have just one holistic, organisation-wide information system, delivering business intelligence. This means that the same information management system can be used by everyone around the organisation – with no conflicting data produced by different departments! Decision making can be based on one set of good, reliable information to reduce risk, facilitated by the new breed of finance professionals, who are now devoting large amounts of time to this crucial activity.

The role of Chief Information Officer (CIO) in the modern organisation must be held by a professional who understands how the whole organisation operates and can facilitate the production of information, that combines financial and non-financial, internal and external, qualitative and quantitative data. The CIO must be able to facilitate the design of an enterprise-wide integrated performance and information management system using the latest web-enabled technological developments including ERP, CRM, SCM, business intelligence software, like data mining, OLAP and enterprise portals. In addition, the CIO needs to be able to access the wealth of external information available through the web using online software.

Many organisations are now taking steps to identify all knowledge and information so that it can be recorded, managed, retained and used by everybody within the company. However, care must be taken to ensure that the end result is not 'information overload'. The key is to identify and filter the useful information and utilise such tools as alerts, exceptions, rules, traffic lights and trend analysis, to present and highlight only those areas needing attention.

According to CIMA (2000):

> Information management is the process of managing data so as to deliver information that adds insight, understanding and value for users by providing management information for:
>
> • Organisational effectiveness – performance.
>
> • Developmental activities – looking to the future.
>
> • Operational efficiency and economy – improvement.
>
> 'Information x (Knowledge + Understanding + Experience) = Decisions'
>
> The Information Manager needs to:
>
> • Understand how organisations operate in order to identify information critical to success.

- Appreciate that principles remain applicable over time although techniques and technologies may change.

- Be able to use the range of techniques to provide information to meet users' specific needs.

- Understand different contexts, needs, perceptions, attitudes and motives of users.

- Be able to select and utilise the most appropriate tools and technology.

- Be able to promote a broad and balanced perspective on how the organisation is achieving its objectives.

Typically, companies spent tens of millions on large-scale system changes driven in haste by the need to replace old equipment to beat the Millennium bug and often failed to take the necessary steps to ensure that they have properly thought through the massive investments. The all-too-frequent failure of IT to deliver on business goals means that in future the crucially important role of information management is more likely than ever to form part of the newly transformed finance operation.

52:2 Defining the Business Requirement

Traditionally, companies have had scores of independent IT systems, often dependent on, and driven by, individual functions, built up over decades. They usually consist of a raft of different technologies, making integration very difficult and expensive or sometimes even impossible. The 1990s became the decade when companies came to realise the importance of breaking down their functional boundaries and viewing their organisations through streamlined processes. With this realisation, there is not only an appreciation of the need for a process-oriented, enterprise-wide decision-support system, but an urgent demand for its implementation, to enable companies to maintain their competitive advantage. In the modern organisation, these processes will extend far beyond old company and geographic boundaries to link their IT systems with those of their suppliers, partners and customers worldwide.

The days are over when managers produced their own set of business information and time at meetings was wasted, arguing over whose figures were correct. No longer is it acceptable to take management decisions relying on 'gut feel', or to spend time 'fire-fighting' problems rather than eliminating the causes. Technology can now provide real-time access to decision-support information that combines quantitative and qualitative, financial and non-financial data, from internal and external sources.

Main areas of input to an information system will include:

(a) *data from companies' ERP, CRM, SCM and other legacy systems;*
(b) *specific external data on such areas as competitors, customers, partners, suppliers and benchmark data;*
(c) *general relevant external information on the economy and the stock markets;*
(d) *the organisational objectives with links to other sources of information to show how these are being met, for example, balanced scorecard and forecasts.*

The primary role for a company's information system (Dilton-Hill, 1993) is to provide an integrated understanding of the financial and operational position of the company in a dynamic business environment and should have the following characteristics:

(a) *be flexible enough to change as the business does;*
(b) *support the company's strategy;*
(c) *provide multiple views of the same data;*
(d) *provide a balanced scorecard of operational and financial performance measures;*
(e) *support a process/activity view of the business, in addition to a functional view;*
(f) *provide for the fast collection and dissemination of data;*
(g) *utilise exceptions, alerts, rules, trend analysis and other such tools to guard against information overload.*

Figure 52:1, Web-enabled information management, shows how a modern IT environment would cope with transaction processing and then pass this to a data warehouse. On top of which would sit business intelligence tools, which in turn would analyse the data and disseminate the information electronically via such tools as EIS, portals, internet and the intranet. The process of designing such a system along with some of the technology available is explained in the sections below.

Figure 52:1 **Web-enabled Information management**

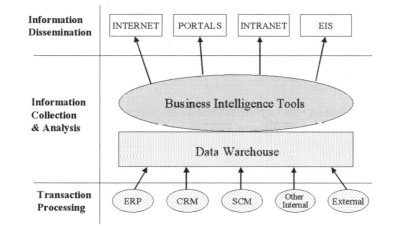

52:3 Understand the Latest Technological Developments

- Enterprise-wide systems, e.g. Enterprise Resource Planning (ERP), Middleware.

- Company-wide desktop personal tools operating as self-service centres, like Microsoft Office and Lotus SMARTSuite products, including such applications as word-processing, spreadsheets, databases, mapping tools, project management, shared diaries, organisers, internal mail, compression software, web browsers and presentational tools.

- Personalised portals enable employees to access selected data, information and services, from internal and external sources – both to help them with their jobs and to enable inputting of source data into the integrated company-wide systems. Examples would include: direct input of hours worked into payroll system (manually or by reader); interactive learning systems. Business to employee (B2E) systems are an important component of the web-enabled organisation.

- The internet has revolutionised the way in which organisations can conduct their business through end-to-end, web-enabled systems linking directly to suppliers and partners (B2B), and customers (B2C). Business Community Integration and Electronic Application Integration (EAI) Middleware; Supply Chain Management (SCM); Customer Relationship Management (CRM), internet standards and security; web services; Application Service Providers (ASP); telecommunications services, technologies and mobile devices.

- Collaborative Computing – through such tools as Workflow, Document Management Systems and Groupware, making the need for manual intervention in processes redundant.

- Business intelligence tools are essential for organisations to turn the mass of data produced from its ERP and other systems into a form in which it can be accessed and turned into meaningful, relevant, timely information. For example, the Manchester Housing case study has a balanced scorecard, utilising Business Objects and the intranet to display its information to all staff (*see* **para.52:6**).

The other technological developments discussed above have been dealt with in detail in Business Process Management (May 2002).

52:4 Formulating a Company-wide Information Strategy

52:4.1 Set Up a Project Team

The information manager needs to start the process by setting up and leading a project team of colleagues, representative of all parts of the organisation.

52:4.2 Analyse Existing Company, Supplier and Customer Systems

This includes systems local to individual departments, some of which may be PC and some manually based. Look also outside the organisation to possible links into the systems of suppliers and customers. These days the use of electronic commerce and business to business (B2B) integration through Electronic Data Interchange (EDI) and extensible mark-up language (XML) standards, working in partnership with suppliers and customers, often removes the need for paper and duplicate keying of data as well as speeding up such processes. Analyse the key features of these systems, including:

- inputs;

- outputs;

- frequency of use;

- purposes;

- interfaces with other systems;

- technical requirements.

52:4.3 Analyse 'Future' Business Needs

Although it is not the intention when setting out, often under pressure of time constraints far too many IT implementation teams simply end up replacing legacy systems with new ones, which operate in exactly the same way as the old ones. It is essential to re-engineer processes and design in new high-level management techniques that allow the organisation to add value continually. Examples include:

- value-based management (*see* **Ch.37A**);

- process-based management;

- balanced scorecard (*see* **Ch.49, para.49:2.3**);

- integrated performance-management;

- decision-support;

- business intelligence;

- improved and standardised end-to-end community-wide processes;

- benchmarking (*see* **Ch.53**);

- business process re-engineering (*see* **Ch.32**);

- priority-based budgeting;

- forecasting and resource allocation.

52:4.4 Consult Independent Experts

These may be specialists and/or potential outsourcers/partners. Remember that this is one of the most important decisions that the organisation will make, not just in terms of an IT investment strategy costing tens of millions but in making an essential contribution to the company's future ability to compete successfully.

52:4.5 Prepare the Business Case

Compile a detailed and compelling business case, evaluating all the benefits, costs and risks of all the elements of the proposed implementation project. Following the very large IT projects at the end of the 1990s driven by Y2K, many of which overran in terms of budget and time and often failed to deliver on promised objectives, organisations are being far more cautious in their approval of IT spending in the 21st century. Projects are often smaller and targeted to a specific improvement/development that is deliverable and certain to pay off in the short term. It is no longer acceptable for IT to be mismanaged and it is more likely than ever that it will be put under the overall control of the finance function.

52:4.6 Consult Widely

While time is of the essence in moving towards new technological advantage, remember that the new transformed finance function no longer prescribes what information the business needs but facilitates the provision of relevant information for operational managers. It is they who will be using it and therefore they who can offer constructive thought on the design. It is, therefore, strongly advisable to win support from all parts of the enterprise before proceeding with implementation. This will lessen the pain later.

52:4.7 Continuous Improvement

Once the system is installed, it is important that a culture of continuous review and improvement is adopted. It is recommended that, at a minimum, an annual audit should be undertaken.

52:5 Knowledge Management

Figure 52:2, From information to business intelligence, shows that information is about understanding relationships, knowledge is about understanding patterns and trends and wisdom about understanding principles. However, a collection of data is not information, a collection of information is not knowledge, a collection of knowledge is not wisdom and a collection of wisdom is not truth.

Figure 52:2 **From information to business intelligence**

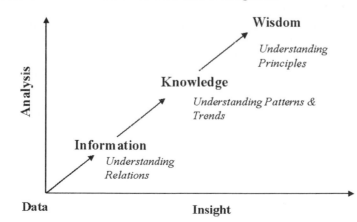

Research (*Sloan Management Review*, 2000) reveals that Chief Knowledge Officers have two principal design competencies:

1. *they are technologists, able to understand which technologies can contribute to capturing, storing, exploring and sharing knowledge; and*
2. *environmentalists, able to create social environments that stimulate and facilitate arranged and chance conversations or to develop events and processes to encourage deliberate knowledge creation and exchange.*

Characteristics include breadth of career experience, familiarity with their organisations and infectious enthusiasm for their mission. Knowledge management (KM) initiatives need to address the basic cultural and organisational issues of how knowledge is shared, distributed and created and how these processes relate to key business goals. The success of an IT solution in KM is in how well it encourages the necessary interaction between people and knowledge sharing culture within the organisation.

Cap Gemini Ernst & Young (Matthews, 2000) has one of the largest knowledge infrastructures in the world, and needs to use this knowledge daily to win work and improve its service to its clients. E&Y's intranet the KnowledgeWeb or KWeb is used by its 85,000 professionals based all over the world. The KWeb, which was developed and maintained by its Centre for Business Knowledge, consists of a web-based front-end, which is linked to an extensive back-end that includes information retrieval technology from Verity, Lotus Notes/Domino databases, web pages and others. The challenge was to bring all the discrete repositories of knowledge content together in one architecture that could be searched by an engine similar to those available on the public internet in that it uses key words or phrases. Since information is classified into information directories organised by familiar business categories, taxonomic searches are also possible, allowing users to navigate information directories easily and combining searching and browsing for more intuitive knowledge discovery.

Law firms are also reliant on large amounts of paperwork and by adopting document management systems can become more productive and competitive. Legal firm McGrigor Donald, uses iManage as it provided a solution with a minimum amount of tailoring and support at a price affordable to a smaller firm that has all transactions now wholly electronic and automated. The features that were most valued are its sheer speed of searching for data across the database, the accuracy of that data and the overall resilience of the system.

52:6 Decision Support and Business Intelligence Tools

Business intelligence (BI) systems enable a business professional to access the information which describes the enterprise – to analyse it, to gain insight into its workings and take action based on its findings. The aim is not just to gather large volumes of data from systems but to turn them into business intelligence to gain competitive advantage. The importance of having one integrated company-wide information system to support the performance management and decision-making process is the objective and it can be achieved with modern IT and provide good business intelligence. Gartner predict the market for BI software to grow to $7 billion by 2003 with over half the top companies having an e-intelligence capability. The growth is partly due to the internet, which allows companies to gather more information about customers and suppliers and share it with employees around the world, but equally driven by the demand of business to receive relevant timely information in place of volumes of data. Modern BI is simpler to use for both query and drill-down and no longer needs specialists. Many have added charting features, like drill-down, web maps and dashboard representations with a move to wireless technology enabling field workers to use a variety of devices. Intelligence is now in-built into the technology so that it can alert the user if a key performance indicator (KPI) is under-performing or calculate the likelihood of cross-selling to a given customer. Tools vary from OLAP and data-mining tools enabling companies to create their own BI systems to packaged applications like Cognos, InterBiz, Brio and Business Objects.

52:6.1 Data Warehousing

Data warehousing (Newing, 1996) allows companies to build, maintain and manage large amounts of data and query them at will. Data entering the warehouse from multiple sources are placed in a common format and then 'mined' for important information. The database software itself operates in a client/server architecture, usually needing very powerful servers. Features of data warehouses include:

(a) *transactional-level database, usually a relational database;*
(b) *the data warehouse holds a copy of data from other systems;*
(c) *used in conjunction with ERP, SCM, CRM and other packaged software to avoid degradation through excessive querying on the live system;*
(d) *its purpose is to optimise enquiries rather than data entry;*
(e) *it is time variant, i.e. date-stamped historical data;*
(f) *non-volatile data (static);*

(g) *often consisting of one or more data marts – a subset of the data warehouse or standalone covering, say, one function;*

(h) *it is organised by subject or entity not application;*

(i) *it can feed a multi-dimensional database, i.e. OLAP.*

See **Figure 52:3**, Advantages of data warehousing, which shows how it can improve quality while reducing costs.

Figure 52:3 **Advantages of data warehousing**

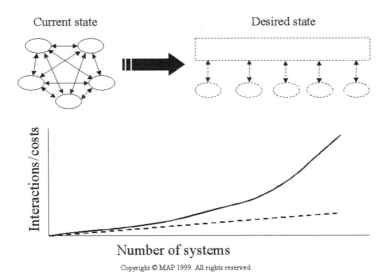

52:6.2 Online Analytical Processing (OLAP) and Decision-support Systems (DSS)

OLAP is a technology that enables users to gain insight into data through fast, consistent and interactive access to a wide variety of possible views of enterprise-wide information. OLAP products, such as iTM1, Essbase and Microsoft SQL, transfer the data to a separate multi-dimensional database for accounts using a spreadsheet link, like Visual Basic. OLAP occurs in many forms with greatly varying features and functionality, offering different advantages and disadvantages for both IT and end users. These include:

- cost;

- level of detail;

- data capacity;

- speed of operation;

- types, e.g. Desktop OLAP (DOLAP) and JOLAO (Java OLAP).

The terms decision-support systems, enterprise information systems (EIS) and management information systems (MIS) appear interchangeable and refer to end-user information-delivery systems that come in all shapes and sizes, offering simply managed queries or more complex drilling and simulation. These tools often incorporate OLAP. Most of the DSS tools could be used to access data directly from source applications, but the data warehouse provides the ideal foundation for integrating the data and taking it off-line, and as such is becoming increasingly popular as part of modern IT architecture.

Global Networking giant, 3Com (Longworth, 2000), has implemented a SAP & Peoplesoft ERP system, which feeds a massive data warehouse containing sales, service, manufacturing, distribution and financial information with daily snapshots. For analysis and reporting 3Com uses both Hyperion Essbase and multi-dimensional OLAP. This allows drag and drop and moves things into Excel and Business Objects, which is a desktop reporting tool creating links to a cube of data, which it stores in memory and then pulls answers to queries from the main database.

52:6.2.1 Process/activity-based DSS

Organisations have recognised the need to link strategy to operational performance through identifying those drivers that create value. Integrated performance management illustrates the necessity of linking any value-based management initiative, to strategy with a balanced scorecard, and underpinning it with detailed process/activity-based management information, that drills down through the organisation to ensure that all decision-making is properly informed. Having established the need for process/activity-based information, this should be designed into the heart of the IT systems, not treated as a 'bolt-on extra'. Most ERP systems are process based.

Specialist vendors produce linked modules for process mapping, activity-based costing, customer profitability, process-based management (May, 2002), priority-based budgeting, performance measurement and balanced scorecards, in addition to link engines to manipulate data between external systems and report-writing tools. These modules are linked to a common database, which holds the central process/activity analysis, integral to most ERP solutions around which all the other techniques are based. Full integration of DSS tools with ERP or other packaged software must be the best solution and at the start of the new millennium most software vendors have developed these tools or formed alliances with specialist DSS vendors. A review of the functionality provided by the top 18 accounting software vendors (*Top 18 accounting software vendors review*, 2000), shows that all either have their own module or a recognised partnership to deliver ABC analysis. **Figure 52:4**, DSS and ERP alliances, shows some of these links between products.

Figure 52:4 **DSS and ERP alliances**

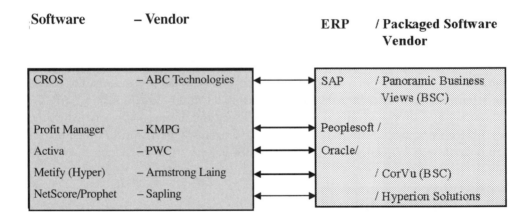

52:6.2.2 DSS Selection Criteria

- User-friendly – providing ease of use and accessibility and graphical presentation.

- Integrated – providing the ability to access information which is financial, non-financial, internal, external, quantitative and qualitative from many different base systems and applications.

- Integrity – the data held must be consistent, robust and inspire confidence.

- Multi-user capabilities – providing information to all users across the organisation.

- Multi-dimensional – provide the ability to view information across multiple dimensions, e.g. by department, by process, by channel, by SBU, etc.

- Responsive – needs to be interactive and responsive to changing conditions.

- Size – must be able to cope with volumes of data, calculations and number of users.

52:6.2.3 Enterprise Business Planning Tools

Many of the new planning and budgeting applications use complex databases designed to help firms monitor, report, analyse and react to developments in their business in a timely manner. Latest developments in this area include support for activity-based budgeting, continual planning and web-based collaboration. Packages include:

- *SAS CFOVision* – web-based financial consolidation, analysis and reporting together with budgeting and planning.

- *Adaytum e Planning 2.2* – web-based solution for enterprise business planning, providing an online forecast into likely future operating performance. It contains modules with financial analysts, line managers, executives and administrators in mind and combines planning and modelling with budget, sales forecasting and workflow.

- *Comshare MPC 4.0* – planning, budgeting, consolidation, management, reporting and analysis application that runs over the web.

- *Hyperion Planning and Modelling 2.0* – the solutions align day-to-day operations with more strategic tasks to aid more informed decision making, providing organisations with the ability to move beyond traditional budgeting.

52:6.3 Enterprise Information Portal (EIP)

Enterprise Information Portal (EIP) technology utilises a web browser interface to give employees access to various data and information systems. They are modelled on internet portals, like Yahoo and Ask Jeeves, which enable a search to be carried out to extract the relevant information. Most EIP products will allow search, retrieval, filtering, knowledge mapping, document management, workflow and personalisation. Portals do not solve the incompatibility problems of proprietary software; they simply avoid them – they provide a gateway to look at things. By embedding application program interfaces (API) into the portals, often dubbed pagelets, portlets or gadgets, the need for complicated back-end integration between programs is eliminated – data gets integrated at the portal level. Vendors, like Peoplesoft's CFO Portal and Plumtree, have developed finance-specific packages, although many organisations have developed their own in house via their employee portals. The use of portals by the largest organisations is expected to rise from 50% in 2001 to 85% in 2003.

Hewlett Packard spent $20m constructing its employee portal (B2E) in 2000 providing a gateway, called @HP, to 90,000 employees in 150 countries to, among other things, update human resources records, change benefit electives and book business trips. Hewlett Packard claims that in its first year it has delivered a ROI of $50m.

Ford Motor Company replaced about 1,000 intranets, each serving individual business units around the world, with a single portal for the whole organisation, using Plumtree. This enables staff in any part of the organisation to retrieve information from other parts in addition to removing the need to maintain duplicate data on local intranets. One example of savings made by Ford is the use of its portal to display and access pay-slips, which are estimated at $18m a year.

52:6.4 Website and CRM Analytics

E-commerce has enabled the collection of vast amounts of customer data that can be analysed. So-called web-mining enables companies to measure site usability, gain a better understanding of user behaviour and make significant improvements to their web-sites. internet server logs provide data that when combined with personal data obtained from customers builds up highly detailed marketing intelligence. This in turn informs customer support and service strategy decisions to improve user experience and sales. Methods of data collection include:

(a) *HTTP server log analysis – log entry for each HTTP request containing details of number of hits, number of visitors, visitor duration, visitor origin, visitor IP address, platform, browser type and version.*
(b) *Server monitors through Application Programmer Interface (API) – unique visitor IDs, referrer pages.*
(c) *Network monitors – client requests, server responses, cookies, stop requests, server response times, form data transmitted and HTML files.*

These data then need to be fed into a relational data warehouse to permit analysis through web-mining and analytics tools like Hyperion's Web Site Analysis suite. This service is also available through ASP, e.g. IBM's web traffic analysis service Surfaid, specialises in the collection and integration of very high volume data and was used during the Sydney Olympics. Xelector, a Dublin-based financial service operation calls itself a B2B2C operator, sitting between product providers and portals like First-e, the internet bank. Its aim is to collect information in the financial services industry and analyse it to remove the need for 'gut feel' decisions. The company uses SAS e-intelligence suite and Questor reporting tools.

Pharmaceutical outsourcing company Innovex (Longworth, 2000), has 600 representatives collecting data electronically using electronic territory management system (ETMS). BO WebIntelligence is used to disseminate the information to low-level users. A cube satisfies 95% of the need for standard reporting, which includes 40 key business measures pre-calculated across six dimensions – time, geography, product, etc. – on a weekly basis. For those that need more flexibility they can carry out ad hoc enquiries.

Whitbread Beer Company has installed a web-based Informix database management system which resides on an IBM RS/6000, with over 100 sales and marketing cubes created by Cognos Powerplay and Impromtu. Staff use laptop computers running Windows NT to access the data through the web.

52:7 Case Study: Data Warehousing at Nationwide[1]

52:7.1 Background

Nationwide Life and Nationwide Unit Trust Managers were formed as the regulated financial services subsidiaries of Nationwide Building Society. They began trading in January 1996, offering good-value products to customers introduced through the society's branch network. Development of the systems and processes took over two years, from a greenfield site in Swindon. A substantial part of the operation was outsourced to third parties.

It was obvious that implementation of a management reporting function faced a number of challenges. As requirements specification was taking place while the full management team was still being recruited, requirements were changing and the systems architecture was still developing, an adaptive approach was essential. With around a dozen production systems being developed, a client/server data-warehousing approach was chosen for the provision of management information. Although this was a high-risk approach relative to the traditional method of report production from production systems, the advantages far outweighed the downside. Those advantages are:

(a) ability to produce ad hoc reports;
(b) local control of reporting;
(c) low development costs;
(d) flexibility of reporting;
(e) ability to analyse data across diverse systems;
(f) ability to produce operational reporting.

52:7.2 The Specification

The system was developed around a high-specification central server, with distributed report access available from around 50 local client PCs using a graphical query tool. This allowed access to pre-defined reports where the user chose report parameters and provided the ability to produce ad-hoc queries with 'super user' training – no reports are produced centrally for paper distribution to these users. Furthermore, the system allows different data views to different categories of user.

The system was built from the bottom upwards – including tackling the issues of data integrity, quality, consistency and control across different platforms. This approach to data warehouse development permits the system to be used as the basis of an executive information system. Data warehousing permits analysis of the complete lifecycle of a product sale, from initial customer contact to post-sale events.

The data warehouse approach represents an ideal solution in a multi-platform systems environment, allowing consolidation of atomic-level business data from diverse systems on to a central relational database. Such an implementation requires less analysis of data, but carried a greater overhead in future development of the system, which can largely be carried out locally by the system administrator.

52:7.3 Management Reporting Solution

Delivery of a system was a small (but key) part of the development of the management reporting solution. This involved addressing cultural and educational issues around implementation of a solution, addressing data and information ownership, development of critical success factors and key performance indicators and a monitoring basis for all business areas.

An integrated balanced business scorecard approach was adopted for management reporting, aligning the corporate vision with guiding principles and a balanced business plan. The emphasis was not on just the traditional financial measures but also on non-financial business measures (*see* **Fig.52:5**, Nationwide balanced scorecard).

Figure 52:5 **Nationwide balanced scorecard**

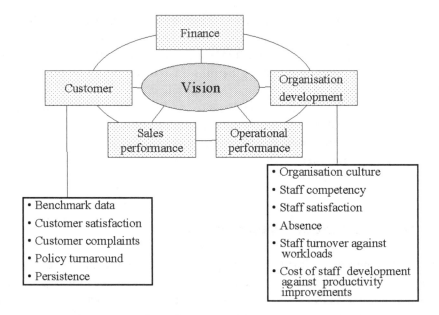

The objective was to divide company reporting to monitor performance against the corporate vision and values (customer perspective, organisation development, sales performance and operational performance). These are the business determinants that deliver financial performance, the ultimate consequence of corporate success. Although traditional monthly management accounts have tended to focus on financial measures alone, they have not monitored the 'levers' that drive corporate performance.

The board information pack is a largely graphical balanced scorecard of mainly non-financial measures, providing information and detailed analysis of results. This includes a section on organisational development, measuring a number of human resources performance measures:

(a) organisation culture;
(b) staff competency;
(c) staff satisfaction;
(d) absence and staff turnover against workloads;
(e) costs of staff development against productivity improvements.

Benchmark data are used to measure performance against the industry.

The customer perspective covers the following areas:

- customer satisfaction;

- customer complaints;

- policy turnaround;

- persistence.

52:7.4 Transformation of the Finance Function

With a high level of automation of reporting, the management accounting function can devote resources to providing value-added support to the business, as opposed to the traditional view of the finance function as a group of 'beancounters' producing historical financial information. This transformation of management accounting needs to be implemented in a number of ways:

(a) development of a vision for the finance function;
(b) establishment of guiding principles;
(c) alignment of objectives with corporate goals;
(d) measurement of team performance, including customer satisfaction;
(e) benchmarking against best practice;
(f) measurement of productivity;
(g) application of quality processes and standards.

Traditionally, the management accounting function has measured performance of the operation, but has rarely had the confidence to measure its own performance. The result of such a focus has been to stifle continuous improvement and limit the influence of finance within the organisation. The alternative is to establish metrics to monitor performance, measuring performance and implementing a development plan to improve the service provided by finance.

The measurement of finance performance exposes the function to the same disciplines that operational areas of the company have. Priorities of the finance function can be easily established through consultation with its customer areas: what are the key corporate objectives and how can finance help the company achieve these?

52:7.5 Conclusion

Corporate priorities can be ranked in terms of both short- and long-term importance to establish a comprehensive strategic plan for the organisation, resulting in an action plan for future development. A formal monitoring framework will allow progress reporting against the action plan.

It is important to manage resource to minimise the part of that resource dedicated to operational activities and increase the amount of time available to perform value-added tasks. This involves managing the balance between 'urgent' and 'important' – investment in the latter produces significantly greater returns.

In conclusion, management reporting has developed into a proactive commercial management function, committed to adding maximum value to the business through the implementation of leading-edge solutions to business problems. The emphasis has moved from reporting historical financial statistics to analysing the full range of business determinants and influencing corporate strategy.

Note

[1] Nationwide case study written by Abhai Rajguru, former Nationwide Management Information Controller, published in *Management Accounting* and by IFAC in 1997, as part of a piece of research by Margaret May entitled *Preparing organisations to manage the future*.

References

CIMA Technical Services (2000) *Information management – the fundamentals, CIMA,* 2000.

Dilton-Hill, Kevin G. (1993) 'Management information to support a world-class company', *Accountancy SA,* May.

Longworth, David (2000) 'High standards', *Computers and Finance,* April.

Matthews, Guy (2000) article in *Management Consultancy,* December.

May, Margaret (2002) *Business process management, integration in a web-enabled environment.* Pearson FT Executive Briefing.

Newing, Rod (1996) 'Data warehousing', *Management Accounting,* March.

Sloan Management Review (2000) Chief Knowledge Officers.

Top 18 accounting software vendors review (2000) CFO Europe, May.

53. Benchmarking

53:1 Introduction

This section explains what the term 'benchmarking' means and why the practice is so popular. There then follows some simple guidelines on the range of costs and time a project can take.

53:1.1 What is Benchmarking?

In the Chambers Twentieth Century Dictionary, the term 'benchmark' has the following explanation: 'A surveyor's mark cut on a rock, etc. indicating a point of reference in levelling (from its horizontal line forming a bench for a levelling instrument)'.

Benchmarking is a technique that is used to identify appropriate best practice, which leads to superior performance. The most commonly used definition for it is that given by David T. Kearns, Chairman of the Xerox Corporation between 1982 and 1990, which is, that benchmarking is: 'the continuous process of measuring our products, services and practices against our toughest competition, or those renowned as leaders'.

Benchmarking is often viewed as a tool, which compares and measures performance. In one sense this is correct if comparing benchmarks as set out in the dictionary. However, using the findings merely to compare results at a given time does not justify the resources used to achieve the results; or make full use of the benefits that can be obtained if the results are used to identify areas for performance improvement. This is shown in **Figure 53:1**.

Figure 53:1 *Benchmarking and performance*

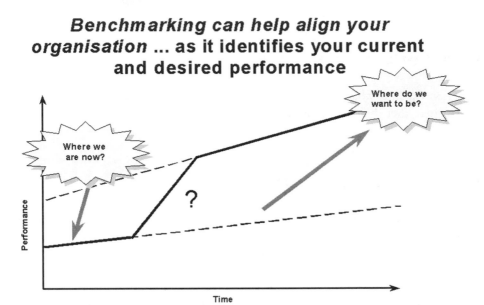

Benchmarking can help align your organisation ... as it identifies your current and desired performance

To demonstrate this application of benchmarking, the difference between *benchmarks* and *benchmarking* should be considered. Benchmarks are measures, usually shown as a percentage, ratio or cost – for example, return on sales or cost per invoice. Benchmarking is the process of comparing and learning how a process is undertaken in a better way. This is extremely interesting in pointing out to an organisation how it compares with others, however it will only identify the performance gaps, not provide the answers to why there is a gap or how those organisations who perform better have achieved their position. Following a series of steps, benchmarking can identify the qualitative practices that explain better or best practice.

Two examples illustrate this point. The first example is of a global organisation producing consumer products. The Executive Board set a benchmark of closing the management accounts within three days of the month end. This was achieved but at the expense of putting aside other activities such as reconciling the tax accounts. The second example is from the Italian branch of a retailing group. Their senior management did not wish to appear at the bottom of the group for transaction processing and therefore reverted back to processing invoices individually rather than in batches. This resulted in a very high productivity per employee and low cost per invoice but of course, this was not sustainable over a period of time and did not truly reflect high performance.

53:1.2 Why Is It So Popular?

Leading-edge organisations continually benchmark for the following reasons. To:

(a) *have a better awareness of what, how and how well they are performing;*
(b) *have a better awareness of what, and how well competitors, industry and best-in-class are performing;*
(c) *gain an external perspective and create internal team spirit;*
(d) *respond to outside pressures such as losing market share, dissatisfied customers, uncompetitive performance, impending privatisation;*
(e) *validate strategy or provide empirical evidence to substantiate perceptions;*
(f) *cure denial problems;*
(g) *identify what needs to be improved, why and how.*

These are some of the reasons and indeed benchmarking can bring many types of benefits such as those outlined below.

53:1.2.1 Cost Reduction

A project can identify and quantify the potential financial savings in implementing what has been learnt through benchmarking. A major retailer benchmarked their finance function across Europe and identified savings representing 0.4% of sales through improving three of their processes. This represented £2.2m for this particular organisation. Improvements included standardisation of processes, adoption of standard software packages and rationalisation of suppliers.

53:1.2.2 Customer Satisfaction

By improving those processes that have an impact upon the customer, customer satisfaction can be directly improved. A pharmaceuticals organisation started its performance improvement activities by first benchmarking customer requirements. They identified what was important to the customer and how their performance was perceived relative to competitors. This highlighted what the organisation needed to improve and maintain and what processes could be streamlined to improve efficiency. The customer requirements benchmarking identified that a large product range was not perceived to be that important and that customers were prepared to wait for delivery provided that they knew the delivery date and could depend upon the product arriving on the due date. This enabled the organisation to outsource delivery moving from six warehouse operations to arrangements with three third-party distributors. The benefits included the reduction of products from 1,000 to 350 products with no loss of revenue together with cost savings estimated at almost $10 million over a five-year period.

53:1.2.3 Increased Efficiency

Benchmarking can help to streamline processes. For example, introducing BACS and instituting minimum expense claim levels can improve the accounts payable process.

53:1.2.4 Increased Effectiveness

Benchmarking can identify how to deliver a better service by identifying better practices adopted by other companies. A company, for instance, introduced a simple form for every new employee which asked them to specify what training courses they had attended and which software skills they had. They entered this onto a database, creating a resource pool of capability, thereby increasing the effectiveness of their staff.

A benchmarking project which links to the organisation's objectives, is managed well and creates a willingness to change can reap considerable benefits. One of the earliest examples of the benefits benchmarking can bring starts with Xerox. Xerox recognised that Japanese competitors were selling copiers in the US at a lower price, and Xerox lost over half of its market share by the early 1980s. It then used benchmarking to reduce its manufacturing costs by 50% and cut product development cycles by 25%. Rover benchmarked itself against Honda and subsequently halved its test times. Other cases include British Rail and British Airways, Rank Xerox and LL Bean, General Motors and AC Deco Systems.

In conclusion, benchmarking can answer the following questions for an organisation:

(a) *How good are we?*
(b) *How good can we be?*
(c) *From whom can we learn?*
(d) *How can we improve?*

53:1.3 How Much Will It Cost And How Long Will It Take?

Obviously benchmarking projects vary considerably both in terms of cost and length of time to complete. A brief comparative study of measures can be undertaken in a matter of weeks, although a minimum of three months should be allowed to successfully plan, communicate and carry out a project. The highest cost element will be the time that the project team puts into the exercise. However there is also the associated time for employee and senior management involvement. Simple exercises using publicly available data, published reports or the internet can be undertaken for as little as £500 but typically, the costs are more in the region of £5,000 upwards. It is advisable therefore to prepare a business case outlining the benefits and potential financial savings that could be achieved. Here, some case study information about the achievement of leading-edge organisations is generally useful. For example, citing empirical evidence such as the two examples that follow will demonstrate there could be significant functional and performance gains in benchmarking. The first example is the computer manufacturer that adopted electronic payments with Oracle and created a shared service centre, therefore reducing the cost of finance from 1.7% to 1% of revenue. The second example is the chemical manufacturer that centralised two processes and adopted SAP, saving $20m across their operations (source, KPMG).

53:2 What to Measure

This section describes how to select a subject to benchmark. By describing the various levels and approaches, a clear understanding of which areas will provide the most opportunity for performance improvement can be selected. The components of each element of this section are illustrated in **Figure 53:2**. This illustration can be used to design and tailor a benchmarking project and the Figure shows the various selection points in the process.

Figure 53:2 **Approaches**

Designing the benchmarking project

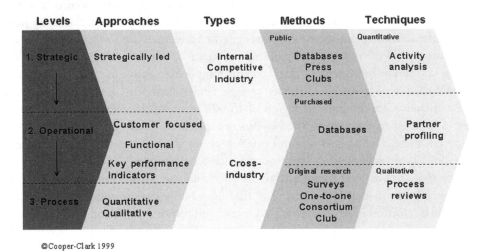

©Cooper-Clark 1999

Sometimes it is quite clear which areas should be compared. This may be because they have high costs or they may be the cause of poor performance across the organisation. An easy way to make a selection based on profit improvement potential would be to analyse the operating expenses and create a pie chart showing the relative costs as a percentage of revenue. Then, carry out industry comparisons and identify those operating costs which are significantly higher than the industry.

The areas that may benefit most from comparison with other organisations may be less clear and there are a number of different approaches, which may help with this selection.

53:2.1 Levels of Benchmarking

There are three levels of benchmarking, namely strategic, operational and process. Strategic focuses upon issues such as market share, shareholder value or organisational structure. Projects at this level will compare the organisation in its entirety.

Operational benchmarking involves comparing organisational performance in areas such as customer satisfaction, supply chain or overheads. There will be a number of functions contributing to the performance.

The third level is process benchmarking. A process is a group of activities that can be linked together for example, accounts receivable or accounts payable. Very often a process runs across many functions and some organisations have structured themselves to take this into account. One example is the purchase to pay process.

An illustration of the levels of benchmarking is shown in **Figure 53:3**.

Figure 53:3 **Levels of benchmarking**

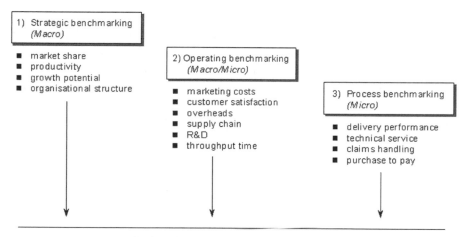

```
┌─────────────────────────────┐
│ 1)  Strategic benchmarking   │
│     (Macro)                  │
└─────────────────────────────┘

  ▪ market share
  ▪ productivity              ┌──────────────────────────────┐
  ▪ growth potential          │ 2) Operating benchmarking     │
  ▪ organisational structure  │    (Macro/Micro)              │
                              └──────────────────────────────┘

                                ▪ marketing costs           ┌──────────────────────────────┐
                                ▪ customer satisfaction      │ 3)  Process benchmarking      │
                                ▪ overheads                  │     (Micro)                   │
                                ▪ supply chain              └──────────────────────────────┘
                                ▪ R&D
                                ▪ throughput time             ▪ delivery performance
                                                              ▪ technical service
                                                              ▪ claims handling
                                                              ▪ purchase to pay
```

Goal: Achieve competitive advantage

← Benchmarking can be applied across all levels and activities →

Benchmarking should start at the highest level that can be managed. For example, benefits will be limited if delivery performance is dramatically improved but the product delivered is not what the customer requires. This was demonstrated in practice with a photocopier organisation that decided to improve their repair call-out time. They invested substantial resources and managed to reduce significantly the time from call to operator arrival. The sales team visited the customers and asked for their perceptions on the service improvement. The customers' response was 'that's all very well but what I really want is for the machine not to break down, similar to what your competitors are offering'. What the team should have selected was product reliability. This would have been identified if the team had first benchmarked customer satisfaction to identify the customers' requirements.

53:2.2 Benchmarking Approaches

53:2.2.1 Strategically Led Approach

If the organisation's strategy, objectives and relative market position are well understood, then the strategically led approach is an ideal way to identify what to measure. All approaches to benchmarking should be aligned to the strategy and objectives of the business. By linking the benchmarking study to the company's strategy the project can identify areas for improvement which will make significant contributions to the organisation's ability to meet its goals. The approach is illustrated in **Figure 53:4**.

Figure 53:4 **Strategically led approach**

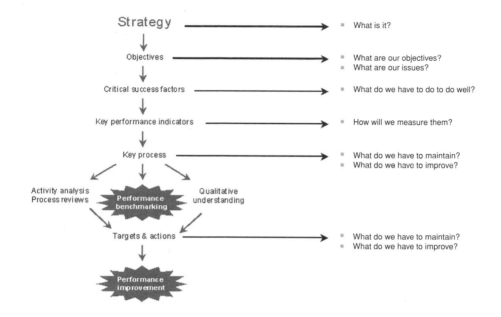

This approach has the following steps.

(a) *Understand the strategy using such tools as Porter's five-forces framework, namely viewing the organisation from perspectives of existing competition, new competition, substitution of products or services, customer power and supplier power. Alternatively, another framework is PEST analysis with political, economic, social and technological perspectives.*

(b) *Understand the objectives arising from the strategy.*

(c) *Translate the objectives into critical success factors (CSF), also known as 'Do Wells'. These are the activities that must be undertaken well to achieve the objective. For instance customer satisfaction is critical to increasing market share and appropriate stock levels would contribute to cost reduction.*

(d) *Identify the processes which link to the critical success factors and are therefore key to the success of the business. Processes that link to customer satisfaction would be all of those that form 'points of contact' with the customer. These would be the potential processes to benchmark.*

53:2.2.2 Operational Benchmarking Approaches

(*See* **Chs** 48 and 49.)

There are three operational approaches, namely the key performance indicator, functional and customer-focused approaches.

53:2.2.2.1 Key Performance Indicator Approach

This approach · reviews all of the organisation's operations, comparing performance against a number of benchmarks called key performance indicators (KPI). These indicators will cross a number of operational areas. The steps involved are as follows.

> (a) *Identify the key performance indicators that relate to the organisation. These can be related to the critical success factors identified in the strategically led method. For example, if the CSF were customer satisfaction, one of the KPIs would be delivery time.*
> (b) *Compare the organisation's performance on the KPIs with similar operations using the chosen approaches (see* **Fig.53:2***) and identify those with a performance gap.*
> (c) *Identify the processes that contribute to the chosen KPIs.*

53:2.2.2.2 Functional Approach

This approach assumes that the function, or functions, has been identified as having improvement potential. Very often the functional head wishes to understand current performance or is responsible for performance improvement in the organisation and wishes to use a function which is easy to benchmark as a pilot study.

The approach is similar to that described under process benchmarking (*see* **para.53:6**) but will compare performance at a higher level. For example function costs as a percentage revenue and number of functional employees/total employees.

53:2.2.2.3 Customer-focused Approach

This approach identifies what is important to the customer and how the organisation performs on these priorities relative to competitors. It then identifies what needs to be improved to increase customer satisfaction. The approach takes the following steps.

(a) *Hold a workshop with key managers to allocate the customers into segments based on buying attributes. The managers then identify what is important to the customer and how the organisation performs relative to its competitors. This step forms the framework for subsequent customer research and obtains a consensus of customer requirements within the organisation.*

(b) *Repeat the process with a number of key customers in each segment.*

(c) *Identify the product and service attributes which are important to the customer and where performance is weak relative to competitors.*

(d) *Link attributes to processes. For example, performance on delivery times is an output of purchasing, stock levels, manufacturing, warehousing and distribution. This step identifies the processes that would be most beneficial to benchmark.*

The customer-focused approach is a useful way to test and validate strategy with customers before proceeding with customer service changes. The results can sometimes be surprising as illustrated in the following two examples.

A pharmaceuticals organisation wished to develop a European supply-chain strategy. The customer-focused method was used and the findings identified that customers in France, Germany and Italy had the same priorities, namely speed to market. The processes relating to delivery were benchmarked and better practices were found for production scheduling and distribution. Another pharmaceuticals organisation used the same approach but found that each of the local markets had different priorities. The priority for one market was delivery time. For another it was product innovation and for the third it was responsiveness. The findings for this organisation were that they should develop a standard European supply chain, but build in sufficient flexibility to meet the different local market requirements.

53:3 How to Measure

This section outlines the different types of benchmarking, for instance, industry, competitive or cross-industry. The various approaches are then covered, such as publicly available data, finding benchmarking partners or using consultants. The section then reviews the types of measure, both quantitative and qualitative and what is meant by best practice.

53:3.1 Types of Benchmarking

Once the method has been agreed there are a number of options for whom to benchmark with. The focus could be internal, competitive/industry or cross-industry. These are not mutually exclusive and successful benchmarking projects have been carried out which use all three types (*see* **Fig.53:2**).

53:3.1.1 Internal

This usually applies to larger organisations but if there is any duplication of processes, it is sometimes useful to compare how they are undertaken and identify and share internal better practices. This is particularly useful if the organisation is new to benchmarking, as it will use existing definitions and terminology.

Enabling technology can facilitate internal benchmarking through the use of systems that collect the quantitative information directly from data warehouses and ERP systems. This, however, does depend upon the level of standardised reporting across the organisation.

The prevailing culture has to be assessed when considering internal benchmarking. Nobody wishes to appear at the bottom of a league table and it is often easier to market a study by using external in addition to internal benchmarking.

53:3.1.2 Competitive/Industry

(*See* **Ch.7.**)

A number of industry associations and consultancies now facilitate regular benchmarking projects. The advantages are that you do not need to analyse market or operating characteristics to such a degree as all participants will be facing similar issues. As such, agreement on what to benchmark may be easier as they will focus on industry priorities. Any industry better practices will clearly demonstrate that the improved performance can be achieved in that market.

There are, however a number of issues to address. The first is whether competitors are willing to share information, particularly if they are market leaders. The benefits for each participant need to be clearly outlined. Another issue is concern over the confidentiality of data. The most popular solution is to use external consultants who can gather the data and feed back the information as ranges of performance without identifying particular organisations. With increased technology, another option is to develop a secure web page, managed by third-party consultants. Participants enter data using their own customised web page and reports are automatically generated online without the need for time-consuming and expensive workshops and meetings. This method does of course require in-built validation of the data and general maintenance by a contractor. The final consideration is that identification of an industry's best performance may not necessarily represent best practice. Above all, the Benchmarking Code of Conduct should be followed to ensure compliance with competition and anti-trust laws.

53:3.1.3 Cross-industry

This is probably the easiest method to consider if larger quantities of information are required. It can also identify practices that may not have been adopted within an industry and could thus lead to step change. It does, however, require some planning to ensure that issues such as industry drivers are taken into account. For example, the speed of growth within an industry could drive the rate of product or service innovation. Similarly, the concentration of competition could cause a focus on prices. These drivers need to be taken into account to ensure that comparisons are valid.

This technique, called 'partner profiling' as suggested in **Figure 53:2**, is illustrated in **Figure 53:5**. It involves identification of those operating characteristics that may impact upon performance. Drawing up the profile of the organisation assists in the identification of similar benchmarking partners.

Figure 53:5 **Drivers of performance**

Examples of drivers of performance

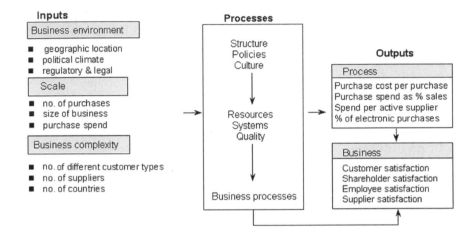

53:4 Benchmarking Methods

Once the level, approach and type of benchmarking have been selected, there are a number of data collection methods, which need to be considered (*see* **Fig.53:2**). These focus upon finding data and are grouped into categories: public, purchased and original research.

53:4.1 Public Data Method

There are a number of data sources available in the public domain and with the growth of the internet the range is expanding. A list of information sources is shown in **Appendix 53:2**. They include:

- library and database searches, including academia;

- company publications and websites;

- conferences;

- customers and suppliers.

53:4.2 Purchased Data Method

Consultancies hold databases along with analyst services such as Gartner and Forrester. The analyst services will provide a listing of reports with brief summaries of their contents. These have a fixed price and are readily available. Consultancies, however, usually offer a benchmarking service that includes collecting client data and benchmarking it with their own database. Obviously this is more expensive but it can be more detailed and prescriptive, that is, the data will be put into context with some conclusions and recommendations for future action.

53:4.3 Original Research Method

If there are insufficient data readily available or more detail is required, then original research should be considered.

The projects will take more time, however the level of detail and benefits in forming benchmarking partnerships with other organisations usually makes the exercise worthwhile. There are a number of different ways to use original research.

Original research offers a choice on the number of participants. The organisation could choose a one-to-one relationship with one or two partners. Alternatively a consortium, which is made up of a number of participants, which meet just for the purpose of the project, could be considered. The final choice would be developing a club, which meets on a regular basis on a number of different projects. One easier method is to join a benchmarking club or an industry association which facilitates benchmarking. A number of benchmarking organisations exists and they can provide member directories which a member can use to source potential partners. Alternatively, another easy method is to use external advisers. Consultancies often facilitate benchmarking projects, often finding other appropriate partners and comparing the findings with their own databases.

Detailed steps on how to conduct a benchmarking project using the original research approach is included in **paragraph 53:6**. This also includes elements on selecting appropriate partners.

53:5 Types of Measures

Once the approach has been selected (*see* **Fig.53:2**), some consideration should be given to the type of information required. This can be divided into two types: qualitative and quantitative.

53:5.1 Quantitative Data

This form of information is that usually shown in pie charts, histograms and league-tables and can be identified as a number, ratio, cost or percentage. For example, cycle days to complete an order or number of invoices per accounting employee. Successful benchmarking incorporates an element of both quantitative and qualitative measures. The advantages of quantitative data are that they are universally understood, easy to compare and logical. Quantified evidence forces an organisation to question its performance and can gain consensus amongst employees. Everyone understands the goal and progress towards this goal can be tracked and measured. The disadvantage is that quantitative data do not explain what is 'good' or 'bad' practice. They identify what the performance is but do not explain the cause of poor or excellent performance. Quantitative data also fail to indicate how to improve performance. League-tables will not identify which organisations are managing well despite their levels of complexity or are not benefiting from advantages such as economies of scale.

An example that illustrates this point is the Standard Chartered Bank (SCB). One of the recognised broad benchmarks for the efficiency of internal process in the banking sector is the cost/income ratio. In 1996, SCB had a ratio of 60% against an overall industry average of 50%. However, comparisons such as these can be misleading. Before drawing any conclusions about internal efficiency from comparative cost/income ratios, there are a number of operating characteristics which should be taken into account. At that time Standard Chartered's business spanned the globe. Its operations included a low-tech business in Africa, a spread of small branches and subsidiary operations in the Middle East to its core business in an emerging market in Asia. These were difficult to manage. To what extent does operating in 52 different countries drive up infrastructure costs compared to a business that operates in a single country? They did not have the benefits of standardised regulations and centralised processing. They also had relatively high environmental changes and a range of differing cultures. When these business characteristics are considered, it can be appreciated that a ratio of 60% showed that Standard Chartered was in fact managing its complexity very well.

53:5.2 Qualitative Data

Qualitative information describes a practice and explains how high performance is achieved. This is often referred to as best practice. For example, the use of e-commerce, integrated IT systems, supplier, customer or even competitor alliances.

Once the attributes of excellent performers are understood, action plans can be developed to implement the required changes. Qualitative comparison is very popular for self-assessment benchmarking exercises. Participants complete a form, which contains qualitative questions, linked to a scale, for example, one equals totally, five equals not at all. The rankings then show the range of replies and although there is an assumption that a certain score is good, there is no link between the operating characteristics, also known as performance drivers, and performance. There is, however, no quantified evidence of the impact of better practices on the bottom-line. Some may have a stronger, more direct impact than others. Using purely qualitative benchmarking to persuade Board members, management and employees that a radical change is required can be challenging. Qualitative information on how high performance is achieved is usually referred to as 'best practice'.

53:5.3 Best Practice

It is also worthwhile considering the term 'best practice'. First, to be given this term, there are a number of criteria which have to be fulfilled. These are that a best practice:

    (a) *must be sustainable over time and therefore will have a proven track record;*
    (b) *will have quantifiable benefits;*
    (c) *will be innovative and will be recognised by its peers as being creative;*
    (d) *will have a recognised positive outcome, recognised by other organisations and the press, having perhaps won an award.*

Secondly, the term implies a description of how an activity is undertaken in the best possible way. That is, at greatest speed, lowest cost and highest quality. However best practice is not necessarily generic. For example, a recognised best practice is the adoption of a shared service centre. This is a central processing unit which will undertake a number of activities for a group of businesses (e.g. financial processing, handling calls, payroll, etc.). Obviously implementing a shared service centre is inappropriate for either a small organisation or one with little transaction processing. Similarly, the adoption of e-commerce for customers may be inappropriate if the organisation has a small customer base who purchase single large-value items on an infrequent basis. Best practice examples should be viewed as a pool of empirical evidence of what can be achieved. The organisation then needs to consider the adoption of these practices in the light of whether they are within the control of the organisation, how the practice will contribute to the organisation's goals, the investment required to implement the best practice and the scale of the benefits the practice will bring to the organisation's performance.

For instance, it may be inappropriate to consider making large investments in IT if the organisation is restructuring, considering mergers or acquisitions or changing customer channel strategies.

53:6 How to Conduct an Exercise

The third level shown in the benchmarking approach (*see* **Fig.53:2**) refers to process benchmarking. A process is a series of linked activities, for example, accounts payable, or recruitment. The higher levels of strategic and operational will identify one or a number of processes, which require more detailed study. This is when a full benchmarking project should be considered. It may be that the organisation has already identified a process, which is clearly inefficient, generates high cost or, because it does not perform well, affects the organisation's objectives. If this were the case, then starting at this level would be appropriate. The project process is based on ten steps.

53:6.1 Agree Subject Scope

There are four activities related to the first step of scoping the project. These include selecting the process, reviewing the process, selecting the performance measures and designing a questionnaire.

The first action is to gain agreement on the objectives of the project and the level of expected change. Then, the level, approach, method and type as outlined in **paragraph 53:3** should be determined. The process should then be selected.

53:6.1.1 Process Selection

A process should always be defined across an organisation rather than within a function. Accounts payable involves the receipt, processing and subsequent payment of an invoice in the finance function. However the efficiency and effectiveness of this process may be related to other activities under the control of, for example the purchasing function. Therefore, when selecting a process it would be better to consider the purchase to pay process.

53:6.1.2 Process Review

The second activity in step one is to undertake a full review of the selected process. This should include flowcharting the process and identifying the resources involved in each step. This will provide an illustration of the activities and relationships with other functions.

53:6.1.3 Select Performance Measures

The third activity is to select the performance measures. Measures should be a balance of quantitative and qualitative. The quantitative should include:

(a) *cost: this will negate any potential conflict in comparing cost of living rates, exchange rates (if cross-country comparisons are made) and salary scales;*
(b) *cycle time: for example, number of days from customer order to delivery;*
(c) *productivity: for example, number of telephone calls per operator;*
(d) *quality: this may be more difficult but examples are percentage of invoices which require adjustment, returns as a percentage of deliveries, number of customer complaints and customer satisfaction ratings.*

53:6.1.4 Design Questionnaire

The final activity in step one is to design a questionnaire. Even if only one or two partners are considered, a structured questionnaire, with definitions, will ensure that the information is comparable. It will also demonstrate to partner organisations that the information requirements have been clearly identified and communicated. The questionnaire should not be more than six to ten pages.

53:6.2 Identify Appropriate Partners

Identifying appropriate partners is probably the most important step. Consideration must be given not just to those organisations that are noted to have high performance but also those who have similar objectives and operating characteristics. For instance, targeting Marks and Spencer may not be appropriate if the number of employees only totals 20,000 or the organisation only trades in one country. It should also be accepted that there are very few organisations that have best practice in every area of their business.

The most successful way to identify potential partners is to first select a potential list and then draw up the similarities by process. Similarities can be grouped under two headings, namely scale and complexity. For example scale will include turnover, number of employees, number of locations, number of customers, number of markets, market share, number of products. Complexity will relate to characteristics such as product range, distribution channels, customer segmentations, etc. that will affect how the activities are carried out. These similarities will also affect the process. For example number of applications will have an impact upon the recruitment process. Therefore, consideration should be given at both the strategic and process levels.

53:6.2.1 The Benchmarking Code of Conduct

The American Productivity and Quality Center and its subsidiary have developed this code with the International Benchmarking Clearinghouse and in association with several of its corporate members. Organisations who benchmark regularly are familiar with the Principles and will expect new partners to comply with them. They are as follows:

(a) *Principle of legality: this principle relates to the inappropriate use of data or activity, which could be improper and illegal. For instance, activities which may lead to an improper knowledge of a market or pricing, or trade secrets or sharing findings without permission from the source are strongly discouraged. If in doubt about the legality of an activity, avoid doing it.*

(b) *Principle of exchange: communicate fully and early to clarify expectations in the benchmarking exchange. Being honest and complete will provide the type and level of information that is required by your benchmarking partner.*

(c) *Principle of confidentiality: confidentially should be maintained throughout the benchmarking interchange, unless prior permission is granted to communicate externally.*

(d) *Principle of use: contact lists provided by external sources in any form should not be used for marketing without permission from the original source. In addition, information gained during the benchmarking project should only be used as agreed in the scope of the study.*

(e) *Principle of first party contact: respect the corporate culture of partner companies and work within mutually agreed procedures.*

(f) *Principle of third-party contact: avoid communicating a contact's name in an open forum without his or her prior permission.*

(g) *Principle of preparation: be prepared prior to making an initial benchmarking contact. Providing a questionnaire and agenda prior to the benchmarking visits can help this.*

(h) *Principle of completion: each commitment made to your benchmarking partners should be made in a satisfactory and timely manner as mutually agreed.*

(i) *Principle of understanding and action: understand how benchmarking partners would like to be treated and how they would like the information handled and used.*

For further details contact the American Productivity and Quality Center, 123 North Post Oak Lane, 3rd Floor, Houston, Texas 77024-7797.

53:6.3 Gather Data

The third step of the exercise is to gather data. If questionnaires have been used, it is useful to allow some time for consideration of the responses before arranging interviews. A subsequent interview is then recommended to gather qualitative information and supporting data for the answers provided in the questionnaire.

The options for gathering the data could include telephone surveys, mail surveys or personal interviews. Some guidelines are:

(a) *telephone surveys: questions should be prioritised and the interview should not take longer than 15 or 20 minutes. In this type of interview, it is usually difficult to obtain any quantitative data;*
(b) *mail surveys: the most successful surveys are short, simple and focused and it is advisable to telephone and identify the appropriate respondent before sending the questionnaire.*

53:6.4 Analyse Performance Gaps

Simple spreadsheet analysis is useful to identify the differing performance levels of the participants. Analysis can include comparison of each practice and the range of performance can be subsequently displayed for each of the agreed measures. Current performance can be compared to the best practice partner's performance with primary identification of activities that can be improved. This analysis should also include any identified future trends or objectives that the organisation foresees. The findings should provide management with a clear idea of the options and provide a realistic view of the potential benefits of adopting the practices.

53:6.5 Project Future Performance

The objective of this step is for the management team to examine the organisation's past performance in relation to the identified best practice, forecast potential change and project future performance both with and without the proposed changes. This activity will provide a clear idea of the options and any required investment which will in turn provide a realistic view of the potential benefits of adopting the benchmarking practices.

53:6.6 Communicate Results

The most successful benchmarking projects are those that have planned for and allowed sufficient time to communicate the objectives, progress and findings of the project. The audience should be everyone in the organisation who will be involved in any changes that are recommended. Communicating results will help to develop learning and sharing culture and will generate a willingness to carry out any proposed recommendations.

53:6.7 Revise Performance Goals

After presenting the findings, there may be some valid requests for further information or adjustments to the results. These adjustments rarely alter the overall findings and are vital to ensure that all objections are tackled before the next step. The organisation may not like the results but they must believe that they are accurate and valid.

53:6.8 Develop Action Plans

This step is extremely important. Too often benchmarking stops at identifying current performance without moving forward to recommendations for performance improvement. It may be helpful to divide the action plan into a timescale, for example, short-term actions which can be undertaken within three months and will generate 'quick wins'. This is particularly useful if the quick wins will generate resources for any investment that may be required in later phases of the action plan. The second term could be for actions to be completed within 18 months. The final phase could be long-term action steps that may require investment in technology, or perhaps partner alliances that will take time to organise and develop.

Each of the phases should have target benchmarks to measure and assess the benefits gained.

53:6.9 Monitor Implementation

Once the action plan has been agreed, performance should be monitored and rewarded. A clear benefit from a benchmarking project is a performance measurement framework using a range of key performance indicators which can be included in an organisation's management reporting.

53:6.10 Recalibrate Benchmark

Leading-edge organisations benchmark on a regular basis. The regularity should be determined by the speed of change within the market or the organisation. Therefore once improvements have been made, plans should be made for the next project.

53:7 How to Make a Benchmarking Project Successful

This section identifies some of the usual barriers that may be encountered when first introducing a benchmarking project and may also be experienced when presenting the findings. Potential solutions are described for each barrier. The section then identifies the golden rules to ensure that a benchmarking project is successful.

53:7.1 Barriers to Benchmarking

There will be many barriers to both the benchmarking activity and also to the subsequent acceptance of the findings. These need to be addressed as soon as they are identified. The following are a few of the most frequently cited obstacles.

53:7.1.1 Our Business Is Different Or Unique

Many people in the organisation may legitimately feel that the organisation or the business may be unique in some way. The response is that it may well be unique but it is the impact that the uniqueness has on the business that can be compared. Very often this points to benchmarking a process rather than the whole organisation. Past experience can demonstrate how seemingly different organisations have been able to compare their operations.

The following example provides an illustration of how two very different organisations were able to form a successful benchmarking partnership. These organisations had a profitable exchange of information on the capital-planning process.

One partner operated in a market with rapid technological and service requirement change. The other organisation operated in an industry which had just been through de-regulation. The impacts on the capital planning process were the same. There was an increasing need to re-evaluate and prioritise the planning projects. The first organisation tried to use technology to speed up their existing process, rapidly evaluating each project. The second had reviewed the demand for re-evaluation and asked themselves, 'will this change?' The answer was 'no'. They then developed a new flexible process to deal with this need. For example, every capital project had to directly link to the organisation's objectives. If it did not then it received a lower priority rating and the capital planning executives could question its inclusion. Every aspect of the process was linked to the organisational strategy and critical success factors. The result was a much shorter, faster and less expensive capital planning process for the second organisation. The first organisation learnt that rather than trying to speed up the process, they needed to develop a new flexible process to meet the new needs of their business.

53:7.1.2 Now Is the Wrong Time

Every organisation is in the midst of change. Measuring and comparing will provide a quantified starting point and a performance measurement framework, which can track progress and adapt to the changes. The financial and operational impact of all potential changes must be considered and included within the project.

The following example illustrates that benefits can be forthcoming when benchmarking in a period of organisational change.

A national government authority was in the process of defining and setting up outsourcing arrangements for many of its administrative processes. Many of the managers felt that benchmarking should wait until the new processes were in place. Senior management disagreed and took time to explain the reasons why. The benchmarking would provide an understanding of current cost and service levels. This would help to set targets for the external service providers. It would also identify performance improvement opportunities that could be developed with the external service providers. Some of the management remained unconvinced. During the process several of them identified other practices which helped them immediately to improve and release internal resources. The process of communication led to the creation of an internal best practice club to share information on activities and act as a forum for the management of the external service providers. It also highlighted those practices that needed to be redesigned before the hand-over.

53:7.1.3 We Do Not Wish to Share Our Data

The solution to overcoming this barrier is to consider benchmarking less sensitive areas first. Find a champion and manage a small project to demonstrate the benefits of a sharing culture. Apart from some functions such as R&D, practices are generally already well known in the industry through the transference of employees, mutual customers and mutual suppliers. The following example illustrates the level of knowledge that can be recognised within an industry.

An industry breakfast meeting was held which was attended by all of the leading retailers and fast-moving consumer goods giants. Most of them attended knowing who else would be at the meeting. During the meeting there was clear identification of each other's practices, which resulted in more sharing and learning. For example, one retailer cited the different warehousing and distribution practices that his competitor had adopted and explained why that was appropriate for them but not for his organisation.

Another solution to overcoming this barrier is to take a cross-industry approach. There will be less sensitivity in comparing practices outside the industry and therefore not sharing information with competitors.

53:7.1.4 We Do Not Have the Time Or Resources

Very often the results of a benchmarking exercise will identify how to save time and work more productively. However, it is sometimes difficult to convince extremely busy people that the additional effort expended in participating will identify productivity improvements in the future. One potential solution is to produce high-level performance league-tables from publicly available data. If these findings identify any large performance gaps, then the potential benefits of benchmarking will be more difficult to ignore. High-level league-table benchmarking using public data can identify any large performance gaps. This will demonstrate that the potential benefits cannot be ignored.

The following example illustrates this approach. A large public organisation found that a simple form of sharing better practices freed up resources to participate in a benchmarking exercise. The organisation's executive management decided to benchmark their administrative processes. One of the process owners could not attend the meetings due to the high level of expense-claims processing she had to manage. She did, however, manage to attend a training course and talk to one of the other participants. She explained that she could not attend due to the scale of claims and asked how the other participant managed to cope. The other participant told her that the number of claims she dealt with was far fewer since she had persuaded senior management to put in a few procedures. For instance, claims had a minimum financial value and settlement was automatically paid into employees' bank accounts, rather than by cheque. The first participant was processing individual claims put forward with values of less than £10. She shared what she had learnt with her senior management and explained the procedures. They implemented the changes, including advances for those employees who could not afford the financial outlay, and she managed to halve the number of claims in the first year and again in the second year.

Many of these barriers hide a number of underlying concerns. The first is that benchmarking is about reducing head count. This is a difficult barrier to overcome and there are only two responses. The first is to stress that the exercise will focus upon performance improvement by identifying smarter ways of working. This should free up resource to undertake more activities which will directly contribute to the organisation's success. Of course, there has to be the consideration of whether the employees are capable of, or wish to, take on more proactive roles.

This was not the case for the Managing Director of a large manufacturing plant who experienced the difficulty in trying to empower his employees. Basically, some employees welcomed the opportunity to become more involved in the business, however others were purely concerned with their own efficiency and did not want additional responsibility. They perceived their contribution to be high performance during their working day, which ended after they had completed their contracted hours.

The second obstacle to address is the concern that the benchmarking will highlight poor performance. Nobody wishes to be at the bottom of a league table. It is therefore the benchmarking team's responsibility to ensure that the focus is about improving current performance, rather than analysing historical results. Solutions include not identifying individuals or teams in the results and only reporting the range of performance. Alternatively, only identify those with better practices, taking care to allow sufficient scope and detail to show each participant they have some better practice to share. Finally, avoiding the use of numbers entirely by perhaps using a symbol approach. This will ensure that the focus is not upon a specific detailed result such as 0.30p per transaction, but that the focus is upon the fact that there is a performance improvement opportunity.

The ultimate response is to highlight that in today's complex and changing environment where there is increasing pressure to reduce costs and improve customer service, organisations will flounder if they do not keep up with the competition. Benchmarking is one way to do this and will ensure that business results will ensure rewards for customers, shareholders and employees. It is particularly valuable to consider allocating part of any financial improvements to a bonus scheme so that those who have demonstrated best practice and those who have significantly improved their practices are rewarded. Care must be taken in not being seen as rewarding employees for previous poor performance purely because it is easier to improve from a poor performance position than a high-performing one.

53:7.2 'Golden Rules' of Benchmarking

There are number of 'golden rules' which, as with most projects, need to be followed to reap the most rewards from benchmarking.

53:7.2.1 Senior Commitment

Benchmarking can be seen as a cost reduction exercise and sometimes generates fear and unwillingness to participate. Senior management can help to dissipate this fear by demonstrating commitment. For instance, they could stress that the project's focus is on performance improvement not headcount; that objectives are to reduce the time spent on activities such as transaction processing and to realign employees to more productive business support.

One of the ways in which senior management can ensure that change is implemented is by adopting a performance measurement framework which tracks progress towards identified benchmarks, as identified in step 10 of the benchmarking process.

The success of any project depends upon management commitment to its objectives and process. This also holds true for a benchmarking project. The role of senior management is to stress the importance of the project, clearly articulate how it fits into organisational objectives and to support the process whenever required. This may include, for example, direct involvement if full co-operation is not received, allocation of resources as required and representation, communication and clear 'ownership' of the initiative.

The most important contribution however is communication. This must stress that the focus of the project is upon identifying performance improvement opportunities and the subsequent change that the exercise will identify.

Senior management can ensure the project's success by confirming that the findings will not focus upon past performance and that the project is not just a 'nice-to-know' exercise. If this is not clearly communicated then the organisation will not fully participate and inaccurate or incomplete data will be forwarded, results will be ignored and the findings will be filed away without further action.

53:7.2.2 Scope

Do not choose too many processes or areas to benchmark. As a guide, it is advisable not to try more than five at any one time, in any depth. In fact, the fewer the better, which is why planning is so important to identify the best place to start. If the scope of the project is too large, resources are stretched and this leads to a longer project time with less effective results. This is particularly important if the exercise is a pilot study and success is crucial to any continuous improvement activities in the organisation.

53:7.2.3 Process Selection

Processes that have the largest performance improvement potential should be identified rather than those that may just be popular. Selection of an area under these criteria will provide a logical reason for the project and will increase the chances of success. It may well be feasible to gather some publicly available league-table benchmarks to demonstrate the potential in benchmarking the chosen activities. This is covered in more detail in the next section.

53:7.2.4 Identify Quick Wins

During the project process, look for quick wins. These are those areas that will be easiest to improve and can demonstrate that the project is worthwhile. This is particularly important if the project is used as a pilot exercise.

53:7.2.5 Link Findings to Actions

The most successful projects are those which align the findings and recommendations into an action plan with qualitative and quantitative targets with individual responsibilities.

53:7.2.6 Team Involvement

Everyone who will be affected by the process in the benchmarking project should be involved. The objectives and actions steps should be explained, together with the commitment required by employees. The greatest challenge for a project is the adoption of new practices and changes to existing ways of working. Everyone who is responsible for implementing any recommended changes has to agree to the objectives and what is required. A few timely meetings can help generate a sense of ownership of the project.

53:7.2.7 Communication

As mentioned under **paragraphs** 53:7.2.1 and 53:7.2.6, wide and frequent communication is vital to the success of benchmarking. Communicate at each and every stage of the process; at the outset to gain commitment; during the project to create a culture that is open to change; and at the end to demonstrate the success of the exercise.

53:7.2.8 Time Required

There is a misconception that benchmarking can easily be carried out in a short number of weeks as it merely involves gathering and comparing some data. In fact, finding comparable data, analysing and interpreting the results so that meaningful conclusions can be drawn will usually take a minimum of three months from start to finish. Inevitably there will be questions after preliminary findings are published and it may take time to find the appropriate answers. If external organisations are invited to participate in a sharing exercise, it will take time to gain their agreement, agree definitions and collect the information. Benchmarking partners may well not have the same priorities as the benchmarking project team.

53:7.2.9 Share Information

If you are seeking information from other organisations, always be prepared to share findings. Consider what you are prepared to share in advance of the exercise.

Nobody likes change, and the desire to change can be particularly hard to develop in more traditional markets. Benchmarking will help the organisation develop an external perspective and highlight the need for change. One of the most frequent benefits cited from benchmarking is the internal understanding that it can bring to the organisation. The process demands an operational overview of activities and resources which very often is put aside for more pressing day-to-day activities.

Appendix 53:1 Benchmarking Terms

The following terms are frequently used and a consistent definition is useful to aid discussions with potential benchmarking partners.

(a) *Best practice: Best practice is the specific process and environment that yielded the benchmark. It is worthwhile considering the term 'best practice' in a little more detail.*

(b) *Metrics: Metrics are quantified measures of process performance. They are usually shown as a number, ratio or percentage. For example, cost per invoice, number of employees recruited per human resource employee, cost as a percentage of sales, professional/administrative employees.*

(c) *Baseline: The baseline is current performance. It is the starting position prior to any improvements.*

(d) *Benchmark: A benchmark is the best possible sustained performance.*

(e) *Process: A process is a structured set of activities to produce an output for a customer. For instance accounts payable, where the activities, sometimes referred to as sub-processes include:*

(i) receiving a request for a product or service;

(ii) sourcing suppliers;

(iii) negotiating terms with the supplier;

(iv) sending the official order;

(v) receiving the invoice;

(vi) authorising the invoice for payment;

(vii) raising and sending payment.

Appendix 53:2 Sources of Information

1. Useful Reading References

Boxwell, R.J. (1994) *Benchmarking for competitive advantages*. Maidenhead: McGraw Hill.

Camp, R.J. (1995) *Business process benchmarking, finding and implementing best practices*. Wisconsin: ASQ Quality Press.

Camp, R.C. (1998) *Benchmarking: The search for industry best practices that lead to superior performances*. New York: American Society for Quality Control (ASQC) Quality Press.

Camp, R.C. (1998) *Global cases in benchmarking*. Wisconsin: ASQ Quality Press.

Codling, S. (1992) *Best practice benchmarking: The management guide to successful implementation*. Bedford: Industrial Newsletters Ltd.

Fuld, L.M. (1988) *Monitoring the competition*. London: John Wiley & Sons.

Karlof, B. and Ostblom, S. (1993) *Benchmarking: A signpost to excellence in quality and productivity*. London: Wiley.

McNair, C.J. and Leibried, K.H.J. (1992) *Benchmarking: A tool for continuous improvement*. London: Harper Business.

Spendolini, M.J. (1992) *The benchmarking book*. New York: Amacom.

Watson, G.H. (1993) *Strategic benchmarking: How to rate your company's performance against the world's best*. London: Wiley.

Zairi, M. (1992) *Competitive benchmarking: An executive guide*. London: Technickal Communications (Publishing) Ltd.

Zairi, M. and Leonard, P. (1994) *Practical benchmarking: A complete guide*. Cambridge: Chapman & Hall.

2. Information from Trade Associations

Trade Associations are listed in *Henderson's Directory of British Trade Associations* (CBD Research, 11th edition, 1992); *Trade Associations and Professional Bodies of the United Kingdom* (I.P. Millard (ed.) 10th edition, Gale Research, 1991); and *Directory of European Industrial and Trade Associations* (CBD Research, 5th edition, 1991). By no means all Trade Associations produce comparative data: in a survey conducted in 1980 roughly one in five did so. The type of data varies enormously and is usually available only to members. It is well worth a call to the relevant association to make enquiries about current practice.

3. Sources of Marketing Information

This guide is based on a pamphlet prepared by the City of London Business Library for its users. We are very grateful to the library for permission to make this use of their pamphlet.

(a) Guides to existing surveys

(i) *Industrial Aids Ltd* – Published data on European industrial markets. List of market reports freely available for purchase with guide to other sources of information on industrial markets.

(ii) *International directory of published market research* (British Overseas Trade Board, now British Trade International).

(iii) T. Walters – *Market research source book* (Headland Press, 1984).

(iv) K.P. Hilton – *Stockbrokers' research and information services* (Oxford Centre for Management Studies, 1985).

(v) *World sources of market information*, 2 vols (Gower, 1982).

(b) Statistics – general guides

(i) CSO – Guide to official statistics, no. 5 (HMSO, 1986). Recent developments are reported in the quarterly Statistical News. NEDO publishes a series of specialised guides, e.g. Distributive trade statistics, Motor industry statistics.

(ii) Government statistics – a brief guide to sources is updated annually and available free. See the National Statistics website at *www.statistics.gov.uk*.

(iii) J.M. Harvey – Sources of statistics (Clive Bingley, 1971). Lists with brief descriptions, the principal sources of statistics in UK, USA, and from main international organisations.

(iv) UN – Directory of International statistics. Guide to series published by the UN and other international agencies.

(v) W.F. Maunder – Reviews of United Kingdom statistical sources (Heinemann Education). Thirteen volumes so far published, each detailing sources in a given subject area.

(vi) R.A. Critchley – Quick reference guide to statistical sources in consumer marketing.

(vii) John Fletcher – Information sources in economics (2nd edn, Butterworths, 1984). Has helpful chapter on economic statistics sources.

(viii) Bernard Edwards – Sources of economic and business statistics (Heinemann, 1972).

(ix) Pamela Foster – Business statistics index (Headland Press, 1983).

(x) SIS CIS (Subject index to sources of comparative statistics) (CBD, 1978). Guide to international statistical sources.

(xi) *Sources of European economic information* (Gower, 1982).

(xii) The Union of International Associations (*www.uia.org/services/*) has links to statistical databases.

(c) Statistics and surveys – UK market

(i) Office of Population Census and Surveys – Census. Official statistics on population, occupations, socio-economic groups, etc. in England and Wales. Separate publications are available for Scotland and Northern Ireland. The OPCS also publish annual population estimates and population trends. See *www.statistics.gov.uk/census/*.

(ii) HM Revenue and Customs – Survey of personal incomes (*www.hmrc.gov.uk/stats/income_distribution/pi_b_1.htm*)

(iii) Office for National Statistics – Family expenditure and food survey (*www.esds.ac.uk/government/fes/*)

(iv) MGN Marketing manual of the UK. Survey of UK social and economic conditions with market-place data on over 90 product fields. Useful feature is citation of sources of statistics. Section C is an analysis of advertising expenditure by product brands and media. A companion volume covers industrial marketing. (Last published 1979).

(v) GfKNOP – Political, social, economic review. Monthly bulletin recording reactions to controversial political and social topics, as well as surveys of individual UK markets (*www.gfknop.co.uk/*).

(vi) A–Z of UK marketing data (Euromonitor Publications Ltd at *www.euromonitor.com/*).

(vii) UK market size guide (Imac Research).

(d) Abstracts and indices

There are few abstracting services covering marketing information. Most services concentrate on technical aspects and contain few, if any, commercial references.

(i) Market research abstracts. Semi-annual publication from the Market Research Society. Concerned more with the theory of marketing, but articles on actual markets sometimes included.

(ii) Anbar abstracts. Series covers: accounting and data processing; marketing and distribution; personnel and training; top management; work study and O & M.

(iii) Marketing information guide. Monthly annotated bibliography, published in the USA, of books, reports and articles on domestic and foreign markets.

(iv) Business periodicals index. Monthly service, cumulating annually, indexing articles by specific subject from a wide range of economic and commercial publications.

(v) Funk & Scott indexes – Europe and International. Monthly indexes, with quarterly and annual cumulations, of articles from major commercial journals and most non-US countries. Both product and country approaches are catered for on the blue and yellow pages respectively.

(vi) Research index. Fortnightly index of articles appearing in the UK press and selected periodicals. Pink pages index by subject items of industrial and commercial news. Companion Reports index for surveys, reports, etc.

(vii) Newspaper indexes. Monthly cumulative indexes, to The Times and Financial Times.

(e) Advertising and readership surveys

  (i)   NRS – National readership survey (*www.nrs.co.uk/*).

  (ii) National businessman readership survey. Analysis of readership of newspapers and journals among different categories of businessmen.

  (iii) MEAL (Media Expenditure Analysis Ltd). This principal source of advertising expenditure data is not available for purchase by libraries.

  (iv) Advertising Association statistical yearbook.

4. Companies Providing Marketing Data

Economist Intelligence Unit Ltd, 24 Red Lion Square, London WC1R 4HQ, tel: +44 (0)20 7576 8181, fax: +44 (0)20 7576 8476, email: *london@eiu.com,* www: *www.eiu.com* issues the following business publications:

The Business Economist: The Society's well respected journal is published three times a year and is free to members. It features articles on practical research, recent theoretical advances and contains an extensive book review section. Articles include contributions from members and other economists. Members are encouraged to submit their own articles.

The Newsletter: The monthly newsletter keeps members informed of all the Society's activities. There is regular news of related groups and developments of interest to the business economist. Recruitment advertisements are often circulated.

Surveys: Regular surveys are carried out, assessing members' views of important issues such as the Budget and the economic outlook. There is also an annual salary survey.

Yearbook: The SBE Yearbook contains a full listing of the over 600 members, by name and by organisation. This is distributed only to members.

Euromonitor Publications Ltd, 60–61 Britton Street, London EC1M 5UX. Publishes UK Market Reports which contain statistical data on consumer markets in the UK. Other publications include UK Retailing Industry Reports, Factfinders and Market Direction Reports as well as a wide range of marketing and business information publications (*www.euromonitor.com*).

Mintel Publications Ltd 18–19 Long Lane, London EC1A 9PL (email: *info@mintel.com*). *Market Intelligence* (monthly reports on five consumer goods markets and marketing using original research).

Retail Intelligence (quarterly journal devoted to aspects of distributive trade with original research).

Leisure Intelligence (quarterly journal reporting on leisure market/activities with original research).

Personal Finance Intelligence (a quarterly journal concentrating on developments in the area of financial services).

Daily Digest (senior management guide compiled from national press and specialist journals).

Monthly Review (a list of key appointments and a wide variety of market sizes).

Monthly Digests. Mintel Information Service (for desk or original research); Mintel library (access to files and journals), fees on request; Mintel client report service (reports tailored to client's requirements), fees on request.

A.C. Nielsen Media International – 2nd Floor, Kings Court, 185 Kings Road, Reading, Berkshire RG1 4EX.

- Continuous national and regional measurements of consumer sales and sales influencing factors at the retail and wholesale outlet for manufacturers of packaged consumer goods.

- Other market and consumer research services (fees on request). Nielsen Researcher and Neilsen Marketing Trends issues periodically covering topics of general marketing interest are available from Sales Office, address as above.

5. Sources Needing a Computer to Access

There is a growing number of online databases of relevance to the businessman. These databases hold detailed information on large numbers of UK companies that is constantly updated.

FAME (Financial Analysis Made Easy) provides financial information about UK public and private companies. Searches can be made by company name or by criteria such as location, turnover size and number of employees. Company information includes: trade description; directors' names; subsidiaries; company accounts. Access is by subscription and may be available in your local library. Contact the publishers, Bureau van Dyk, through Northburgh House, 10 Northburgh Street, London EC1V 0PP, tel: 44 20 7549 5000, fax: 44 20 7549 5010, email: *london@bvdep.com*.

Datastream provides a wide range of statistical information on companies, financial markets and economics. Most of the data can be downloaded into an Excel-compatible format. More information is now available through Thomson Financial: *www.thomson.com/content/financial/brand_overviews/Datastream_Advance*.

The Companies House web site is the foundation of company information exchange in the UK: helping businesses, informing the public and benefiting the economy. It offers a range of searchable databases, which provide information on companies and directors: *www.companieshouse.gov.uk/*.

6. Other Information Sources

The Centre for Interfirm Comparison. The Centre publishes a brochure about its services, which may be obtained on request from its offices at 32 St Thomas Street, Winchester, Hampshire SO23 9HJ or at *www.cifc.co.uk.*

Most of the projects are carried out on an annual basis. For some sectors an 'Appraisal Service' is in operation, which enables a firm to send in its data at any time, and quickly receive in return a written appraisal of its performance as measured against the existing databank for that sector.

Aslib. It may be worth subscribing to an information service such as that offered by one of the membership benefits. Aslib offers referral assistance to inquiries on any subject by advising on appropriate information sources, and will carry out online searching on request. They can also give informal advice on all aspects of information management, from the selection of equipment to the automation of a company information centre. Aslib, The Association for Information Management, Holywell Centre, 1 Phipp Street, London EC2A 4PS, tel: +44 (0) 20 7613 3031, fax: +44 (0) 20 7613 5080, email: *aslib@aslib.com*, www: *www.aslib.co.uk/*.

Aslib directory of information sources in the United Kingdom, edited by E.M. Codlin. Two volumes: Vol.1 – Science, technology and commerce, 5th edn, 1982; Vol.2 – Social sciences, medicine and the humanities, 5th edn, 1984.

The British Library. One of the major parts of the British Library whose stock and services specifically cater for the needs of industry and commerce is the Business and IP Centre. It holds one of the most comprehensive collections of business and intellectual property information in the UK. The information is practical rather than theoretical in nature. It is particularly useful for UK and overseas market, company and product information. It includes: 7,000 current market research reports; 3,000 trade directories; business journals, company annual reports, house journals and trade literature; over 50 million patent specifications from 40 countries worldwide; official gazettes on patents, trade marks and registered designs; law reports and other material on litigation. See their website for further information: *www.bl.uk/services/reading/bipcentre.html.*

London Business School Information Service, Sussex Place, Regents Park, London NW1 4SA. The LBS service offers a comprehensive range of research and library facilities for a corporate subscription to use the library and hourly research fees. The library is located at: 25 Taunton Place, London NW1 6HB, tel: +44 (0)20 7000 7620, fax: +44 (0)20 7706 1897, email: *library@london.edu*.

London Chamber of Commerce and Industry, 33 Queen Street, London EC4R 1AP. For a fee the LCCI will search through its computerised files to see if there are businesses using the same or similar names registered with the LCCI, or which appear on the 'modern index' previously controlled by the Department of Trade. For information, telephone: +44 (0)20 7203 1884, email: *info@londonchamber.co.uk* or visit *www.londonchamber.co.uk/*.

The Institute of Administrative Management, Caroline House, 55-57 High Holborn, London WC1V 6DX, tel: +44 (0) 207 841 1100, fax: +44 (0) 207 841 1119, for General Enquiries, email: *info@instam.org*. Publishes surveys of administrative and overhead costs, office salaries, holidays and bonus, etc.

Car running costs
Information on this subject may be obtained from:
- *Fleet Facts*, Telepress Ltd, Strand House, Great West Road, Brentford, Middlesex TW8 9EY.

- *Car Fleet Management*, Business Press International Ltd, Quadrant House, The Quadrant, Sutton, Surrey SM2 5AS.

- *Fleet Car Comparisons*, Masterlease, International House, Bickenhill Lane, Birmingham, West Midlands, B37 7HQ, tel: +44(0) 870 732 4444 or visit *www.masterlease.uk.com/carcomparison/index.html*. Gives overall operating costs for every car available in the UK today.

- *Automobile Association:*
  www.theaa.com/allaboutcars/advice/advice_rcosts_petrol_table.jsp.

7. Benchmarking Clubs and Associations

The Best Practice Club (www.bpclub.com)
The Atrium
Curtis Road
Dorking
Surrey
RH4 1XA
United Kingdom

Email: enquiries@bpclub.com
Tel: +44 (0)1306 646555
Fax: +44 (0)1306 646556

Global Benchmarking Council (www3.best-in-class.com/gbc)
Best Practices, LLC
6320 Quadrangle Drive, Suite 200
Chapel Hill, NC 27514-7815

The Benchmarking Exchange (www.benchnet.com)
437 Coates Drive
Aptos, California
USA
95003

EFQM (www.efqm.org)
EFQM Representative Office
Avenue des Pléiades 15
B-1200 Brussels
Belgium

APQC (www.apqc.org)
123 North Post Oak Lane
3rd Floor
Houston, Texas 77024

54. Implementing a Balanced Performance Measurement System

54:1 Introduction

This chapter takes a practical approach to the design and implementation of a performance measurement system. It starts by looking at why we measure performance before going on to describe three practical steps you should take in designing and implementing a performance measurement system. The tools and techniques described here are not simply theoretical models, they have been tried and tested and the chapter includes practical advice based on experience from doing this in real companies.

54:1.1 Why Implement a Performance Measurement System?

The ultimate aim of implementing a performance measurement system has got to be 'improving the performance of the organisation' and there is evidence that performance measurement systems do just this (Lingle and Schiemann, 1996). However, there are five underlying reasons for measuring performance which will help you achieve the ultimate goal. These are:

1. *establish position;*
2. *communicate direction;*
3. *stimulate action;*
4. *facilitate learning;*
5. *influence behaviour.*

54:1.1.1 Establishing Position

Establishing the current level of performance is an important first step before doing anything else. You need to know where you are to establish:

(a) *basic health (are you profitable, solvent, etc.?);*
(b) *a base level of performance against which to judge improvement;*
(c) *levels of performance to make meaningful internal comparisons (e.g. between departments);*
(d) *levels of performance to make meaningful external comparisons (e.g. before benchmarking).*

Performance measurement therefore allows you to establish a sound base from which to develop.

54:1.1.2 Communicating Direction

Having established where you are, the next step is to communicate where you are going and performance measures enable you to do this by:

(a) *communicating between the members of the management team. It is quite surprising how a well-designed set of performance measures transforms a wordy strategic plan into a focused, measurable and time-bound set of goals which the team can all understand;*
(b) *directing, through communicating standards, targets and goals down the organisation;*
(c) *directing, through explicitly measuring what is important;*
(d) *communicating goals, standards, expectations and service levels between departments or between customers and suppliers.*

In this way, performance measures can be used to precisely communicate direction.

54:1.1.3 Stimulate Action

Having established the current level of performance and set the target, action needs to be taken to close the gap. Performance measures allow you to do this by:

(a) *providing feedback to stimulate corrective action;*
(b) *highlighting areas of poor performance stimulating management review, process redesign, reallocation of resources;*
(c) *providing information for objective decision making.*

54:1.1.4 Facilitate Learning

Action may be one of the keys to improving performance through performance measurement, but it is also important to reflect on what the measures are telling you and to learn from the experience. You need to consider the appropriateness of the action being taken, check that the action being taken is delivering the results you expected and use the performance measures to understand better how the organisation works and interacts with its environment. This is done by:

(a) *learning through a change of perception brought about simply by measuring and being cognisant of the results;*
(b) *learning through making connections between performance in one area and performance in another;*
(c) *learning through using the measures to test assumptions made about the internal and external business environment;*
(d) *learning through the debate the performance measures engender.*

54:1.1.5 Influencing Behaviour

There are a number of adages, 'what you measure is what you get', 'what gets measured gets done', and 'what gets measured gets managed'. Implementing measures influences behaviour whether it is through tying the recognition and reward system to the performance measures or simply by focusing management attention on the results. Therefore, do not be surprised if you find that badly designed measures do not produce the behaviour you expected (designing measures is covered in **para.54:2.2**).

Performance measurement should contribute to improved organisational performance through:

(a) *motivating people to achieve the organisation's goals and targets;*
(b) *encouraging appropriate actions;*
(c) *discouraging inappropriate actions.*

54:1.1.6 Summary

Improving organisational performance may be the ultimate goal in implementing a performance measurement system, but remember that there are a number of steps on the way. First, establish your position through measurement. Then communicate the direction in which you want to go through appropriate measures and targets. Use the results of the measures to stimulate action, but do not forget to reflect on what the measures are telling you and to learn from this. Finally, remember that the measures will influence behaviour and whether that behaviour is the behaviour you want will depend largely on how well you have designed the measures.

54:1.2 The Problem with Pure Accounting Measures

Pure accounting measures have been criticised for, among other things:

(a) *encouraging short-termism – in the short term it is easier to increase profits by reducing costs rather than increasing revenues. Often R&D spending and other projects which are important for the future are the first to be hit;*
(b) *being backward-looking – they tell you how well you performed last month, quarter or year, not how you will perform in the future;*
(c) *being internally focused, concentrating attention on internal efficiencies rather than on what is happening in the market place;*
(d) *encouraging local optimisation through achieving the overhead recovery rate at the expense of satisfying the customer;*
(e) *encouraging minimisation of variance rather than continuous improvement;*
(f) *lacking strategic focus.*

Accounting measures are result measures, they tell you what you have achieved rather than how you achieved it (*see* **Ch.48**). They emphasise the outcome of the business activity rather than focus on the drivers of performance.

Consequently it is useful to consider financial measures as one dimension of a balanced performance measurement system rather than as the only tool for managing the organisation.

54:1.3 The Concept of a Balanced Performance Measurement System

In an attempt to overcome the shortcomings of purely financial performance measurement systems, the late 1980s and early 1990s saw the development of the concept of balance. For example:

(a) *Keegan et al. (1989) propose a balance between internal and external measures and between financial and non-financial measures;*
(b) *Cross and Lynch (1988/9) describe a pyramid of measures which integrates performance through the hierarchy of the organisation;*
(c) *Fitzgerald et al. (1991) distinguish between the results (financial performance and market competitiveness) and their determinants (service quality, flexibility, resource utilisation and innovation), see **Chapter 49, paragraph 49:2.1;***
(d) *Kaplan and Norton (1992) identified the four perspectives of the balanced scorecard (financial, external customer, internal process, innovation and learning), see **Chapter 49, paragraph 49:2.3.***

However, although performance measurement frameworks help us understand the different perspectives of the performance measurement system and the balance between the measures, they do not tell us exactly what the measures should be. To do this we need a management process.

54:1.4 The Management Process

What is a management process? It is a process which helps managers review the business, improve other processes and make decisions. It is usually structured into a number of workshops where specific tools (such as SWOT analysis or business process mapping) are used. The structure of the process enables each part of the problem to be considered sequentially and a good process will focus on specific aspects at each stage. The workshop format allows a number of managers to participate, making their contribution based on the personal or functional experience, having their personal views heard as well as participating in the debate and decision making. Usually, such a process is facilitated.

The role of the facilitator is not to make a contribution to the content of the work being done or the decision being made, but to manage the process.

There are a number of advantages of adopting a process for the design of a performance measurement system. In summary the process should:

(a) *structure thinking by focusing attention on the key questions to be asked and decisions to be made;*
(b) *elicit input from a wider group rather than simply the views of a single individual;*
(c) *make trade-offs explicit through the debate;*
(d) *engender through the process a sense of fairness, making it more likely that unpopular decisions will be accepted;*
(e) *create a shared understanding of what is to be achieved;*
(f) *build commitment to achieving it.*

This is why companies and consultancies are increasingly adopting a management process approach.

54:2 Three Steps to Designing and Implementing a Performance Measurement System

A simple three-step management process is described here for designing and implementing a performance measurement system.

Step 1: Define and agree the objectives the business is trying to achieve.
Step 2: Design measures which stimulate actions and behaviour in support of those objectives.
Step 3: Manage the measures in an appropriate manner.

54:2.1 Step 1: Defining Business Objectives

Many strategies have a visionary element, but to make the strategy actionable, the vision needs to be broken down into specific business objectives. Three different approaches to doing this are described here.

54:2.1.1 The Customer/Stakeholder Approach

The approach developed by Cambridge University (*Getting the measure of your business*, Neely *et al.* 1996) uses customer and stakeholder needs as the basis for generating the top-level business objectives.

Business objectives are developed in a facilitated workshop with the senior managers or directors of the organisation.

First, customer needs are identified under the headings of quality, time, cost/price and flexibility. Managers are asked to articulate precisely what their customers are looking for and are made to distinguish between order qualifiers (the things you need to do to be considered as a potential supplier to the customer) and order winners (the things you need to do to win the order). The result is a clear list of customer needs which the organisation has to meet.

Secondly, stakeholder needs are identified. Stakeholders are any group whose needs the organisation wishes to take into account when setting the business objectives. The stakeholders usually consist of the organisation's owners, the senior managers and often the employees. However, it may also include the organisation's suppliers and local community. Stakeholder needs are also identified under the quality, time, cost/price and flexibility heading.

The two lists are then compared, balanced and blended into a set of objectives which meet the requirements of both the customer and the stakeholders.

Some of these needs will obviously match. The customer may need high product reliability to minimise the inconvenience when the product goes wrong. The company may well have the same objective to minimise warranty costs. Here there is no conflict.

Some of these needs will appear at first sight to conflict. Customers may well be looking for quick delivery. The company may being looking to meet return on investment targets (ROI) and reducing stockholding may be seen as critical to achieving this. The customer lead-time need and the stock reduction objective may therefore conflict. As a consequence, one of the resulting objectives may be to reduce production lead-times drastically.

Figure 54:1 shows an example of how the customer and stakeholder needs described above are translated into business objectives.

Figure 54:1 **Developing business objectives**

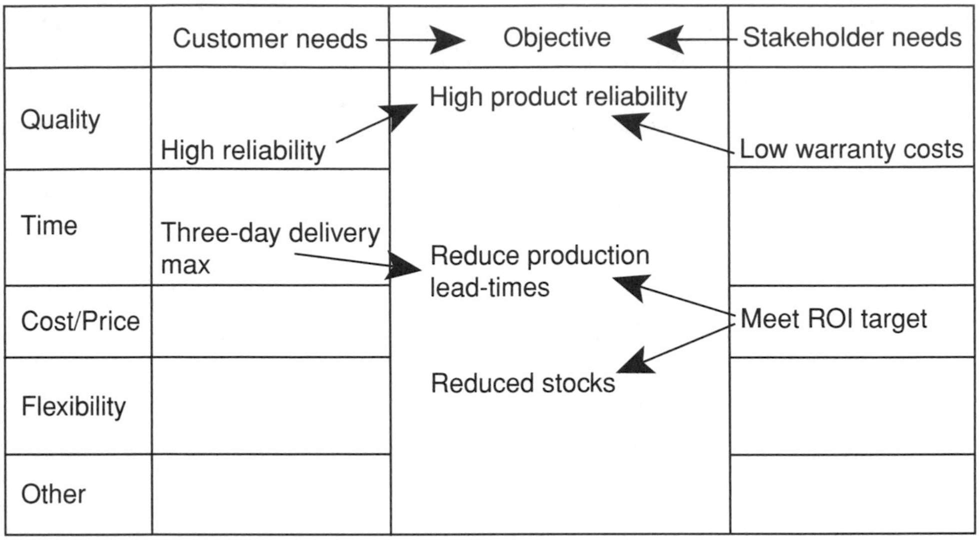

	Customer needs ⟶	Objective ⟵	Stakeholder needs
Quality	High reliability	High product reliability	Low warranty costs
Time	Three-day delivery max	Reduce production lead-times	
Cost/Price			Meet ROI target
Flexibility		Reduced stocks	
Other			

In this way a top-level set of organisational objectives are developed which meet both the customer needs and the needs of the stakeholders.

54:2.1.2 The 'What/How' Approach

The what/how approach is a simple technique for translating a top-level business goal into the series of subobjectives necessary to achieve this goal. It is the approach adopted by Kaplan and Norton (1996) and has been used by companies such as BT.

The job of the facilitator is to encourage debate between the members of the senior management team around the core objective of the organisation. Once this has been agreed, the facilitator steers the debate from 'what is to be achieved' to 'how this should be achieved'.

For example, a company wishes to increase its financial returns. Having agreed the 'what', the debate moves on to 'how' this should be achieved. The management team sees two main methods – growing revenues and reducing costs. After debating the exact meaning of these concepts for their business, these two become the main 'hows' for implementing the strategy (*see* **Fig.54:2**).

Figure 54:2 **A 'what/how' example**

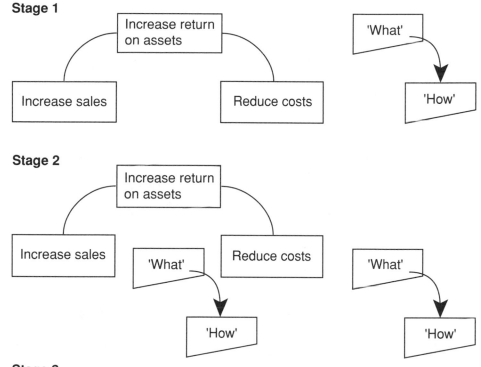

The question now turns to how the revenue will be increased and how costs will be cut. The 'hows' for increasing returns now become the 'whats' for the next level down. The facilitator will state 'what we are trying to achieve is an increase in revenue, how are we going to achieve this?'

In this way the 'hows, and 'whats' of achieving the strategy are cascaded down the business. The result is what Eccles and Pyburn (1992) call a 'business model'. The model encapsulates the management belief of how action at one level affects outcomes at the next level, drawing the belief into a cause and effect diagram which communicates the strategy.

Kaplan and Norton (1996) have developed this concept into a structure incorporating their balanced scorecard and the approach is shown in **Figure 54:3** as it was applied to one of the Institute of Management's training profit centres.

Figure 54:3 **The Institute of Management non-accredited programmes balanced scorecard**

**Revenue growth
strategy**
To grow by attracting new customers
and broadening sources of revenue
from current customers

**Internal efficiency
strategy**
To improve operating efficiency:
increasing marketing response rate
and concentrating on key return areas

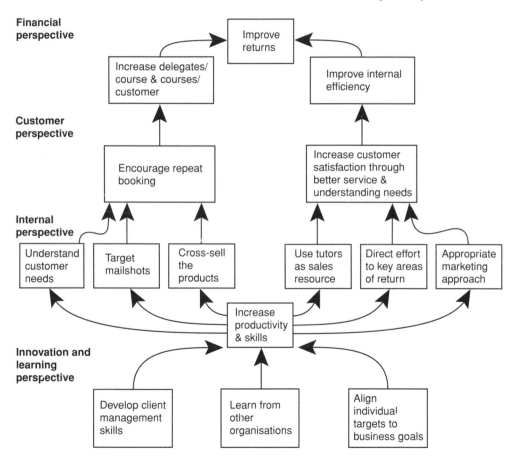

Each of these objectives is then taken and translated into performance measures (*see* **Para.54:2.2**).

54:2.1.3 The Five-year Vision Approach

This approach involves the senior management team in developing a vision of what the business will look like five years from now. Ideally, it is done through a series of workshops that start by developing the different business perspectives which need to be considered. The next step is to describe what the business will look like in the future under each of these perspectives before debating how the organisation will get there.

The outcome includes:

(a) *an articulated vision of the future;*
(b) *a set of high-level business objectives;*
(c) *a series of actions or projects which underpin the achievement of the objectives;*
(d) *a set of measures to manage the business today and gauge progress towards achieving the objectives.*

This type of approach has been used by DHL (Morris, 1996). Their vision of the future was developed over a 12-month period by the board of directors spending one day per month in workshops. They started by considering the business under the four perspectives of the balanced scorecard: financial, external customer, internal process and innovation and learning. However, the board of directors wanted the language they used to be accessible to the whole business. To achieve this, they articulated their performance management framework as follows: 'We have customers, to whom our people provide a service, through following processes, which, when successful, produce results'. Subsequently, they split the customer perspective into the two elements the customer sees, the core service and the ease of use of that service.

The result was a vision of what the company will look like in the future for each of the five perspectives. This was brought together with a specific set of high-level actions and underpinning projects to take the company forward. These were supported by measures and targets which monitored progress towards the visions as well as measures to run the business day to day.

Figure 54:4 **The DHL vision**

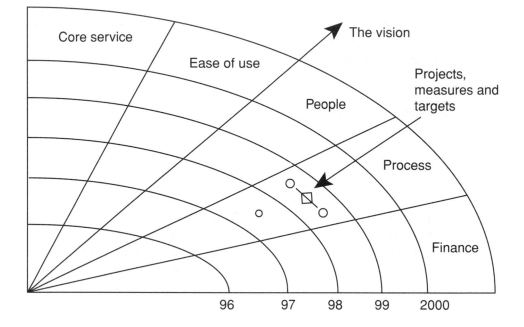

Source: Adapted from Morris, 1996

54:2.1.4 Summary
Three alternative approaches for developing business objectives have been outlined here. Each approach is very different in the way it develops the objectives but they have some core similarities. These are:

(a) they are all participative workshop approaches involving the whole senior management team;

(b) they all structure the discussion;

(c) they all encourage debate of the key factors;

(d) they are all simple and understandable techniques;

(e) they all result in agreement on the key objectives to be met.

The process of debate, understanding and agreement is considered by many as being the most important aspect of any strategy development or performance measurement system design. To quote Drew Morris (1996):

As a board, we got almost as much benefit working through this as we did in terms of output. There isn't any substitute for that. Nobody will give you one of these and stick it in the company and find it will work.

54:2.2 Step 2: Designing Performance Measures

Setting business objectives by itself is not enough. Well-designed measures are required to support the implementation of the objectives and to measure achievement. This vital step is often missed and the approach described in this section is taken from the Neely *et al.* (1996) process.

54:2.2.1 The Factors to Consider in the Design of Performance Measures

If you ask managers about performance measures they will describe them in terms of their title and formula, for example, 'on-time delivery' – the percentage of orders delivered in the month on the day they were required.

To design a good performance measure, the definitions need to be precise. Using the example above:

- often the measure does not include all orders:

  'we don't include spares orders';

- often the language is used imprecisely:

  'we only measure the actual delivery on the orders we deliver ourselves. The date the courier collects the orders is used for the rest', and

  'the date the order is required is the delivery date we originally advised to the customer and this is taken from the computer system. The advised delivery date is not necessarily the date the customer wanted it';

- or is even misleading:

  'we measure using the orders delivered as the base for the calculation. If the order isn't delivered during the month, it doesn't appear in the figures as a late delivery. This will only happen in the month it finally gets delivered'.

There are a number of factors to be considered when designing a performance measure:

(a) *Why are you measuring this? Make the purpose explicit (communicate direction and facilitate learning).*

(b) *What top-level business objective does this measure relate to? Measures need to be aligned to the business objectives or at best, the measure will produce sub optimality, at worst it can completely thwart the achievement of the original objective (communicate direction).*

(c) *What is the target to be achieved (communicating direction)?*

(d) *How should this be measured? This should include a precise and detailed formula as well as the frequency of measurement and review (establishing position).*

(e) *How do we ensure consistency of measurement? This is required for comparability between periods and to ensure that motivation is not destroyed by changing the goalposts (influencing behaviour).*

(f) *How do we ensure that measurement leads to action (stimulate action)?*

54:2.2.2 The Performance Measure Framework

Figure 54:5 **The performance measure record sheet**
Source: Neely *et al.*, 1996

Measure	A good self-explanatory title.
Purpose	Why are we measuring this?
Relates to	To which top-level business object does this relate?
Target	What is to be achieved and by when?
Formula	How is this measured? Be precise.
Frequency	How often is this measured and reviewed?
Who measures?	Who collects and reports the data?
Source of data	Where do the data come from?
Who acts on the data?	Who is responsible for taking action?
What do they do?	What are the general steps which should be taken?
Notes and comments	

The value of the record sheet is that it:

(a) *helps structure the design of the measure;*
(b) *fully documents measures;*
(c) *identifies who is responsible for improvement;*
(d) *identifies what should be done;*
(e) *communicates why this is measured.*

54:2.2.3 The Questions to Ask When Agreeing Measures

For each individual measure you should ask:

(a) *Is the meaning and formula clear and precise?*
(b) *Have different departmental perspectives been identified and conflicts resolved?*
(c) *What behaviour will this encourage?*
(d) *Is this behaviour desirable?*
(e) *Has the target been agreed?*
(f) *Is the target realistic?*
(g) *How does this target fit in with the achievement of other measures, budgets or plans?*
(h) *Who will own the measure?*

For the group of measures as a whole, you should ask:

(a) *Is the set of measures balanced (such as in the balanced scorecard, for example)?*
(b) *Have conflicts between measures been eliminated or the trade-off made explicit?*
(c) *If this set of measures is successfully implemented, will they drive the organisation forward in the way you desire?*

Before implementation, you should ask:

(a) *What are the barriers to implementation?*
(b) *What resources are required?*
(c) *Does the organisation's reward system align with the new measures?*

54:2.2.4 Considering the Behaviour

The questions 'what behaviour will this encourage?' and 'is this behaviour desirable?' are very important. If you have difficulty with this, try and reconstruct the performance measure which resulted in the behaviour described below.

> An airline was concerned that an important aspect of customer satisfaction was determined not by the flight itself, but by how quickly the passengers received their luggage after landing. As a result, the company introduced a new performance measure to improve the baggage delivery performance.
>
> After this new measure was introduced, a team of baggage handlers were observed in action. They stood around chatting and smoking in a group awaiting the tractor pulling the cars with the bags from the plane. As the tractor arrived, the team leader grabbed a small bag off the first car and threw it to the youngest member of the team. He caught the bag and then sprinted across the tarmac, throwing the bag onto the conveyer as he reached it. Having done this, he sauntered back to the rest of the group who were still engrossed in their conversation which they continued, until they had finished their cigarettes.

54:2.3 Step 3: Managing Through Measurement

54:2.3.1 Barriers to Implementing the Measures

In the author's experience there are four main barriers to implementing a performance measurement system. These are:

1. *Insufficient time and effort. Managers are usually busy and the performance measurement initiative creates further work. If the project does not take a high priority, there will be serious delay during implementation.*
2. *An underestimation of the IT resource required to implement the measures, leading to a delay which can cause the project to stall.*
3. *A fear of being measured. Invariably change is resisted but in some companies past management practice creates a fear of measurement. This makes the introduction of new measures very difficult. Resistance usually surfaces during implementation.*

4. *Business objectives being set by the wrong level of management. As a result, changes in strategy at divisional or parent company-level can undermine the objectives set and group-wide initiatives can swamp the performance measurement initiative.*

To overcome these problems:

(a) *sustained senior management commitment is essential and the project needs to be given priority;*
(b) *the project needs to be adequately resourced, especially with IT support for implementing the measures;*
(c) *the number of other concurrent initiatives should be managed;*
(d) *the project needs to be managed in a way which recognises the cultural and management change implications;*
(e) *the project must involve the management team who have the authority to agree the business objectives and should be done with the full support of the next level of management;*
(f) *the reward and recognition system should be aligned with the performance measures (or at least be neutral in its effect).*

54:2.3.2 Reviewing the Measures

It is important to get into the habit of regularly reviewing the performance measures. This can be difficult at first as it takes time to set up the measures. Often the first couple of meetings can be frustrating when the data simply are not available. Persistence will usually overcome this hurdle.

The review of an individual measure should develop over time.

(a) *How does actual performance compare with the target set?*
(b) *What are the main reasons why the target is not being met?*
(c) *What is the plan for corrective action?*
(d) *Has the action been taken?*
(e) *Does the action have the desired impact on the performance of the measure?*

A useful visualisation for managing reviews in this way has been developed by Ford.

Figure 54:6 **The Ford QOS measure visualisation**

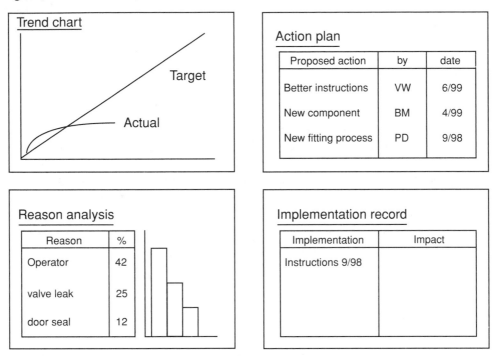

Besides managing the review of measures independently, their interdependence needs to be considered. In particular:

(a) *Is improvement in one area being made at the expense of performance in another?*
(b) *Do improvements in performance drivers (such as service quality) result in the expected improvements in outcome measures (such as financial results and market performance)?*
(c) *Do some measures predict performance in others (e.g. the current value of quotations may predict the future order intake)?*
(d) *Does the business model match the reality of the measures?*

54:2.3.3 Displaying the Measures

The author believes that going public with the measures is the defining point in the implementation of the performance measurement system. Up until then, it is no more than a management toy.

Making the measures public by displaying them widely throughout an organisation makes a strong statement about the management commitment to the performance measurement system. Measures:

(a) *have to be kept up to date, and it is soon noticed if this does not happen;*

(b) *show a commitment to sharing at least some of the management information with the rest of the organisation;*

(c) *show good news as well as bad and demonstrate that the organisation is mature enough to consider its shortcomings;*

(d) *also show where improvement is being achieved and where it is not.*

54:2.3.4 Driving Performance Through Measurement

A lot of managers see performance measurement as a way of driving up performance. The measures will influence behaviour, but performance can be driven through performance reviews, appraisal systems and bonus schemes. This type of approach will work in situations where performance is highly dependent on the effort of individual employees, where that effort will be directly reflected in performance and where you can measure accurately and precisely the performance. This may be considered the 'McGregor theory X' of performance measurement.

In many organisations today, there are problems in adopting this approach. First, it is not just the level of effort required, but the quality. We want people to work smarter rather than harder. Often there are a number of people involved. The practice and processes need to be changed to make the improvements required. Also, there is usually a time gap between the action and the result. This may be a few weeks in terms of an operating process improvement, but several years in terms of a new product introduction.

Besides influencing behaviour, performance measures can have a much wider use. They can communicate direction, allowing co-ordination between people, processes and functions. They can stimulate appropriate action, be it process redesign, staff retraining or resource reallocation. They can also be used to facilitate learning throughout the whole organisation. This may be considered the 'McGregor theory Y' of performance measurement.

Therefore, there is a choice in the way you use a performance measurement system. Do you:

(a) *Focus on the individual or the process?*
(b) *Apportion blame or look to improve the situation?*
(c) *Celebrate success or punish failure?*
(d) *Learn from your mistakes or sack the individual to make sure it does not happen again?*

As a result, do your people:
(a) *Try their best or try to do nothing wrong?*
(b) *Ask for help or pretend the poor performance is not happening?*
(c) *Provide excuses or ideas for improving performance?*
(d) *Debate the issues or move on to someone else's problem as soon as possible?*
(e) *Fiddle the measures or improve the measures to make them more appropriate for the business?*

Remember, you cannot increase the speed of your car just by pushing up the needle on the speedometer.

54:2.3.5 Developing the Performance Measurement System

Finally, like anything else, if the system is not developed it will stagnate and die. Some of the steps involved in continuing to develop the system should include:

(a) *reassessing and resetting the targets as performance improves and needs change;*
(b) *redesigning the measures in light of experience;*
(c) *introducing new measures and deleting old ones to reflect changes in strategy and business objectives;*
(d) *using the measures to challenge the assumptions underpinning the strategy and even the strategy itself.*

References

Cross, K.F. and Lynch, R.L. (1988/9) 'The SMART way to sustain and define success', *National Productivity Review*, 8(1): 23–33.

Eccles, R.G. and Pyburn, P.J. (1992) 'Creating a comprehensive system to measure performance, *Management Accounting [US]*, October, 41–4.

Fitzgerald, L., Johnston, R., Brignall T.J., Silvestro, R. and Voss, C. (1991) *Performance measurement in service businesses*. London: The Chartered Institute of Management Accountants.

Kaplan, R.S. and Norton, D.P. (1992) 'The balanced scorecard – measures that drive performance', *Harvard Business Review*, January/February 71–9.

Kaplan, R.S. and Norton, D.P. (1996) *The balanced scorecard – translating strategy into action*. Boston, MA: Harvard Business School Press.

Keegan, D.P., Eiler, R.G. and Jones, C.R. (1989) 'Are your performance measures obsolete?', *Management Accounting*, June: 45–50.

Lingle, J.H. and Schiemann, W.A. (1996) 'From balanced scorecard to strategy gauge: Is measurement worth it?', *Management Review*, March: 56–62.

Morris, D. (1996) 'Integrating improvement programmes to harness and direct company wide initiatives', *Business performance measurement conference*, Business Intelligence, 22 and 23 October, London.

Neely, A.D., Mills, J.F., Gregory, M.J., Richards, A.H., Platts, K.W. and Bourne, M.C.S. (1996) *Getting the measure of your business*. London: Findlay.

Appendix I. **Discounted Cash Flow Tables**

Using DCF Tables

The tables enable the calculation of:

(a) *the present value of a sum to be received in the future; or*
(b) *the current investment needed to accumulate to a given sum at the end of a number of years.*

Example

A company has to pay £58,000 six years hence; the current interest on invested funds is 9%. To meet the future requirement it must invest £58,000 times the factor against the six year figure in the 9% column of the tables – 0.5963.

Year	Percentage					
	1	*2*	*3*	*4*	*5*	*6*
1	0.9901	0.9804	0.9709	0.9615	0.9524	0.9434
2	0.9803	0.9612	0.9426	0.9246	0.9070	0.8900
3	0.9706	0.9423	0.9151	0.8890	0.8638	0.8396
4	0.9610	0.9238	0.8885	0.8548	0.8227	0.7921
5	0.9515	0.9057	0.8626	0.8219	0.7835	0.7473
6	0.9420	0.8880	0.8375	0.7903	0.7462	0.7050
7	0.9327	0.8706	0.8131	0.7599	0.7107	0.6651
8	0.9235	0.8535	0.7894	0.7307	0.6768	0.6274
9	0.9143	0.8368	0.7664	0.7026	0.6446	0.5919
10	0.9053	0.8203	0.7441	0.6756	0.6139	0.5584
11	0.8963	0.8043	0.7224	0.6496	0.5847	0.5268
12	0.8874	0.7885	0.7014	0.6246	0.5568	0.4970
13	0.8787	0.7730	0.6810	0.6006	0.5303	0.4688
14	0.8700	0.7579	0.6611	0.5775	0.5051	0.4423

Year	Percentage					
	1	2	3	4	5	6
15	0.8613	0.7430	0.6419	0.5553	0.4810	0.4713
16	0.8528	0.7284	0.6232	0.5339	0.4581	0.3936
17	0.8444	0.7142	0.6050	0.5134	0.4363	0.3714
18	0.8360	0.7002	0.5874	0.4936	0.4155	0.3503
19	0.8277	0.6864	0.5703	0.4746	0.3957	0.3305
20	0.8195	0.6730	0.5537	0.4564	0.3769	0.3118

Year	Percentage					
	7	8	9	10	11	12
1	0.9346	0.9259	0.9174	0.9091	0.9009	0.8929
2	0.8734	0.8573	0.8417	0.8264	0.8116	0.7972
3	0.8163	0.7938	0.7722	0.7513	0.7312	0.7118
4	0.7629	0.7350	0.7084	0.6830	0.6587	0.6355
5	0.7130	0.6806	0.6499	0.6209	0.5935	0.5674
6	0.6663	0.6302	0.5963	0.5645	0.5346	0.5066
7	0.6228	0.5835	0.5470	0.5132	0.4817	0.4523
8	0.5820	0.5403	0.5019	0.4665	0.4339	0.4039
9	0.5439	0.5002	0.4604	0.4241	0.3909	0.3606
10	0.5083	0.4632	0.4224	0.3855	0.3522	0.3220
11	0.4751	0.4289	0.3875	0.3505	0.3173	0.2875
12	0.4440	0.3971	0.3555	0.3186	0.2858	0.2567
13	0.4150	0.3677	0.3262	0.2897	0.2575	0.2292
14	0.3878	0.3405	0.2992	0.2633	0.2320	0.2046
15	0.3624	0.3152	0.2745	0.2394	0.2090	0.1827
16	0.3387	0.2919	0.2519	0.2176	0.1883	0.1631
17	0.3166	0.2703	0.2311	0.1978	0.1696	0.1456
18	0.2959	0.2502	0.2120	0.1799	0.1528	0.1300
19	0.2765	0.2317	0.1945	0.1635	0.1377	0.1161
20	0.2584	0.2145	0.1784	0.1486	0.1240	0.1037

Year	Percentage					
	13	14	15	16	17	18
1	0.8850	0.8772	0.8696	0.8621	0.8547	0.8475
2	0.7831	0.7695	0.7561	0.7432	0.7305	0.7182
3	0.6931	0.6750	0.6575	0.6407	0.6244	0.6086
4	0.6133	0.5921	0.5718	0.5523	0.5337	0.5158
5	0.5428	0.5194	0.4972	0.4761	0.4561	0.4371
6	0.4803	0.4556	0.4323	0.4104	0.3898	0.3704
7	0.4251	0.3996	0.3759	0.3538	0.3332	0.3139
8	0.3762	0.3506	0.3269	0.3050	0.2848	0.2660
9	0.3329	0.3075	0.2843	0.2630	0.2434	0.2255
10	0.2946	0.2697	0.2472	0.2267	0.2080	0.1911
11`	0.2607	0.2366	0.2149	0.1954	0.1778	0.1619
12	0.2307	0.2076	0.1869	0.1685	0.1520	0.1372
13	0.2042	0.1821	0.1625	0.1452	0.1299	0.1163
14	0.1807	0.1597	0.1413	0.1252	0.1110	0.0985
15	0.1599	0.1401	0.1229	0.1079	0.0949	0.0835
16	0.1415	0.1229	0.1069	0.0930	0.0811	0.0708
17	0.1252	0.1078	0.0929	0.0802	0.0693	0.0600
18	0.1108	0.0946	0.0808	0.0691	0.0592	0.0508
19	0.0981	0.0829	0.0703	0.0596	0.0506	0.0431
20	0.0868	0.0728	0.0611	0.0514	0.0433	0.0365

Year	Percentage					
	19	20	21	22	23	24
1	0.8403	0.8333	0.8264	0.8197	0.8130	0.8065
2	0.7062	0.6944	0.6830	0.6719	0.6610	0.6504
3	0.5934	0.5787	0.5645	0.5507	0.5374	0.5245
4	0.4987	0.4823	0.4665	0.4514	0.4639	0.4230
5	0.4190	0.4019	0.3855	0.3700	0.3552	0.3411
6	0.3521	0.3349	0.3186	0.3033	0.2888	0.2751
7	0.2959	0.2791	0.2633	0.2486	0.2348	0.2218
8	0.2487	0.2326	0.2176	0.2038	0.1909	0.1789
9	0.2090	0.1938	0.1799	0.1670	0.1552	0.1443
10	0.1756	0.1615	0.1486	0.1369	0.1262	0.1164
11	0.1476	0.1346	0.1228	0.1122	0.1026	0.0938
12	0.1240	0.1122	0.1015	0.0920	0.0834	0.0757
13	0.1042	0.0935	0.0839	0.0754	0.0678	0.0610

Year			Percentage			
	19	20	21	22	23	24
14	0.0876	0.0779	0.0693	0.0618	0.0551	0.0492
15	0.0736	0.0649	0.0573	0.0507	0.0448	0.0397
16	0.0618	0.0541	0.0474	0.0415	0.0364	0.0320
17	0.0520	0.0451	0.0391	0.0340	0.0296	0.0258
18	0.0437	0.0376	0.0323	0.0279	0.0241	0.0208
19	0.0367	0.0313	0.0267	0.0229	0.0196	0.0168
20	0.0308	0.0261	0.0221	0.0187	0.0159	0.0135

Year			Percentage			
	25	26	27	28	29	30
1	0.8800	0.7937	0.7874	0.7813	0.7752	0.7692
2	0.6400	0.6299	0.6200	0.6104	0.6009	0.5917
3	0.5120	0.4999	0.4882	0.4768	0.4658	0.4552
4	0.4096	0.3968	0.3844	0.3725	0.3611	0.3501
5	0.3277	0.3149	0.3027	0.2910	0.2799	0.2693
6	0.2621	0.2499	0.2383	0.2274	0.2170	0.2072
7	0.2097	0.1983	0.1877	0.1776	0.1682	0.1594
8	0.1678	0.1574	0.1478	0.1388	0.1304	0.1226
9	0.1342	0.1249	0.1164	0.1084	0.1011	0.0943
10	0.1074	0.0992	0.0916	0.0847	0.0784	0.0725
11	0.0859	0.0787	0.0721	0.0662	0.0607	0.0558
12	0.0687	0.0625	0.0568	0.0517	0.0471	0.0429
13	0.0550	0.0496	0.0447	0.0404	0.0365	0.0330
14	0.0440	0.0393	0.0352	0.0316	0.0283	0.0254
15	0.0352	0.0312	0.0277	0.0247	0.0219	0.0195
16	0.0281	0.0248	0.0218	0.0193	0.0170	0.0150
17	0.0225	0.0197	0.0172	0.0150	0.0132	0.0116
18	0.0180	0.0156	0.0135	0.0118	0.0102	0.0089
19	0.0144	0.0124	0.0107	0.0092	0.0079	0.0068
20	0.0115	0.0098	0.0084	0.0072	0.0061	0.0053

Appendix II. Compound Interest Tables

Using Compound Interest Tables

The factors in the tables relate to the value, at a given rate of interest, on the last day of a year of an investment made on the first day of that year.

Example

An investment made of £45,000 at 7% for five years will produce £45,000 *times* the factor against the five year figure in the 7% column – 1·4026.

Year	Percentage					
	1	*2*	*3*	*4*	*5*	*6*
1	1.0100	1.0200	1.0300	1.0400	1.0500	1.0600
2	1.0201	1.0404	1.0609	1.0816	1.1025	1.1236
3	1.0303	1.0612	1.0927	1.1249	1.1576	1.1910
4	1.0406	1.0824	1.1255	1.1699	1.2155	1.2625
5	1.0510	1.1041	1.1593	1.2167	1.2763	1.3382
6	1.0615	1.1262	1.1941	1.2653	1.3401	1.4185
7	1.0721	1.1487	1.2299	1.3159	1.4071	1.5036
8	1.0829	1.1717	1.2668	1.3686	1.4775	1.5938
9	1.0937	1.1951	1.3048	1.4233	1.5513	1.6895
10	1.1046	1.2190	1.3439	1.4802	1.6289	1.7908
11	1.1157	1.2434	1.3842	1.5395	1.7103	1.8983
12	1.1268	1.2682	1.4258	1.6010	1.7959	2.0122
13	1.1381	1.2936	1.4685	1.6651	1.8856	2.1329
14	1.1495	1.3195	1.5126	1.7317	1.9799	2.2609
15	1.1610	1.3459	1.5580	1.8009	2.0789	2.3966
16	1.1726	1.3728	1.6047	1.8730	2.1829	2.5404
17	1.1843	1.4002	1.6528	1.9479	2.2920	2.6928
18	1.1961	1.4282	1.7024	2.0258	2.4066	2.8543
19	1.2081	1.4568	1.7535	2.1068	2.5270	3.0256
20	1.2202	1.4859	1.8061	2.1911	2.6533	3.2071

Year			Percentage			
	7	8	9	10	11	12
1	1.0700	1.0800	1.0900	1.1000	1.1100	1.1200
2	1.1449	1.1664	1.1881	1.2100	1.2321	1.2544
3	1.2250	1.2597	1.2950	1.3310	1.3676	1.4049
4	1.3108	1.3605	1.4116	1.4641	1.5181	1.5735
5	1.4026	1.4693	1.5386	1.6105	1.6851	1.7623
6	1.5007	1.5869	1.6771	1.7716	1.8704	1.9738
7	1.6058	1.7138	1.8280	1.9487	2.0762	2.2107
8	1.7182	1.8509	1.9926	2.1436	2.3045	2.4760
9	1.8385	1.9990	2.1719	2.3579	2.5580	2.7731
10	1.9672	2.1589	2.3674	2.5937	2.8394	3.1058
11	2.1049	2.3316	2.5804	2.8531	3.1518	3.4785
12	2.2522	2.5182	2.8127	3.1384	3.4985	3.8960
13	2.4098	2.7196	3.0658	3.4523	3.8833	4.3635
14	2.5785	2.9372	3.3417	3.7975	4.3104	4.8871
15	2.7590	3.1722	3.6425	4.1772	4.7846	5.4736
16	2.9522	3.4259	3.9703	4.5950	5.3109	6.1304
17	3.1588	3.7000	4.3276	5.0545	5.8951	6.8660
18	3.3799	3.9960	4.7171	5.5599	6.5436	7.6900
19	3.6165	4.3157	5.1417	6.1159	7.2633	8.6128
20	3.8697	4.6610	5.6044	6.7275	8.0623	9.6463

Year			Percentage			
	13	14	15	16	17	18
1	1.1300	1.1400	1.1500	1.1600	1.1700	1.1800
2	1.2769	1.2996	1.3225	1.3456	1.3689	1.3924
3	1.4429	1.4815	1.5209	1.5609	1.6016	1.6430
4	1.6305	1.6890	1.7490	1.8106	1.8739	1.9388
5	1.8424	1.9254	2.0114	2.1003	2.1924	2.2878
6	2.0820	2.1950	2.3131	2.4364	2.5652	2.6996
7	2.3526	2.5023	2.6600	2.8262	3.0012	3.1855
8	2.6584	2.8526	3.0590	3.2784	3.5115	3.7589
9	3.0040	3.2519	3.5179	3.8030	4.1084	4.4355
10	3.3946	3.7072	4.0456	4.4114	4.8068	5.2338
11	3.8359	4.2262	4.6524	5.1173	5.6240	6.1759
12	4.3345	4.8179	5.3502	5.9360	6.5801	7.2876
13	4.8980	5.4924	6.1528	6.8858	7.6987	8.5994

Year			Percentage			
	13	14	15	16	17	18
14	5.5348	6.2613	7.0757	7.9875	9.0075	10.1472
15	6.2543	7.1379	8.1371	9.2655	10.5387	11.9737
16	7.0673	8.1372	9.3576	10.7480	12.3303	14.1290
17	7.9861	9.2765	10.7613	12.4677	14.4265	16.6722
18	9.0243	10.5752	12.3755	14.4625	16.8790	19.6733
19	10.1974	12.0557	14.2318	16.7765	19.7484	23.2144
20	11.5231	13.7435	16.3665	19.4608	23.1056	27.3930

Year			Percentage			
	19	20	21	22	23	24
1	1.1900	1.200	1.2100	1.2200	1.2300	1.2400
2	1.4161	1.4400	1.4641	1.4884	1.5129	1.5376
3	1.6852	1.7280	1.7716	1.8158	1.8609	1.9066
4	2.0053	2.0736	2.1436	2.2153	2.2889	2.3642
5	2.3864	2.4883	2.5937	2.7027	2.8153	2.9316
6	2.8398	2.9860	3.1384	3.2973	3.4628	3.6352
7	3.3793	3.5832	3.7975	4.0227	4.2593	4.5077
8	4.0124	4.2998	4.5950	4.9077	5.2389	5.5895
9	4.7854	5.1598	5.5599	5.9874	6.4439	6.9310
10	5.6947	6.1917	6.7275	7.3046	7.9259	8.5944
11	6.7767	7.4301	8.1403	8.9117	9.7489	10.6571
12	8.0642	8.9161	9.8497	10.8722	11.9912	13.2148
13	9.5964	10.6993	11.9182	13.2641	14.7491	16.3863
14	11.4198	12.8392	14.4210	16.1822	18.1414	20.3191
15	13.5895	15.4070	17.4494	19.7423	22.3140	25.1956
16	16.1715	18.4884	21.1138	24.0856	27.4462	31.2426
17	19.2441	22.1861	25.5477	29.3844	33.7588	38.7408
18	22.9005	26.6233	90.9127	35.8490	41.5233	48.0386
19	27.2516	31.9480	37.4043	43.7358	51.0737	59.5679
20	32.4294	38.3376	45.2593	53.3576	62.8206	73.8641

Year			Percentage			
	25	26	27	28	29	30
1	1.2500	1.2600	1.2700	1.2800	1.2900	1.3000
2	1.5625	1.5876	1.6129	1.6384	1.6641	1.6900
3	1.9531	2.0004	2.0484	2.0972	2.1467	2.1970
4	2.4414	2.5205	2.6014	2.6844	2.7692	2.8561
5	3.0518	3.1758	3.3038	3.4360	3.5723	3.7129
6	3.8147	4.0015	4.1959	4.3980	4.6083	4.8268
7	4.7684	5.0419	5.3288	5.6295	5.9447	6.2749
8	5.9605	6.3528	6.7675	7.2058	7.6686	8.1573
9	7.4506	8.0045	8.5948	9.2234	9.8925	10.6045
10	9.3132	10.0857	10.9153	11.8059	12.7614	13.7858
11	11.6415	12.7080	13.8625	15.1116	16.4622	17.9216
12	14.5519	16.0120	17.6053	19.3428	21.2362	23.2981
13	18.1899	20.1752	22.3588	24.7588	27.3947	30.2875
14	22.7374	25.4207	28.3957	31.6913	35.3391	39.3738
15	28.4217	32.0301	36.0625	40.5648	45.5875	51.1859
16	35.5271	40.3579	45.7994	51.9230	58.8079	66.5417
17	44.4089	50.8510	58.1652	66.4614	75.8621	86.5042
18	55.5112	64.0722	73.8698	85.0706	97.8622	112.4554
19	69.3889	80.7310	93.8147	108.8904	126.2422	146.1920
20	86.7632	101.7211	119.1446	139.3797	162.8524	190.0496

Appendix III. **Annuity Tables**

Using Annuity Tables

The tables provide a means of calculating the present value of an annuity (money payable at the end of each year at the stated rate of interest).

Example

A 10-year lease on an office block produces an annual rent of £30,000. An alternative investment at current rates would produce a return of 9%. The present value of the 10-year lease is thus £30,000 *times* the factor against the 10-year figure in the 9% column of the tables – 6.4177.

Year			Percentage			
	1	2	3	4	5	6
1	0.9901	0.9804	0.9709	0.9615	0.9524	0.9434
2	1.9704	1.9416	1.9135	1.8861	1.8594	1.8334
3	2.9410	2.8839	2.8286	2.7751	2.7232	2.6730
4	3.9020	3.8077	3.7171	3.6299	3.5460	3.4651
5	4.8534	4.7135	4.5797	4.4518	4.3295	4.2124
6	5.7955	5.6014	5.4172	5.2421	5.0757	4.9173
7	6.7282	6.4720	6.2303	6.0021	5.7864	5.5824
8	7.6517	7.3255	7.0197	6.7327	6.4632	6.2098
9	8.5660	8.1622	7.7861	7.4353	7.1078	6.8017
10	9.4713	8.9826	8.5302	8.1109	7.7217	7.3601
11	10.3676	9.7869	9.2526	8.7605	8.3064	7.8869
12	11.2551	10.5753	9.9540	9.3851	8.8633	8.3838
13	12.1337	11.3484	10.6350	9.9856	9.3936	8.8527
14	13.0037	12.1062	11.2961	10.5631	9.8986	9.2950
15	13.8651	12.8493	11.9379	11.1184	10.3797	9.7122
16	14.7179	13.5777	12.5611	11.6523	10.8378	10.1059
17	15.5623	14.2919	13.1661	12.1657	11.2741	10.4773

Year			*Percentage*			
	1	*2*	*3*	*4*	*5*	*6*
18	16.3983	14.9920	13.7535	12.6593	11.6896	10.8276
19	17.2260	15.6785	14.3238	13.1339	12.0853	11.1581
20	18.0456	16.3514	14.8775	13.5903	12.4622	11.4699

Year			*Percentage*			
	7	*8*	*9*	*10*	*11*	*12*
1	0.9346	0.9256	0.9174	0.9091	0.9009	0.8929
2	1.8080	1.7833	1.7591	1.7355	1.7125	1.6901
3	2.6243	2.5771	2.5313	2.4869	2.4437	2.4018
4	3.3872	3.3121	3.2397	3.1699	3.1020	3.0373
5	4.1002	3.9927	3.8897	3.7908	3.6959	3.6048
6	4.7665	4.6229	4.4859	4.3553	4.2305	4.1114
7	5.3893	5.2064	5.0330	4.8684	4.7122	4.5638
8	5.9713	5.7466	5.5348	5.3349	5.1461	4.9676
9	6.5152	6.2469	5.9952	5.7590	5.5370	5.3282
10	7.0236	6.7101	6.4177	6.1446	5.8892	5.6502
11	7.4987	7.1390	6.8052	6.4951	6.2065	5.9377
12	7.9427	7.5361	7.1607	6.8137	6.4924	6.1944
13	8.3577	7.9038	7.4869	7.1034	6.7499	6.4235
14	8.7455	8.2442	7.7862	7.3667	6.9819	6.6282
15	9.1079	8.5595	8.0607	7.6061	7.1909	6.8109
16	9.4466	8.8514	8.3126	7.8237	7.3792	6.9740
17	9.7632	9.1216	8.5436	8.0216	7.5488	7.1196
18	10.0591	9.3719	8.7556	8.2014	7.7016	7.2497
19	10.3356	9.6036	8.9501	8.3649	7.8393	7.3658
20	10.5940	9.8181	9.1285	8.5136	7.9633	7.4694

Year			*Percentage*			
	13	*14*	*15*	*16*	*17*	*18*
1	0.8850	0.8772	0.8696	0.8621	0.8547	0.8475
2	1.6681	1.6467	1.6257	1.6052	1.5852	1.5656
3	2.3612	2.3216	2.2832	2.2459	2.2096	2.1743
4	2.9745	2.9137	2.8550	2.7982	2.7432	2.6901
5	3.5172	3.4331	3.3522	3.2743	3.1993	3.1272
6	3.9975	3.8887	3.7845	3.6847	3.5892	3.4976
7	4.4226	4.2883	4.1604	4.0386	3.9224	3.8115
8	4.7988	4.6389	4.4873	4.3436	4.2072	4.0776

Year	Percentage					
	13	14	15	16	17	18
9	5.1317	4.9464	4.7716	4.6065	4.4506	4.3030
10	5.4262	5.2161	5.0188	4.8332	4.6586	4.4941
11	5.6869	5.4527	5.2337	5.0286	4.8364	4.6560
12	5.9176	5.6603	5.4206	5.1971	4.9884	4.7932
13	6.1218	5.8424	5.5831	5.3423	5.1183	4.9095
14	6.3025	6.0021	5.7245	5.4675	5.2293	5.0081
15	6.4624	6.1422	5.8474	5.5755	5.3242	5.0916
16	6.6039	6.2651	5.9542	5.6685	5.4053	5.1624
17	6.7291	6.3729	6.0472	5.7487	5.4746	5.2223
18	6.8399	6.4674	6.1280	5.8178	5.5339	5.2732
19	6.9380	6.5504	6.1982	5.8775	5.5845	5.3162
20	7.0248	6.6231	6.2593	5.9288	5.6278	5.3527

Year	Percentage					
	19	20	21	22	23	24
1	0.8403	0.8333	0.8264	0.8197	0.8130	0.8065
2	1.5465	1.5278	1.5095	1.4915	1.4740	1.4568
3	2.1399	2.1065	2.0739	2.0422	2.0114	1.9813
4	2.6386	2.5887	2.5404	2.4936	2.4483	2.4043
5	3.0576	2.9906	2.9260	2.8636	2.8035	2.7454
6	3.4098	3.3255	3.2446	3.1669	3.0923	3.0205
7	3.7057	3.6046	3.5079	3.4155	3.3270	3.2423
8	3.9544	3.8372	3.7256	3.6193	3.5179	3.4212
9	4.1633	4.0310	3.9054	3.7863	3.6731	3.5655
10	4.3389	4.1925	4.0541	3.9232	3.7993	3.6819
11	4.4865	4.3271	4.1769	4.0354	3.9018	3.7757
12	4.6105	4.4392	4.2784	4.1274	3.9852	3.8514
13	4.7147	4.5327	4.3624	4.2028	4.0530	3.9124
14	4.8023	4.6106	4.4317	4.2646	4.1082	3.9616
15	4.8759	4.6755	4.4890	4.3152	4.1530	4.0013
16	4.9377	4.7296	4.5364	4.3567	4.1894	4.0333
17	4.9897	4.7746	4.5755	4.3908	4.2190	4.0591
18	5.0333	4.8122	4.6079	4.4187	4.2431	4.0799
19	5.0700	4.8435	4.6346	4.4415	4.2627	4.0967
20	5.1009	4.8696	4.6567	4.4603	4.2786	4.1103

Year	Percentage					
	25	26	27	28	29	30
1	0.8000	0.7937	0.7874	0.7813	0.7752	0.7692
2	1.4400	1.4235	1.4074	1.3916	1.3761	1.3609
3	1.9520	1.9234	1.8956	1.8684	1.8420	1.8161
4	2.3616	2.3202	2.2800	2.2410	2.2031	2.1662
5	2.6893	2.6351	2.5827	2.5320	2.4830	2.4356
6	2.9514	2.8850	2.8210	2.7594	2.7000	2.6427
7	3.1611	3.0833	3.0087	2.9370	2.8682	2.8021
8	3.3289	3.2407	3.1564	3.0758	2.9986	2.9247
9	3.4631	3.3657	3.2728	3.1842	3.0997	3.0190
10	3.5705	3.4648	3.3644	3.2689	3.1781	3.0915
11	3.6564	3.5435	3.4365	3.3351	3.2388	3.1473
12	3.7251	3.6059	3.4933	3.3868	3.2859	3.1903
13	3.7801	3.6555	3.5381	3.4272	3.3224	3.2233
14	3.8241	3.6949	3.5733	3.4587	3.3507	3.2487
15	3.8593	3.7261	3.6010	3.4834	3.3726	3.2682
16	3.8874	3.7509	3.6228	3.5026	3.3896	3.2832
17	3.9099	3.7705	3.6400	3.5177	3.4028	3.2948
18	3.9279	3.7861	3.6536	3.5294	3.4130	3.3037
19	3.3924	3.7985	3.6642	3.5386	3.4210	3.3105
20	3.9539	3.8083	3.6726	3.5458	3.4271	3.3158

This index is arranged alphabetically, in word-by-word order. All references in the index are to chapter number, in bold, followed by section number. Chapter 1 is an introduction to the contents and use of the handbook and should be read before using the book. Publications listed at the end of chapters are not included in the index.

App = Appendix
Fig = Figure
Tab = Table

D

E

N

P

Q

U